PROFESSIONAL

SPORTS TEAM

HISTORIES

BASKETBALL

BASKETBALL

PROFESSIONAL

SPORTS TEAM

HISTORIES

MICHAEL L. LaBLANC, **Editor**

MARY K. RUBY, Associate Editor

 Gale Research Inc. *DETROIT • WASHINGTON, D.C. • LONDON*

♾™ This book is printed on acid-free paper that meets the minimum requirements of American National Standard for Information Sciences— Permanence Paper for Printed Library Materials, ANSI Z39.48-1984.

Printed in the United States of America
Published simultaneously in the United Kingdom
by Gale Research International Limited
(An Affiliated company of Gale Research Inc.)

ISBN 0-8103-8860-X

10 9 8 7 6 5 4 3 2 1

I(T)P

The trademark **ITP** is used under license.

STAFF

Michael L. LaBlanc, *Editor*
Mary K. Ruby, *Associate Editor*
George W. Schmidt, *Indexer*
Marilyn Allen, *Editorial Associate*
Michael J. Tyrkus, *Assistant Editor*

Barbara Carlisle Bigelow, Suzanne M. Bourgoin, Kathy Edgar, Nicolet V. Elert,
Marie Ellavich, Kevin Hillstrom, Laurie Collier Hillstrom, Anne Janette John-
son, Janice Jorgensen, Denise Kasinec, Paula Kepos, Jane Kosek, Mark Kram,
Mary P. LaBlanc, L. Mpho Mabunda, Tom McMahon, Louise Mooney, Les
Ochram, Terrie Rooney, Mary Ruby, Julia Rubiner, George W. Schmidt,
Debbie Stanley, Aarti Stephens, Les Stone, Roger Valade, Cathy Wilson,
Contributing Editors

Kevin Hillstrom, Keith Reed, Mary K. Ruby, *Photo Editors*

B. Hal May, *Director, Biographies Division*
Peter M. Gareffa, *Senior Editor, Contemporary Biographies*
David E. Salamie, *Senior Editor, New Product Development*

Jeanne Gough, *Permissions Manager*
Margaret A. Chamberlain, *Permissions Supervisor (Pictures)*
Pamela A. Hayes, Keith Reed, *Permissions Associates*
Susan Brohman, Arlene Johnson, Barbara A. Wallace, *Permissions Assistants*

Mary Beth Trimper, *Production Director*
Mary Kelley, *Production Assistant*
Cynthia Baldwin, *Art Director*
Mark C. Howell, *Cover Designer*
Kathleen Hourdakis, *Page Designer*
Michael L. LaBlanc, *Typesetter*

Cover photo by arrangement with AP/Wide World Photos

v

Contents

Introductory Essay

Eastern Conference

Atlantic Division

Central Division

Western Conference

Midwest Division

Pacific Division

Introduction

Professional Sports Team Histories is a multivolume reference series that chronicles the evolution of four major U.S. spectator sports: basketball, baseball, football, and hockey.

Basketball, the most recent of the four sports to achieve full professional status, has quickly attained unimagined--and unrivaled--popularity in the United States, while securing a spot in the hearts of fans around the world.

Professional Sports Team Histories: Basketball traces the development of the sport from its humble beginnings in late nineteenth-century Massachusetts to its current domination of the American sports scene. The brainchild of Canadian teacher James Naismith, basketball began as a wintertime diversion for unruly students. Over the past hundred years, the rough-and-tumble battle to sink the most balls into the opposing team's peach basket has been transformed into a highly structured game of skill, speed, accuracy, and athletic prowess.

With an extensive prose entry on each National Basketball Association (NBA) team, *Basketball* focuses on the formation and growth of each franchise and highlights the accomplishments of significant players and members of management. The volume also charts the creation of the NBA in the summer of 1949, the history of the league's precursors, the pioneering teams that engaged in post-World War II play, and the refinement of the game into the sport of the 1990s.

A Source of Convenient Reference *and* Interesting Reading

· **Informative historical essays,** many written by specialists in the field, offer an overview of each team's development from its inception through the 1992-93 season, with coverage of franchise moves, name changes, key personnel, and team performance.

· **A special entry on the history of the sport** follows the development of the game over the years and presents a thorough analysis of the factors that have led to changes in the way it is played.

· **Designed with a broad audience in mind,** the information in *Professional Sports Team Histories* is accessible enough to captivate the interest of the sports novice, yet comprehensive enough to enlighten even the most avid fan.

· **Numerous photos**--including shots of Hall-of-Famers--further enhance the reader's appreciation of each team's history.

· **Easy-to-locate "Team Information at a Glance"** sections list founding dates for each team; names, addresses, and phone numbers of home stadiums; team color/logo information; and franchise records.

· **Additional eye-catching sidebars** present other noteworthy statistics, interesting team-related trivia, close-up profiles of important players and management figures, and capsulized accounts of events that have become a permanent part of sports folklore.

Helpful Indexes Make It Easy to Find the Information You Need

Each volume of *Professional Sports Team Histories* includes a detailed, user-friendly index, making it easy to find information on key players and executives.

Available in Electronic Formats

Diskette/Magnetic Tape. *Professional Sports Team Histories* is available for licensing on magnetic tape or diskette in a fielded format. Either the complete, four-sport database or a custom selection of entries may be ordered. The database is available for internal data processing and nonpublishing purposes only. For more information, call (800) 877-GALE.

We Welcome Your Comments

The editors welcome your comments and suggestions for enhancing and improving any future editions of the *Professional Sports Team Histories* series. Mail correspondence to:

The Editor
Professional Sports Team Histories
Gale Research, Inc.
835 Penobscot Bldg.
Detroit, MI 48226-4094
Phone: (800) 347-GALE
FAX: (313) 961-6599

ACKNOWLEDGEMENTS

Professional Sports Team Histories represents the culmination of nearly three years' effort by a large and diverse group of people. The editors wish to acknowledge the significant contribution of the following individuals and organizations:

• The fine pool of sportswriters and historians who wrote the individual entries, especially author Richard Cohen and Jack Pearson, editor of Milwaukee's *Exclusively Yours* magazine, for sharing their considerable wealth of knowledge on the subject matter. In cases where the writers have drawn on reference materials in addition to their own archival resources, we have included a Sources section at the end of the entry. These sources contain a wealth of additional information, and we urge the interested reader to consult these sources for a more detailed understanding of the subject.

• Mr. Wayne Patterson of the Naismith Memorial Basketball Hall of Fame and Museum, for assistance in securing photos of and information on its members. The Naismith Memorial Hall of Fame and Museum is an organization dedicated to the collection and preservation of information, records, and artifacts relating to the people who have performed outstanding services to the sport. The Museum is open to the public and features numerous displays, an extensive library, and a gift shop. For more information about the Hall, its Museum, or its publications, contact:

> The Naismith Memorial Basketball Hall of Fame and Museum
> 1150 West Columbus Ave.
> PO Box 179
> Springfield, MA 01101
> Phone: (413) 781-6500

• The media relations departments of the various teams, for their valuable cooperation and assistance in providing photographs, historical materials, information on current players, and for directing us to local sports historians and sportswriters.

• Lauren Fedorko and Diane Schadoff of Book Builders Incorporated, and to Jim Evans of Deadline Inc., for their help in securing knowledgeable and entertaining contributors of team essays.

• The talented and dedicated in-house Gale staff—especially Mary K. Ruby and the Contemporary Biographies and the Biographical References Group staffs; Keith Reed of Picture Permissions; Marilyn Allen, Mike Trykus, and Laura Standley Berger of the *Contemporary Authors* Autobiographical Series; Mark Howell and Cindy Baldwin of the Art Department; Patrick Hughes of PC Systems; MaryBeth Trimper, Dorothy Maki, Mary Winterhalter Kelley, and Eveline Abou-El-Seoud of Production; Don Wellman and Maggie Patton of Creative Services; and the entire Marketing and Sales departments—for their invaluable contributions to this series.

HISTORY OF THE NBA

Like many great sports stories, the history of the National Basketball Association (NBA) is the story of an underdog that won despite very long odds. In a country that had enshrined baseball and football as its national pastimes, the NBA gave structure and legitimacy to the professional version of a game played by millions but rarely considered worth the time of serious sports fans. It was hardly an easy victory though, and it was won only recently.

In 1946, when the Basketball Association of America (BAA)—the NBA's precursor—was founded, professional basketball was a game of questionable repute played by men in cages, often marked by tremendous violence and boring play. Since then, the NBA has struggled constantly against negative influences from both outside the league and within it to change the image of the game and even the game itself.

Competing leagues, financial difficulties, the ups and downs of fan interest and how the game was played at times have all challenged the NBA, but the league has always learned and adjusted at the crucial moment.

By turning a once sluggish and slow game into one that blends speed and accuracy, team play and personal innovation, finesse and force, the NBA has matched the pace of post-World War II America and hit levels of popularity never dreamt of by its founders. Now it is on the cutting edge of sport and the driving force behind basketball's new position as rival to soccer for the title of the most popular sport in the world.

Basketball is Born at the YMCA

Basketball can proudly claim that, unlike baseball and football, it knows exactly who its father is. Canadian James Naismith was thirty years old in 1891 and an instructor at the School for Christian Workers, an institution created to supply the then-growing Young Men's Christian Association (YMCA) movement with leaders who could advance its ideal of "muscular Christianity," when he was handed a problem.

Since the school was in Springfield, Massachusetts, the snowy winter months meant that the students were forced to take gym class indoors. Weightlifting, calisthenics and the like were wearing thin and the class of 18 was becoming troublesome. The directors asked Naismith to come up with something to give the students exercise and the challenge they needed indoors. After two weeks of thinking, Naismith had two peach baskets nailed to the track railing around the gym and introduced his new sport.

Though the essential goal of the game was the same, it was quite different from what is played now in the NBA. First, there was no limit on how many players each side could have. Second, one could only catch and then throw the ball; running was not allowed and dribbling hadn't been invented. Third, fouls were only called on particularly violent actions and three consecutive fouls without an intervening one by the other team counted as a goal. Finally, the first player to touch the ball out of bounds threw it back in. Clearly, early basketball must have looked like a game of "Pick Up the Ball and Slaughter." That December a member of the class told Naismith it should be called "basketball" and a new sport was born.

The students loved basketball and the game quickly spread to other YMCAs as an endorsed sport for play in their gyms. As the game evolved in the 1890s, Naismith recommended certain rules such as nine men to a side, but changes such as goals being worth two points, the introduction of foul shots and their value of one point, and the invention of dribbling as a way to elude defenders all developed from the players. Backboards were put up so fans wouldn't interfere with shots, but they did not become standard for decades.

Scores were usually under ten points for each side and five to a side was soon recognized as the optimum number of players. Though Naismith had intended basketball to be non-contact, it turned into a highly physical game, so much so that by 1897, YMCAs were debating whether basketball should be banned from their gyms because of its violent nature. Some went as far to do so, but basketball had already become the property of those who played it.

NBL First Professional League

As the YMCA stepped away from the sport it helped to create, players looked for new places to play both for fun and for pay. The Trenton Basketball Team was probably the first professional basketball team. Originally a YMCA team, they began to receive pay to play in 1896 as they took on other teams from Philadelphia and points north.

The team invented the cage, from which the term "cager" comes from, as a way to protect spectators from players diving to get loose balls and also to speed up play by keeping the ball always inbounds. The first professional league started in 1898 around the Trentons. It was called the National Basketball League (NBL) and though short-lived, it spawned many more leagues in the Northeast.

Up through the 1920s there were at least twelve different professional leagues in the east, none of which gained any national profile. No league had teams west of Ohio, the schedules were unreliable, as were the players, who suited up for whichever team would pay them the most money on any given night. The Original Celtics, based in New York, made the first big move to national recognition for the game by dominating the various leagues they played in and by barnstorming through the decade.

Innovators like Nat Holman and Dutch Dehnert invented standard moves like the pivot play and the give and go and helped establish the eastern style of play as a half-court, methodical game based on set plays. They also stressed strong defense. On the down side, the professional game as they played it had a shady reputation as a sport that could be easily fixed by bettors and that was too violent for most tastes.

College Basketball Catches On

At the same time, the game continued to develop on the amateur side. College basketball thrived and the Amateur Athletic Union of the United States (AAU) sponsored many leagues throughout the country, especially in the Midwest. The AAU did not use cages, or allow double dribbling, and the hoops were only six inches from the backboard, as opposed to twelve. Even the professional leagues that developed in the Midwest tended to use amateur rules and as the professional leagues in the east failed over and over again to take hold, the faster, cleaner amateur game spread.

In 1925 the first true national basketball league, the American Basketball League (ABL), started and adopted AAU rules almost completely. For the first time, teams from the Midwest and the East played against each other and differences were apparent that still remain. Eastern teams played a slower, defense oriented half-court game, while the teams from the West liked a full-court running game high on scoring and low on defense, a difference that is still generally the rule in the NBA. The ABL lasted until the early 1930s.

Though the two styles of play would continue to battle for pre-eminence in professional basketball, the old, bruising, cage-enclosed game was over and the gradual move towards a faster professional style had begun. Other barnstorming teams like the Harlem Rens and the Globetrotters and a reborn ABL continued basketball's rise in the 1930s, playing in dance halls, on stages, in ratty gyms; wherever there was space for a game and paying fans.

More college players entered the pros as a way to make extra money during the Depression, which furthered the amateur style of play in the pros. A few rules were changed too. Players would now have to bring the ball upcourt within ten seconds and the center jump after each basket was eliminated. Now the game would not have to stop after each hoop was scored.

As industry-sponsored professional leagues emerged in the Midwest, like the National Basketball League (no relation to the earlier one of the same name), college basketball swept the nation in the 1930s and 1940s to a degree the game never had before. Madison Square Garden became the Mecca of the sport with its college doubleheaders. The professional game lumbered to keep up, but it had not yet shed its bad image as a slow, thuggish sport.

A group of arena owners headed by Madison Square Garden promoter Ned Irish, Boston Gardens president Walter Brown and Al Sutphin of the Cleveland Arena united to form a new professional basketball league to compete with the NBL, at that point the major professional league.

Whereas earlier leagues were primarily created by players as a way to make some money playing ball or sponsored by businessmen and companies as means of advertising, this new league, called the Basketball Association of America, was born to make money for the arena owners, most of whom already had professional hockey teams.

The BAA would play college-style ball and try to draw players just graduated from college for their teams. Also, instead of having teams in places like Fort Wayne and Oshkosh, as the NBL did, the BAA would play in cities like New York, Boston and Philadelphia.

Business Meets Basketball in BAA

Eleven teams began the first season in 1946: the Boston Celtics, New York Knickerbockers, Philadelphia Warriors, Chicago Stags, Cleveland Rebels, Detroit Falcons, Pittsburgh Ironmen, Providence Steamrollers, St. Louis Bombers, Toronto Huskies and Washington Capitols. Most of the players were older professionals from the NBL and the ABL, kids out of college and men who had played in the service during the war.

The rules were those of the college game, with a few changes. The games were 48 minutes long, as opposed to 40 in the NBL; six fouls were permitted instead of five because of the longer games; and zone defense was not allowed. Though the rules meant to stress college play, most coaches and players tended towards a more physical style because it was simply more effective; also, the owners knew from their experience with hockey that a little fight now and then was good for business. Rough stuff was quietly encouraged along with the faster play.

The Knicks and the Huskies played in the league's first game on November 1, 1946. The Knicks won 68-66 in Toronto and went on to a 33-27 season overall. New York's success was crucial for the league because of the publicity a good team there could draw for the league. The league's best team that first year was the Washington Capitols, coached by Red Auerbach. Their 49-11 record stood for decades as the highest winning percentage ever, but the Philadelphia Warriors took the first BAA title behind their big scorer, Joe Fulks.

Fulks is credited with inventing the jump shot. Though it's hard to imagine a basketball game without jumpers, up until Fulks, shots were either layups or set shots put up with two hands. Teams had trouble defending this new wrinkle to the game and he led the league in scoring with a 23.2 points a game average at a time when a high point man might average ten or twelve a game.

Fulks was the BAA's first big star, but the NBL had the best player in the game—George Mikan. While at DePaul in his college years, Mikan had dominated the college game by being the first true tall center in the game. In the 1920s Original Celtic great and later Knicks coach Joe Lapchick was called a giant because he was 6-foot-5; Mikan was 6-foot-10 and a great rebounder and shooter.

Opting for the Chicago American Gears of the NBL when he graduated in 1946, Mikan brought interest in basketball to a new level. At first this was fine for the BAA. To them any interest in professional basketball could only help. But soon the absence of the one real basketball superstar began to hurt the league.

The BAA's initial year was successful on a purist's level. The games were good, clean and fairly exciting. The problem was money. Operating in big arenas with lots of seats to fill and thousands of miles of expensive travel between cities, BAA franchises had high overheads. By the end of the season, Cleveland, Detroit and Pittsburgh couldn't last any longer. They folded, as did Toronto. The remaining teams were barely hanging on.

Ned Irish of the Knicks was willing to continue losing money in order to assure that the game would stay first-class so that it would eventually become a big league, but some of the owners that came in without a lot of money wanted to do whatever they had to in order to stay afloat.

A rift developed between Irish and most of the other owners that, while keeping the Knicks from getting a little extra help from the league when they needed it, acted as a checks and balances system. Irish's insistence on the best possible game played in the best venues evened out the strong business imperatives of the weaker teams, as represented by league commissioner Maurice Podoloff.

Troubles for Both Leagues

Before the 1947-48 season, the league made more changes. The Baltimore Bullets entered the league from the ABL and the two divisions were reorganized to cut down on travel. Second, the schedule was reduced from 60 games to 48. Third, the BAA instituted a draft of college players. This would keep the league out of intra-league bidding wars. They also added something called "territorial draft picks" so teams could fully exploit home-grown talent to increase interest.

The results were mixed. Fewer games meant less income as well as lower expenses and a draft didn't mean much when the players had other professional options available to them. On the plus side, the play itself was strong. The teams were close all season. New York added legend Joe Lapchick as coach to shore up this key franchise and the Warriors won the title again by beating the Bullets in six games.

Max Zaslofsky of the Stags and the Knicks' Carl Braun, who set a league record with 41 points

Naismith Memorial Basketball Hall of Fame

Adolph Schayes

From the start, the NBL and BAA had enjoyed relatively friendly relations. Between the 1946-47 and 1947-48 seasons, the leagues had agreed to a uniform contract for both leagues, a joint draft, trading between leagues and a championships series were resolved amiably during 1947-48, among with other issues.

Then Maurice Podoloff stirred things up. He convinced the Kautskys and the Pistons of the NBL that they should join the BAA. The Lakers, who had been building a dynasty in the NBL, jumped too, followed by the Rochester Royals, the other elite NBL team. For all practical purposes, the NBL was finished.

With its best teams gone, along with the mutually agreed upon non-raiding policy, the NBL continued, but on very wobbly legs. The BAA, though, went into the 1948-49 season as "the" major professional basketball league. The addition of four powerful teams and the sport's biggest name saved the league.

The only major college player that went to the NBL was Dolph Schayes, and even Schayes would have chosen the Knicks over the Syracuse Nationals if they had offered him a touch over the rookie salary cap.

The BAA now had twelve teams, so it returned to a 60-game schedule to accommodate the new franchises and maximize Mikan's exposure. Mikan led the league in scoring with 28.3 points a game to Fulks's 26 and other former NBL players made immediate impacts as well.

Bob Davies of Rochester topped everyone with 321 assists and teammate Arnie Risen had the best shooting percentage at .423. Rochester and Minneapolis had the two best records, but the Lakers eliminated the Royals in the division championship and then beat the Capitols to win the BAA title.

That summer, the NBL gave up and on August 3, 1949, the NBA was created. The BAA accepted six NBL teams—Syracuse, Tri-Cities, Sheboygan, Waterloo, Denver, and Anderson—as well as the Indianapolis Olympians, who were really the graduating University of Kentucky team gone professional together. With Providence and

in one game against Providence, emerged as new stars to watch. Still, the financial problems outweighed the on-court successes and the often public friction between Irish and Podoloff made the league look less first class than it aspired to be. Something more drastic had to happen if the BAA was to stay alive.

The situation in the NBL wasn't promising either. The owner of the American Gears pulled his team prior to the start of the 1947-48 season to start another league, which promptly collapsed.

The players were parcelled out to the other teams in the league—Mikan to the Minneapolis Lakers—and while this was probably the biggest year for the NBL, with more teams than it ever had and its best player rising in popularity, it was also clear that it could not expand very far with franchises in towns like Syracuse, Rochester and Sheboygan. The bottom line was that the NBL had the best players and the BAA had the best venues. A merger was obviously on its way.

the BAA's first Indianapolis team, the Jets, folding, the NBA had 17 teams. Finally, all the pieces were joined for one true professional basketball league.

Unfortunately, this one true league had 17 teams of varying levels of market, talent and fan support. One couldn't expect fans in New York to get excited about the Waterloo Hawks coming to town, and neither could one expect that the Hawks would be able to pay the expenses involved in travelling to New York. Ned Irish wasn't happy with this mix of big cities and small towns, but he was mollified by the way the teams were folded into the league.

Three divisions were formed and the NBL teams were inserted in ways that would force some of the smallest and least financially stable teams to incur the highest expenses. The scheduling was a mess though, and almost cost the league some of its hard won credibility. Teams in the Eastern and Central Divisions would play 68 games and teams in the Western would play 62. This was supposedly done to save the Western teams, like Anderson and Sheboygan, travel money, but it was more to preserve old BAA rivalries.

The anomaly was Syracuse, who played a Western schedule, but its record counted in the Eastern Division. Syracuse and Tri-Cities also played two extra games apiece versus Indianapolis and Anderson, respectively. In the end, ten teams played 68 games, four played 64 and three had 62 games.

The Minneapolis Lakers Take First NBA Title

The whole thing was so complicated that few fans cared to investigate, despite the fact that some good basketball was played. Mikan led all scorers with 27.4 points a game. Alex Groza of Indianapolis followed with 23.4. Joe Fulks, who only three years earlier was thought untouchable as a scorer finished eleventh. Dolph Schayes's Nats, Mikan's Lakers and Groza's Olympians won their divisions and in a tortuously involved playoff sys-

Naismith Memorial Basketball Hall of Fame

Bob Davies

tem, the Lakers came out on top again, winning their second straight championship and the first ever NBA title.

More stars were beginning to capture the public eye. As well as Mikan, Ed Macauley in St. Louis, Jim Pollard and Ken Sailors in Fort Wayne, and Ralph Beard in Rochester were responsible for drawing fans.

The first major repercussion of the 1949-50 season was the loss of six franchises that simply couldn't make it. Anderson, Sheboygan, Waterloo, Denver, Chicago and St. Louis all folded prior to 1950-51, and Washington called it quits during the season. This shakeout helped to concentrate quality players and build the teams that would guide the game all the way into the late 1960s.

Center Ed Macaulay went to the Celtics, now coached by Red Auerbach, and Bill Sharman came in the draft. Though they didn't pick college star Bob Cousy, the Celtics ended up with him when the Stags closed shop in October. Max Zaslofsky went to New York and playmaker Andy Phillips moved to Philadelphia.

The NBA was down again to a manageable eleven teams and two divisions, so they returned to a more normal schedule that was thrown askew somewhat by Washington's demise in January 1951.

Despite the inroads the NBA was making, college basketball was still king. Fans around the nation followed teams like City College of New York (CCNY), Long Island University (LIU), New York University (NYU), Bradley and Kentucky and doubleheaders at Madison Square Garden remained the game's biggest attraction. Professional ball was still a distant second in the public's mind. Then scandal shifted the balance.

In January of 1951, a college point shaving scandal broke. Players from Manhattan College, national champions CCNY, and LIU were indicted for altering the scores of games to help bettors, who in turn kicked back money to the players. Further investigations revealed many recruiting violations at the schools as well. Suddenly college basketball was seen as the dirty game and everyone involved with the NBA held their breath, waiting to see if the league would be implicated too.

And so they played on, with a storm on the horizon and something to prove. Minneapolis again had the best record at 44 and 24 to take the Western Division. Philadelphia won the Eastern with a 40-26 mark, but the Rochester Royals, who finished second to the Lakers, were a better team and proved it by making it to the finals against the Knicks. Dolph Schayes, the inventor of the high-

five, led the league with 16.4 rebounds a game and Mikan and Groza again finished one-two in scoring, with Ed Macaulay third.

By April, as the finals started, still no scandal had broken in the NBA. The Knicks, a strong team in the game's biggest market, had finally emerged as contenders and their series with Rochester was crucial to the league. It was hard fought, went seven games and caught the imagination of New Yorkers. Rochester took the deciding game in a 79-75 squeaker. The NBA made it through the year without taint from the college troubles and had managed to put on a great show. The fans did not come running immediately, but the league's credibility was now beyond question.

On October 31, 1950, Earl Lloyd of the Capitols became the first African-American to play in an NBA game. Chuck Cooper and Sweetwater Clifton also played regularly that season. Though blacks certainly faced problems in hostile cities like St. Louis, they would change the game forever and in time become its driving force.

Naismith Memorial Basketball Hall of Fame

Ed Macauley

Aside from its being first season of the NBA, 1950 was a watershed for professional basketball for another reason. As the NBL and BAA emerged as the dominant leagues in the mid- to late-1940s, African-American teams were left with fewer teams with which to play and fewer paying venues at which to play.

Barnstorming teams like the Rens found it harder to make money, and their one season in a "white" league was the NBL's last. The Globetrotters had an association with the BAA which took the place of any stated policy to exclude black players from the league. With Jackie Robinson playing for the Dodgers though, it was only a matter of time before African-Americans would be accepted, however belatedly, into the NBA.

On April 25, 1950, the first African-Americans were drafted by NBA teams. Walter Brown of the Celtics chose Chuck Cooper out of Duquesne and the Capitols picked Earl Lloyd of West Virginia State. Abe Saperstein, the founder and owner of the Globetrotters, was incensed, feeling that the NBA was stepping on his turf. Other owners were also unhappy because a Trotter warm-up game helped improved box office for the regular game and Saperstein threatened to boycott them. This only firmed Brown's resolve to break the color barrier.

Though the perception now is that the Celtics are somehow a "white" team, they have been a positive force for African-Americans in basketball throughout their existence. A few months after the draft, the Knicks bought Sweetwater Clifton's contract from the Globetrotters. The next season would finally see African-Americans playing professional competitive basketball in major arenas.

The Mikan Era

The years between 1948 and 1954 are often called the Mikan Era. The Minneapolis Lakers won the championship five times in that period, with the only interruption being the Royals in 1951. Mikan anchored the team at center and had other big men like Jim Pollard, Clyde Lovellette and Vern Mikkelsen around him. They were virtually unstoppable.

The Rochester Royals were the other elite team and featured Bob Davies, Arnie Risen and Bob Wanzer. They too dominated the rest of the league, but the one team they couldn't beat was the Lakers. Minneapolis had too much of a height advantage for the faster, more balanced Royals.

There were certainly other strong units. Fulks' Phillip and new scoring threat Paul Arizin led a tough Warriors squad. The Knicks made the finals three straight years from 1951 to 1953, but could never crack Minneapolis or Rochester.

Schayes and the Nats also were perennial contenders. Cousy and Sharman pulled the Celtics out of the cellar and pointed them towards the future. Still, it was the big men of the Lakers that set the pace for how the game was played.

It should have been a golden period for the league, with great talent and only two players—Alex Groza and Ralph Beard of the Olympians, formerly of Kentucky—involved in the college scandals from their school days, but the style of play that created the Laker dynasty had a detrimental effect on the game.

First, the tall Laker team meant that all the other teams were going bigger in order to match up with them. This in itself was not negative. As time went by, tall men in high school and college were developed more and proved that they were as capable athletes as any of the spunky, smaller players that dominated the game in its early years. The biggest problems came out of the style of play that emerged.

Unlike many of the other centers who would headline the NBA in later years, Mikan and his imitators, though fine athletes, had fairly limited games. They weren't great leapers, playmakers or shooters. The offense focused on dumping the ball into the big man for a layup. With no time restraint at this point on how long the offensive team could hold the ball, they could wait minutes for a good opportunity. This made for some very boring play.

Second, if a team couldn't match up in size or skill with a Mikan, they would try to get physical. Basketball in the Mikan Era was a very rough game and harkened back to the old style professional game. Players tried to earn respect quickly by showing that they couldn't be pushed around. Others tried to take other players out of their game with forty-eight minutes of shoving, hacking, hitting and so forth. Fistfights were common.

This could have been avoided had the referees been given any real power, but they were under orders from the owners to let the players play as much as possible in order to keep the action fast. "No blood, no foul" became the basic rule. When the refs did try to create some order, coaches, players and even owners would routinely berate them on the floor. Baiting refs was completely accepted. They had virtually no support from the league, and so they had little actual authority on the court. The image of thuggish basketball players that many thought had gone the way of cages was coming back.

The final, and most devastating, issue was deliberate fouling. When a game moved into the last minutes with a close score, the teams would usually foul opposing players on purpose in order to trade the one foul shot and get the ball back for a chance at a two point basket.

Obviously, the other team was on to this too and what should have been close, hotly fought games became free throw contests. The league tried to cut back on this in 1950-51 by putting in a jump ball after each free throw in the last three minutes of the game. All this did was start the fouling before the last three minutes. The league moved it down to two the next year, but that didn't have an appreciable effect.

Time to Change Some Rules

Though not every game fell apart because of these problems, enough did at crucial points for the league to get worried. In 1950, Minneapolis and Fort Wayne played a 19-18 game. The Pistons stalled the entire game and won in the final seconds. Four points were scored in the fourth quarter.

That same season, the Olympians beat the Royals 75-73 in triple overtime. It sounds exciting, but in the overtimes, each team held the ball for the length of the extra session to take a shot in the last seconds.

Fans got up and walked out after booing as much as they could. The Knicks and Celtics had a nationally televised foul-trading travesty that the network cut away from in the last minutes because it was so tedious. The league had to make rule changes, and fast.

Up through 1954, the league did try some new things. One important change was to expand the width of the free-throw lane from six feet to twelve. Big centers, namely George Mikan, had to post up further out and make a move to the hoop instead of just standing under it. Driving was also encouraged without a lane constantly jammed with bodies.

The league made the post-foul jump ball between the player who was fouled and his normal match up, since teams had their big men switch to and then foul smaller players to have the advantage at the tip. This didn't cut to the core though. After the Knicks-Celtics fiasco in the 1954 playoffs mentioned above, the league looked for a more drastic solution.

Danny Biasone, owner of the Nationals, had the answer. Biasone divided the average number of shots in a game by the length of the game and arrived at 24 seconds. This would give each team approximately 60 shots a game.

The ten-second limit on bringing the ball over was already in place and few players took all of that. There would be more than enough time for a team to execute. If they didn't, the ball would go over to their opponents.

To take care of the fouling problem, the league put in a limit on team fouls. Now, if a team had more than six fouls in a quarter, an extra shot would be added. What had been a one shot foul would now be a two shot one, and a two shot foul would become a three to make two. Offensive fouls were not counted against the team total and backcourt fouls became two shot fouls.

The NBA and professional basketball had made just the right move, with not a moment to spare. Tri-Cities had moved to Milwaukee in 1951, but the arrival of the baseball Braves had taken attention away from the city's first major league team and now the Hawks were in trouble. Indianapolis had folded in 1953. The bad experiences television had had with basketball kept them off what was slowly becoming a valuable outlet for exposure.

Ironically, George Mikan retired before the 1954-55 season ever started, possibly to some measure because of the new rules. The Lakers' deliberate offense would be impossible to execute under them and Mikan's best playing days were behind him anyhow.

Two new players entered the league from the draft: center Bob Pettit went to Milwaukee and high scoring Frank Selvy joined Baltimore, only to end up in Milwaukee as well after Baltimore folded three games into 1954. The NBA anxiously watched the 1954-55 season to gauge the effect the new rule changes would have.

What they saw was a game transformed. Four men—Neil Johnston of the Warriors, Arizin, Cousy and Pettit—all averaged over twenty points a game. Scores jumped and the games stayed exciting all the way through to the end. Running teams like the Celtics were suddenly racking up wins.

To finish the season with some poetic justice, Biasone's Nationals won the title by beating the Pistons 92-91 in a thrilling seventh game. The league had not just been saved; it had turned its product into a game that could start to dream of competing with the other major spectator sports.

The league was still riding through some tough financial times. The Milwaukee Hawks moved to St. Louis and Rochester was on the ropes, and the Lakers and Knicks were at the beginning of their long declines.

The Warriors won the 1955-56 title and generally things were looking up, but the game was still in transition. No team had really stepped up into the new rules and made the game their own as the Lakers had done earlier. Then Boston's Red Auerbach made a deal in the summer of 1956 that would make sports history.

Auerbach and the Celtics Dynasty

Red Auerbach grew up in Brooklyn and had all the fiesty toughness that the borough prides itself on. He was never particularly loved; he fought everyone from players to refs and he annoyed just about anyone with whom he came in contact, but he was a basketball genius. Auerbach had put together a good Celtics team, but they lacked height. Ed Macaulay was a fine player, but he wasn't a strong enough to compliment the fast backcourt of Cousy and Sharman. Auerbach wanted Bill Russell.

Russell was a 6-foot-9 center at the University of San Francisco who had led his team to 55 straight wins and two national championships. He was thin, unlike the meaty Mikan and Lovellette, and he had drive. He didn't score a lot of points in school and never did in his professional career either, but he was the kind of man that centered a team both as a player on court and as a man off the court. Auerbach wrangled a deal with the Hawks, sending them Macaulay and rookie Cliff Hagan for the rights to draft Russell, and the Boston Celtics dynasty began.

Russell played for the 1956 United States Olympic basketball team so he didn't join the Celtics until December, but Boston had already jumped to a 13-3 start by the time he came on board. Auerbach had also picked up forward Tommy Heinsohn in the draft and had added Arnie Risen from Rochester, so Russell wasn't the only improvement to the team, but he was the clincher. Russell's presence in the middle did two things for the Celtics.

First, on defense he was the most active and intimidating big man the game had ever seen. Russell was a master at blocking shots, something which hadn't figured prominently in the game before. What was more, Russell didn't just knock the ball into the stands; he blocked it towards his teammates. This powerful new element took stress off the less defensively minded Cousy and Sharman and also made opposing offenses more tentative. Russell also cleaned the boards in a way no one ever had. In his 48 games, Russell averaged 19.6 rebounds a game, which was 2.2 boards more per game than Maurice Stokes, whose 1256 were the most in the league.

Once Russell either rebounded the ball or blocked it, he became an offensive weapon by triggering the fast break. He would toss the outlet pass to Cousy, who thrived on the transition game. Cousy would then either take the shot——he aver-

aged 20.6 points a game in 1956-57—or dish to Sharman or Heinsohn. Russell was as dominating on the offensive boards as he was on the other end, which also helped the Celtics' scoring. Russell was a new kind of center. He didn't rely on his physical gifts; he used them. He was a great athlete who happened to be tall.

The Celtics never looked back. At least not until the finals. They finished the season at 44-28 and blew past Syracuse to face the St. Louis Hawks in the finals. With Bob Pettit already at center, the Hawks had picked up Slater Martin from the Knicks to run the team from the point. Though they wound up 34-38 in the Western Division, they shone in the playoffs and reached the finals. No one thought the Celtics would have trouble dispatching St. Louis, but the series went down to the seventh game, carried live on television.

Boston appeared to take control any number of times and then the Hawks would fight back.

AP/Wide World Photos

Red Auerbach (left, with cigar)

Two free throws by Pettit in the waning seconds put the game into overtime at 103 all. At the end of the first overtime, it was knotted at 113. With only two seconds left in the second overtime, the Celtics led 125-123. The Hawks had one last shot. The ball went in to Pettit, whose shot bounced off the rim. The Celtics won and won beautifully before a national audience. The NBA was very happy.

So were the Celtics, and they would remain happy for many years to come. From 1957 to 1969, the Boston Celtics won eleven NBA titles, including eight in a row. Their accomplishments showed that basketball had an almost unlimited potential, that a standard of excellence could be established against which all other teams would be judged. The Yankees did it for baseball and the Montreal Canadiens did it for hockey. With their unprecedented hold on the NBA crown, the Celtics raised basketball one more notch in the public's estimation.

No one thought a dynasty was in the offing during the 1957-58 season. The Hawks wanted revenge for their heartbreaking loss the year before and got it, defeating the Celtics four games to two in the finals, due in large part to an ankle injury to Russell. Other shifts took place as well. Fort Wayne and their tiny auditorium couldn't keep up with the bigger clubs and finally moved to Detroit. Rochester fell to the same fate and became the Cincinnati Royals.

The Celtics sent the message in 1958-59 that they were at the top for good. Russell led the league in rebounds with 23 a game; Cousy led in assists with 8.6. No Celtic cracked the top five in scoring, but all the starters were among the top twenty. Their record was 52-20 and they blanked the Lakers four games to none in the finals.

The Lakers got as far as they did with an aging team mostly on the strength of their rookie forward Elgin Baylor. Baylor's acrobatic style pioneered the kind of high flying, above the rim game we are used to today. After this cakewalk season, teams started to wonder if the Celtics could be stopped. Was there anyone who could match up against Russell? And Cousy? And Heinsohn?

The Chamberlain/Russell Rivalry

If ever there was one man who could take on a whole team, it was the next force to enter the NBA—Wilt Chamberlain. The Philadelphia Warriors selected Wilt as a territorial draft pick while he was still in high school. Chamberlain went to Kansas for college, where his commanding play took the Jayhawks to the National Collegiate Athletic Association (NCAA) finals.

North Carolina beat Kansas by overplaying Chamberlain to an almost embarrassing level and Wilt was branded a loser, a name he was never able to escape throughout his career. After leaving Kansas in his junior year, he toured with the Globetrotters for a year and then came to the Warriors for the 1959-60 season. The Celtics would still dominate the NBA, but Wilt was the one man who could take on Russell and the two began a rivalry that Magic and Bird never approached for intensity and ferociousness.

Given his size, his talents and his boundless ego, Wilt was born to be at the center of things all his life. Unfortunately, he was at the center of more controversy than he was celebration. Throughout his career, Chamberlain was compared with Russell and was usually judged the lesser of the two.

His talents were awesome. No one had ever scored the way he did. He could do anything he set out to do. When he was blasted for not passing enough, Wilt went out and led the league in assists. Whether or not this was good for the team was another issue, and that was, and remains, the point that put Russell over Wilt. Chamberlain didn't play on winners.

In fairness, it must be said that the Celtics were better than just about every team Wilt played on. Many feel that Wilt never understood the concept of team basketball. It seemed that he saw a successful team as the aggregate of its talent, not as a product of five men playing together. Another, future, superstar, Michael Jordan, learned this lesson and assumed the role not only as scorer but as team leader as well, something Wilt was late in becoming.

All of these issues aside, Wilt Chamberlain was to rewrite the record books. In his rookie year, Wilt averaged 27 rebounds and 37.6 points a game. He had seven games with 50 or more points. Plus, he played all 48 minutes of almost every game he played. Wilt was both Rookie of the Year and Most Valuable Player (MVP). Philadelphia improved to a 49-26 record, but Wilt's team went down against Boston in the Division finals, an occurrence that was to become common in the next decade. Boston went on to win the title again over the Hawks, but everyone wanted to see more of Chamberlain versus Russell.

Now that the underlying problems with the NBA had been solved, the two huge names of Russell and Chamberlain became only the first of many great young stars to emerge in the early 1960s that basketball fans could concentrate on.

Smooth, controlled guard Oscar Robertson joined the Royals in 1960 after his senior year at Cincinnati. He scored 30.5 a game and led the league with 690 assists. He was the ultimate guard and many feel the game's finest all around player ever.

In the same year, Jerry West graduated and went to the Lakers, who had just moved to Los Angeles from Minneapolis. West, a guard, became "Mr. Outside" to Baylor's "Mr. Inside" and started the Lakers' climb back up to contention.

The next season, Walt Bellamy signed with the new Chicago Packers and averaged 27.9 points in his debut year. Clearly the level of play in the NBA was stepping up. Jump shooters finally took over as the prime offensive threat, sending the two-handed set shot into retirement.

Fifteen players scored over 19 points a game in 1959-60, aided in part by the speeded up game produced by the 24-second clock. But the story remained the Celtics and Wilt. In 1960-61, the Celtics took the title again, topping the Hawks four games to one. Wilt upped his scoring to 38.4 points a game and hauled in 55 rebounds in a game against Boston. The schedule expanded to 80 games.

1961-62 saw few changes in the standings. The Celtics won the title. Wilt's Warriors finished second in the East and the Knicks were last for the third year running. The Chicago Packers were added, came in last and changed their name to the Zephyrs.

The real news was Wilt, who put on the greatest show of offense over a season the game has ever seen. Chamberlain averaged 50.4 points a game, scoring 4029 points, and still brought down 25.7 rebounds. On March 2, 1962 in Hershey, Pennsylvania, Wilt poured in 100 points against the Knicks, winning 169-147. The next season Wilt slipped down to a 44.8 average for the Warriors, who had moved to San Francisco during the summer.

As he continued to post numbers that may never be reached again in the NBA, Chamberlain heard more and more criticism that he was selfish, took too many shots, and didn't always try hard.

Since Wilt's shooting percentage was 12 points better than the rest of the team, his team would have had no chance at all if he passed up shots. And those who rapped Chamberlain for not trying often felt he was ruining the game with his big numbers. Wilt's strident nature only fueled the debate.

Bob Cousy announced his retirement in 1962-63 and made his farewell tour of the NBA as the Celtics broke in another blue-chip player named John Havlicek en route to winning their fifth straight title.

The Zephyrs' new name did not help; they went 25-55 and became the Baltimore Bullets after the season's finish. The Syracuse Nationals also gave up and were bought by two businessmen who renamed them the 76ers and brought the team to Philadelphia to fill the void left by the Warriors.

With the Nationals gone, an era had ended. The NBA was now playing in only major metropolitan areas of the country and Maurice Podoloff was able to stitch together a new television deal during the 1962-63 season. Attendance at NBA games continued to rise and when Podoloff finally decided to retire in 1963, he left a game that had weathered some very difficult years and was looking ahead to better ones.

All-Star Game Threatened by Labor Dispute

In truth, Podoloff was also leaving some major problems for his successor, Walter Kennedy. The television situation needed to be addressed. Throughout the NBA's history, television had run hot and cold on the game. After the Celtics' dramatic win over the Hawks in 1957, television came running. But when Boston seemed to have a lifetime hold on the championship and the game had so many high scorers besides Wilt, like Robertson, Bellamy and Baylor, contests were considered too fast and too high scoring. And television networks were skittish again. Podoloff's make-shift network was not enough.

Even more important were some looming labor disputes between the players and the owners. The players had been asking for a pension plan for years and the league had never fully addressed the issue. With revenues increasing for owners and the workload increasing for the players, the men who played the game wanted to share in the financial security that they had helped to create for the owners. As the years went by and Podoloff did not advance the discussion, the players finally decided to take action, action which would test Kennedy's resolve, power and integrity.

The league had put together another loose network of television stations to carry the 1964 All-Star game in hopes that it would draw in major network interest in the playoffs. A few hours before the game, Chamberlain, Baylor, Russell, West, Robertson and the other great names threatened to strike the All-Star game if they didn't get a pension agreement right then and there. Panic ensued. Not all the owners were there and the stations climbed the walls, waiting to see if they'd have a show or not.

Finally, with just minutes to go before the tip off, Kennedy walked into the locker room and said that while he couldn't contact all of the owners, he gave the players his personal word that pensions would be addressed at the next owners' meeting. The players gave in and Kennedy kept his word. After the season, a pension plan was created.

With Cousy gone, the other teams looked for chinks in the Celtics' armor but found none. Boston loped to a 59-21 record and took a sixth NBA championship. K. C. Jones took over the play-making role from Cousy, finishing third with 5.1 assists per game to Oscar Robertson's leading 11. Forward John Havlicek was now the high point man for Boston. Russell's older legs started to show despite his 24.7 rebounds a game, as Chamberlain overpowered him in the Finals but couldn't overpower the whole team.

Television was back on board for 1964-65, but the fans were watching a high school kid in New York named Lew Alcindor who was 7-foot-1 and winning everything. Who could blame them? The script was the same every year—Boston would roar out to a lead in the standings, no one could catch them, then they'd destroy whoever won the West in the Finals. Then San Francisco cut a deal with the Sixers that made everything exciting again.

Right after the All-Star game, the Warriors sent Wilt Chamberlain back to Philadelphia for $150,000 and three players. Now Wilt and Russell would be face to face again and this time Chamberlain would have a better team around him. The Warriors weren't winning, or drawing crowds, with Wilt, so they had a chance to cut their payroll and rebuild. The Sixers now had a chance to challenge the Celtics.

Philadelphia had a slow first half, but Wilt pushed them over into the playoffs and the matchup everyone was waiting for—the Celtics and Sixers in the Eastern Division Finals. It went seven games and came down to the last seconds. Wilt Chamberlain's growing advantage over Russell let him pull the Sixers to within one point, but he dropped a pass with only seconds to go and Celtics had the ball. All Bill Russell had to do was inbound the ball and let his team kill two seconds.

Russell threw the ball in, hitting a support wire behind the basket. Sixers' ball. Philadelphia set up for their last shot. Hal Greer tossed the ball towards Chet Walker, but John Havlicek zipped in front and stole the pass. Boston won again and Celtics' announcer Johnny Most's call—"Havlicek stole the ball!"—has become immortal. Though the Celtics did it for a seventh time, they were showing signs of weakness. It was time for a new champion.

The drama carried over in 1965-66. Red Auerbach announced that this would be his last season coaching the Celtics, so Boston had some very strong emotional reasons for gunning hard at their eighth straight championship. Heinsohn was gone and Havlicek stepped up to his place. The Sixers picked up hot rookie Billy Cunningham to shore up the backcourt and, more importantly, they had Wilt for all 80 games. Chamberlain had a new contract for $100,000 and Russell literally one upped him by asking for $100,001. The lines were drawn.

Boston moved out to an early lead in the East and held a three game lead in the loss column in mid-February. Then the Celtics dropped three in a row. The Sixers jumped on the opening. They won three straight, then pounded the Celtics in back to back games. Philadelphia finished the season 55-25, one game up on the Celtics.

Someone had finally knocked Boston off the hill. That was only one battle though; the war wasn't over. In the second round of the playoffs, the Celtics got revenge and downed the Sixers in five games to face Los Angeles in the finals.

The Lakers had added two rookies from University of California, Los Angeles (UCLA), Walt Hazzard and Gail Goodrich, who picked up some of the slack for Elgin Baylor and his deteriorating knees. Los Angeles surprised everyone by taking the first game. Then Red Auerbach surprised everyone even more by naming his successor—Bill Russell.

Russell would become the first African-American to coach not only a basketball team, but any major league sporting team. Fired up by the announcement, the Celtics went on to win the series and the last of their eight consecutive championships. The league would have to wait another year for a new champion.

The 1966-67 season was a new start for the NBA and for some of its players. Chicago came back into the league for good with the Bulls, who

were solid enough to make the playoffs in their first year. Russell now wore two hats and Wilt learned how to wear his one to best effect. After leading the league in scoring for seven straight years, Chamberlain finished third behind sophomore star Rick Barry of San Francisco and Oscar Robertson. Wilt did win his second MVP award in a row because he was finally surrounded by winners.

New coach Alex Hannum, a veteran of the early days of the BAA and NBL, convinced Larry Costello to come out of retirement to help the backcourt and added another promising guard, Wally Jones. The Sixers powered out to one of the NBA's greatest seasons ever, winding up 68-13.

Wilt's job was to score of course, but he could now concentrate on rebounding—in which he led the league with 24.2 a game—and on passing. Wilt actually led the Sixers in assists and was third in the league. Plus, Chamberlain played a level of defense he had never played before.

While the Sixers thrived, the Celtics were thriving too, but not enough. Their 60-21 record was not enough to catch Philadelphia. Their meeting in the Division Finals had all the electricity of a championship series. The Sixers took a three games to none lead, then the Celtics struck back in Game Four. If the Sixers blinked, Boston was still dangerous enough to come back.

Game Five was a blow-out. The Sixers demolished Boston and the streak was over. Philadelphia wiped out the newly resurgent Warriors, with Barry, Jeff Mullins and center Nate Thurmond, four games to two in the finals and for the first time since 1957, the NBA had a new champion.

Other teams were now making noises around the league that they were ready to challenge. The post-Wilt Warriors had made it to the finals and looked to be a force in the future. The Knicks and their young center Willis Reed would also have college sensation Bill Bradley back from Oxford on his Rhodes Scholarship to add to their maturing team. Blazing rookie Earl Monroe was ready to help turn the Bullets into contenders too. But talent was not the only aspect of the league that was expanding. The NBA was expanding for the 1967-68 season, and so was the entire professional basketball scene.

NBA Gets Competition

In the late 1960s, interest was high in professional basketball and it was clear that the pool of available talent was growing larger. A group of California businessmen saw an opportunity. If they could put together a rival league and hold on long enough to draw both some money and some attention away from the NBA in markets where the NBA did not have a presence, the league would invite them into the big show where the real money was.

Rumors of a competing league swirled around the NBA in the mid-1960s, so when the American Basketball Association (ABA) announced its existence in February 1967 for the 1967-68 season, the league was not surprised nor unprepared. The NBA added two new West Coast teams, the Seattle SuperSonics and the San Diego Rockets, and planned two more for the year after that for Phoenix and Milwaukee.

The ABA forced the NBA into expanding, which it was planning to do anyway, but it had a number of other serious effects on the league and the game. First, by increasing the number of jobs available playing basketball and offering the majority of those jobs to African-American players, the ABA allowed the black aesthetic which had usually been just one aspect of the NBA game to be the dominant style of play throughout the league.

By the late 1960s, NBA basketball was an up-tempo game. The end of the Celtics and the rise of the quick, bench-deep, role-playing Warriors proved that things would only get faster. With new players like Monroe, Walt Frazier, Walt Hazzard and other creative men on the floor, moves were becoming more important as well.

The ABA didn't grow into that kind of game, though. It started out fast and showy. Going above the rim was not the privilege of a few superstars; it was the norm. The three-point shot, 30 second

Naismith Memorial Basketball Hall of Fame

Red Holzman

clock, red, white and blue ball and forward oriented play contributed to a way of playing that stressed style. Style seeped across the line into the NBA very quickly and accelerated a change that was already coming.

As well as changing the style of play, the increased participation of African-Americans in the ABA began a higher level of identification of blacks with the sport. As the civil rights movement forged ahead, the existence of a professional league that focused primarily on black talent became a source of pride.

During the Chamberlain-Russell years, the NBA had presented two kinds of African-American role models. Wilt was an individualist and a Republican while Russell came to represent the consummate liberal team player. In their own way, each had become valid and powerful images of

ALL-TIME WINNINGEST COACHES

	Wins	Losses	Pct.
Red Auerbach	938	479	.662
Jack Ramsey	864	783	.525
Dick Motta	856	863	.498
Bill Fitch	845	877	.491
Lenny Wilkens	815	721	.531
Cotton Fitzsimmons	805	745	.519
Gene Shue	784	861	.477
Don Nelson	719	493	.593
John MacLeod	707	657	.518
Red Holzman	696	604	.535

black success, but even that appeared to be within a white structure. The ABA helped to shift the balance of power in professional basketball to African-Americans by basing its existence on them and not pretending otherwise.

Salaries Begin to Climb

Another long-lasting impact the ABA had was on how players were acquired and signed. A competing league in a sport that was already paying some big numbers to its top players meant bidding wars. Salaries would escalate to a level that exceeded what would be deemed a reasonable reflection of the actual work done by an athlete. This was the starting point for seven- and eight-figure deals for sports figures.

These battles would not be confined to only men already in the NBA; it also meant that NBA teams would have to fight and pay dearly for college draft picks, too. The ABA further complicated this by not holding to the NBA standard which demanded that a rookie could not play until his college class had graduated. By going after college, and even high-school, players, the ABA opened the door for hardship cases in both leagues.

The increased leverage represented by the ABA also gave further bargaining power to those players who intended to stay in the established

league. Even before the ABA was formed, the mere rumor of its existence, along with a threat to strike the playoffs, allowed the NBA players' association to work out an improvement in their pension plan with the owners.

The ABA opened with eleven teams in New Jersey, Pittsburgh, Kentucky, Indiana, Minnesota, New Orleans, Anaheim, Oakland, Dallas, Houston and Denver. Since the NBA considered these off markets and most teams were solvent enough to deal with the challenge of higher salary costs, the league never declared all out war on the ABA. Instead, it tried to ignore the new league, but try as it may, the NBA could not forget about it. Prior to the 1967-68 season one of the NBA's brightest young stars, Rick Barry, announced that he was jumping to the Oakland Oaks of the ABA. A legal battle ensued.

The Warriors held that Barry's contract with them contained an option clause that he had to respect. The judge ruled that Barry had to respect the option by not playing with any team other than the Warriors, but once the year was over he was a free agent. Barry went to the Oaks' broadcasting booth for a year and the ABA had won its first skirmish with the NBA. Other players would jump and some jumped back, even before the season started.

The 1967-68 NBA season had some surprises on the court that kept attention on the senior league's new 82 game schedule. The Sixers were the favorites to win it all again and establish a new dynasty in Philadelphia. Wilt had found himself. His points were down to 24.3 a game, third in the league behind Dave Bing of Detroit and Elgin Baylor, but he led in field goal percentage, rebounds, and assists. The Sixers finished 62-20, eight games up on the second-place Celtics.

In the West, the Barry-less Warriors came in third and weren't able to get past the first round of the playoffs. The Lakers made it to the finals, but they didn't face whom they'd expected. In a hard fought series, the Celtics beat the Sixers in seven games, and then went on to take Los Angeles in six. Just when everyone thought they were dead, the Celtics were champions again.

New players and new teams continued to give the NBA primacy in the professional basketball market. The disappointment of their second round ouster by the Celtics ended the Sixers unit. Chamberlain was traded to Los Angeles for three players and the Lakers had the biggest star of all to put into their new arena, the Forum. The St. Louis Hawks moved to Atlanta and the Phoenix Suns and Milwaukee Bucks took their first shots in the 1968-69 season.

Rookie Elvin Hayes of San Diego won the scoring title but another rookie, Wes Unseld, provided the biggest headlines. The Bullets center was named Rookie of the Year and MVP for his role in leading his team to the Eastern Division title. Unseld was shorter than both Russell and Chamberlain, but his strength and rebounding ability began a cycle of smaller centers.

Once and for all, the Celtics appeared dead. They finished with their worst record in 13 years, 48-34, good only for fourth in the East. Unfortunately for Baltimore, the Knicks wiped them out four straight in the first round of the playoffs. The Celtics, in turn, dispatched with New York in six and the last of the great Russell-Chamberlain confrontations was slated for the finals.

As usual, it was tough all the way, but player/coach Russell had the last word. Boston edged out a 108-106 victory in Game Seven to win their eleventh title in 13 years. Russell retired after the series and the Celtic dynasty finally passed into legend.

The ABA was still trying to settle down into some semblance of the regularity necessary for a professional league. Teams shifted around and the cast of a handful of stars like Barry, Connie Hawkins, Doug Moe and Larry Brown surrounded by journeyman players getting a second chance and lesser known college grads had yet to catch on. The NBA also struck back in a few ways in 1969-70 that seemed to put the ABA on the ropes.

First, Connie Hawkins jumped to the NBA. A brilliant player, Hawkins had not made it to the NBA because of fixing allegations when he was a freshman at Iowa. Though he was never indicted, the controversy destroyed his already tenuous academic career and tarnished his reputation. Hawkins was a journeyman until the ABA picked him up, and he could not pass up the chance to star in the NBA. He led the Suns with 24.6 points a game and 391 assists, and was second on the team with 846 boards.

Knicks Garner New Fans for NBA

Second, the rise of the Knicks gave an enormous boost to the NBA. Since the league's inception, it had been waiting, although trying at times to thwart Ned Irish and the team's best interests, for the Knicks to win a title. A winner in the world's media center would bring huge amounts of publicity to the NBA. Though the Knicks were a power under Joe Lapchick in the first years of the league, they fell into the cellar during the late 1950s and early 1960s. Now, after some years of rebuilding, the Knicks were contenders again.

Crowd favorite Willis Reed, scholar Bill Bradley, stylish Walt "Clyde" Frazier, and Dave DeBusschere along with coach Red Holzman, led the Knicks to a 60-22 season and became the first team that was covered for its personality as well as its play. New York, and the New York press, loved the Knicks and made them the biggest sports story of the year. Their drive to the title, capped by a dramatic seven game final series against Chamberlain and the Lakers, brought more people to the NBA than probably any team before.

Third, Lew Alcindor signed with the Milwaukee Bucks rather than the ABA. Highly touted since his high school days, Alcindor was another dominating big man in the Russell/Chamberlain mold that people would pay to see play. His presence in the ABA would have immediately legitimized the junior league and increased revenues dramatically. Instead, he went to Milwaukee, came in second in scoring to Jerry West and third in rebounding.

Alcindor also had the advantage of being a soft-spoken, introspective man whose personal beliefs later brought him to Islam and the name Kareem Abdul-Jabaar. Alcindor's conversion in

1971 raised some eyebrows, but his sincerity, integrity and intelligence won over any detractors. The NBA had a new, towering drawing card that combined Russell's personal attractiveness with much of Wilt's talents.

The ABA fought back. On the court, the Denver Nuggets signed Spencer Haywood, a college sophomore. Unfortunately for the Nuggets, the NBA decided to soften its rules on hardship cases the next season and Haywood jumped to Seattle for the 1970-71 campaign. Since their goal had always been a merger, the ABA began to press harder for it after Alcindor's choice of the Bucks.

The ABA filed suit against the NBA for antitrust violations, forcing the two leagues to finally sit down and work out a merger agreement. The owners were happy, but the players weren't. They liked having options and they had certainly benefitted from the bidding wars, so the players association blocked the move. Until the league made some serious concessions to the players, the NBA and the ABA would be separate.

The NBA continued its expansion into the 1970-71 season. The Buffalo Braves, Cleveland Cavaliers and Portland Trail Blazers came aboard. The league now had 17 teams and four divisions: Atlantic, Central, Midwest and Pacific.

Though it's common for the champions to be favorites for the next title, Knicks fans saw the handwriting on the wall when Oscar Robertson joined Alcindor and the Bucks in Milwaukee. The Big O was the perfect complement to Alcindor's tough inside game. The Bucks ran off a record 20 straight wins and finished with a 66-16 record. Alcindor's 31.7 points a game was tops in the league and he earned the MVP award, as the Bucks blew past all comers and easily blanked the Bullets in the Finals, four games to none.

All the talk of Alcindor, who now by the 1971-72 season had become Jabbar, stirred up Chamberlain's blood. There were still two big men in the NBA and though getting older, Wilt had something to prove. Around the league, many said that Jabbar's Bucks were one of the greatest teams ever, but they hadn't seen the 1971-72 Lakers. Coached by former Celtic Bill Sharman, the Lak-

ers strung together a 33 game winning streak, scored over 100 points in 81 of 82 games and sprinted to a 69-13 record. All of these marks still stand.

Milwaukee had a fine season too, but Robertson was downed by an injury and didn't play much in the Western Conference Finals versus the Lakers. Los Angeles won four games to two and pasted the Knicks 4-1 in the championship series. Overall, the Lakers went 81-16 for the season and remain to many the finest basketball team ever.

ABA Gets Infusion of New Talent

The ABA seemed to be on its last legs. NBA interest was booming even before the classic Lakers glided to the top, but the interest was not crossing over. Then the Virginia Squires signed a University of Massachusetts sophomore named Julius Erving. Another sophomore, George McGinniss, also joined the league and suddenly the ABA had two of the hottest players in professional basketball. Though Rick Barry returned to the Warriors for the 1971-72 season, the ABA found itself with new life.

A shift was starting. The Knicks took the title in 1972-73, but with little of the fanfare and ink that they had garnered in 1969-70. Boston's new center Dave Cowens, another smaller pivot man in the Unseld vein, along with Jo Jo White and the aging Havlicek sent notice that the Celtics were back with their 68-14 record and looked to take it all until the Knicks stopped them in the Conference Finals.

The Rockets had moved to Houston in 1971 and now the Royals went to Kansas City-Omaha, becoming, more specifically, the Kings.

Young gunners like Pete Maravich and Tiny Archibald posted big numbers and Ernie DiGregorio piled up assists in Buffalo, but Dr. J, Julius Erving, was lighting things up in the ABA. When he moved to the New Jersey Nets in 1973-74, the NBA had to see what was happening. The New York metropolitan area was always hungry for a new star and a player of Erving's calibre there would draw a great deal of attention to the league. Then someone even bigger moved to the ABA—Wilt Chamberlain.

Wilt left the Lakers and signed as player/coach with the San Diego Conquistadors. A legal ruling similar to the one in the Rick Barry case put Chamberlain squarely into a coach's role for the 1973-74 season and he never returned to active play again, but the NBA had lost its greatest star to the upstarts.

Robertson and Willis Reed were retiring after the season, too, and Jerry West was also going to the ABA. The league wasn't panicking, but clearly things could be a lot better.

Walter Kennedy left the commissioner's office prior to the 1974-75 season, replaced by Larry O'Brien. Just as Kennedy had inherited problems from Maurice Podoloff, O'Brien found difficulties waiting for him when he took over. The ABA had never reached the level of financial stability and market share to seriously threaten the NBA for pre-eminence, but it had made inroads and its high-flying extravagance was gaining fans.

Neither the New Orleans Jazz, the NBA's latest expansion team, nor the 1974-75 champion Golden State Warriors managed to excite the basketball world. More and more, the NBA was being perceived as little other than a full court run and shoot game.

Though the NBA was still willing to merge with the ABA and the viable ABA teams were very eager to merge with them, Kennedy and the owners had not solved the labor issues that the players association wanted dealt with before any union would be possible. O'Brien would have to clear these things up before the league could move ahead.

On the court, there were few surprises in 1975-76. Bob McAdoo of the Buffalo Braves won his third straight scoring title and Boston won the championship with Dave Cowens's more working class version of the Celtics. The important things took place off the court. The New Jersey Nets and the Denver Nuggets applied to the NBA for membership. A merger was definitely in the offing.

By February of 1976, O'Brien and league attorney David Stern had hammered out a landmark agreement with the players association. The option clause would be taken out of all rookie contracts starting the next season. For veterans who wanted to solicit better offers when their contracts ran out, the league would allow other teams to tender them offer sheets, which the player's current team would then have the right to match.

Also, starting in 1980, the NBA would eliminate the rule that forced a moving player's new team to compensate his old team with players or cash of a value equivalent to his. Finally, the owners agreed to pay a cash settlement to the players' association for expenses related to these ongoing legal battles. These terms broke new ground in major league sports and helped paved the way for similar agreements in baseball and football.

With this hurdle at last overcome, the NBA and the ABA announced their plans for a merger. In June of 1976, the owners of the Indiana Pacers, New Jersey Nets, Denver Nuggets and San Antonio Spurs all agreed to pay $3.2 million dollars each to the NBA for the right to join the league. Because the Nets would be invading the New York Knicks' turf, the Nets also had to pay an additional $4 million dollars directly to the Knicks. A draft was arranged for the NBA to pick up players from the now defunct ABA. Once again, the NBA was the sole major professional basketball league. The years ahead, though, would show that the ABA was the least of the NBA's problems.

NBA Encounters Some Problems

The NBA now had a new infusion of talent. Moses Malone, George Gervin, Artis Gilmore, and David Thompson were among the new stars that had come over from the ABA, bringing with them the kind of playground basketball that thrilled crowds when it was good and led to poor team play and sloppiness when it was bad. The years between 1976 and 1980 saw the NBA reach new physical heights on the court, but its reputation began to suffer because of a few factors.

ALL-TIME NBA LEADERS

Most Games Played • 1,560
Kareen Abdul-Jabbar

Most Field Goals Made • 15,837
Kareem Abdul-Jabbar

Most Field Goals Attempted • 28,307
Kareem Abdul-Jabbar

Most Minutes Played • 57,446
Kareem Abdul-Jabbar

Most Rebounds • 23,924
Wilt Chamberlain

Most Steals • 2,277
Maurice Cheeks

Most Assists • 9,921
Magic Johnson

Most Blocked Shots • 3,189
Kareem Abdul-Jabbar

Most Personal Fouls • 4,657
Kareem Abdul-Jabbar

Highest Scoring Average • 32.3 ppg
Michael Jordan

The first was the stylish brand of basketball that had taken over the game and was emerging with or without the new ABA men. Although it showcased a player's pure athletic skills and made for some great highlight film clips, this wide open, individual play was antithetical to the structured team play that championship basketball almost always features. It was not uncommon to hear players say after a game that they were happy if they had scored their points, even if their team lost. Not even Wilt at the peak of his arrogance and hunger for statistics ever claimed to not care whether his team won or lost. This rampant self-ishness cast the league in a bad light. It seemed that the players weren't in it to win, and that undermined the concept of the entire league.

Violence also became a serious issue in the late 1970s. Rough, physical play had always been an element of basketball, from the very first contest in Springfield, Massachusetts, to the modern professional game. Rule changes, personnel changes and cycles in the style of play meant that the level of rough play varied from period to period and two incidents in the 1977-78 season made it clear that the NBA had entered a new period of violence; violence at a level which could fatally harm the game if not checked.

In the first, Kareem Abdul-Jabbar knocked out rival center Kent Benson of the Milwaukee Bucks, breaking his own hand in the process. As well as the danger to Benson's well-being, neither the league nor the Lakers management were happy about losing Jabbar for the time it took his hand to heal. With salaries as high as they were, owners did not want to lose stars and therefore fans through extraneous violence.

The second incident was much more dangerous and left a black mark on the game that took years to erase. During an on-court scuffle, Kermit Washington of the Lakers saw Houston's star Rudy Tomjanovich come towards him and believed that Tomjanovich intended to hit him. Washington struck first. He threw a roundhouse punch that shattered Tomjanovich's jaw and sent him to the emergency room. Tomjanovich underwent surgery and his life hung in the balance for days. Washington received a stiff fine and a 60 day suspension.

The NBA had worked so hard in recent years to present basketball as a game of skill, speed and athleticism, to bury its roots as a sport full of fistfights and trashtalking, and now that was called into question. Stricter rules and enforcement of those rule were put in place, but the two fights added to the sense that the NBA was spinning out of control.

The final problem was drugs. No sport has ever been immune to substance abuse. Baseball and football lore abound with stories of players performing drunk and carousing into the night, and the culture of athletics tends to create an aura around sports figures which places them higher than "normal" people and not only forgives but celebrates their excesses as proof of their superiority. This was especially true when their excesses revolved around liquor.

When drugs invaded American society in the 1970s, liquor remained a socially acceptable substance to abuse, but drugs were rightfully condemned. Unfortunately, for all the condemnation, an enormous percentage of the population was using them and this percentage was higher in basketball, a sport with hundreds of young male athletes who made hundreds of thousands, and even millions, of dollars.

Many basketball players had been happy to accept the status and the seeming immunity that their talents had given them through high school, college and now the professional ranks. Unfortunately, fame and financial success had not necessarily made them wiser men. Drug use became widespread and visible. The league began to implement programs to deal with the problem, but the image remained of a sport shot through with stoned players. Tragedies loomed that would eventually force the NBA to break new ground in handling its players' drug use.

The more wide open game of these years meant a greater presence by West Coast teams, since even from the 1930s, the western part of the country played a full court, running style. Portland took the title in 1976-77 on the shoulders of UCLA star Bill Walton and Seattle won in 1978-79.

The Washington Bullets surprised everyone in the 1977-78 season, as Dick Motta, who had guided many great Bulls teams in the early 1970s, led Washington to the title.

With all the teams deeper from the infusion of ABA talent, big centers became important again. Men like Walton, Gilmore, and Jack Sikma took on Jabbar, though none approached him or his predecessors, Russell and Chamberlain. Given the bigger role that forwards took now, centers even at their most dominating would never run the

show the way they had. Top rebounders during these years averaged 14 to 16 a game, as opposed to the mid- and high twenties of Wilt and Russell.

Dr. J, the man who had kept the ABA breathing as long as it had, didn't stay with the Nets when they entered the league. He went to the Sixers and joined one of the period's greatest, most electrifying teams. With Erving, McGinniss, Doug Collins, World B. Free and "Chocolate Thunder" Darryl Dawkins, Philadelphia loved to score points, but they were denied a title until the 1980s.

Other developments included a swap between Boston owner Irv Levin and Buffalo owner John V. Brown. Not happy to just trade players, they traded their entire franchises with each other. Levin promptly moved the Braves to San Diego and renamed them the Clippers.

The Knicks and Nets also continued their battle for supremacy in the New York area, a battle which the Knicks won if not on the court, then in the league offices. The Nets were obliged to pay the Knicks another $4 million dollars for their share of the market.

The Situation Worsens

By 1980, the NBA was in serious trouble. Despite the athleticism displayed on the floors around the league, the problems outlined above had eaten away the public's interest. In 1980-81, 16 out of 23 teams lost money. Attendance was down one million from the year before.

As it had been in the past, television was skeptical about the game. Sponsors expressed concerns that the game was "too black," drug-ridden, and regional. The sixth and deciding game of the 1979-80 finals was not carried live on television, but broadcast on tape after the late news. *Los Angeles Times* published an article saying that 75 percent of NBA players used drugs.

Whether or not this was true was never proven, but the very fact that it could be debated was damaging. Adding the three-point shot in 1979-80 was not the solution that would bring back the fans. On the brink of collapse, the NBA

TOP TEN NBA CAREER SCORERS

	Yrs.	Minutes	Points	Average
Kareem Abdul-Jabbar	20	57,446	38,387	24.6
Wilt Chamberlain	14	47,859	31,419	30.1
Elvin Hayes	16	50,000	27,313	21.0
Moses Malone	16	44,200	27,016	21.7
Oscar Robertson	14	43,886	26,710	25.7
John Havlicek	16	46,471	26,395	20.8
Alex English	15	38,063	25,613	21.5
Jerry West	14	36,571	25,192	27.0
Adrian Dantley	15	34,151	23,177	24.3
Elgin Baylor	14	33,863	23,149	27.4

pinned its hopes on the two brightest rookies it ever seen in one year—Larry Bird and Earvin "Magic" Johnson.

The rivalry between Magic Johnson and Larry Bird went back to college. Magic went to Michigan State and Bird attended Indiana State. By far, they were the best in the college ranks. Both were extremely versatile and large, so they transcended one role on the court. They faced each other in the NCAA finals in 1979, a game which Michigan State won. It was a sad end to Bird's college career, but through the 1980s he would have many chances for revenge.

The Celtics had slipped down to the bottom of the league during the late 1970s and they drafted Larry Bird in the first round. Magic, though only a sophomore, went hardship and the Lakers chose him as the first pick overall in the draft. The matchup that had elevated college basketball would move to the pros.

Their impact was immediate on their teams, if not yet to fans. Magic's presence woke up Jabbar, who had been drifting out of games the last few years, and the Lakers went 60-22. Magic was basically a guard because of his playmaking instincts, but at 6-foot-8 he would have been a big center in earlier days. He could shift to forward or even take the pivot, as he did in the deciding

game of the 1979-80 finals when Jabbar was down with an injury.

Bird did some magic of his own in Boston. The Celtics had been 29 and 53 in 1978-79; in Bird's rookie year they went 61-21. Bird earned Rookie of the Year honors and only Dr. J's Sixers kept the Celtics out of the finals against the Lakers. The Lakers won it all, but it wouldn't count until they did it against the Celtics.

And the Celtics weren't napping. After years of leadership changes in the front office, Red Auerbach returned and took over management of the team. Boston added Kevin McHale at forward and Robert Parish at center. Another historic Celtic team had come together.

One of reasons Bird and Magic made such a difference to the league was the breadth of their abilities. They could dish the ball in ways once only done by the Globetrotters against patsy teams in exhibitions as well as score.

With a great cast of players now surrounding him, Bird could now display all the facets of his game and challenge the Lakers. Unfortunately, the challenge would have to wait another year. The Celtics ran off a 62-20 regular season record, but an injury to Magic held the Lakers to second place in the Pacific with a 54-28 mark. The Lakers couldn't get past the Rockets in the first round of the playoffs and Boston handled Houston easily in the finals.

Now it was the Lakers' turn to adjust. Pat Riley took over as head coach and changed the focus of the team away from Jabbar and onto Magic. "Showtime" had begun, but Riley's Showtime was different from the showtime of the late 1970s. The ABA-influenced, showy game stressed individual play, whereas Riley taught the Lakers how to use their individual games within a team structure.

Magic and Bird get most of the credit for saving the NBA in the 1980s, but coaches Pat Riley and the Celtics' Bill Fitch deserve their share as well. They saw that the talent of the players had gone beyond the offensive and defensive systems NBA teams used. Players were smarter, bigger, and more gifted than ever, which led to free-lancing on the court. Riley and Fitch created systems which made maximum use of their players, to the benefit of their teams, and thereby moved the entire game to a new level.

In 1981-82, Magic led his team in assists, steals and rebounds, which let Jabbar concentrate on scoring. The Sixers ousted the Celtics again from the playoffs, after finishing second to them in the regular season, and the Lakers in turn polished off the Sixers in six in the Finals. The dream final between Boston and Los Angeles would have to wait.

1982-83 was the Sixers' year, a pause in the Magic-Bird battle to let Dr. J finally win his one NBA title. Moses Malone came over from the Rockets and provided the MVP center play, which the team had needed to go over the top.

Malone led the team in points and rebounds, Maurice Cheeks ran the club from the point and Dr. J brought it all together. They dominated the league, going 65-17, and lost only one game in the playoffs. The Sixers capped it all with a 4-0 sweep of the Lakers.

League Experiences a Comeback

The rivalry between Magic and Bird, plus the Dr. J show in Philadelphia, had gone some of the way towards pulling the NBA back up to par with the other major professional sports, but the league was not out of the woods yet. New Orleans moved to Utah to become the oddly named Utah Jazz. Dallas lobbied for and finally won a franchise, dubbed the Mavericks. Rumors flew about other teams folding and possible mergers of franchises.

On the court, teams were simply scoring too many points. The 1982-83 Nuggets had three players—Alex English, Kiki Vandeweghe and Dan Issel—who each averaged over 20 points a game. As a team, Denver scored 123.2 and allowed 122.6. Though entertaining in short spurts, 48 minutes of uncontested shooting became boring fairly quickly.

Other teams were guilty of ignoring defense, too. The Spurs and Bucks played a 171-166 triple overtime game which Denver and Detroit topped in 1983, Detroit winning 186-184, again in triple overtime. 1983-84 was the year the league turned around.

The on court reason was that the Lakers and the Celtics finally met in the finals. For three out of the next four years, Los Angeles and Boston battled over the championship, as Magic and Bird both reached their playing peaks. Boston and Los Angeles each won their divisions in 1983-84 and Boston had the league's best record again at 62-20.

The finals went seven games and featured two overtime contests. The deciding game was carried live on television and drew the largest viewing audience in NBA history. The fans were back and their numbers increased as the Los Angeles-Boston rivalry continued.

The off-court reason was the departure of Larry O'Brien as NBA commissioner. David Stern, an attorney who in 1976 had helped to create the agreement with the players association and the merger plan, became the fourth commissioner of the NBA. Stern did not step away from the issues that faced the league. He saw his primary goal as making money not just for the owners, but for the league, the players, sponsors, television networks and anyone else doing business with the NBA.

ALL-TIME TOP PERFORMANCES

Most Points Scored in One Game • 100
Wilt Chamberlain, March 2, 1962 versus New York Knicks

Most Rebounds in One Game • 55
Wilt Chamberlain, November 24, 1960 versus Boston Celtics

Most Assists in One Game • 30
Scott Skiles, December 30, 1990 versus Denver Nuggets

Most Steals in One Game • 11
Larry Kenon, December 26, 1976 versus Kansas City Royals

Most Blocked Shots in One Game • 17
Elmore Smith, October 28, 1973 versus Portland Trail Blazers

The product was there. Though the perception remained from the high scoring teams like Denver and San Antonio that the game was somehow soft, the fact was that those teams weren't winning like Boston and Los Angeles were and that was beginning to make sense to other teams and to the public.

By marketing a more positive image of the game, revenues would increase and everyone would settle down to present the best possible product, which would create an even better image. The league put through two measures around this time that went a long way in bringing the NBA not only back to the level of the other professional leagues, but actually position it to go beyond them.

First, in 1983, the league put in place a salary cap that would limit the total expenditures a team could make on talent in a given season. This would keep free agency and bidding wars within a reasonable level without restraining a player's right to receive market value for his services. To compensate for any shortfall that might develop between players' values and the revenues they brought in, the league offered to give the players 53 percent of all revenues earned by marketing the league and the sale of broadcasting rights.

Second, the NBA instituted a drug policy. If a player admitted that he had a substance abuse problem, the league would help him find treatment with no recrimination save for it counting as one strike in his records.

If the problem recurred, the player would have one more chance, but if he violated the rules a third time, he would be barred from the league for life. Even though there was an appeal process, no player wanted to lose prime playing and earning years. By setting a firm and fair policy, the NBA led the way in professional sports in handling drug use by athletes and regained a large measure of respectability for facing up to this problem.

Enter Michael Jordan

A new force in the league also appeared in 1984—the one player who would become the cornerstone of the NBA's efforts to repackage itself as the sport of the 1980s and 1990s. His name was Michael Jordan.

The Chicago Bulls drafted him out of North Carolina in the first round of the 1984 draft and he immediately began to electrify crowds with his accurate shooting and seeming ability to defy gravity.

Though not abrasive in the way that Chamberlain could be, Jordan's abilities were on a level with Wilt's and he came in for much of the same kind of criticism during his first seasons in Chicago. Surrounded by a team of inferior talent, Jordan took a huge percentage of the Bulls' shots and made it clear that he didn't trust anyone else to score.

This approach did not work. Chicago improved to a playoff spot in 1984-85, but it would be years before the Bulls would rebuild to a contending level and Jordan would learn to work with his team instead of against it. In the meantime, the marketing of Air Jordan began.

1984-85 was another Celtics/Lakers year. In the Atlantic Division, Philadelphia posed the only threat to Boston's 63-19 record, finishing second on the strength of rookie Charles Barkley, known as "the Round Mound of Rebound" during his college days at Auburn. Barkley's height and bulk would have made him a center in earlier years, but his ability to run the floor and handle the ball put him at forward and showed the remarkable physical level NBA players were reaching.

The Denver Nuggets were the closest challengers to Los Angeles in the West, but they were still ten games back of the 62-20 Lakers. After cruising through the playoffs, the Celtics and Lakers met to decide things in the finals. Boston crushed Los Angeles 148-114 in Game One, but it was all Los Angeles after that. Los Angeles won the series four games to two and had finally beaten Boston head to head.

The Kings moved to Sacramento for the 1985-86 season and Georgetown star Patrick Ewing came to the Knicks to help raise their fortunes, but in 1985 the word was Bird. He led the Celtics in points, assists, rebounds, steals and minutes and finished in the league's top ten in five categories.

Bird captured his third straight MVP award, the first time anyone had done so since Wilt Chamberlain took three between 1965 and 1968, and brought Boston back to the finals.

In the West, a newcomer blocked the Lakers' path to rematch with the Celtics. Second year man Hakeem Olajuwon, a powerful Nigerian center, teamed up with former University of Virginia center Ralph Sampson to create a "twin towers" attack that bested Los Angeles four games to one in the conference finals, despite Los Angeles's eleven game advantage in its regular season record. Bird would not be denied, though, where Magic and Kareem had. The Celtics won the series easily in six.

With the league running more smoothly than it ever had and revenues increasing, the fans, the press and everyone involved with professional basketball hoped to finally sit back and enjoy the game. Hopes for a smooth season were crushed, though, soon after the 1986 draft.

Prior to the season's start, the Celtics knew they were getting older and Red Auerbach had staged a coup by getting an early first round draft pick and using it to select Maryland's Len Bias. Bias would be the key to the next generation of Celtics' dominance. Then tragedy struck.

While celebrating his new job with illegal drugs, Bias suffered a heart attack from cocaine. Other players had been ejected from the league under the anti-drug policy, but the death of this promising star had a deeper impact on the NBA and its players than any punitive action.

Suddenly, taking drugs was not even remotely acceptable. The league cracked down harder on drugs and implemented a program to help rookies, who were often millionaires in their early twenties, adjust to the pressures of playing in the NBA.

The game went on, despite the tragedy, and there were other topics at hand. The discussions had begun as to which team was the team of the 1980s—the Lakers or the Celtics. Each had won three championships in the decade and they had split the two finals they met in. To many, 1986-87 decided it, and in the Lakers' favor.

Though Bird had another great year, it was Magic's turn to have an MVP season. Along with forward James Worthy, Magic guided the Lakers to a 65-17 record. Pat Riley's "Showtime" game hit its peak, playing the finest example of fast paced, Western Conference basketball the league had ever seen.

Pistons' Play Reminiscent of the Early Days

The Celtics faced a strong challenge from a rising Detroit team with a style of its own. The Pistons with smooth Isaiah Thomas at guard and a front line of Bill Laimbeer, John Salley, Adrian Dantley and Dennis Rodman played a rough, physical game of basketball that harkened back to the old days.

Boston just got by them in seven in the Conference Finals to meet Los Angeles, where the Lakers were too much. Los Angeles won four games to two in the last of the great Laker-Celtics matchups. This rivalry between Magic and Bird and their teams had revitalized the game. Never ugly or bitter, the two teams battled with skill and brilliance and consistently displayed the sport at its best.

The Pistons, however, displayed to many the sport at its worst. Their emergence in 1987-88 as the most powerful team in the East was greeted with mixed notices, at best. The Pistons liked to use their bodies and the constant physical contact, though completely legal, felt like a step backwards to those who had appreciated the finesse games of both Boston and Los Angeles.

In truth, Detroit's game was just as valid a way of winning as any, but their swaggering, "Bad Boys" approach was what most bothered their detractors. Detroit dethroned Boston in the Conference Finals but the Lakers weren't done yet. In a hard fought, tight series, Los Angeles won the seventh game 108-105. Los Angeles had now won five of the last nine NBA titles.

As the Pistons had pushed forward as the next team to watch, Michael Jordan had flown over everyone to become the most potent and most visible player in the league. In 1986-87, Jordan racked up Wilt-like numbers with a 37.1 scoring average and came close to matching it the next season with 35 a game. His 63 points in a playoff game against the Celtics that year still stands as a single game playoff record.

Following in the path blazed by Magic and Bird, Jordan was not a one-dimensional player; he had also developed into maybe the best defensive player in the league. With a team that had not yet gelled, Air Jordan was carrying the load for Chicago and for the whole NBA as well as being a goodwill ambassador and symbol of professional basketball. Jordan and the athletic shoe company Nike worked together to fully exploit his stardom and created an image that shot the game into the front of the sports world.

As the Bulls slowly improved, the Pistons took the league by force, finishing with the NBA's best record at 63-19. Chicago had finally climbed to a winning record and made it all the way to the Conference Finals, but Detroit was too tough and won the series four games to two.

The Lakers had a sentimental reason for winning in 1988-89: Kareem Abdul-Jabbar was retiring. Los Angeles's entire season had been a farewell tour for one of the game's greatest players and Magic added an MVP season. The playoffs were almost a crusade. The Lakers swept each of their first three rounds, then ran headlong into Detroit.

The Pistons were never known as a sentimental team. Having been denied the year before, they were not in the mood to let Jabbar leave a winner. They wiped Los Angeles out in four straight. The Laker years were over and the "Bad Boys" were on top.

The start of the 1989-90 season brought proof that the NBA had built to a new level of popularity. The first players from foreign leagues suited up for NBA teams. Serbian center Vlade Divac assumed Jabbar's duties in Los Angeles and had a hand in Los Angeles's league leading 63-19 record, but the hot shooting of Croatian Drazen Petrovic helped Clyde Drexler and the Portland Trailblazers reach the Finals.

Though the Pistons still offended some, their hunger to win and clutch play had to impress. Detroit eased through the first two rounds, then had to battle through seven games with the Bulls to earn a berth in the Finals. Once there, they handled Portland in five and repeated as champions. Detroit had won two in a row, but they were hearing footsteps. Chicago had hired Phil Jackson to coach and he had been the difference in bringing the Bulls to the Conference Finals in 1989-90. While other coaches like Doug Collins and Stan Albeck had tried to actually coach Jordan, Jackson worked more as a co-coach with Jordan.

Controlling Jordan was foolish, but the other players needed help and a liaison to the man who really ran the franchise, whether they liked it or not. Often they didn't. Jackson was a player's coach, who could take care of both sides. The Bulls management wanted Jordan happy and they wanted a winning team. Jackson's hands-off approach was the answer.

The other key was Scottie Pippen. A fabulous open court player, Pippen had seemed to have caved against the physical play of the Pistons. He was labeled soft. Until he could step up to provide the other offensive threat needed to pull some defensive pressure away from Jordan, teams could still smother the Bulls by smothering Jordan.

The league wanted the same things as the Bulls, who had more marketing potential than the Pistons. A championship for Jordan would mean an immense amount of revenues from everything from global television rights to T-shirts. 1990-91 would be the year the Bulls either came together or fell apart.

Bulls Charge to a Championship

The Bulls answered the questions quickly in the regular season. They went 61-21, ten games over Detroit, and Jordan won his second MVP award. The Pistons were a money team, though. Nothing was settled until the playoffs. The Bulls lost only one game in the first two rounds and then faced Detroit in the Conference Finals. Any doubts about Chicago were blown away by their performance. They swept Detroit in four.

In the West, the Portland Trail Blazers built the league's best record at 63-19, but they had a reputation for not winning the big games; a reputation they lived up to when Los Angeles bested the four games to two in the Conference Finals.

Los Angeles still had Magic and Worthy, but they couldn't handle Pippen and Jordan. Pippen had blossomed during the season and played All-Star ball through the playoffs. The Bulls won in five and the game's greatest player had a championship.

During the six years of David Stern's reign as commissioner, the NBA had been transformed. Player salaries were up from a yearly average of $325,000 in 1980 to $900,000. The average franchise was now worth $65 million dollars, three times as much as they were in the early 1980s. While the league had made approximately $110 million dollars a decade before in ticket fees and television rights, 1990-91 brought in $700 million dollars.

Merchandising had exploded. Sales of T-shirts, caps, and other team-logo items had risen from $44 million in 1983-84 to $1 billion dollars in 1990-91. Arenas were running at 89 percent of capacity and the NBA began to discuss ventures in China, Japan and Europe and even the possibility of a World Cup style international championship. The NBA had come a long way from Sheboygan and Syracuse.

The only sad note was a very sad one indeed. Magic Johnson, surpassed only by Jordan as the game's most popular player, announced that he had tested positive for the human immunodeficiency virus (HIV) in 1991 and retired from the Lakers. Magic began working on projects concerning the acquired immunodeficiency syndrome (AIDS) and broadcasting, but he remained in playing form.

Now the question was whether the Bulls were one of the greatest teams ever. Their march through the playoffs in 1990-91 had been impressive, but critics wondered if Jordan and the Bulls had the stuff to do it again. A few months into the season, there was a new question—would the Bulls win 70? Chicago had a mission in 1991-92. They won 67 games and went into the playoffs with momentum. The only scare they had was

**NBA Commissioner David Stern (right)
welcomes Chris Webber to the league**

from a resurgent New York Knicks team, now coached by Pat Riley, who had left the Lakers for the broadcasting booth after the 1989-90 season.

Riley worked with Pat Ewing to create a physical team that stressed defense. Forward Xavier McDaniel handled Pippen, but Pippen adjusted to the physical play well enough to make the difference for the Bulls. Chicago met Portland in the finals and while many claimed Portland had greater depth and better overall talent, the Bulls had faced tougher series within their own conference from New York and Cleveland. Once again, the Bulls won the championship, this time in six.

Now that Jordan had reached the top, the NBA began to look ahead to see which player would carry the banner into the next century. At Louisiana State University, Shaquille O'Neal had played two years of brilliant ball and was coming out hardship in the draft, along with a talented crop of rookies. Orlando won the draft lottery and selected O'Neal first in the 1992 draft.

With his enormous bulk, speed and power, the Shaq immediately became a star before he had ever played a game. Reebok, another athletic shoe maker, signed him to an endorsement deal to rival Jordan's with Nike and the league promoted him as the successor to Jordan's mantle. Basketball fans love big, dominating centers and Shaquille O'Neal may be one of the best ever.

From sweaty gym floors and cages, two-handed set shots and a few random inches in the back pages of the sports section, professional basketball and the NBA had risen to the pre-eminent sport in America. By becoming an effective business, exploiting all income producing venues, and producing a superior game, the league had made the players, owners, sponsors and fans all very satisfied.

Much to the distress of baseball and football, basketball was now the favorite sport of American children, signalling a long run for the NBA at the lead. But the United States was not enough. Professional basketball leagues existed around the world and the game's popularity was rising. Though some of these leagues produced good players, only the very best could ever compete in the NBA. When the International Olympic Committee relaxed its rules on professional participation in the Olympic Games, the NBA was ready. The United States had lost its hold on the gold medal and the NBA wanted to help get it back, as well as promote the league and its players on a global level.

Rather than send another talented group of college stars, the Dream Team was created. The very best basketball players in the NBA—Ewing, Jordan, Barkley, Pippen, David Robinson, Karl Malone and Magic Johnson, who came out of retirement for the tourney, among others—went to Barcelona and showed how well basketball could be played.

No longer just American stars, the Dream Team players became international celebrities and helped spread the game throughout the world. Basketball now challenges soccer as the world's most popular sport because of the efforts of the NBA, a league of humble beginnings that has become a giant.

Basketball was dealt a pair of blows following the 1993 playoffs, which saw Chicago become the first team to win the Championship three years in a row. First, James Jordon, Michael's father and a growing celebrity in his own right, was robbed and murdered while travelling near his North Carolina home. A favorite among players and fans alike, James Jordan's death was felt as a personal loss by the nation.

Then, just prior to the start of the 1993-94 season, Michael Jordan stunned the world by announcing his retirement. Only 30 years old and at the peak of his game, Jordan—considered by many the greatest player in the game's history—had grown weary of the demands and limitations placed on him by superstardom and the attendant constant scrutiny of his every move.

Recognizing the need to regain his focus on life, particularly in view of his father's recent death, Jordan made the difficult decision to leave basketball and celebrity behind in order to resume a measure of normal life. He did, however, leave open the possibility that he might return to the game someday, leaving his legions of fans hopeful that he will one day grace the court again.

SOURCES

BOOKS

Auerbach, Red, with Joe Fitzgerald, *On and Off the Court,* Macmillan, 1985.

Carter, Craig and Sachare, Alex, eds., *The Sporting News NBA Guide 1992-1993,* The Sporting News, 1992.

Clary, Jack, *Basketball'S Great Moments,* McGraw-Hill, 1988.

George, Nelson, *Elevating the Game,* Harper-Collins, 1992.

Hollander, Zander, ed., *The Modern Encyclopedia of Basketball,* revised edition, Four Winds Press, 1973.

Hollander, Zander and Sachare, Alex, eds., *Official NBA Basketball Encyclopedia,* Villard, 1989.

Koppett, Leonard, *24 Seconds to Shoot,* Macmillan, 1968.

Libby, Bill, *Goliath,* Dodd, Mead, 1977.

Neft, David S., and Cohn, Richard M., *The Sports Encyclopedia: Pro Basketball,* third edition, revised and updated by Hogosian and Gill, St. Martin's Press, 1990.

Peterson, Robert W., *Cages to Jump Shots,* Oxford University Press, 1990.

Pluto, Terry, *Tall Tales,* Simon & Schuster, 1992.

Rosen, Charles, *Scandals of '51,* Holt, Rinehart and Winston, 1978.

Russell, Bill, as told to William McSweeney, *Go Up for Glory,* Coward-McCann, 1966.

Ryan, Bob, *The Pro Game,* McGraw-Hill, 1975.

Salzberg, Charles, *From Set Shot to Slam Dunk,* Dutton, 1987.

PERIODICALS

Sports Illustrated, February, 16, 1976; June 28, 1976; June 3, 1991.

—*Tom Dyja* for Book Builders Inc.

Eastern Conference

Atlantic Division

BOSTON CELTICS

In the history of professional basketball one team stands as the very best of the best. That team is the Boston Celtics, sixteen–time champions of the National Basketball Association (NBA). A case can be made that the Celtics are the ultimate professional franchise in any sport. No other team has ever turned in eight consecutive championship seasons or won the crown eleven times in thirteen years. Few others have been so stacked with All–Star talent season after season, and fewer still have been guided so astutely by a single, fervently dedicated man.

"Most professional teams are loved by their hometown fans," writes Bob Ryan in *The Boston Celtics: The History, Legends, and Images of America's Most Celebrated Team.* "Only the Boston Celtics are beloved throughout the world. The Celtics have followings in Italy, Spain, Belgium, France, the Scandinavian countries and throughout South America. Celtics T–shirts have shown up in photographs from the jungles of Nicaragua

to the mountainous regions of the Soviet Union. Other teams have histories: Boston alone has a mystique."

Indeed, "Celtic Mystique" has been a catch–phrase in the NBA since the 1960s and remains a force to be reckoned with today. The mystique— so loved in Boston and so detested in other basketball cities—is best illustrated by the rows of bright championship banners hanging from the rafters in Boston Garden, the home of the Celtics. Visiting players are greeted by a visible, and daunting, reminder of the Celtics' great past even before they confront their confident opponents on the parquet floor.

In *Ever Green,* former Celtic M. L. Carr reflected on the banners and their implications: "Those banners up there are a symbol that men have come together and have won through all kinds of adversity. It's a never–think–quit type situation when you work for the Boston Celtics.... Those banners will wave above you forever to remind you that ... it doesn't matter who fills the [playing] spot. There will always be someone who will try to carve out their piece.... No matter what you do, you can only be a part of it." For many years, being a part of the Boston Celtics was the ultimate dream of any youngster who was able to dribble a basketball.

The Celtics' history divides roughly into three eras. The team first gained prominence in the late 1950s and early 1960s on the playing prowess of Hall–of–Famers Bill Russell and Bob Cousy. As Russell began to age past the peak of his considerable powers, the torch was passed to John Havlicek and Dave Cowens, who brought more banners to the Garden ceiling. Cowens's last year neatly coincided with the rookie season of Celtic superstar Larry Bird, possibly the best forward of all time.

These and numerous other marvelous athletes assured Boston championships in each of four decades, despite the inevitable turnover of personnel and the growing parity between professional teams.

Only one factor has remained constant almost from the dawning of the Celtics franchise. Arnold "Red" Auerbach came to Boston as head coach in 1950 and is still there, now serving as team president. Auerbach was at the helm when the Celtics won eight straight championships and was the significant front-office dealer who assured the team's subsequent success. The arrogant Auerbach, with his tough talk and victory cigars, became the winningest coach in any sport and is nothing less than an icon in Boston today.

"Auerbach endures as the most revered, nonplaying sports figure in Hub history," writes Dan Shaughnessy in *Ever Green.* "In terms of longevity and success, there is no close runner up. Auerbach was lucky *and* good. He met presidents and kings. He took the message of the Boston Celtics around the world."

The Celtics Came to Town

Professional basketball came to Boston just after World War II. It was hardly welcomed in a city devoted to baseball (the Red Sox) and hockey (the Bruins), a city that did not even offer a basketball program in the high schools. The principal reason for bringing a basketball team to town was the idea that it would provide a filler for dark nights at the Boston Garden, the city's premier arena since 1928.

On June 6, 1946, a franchise was awarded to Walter Brown as part of the newly formed Basketball Association of America (BAA). Brown's Boston team joined a league that included New York, Philadelphia, Providence, Toronto, Chicago, Cleveland, Detroit, Pittsburgh, St. Louis, and Washington, D.C., among others. Shaughnessy writes: "Pro basketball hadn't fared well [in Boston] in the past, but the timing seemed right."

Brown might have laughed that the "timing was right" for his new team. Indifference ruled as he established the franchise, dubbed it the Celtics, and clad his players in kelly green and white. The team practiced in the Boston Arena Annex and slept on cots beneath the gym at night. The local newspapers devoted little more than a paragraph per game to each contest, if that, and most nights less than 3,000 fans gathered in the 13,000–plus seat Garden for home games.

The first Boston Celtics team consisted of Harold Kottman, Tony Kappen, Art Spector, Warren Fenley, Wyndol Gray, Red Wallace, Virgil Vaugn, Al Brightman, brothers Connie and Johnny Simmons, Mel Hirsch, and Chuck Connors. For coaching duties Brown recruited John Davis "Honey" Russell, formerly with Seton Hall college. This ragtag band of fellows turned in a 22–38 year in 1947, almost 30 games behind the Washington Capitols, coached by Red Auerbach.

Four BAA teams folded after the first year, and league officials trimmed the season to 48 games. Brown's 1948 Celtics showed little improvement, going 20–28, but the record was sufficient to assure the Celtics a playoff spot. In the first of many post-season series, the Celts met the Chicago Stags and lost a best-of-three series in three games. After the playoffs, Brown gently dismissed Honey Russell and hired Alvin "Doggie" Julian, the coach of a wildly popular Holy Cross college team.

Team Information at a Glance

Founding date: June 6, 1946 (part of Basketball Association of America)
3 years in Basketball Association of America, 45 in National Basketball Association

Home court :
Boston Garden
151 Merrimac Street
Boston, MA 02114
(617) 523–6050

Seating capacity: 14,890 for basketball

Team uniforms: Home—base color white, kelly green trim
Road—base color kelly green, white trim

Team nickname: Celtics

Logo: Stylized Irishman balancing a basketball on one finger

Franchise record	Wins	Losses	Pct.
(1946–1992)	2274	1285	.639

NBA Championship wins (16): 1957, 1959, 1960, 1961, 1962, 1963, 1964, 1965, 1966, 1968, 1969, 1974, 1976, 1981, 1984, 1986

Eastern Conference championships (19): 1957, 1958, 1959, 1960, 1961, 1962, 1963, 1964, 1965, 1966, 1968, 1969, 1974, 1976, 1981, 1984, 1985, 1986, 1987

Reached Conference finals (29): 1952, 1954, 1955, 1957, 1958, 1959, 1960, 1961, 1962, 1963, 1964, 1965, 1966, 1967, 1968, 1969, 1972, 1973, 1974, 1975, 1976, 1980, 1981, 1982, 1984, 1985, 1986, 1987, 1988

Julian was able to attract two of his National Collegiate Athletic Association (NCAA) champion Holy Cross stars, George Kaftan and Dermie O'Connell, but they did little to boost the team's fortunes. The third Celtics team finished 25–35, out of the playoffs and more than $100,000 in the red. The stockholders urged Brown to fold the franchise. In turn, Brown pleaded for one more year. His 1949–50 Celtics performed even more dismally, going 22–46 and attracting only several hundred fans to each home game. That might have been the end of the Celtics. The stockholders insisted upon selling the team, and Brown mortgaged his home and liquidated other assets to assume sole ownership. He was determined to make the Celtics a success.

Auerbach Takes Over

"It would be impossible to guess what might have happened to the NBA if Brown hadn't decided to hang on for one more season, but it can be safely stated that the 1950–51 Boston Celtics forever changed the face of professional basketball," notes Shaughnessy. The turnaround came in the person of Red Auerbach, a pompous, cigar–smoking, veteran NBA coach who wanted nothing more than a chance to coach without interference.

Auerbach arrived in 1950 and almost instantly alienated the few faithful Boston fans by passing on local college hero Bob Cousy in the draft. Auerbach told the newspapers: "I'm not interested in drafting someone just because he happens to be a local yokel." The coach did draft Chuck Cooper, the first black man ever chosen in an NBA draft.

The decision to pass on Cousy might have come back to haunt Auerbach for years, but fate intervened. Due to trades and the folding of other teams, Cousy wound up as one of three players up for grabs in the summer of 1950. Cousy's name was placed in a hat with the other two players, and Brown and three owners met to choose the names from the hat. Brown had last pick, and he won Cousy's services by default.

Auerbach remained adamant: the flashy guard would have to earn his way onto the Celtics. Cousy did that and more. In Boston he became no less than "Mr. Basketball," starring with the Celtics for thirteen years and helping to lead them to their first six championships.

Shaughnessy writes: "From 1951 to 1956 the

AP/Wide World Photos

Red Auerbach (center, smiling)

Naismith Memorial Basketball Hall of Fame

Bill Russell

Celtics were in the waiting room: waiting for a big man, waiting for championships. The team was neither great nor awful. They were entertaining, but they still didn't draw the way Holy Cross was drawing.... The team wasn't making any money for Walter Brown, but with consistent winning and the star power of Cousy, it was a nice additional attraction for the Garden's winter nights."

Cousy was named rookie of the year in 1951, and an improved 39–30 Boston team was eliminated in a best-of-three divisional playoff against New York.

The substantial improvement was only one step in Auerbach's plan for the Celtics. Boston's evolution into greatness is now the stuff of legend. Whole books have been written about Auerbach's basic seven-play system, in which scoring developed off of options within the plays.

Generations of NBA coaches have credited Auerbach with the development of the pro running game, the refinement of the fast break, and the devotion to team ideals over individual prowess. Perhaps equally important, Auerbach was a master of intimidation who taught his players to use psychological tactics wherever possible. The

dreaded victory cigar that Auerbach lit whenever Boston won symbolized Celtic dominance during the 1950s.

Between 1951 and 1956 the Celtics always played better than .500 each season. The team made the division finals in 1953, 1954, and 1955, losing in each year. Far from being frustrated, Auerbach felt confident that his Celtics, including Bill Sharman, Ed Macauley, Frank Ramsey, Jim Loscutoff, and Cousy could ascend to the championship eventually. What the team needed was a big, powerful center who could dominate the game. Auerbach found just such a man in Bill Russell.

A Dynasty Is Born

Russell was a collegiate star with the University of San Francisco. He was not considered much of a scoring threat, but in every other category from ball handling to defense he was brilliant. Under his leadership, San Francisco had won 55 straight games and the NCAA championships in 1955 and 1956.

Unfortunately for Auerbach, Russell's talents were no secret in the NBA. Everyone assumed he would not last past a second or third pick in the first round of the draft.

In what would become the most celebrated of numerous player deals, Auerbach arranged to trade All-Star Ed Macauley and Cliff Hagen to St. Louis for the second pick in the draft. Some have suggested that the St. Louis owner agreed readily because he did not want blacks on his team. On April 20, 1956, the Celtics drafted Bill Russell, one of the greatest players ever to don a jersey in the NBA.

"Red Auerbach would never again have to lead the Celtics without Bill Russell, and the big center helped him fulfill his wildest coaching fantasies," Ryan claims. "A truly superior coach has more than rules, regulations and a playbook. He has a vision of how the game should be played. Only a very few ever see that vision realized.... With Russell as the driving force, Auerbach would see his basketball vision successfully displayed for ten exhilarating years."

A great dynasty was born during the 1956–57 season. The Celtics compiled a 44–28 record and cruised through an easy first round playoff victory against the Syracuse Nationals. In their first-ever championship finals, the Celtics drew the very team—the St. Louis Hawks—that had traded away a chance at Russell.

The best-of-seven series stretched to seven games. In the final showdown, rookie Celtic Tom Heinsohn scored 37 points and pulled down 23 rebounds, and Russell chimed in with 19 points, 32 rebounds, and a marvelous show on defense. The game went into double overtime, and Boston won it 125–123 for the championship.

"It was a triumphant day for all the Celtics veterans who'd struggled through the formative years," Shaughnessy notes. "Cousy, the man who rescued the franchise, finally had a ring. Auerbach had his first title after performing as the NBA's best coach for eleven seasons. For Russell, it was his third crown (NCAA, Olympic gold medal, and NBA) in thirteen months.

But Walter Brown had to be the happiest man in the Boston Garden that day. Brown was the man who sold his house and hocked his furniture because he believed in the dream of professional basketball in Boston. And now he was the proud owner of the finest team in the country." Shaughnessy adds: "No one could have predicted that the Celtics and their fans were in for the greatest ride in the history of professional sports."

The Celtics returned to the championships in 1957 and were beaten by the Hawks. Then, from 1959 until 1966, they won eight straight titles.

The string began in 1959 with a sweep of the Minneapolis Lakers, continued in 1960 and 1961 with revenge matches against the Hawks, moved into 1962 and 1963 with two heated series against the Los Angeles Lakers, extended into 1964 with a victory over San Francisco, and lasted into 1965 and 1966 with two more wins over the Lakers.

That string of championships is unparalleled in the history of American professional sports and was achieved despite the expected turnover of per-

Naismith Memorial Basketball Hall of Fame

Frank V. Ramsey, Jr.

sonnel. Shaughnessy calls the Celtics of this period "the guys with more rings than Zsa Zsa Gabor."

Both the 1959 and 1964 championships featured matchups between Russell and Wilt Chamberlain, the two top basketball superstars of the era. Theirs was a fierce rivalry as Russell won five Most Valuable Player awards and Chamberlain four. Chamberlain was taller and heavier than Russell and could always be expected to score more, but Russell was the consummate team player who could sculpt a game by breaking up plays and ruining an offense's rhythm.

Chamberlain, ever conscious of statistics, compiled better numbers than Russell. As Ryan notes, however, the bottom line belonged to Russell and Boston: "while Wilt played on some truly powerful teams in those years, Boston won 86, or more than 60 percent, of the games."

The Midas Touch

Auerbach was almost the King Midas of basketball in those days. His players were selfless and canny about the game, and his bench was deep.

Naismith Memorial Basketball Hall of Fame

Bill Sharman

One by one the original championship players retired—Sharman in 1961, Cousy in 1963, Ramsey and Loscutoff in 1964, and Heinsohn in 1965. By 1965, only two members of the original championship team remained—Russell and Auerbach. Still the team flourished, because Auerbach's trades and draft choices fit seamlessly into the puzzle.

At one point during the long championship run, Boston's coach had two Hall-of-Famers on the bench as backups: Sam Jones and K. C. Jones. As the starters retired, these able men stepped in to replace them. Cousy's last year coincided with the rookie season of Ohio State player John Havlicek, a key Celtics performer through most of the 1970s.

In 1964, Walter Brown died. It was a great loss to the Celtics. Players had appreciated his forthright generosity during contract talks, and Auerbach had depended upon his help in business matters. After Brown's death Auerbach found himself doing the coaching and all the contract negotiations for an ever–changing cast of owners.

The strain began to tell. Finally, at the start of the 1965–66 season, Auerbach announced that he would retire at season's end. He was still a relatively young man at 47, but he looked—and said he felt—much older.

Auerbach's announcement was almost a challenge to the other teams the Celtics played: if they wanted to beat him, they had one year to do it. On the other hand, his team tried harder than ever to send him out in style. The 1965–66 edition of the Celtics went 54–26. Their regular season record fell one game short of the mark compiled by the Philadelphia 76ers—now hosting Chamberlain in their lineup—and Boston was forced into a first round playoff. That series went the distance, five games, and the Celtics advanced to a round with Philadelphia. It was yet another chance for Russell to square off against Chamberlain. This time the 76ers were favored, but Boston took the best-of-five series in five games.

As the Celtics prepared to meet the Los Angeles Lakers in the finals, Auerbach announced that Bill Russell would be the new Boston coach for 1966–67. Buoyed by the news, the Celtics won three of the first four games and clinched the championship in a seventh game at Boston Garden. Auerbach relinquished his coaching duties with yet another victory cigar and championship ring. Shaughnessy writes: "The word 'great' has been diluted beyond recognition in today's era of instant fame and fortune, but those who patronized the 1959–66 Celtics know what they saw." Nor was the winning over, by any means. Auerbach may have given up the day–to–day coaching chores, but he would still sculpt and refine the team from the front office, collecting more rings along the way.

The winning streak ended in 1967. Russell's team compiled a 60–21 record that only proved a distant second best to the Philadelphia 76ers' 68–13 season tally. Boston took a 3–1 first round playoff victory from the New York Knicks but then met Philadelphia for the divisional final. This time the 76ers and Chamberlain could not be beaten. They rolled over Boston in five games, and the Celtics were out of the running for a champion-

Boston's proud basketball tradition offers an embarrassment of riches for any highlight film. Four generations of fans have watched championship banners ascend to the heights above Boston Garden's parquet floor. If asked, these fans might recall three spectacular steals that helped advance the Celtics in the playoffs—one by John Havlicek, one by Gerald Henderson, and one by Larry Bird.

1965 Division Final versus Philadelphia •

In the seventh game of a tough series, Boston clung to a one-point lead with just seconds remaining in the contest. The problem: Philadelphia had the ball. Sixer Hal Greer prepared to inbound a pass to Chet Walker with plenty of time for a two-point shot. Greer passed; John Havlicek reached out and stole the ball, preserving a Boston victory. Boston earned the right to meet the Los Angeles Lakers for Celtics championship number eight.

1984 Championship Finals versus Los Angeles •

Los Angeles had won the first game of the series and seemed poised to win the second as they led by two points with twenty seconds to go in the game. The Lakers had possession of the ball. Magic Johnson inbounded it to James Worthy, who tried to pass it to a fellow Laker but instead delivered it to Celtic Gerald Henderson, who singlehandedly converted a field goal to tie the game. Boston won in overtime, 124-121, and went on to take championship number fifteen.

1987 Eastern Conference Finals versus Detroit •

The series offered perhaps the quintessential grudge match between an aging Celtics team and a young, hungry group of Pistons. Detroit held a one-point lead in Game Five with just five seconds to go. Piston Isiah Thomas did not hear his coach's frantic calls for a time-out but instead inbounded the ball toward Bill Laimbeer. Bird leaped in front of Laimbeer, grabbed the ball, and passed it to Dennis Johnson, who scored the go-ahead points at the buzzer. The Celtics went on to win the series in seven games.

John Havlicek

Naismith Memorial Basketball Hall of Fame

ship for the first time since 1957. Long–suffering Philadelphia fans chanted, "Boston is dead! Boston is dead!" during the deciding game.

The taciturn Russell, who was never particularly popular in Boston, was greeted with predictions of doom. Was the Celtics' long dominance over forever? Russell and Auerbach thought otherwise. A new superstar was emerging who would bring his talents to future championships. His name: John Havlicek.

Ryan notes: "Havlicek was a superstar without a superstar's ego. Whatever the coach asked him to do, he would try. Start? Fine. Come off the bench? That's fine, too. Guard? OK. Forward? Why not? He was, in some ways, the quintessential Celtic." After years of serving as sixth man for the team, Havlicek emerged in the 1967–68 and 1968–69 seasons as a star in his own right.

Naismith Memorial Basketball Hall of Fame

Sam Jones

The Sweetest of Victories

The 1968 season ended with another playoff matchup between Boston and Philadelphia— again a Russell-Chamberlain showdown. The Celtics had eliminated the Detroit Pistons in six games in the preliminary round. Now Boston braced for another hard- fought series.

The Sixers, essentially the same team that had defeated the Celts in 1967, roared off to a 3–1 lead. Only one of the final three games was scheduled for Boston Garden. Almost everyone assumed Philadelphia would win the series.

Instead, Russell, Don Nelson, and Havlicek brought physical and psychological pressure to bear on the situation. The final three outings were won by the Celtics, 122–104, 114–106, and 100–96. Chamberlain took only two shots in the final half of the seventh game.

Boston went on to defeat the Lakers in six games for their tenth championship crown. Havlicek, for years among the sturdiest of NBA professionals, played 291 of 293 minutes in the final series and scored 40 points in the clincher. Once again a nucleus of older stars—Russell, Sam Jones, Sanders, and Bailey Howell—was aided by

timely production from younger players like Havlicek and Don Nelson.

"The 1968-69 season was perhaps the most magical of all Celtics campaigns," contends Shaughnessy. "Conventional wisdom was that 1967–68 had been a last gasp, or perhaps an aberration. In either event, the Celtics certainly had done as much as they were going to do in this generation, and it was time to yield the throne."

The prediction was based on the age of the team. Russell, in his last year as player–coach, was 35. Sam Jones was 36, Sanders 30, and Howell, 32. The season started slowly, and only later did observers realize that the canny Russell was in essence pacing his teammates so they would be rested for the "second season." The 1968–69 Celtics finished 48–34 for fourth place in their division. They were underdogs going into all three of their playoff series.

Auerbach still wears the championship ring he won from the 1969 finals. It was possibly the sweetest of many Celtic victories. Boston dispatched Philadelphia in a semifinal and the Knicks

Naismith Memorial Basketball Hall of Fame

Tom Heinsohn

in the division finals, only to face Los Angeles—now with an old nemesis, Chamberlain, as a Laker.

With Chamberlain, Jerry West, and Elgin Baylor starting for Los Angeles, the fossils from Boston seemed to have no chance. Indeed, the Lakers won the first two games of the finals. Boston rebounded by taking the next two games at the Garden. In Game Five the Lakers won by 13 points. Game Six belonged to Boston at the Garden. Then the show returned to California for a seventh and decisive game.

Lakers owner Jack Kent Cooke, confident of a home court victory, had prepared a massive celebration for his fans. Thousands and thousands of balloons were held in suspension in the rafters of the Forum.

The University of Southern California marching band was on hand to serenade the crowd. Don Nelson told Shaughnessy: "Red mentioned [the celebration plans] before the game, and you could see the balloons by the thousands, and he just let

his feelings be known. It was definitely a mistake on their part to do that."

Fired up, the Celtics took the floor and won a close game, with Nelson hitting a fluke shot in the last two minutes and Chamberlain removing himself in the fourth quarter with a sore shin. The final score was 108–106, Boston. Lakers fans got treated not to a shower of balloons but to another Auerbach cigar.

The decade of the 1960s began and ended with Celtics championships. The team had won 11 titles in 13 years. Critics predicted the string would end when Cousy retired; it didn't. They predicted it would end when Auerbach left the bench; it didn't. They predicted it would end after Philadelphia trounced Boston in 1967; it didn't. Now Russell was leaving, and the pundits again proclaimed that the Celtics were finished. For awhile they appeared to be right, but Celtic Mystique would surface again as a new crop of players joined the fabled "Green Machine."

New Faces, Same Results

The 1969–70 season—without Russell and Sam Jones—saw Boston dip to 34–48 for a non–playoff finish. The season was disappointing for Auerbach and his new coach Tom Heinsohn, but the two were making moves that would lead to improvement.

New Celtics arrivals in the period included guards Don Chaney and Jo Jo White. A low finish in the 1970 season assured a high pick in the draft, and Auerbach selected six-foot-eight center Dave Cowens from Florida State. Cowens was short for a center, but he was remarkably aggressive and, like Russell, he was left-handed.

Ryan writes: "To say that Cowens was, and is, unique is to say that Everest is a pretty big hill. There has never been a professional basketball player quite like Dave Cowens—on or off the court.

No center has matched his playing style, and his lifestyle was a strange and wonderful blend of personality, intelligence and enthusiasm for a wide

Naismith Memorial Basketball Hall of Fame

Dave Cowens

variety of interests." Cowens, White, and Havlicek became the hub of a new generation of Boston winners.

Rebuilding continued in 1971 and 1972. Paul Westphal and Steve Kuberski were draft picks, and Auerbach traded with Phoenix for the services of forward Paul Silas. Silas, an eight-year veteran, teamed extremely well with Cowens. According to Shaughnessy, Silas "put the Celtics over the top in 1972–74."

The 1972–73 Celtics were back in business. They compiled a 68–14 regular season record—a franchise best. "They ran as much as any Celtics team, no small boast," notes Shaughnessy. "Cowens was Most Valuable Player, and Havlicek, ageless at thirty–three, remained at the top of his game. The city of Boston was turned on by this team.... It was undoubtedly the best Boston team that *did not* win a championship." In the playoffs, Boston beat the Atlanta Hawks in six games but did not survive a series with the New York Knicks.

Those who had written the Celtics off in 1970 were stunned to find them back in the championship finals of 1974. The Cowens-White-Havlicek version of the Celts breezed through the playoffs with a six–game victory over Buffalo and a five-game trouncing of the Knicks. Then they faced the Milwaukee Bucks with their fabulous seven-foot center, Kareem Abdul-Jabbar.

Cowens, who was never intimidated by taller men, used his muscle to compete with Abdul–Jabbar, and the championship series stretched to seven games. In the final Cowens was particularly effective, and Boston won it by a 102–87 margin. Championship banner number 12 was hoisted to the Garden roof.

"The glory was spread around, but no one was happier than Auerbach," recalls Shaughnessy. "For a long time he'd been hearing 'You never won without Russell.' Finally, he won without Russell. He had built a team from bottom to top in five seasons. This stands as one of his great achievements. The 1974 team featured four starters who were Celtics first-round draft picks. He'd done it without the big bankrolls that existed in New York and Los Angeles. The 1974 title also signifies the beginning of a second period of Celtics success."

Havlicek, Cowens, White, Nelson, and Silas played together four full seasons and won championships in 1974 and 1976. After being eliminated in the conference finals in 1975 they advanced again to the championships in 1976. It was altogether timely that the popular Celtics would be playing for a national championship in Boston just as the nation geared up for its bicentennial celebration.

The final series with Phoenix stretched to seven games and included a triple-overtime sixth game that the Celts won with help from little-used benchman Glenn McDonald. Boston won the final 87–80 and brought a thirteenth championship home from Arizona. "This was a true team championship," claims Ryan. "Havlicek struggled through the playoffs despite a torn plantar fascia in his left foot.... But the Celtics received timely contributions from every starter, and from little-named substitutes such as Jim Ard, Kevin Stacom, and McDonald." One particular standout was Charlie Scott, who scored 25 points and grabbed 11 rebounds in the clincher.

Troubled Times

Little did the Celtics know that they were entering another down period as the 1976–77 season dawned. Nelson retired, and Silas departed over a salary dispute. The loss of Silas was particularly disheartening to Cowens, who took a leave of absence that stretched to two months. New owner Irv Levin brought in Sidney Wicks and Curtis Rowe, two former UCLA stars who never meshed well with the Celtics' system. After finishing 44–38 in 1977 and being eliminated in the second round of the playoffs, the Celtics turned in a 32–50 season in 1977–78 and a dismal 29–53 season in 1978–79.

Team fortunes hit rock bottom in a one-year period between the spring of 1978 and the spring of 1979. Tom Heinsohn was fired mid-season in 1978—the first Celtics coach to be so dismissed in 22 years—and was replaced by Satch Sanders. Just a dozen games into the 1978–79 season, Sanders was replaced by a reluctant Dave Cowens as player-coach.

Havlicek retired in 1978 to end a 16–year career. The most desperate moment in the history of the franchise occurred when the team became the property of Kentucky businessman John Y. Brown in a 1978 franchise swap. Terms of the deal included a personnel swap with the Buffalo Braves, a transaction Brown finished without consulting Auerbach. "John Y. Brown was the antithesis of his [unrelated] namesake, Walter Brown," writes Shaughnessy. "John Y. was in it for the short haul, for the money, for the glory."

Auerbach was humiliated by Brown's autocratic behavior. The popular Boston general manager seemed prepared to jump ship for a job with the Knicks, but Brown convinced Auerbach to stay. Then, in February 1979, Brown unilaterally traded three Boston first-round draft picks to New York for Bob McAdoo. Auerbach fumed.

Years later, Red told Shaughnessy of John Y.: "He made one great big deal that could have destroyed the team, without even consulting me. He did ruin it. We just happened to put it back together again, luckily. One wrong guy can ruin it so fast your head will swim." Auerbach concluded that he threatened to quit if John Y. did not sell the team, and the owner complied. McAdoo played only 20 games with the Celtics before becoming trade bait in Auerbach's hands.

Through this dark period in Celtics history, a bit of light remained on the horizon. On June 9, 1978, Auerbach had selected Larry Bird of Indiana State University as the sixth pick in the first round of the draft. The choice was especially remarkable because Bird had announced that he intended to stay in college another year—he was eligible for the draft but only a junior in class standing.

Auerbach hoped Bird would be a dividend that paid later, and as the Celtics sagged—and Bird's college team made the 1979 NCAA Final Four—the eyes of Boston fans turned west toward their promising draft choice.

"Larry Legend"

Ryan writes: "Bob Cousy saved professional basketball in Boston. Bill Russell was the most valuable team player in the history of American sports.... Dave Cowens was the team's Everyman, bringing unrivaled passion to his job. John Havlicek retired in 1978 as the most complete ball player the game had yet known. But of all these Celtics, none touched the Boston fans the way Larry Bird has. The people who love the game recognize that he is the purest practitioner of the art of basketball they've ever seen."

Bird came to Celtics training camp in 1979, after having lost a heartbreaker in the NCAA finals to Michigan State and its star, Earvin "Magic" Johnson. Expectations ran high for Bird, who had won the highest salary ever awarded to an NBA rookie. The moment he hit camp—and submitted

AP/Wide World Photos

Larry Bird (33)

himself to the tutelage of new Celtics coach Bill Fitch—the taciturn Indiana native blossomed into a bona fide superstar.

"Bird was such an instant success that people tend to give him all the credit for the team's dramatic 32–game turnaround [in 1979–80]," notes Ryan. "Yes, the Celtics won 61 games in Bird's rookie season, and he deserves much or perhaps even most of the credit. But he wasn't the only fresh influence."

As coach, Fitch established new standards of discipline and conditioning. He and Auerbach had transformed the roster, trading McAdoo for Detroit's M. L. Carr. Carr, a versatile two-way player, boosted spirits in the locker room with his lighthearted antics.

Fitch also received the benefits of revitalized performances from Cowens, Tiny Archibald, and Cedric Maxwell, the first round pick from 1977. All eyes were on Bird, however, as the Celtics went 61–21 during the regular season and downed Houston in the semifinals in four straight games.

"The fans ... fell in love with Bird immediately," claims Ryan. "His numbers weren't what they would one day be, but they were good enough. And they didn't really tell the story. He was not only a scorer, but a wondrous passer. He made look-away passes, touch passes, behind-the-back passes, 50–foot outlet passes, 80–foot baseball passes and all sorts of bounce passes.... Bird delivered the ball only when the intended recipient was ready and in the best position to take his shot....

"Bird was hired as a scorer, but his offensive game proved to be far more versatile than that label indicated. His jump shot was textbook perfect, his range was astounding ... and he was equally comfortable facing the basket or playing with his back to it. Fouling him was a waste of time, because he arrived an 85 percent foul-shooter and developed into a 90 percent shooter and three-time league leader. Most of all, Bird lived to play the game, and never stopped trying to improve his performance. His work habits soon became the stuff of legend."

Few great expectations in life are fulfilled as brilliantly as those attending the arrival of Larry Bird in the NBA. In Bird's rookie year, however, the momentum ran out in a conference final series with the Philadelphia 76ers.

The Sixers, led by Julius "Dr. J" Erving, drew upon their wider experience to defeat the Celts in five games. At season's end, Cowens retired, confident that he had passed the torch of Celtic Mystique on to Bird. For his part, Bird vowed to play with even more ferocity in next year's postseason.

Parish and McHale

Draft day in 1980 provided another important pivotal moment in the history of the Celtics.

Boston had earned a first-round draft pick from the Detroit Pistons, and since the Pistons had finished 16–66 on the season, the Celts had the number one pick. Fitch and Auerbach traded this pick to the Golden State Warriors for center Robert Parish.

This still left the Celtics with the number three pick in the first round, and Boston called upon University of Minnesota forward Kevin McHale. Parish, at seven feet, brought needed height to the center position, and McHale—after some initial disappointment over salary—settled in to become yet another Celtic superstar.

The 1980–81 Celtics went 62–20, matching Philadelphia for the best regular season record. A victory over the 76ers in the Garden on the last day of the regular season guaranteed the Celtics home-court advantage throughout the playoffs. Boston beat Chicago in four straight games to advance to the conference finals against Philadelphia. An old and bitter rivalry continued in this hard-fought series.

The Sixers won three of the first four games and led game five by six points with less than two minutes to play. In dramatic fashion Boston rallied and won by two points, 111–109. The series extended to seven games, with the final in the Boston Garden. Again the Celts trailed by nine points with only five minutes to play, and again they rallied to win 91–90 on a crucial Bird three-pointer. The Garden crowd—an important factor throughout the game—went wild.

In an anti-climactic championship final series, Boston beat Houston in six games. Banner num-

AP/Wide World Photos

Kevin McHale (32) drives to the basket against the Indiana Pacers

ber 14 ascended to the Garden roof. It was hard to believe that in just two years a team that had been 29–53 had won another championship. The celebration that was held in Boston lasted throughout the night.

Amidst the growing parity between NBA franchises, it had become much harder to string together back-to-back championships. The Celtics discovered this after the 1981 title when they lost a seven–game conference final to the 76ers (with Moses Malone) in 1982 and, the following year, completed an even more dismal post–season showing with a four-game semifinal loss to the Bucks.

One of the casualties of this disappointing downturn was coach Fitch. Fitch was the rare Celtics coach who had not played for the team under Auerbach. He chafed under Auerbach's interference and was annoyed when Red reaped credit for trade deals and draft choices.

By the end of the 1982–83 season Fitch had lost control of the team. Players who had once welcomed his zealous coaching now mocked him behind his back. When team owner Harry Mangurian, Jr., sold the club soon after the Milwaukee debacle, Fitch resigned.

K. C. Takes the Helm

Auerbach moved quickly to find another coach from the Celtics' "family." He chose K. C. Jones, a former member of his glory-years team who had been assistant coach under Fitch. "It was clear from the start that the veteran Celtics would play harder for Jones than they did for Fitch," contends Shaughnessy. "K. C. was much closer to the players ... and many resented the way Fitch had treated Jones.... Jones's laid-back personality was exactly what the Celtics needed and wanted at this point. The goose step was out. It was time for a little soft shoe."

Players added during this period also contributed to an improved Celtics team. Guard Danny Ainge arrived after having played some 200 games with baseball's Toronto Blue Jays. Auerbach also traded backup center Rick Robey to Phoenix for All-Star guard Dennis "DJ" Johnson. Ryan writes: "Johnson was an immediate hit in Boston. He brought an element of toughness and professionalism to the Celtics backcourt.

Though never billed as a playmaker, he adapted quickly and well to that role, and his reputation for defensive prowess was deserved. Nobody appreciated the new Celtic more than Larry Bird. By the end of their second season together, Bird was calling DJ 'the best player I've ever played with.'"

With the additions of Johnson, Ainge, and guard Gerald Henderson, the Celtics leaped back into contention in 1983–84. Boston finished 62–20 during the regular season and defeated Washington and New York in early playoff rounds.

The Eastern Conference championship provided a welcome opportunity to pay the Bucks back for the four-game humiliation in 1983. Boston won the conference final in five games. This advance brought about the first world championship confrontation between Bird's Celtics and Magic Johnson's Los Angeles Lakers.

Bird vs. Magic

Basketball aficionados had been comparing Bird and Magic since the two were in college. The finals brought the men's friendly rivalry to a worldwide audience. Unlike Russell and Chamberlain—who had eventually come to dislike each other personally—Bird and Magic kept their competition on a professional level and remained friends through the decades. Still, they provided some of the most riveting basketball spectacles of the 1980s in various playoff encounters.

The 1984 championship series looked like a Laker lock early on. Los Angeles won the first game 115–109 and seemed to have the second in hand as well.

Late in the second game, however, Laker James Worthy lofted a pass that was snatched by Gerald Henderson and turned into a Boston two–pointer. Boston won the game in overtime, 124–

121. The Lakers rebounded to win the third game easily, 137–104. Boston tied up the series in another overtime shocker, 129–125. Then Mother Nature intervened on behalf of the Celtics.

Game Five was scheduled for Boston Garden, which is not air-conditioned. Boston was suffering from an unusual early summer heat wave, and the temperature in the Garden soared to 97 degrees by game time. The Lakers wilted and lost 121–103. Afterwards, Lakers center Kareem Abdul-Jabbar described the playing conditions: "I

suggest you go to the local steam bath, do one hundred push–ups with all your clothes on, and then try to run back and forth for forty–eight minutes."

Los Angeles evened the score again with a sixth game, 119–108 victory at the Forum, but the Celtics finished the series with a 111–102 win at the Garden. A fifteenth championship went into the record books for the Celtics, and the team was invited to meet President Ronald Reagan at the White House.

Naismith Memorial Basketball Hall of Fame

K.C. Jones (25) during his playing days with the Celtics

The 1984–85 season began on a sour note. Cedric Maxwell and Gerald Henderson both missed training camp in contract disputes. Shortly after signing Henderson, Auerbach traded the playoff star to Seattle. Ainge took Henderson's place in the lineup and blossomed into a reliable star. Once again the Celtics advanced to the 1985 finals with victories over Cleveland, Detroit, and Philadelphia. The stage was set for another finals series against the Lakers.

This time Bird was slightly injured, and so was Maxwell. Try as they might, the Celts could not repeat. They lost in six games. At the end of the final encounter, Lakers co-owner Jerry Buss told reporters: "This removes the most odious sentence in the English language. It can never again be said that the Lakers have never beaten the Boston Celtics."

Walton Trade Spurs Controversy

The Celtics began 1985–86 with numerous roster changes. M. L. Carr retired, and Maxwell was traded for Clippers center Bill Walton. "The arrival of Walton put Celtics fans in hardwood heaven," claims Shaughnessy. "Walton was *the* player of the mid–1970s, and basketball aficionados from coast to coast regarded him as the consummate team center."

The trade of Maxwell for Walton—and other personnel moves by Auerbach and Celtics general manager Jan Volk—have led some to charge the Boston front office with racist hiring practices stretching over its entire history. The charges were loudest in 1986, when the Celtics offered a team with eight white players and four blacks in a league that was 72 percent black.

In their book *The Selling of the Green: The Financial Rise and Moral Decline of the Boston Celtics,* Harvey Araton and Filip Bondy suggest that the Celtics management stacked the team with white players whenever possible to appease racist fans, searched aggressively for white superstars, and retained these stars on the roster while trading blacks who had passed their prime.

"Beyond the Celtic Mystique and the sixteen championships, there was another legacy passed on," the reporters conclude. "The Celtics were a basketball franchise with few or no ties to a black community.... In no other city haunted by the misery and tragedy of urban America was professional basketball such an exclusive province, such a country club, for the white fan.... The Boston Celtics are still for whites. Whites are still for the Boston Celtics."

Auerbach and company might counter that Boston has given a raft of "firsts" to blacks in basketball. The Celtics were the first team to draft a black player, the first to play five blacks on the floor at the same time (during the Russell era), and the first to hire a black head coach (Russell).

Celtics teams have been coached by three African-Americans: Russell, K. C. Jones, and Satch Sanders. Still, the favored status of white players in Boston has been obvious since the days when attendance dropped at the Garden in the wake of Cousy's retirement. It is entirely possible that the careers of some of the 1980s Celtic superstars were shortened by the lack of depth on the mostly-white bench.

Red Auerbach bridles when the subject of racism comes up. The team president told Shaughnessy: "Ever since Walter Brown owned the team, and he and I saw eye to eye, every player we get is a player we feel can do the best for this team. We don't care anything about his religion, his color, or anything, and that's where it's at. People are always trying to start trouble and look for trouble. I don't pay any attention to that. I refuse to even discuss it."

Sweet Sixteen

The 1985–86 Celtics won a phenomenal 67 games, just one less than the franchise record. Parish, McHale, Bird, and Johnson were all in peak form, and Walton performed admirably off the bench. The team won 29 straight games at the Garden and finished with a 40–1 home record. In the playoffs, the Celts beat the Chicago Bulls and their ace rookie Michael Jordan in three, knocked the Hawks out in five, and swept the Bucks in the conference finals.

The only disappointment came in the championship finals matchup: the Lakers had not returned. In their place stood the Houston Rockets, coached by Bill Fitch. The series was very physical, with fights and injuries, and Boston won it in six games. Shaughnessy writes: "The Celtics were at the top for the sixteenth time. Sweet Sixteen. In many ways, this Celtics edition was more pleasing to the eye than any other. They had the full complement of weapons, and they passed and played defense as well as any championship entry....

"Bird has said it was his favorite team. It spawned a new generation of Celtics fans and gave them something in common with the two generations preceding them. Rooting for the Celtics became chic, and pockets of Green people suddenly started appearing in hotel lobbies and arenas across the land. It would be a while before the Celtics would win again, but after sixteen championships in thirty years, the Celtics had earned their status as an American institution."

The Len Bias Tragedy

The world champion Celtics were beginning to show their age by draft day in 1986. Parish was 33, Walton 34, DJ 31, Bird 29, and McHale 28. Auerbach and Volk had anticipated this state of affairs and had dealt with Seattle for a high pick in the first round of the 1986 draft. As it turned out, Boston got the second pick overall, and the choice was quite obvious.

The Celtics drafted University of Maryland forward Len Bias, an athlete in the Michael Jordan mold whose college career showed great promise. Bias was thrilled. "Praise the Lord," he sighed as the news reached him. Within hours he had signed a million-dollar sneaker deal with Reebok. Bird told reporters that he would personally work with Bias at rookie camp the way Cowens had worked with him. The Celtics' future never looked brighter.

Within days all of that promise, all of those great expectations vanished. Bias died of cocaine intoxication while celebrating with friends at the University of Maryland campus. Auerbach called Bias's death "one of the biggest disappointments of my career." The tragedy had both immediate and lasting implications for the Celtics as they tried to regroup without their best draft pick in years.

The immediate implications began to show in the 1987 playoffs. Boston compiled a 59–23 regular season record, relying heavily on the aging starters, and won an easy first-round playoff series against Chicago. Then the going got tough. The Celts battled through seven games in the semifinal with Milwaukee and endured an even more physical seven-game conference final against Detroit.

"The Pistons were young and hungry, and they believed they were better than the Celtics," Shaughnessy writes. "Like so many other losers over the years, they felt Boston always got the benefit of the doubt from the media, the officials, and the networks." Fighting between the two teams was almost commonplace.

In Game Three of the series, Bird and Detroit center Bill Laimbeer were ejected. In Game Five, Parish slugged Laimbeer. Parish had to sit out Game Six, and the Pistons won. Game Seven belonged to Boston, in the Garden. The Celts were helped considerably by a fluke collision between Pistons Vinnie Johnson and Adrian Dantley that sent Dantley to the hospital with a concussion.

The charges of racism came home to roost after that bitter showdown. In the Pistons' locker room after the final, Dennis Rodman and Isiah Thomas complained that Bird was overrated because he was white. Thomas said of Bird, "If he was black, he'd be just another good guy." The comment caused a tempest, and days later Thomas found himself apologizing publicly to a gracious Bird.

In the meantime, the Celtics were back in the championship finals against the Lakers. Here the loss of Bias was felt most painfully. Los Angeles had Magic Johnson in his first MVP season and a deep bench. The Lakers won the first two games at the Forum. Boston took Game Three in the Garden. The series turned when the Lakers won Game Four in Boston after the Celts blew a 16–point third quarter lead. Boston, faced with the daunting task of taking three straight games—two of them in Los Angeles—folded in Game Six.

"Boston has been to the NBA finals nineteen times, winning sixteen and losing only three," Shaughnessy concludes. "No one can safely predict how long it'll take to get back to the championship series. It looks like it's going to be a long time, but that's been said before about the Celtics."

The Changing of the Guard

The days of NBA championship dynasties may well be over. For Boston they ended in the late 1980s with the inevitable aging of Bird, Parish, McHale, and Johnson. Since 1988 the team has been unable to advance past the conference finals, and since 1989 they have been eliminated in or before the semifinals.

This is the lasting legacy of Len Bias and, perhaps, of that mostly-white championship team. Once Auerbach could choose fine players from his bench to replace his ailing or aging starters. In the late 1980s, those starters—popular, yes, but still aging and ailing—continued to reap the lion's share of the playing time.

A new generation of Celtics talent is represented by guard Dee Brown, the 1990 first-round draft choice; veteran forward Xavier McDaniel; and Parish, the only remaining Celtic from the 1980s championships. Ainge was traded in 1989. Bird retired at the end of the 1992 season, and McHale stepped down in 1993.

Another big disappointment for Celtics fans was Brian Shaw, the first round draft pick in 1988. Shaw quarreled with the Celtics front office about his salary, then accepted an offer from the Italian basketball team Il Messaggero. After a season in Italy, Shaw re-signed with the Celtics but changed his mind about returning to Boston before the season began. Eventually a court ordered him to

AP/Wide World Photos

Reggie Lewis

honor his Celtics contract; he did so grudgingly but is no longer with the team. The disappointment over Shaw, however, paled in comparison to the sorrow that accompanied the death of Celtic forward Reggie Lewis in 1993.

On April 29, 1993, Lewis, a graduate of Boston's Northeastern University, the Celtics' captain, and an emerging NBA superstar, collapsed during a playoff game against the Charlotte Hornets. A cardiological team headed by Celtic team physician Arnold Scheller determined that Lewis was suffering from ventricular arrhythmia, a potentially fatal heart condition, and Scheller announced that Lewis might have to retire from basketball.

After receiving a second, more optimistic opinion from Boston cardiologist Dr. Gilbert Mudge, who diagnosed Lewis as having a benign fainting condition, Lewis traveled to Los Angeles to meet a third team of doctors for another series of tests. The results showed an abnormality in Lewis's heart, and the medical team recommended that even more tests be conducted under simulated game conditions.

Lewis continued to work out on his own, though, and on July 27, 1993, while shooting baskets at Brandeis University, Lewis collapsed again, lapsing into unconsciousness. Paramedics rushed Lewis to the hospital but were unable to revive him. The cause of death was a heart attack.

In the days that followed, questions arose over the ethical and legal ramifications of Lewis's death. As E. M. Swift wrote in *Sports Illustrated,* "Surely all who knew him must have wondered ... whether Lewis's death was preventable. If Lewis had not been a professional athlete, would his treatment and prognosis have been the same? Had doctors worked too hard to keep him on the basketball court?" Swift added, "Or had all parties exercised reasonable caution? Was no one to blame but cruel fate?" The answers to those questions may never be known.

Looking to the Future

The fortunes of the Celtics have been guided since 1990 by senior executive vice president Dave Gavitt. A former NCAA Final Four and U.S. Olympic Team coach, Gavitt has earned the respect of players and agents as firm but fair in negotiations. He is helped in the front office by Volk—who has spent his entire professional career in Celtics management—and by the continued presence of Auerbach, albeit now in a more symbolic role. Chris Ford, another former Celtics player and assistant coach, assumed head coaching duties in 1990.

The Celtics changed head coaches 11 times between 1947 and 1993. Ownership of the team has changed a phenomenal 14 times in the same period. Walter Brown bought the team with an investment group in 1946 and assumed sole ownership in 1948. Two years later, Brown sold an interest to Lou Pieri. After Brown's death in 1964, Pieri and Brown's widow owned the team until 1965. The Celtics were then bought by Marvin Krattner and National Equities, who in turn sold to Ballantine Brewery in 1969. After just a year, Ballantine turned the property over to E. E. Erdman and Trans-National Communications. A group called Investors' Funding Corporation bought the Celtics in 1971. The next year the franchise became the property of Bob Schmertz and Leisure Technology.

Leisure Technology sold out its interest in 1974 to Irv Levin. Levin was sole owner from 1975–78 and then sold the team to the hated John Y. Brown. Brown passed the franchise on in 1979 to Harry Mangurian, Jr. who, in 1983, sold it to the current owners: Don Gaston, Paul Dupee, Jr., and Alan Cohen.

The complicated ownership history is further muddied by a stock sale that Gaston, Dupee, and Cohen initiated in 1984. The three owners offered a portion of the Celtics as public stock that year. Forty percent of the team went up for grabs at about $18 per share. The response was phenomenal. Everyone, it seemed, wanted a little bit of the Celtics.

Most stocks sold individually, and the certificates were framed and hung in fan bedrooms. The constant turnover at the top notwithstanding, the Celtics have proven immensely profitable. Brown founded the team for $10,000. At the time of the public stock sale, the appraised value of the Celtics was $120 million. The team had increased in value more than one million percent in forty years and is still climbing.

The NBA may never produce another franchise as consistently successful as the Boston Celtics. Even though the last championship is now consigned to a previous decade, Celtic Mystique still clings to the team—a legacy of Cousy, Russell, K. C. Jones, Havlicek, Cowens, Bird, Parish, and McHale.

Ryan writes: "History has taught the people of Boston that the wait for the proud Celtics tradition to continue is never a long one. Continuity is the team's hallmark.... The famous flags overhead are a testament—like no others in sport—to those who have gone before. Red Auerbach still sits in his midcourt seat, his mind focused on the future; leave the reminiscing to the writers and the fans."

Ryan concludes: "No glittering new arena will ever quite match the atmosphere of the old Boston Garden. The emphasis here has always been on the game, first and foremost. And the best basketball ever seen anywhere has been played in Boston. There is every reason to expect that it will be again."

Sources

BOOKS

Araton, Harvey and Filip Bondy, *The Selling of the Green: The Financial Rise and Moral Decline of the Boston Celtics,* Harper/Collins, 1992.

Auerbach, Red and Paul Sann, *Red Auerbach: Winning the Hard Way,* Little, Brown, 1966.

Auerbach, Red and Joe Fitzgerald, *Red Auerbach: An Autobiography,* Putnam, 1977.

Bird, Larry, *Drive,* Doubleday, 1989.

Cousy, Bob and Bob Ryan, *Cousy on the Celtic Mystique,* McGraw-Hill, 1988.

Fitzgerald, Ray, *Champions Remembered,* Stephen Greene Press, 1982.

Havlicek, John and Bob Ryan, *Hondo,* Prentice Hall, 1977.

Heinsohn, Tom and Joe Fitzgerald, *Give 'Em the Hook,* Prentice Hall, 1988.

Russell, Bill, *Go Up for Glory,* Macmillan, 1966.

Russell, Bill and Taylor Branch, *Second Wind,* Random House, 1979.

Ryan, Bob, *The Boston Celtics: The History, Legends and Images of America's Most Celebrated Team,* foreword by Red Auerbach, photographs by Dick Raphael, Addison-Wesley, 1990.

Schron, Bob and Kevin Stephens, *The Bird Era,* Quinlan Press, 1988.

Shaughnessy, Dan, *Ever Green,* St. Martin's, 1990.

Sullivan, George, *The Picture History of the Boston Celtics,* Bobbs-Merrill, 1981.

PERIODICALS

Sports Illustrated, August 9, 1993.

—*Mark Kram*

MIAMI HEAT

South Florida has recently acquired top-level professional sports teams in two sports: basketball and baseball. The basketball entry is the Miami Heat, an expansion team created in 1987. One of four expansion franchises admitted to the National Basketball Association (NBA) in the late 1980s, the Heat boasts an active ownership group, one of whose partners is Billy Cunningham, a member of the Basketball Hall of Fame.

Cunningham's participation as an owner of the Heat brings him full circle in the sport: he has been a respected player, a highly successful coach, and now a team co-owner. His influence has helped to bring the Heat slow but steady success toward eventual playoff contention.

The drive to bring an NBA team to South Florida began in earnest in 1986, when business-man Zev Bufman—a producer of Broadway shows and owner of dinner theaters—contacted Cunningham merely by calling the former coach on the telephone. At the time Cunningham was living in Philadelphia and working as a broad-caster for televised NBA games in the wake of a 454-196 head coaching career, primarily with the 76ers.

For years Cunningham had nursed the idea of owning an NBA franchise, so he teamed up with Bufman. Shortly thereafter the pair also recruited Cunningham's childhood friend Lewis Schaffel, an experienced NBA executive then with the New Jersey Nets. Further financial backing came from entertainer Julio Iglesias and other limited part-ners.

Cunningham and Bufman announced their pursuit of an NBA franchise for Miami in June of 1986. One stipulation made by the NBA Expan-sion Committee was that potential sites needed a state-of-the-art basketball arena for home games. Within months of the Cunningham/Buf-man an-nouncement, ground was broken for a brand-new Miami Arena to house the team should it arrive. The city's chances for a team were also enhanced by the entry of a new financial partner, Ted Arison. The owner of Carnival Cruise Lines—and vast real estate holdings in Florida—Arison became the big-money man the city needed to comfortably bankroll the $32 million franchise.

The name "Heat" was chosen from a "name that team" contest that drew a phenomenal 20,000 entries. Another contest was held to provide the logo, and the winning design was a flaming basketball passing through a hoop. Team colors of red, orange, and white seemed an appropriate extension of the "heat" theme.

On April 22, 1987, the board of governors of the NBA officially granted Miami an expansion team. Other franchises granted the same day were the Charlotte Hornets, the Minnesota Timberwolves, and the Orlando Magic. It was decided that Miami and Charlotte would begin play in 1988, with the other two teams set to start in 1989.

This gave the Heat executives slightly more than a year to prepare for the special expansion draft and the regular 1988 college draft. Stu Inman, director of player personnel for the Milwaukee Bucks, agreed to take the same responsibilities for the Heat. He and Cunningham set out to craft a team and choose a head coach.

The expansion draft was held on June 23, 1988, and was conducted by conference telephone call. Miami drew the first choice in the draft and picked Arvid Kramer from the Dallas Mavericks. As a bonus on the pick, Miami also received a first round college draft choice from Dallas for not selecting Bill Wennington, Uwe Blab, or Steve Alford.

Other Heat players chosen that day included Lakers forward Billy Thompson, Celtics forward Fred Roberts, Atlanta forward-center Scott Hastings, and San Antonio guard Jon Sundvold. The college draft a week later brought the services of center Rony Seikaly, guard Kevin Edwards, and forward Grant Long.

A sellout crowd greeted the Miami Heat at its first home opener on November 5, 1988, at the Miami Arena. The Heat lost the game 101-80 to the Los Angeles Clippers. In the following weeks, Miami compiled a record-setting streak, losing its

AP/Wide World Photos

Rony Seikaly (with ball)

first 16 consecutive games. An 89-88 victory over the Clippers in Los Angeles halted the streak, but the team still suffered as the butt of jokes for some two years after its arrival in the league. By the end of its second season, the Heat had won only 33 of 131 contests.

The slow start was misleading, however. As early as 1991, a *Sports Illustrated* poll of NBA team executives picked Miami to be the most successful expansion franchise of recent years. The executives highlighted the way Miami had built its team and the slow but sure progress it was making.

A year later, in 1992, *New Miami* magazine contributor Gary Ferman wrote of the Heat: "There have been many fine moments and plenty of mistakes these first four seasons. Triumph—the development of players like Glen Rice and Rony Seikaly. Pitfall—original coach Ron Rothstein lasting just three years. Triumph—uncovering hidden gems like Bimbo Coles and Grant Long in the

Team Information At a Glance

Founding date: April 22, 1987
Home court: Miami Arena
Miami, FL 33136-4102
Phone: (305) 577-4328

Seating capacity: 15,008 for basketball

Team colors: Orange, red, black, yellow, and white.
Team nickname: Heat
Logo: Flaming basketball

Franchise record	Won	Lost
(1988-1993)	131	279

second round of the draft. Pitfall—the lack of development by first-round draft picks Alec Kessler and Willie Burton, and the Sherman Douglas contract problems that led the Heat to trade their 1991 Most Valuable Player in a deal with the Boston Celtics."

Ferman added: "That's the business of basketball in the NBA. Dealing with players, the agents, the league executives, men like Cunningham handle countless uncontrollable situations. There is a high margin of error.... But through it all, Cunningham has been having the time of his life.... The experience of team ownership has been particularly sweet.".

Sources

New Miami, April 1992.
Sports Illustrated, February 18, 1991.

—Anne Janette Johnson

NEW JERSEY NETS

Begun as the New Jersey Americans in 1967-68 in the new-born American Basketball Association, the team became the New York Nets for its next four seasons, then turned into the New Jersey Nets for good in 1972-73 to herald its 1973-76 run of ABA success.

One of four ABA survivors taken in the NBA in the 1976 merger—the NBA officially called the Nets, Denver Nuggets, Indiana Pacers, and San Antonio Spurs "expansion teams"—the Nets paid a heavy price for absorption; it was ruled that they infringed on the New York Knicks territory, and they had to pay not only a fee to enter the NBA, but also had to compensate the Knicks for infringement. As a result, the Nets had to sell their best player, Julius Erving, to the highest bidder (Philadelphia) and have spent their entire NBA existence, 17 years, trying to recover from the price paid in 1976.

The Nets have been overshadowed by the midtown Manhattan Knicks from their very start and now play at the Meadowlands Complex's Brendan Byrne Arena, an exit slot on the freeway. The Nets have also been the victim of unfortunate circumstances throughout their history, beginning with the forfeiture of a playoff game at the end of their first ABA season in 1967-68 when a game was moved to another site and the teams arrived to find the floor unplayable.

New Jersey's Americans made their American Basketball Association debut on October 23, 1967. It was a year in which they averaged 2,008 in attendance and lost a reported $500,000 playing at the Teaneck, New Jersey, Armory. Former Bradley University guard Lavern (Jelly) Tart, acquired in mid-season from the Oakland Oaks for Barry Liebowitz—who had been traded by Pittsburgh to the Americans for Art Heyman—led the Nets in scoring (23.6) and was third in the ABA.

Dan Anderson, in his first of two Nets seasons, was fourth in field goal shooting at .494. A trio of Americans, guard Bob Lloyd (.854), forward Tony Jackson (.829), and guard Mel Nowell (.826), ranked second, fourth, and fifth in foul shooting, respectively. Longtime NBA guard Max Zaslofsky, a 10-year veteran with five teams and a 1947-48 scoring champion (21.0) in Chicago, was the coach. Tart briefly held the ABA single-game scoring record of 49 points until Denver's Larry Jones, Tart's former Eastern League (now CBA) teammate at Wilkes-Barre (Pennsylvania), notched 52.

New Jersey tied Kentucky at 36-42 for the fourth playoff spot in the East. (Eight of the 11 teams made the playoffs.) The Americans were the home team in the one-game playoff, the winner to meet second-place Minnesota. The game was originally scheduled for the home Teaneck Armory, but the circus—the big-top type—was scheduled for the building. The game was moved to the Commack (New York) Arena on Long Island.

However, when the teams arrived, the floor was a shambles: pieces of wood were sticking out, and there were loose bolts and nuts all over the place. Both teams placed calls to Commissioner George Mikan to tell their side of the story since the floor was unplayable. Mikan listened, then forfeited the game to the Colonels.

The Americans used 16 players that first season, 13 of whom were playing their first pro season, though many had been out of college four or five years. For six players, it was their only season in the pros.

How impressed were the Americans with that final non-game? Quite a bit, apparently. Owner Arthur Brown of New York City's ABC Freight, who had originally wanted to name the team the Freighters, re-named the team the Nets (to rhyme with Mets and Jets) and moved them on July 15, 1968, to—where else—Long Island's Commack Arena.

The floor was fixed for year two; the team was not. It went 17-61, the fewest wins for any ABA team until Virginia won only 15 games each in 1974-75 and 1975-76, and did not make the playoffs. Guard Willie Somerset, acquired during the season from Houston, averaged 23.8 to finish

seventh in ABA scoring. He was also fifth in free-throw shooting (.830), while Bob Lloyd shot .886 at the line and ranked third to Rick Barry (.888) and Tony Jackson (.887), who was traded away. Lloyd also set an ABA mark by making 49 straight free throws over 13 games, just shy of Bill Sharman's 56 in a row in 1959's NBA playoffs. Houston sank all 36 of its free throw shots in a game against the Nets, the first perfect game in any major pro league by a team with more than 10 attempts. The Nets drew only 43,195 fans (averaging 1,108 per game) for the season.

It's uncertain how many of the Nets' hopes in 1969 were pinned on obtaining three-time College Player of the Year Lew Alcindor (later Kareem Abdul-Jabbar). The ABA draft rights were awarded to the Nets so that Alcindor, a New York City native, could play close to home and be a Nets drawing card. Milwaukee won an NBA coin flip with Phoenix.

Alcindor told the two leagues he would accept one sealed bid from each league. All of the ABA teams agreed to share in the cost of his contract, and a fabulous offer was readied. Nets owner Brown and ABA Commissioner Mikan submitted a lower bid, intending to raise it when needed. True to his word, Alcindor took the Bucks' better offer as the Nets rushed back with a counter-offer and a certified check for one million dollars, which later became a collector's item. Mikan then resigned. The Nets used 23 players that season, their most ever.

Boe Buys Team

In the 1969 off-season clothier Roy Boe bought the team from Brown and moved their playing site again. This time the Nets went to the Island Garden in Hempstead, Long Island, New York. At the same time, Boe promised to push for a new Long Island arena. Zaslofsky was replaced as coach by York Larese, a 6'4" swing-man who played one NBA season in 1961-62. With Lavern Tart finishing seventh in scoring (24.1) and leading the Nets for the second time, and play-mak-

TEAM INFORMATION AT A GLANCE

Founding date: 1967 (ABA); 1977 (NBA)

Home court: Meadowlands Arena
East Rutherford, NJ 07073
Phone: (201) 935-8888
FAX: (201) 935-1088

Seating capacity: 20,039

Team colors: Red, white, and blue.
Team nickname: Nets
Logo: Word "Nets" on top of a basketball.

Franchise record	Won	Lost
(1967-89)	844	1,129

ABA Championships (1): 1976

ing guard Bill Melchionni lured from the NBA Philadelphia Warriors to tie for second in ABA assists at 5.7, the Nets went 39-45 and made the playoffs for the first time.

Lloyd (Sonny) Dove, the team's top college draft pick in 1967, came from the NBA Pistons, where he'd scored just 174 points in 57 games over 398 minutes in two seasons. He became a 14.4 scorer with 6.8 rebounds, closer to his St. Johns (New York) roots. In the playoffs, the Nets went up, 1-0, 2-1, 3-2, over Kentucky, which won the last two games to advance to the Eastern Finals.

The Nets used 18 players, only one of whom was a 1969 draft pick: Billy Evans, picked in the second tier of five rounds. Attendance climbed past the 4,000 plateau. Larese was out and St. Johns coach Lou (Looie) Carnesecca, who had signed a 3-year contract before the 1969-70 season, took over after finishing out his St. Johns pact.

Owner Roy Boe added a significant playing face, too, when he got Rick Barry from Virginia. The Oakland Oaks had moved to Washington for their third season and now planned to go to Virginia. Barry did not want to live in the South. "I don't want my kids growing up saying, 'Hi y'all, Dad'," he said in a *Sports Illustrated* feature. Barry led the Nets with 29.4 ppg, second in the ABA to Dan Issel's 29.8. He also led the ABA in free throw percentage for the second time at .890 and was the first Net named to the All-ABA Team. Melchionni was first in assists at 8.3 per game.

Rookie Billy Paultz, a 6'11" center who came with Carnesecca from St. Johns, was second in field goal percentage at .524. The Nets, with all of that, improved one victory to 40-44, good for third place in the East. In the ABA's screwy playoff matchups, the first- and third-place teams met in one Conference semifinal while the second- and fourth-place teams were matched in the other.

Barry, who had been acquired from Virginia for cash ($25,000 or $75,000 said varying sources) and a draft choice, couldn't carry the Nets past Virginia, who had finished 15 games ahead of them in the regular season, bowing 4-2. The foundation for future success was being laid. New York, Indiana, Virginia, and Denver played a double header before 12,252 at the new Madison Square Garden. About 6,000 red, white, and blue basketballs were given away as a promotion, with an ABA record $80,000 gate reported.

The 1971-72 season marked the first time that every team was in the same spot as the year before. The Nets stayed on Long Island and as of February 11th were housed in the new Nassau Veterans Memorial Coliseum in Uniondale. In year five of the ABA and Lou Carnesecca's second, the Nets reversed their record of 1970-71, improving to 44-40, still finishing third in the East. The team had stability, using a record-low 15 players, seven of them returnees.

Rick Barry was second in scoring again, this time averaging 31.5 in his final ABA season, his second-best ABA average to his league-leading 34.0 in Oakland in 1969. Barry repeated as free throw shooting champ (.878), and Melchionni was again the assists leader (8.4). Power forward Tom Washington was second in field goal percentage (.571). Barry and Melchionni made the All-League Team.

John Roche made the All-Rookie Team and with Barry helped the Nets oust 68-game winner Kentucky 4-3 in the first round of the playoffs and Virginia 4-3 in the Eastern Finals. The Pacers claimed their second title in three years 4-2 over the Nets. Roche had averaged 32 points in the Kentucky series.

Attendance averaged more than 12,000 in the playoffs at the new arena, and two games with Indiana drew 15,000. With its first winning season behind them, optimism was at an all-time high, even though a judge ordered Barry to return to the Golden State Warriors (a native of Elizabeth, New Jersey prefered playing nearer his home). However, the team announced it had signed 6'11"
Marquette (Michigan) center Jim Chones, who, along with Princeton's Brian Taylor, were taken as "hardships" in the 1972 draft during the playoffs.

Imagine what the Nets might have been in 1971-72 had they not decided against trying to sign little-known forward Julius Erving, who was leaving the University of Massachusetts after his junior season and was a Roosevelt, New York, native. He became Co-Rookie of the Year when he was sixth in scoring and third in rebounds.

The Nets did get the Rookie of the Year in 1972-73 in Brian Taylor, a classy point guard, and he and Jim Chones made the All-Rookie Team. Barry went back to the West Coast. George Carter, a well-traveled forward led the team in scoring at 19.0 as the Nets sagged to 30-54 in Lou Carnesecca's final season.

The Nets made a fourth straight playoff appearance, but bowed to the Carolina Cougars in five games. Larry Brown, who would coach the Nets a decade later, was Carolina's rookie coach. Utah guard Jimmy Jones said of the Nets, "Sometimes they stand around like they are waiting for Rick Barry to come back."

Bill Melchionni led the ABA again with 7.5 assists while Billy (Whopper) Paultz was third in rebounding at 12.5, his highest average. During the season, Nets legal counsel Bob Carlson replaced Jack Dolph as commissioner of the ABA. Carlson had been one of the people working in behalf of the ABA toward a merger with the NBA.

Erving and Loughery

The 1973-74 season brought a lot of "new" to the Nets. Carnesecca had missed college ball very much and it was no surprise that the future Hall-of-Fame coach returned to alma mater St. Johns. Kevin Loughery, who had finished out the woeful 1972-73 Philadelphia 76ers 9-73 season as head coach for the last 32 games (5-26), came over as the new coach when his agent and the 76ers couldn't agree on a "coach-only" contract and Roy Boe offered him $35,000 to coach the Nets.

Julius Erving: The Doctor

Although he was only with the team for three seasons (1973 to 1976), Julius Erving was inarguably the greatest player in Nets history. The Nets paid Julius Erving the supreme compliment on his 1986-87 farewell tour by retiring his number 32 uniform on his final Meadowlands appearance.

In his three Nets seasons, New Jersey won two of the last three American Basketball Association Championships. Erving was the ABA's MVP in each of his three Nets seasons (tying with Indiana's George McGinnis in 1975). He won three ABA scoring titles, including two during his Nets tenure, in 1974 and 1976.

The Nets acquired him from Virginia, which was in financial trouble at a time when Erving was eyeing the NBA after signing with the Atlanta Hawks. The Nets lost him because owner Roy Boe was in financial trouble after the 1976 merger and needed cash to pay the NBA $3.2 million entry fee and a $480,000 annual indemnity to the Knicks.

As much as for his on-floor presence, Doctor J was admired for his locker-room leadership, his practice ethic, and his ability to deal with the media and pump up teammates who needed a boost. He was the ABA's goodwill ambassador in the 1970s after leaving the University of Massachusetts following his junior season.

Naismith Memorial Basketball Hall of Fame

And he was the NBA's ambassador following the merger until his 1987 retirement as the third-most-prolific scorer (ABA/NBA combined) in pro basketball history with 30,026 points. The Nets went 168-84 (.667) during his three-year stay, still New Jersey's best run of success and its only 50-plus win seasons. In addition, the team was 21-11 in the play-offs. It was the "Era of Erving."

Julius Erving was purchased from the Virginia Squires in the summer after he tried to jump to the NBA Atlanta Hawks. Boe paid off both the Squires and the Hawks. Then Boe signed Larry Kenon from Memphis State, whose draft rights were held by the Memphis Tams.

Tams owner Charlie Finley—yes, the baseball and hockey Charlie O.—did not have enough money to sign "Mr. K.," and the ABA approved the deal because it didn't want him to go to the NBA. The Nets also grabbed another underclassman in "Super John" Williamson, who would step into the starting lineup with Brian Taylor at guard after a 4-1 start became 4-10. Williamson and Kenon both averaged 15 ppg.

Erving was the ABA scoring champ at 27.4, third in steals at 2.27, and tied for fourth in assists at 5.2 in winning the regular season MVP Award.

He also claimed the Finals MVP crown as the Nets downed Utah in five games.

The Nets had gone 55-29 in regular season play, the ABA's best, and scuttled Virginia 4-1 and Kentucky 4-0 in earlier rounds. Lou Dampier shattered Lloyd's old consecutive free throws record with 55 straight.

The Nets won despite rebound woes. Artis Gilmore set an NBA mark with 40 and George McGinnis fashioned a 52-point, 37-rebound game against them. Loughery contributed to ABA technical foul lore in capping off a two-week span in which Memphis's Bill van Breda Kolff picked up four in a game, Indiana's Bob Leonard got three and a two-game suspension for throwing a ball rack at an official, and Loughery got three when he threw a paper cup full of water on the floor. The Nets led the ABA in attendance with an 8,923 average, a long way from 1967-68, when they had 50 season ticketholders at 4,800-seat Teaneck Armory.

The Nets made few changes for 1974-75, using just 13 players, the franchise's all-time record low. Coach Kevin Loughery retained the title lineup of Erving, Kenon, Paultz, Taylor, and Williamson, all of whom had left college early, and went 58-26 in the regular season to tie Kentucky in the Eastern Division. Still, the team lost a one-game playoff in Kentucky 109-99 for the title and playoff seeding.

In 1972-73, the ABA had switched to 1-4 and 2-3 matchups. Denver, with new coach Larry Brown, was revitalized with a 65-19 mark. Erving lost the scoring title to George McGinnis, the previous year's runner-up, 29.8 to 27.9. Taylor led in steals at 2.80, with Erving fourth at 2.21, and Doc was fourth in blocked shots at 1.87. Erving set an ABA record and personal pro best with 63 points in a four-overtime game at San Diego.

New York had gone 12-0 versus St. Louis in the regular season, but the Spirits won in the playoffs 4-1. Erving and McGinnis shared the league MVP Award. Dave DeBusschere, who had retired from the Knicks after the 1973-74 season, spent the year as Nets GM before becoming ABA commissioner to preside over the merger.

Shortly after the season ended, the Nets started making changes. DeBusschere replaced Tedd Munchak as ABA commissioner. On June 3rd, in separate deals, the Nets sent Larry Kenon and Mike Gale to the Spurs. On June 24th, journeyman forward Wendell Ladner was killed at age 26 in a plane crash in Mississippi, and his number, four, was the first retired by the Nets. On September 8th, Paultz went to the Spurs as well.

In return, the Nets had acquired Tim Bassett, Kim Hughes, Rich Jones, Ted McClain, Swen Nater, and Jim Eakins. Most importantly, they still had Erving, Taylor, and Williamson, and the veteran Melchionni was still on hand.

Before the start of the 1975-76 season, the Nets and Nuggets applied separately to join the NBA, a move that shocked the players and was opposed by the NBA Players Association because they felt it would constitute a merger, end the ABA, and create just one league.

Erving dominated the league, winning the scoring title at 29.3 and then averaged 34.6 in the playoffs. He was the regular season and playoff MVP as the Nets went 55-29 to finish second in what had become a seven-team ABA (no divisions) due to three teams folding. Erving was fifth in rebounding (11.0) and third in steals (2.46). Taylor led the league in three-point shooting (.421) and was fourth in steals (2.31). Eakins was second in free throw percentage (.888), and Hughes was third in field goal percentage (.530) while hitting a career-best .455 at the foul line as a rookie.

The Nets ousted third-place San Antonio in seven games, then claimed the final ABA title over Denver in six games as no game was decided by more than nine points. Erving's game-winning jumper at the buzzer in Game One's 120-118 win set the tone for the series.

Erving had made an impact in Denver at the All-Star Game when he won the first-ever All-Star Slam-Dunk contest over Nugget David Thompson, who was the All-Star Game's MVP. Erving showed what would become his legendary dunk when he took off at the foul line and soared to the hoop.

In Game Six, Denver led by as much as 22 in the third period before Erving led a 34-14 fourth-quarter comeback in the series's fifth sell-out. He had 31 points and 19 rebounds. He had scored 45 in Game One. "If this is going to be it, I wanted to go out a winner," Erving said. It was it. It also marked the last appearance of the red, white, and blue ball, the 30-second shot clock, and the three-point field goal, which would be adopted by the NBA in 1979.

In its final year, the Nets and ABA played with a 24-second clock in preparation for a merger. When the NBA players approved the settlement of the Oscar Robertson suit at the All-Star Game, the way was paved for a merger. The questions remained: how many teams would get in and at what price?

Hello NBA, Goodbye Dr. J

On June 17, 1976, the Nets were accepted into the NBA along with Denver, Indiana, and San Antonio, but the price was steep; they had to pay $3.2 million to the NBA by September 15th and had to pay the New York Knicks $480,000 per year for 10 years as a territorial indemnity.

Then, Julius Erving revealed that he felt he had been promised a new contract, though he had years to go on a $350,000 deal according to owner Roy Boe. Strapped for cash, Boe first offered the Doctor to the Knicks in lieu of the indemnity fee. They refused. Philadelphia offered $3 million in cash for Erving and gave him a $3 million contract over five years in a deal finalized October 20th—just days before the season began.

The Nets were in the NBA, but their team was in tatters. In addition, they would not share in the TV revenue for the first three seasons and would not take part in the 1976 college draft. They could keep their own players, but the other players from disbanded teams were placed in a dispersal draft. The Nets selected 11th and grabbed Jan van Breda Kolff for $60,000.

Brian Taylor was dealt away to the Kansas City Kings September 10th, along with a pair of first-round picks, for Nate (Tiny) Archibald, the only player ever to win scoring and assists titles in the same season, in 1972-73, with the Kings. Archibald would average 20.5 ppg in 34 games before breaking an ankle to finish his season.

Williamson was swapped to the Pacers January 31st for a first-round pick and Darnell Hill-man. Guard Robert (Bubbles) Hawkins came on after being waived by Golden State to lead the Nets in scoring at 19.3 in 52 games, but the team limped in 22-60 and last in the Atlantic Division with the NBA's worst record.

The Nets went 10-21 at home, worse than their 17-win ABA Year Two. Veteran Bill Melchionni retired to become GM before the season began. Van Breda Kolff was 10th in free throw percentage (.855), the lone Net among league leaders. Attendance dipped to 6,928 per game.

Milwaukee won the 1977 draft coin flip, and Kansas City used the Nets' pick to select Otis Birdsong, who would become a Net four years later. The Nets picked seventh with the Pacers' choice and grabbed underclassman Bernard King.

On September 12th the Nets moved to New Jersey, playing at the Rutgers Athletic Center in Piscataway. It was a hard-to-find location and locals adopted the phrase "thataway to Piscataway." Archibald had been traded to Buffalo, and Hawkins held out, returning to play just 15 games.

But Bernard King was a sensation with 24.2 ppg, tenth in NBA scoring, and 9.5 rebounds. John Williamson, reacquired from Indiana less than a year after being sent away, wound up 11th in NBA scoring (23.7). Kevin Porter, obtained from Detroit, averaged 10.2 assists to lead the NBA and broke a 19-year-old NBA record set by Bob Cousy

---

RETIRED NETS NUMBERS

4: Wendell Ladner
23: John Williamson
25: Bill Melchionni
32: Julius Erving

PROFILE — Super John Williamson

Super John Williamson, a 1973 Nets ABA "hardship" draft selection from New Mexico State, may have been the Nets player most loved by coach Kevin Loughery. Julius Erving was the best player and the most respected, but Williamson earned a special place in Loughery's heart and the hearts of Nets fans with his big-play heroics during the team's two championship seasons. Williamson was also the only Nets player ever traded away and then brought back.

Williamson was a kid, a rookie who had just turned 21, when he was inserted in the Nets starting lineup with the team at 4-10 after a 4-1 start. He and Brian Taylor replaced three-time all-Star Bill Melchionni and John Roche, who was later traded away, and the Nets soared. Williamson was a physical player who took too many shots, some of them bad. He could score, though, and gave the team another key weapon. At that time, the Nets lineup consisted of Taylor, Williamson, Julius Erving, Larry Kenon, and Billy Paultz, all of whom left college early for the ABA.

During his fourth Nets season, the team's first year in the NBA, Williamson was dealt to the Indiana Pacers, then brought back five days short of a year later. Two years later he was sent to Washington and finished up in the 1980-81 season, just past age 28.

In poor health in recent years, Williamson was brought back by the Nets for a night in 1992, when his uniform, number 23, was retired—the fourth set aside by the franchise. Williamson averaged 20.1 in five NBA seasons and 14.1 in three ABA campaigns. His best three years came in 1976-77, 1977-78, and 1978-79, when he averaged 20.8, 23.7, and 22.2, respectively.

(tied by Guy Rogers) with 29 assists February 24th against Houston. George (Swat) Johnson led the league in blocked shots (3.38).

But the Nets improved just two wins to 24-58, still last in the Atlantic Division, with the NBA's worst record. Kevin Loughery was in the first year of a three-year contract and secure.

Nets Sold

A partnership led by Joseph Taub and Alan Cohen purchased the Nets franchise August 28, 1978 and made certain it was financially secure. Boe had been drained by the Nets and the NHL Islanders, as well as the indemnity to the Knicks, which would run through the 1985-86 season.

On the court, the Nets improved by 13 wins to 37-45 and made the NBA playoffs for the first time. However, they were eliminated by the 76ers in two games in the first round. The season was nonetheless a success since they finished six games

ahead of the across-the-river Knicks. John Williamson ranked 13th in NBA scoring (22.2), and Bernard King was 19th (21.6). George Johnson finished second in blocked shots (3.24).

Second-year guard Eddie Jordan, from Rutgers, ranked second in steals (2.45). Kevin Porter had been sent back to Detroit, where he set an NBA record with 1,099 assists (13.4). First-round pick Winford Boynes made the team but contributed little in his two seasons. But there was now promise for the future, with Charlie Theokas having taken over as General Manager.

In the 1979 draft the Nets grabbed forwards Calvin Natt from N.E. Louisiana and undergraduate Clif Robinson from USC in the first round. In the tenth round, they selected a non-player from Tulane, Eric Fleisher, son of NBA Players Association head Larry Fleisher and later a player agent like his father.

Bernard King was sent to the Utah Jazz October 2nd for center Rich Kelley. This opened a starting spot for Natt, who, on February 9th, was traded to Portland for Maurice Lucas and two first-round picks. Natt wound up on the All-Rookie Team while Robinson, recovered from early-season injuries and illness, made the Second Team while scoring 13.6 with 7.2 rebounds. Kelley was moved to Phoenix February 15th for a 1982 first-round choice. Eleven days earlier, Williamson was traded to Washington for long-range shooter Roger Phegley, who would be gone at season's end.

On December 16th, newly acquired Mike Newlin (from Houston) set a Nets NBA record with 52 points. He finished 17th in scoring at 20.7 and fifth in free throw shooting (.884) in his finest pro season, while George Johnson was again second in blocked shots (3.19). Eddie Jordan finished second in steals (2.72) and ninth in assists (6.8). Still, the team stumbled home 34-48, last in the Atlantic Division, five games behind the Knicks and 27 out of first as Rookie of the Year Larry Bird led a 29-game Celtics turnaround, best in the NBA to date.

The Nets picked 6-7 in the 1980 college draft and grabbed Atlantic Coast Conference products Mike O'Koren (North Carolina) and Mike Gminski (Duke). They also got a sleeper, fourth-round choice Rory Sparrow, who twice came back from the CBA to last 12 NBA seasons but only one in New Jersey.

The best pickup might have been Darwin Cook, a fifth-round pick waived by the Detroit Pistons in the Summer League and signed by the Nets to play six seasons. Mike Newlin scored 21.4 to lead the team again and ranked 15th in the NBA. He was third in free throw shooting (.888), the Nets' only other league ranking. Kevin Loughery resigned as coach in December after a 12-23 start with a 297-318 mark for his seven-plus Nets seasons.

Assistant Coach Bob MacKinnon took over. Larry Brown was hired away from UCLA in March to take over in 1981-82. The team finished 24-58, last in the 5-team Atlantic Division, with the NBA's third-worst record and 20 games out of the playoffs. It was a dismal end to the team's stay at the Rutgers Athletic Center.

Brown and First-Rounders Arrive

Larry Brown took over as coach in 1981-82, and the Nets, with the third pick in the college draft, grabbed Maryland underclassman Buck Williams, who went on to win the NBA Rookie of the Year Award and make the All-Rookie Team. The Nets, for only the fifth time in NBA annals, had three first-round choices; they also snagged Williams's Maryland teammate Albert King, brother of Bernard, and forward Ray Tolbert.

In preparation for playing in the Meadowlands's Brendan Byrne Arena and hosting the 1982 All-Star Game—in which Buck Williams would become the first Net to play in an NBA All-Star Game—the Nets engaged in active trading. Maurice Lucas and Mike Newlin were sent to New York just before the season for Ray Williams.

In the summer, Otis Birdsong came from Kansas City for Cliff Robinson. Early in the season, Mike Woodson moved to the Kings for Sam Lacey while Tolbert went to Seattle for former Rutgers forward "Jammin'" James Bailey.

The Nets started 3-12 before coming on to finish 44-38, the team's first winning year in the NBA. The 20-win improvement was the season's best, but New Jersey, which gained the fourth of six playoff spots, was upset by fifth-seed Washington in two straight. Ray Williams was 19th in NBA scoring at 20.4, while Buck Williams was third in rebounding (12.3) with his first of five 1000-rebound years in his first six seasons. He was also third in field goal percentage (.582), thanks to his strong inside play.

Ray Williams was fifth in NBA steals (2.43). Buck Williams had ten rebounds and four points in the All-Star Game, which had originally been ticketed for the Knicks and Madison Square Garden but was switched to the Meadowlands. The Nets ranked fourth in NBA attendance at 13,875. In the final week of the season, Ray Williams tied Newlin's club record with 52 points against Detroit. That was his single individual highlight of his only Nets season. He was in Kansas City with the Kings in 1982-83.

In a season strange even by Nets standards, turmoil and change were the norm. Phil Ford came from Kansas City in the Williams deal in the 1982 summer and was installed as the Nets point guard. Seven games into the season, he was traded to the Bucks for Mickey Johnson. Johnson helped the Nets go on a franchise-record 11 straight wins from December 23rd to January 12th.

On February 6th, he and 1982 Nets first-rounder Eric (Sleepy) Floyd were dealt to Golden State for ex-Knick Michael Ray Richardson. Darryl Dawkins was acquired over the summer from the 76ers. Buck Williams and Albert King led the Nets scoring (17.0). Williams was second in NBA rebounding (12.5) and fifth in field goal accuracy (.588), while Dawkins was third (.599). Richardson led the NBA in steals (2.84), and Darwin Cook was fifth (2.37).

The Nets won their all-time NBA best 49 games, but the season was marred when Larry Brown was fired with six games left for accepting the University of Kansas job for 1983-84. Assistant Bill Blair went 2-4 the rest of the way, and the Nets were eliminated by the Knicks, who finished five wins behind them, in two straight games. Buck Williams played in the All-Star Game, his second straight.

Albeck Promises Playoff Win

Stan Albeck, an ABA and NBA coaching veteran, left San Antonio after a three-season 153-93 stay to coach the Nets. While the Nets made no trades, they had to compensate the Spurs for Albeck jumping his contract and gave them the rights to forward Fred Roberts, who had played overseas in 1982-83, and cash. The Nets won 19 of 25 games down the stretch to gain a third straight playoff berth with a 45-37 record.

In the first round, New Jersey ousted defending NBA Champion Philadelphia 3-2, with the visiting team winning every game. It was the first year that 16 teams made the NBA playoffs and first-round byes were eliminated, but the Nets as the sixth seed would have qualified anyway.

Darryl Dawkins had his best NBA season with 16.8 points and 6.8 rebounds while ranking fourth in field goal percentage (.599). Buck Williams became the ninth player to grab 1000-plus rebounds in each of his first three seasons, ranking second (12.3) again. Darwin Cook rated eighth in steals (2.00). Michael Ray Richardson was held to 48 games, 12.0 points, and 103 steals. Otis Birdsong topped the scoring at 19.6, missing 13 games. Third-round pick Bruce Kuczenski was the only pick to play, getting into seven of his 15 career NBA games before being let go.

Stan Albeck took the Nets back to the playoffs again in 1984-85, but the fifth-seeded Nets were bounced by Detroit in three straight games after a 42-40 regular season. Birdsong (20.6) and Richardson (20.1) formed a formidable starting backcourt. Richardson led the NBA in steals (2.96) and was sixth in assists (8.2), while Buck Williams was third in rebounding (12.3). He was the 8th player and first forward to grab 1,000 rebounds in each of his first four seasons.

The team's top draft pick was southpaw forward Jeff Turner, a 1984 Olympian. Injuries (223 lost games) hurt the Nets as Birdsong (26), Darwin Cook (24), Darryl Dawkins (43), Albert King (40), and Mike O'Koren (38) were key casualties, and the team used 13 different starting lineups. Richardson was selected for the All-Star Game in Indiana and was voted Comeback Player of the Year, an award since discontinued. Albeck resigned June 13th to coach the Chicago Bulls.

Wohl Hired as Coach

Dave Wohl, a Nets player in the team's first two NBA seasons, was selected as the new coach and his running game had the team off to a 23-14 start when Michael Ray Richardson suffered a drug relapse and later was banned from the NBA as a third-strike offender.

Darryl Dawkins's back injury kept him out of 31 of the last 32 games, but Mike Gminski blossomed and led a balanced scoring sheet (16.5). He was third in NBA free throw shooting (.893), and

---

PROFILE | **Kevin Loughery**

Kevin Loughery made his coaching mark with the New Jersey Nets—for better <u>and</u> worse. After a 31-game (5-26) breaking-in stint with the woeful 9-73 Philadelphia 76ers in 1972-73, Loughery came to the nets when his agent and the 76ers management could not agree on a "coach-only" contract. His deal had been as player-coach, but his playing career was done.

Nets owner Roy Boe offered Loughery $35,000 a year for five years just to coach and then brought in Julius Erving to build a team around. The Nets improved 25 wins that first season and won the 1974 ABA title. They won a second title in 1976, the ABA's final season.

When Erving left, Loughery's coaching became subject to disparagement, but Dr. J was not the only loss; the financially strapped Nets lost other players, made some questionable acquisitions, and could not recapture their glory days.

In their nearly seven and a half seasons with Loughery as head coach, the Nets were 297-318. A feisty player for 11 seasons with the Pistons, Bullets, and 76ers, Loughery was a sideline battler adept at working the officials and was annually among the league coaching leaders in technical fouls and ejections. His 1992-93 stay in Miami was a marked contrast.

After leaving the Nets, Loughery coached in Atlanta (1981-83), Chicago (1983-85)—where the general manager was his longtime teammate and assistant Rod Thorn—and Washington (1985-88), then spent time broadcasting and scouting until the Miami Heat called. He is recalled as the Nets' winningest coach.

Williams was third in rebounding at 12.0, while Richardson rated second in steals (2.66).

The Nets ended a string of four straight winning seasons with a 39-43 slate and lost to Central Division champ Milwaukee in three straight in a fifth consecutive playoff appearance. Williams scored 13 in his third All-Star Game appearance. Top draft pick Yvon Joseph, a second-rounder, got into one game and was gone.

The Nets injury jinx continued as 252 player games were lost to injury in 1986-87 and the Nets plummeted to a 24-58 record and missed the playoffs after five straight appearances. Darryl Dawkins was lost after six games, and Otis Birdsong left with a leg injury after 13.

Orlando Woolridge was the first forward to lead the team in scoring (20.7) since 1978-79. Buck Williams was third in rebounding (12.5) and sixth in field goal shooting (.557), and Kevin McKenna was sixth in three-point shooting (.419). Harry Weltman, formerly of Cleveland, was hired to head basketball operations, and Wohl received

a contract extension. Top draft pick Pearl Washington shared the point, ranking second in team assists.

Amazingly, the Nets set an NBA mark with 348 player games lost to injury in 1987-88. After a 2-13 start, Coach Dave Wohl was let go, and after a 12-week search, Hall-of-Famer and former Knick All-Star center Willis Reed was named captain of the Nets. Bob MacKinnon coached the injury-riddled team on an interim basis.

After more than six seasons, Buck Williams missed his first games (12), but was still fifth in NBA rebounding and seventh in field goal accuracy. He scored a career-best 18.3 to lead the team. Roy Hinson, acquired from the 76ers for Mike Gminski, was tenth in blocked shots (1.82). Keith Lee, John Bagley, and Tim McCormick also came in trades.

Attendance climbed for the first time since the inaugural Meadowlands season. The team was 10-29 under MacKinnon and 7-21 under Reed, an overall 19-63, worst in the Eastern Conference and

---

the franchise's worst yet in the NBA. Top draft pick Dennis Hopson debuted to mixed reviews, scoring 9.6.

The 1988-89 season, Willis Reed's only full season as coach, saw the Nets improve to 26-56, but with the NBA's fifth-worst mark and out of the playoffs. The team obtained seven new players, chief among them Joe Barry Carroll and ex-Laker guard Mike McGee. New Jersey started 5-3, but Carroll's loss triggered a 6-game loss skein and despite some later key wins over top foes, the improvement was slight.

Roy Hinson led team scoring (16.0). Buck Williams was seventh in field goal accuracy (.560) but finished out of the Top Ten in rebounding and under 10.0 (9.4) for the first time. The Nets had five sellouts, and attendance increased again. First-rounder Chris Morris scored 14.1.

Fitch Begins Reign

In August of 1989, Willis Reed gave up coaching to become senior vice-president of basketball operations, and Bill Fitch was hired as head coach. In June the Nets sent Buck Williams to Portland for oft-injured Sam Bowie and first-round point guard Mookie Blaylock. The Nets hit bottom with a franchise-worst 17-65 record, the poorest record in the NBA, a game behind expansion Miami in the Atlantic Division.

Dennis Hopson (15.8), Chris Morris (14.8), and Bowie (14.7) led the scoring, and Bowie managed 10.1 rebounds and 1.78 blocks after almost two idle years. In a late-season home win over Boston, the Celtics were held to a franchise-low 77 points—six in one quarter. Attendance fell 500 a game.

Optimism surged when the Nets won the 1990 May draft lottery. In June, they selected Syracuse forward Derrick Coleman, who would go on to become 1990-91 Rookie of the Year. He ranked tenth in NBA rebounding and was second in Nets scoring (18.4) to Reggie Theus (18.6), who came from Orlando. Theus reached 19th on the NBA points list (19,015), while Coach Bill Fitch

AP/Wide World Photos

Derrick Coleman

posted his 800th NBA win, against Washington, March 15th. In-season trades brought Terry Mills from Denver and Drazen Petrovic from Portland.

The record improved to 26-56 as the Nets led the NBA with 600 blocked shots, but attendance sagged to 11,949 per game. The Nets got another high pick in the 1991 draft and picked underclassman Kenny Anderson (Georgia Tech) from nearby Queens in what by all accounts was not a unanimous choice among Nets leaders. Signed four games into the season, Anderson got just 17 minutes per game, netting 7.0 points and 3.2 assists.

With Reggie Theus gone, Drazen Petrovic was the top scorer (20.6), 17th in the NBA. Derrick Coleman averaged 9.5 rebounds but missed 17 games and did not qualify for the NBA leaders list. Mookie Blaylock was fourth in steals (2.36). Petrovic ranked second in three-point shooting (.444) and was fourth in the All-Star Weekend Long Distance Shootout.

The team improved 14 wins to 40-42, making the playoffs for the first time since 1986 despite late-year turmoil that put Coach Bill Fitch's job in jeopardy. The Nets closed 33-24 (21-14 after the All-Star break) after a 7-18 start and got the sixth seed on a tie-breaker but lost to the Cavs in four. On May 12th, an embattled Fitch resigned. The Nets had led the NBA in rebounding (47.6) and set an NBA one-game blocks mark (22) as attendance surged.

Daly Takes Over

The Nets ended a string of seven losing seasons with a 43-39 mark in Chuck Daly's first season as head coach. They made the playoffs again and this time took Cleveland to five games in the first round before losing. Mookie Blaylock was traded before the season, opening the point guard slot for Kenny Anderson, who missed the last 27 games after hurting his wrist but still ranked ninth in assists at 8.2.

Drazen Petrovic made the All-NBA Third Team after finishing 11th in scoring at 22.3, third in three-point percentage (.449), ninth in free throw shooting (.870), and 20th in field goal accuracy (.518). Derrick Coleman's 20.7 average was good for 17th. He was tenth in rebounding (11.2) and also made the All-NBA Third Team.

The NBA and international basketball communities were stunned when Petrovic was killed in an auto crash in Germany on June 7, 1993.

SOURCES

BOOKS

Bell, Marty, *The Legend of Dr. J,* Coward McCann & Geoghegan, 1975.

Carter, Craig, and Alex Sachare, *The Sporting News NBA Guide,* 1992-93 edition, The Sporting News, 1992.

Hollander, Zander, editor, *The NBA's Official Encyclopedia of Pro Basketball,* New American Library, 1981.

Hollander, Zander, and Alex Sachare, editors, *The Official NBA Encyclopedia,* Villard Books, 1989.

Hollander, Zander, editor, *The Pro Basketball Encyclopedia,* Corwin Books, 1977.

Mertz, John, and John Tudhope, editors, *The New Jersey Nets 1992-93 Media Guide,* New Jersey Nets, 1992.

Pluto, Terry, *Loose Balls: The Short, Wild Life of the American Basketball Association,* Simon & Schuster, 1990.

Sachare, Alex, and Mark Shimabukuro, *The Sporting News NBA Register,* 1992-93 edition, The Sporting News, 1992.

NEW YORK KNICKS

Basketball is a city game, and no city has taken to basketball like New York. Fans follow hundreds of high school and college teams that make their home in the Big Apple, but when the Knicks are hot, every other team takes second place in New York's heart. From their early days as a quick, scrappy unit under coach Joe Lapchick to the championship years between 1969 and 1973, to Pat Riley's physical squads of the 1990s, the Knicks have always played a tough, defensive brand of basketball that New Yorkers appreciate.

Though the Knicks have certainly had their long streaks of bad play and last-place finishes, few events in New York have the electricity and glamour of a Knicks' game on a Saturday night at their home, the legendary "Mecca of basketball," Madison Square Garden.

Given the competition from college basketball and the other pro basketball league at the time—the National Basketball League—few people in 1946 had high hopes for the Knickerbockers and the Basketball Association of America (BAA). The Knicks' general manager of the era, Ned Irish, stood firm, though, behind his dream of a pro game as fast, clean and exciting as the college game was then.

By signing some of the best local players from New York, the city with the deepest reserve of basketball talent in the world, Irish built a winner that reached the playoffs nine straight years and the finals three times in a row during the late 1940s and early 1950s and garnered a strong following among the New York fans.

The Knicks' fortunes took a turn for the worse in the mid-1950s. Except for a good 40-32 season and brief playoff appearance in 1959, the Knicks stayed at the bottom of the league from 1955 through 1966. Consistently poor personnel decisions kept the club down, and draft pick after draft pick turned out to be a washout until 1964, when the Knicks selected Willis Reed. Reed proved to be the cornerstone of the team's rebuilding effort.

The Knicks added to the roster such luminaries as Bill Bradley, Walt Frazier, and Phil Jackson over the next few years. When Red Holzman came on board to coach in 1968, the Knicks were ready to take over the league.

Knicks fans still talk about the championship teams of 1969-70 and 1972-73 and compare every current Knick squad to them. The old Knicks win every comparison and easily stack up as one of the greatest teams ever to play under the banner of the NBA. Holzman stressed defense, crisp passing, and smart play, and he created a team and a style that drew the best out of every man on the floor and captured the imagination of basketball fans not only in New York, but all over the country.

These were the original "Showtime" teams, long before the Lakers of Pat Riley and Magic Johnson. Willis Reed's courage, Clyde Frazier's cool, Bill Bradley's brains, Earl Monroe's skill, and Dave DeBusschere's toughness combined to make the Garden a focal point of interest for sports fans everywhere.

During the 1970s many of the great Knicks retired or were traded and the team entered another long period of rebuilding. They failed to make the playoffs in 1976 and, save for a couple teams anchored around the great forward Bernard King in the early 1980s, the Knicks continued to live off the fading glory of the championship years.

But in 1984, just as 20 years before the acquisition of a big man had changed the team, the Knicks chose Georgetown star Patrick Ewing as the number-one pick in the draft and a new era began. 1987 brought guard Mark Jackson, that season's Rookie of the Year, and Rick Pitino, a young coach who reinstilled the kind of hustle and defense that has always marked a good Knick team.

Though Pitino only stayed a few years, the Knicks rose to a higher level during his stint and showed that the club had the raw talent to win it all. The arrival of highly regarded coach Pat Riley in 1991 and some crucial personnel changes made the Knicks the surprise team of that season and, as Knick fans hope, might mean the start of an-

other string of glory years that will equal the ones enjoyed during the era of Holzman, Reed, and Frazier.

The Early Years

After World War Two, America wanted to have fun again. The soldiers were back home and suddenly both the number of people interested in sports and the quality of athletics shot up. College basketball was booming and Madison Square Garden was the center of the boom, scheduling games all winter and hosting the NIT Tournament, then the biggest college tournament in the game.

At the same time, pro basketball in the NBL, though played by talented players, had a reputation as a dirty, violent game. On June 6, 1946, arena owners from 11 cities around the country formed the Basketball Association of America, a new league that would play a style of basketball more like the college game and draw on recently graduated collegians for players.

New York sportswriter Max Kase came up with the idea, but in order to secure a place for a New York franchise to play, he sold his rights to Madison Square Garden, which in turn sold the rights to Ned Irish. Irish ran the enormously successful college basketball program for Madison Square Garden and represented the newly born Knickerbockers at that first meeting in June.

From the club's inception, the Knicks were a business venture meant to put fans in the seats. Ned Irish was aware, though, that the club was unproven in both its ability to play and to attract fans, and so Irish only booked six home games for his new team at Madison Square Garden. The rest were played at the 69th Regiment Armory at Lexington Avenue and 34th Street. Neil Cohalan, who coached the Manhattan College team from 1929 through 1942, ran the team, led by CCNY grad Sonny Hertzberg and the classy John "Bud" Palmer.

The young league presented its first game on November 1, 1946, in Toronto in a battle that pitted the hometown Huskies against the Knicks. A

TEAM INFORMATION AT A GLANCE

Founding Date: June 6, 1946

Home Court: Madison Square Garden
Two Pennsylvania Plaza
New York, New York 10121
Phone (212) 465-6499.

Seating Capacity: 19,763, built in 1968

Team Uniforms: Home—Base color white, trimmed in orange and blue
Away—Base color blue, trimmed in orange and white

Team Nickname: New York Knickerbockers; Knicks

Franchise Record: Wins—1760 Losses—1795
Playoff Record: Wins—113 Losses—118
World Championships: 1969-1970, 1972-73
Division First Place Finishes: 1952-53, 1953-54, 1969-70, 1970-71, 1988-89, 1991-92 (tie)

Division Last Place Finishes: 1956-57, 1957-58, 1959-60, 1960-61, 1961-62, 1962-63, 1963-64,
1964-65, 1965-66, 1975-76, 1981-82, 1984-85, 1985-86, 1986-87

crowd of 7,090 watched the Knicks win 68-66, but no one back in New York paid much attention. The press gave the Knicks little coverage and, despite a nine-game win streak—a team record until 1968-69—fans preferred the college game. The Knicks fell off some after the streak, but still finished 33-27, losing in the second round of the playoffs to the Philadelphia Warriors, the eventual champion.

Irish believed in the Knicks. What he needed was more local interest and a proven winner, so he hired Joe Lapchick to coach the 1947 Knicks. Lapchick was one of the original Celtics and had taken St. John's to 181 wins against 53 losses as their coach. Irish had actually wanted Lapchick from the start, but waited until the St. John's legend fulfilled his contract with the university. With the additions of Sid Tannenbaum, a New York

University favorite, and Carl Braun from Colgate, Irish was finally close to the kind of Knicks team he had always envisioned.

Braun showed signs that he would be a star early by scoring 47—then the league record—against Providence in December of 1947. The Yankees had signed Braun to pitch, but a sore arm forced him to leave baseball and allowed him to make the Knicks competitive for years. That first season he averaged 14.3 points a game, sixth in the league, and the Knicks finished second. In the playoffs the Knicks blew a lead with under two minutes left in the third and deciding game of their series against the Washington Bullets and were eliminated in the first round.

In 1948 the NBL and the BAA began the merger that resulted in the NBA the following year. Although it's hard to believe now, the NBA was a tough sell in those days. For years to follow, teams folded, sprouted up, and folded again around the league, but the Knicks remained. Fan loyalty was slowly building, and the Garden had the money to stick it out during the lean periods of the league. In any case, Lapchick's brilliant coaching had the Knicks playing solid ball.

Rookie Harry Gallatin joined the club eight games into the season at forward and played every game until he retired in 1958—746 straight games. Though his 8.3 points a game wasn't All-Star caliber, he stepped up his play and became pivotal as the Knicks moved toward their first period of real excellence.

Ned Irish made one mistake, though, in 1948. Dolph Schayes, the most sought after college player of the period, wanted to play with the Knicks, but asked for $1,000 over the salary cap agreed upon by the owners for rookies. Irish wouldn't give it to him, so Schayes went to Syracuse and took with him the chance for the Knicks to dominate the NBA as Russell's Celtics and Magic's Lakers did in later years.

Bud Palmer quit before the start of the 1949-50 season to become a broadcaster, but the addition of four new players proved to be the final piece needed to form the championship caliber Knick teams of the early 1950s.

Dick McGuire was a superb ball-handler and led the league in assists with 386, in part, perhaps, because of his aversion to shooting the ball. Garden fans often yelled, "Shoot, Dick! Shoot!" when he held the ball, and Ned Irish once even offered him $10 for every shot over five he took in a game. McGuire only made $30.

Vince Boryla was the team's best clutch player at forward; Connie Simmons came from Baltimore in a trade for Sid Tannenbaum and put in 11.3 points a game. Finally, Ernie Vandeweghe, a medical student at Columbia University, played part-time as sixth man. Braun upped his scoring average to 15.4 and the Knicks improved to 40-28. That was 13 games behind Schayes' Syracuse team, but the Knicks were clearly on the move.

1951 was a turning point in many ways for the Knicks and the NBA. The NBA featured its

Naismith Memorial Basketball Hall of Fame

Harry Gallatin

first African-American players. The Knicks signed Nat "Sweetwater" Clifton, the former Harlem Globetrotter, and the Celtics added Chuck Cooper. Though neither man became a superstar, their role as pioneers in breaking the color barrier in the NBA was vital to the game and the nation as a whole.

Second, a point shaving scandal broke in 1950 that changed the balance of power between college and pro basketball. College players from CCNY, Long Island University, and NYU were discovered to have affected the outcome of games in order to win bets they had placed on them. The news racked the previously pristine image of college basketball. Ned Irish and Madison Square

Naismith Memorial Basketball Hall of Fame

Dick McGuire

rebounds and fifth in field-goal percentage at .416. McGuire tallied 400 assists over the course of the season, trailing only the Warriors' Andy Phillips.

The Knicks finished third in the Eastern Division, but shocked the Celtics and the Syracuse Nationals in the playoffs to reach the finals against the Rochester Royals. Rochester outplayed the Knicks early and took a commanding three game lead, but the Knicks came back. They won Game Four 79-73 in New York, then squeaked out a 92-89 victory two days later at Rochester.

An 80-73 win in Game Six at the Armory took the series back to Rochester for a seventh game and a chance for New York's first title. Game Seven was close, tied 75-75 with under a minute left, but Rochester pulled it out 79-75. The Knicks lost the championship, but their furious comeback, coupled with the college scandals, enabled them to win over the city of New York. Now the Knicks were really New York's team.

The next season was a virtual repeat of 1950-51. Lapchick's running team had no big stars, but they were a solid, deep unit. Lapchick believed you could never lose a game in the first eight or ten minutes, so he often started three substitutes and then blended in his first line players as the game went on.

Boryla's outside shooting and strength made up for his lack of elevation and Simmons' hook shot proved hard to stop. Zaslofsky led the team with a 14.1 per game scoring average. McGuire did his part, too, setting a team record with 17 assists versus Milwaukee.

At season's end the Knicks were in third, 37-29, three games behind Syracuse. After an 88-87 overtime win over the Celtics in Game Three of their three-game first round set, the Knicks polished off the Nats three games to one and tried again to take the crown, this time versus George Mikan and the Minneapolis Lakers.

A blown call marred Game One as Knick Al McGuire drove to the hoop with seconds left in overtime and was fouled. The foul was called, but both refs missed seeing the ball go in! Everyone at the game saw the shot was good, but the refs disallowed the basket. McGuire missed the free

Garden took much of the blame for their part in making the college game such a big business and at first the pros were found guilty by association.

As the season continued, though, no evidence could connect the pros to the scandal and suddenly the rough young league became the more respectable version of the sport. Another wave of charges about fixing came out in the spring. Thus, through some very unfortunate circumstances, the NBA came of age.

The Knicks came of age during that turbulent season as well. The army called Carl Braun away for two years, but New York picked up Max Zaslofsky from the defunct Chicago Stags to take his place. Gallatin was third in the league with 800

Madison Square Garden has over the years actually been four different buildings, but it has always been America's premier arena. In 1879 William Vanderbilt took over the lease on a former railroad shed that P.T. Barnum used as a "hippodrome" and renamed it "Madison Square Garden" after its location on Madison Square. Poor attendance at Vanderbilt's boxing shows and other events forced him to raze the first Garden, but a syndicate of investors convinced him to build a second Garden on the spot, to be designed by Stanford White.

White's Garden was a marvel of the turn of the century and hosted circuses, political conventions, dog shows and, of course, boxing matches. Tex Rickard expanded its attractions in the 1920s to include bicycle racing, track and field, and some of the biggest fights of all time. He made the Garden the place where New York plays and its success encouraged Rickard to build a third Garden uptown in 1925.

The National Hockey League Rangers arrived in the 1920s, closely followed by college basketball. Along with the old favorites, these two sports kept the fans coming until the Knicks took up residence in the 1950s.

In 1967 the fourth and present Garden opened over Penn Station and the proud tradition of memories—sporting and otherwise—continues over 100 years after its birth with recent events such as the Democratic National Convention in 1992.

throws and the Lakers won 83-79. The call made all the difference. The Knicks and Lakers split the remaining six games and the Lakers were the new champs.

1952-53 was the Knicks' high water mark for a long time to come. Despite injuries to key players, including a broken leg for Max Zaslofsky, the Knicks won the Eastern Division title at 47-23, a .671 winning percentage that stood as a record until 1970. Carl Braun came back from the army and poured in an average of 14 points a game. Harry Gallatin's 33 rebounds against Fort Wayne on March 15 set a team high. After cruising through Baltimore and Boston, the Knicks faced the Lakers again in the finals.

Game One in St. Paul was a grudge match for the Knicks. They won a dramatic 96-88 game but then collapsed. The Lakers took them to school afterward, sweeping the next four games to repeat as champs. 17 years would pass before the Knicks reached the finals again.

Losing the championship three straight years makes it very hard to keep going, but the Knicks persevered. They finished on top in the East again in 1954 after receiving an exceptional season from Harry Gallatin.

Gallatin's 1,098 rebounds led the league and made him the first Knick to pull in over 1,000 boards in a year. He was the first Knick named to the first string of the All-NBA team. He was supported by Braun, who was ninth in scoring with a 14.8 average and McGuire, whose 354 assists put him fourth in the league.

The Knicks were ready for a fourth shot at the finals, but the league had a surprise for them. Instead of the usual playoff system, the first round would be a round robin tournament; the teams with the best records in the tournament would advance to the series.

Game One, the Knicks versus the Celtics, is historic. The NBA believed that it was time to establish itself on television, so Game One was to be broadcast nationwide and turn everyone into instant NBA fans. What America got was 95 fouls and one of the worst basketball games ever played.

The Celtics won 49-46, but not many people

knew the outcome because the network had switched away in disgust before the game's end. The strong reaction against the display forced the league to introduce the 24-second clock for the 1954-55 season. The round robin format did not return. The Knicks did not recover, either. They were eliminated in the first round and began the long descent to the cellar.

On paper, the 1954-55 Knicks looked good. Braun, Gallatin, Jim Baechtold, and newcomer Ray Felix, a very tall though physically limited player, all scored over 1,000 points—the first time an NBA team had four 1,000+ scorers. The team's scoring average leapt to 92.7 points a game from 79.6 the year before. Of course, the introduction of the 24-second clock made these numbers possible.

The Knicks lost Boryla, Fred Schaus, and Ernie Vandeweghe to retirement that year, though, and traded Connie Simmons and Al McGuire. Gallatin, Clifton, and Braun were still there, but replacements Gene Shue, Jack Turner, and Felix were unable to wholly fill the resulting void or show the drive that powered the Knicks before them.

The team hit its low point that season in a game played on December 31 in which they shot only 24 for 102 from the field—a .235 percentage and the second lowest posted in a game. They finished in second place, five games behind Syracuse, and went out in the first round of the playoffs against Boston.

The stress of coaching a faltering team in the toughest sports town in the country finally began to wear down Joe Lapchick in 1955. He sat out a number of games, felled by a recurring illness, and scout Sonny Hertzberg sat in for him. The Knicks played reasonably well until January, going 21 and 20 despite disappointing performances from new big men Kenny Sears and Walter Dukes.

On January 27 Joe Lapchick announced that he was quitting. Ten games later he was gone. His 356-277 career record hung heavily over 29-year-old replacement Vince Boryla, who guided the team to a 35-37 close and a third-place tie with Syracuse. Given the level of play displayed by the club over the course of the season, it was no surprise when they lost the one game playoff with the Nats for the remaining spot in the tournament and sat out post season play for the first time in the team's history. The dark days had settled in at Madison Square Garden.

Between 1957 and 1967, the Knicks finished in last place nine out of ten seasons. There are many reasons for their decline. First, the front office made poor moves such as trading proven star Dick McGuire to Cleveland, where he continued to play good ball, in order to feature rookie bust Brendan McCann in 1957, the same year they sent Gallatin and Clifton to the Pistons for center Charlie Tyra and forward Mel Hutchins.

Draft selections such as Ronnie Shavlik, Gary Berger, and Darrall Imhoff proved less than stellar, while other selections, such as the one of Kenny Sears over Bill Russell in 1955 and Paul Hogue instead of the available John Havlicek, Chet Walker, or Zelmo Beaty in 1962 were simply mistakes.

Suspect coaching over the decade also exacerbated the problems. There were some bright spots. Richie Guerin started in 1956 and put in seven solid years, while Willie Naulls played consistently well for six seasons. Still, the Knicks seemed entangled in a perpetual state of rebuilding.

Vince Boryla's tenure lasted until 1958. His teams came in last both full seasons he coached, despite the presence of seven players that averaged double figures in scoring in 1957-58. Their 112.1 points a game was a record as well, but it wasn't enough to keep up with the Celtics. A pattern of rotating coaches ensued.

Assistant coach Andrew "Fuzzy" Levane came in for the 1958-59 season and at first it seemed like they'd turned the corner. The Knicks took the first ten of eleven games, Kenny Sears averaged 21 a game and Guerin posted a Knick record 57 points against Syracuse, but their lack of rebounding eventually beat them. They played .500 ball after the hot start and came in second. The Nats brushed them away two games to none in the first round of the playoffs.

Twenty-seven games into 1959 Levane was out and Carl Braun was in as player-coach. Braun was born to play basketball, but he proved that he was not born to coach it. He only lasted a season and a half with 40 wins against 87 losses. One player—Johnny Green—best represents these hapless Knicks.

Green was a remarkable leaper. Though only six-foot-five, he often jumped above the rim and out of position for the rebound. He appeared to be in a constant state of befuddlement, which is not a good way to appear in New York City. Despite his obvious lack of basketball skills, Green was among the team leaders during his years with the Knicks from 1959 to 1966.

The Knicks handed the coaching job to former St. Bonaventure coach Eddie Donovan for the 1961 season. The dismal campaign of 1960-61, during which they lost 11 games in a row and served as victims of Wilt Chamberlain's 100-point game, earned the Knicks, or so they thought, first shot at college star Walt Bellamy and a fresh start at respectability with Guerin, Naulls, and the promising rookie.

The NBA thought otherwise. The league gave the first pick in the draft to a new franchise, the Chicago Packers, who snatched up Bellamy and left the Knicks with Tom Stith of St. Bonaventure. A Brooklynite and crowd-pleaser, Stith came down with tuberculosis and only logged 57 games in a Knick uniform. Stith's shortened career was a tremendous disappointment to the organization, and the ensuing three and a half years under Donovan were not good ones for the Knicks.

Richie Guerin tried his best, setting Knick records for points (2,303) and average (23.5) in 1961 and reaching 10,000 career points in 1963 before the team traded him to the Hawks the following season. Still, a porous Knick defense allowed in 1962-63 alone a 73-point game to Wilt, a 71-pointer for Elgin Baylor, and 63 points at the hands of Jerry West. Midway into the 1964 season, headed for another summer in the cellar, the Knicks replaced Donovan with Harry Gallatin.

Even with Rookie of the Year Willis Reed averaging 19.5 a game and snagging 1,175 re-

Naismith Memorial Basketball Hall of Fame

Walt Bellamy

bounds, Gallatin and his disciplinary style did little to motivate the team. Another last place finish in 1965 meant another good pick in the draft and for the second year in a row, the Knicks made a smart choice.

The addition of Bill Bradley, though they had to wait two years for him to complete his studies at Oxford, meant that the second championship element belonged to New York. The talent was slowly trickling in, but the team's performance wasn't improving.

The Knicks traded three players to the Bullets to finally get Walt Bellamy early in the 1965-66 season. The addition of Bellamy enabled New York to shift Reed to forward, but they still plodded off to a 6-15 start. Gallatin was given his walking papers and Dick McGuire took his place, where he lasted until December of 1967.

Just as Gallatin's tough playing style translated into tough coaching, the self-effacing nature that made McGuire a perennial assist leader shy about shooting seemed to contribute to his weakness as a coach.

During the parts of three seasons McGuire ran the team, the Knicks added Cazzie Russell, Walt Frazier, Phil Jackson, Dick Barnett, and Bill Bradley, yet McGuire was unable to bring these great players together. He did not enforce discipline and the team spun apart, finishing last in 1964-65 and 1965-66. Substitute Freddie Crawford even fell asleep once on the bench during a game!

The sheer talent of the roster brought the Knicks out of last place in 1966-67. The club's 36-45 record got them into the playoffs for the first time since 1959. The Celtics sat the Knicks down quickly three games to one, but something had definitely changed. The Knicks had posted 77 straight 100+ point games. Bellamy, Reed, and Barnett were in the top ten in field goal percentage. The talent was there. Yet the Knicks needed two more vital changes to create a championship unit.

Holzman Takes The Reins

In December of 1967 the underperforming Knicks lost another game they should have won, which dropped them to a 15-22 record. Ned Irish removed Dick McGuire and named Red Holzman as head coach. Red had compiled an undistinguished 83-120 pro coaching record prior to joining the Knicks as chief scout in 1958, but he immediately turned the team into a winner. Holzman emphasized defense and a passing game on offense centered on hitting the open man. He also demanded respect and a team spirit that built pride in the Knicks.

Under Red, the Knicks began to give their all, as the entire roster contributed to the team's new success. Frazier and Jackson made the all-rookie team; Reed and Barnett were All-Stars. Willis scored 53 against LA. Cazzie hit for 42 versus the Pistons. Bellamy's shooting percentage reached .541.

The Knicks ended the season with a 43-39 record, in third place. The 76ers, led by Billy Cunningham and Chet Walker, won the first round series 4-2, but it was apparent that the Knicks had shaken off the lethargy that had settled over them for so long. All of New York spent the summer talking about its Knicks.

Unfortunately, at least at first, their high expectations were crushed by a 6-13 record at the beginning of the 1968-69 season. Problems within the team involving Bellamy, a moody, inconsistent player who never provided the maturity the Knicks had to have, and the hustling but abrasive Howard Komives had to be solved.

On December 20, the Knicks sent Bellamy and Komives to the Pistons for Dave DeBusschere and the championship Knicks were all in place. Reed went back to center; Frazier played full time at guard and DeBusschere's strength, agility, and toughness added a new dimension to the Knick frontcourt. The Knicks ran off 11 straight wins and 20 straight victories at the new Madison Square

Naismith Memorial Basketball Hall of Fame

Bill Bradley

Garden en route to a team record 54 wins and third place in the Eastern Division. All of this was accomplished without Phil Jackson and Russell, both of whom missed much of the season due to injuries.

Maybe Holzman's most important accomplishment was to form a special relationship with Walt Frazier. The talented guard, known as Clyde, was known for his shyness, but Red knew how to encourage the competitor in him. Frazier's assists doubled from 305 in 1968 to 635 in 1969, as double-digit assist games from the young talent became commonplace. He was also ferocious on defense and, along with DeBusschere, was named to the NBA's First Team All Defensive squad.

The Knicks felt ready to win in 1969. They swept the Eastern champion Bullets four straight in the first round and then ran square into the Celtics. John Havlicek was in his prime; coach Bill Russell was playing his last season. The Celtics would not be denied. They beat the Knicks four games to two and then moved on to defeat the Lakers for their 11th title in 13 years. With the retirement of Bill Russell for the 1969-70 season, the Celtics ended their greatest years and made room for the Knicks.

Everyone knew the Knicks were the favorites going into 1969-70, yet memories remained of their slow start the year before. A quick five wins calmed New York's nerves and, after a loss to the Warriors, they started a new streak. When it hit ten games, the squad set a new record for the best start ever—15-1. When it finally ended at 18, the Knicks were 23-2 and the rest of the league might as well have quit then. The Knicks were close to unbeatable.

Their balanced attack featured a hard, pressing defense that held opponents to under 100 points 25 times. Frazier ran the show on offense with 629 assists, but no one player dominated. Reed's team-leading 21.7 points a game was only good for 15th in the league, and his 1,755 rebounds ranked him sixth. As Clyde said in his book, *Walt Frazier*, "We weren't the tallest, fastest or best jumpers. We were just the most intelligent team I've ever seen." New York couldn't get enough

Naismith Memorial Basketball Hall of Fame

Walt Frazier

of them. They were an enormous media attraction. Movie stars crushed into the Garden with cabbies and businessmen and cheered the Knicks to a 60-22 season.

The Knicks stole a fast 2-0 edge in the first round of the playoffs before the Bullets, led by Wes Unseld, tied the series. Even with Unseld and Earl Monroe, though, the Bullets couldn't match up against the Knicks and dropped the hard fought series 4-3. The Bucks posed less of a challenge, going down 4-1 in the Eastern Finals. The Knicks thus found themselves back in the Championship Series after 17 years. Their opponents—the Lakers, featuring Wilt Chamberlain, Elgin Baylor, and Jerry West.

Game One was all Willis Reed. He scored 37 points and pulled down 16 rebounds while holding Wilt to 17 points. The Knicks won 124-112. Game Two wasn't as easy. Chamberlain, whose defense was spotty throughout his career, decided to play tough inside and denied the Knicks room to drive. The Lakers cut off the Knicks' perimeter game and that left the New Yorkers with little to

Naismith Memorial Basketball Hall of Fame

Dave DeBusschere

ing to go big against Wilt, Red Holzman fielded a small and fast group and the Knicks escaped 107-100.

The Lakers were nevertheless confident of securing the championship. The Knicks, it was felt, could not win the series without the services of Willis Reed and the Lakers proved that by stomping them 135-113 in Game Six. Wilt scored 45 and pulled in 27 rebounds. The stage was set for Game Seven.

Madison Square Garden was buzzing in anticipation for the biggest game in Knick history, but it roared when the announcer introduced Willis Reed as a surprise starter at center. Barely able to walk, let alone run, Reed hit his first two shots and the Knicks raced out to a 9-2 lead. The Lakers never recovered.

The Knicks won 113-99 and New York had its first NBA championship. Willis Reed's historic courage and dominating play earned him places on the All-Defensive team and the All-NBA team, the MVP of the playoffs, and the MVP of the All-Star game. No Knick has ever matched the honors reeled in by Reed that banner season.

1970-71 was Walt Frazier's year. He led the team with 21.7 points a game, 536 assists, and over 500 more minutes played than any other Knick. Everyone else had solid years, but there was a let-

work with. Jerry West put in 34 for the Lakers as they edged the Knicks, 105-103.

Game Three was a nail-biter. Reed's free throw with 50 seconds to go put the Knicks up 98-97. Then Jerry West popped a jumper with 38 seconds left—99-98, Lakers. 18 seconds to go and Dick Barnett hits from 18 feet. The Knicks led 100-99 and fouled Wilt as soon as he touched the ball. He made one of two to tie the score. With three seconds on the clock, DeBusschere scored and it looked as if the Knicks would emerge victorious.

Chamberlain inbounded to West in the waning seconds, however, and West flung a 55-foot prayer that went in! Overtime. The contests remained close all the way until Barnett hit another clutch shot with four seconds left to ice a 111-108 victory for the Knicks. Game Four went to overtime too, but the Lakers walked out with a 121-115 win.

Game Five was all about Reed again. With the score 25-15 Lakers, Reed torn his right thigh muscle and had to leave the game. Instead of try-

---

KNICKS HALL-OF-FAMERS

Ned Irish - 1964
Joe Lapchick - 1966
Tom Gola - 1975
Jerry Lucas - 1979
Willis Reed - 1981
Slater Martin - 1981
Bill Bradley - 1982
Dave DeBusschere - 1982
Red Holzman - 1985
Walt Frazier - 1986
Earl Monroe - 1990
Harry Gallatin - 1991
Al McGuire - 1992

---

down after the last incredible season. Though the Knicks' defense stood tough, leading the league for the third straight year, and they won the new Atlantic Division with a 52-30 record, the Milwaukee Bucks with Kareem Abdul-Jabbar and Oscar Robertson emerged as the best team in the league during the regular season.

The Knicks took the Hawks easily 4-1 in the first round, but Wes Unseld, Earl Monroe, and the rest of the Bullets waited for them in the second round.

The 1969-70 series versus the Bullets had been a tough hurdle for the Knicks, and this year's encounter was an obstacle that New York proved unable to overcome. The Bullets took revenge on the Knicks, knocking the defending champs out in seven games. It was time for some tinkering at the Garden.

Willis Reed's bad knees were a source of growing concern, so the Knicks traded Cazzie Russell to the Warriors for Jerry Lucas, a quality rebounder with a nice outside touch, who was anxious to play for a champion. This let Reed rest for all but eleven games of the 1971-72 season. Lucas averaged 16.7 points a game and filled in well on the boards, snaring 1,011 caroms over the course of the season.

An even more dramatic trade took place in November, when the Knicks sent subs Dave Stallworth and Mike Riordan and a lot of cash to the Bullets for Earl "The Pearl" Monroe. Monroe had trouble getting into the New York flow at first. Some thought he would compete with Clyde for control of the floor and resent a system that sacrificed high individual numbers for team play. Just like Lucas, though, Monroe wanted a championship ring, and he worked to integrate himself into a proven system.

Holzman made 1971-72 a learning year, a year to get ready, much like 1968-69 had been. Even though this squad had not fully come together, their talent pulled them through the first two rounds of the playoffs versus Baltimore and Boston and put them back in the finals against the Lakers. The Knicks won the first game, but Dave DeBusschere injured his hip in the second. With Reed and DeBusschere on the sidelines, the Lakers romped over the Knicks in four straight games to win the title.

The 1973 Knicks won it all with the same combination of determination, unselfish offense, and intense defense that worked in 1970. One game in November shows just how determined this team was. Abdul-Jabbar and the Milwaukee Bucks strode out to a lead early and controlled the game.

With less than six minutes remaining in the contest the Bucks had a comfortable lead of 18 points, 86-68. From that point on, the Knicks took over. They scored the final 19 points of the game, shutting the Bucks down completely, and won the game, 87-86.

During the course of the season, Monroe found his place in the Knick offensive flow and Reed and Lucas combined to average 20 points at center. Again, like the 1970 champs, no individual player posted huge numbers. The club won on the strength of team play and the league's leading defense.

Given all of this, the Knicks still did not dominate the regular season. 57-25 was good enough for second behind the resurgent Celtics' splendid 68-14 season. The Knicks beat the Bullets in the first playoff round four games to one to move on to the first real test of the playoffs, Dave Cowens' Celtics, in the division finals.

Geographic proximity and longstanding traditions make for a great sports rivalry and the Knick/Celtic one really took flight in this series. The Celtics hammered the Knicks in Game One 134-108. The Knicks charged back with three straight victories, forcing Boston to the ropes, but the Celtics wouldn't go down. They squeaked out a 98-97 win in Game Five and evened the series by taking Game Six at Madison Square Garden. With momentum behind the Celtics, the Knicks went into Boston Garden and broke them down 94-78, setting the stage for another match up in the finals against the Lakers.

The Knicks and Lakers had their own rivalry going, each having beaten the other in the finals. Implicit in this third match-up was the sense that

| PROFILE | Great Coaches |

Joe Lapchick

Joe Lapchick spent his whole life in basketball. Born in Yonkers in 1900, he started playing for amateur teams in the New York area at the age of twelve and in 1923 joined the original Celtics at their request. He took over as coach of St. John's University and led them to the NIT seven straight times between 1936 and 1947, winning the championship in 1943 and 1944. Ned Irish lured Lapchick to the Knicks in 1947 and the Knicks never had a losing season while he was at the helm. Players remember him as a decent man as well as a great coach. The stress of pro ball wore on him, though, and he returned to St. John's in 1956. Lapchick's Redmen won the NIT two more times (1959 and 1965) and he retired after this last taste of glory. He was inducted into the Naismith Memorial Basketball Hall of Fame in 1966.

Red Holzman

William "Red" Holzman was born and raised on New York's Lower East Side. He played college ball at CCNY in the early 1940s under coaching legend Nat Holman and entered the Navy in 1942. After World War II, Red played for the Rochester Royals and Milwaukee Hawks through 1954, when he replaced Andrew "Fuzzy" Levane as Hawks coach. He in turn was fired during the 1956-57 season. In 1958 the Knicks hired him as chief scout and assistant coach and in December 1967 he rose to head coach of the team.

Red immediately took the great talent of the Knicks and molded the club into a championship unit. Knick fans loved his phrases, "See the Ball!" and "Hit the Open Man!" and his emphasis on defense. Red's wry humor and low-key style made him very popular in the glory years and kept him on the good side of the press long after his best coaching years had passed. He retired in 1977, but returned to coach again from 1979-82. His lifetime record of 696-604 is the best in Knicks history.

Pat Riley

Prior to coaching, Pat Riley played with the Rockets, Lakers, and Suns, but he made his greatest impact on the game with his clipboard. He guided the Lakers for nine years—from 1981 to 1990—leading them to NBA titles in 1982, 1985, 1987, and 1988. His 108 playoff wins and .722 (584-225) winning percentage are league records. Each year he has coached, his team has won at least 50 games. Riley's style extended beyond tough defense and a dynamic offense; his slicked-back hair and expensive suits became trademarks in Los Angeles during the Showtime years and have taken New York by storm since he arrived on the East Coast in 1991.

---

this series would settle the question of primacy. The Lakers edged the Knicks in Game One 115-112. After that contest, however, it was all Knicks. New York clamped their defense down hard on Chamberlain and West. The Lakers proved unable to break the century mark for the rest of the series and the Knicks won the next four games to bring their second title back to New York. The club hasn't been to the finals since.

Red Holzman's team had gotten older and injuries began to pull them down in 1973-74. They still played tough defense, assuming their perennial spot as the league leaders in that aspect of the game. Willis Reed played only 19 games, though, and Lucas and John Gianelli weren't able to make up the missing scoring punch. Monroe had a leg operation, so he saw only 41 games that year. DeBusschere made the All-Defensive team yet again, but he was 33 years old and in the latter stages of his career. The Knicks closed out the year with a 49-33 record, polished off the Bullets in seven games, then squared off against the Celtics. Boston was happy to embarrass the Knicks 4-1 in the conference finals.

After the season Willis Reed, Jerry Lucas, and Dave DeBusschere all retired. Though Clyde, Bradley, Earl the Pearl and Phil Jackson remained, this second great period of Knick basketball had ended. Another era ended as well that year when Ned Irish stepped down and Mike Burke became

Naismith Memorial Basketball Hall of Fame

Earl "The Pearl" Monroe

president of the Knicks. It was time to rebuild again.

At first the 1975 Knicks looked like the surprise team of the league. With fan favorite Harthorne Wingo coming off the bench, the Knicks rolled out to an 18-8 start. Frazier and Monroe both averaged over 20 points a game and Clyde was second in the league with 190 steals, but the strength on the boards wasn't there. No one broke 700 rebounds; John Gianelli's 689 were team high. The Knicks slipped away after the good beginning and finished 40-42, the club's first sub-.500 season under Holzman. The Knicks' slide to eighth place in defense was further indication that the good times were over. New York snuck into the playoffs on the last day of the season and bowed out in the first round to the Houston Rockets.

To the credit of the front office, the Knicks did not sit idly by and watch their team crumble in the 1976 season. After the team stumbled to an 8-19 start, the Knicks bought Spencer Haywood from Seattle on October 23, 1975, to provide some new spark on offense. Haywood was definitely a scorer. He averaged 19.9 a game, but his play focused on his own abilities and not the team system Holzman had built up. In 71 games with the Knicks that year he dished only 82 assists.

The Knicks also tried to sign high scoring George McGinniss out of the ABA. Instead, they found themselves immersed in controversy. NBA commissioner Larry O'Brien claimed the 76ers held draft rights to McGinniss and voided the contract. Red's system was collapsing because of age, lack of talent, and talent that couldn't work in the system. The Knicks dropped 22 of their final 33 games and finished last in the division.

Knick management kept trying. Bob McAdoo came over from Buffalo, as did Jim McMillan. McAdoo averaged 26.7 points a game for the Knicks and Monroe added 19.9. Frazier's numbers began to slip, though, and Haywood played in only 31 games because of a leg injury.

The core of the old Knick squads—Bradley, Frazier, Jackson, and Monroe—did their best to maintain a disciplined, effective team, but the Knicks had changed. Their 40-42 record and third place finish in 1977 meant the end of an era. Red Holzman stepped down as coach, Frazier was traded to Cleveland, and Bill Bradley retired.

Willis Reed became the Knicks' new coach. Under Reed the Knicks looked more to scoring and less to defense for their wins. McAdoo was third in the league in 1978 in scoring with a 26.5 average, and his 1,010 boards placed him eighth in the NBA. As a team the Knicks' 113.4 points a game average was the third highest in the league. Assists were balanced, with Monroe, Ray Williams, and Butch Beard each dishing out more than 300. Lonnie Shelton contributed more than any Knick rookie had in years.

On the negative side, the Knick defense grew increasingly porous, ranking last in the league. Second place and a 43-39 record was a pleasant surprise. In the playoffs, the Knicks ousted Clyde and the Cleveland Cavaliers 2-0 in the first round before losing four straight to the Sixers in round two.

That summer Sonny Werblin took over as president of Madison Square Garden. Werblin and Reed never got along and after going 6-8, the Knicks found themselves with a new coach—Red Holzman. Red had little to work with. Newcomer Marvin Webster led the team with 655 rebounds, but he missed 22 games with a knee injury. Monroe was hurt, Werblin sent McAdoo to Boston for three draft picks, and Spencer Haywood went to New Orleans for Joe Merriweather. Red had an impact anyway. The Knicks won six of their first seven under him and failed to hold the opposition to under 100 points only once.

Guard Ray Williams stepped up a notch during the season, posting 504 assists and a 17.3 scoring average. Michael Ray Richardson showed his promise by stealing the ball 100 times in only 1,218 minutes. Richardson was to become the Knicks' playmaker in years to come. He was a good draft pick, although Larry Bird was still available when they chose him. In the end, Red could only do so much magic. The Knicks stayed home for the playoffs after recording a fourth-place finish in the Atlantic Division.

1979-80 was Earl Monroe's last season. He

a3veraged only 7.4 points in his 51 games and passed the torch on to the new, young Knicks of Ray Williams and "Sugar" Richardson. Williams and Richardson took charge of the Knicks, along with rookie center Bill Cartwright. Richardson, a temperamental player with attitude to spare, tied for a spot on the All-Defensive team and led the league with 832 assists and 265 steals.

Cartwright garnered Rookie-of-the-Year honors on the strength of his 21.7 points a game. Williams added 20.9 and Toby Knight 19.1. Still, the Knicks were a young team. They finished out of the money again, 39-43, 22 games behind Larry Bird's Celtics.

1981 was Red Holzman's last great year. The Knicks clawed their way to a 50-32 regular season mark. Richardson kept up his strong defensive play and new addition Campy Russell meshed well with Red's passing style offense. They made the playoffs but were ushered out quickly by the Bulls in the first round. Ray Williams left the Knicks via free agency and joined the Nets that summer. The team dropped to last place in 1982

Naismith Memorial Basketball Hall of Fame

Jerry Lucas

HARRY GALLATIN

From the time the Knicks drafted Harry "The Horse" Gallatin out of Northeast Missouri State Teacher's College in 1948 until they traded him to the Pistons in 1957, the forward anchored the Knicks. At 6'6", 210 pounds, Harry was certainly not the biggest player on the court in any game. He was not a great ball handler and at first some even doubted that he was a bona fide pro ballplayer, but Gallatin proved all the doubters wrong.

Eight games into the 1948-49 season, Harry Gallatin played his first minutes for the Knicks and he just kept on playing. In his 682 straight games in New York, Gallatin led the team in rebounding every year but one, setting a team record in 1953-54 of 1098 that stood until Willis Reed came along. His skills at boxing out, opportunistic play in the paint, and reliability made Gallatin one of the toughest competitors in the NBA. Throughout his career Gallatin invariably finished among the league's leaders in boards, field goal percentage, and points. He made first team All-NBA in 1953-54 and second team in 1954-55. The Hall of Fame added him to its roster in 1990.

WILLIS REED

New York sports fans hold a few athletes beyond question—Ruth, DiMaggio, Gehrig, Seaver, and Namath among them. Willis Reed is regarded with the same reverence. When he hobbled out on to the Garden floor for the seventh game in the 1969-70 Finals against the Lakers, Willis Reed entered sports legend. The determination he displayed that night, as well as his dominant play before tearing his thigh muscle in Game Five, earned him the MVP award for the finals and established a standard for courage in sports.

After a strong college career at Grambling that included an NAIA championship and tournament MVP honors, the Louisiana native was initially disappointed that the Knicks selected him in the second round of the 1964 draft, but he never let it affect his play. He scored and rebounded his way to the Rookie of the Year award in 1964-65, leading the Knicks in both categories that year and almost every year until knee problems forced him to retire in 1974. In 1966-67 Reed emerged as the team leader. He was the heart of the Knicks and his greatest seasons were the Knicks greatest seasons. He garnered the league MVP award in 1969-70 and was named MVP of the finals in both 1969-70 and 1972-73. After Willis Reed retired he moved to coaching. He is now the general manager of the New Jersey Nets.

BILL BRADLEY

Senator Bill Bradley has been in the spotlight since his college years at Princeton, where he was a three-time All-American and a Rhodes Scholar. He was constantly in the news and even had a book written about him. A *New York Post* writer said about the then 20-year-old Bradley that in those troubled times, he was comforted that Bill Bradley could run for president in 25 years.

All the attention, coupled with his proven basketball ability, combined to convince the Knicks to draft him in the first round in 1965, even though he would not be available immediately. When he finally joined the Knicks in 1967 after his two years of study at Oxford, he was rusty. Bradley came off the bench until Cazzie Russell broke his leg and permanently surrendered his starting spot.

His clever, determined style and unparalleled practice ethic made him a great team player, though he never dominated the sport the way many expected him to. He was the most cerebral of the championship Knicks and it was no surprise that he won a seat as a Democratic junior senator from New Jersey in 1978 after he retired. In his 15 years in office,

WALT FRAZIER

To many fans, Walt "Clyde" Frazier was the consummate Knick. Born the oldest of nine brothers and sisters, Frazier grew up in Atlanta and attended Southern Illinois University. While Frazier was there, the Huskies won the NIT and he won the tournament MVP award. The Knicks picked the playmaker first in the 1967 draft. He started his first season, but it wasn't until Red Holzman came mid-season to coach that Frazier's great defense, dribbling, passing, and stealing abilities began to shine.

In 1968 the movie "Bonnie and Clyde" premiered and teammates nicknamed him "Clyde" after Clyde Barrow because of his taste for flashy clothes. His smart playing and smooth, cool demeanor soon ensured his status as a fan favorite. The Knicks traded him to the Cleveland Cavaliers in 1978 for Jim Cleamons and Clyde only played two more seasons, retiring in 1979. His accomplishments are Knick legends. 1967-68 All-Rookie team. First Team All-Defensive team six straight years. First team All-NBA four times (and second team All-NBA, twice). Frazier was inducted into the Hall of Fame in 1986 and now serves as a broadcaster and analyst for the Madison Square Garden cable network.

PATRICK EWING

Patrick Ewing was born in Jamaica, but was raised by his mother in Boston, where he attended Boston Latin High School. Patrick was a phenomenon even during his prep years and John Thompson and the Georgetown Hoyas won the heavily contested recruiting battle. Thompson's intense defensive philosophy placed Ewing at its center, where the towering center rose to the constant challenge of playing the bad guy for four years.

Ewing graduated with one NCAA championship and the Knicks drafted him as soon as they won the first NBA draft lottery. From the start, it was clear that Ewing would live up to his reputation. Though he sat out a portion of the year with a knee injury, Ewing was named Rookie of the Year in 1986 and has since established himself as one of the premier centers of the game.

with a poor 33-49 record. Red had stayed one season too long. He stepped down a second time, and this time for good.

Holzman's successor, Hubie Brown, brought a slow, deliberate style of offense to the Knicks centered around Bernard King, a scoring machine acquired from Golden State for Michael Ray Richardson. Brooklyn-born King became an immediate New York hero despite his earlier problems with substance abuse.

The new, clean, Bernard King redeemed himself while with the Knicks. Knee injuries allowed King to play in only 68 games in the 1983 season; he still averaged 21.9 points a game when he was healthy. Guards Rory Sparrow and Paul Westphal, the former Phoenix Sun All-Star, powered the ball down low to either King or Cartwright in the post. Truck Robinson, a tireless rebounder, rounded out the starting lineup.

After a shaky start under Brown, the Knicks gelled and closed strong, winning 27 of 38. New York was back over .500 at 44-38 and faced their cross-Hudson rivals, the New Jersey Nets, in the first playoff round. Two wins sent the Knicks on to Philadelphia for a quick and painful appointment with Dr. J. The Knicks dropped four straight and Julius Erving moved on to secure his one NBA championship.

The 1984 Knick squad was one that veered tantalizingly close to greatness. Rookie Darrell Walker added defense and tied for a spot on the All-Rookie team. Hubie Brown's methodical style helped Bernard King to a spot as the fifth-leading scorer in the league (including two consecutive 50+ point games), and an all-around season that earned him the *Sporting News* Player of the Year award in a poll of NBA players.

King's greatest streak that year—and maybe ever—took place against the Pistons in the first round of the playoffs. Bernard ruled the floor. He scored 40 or more points in four straight games and seemingly sent the Pistons home by himself. The Knicks stretched the Celtics to seven games in the Eastern semifinals but the Celtics triumphed. Hubie's one opportunity to take the Knicks all the way was over.

Injuries dropped the Knicks from 47 wins in 1984 to 24 in 1985. King missed 27 games with chronic knee problems and Cartwright and Marvin Webster missed the whole season. King still managed to set a new Knick record by scoring 60 against the Nets on Christmas Day and Trent Tucker's .403 percentage from 3-point range kept some excitement at the Garden. By the end of the season, though, fans cheered for Knick losses— and they had a team record 12 in a row to cheer in March—because Patrick Ewing, the overpowering Georgetown center, was the prize for the lottery winner that summer.

Knicks Snag Ewing

After years of dreadful draft picks, Knicks fans finally received their due. General manager Dave DeBusschere got the first pick in the draft and chose Ewing. Ewing's knees kept him down 32 games his rookie year; Cartwright saw action twice, while Bernard King was out for the season; indeed, many NBA observers mistakenly came to the conclusion that King's career was over.

Ewing's Rookie of the Year award and the team's finish as the NBA's best defensive team seemed less important next to the fact they were last offensively and finished 23-59. The Ewing era began with a clank, and 16 games into the 1986-87 season, Hubie Brown was fired. Somehow the Knicks had sunk to 4-12 and wallowed at the bottom of the league.

King's unexpected return failed to rouse the Knicks and the front office engendered some ill-will from fans by cutting King loose after six games. Interim coach Bob Hill squeezed 20 more wins out of the crew the rest of the way, but given the presence of the already-dominating Ewing, such a performance was simply unacceptable.

The Knicks found the new leadership they needed in Rick Pitino, a young coach who related well to his players. DeBusschere's successor, Scotty Sterling, had signed Pitino before he himself was replaced by Al Bianchi. As with Werblin and Reed, Pitino and Bianchi never got along and

AP/Wide World Photos

Patrick Ewing

because of that, Pitino's dynamic stay in New York ended quickly.

Pitino saw the young players he had—Ewing, rookie Mark Jackson, Gerald Wilkins, Kenny Walker—and he knew their speed, enthusiasm, and endurance could win games. He instituted a running game that utilized a full court pressing defense. The game was fun again for the players, finally free of Brown's slow, half-court offense, ill-suited for the team's personnel.

Jackson, another Knick out of St. John's, took Rookie of the Year honors and his 868 assists were a rookie record. The Knicks upped their record by 13 games and though they lost three games to one in the playoffs against the Celtics, they were very happy to be there.

Pitino had the Knicks primed for 1988-89. Bill Cartwright, who had been playing forward,

went to the Bulls in exchange for Charles Oakley, a natural power forward. Rod Strickland, another creative guard, came in the draft. Everything fell into place. If anything, the Knicks were too primed and too cocky. They cruised to 52 wins and, after sweeping the Sixers in the first round, some of the players brought out a broom and "swept" Philly off the floor of the Spectrum. Their joke was not well received.

A four games to two drubbing by the Bulls brought the Knicks down to earth. Still, most saw this as a year of preparation. Their hopes fell, however, when Rick Pitino left New York to coach the University of Kentucky Wildcats, in large part because of differences with Bianchi.

Stu Jackson, a highly regarded assistant coach, replaced Pitino but he never had the same command of the team, nor did he energize them the same way Pitino could. He was often tentative and players like Mark Jackson became increasingly difficult to control.

Much of the star guard's anger stemmed from a rivalry between Jackson and Strickland. Jackson's production slumped. Strickland was dealt to the Spurs and Maurice Cheeks brought in to stabilize the backcourt. Neither Jackson's play nor attitude improved. A fast, powerful team was just treading water.

The only positive note was Ewing's team record 2,347 points through a 45-37 campaign. Stu Jackson coached another half of a season in 1990-91 before Bianchi brought in John MacLeod. MacLeod had a long, admirable coaching record, but in New York critics charged that it seemed he was counting the days until he could leave. The Knicks finished at 39-43 and Patrick Ewing started to make noises about free agency. MacLeod was gone, and so was Bianchi.

Madison Square Garden cleaned house for 1992. Dave Checketts came in as president and Pat Riley, who had coached the Los Angeles Lakers to several NBA championships in the 1980s, was coaxed out of the broadcasting booth to assume the reins of the Knicks. Free agent Xavier McDaniel promised hustle and points to pick up for Oakley's lost shooting touch.

A remodeled Madison Square Garden saw the Knicks surge back to championship form. Riley taught the Knicks how to play the kind of defense that had won titles for them decades before. Anthony Mason and John Starks provided energy and power off the bench. A leaner, more mature Mark Jackson returned to his rookie year form and took a leadership role. After leading the Atlantic Division most of the season, the Knicks faded at the end and the Celtics edged by them for the top spot. The Knicks got it together in time for the playoffs, however. The Pistons went down kicking, and then the Knicks took the World Championship Bulls to seven games in a physical, sometimes angry, series. The Knicks lost Game Seven 110-81, but they'd given notice that they were a team to watch in 1993.

In 1993 the Knicks stomped through the regular season with a physical, belligerent style that was somewhat reminiscent of the roughhouse methods employed by the Detroit Pistons to win two championships in the late 1980s. Mark Jackson departed to play for the Los Angeles Clippers and Riley filled the point guard spot with Glenn "Doc" Rivers, a tough veteran who proved a valuable acquisition.

Ewing enjoyed another tremendous season and Riley made several personnel moves specifically designed to knock the Bulls off. During playoff time, however, the Knicks once again were unable to wrest the crown from Michael Jordan and his supporting cast in Chicago.

SOURCES

BOOKS

Albert, Marv, with Jim Benagh, *Krazy About the Knicks*, Hawthorne Books, 1971.

Berger, Phil, *Miracle on 33rd Street*, Simon and Schuster, 1970.

Cole, Lewis, *Dream Team*, Morrow, 1981.

Durso, Joseph, *Madison Square Garden*, Simon and Schuster, 1979.

Frazier, Walt, with Neil Offen, *Walt Frazier*, Times Books, 1988.

Goldman, William, and Mike Lupica, *Wait Till Next Year*, Bantam Books, 1988.

Hollander, Zander, ed., *Basketball's Greatest Games*, Prentice-Hall, 1971.

Hollander Zander, ed., *The Modern Encyclopedia of Basketball*, rev. ed., Four Winds Press, 1973.

Holzman, Red, with Harver Frommer, *Red on Red*, Bantam Books, 1987.

Koppett, Leonard, *24 Seconds to Shoot*, Macmillan, 1968.

Reed, Willis, with Phil Pepe, *A View From the Rim*, Lippincott, 1971.

The Sporting News, *NBA GUIDE 1992-93*, The Sporting News, 1992.

—Richard Cohen for Book Builders Inc.

PHILADELPHIA 76ERS

The National Basketball Association has been a frustrating battleground for the Philadelphia 76ers. During any given year since the franchise moved to Philadelphia in 1963, the Sixers have been either hotly-touted championship material or bitter, dispirited also-rans. Other teams have built dynasties and dominated the lengthy NBA play-offs year after year. The 76ers have not been denied all glory, but their championship seasons have been few and far between.

Philadelphia Daily News contributor Phil Jasner notes that the 76ers have gone "from the best of times to the worst of times and back, in 1982-83, to the best of times." Jasner adds: "Depending on whom you ask, they are now on either the high road or the low road. Whichever, they have survived."

Survival has depended upon some of the best names in basketball history. Wilt Chamberlain, Moses Malone, and the legendary Julius "Dr. J" Erving contributed mightily to 76er history. More recently the team was dominated by Charles Barkley, a competitor who backed his tough talk with magnificent on-court skills. These and other memorable stars have created some pinnacles of victory for the team and have given the hard-to-please Philadelphia fans some genuine heroes.

Jasner feels that the 76ers continue to appeal to Philadelphians because, like so many in society at large, "they've been high and they've been low. They've been princes and they've been paupers. They've lived like kings, struggled as common men."

The 76ers were by no means the first professional basketball franchise in Philadelphia. Long before the Sixers moved to town, the City of Brotherly Love played host to the powerful Philadelphia Warriors. The Warriors had been a presence in the city since the days of the Basketball Association of America in the 1940s and were incorporated into the original NBA in 1948-49. By the late 1950s and early 1960s the team was vying for championship laurels on the strength of star player Wilt Chamberlain, a native of Philadelphia who had attended the city's Overbrook High School.

The Warriors found a perennial Eastern Division opponent in the Syracuse Nationals. The Nats had been formed the very year the NBA began, 1948. By the following year, the team reached the championship finals in a rather roundabout way. Although listed with the Eastern Division, Syracuse played most of its games against weaker Western Division opponents, giving it a division-topping record at the end of the season. Even after that disparity was rectified, however, the Nats continued to enjoy modest success in playoff games, reaching the Eastern finals in 1955-56, 1956-57, and 1958-59.

The National Basketball Association was a fledgling enterprise in those years, and towns the size of Syracuse, New York could afford to field a team. As the NBA gained prestige--and owners began to outbid each other for top talent--franchises such as the Nats began to lose money. In the case of Syracuse, the team found itself in dire financial straits by 1961. That same year, the Warriors were bought by a group of San Francisco businessmen and moved out of Philadelphia. One of the biggest cities in America suddenly found itself without a professional basketball team.

The Team Nobody Wants

In an attempt to appeal to Philadelphia's fans after the departure of the Warriors, a masking tape company fielded an American Basketball League squad with the laughable name of Tuck Tapers. Needless to say, the Tuck Tapers bombed. They arrived in town in November of 1962 and were history by January of 1963. In his book *The Philadelphia Story,* Frank Dolson writes of the unfortunate ABL franchise: "There were pickup teams on the Philadelphia playgrounds that attracted more attention and created more excitement. Practically nobody paid to watch the Tapers play, strong evidence that Philadelphia sports fans were smarter than average. The only time the Tuck Tapers made headline news in the Philadelphia papers was when they did the only decent thing they could do: fold."

Irving Kosloff was among the Warrior fans who missed good basketball in Philadelphia. The son of Russian immigrants, Kosloff had grown up poor in Philadelphia. He earned a football scholarship to LaSalle University but could not play much due to knee injuries.

A brief sojourn at Temple University's dental school was cut short by lack of tuition money, so Kosloff went to work as a salesman of cardboard boxes. While still in his early twenties, he began to buy odd lots of surplus paper and sell them to printers and publishers. In 1932 he established Roosevelt Paper Company and managed it into the largest paper conglomerate in the world.

Kosloff had owned season tickets to the Warriors games, but he never considered owning a team until the Warriors left town. In the summer of 1963 he was approached by attorney Ike Richman. Richman had represented Edward Gottlieb, the owner of the Warriors and had thus become an NBA insider.

Richman told Kosloff that the owner of the Syracuse Nationals wanted to sell the team. The two men formed a partnership to bring the Nationals to Philadelphia, with the understanding that Richman would oversee the team while Kosloff bankrolled it. The deal was struck, and the Nats prepared to move south.

For years the Warriors and the Nationals had been fierce enemies. Philadelphia had suffered through an entire season without professional basketball--made poignant by the hapless Tuck Tapers--but still Richman and Kosloff realized that Philadelphians would probably not care to root for the "Nationals."

Richman and Kosloff mounted a contest to pick a new name for the franchise. Several entrants suggested "76ers," because America was founded in Philadelphia in 1776. Despite some grumblings that the name was awkward, "76ers" won the contest. Today the terms "76ers" and "Sixers" are used interchangeably.

TEAM INFORMATION AT A GLANCE

Founded as the Syracuse Nationals;
purchased, renamed 76ers, and moved to Philadelphia, May 22, 1963

Home court:
The Spectrum
Post Office Box 25040
Philadelphia, PA 19147-0240

Seating capacity: 18,246

Team uniforms: Home--base color white,
bold red and blue letters with blue shower of stars
Road--base color red, bold blue letters, similar stars
Team nickname: Sixers and 76ers used interchangeably.
Logo: Basketball with 76ers inside, 7 in bold red with 13 stars in circle above it.

Franchise record	Won	Lost	Pct.
(1963-1992)	1366	1005	.735

NBA Championship wins (2) 1967, 1983
Eastern Conference championships (6) 1967, 1968, 1977, 1980, 1982, 1983
Reached Eastern Conference finals (11) 1965, 1966, 1967, 1968, 1977, 1978,
1980, 1981, 1982, 1983, 1985

The team that arrived in Philadelphia was a strong one that had made it to at least the first round of the playoffs every year of its existence. The coach was player Dolph Schayes, and the starting lineup boasted the talents of guard Hal Greer and forward Chet Walker. Still, the brand new 76ers were greeted with a measure of derision by Philadelphia fans.

Former Sixer Al Bianchi told the *Philadelphia Daily News:* "When we played for Syracuse and would come to Philly to play the Warriors, the fans would hang around the basket during warm-ups and say, 'We wish we had a team like yours, 'cause you pass the ball, you move.' A year later, we move. Now the fans hang around the basket and say, 'You guys ought to go back to Syracuse.'"

To make matters worse, the early 76ers could not get decent press coverage from the *Philadelphia Inquirer,* the city's largest morning newspaper. *Inquirer* owner Walter Annenberg imposed the bizarre rule that games *won* by the Sixers would be accorded *two* paragraphs in the sports section, and games *lost* by the Sixers would earn *three* paragraphs.

Dolson writes: "I remember thinking that if the 76ers lost by a really bad score some night-- you know, by seventy or eighty points--that Mr. Annenberg might soften his stand and permit the paper's pro basketball writer to sneak in a fourth graph. That never happened, however. Two paragraphs for wins, three for losses--no matter how lopsided--was the rule. In fairness, however, it should be pointed out that some of those paragraphs got to be rather long."

For several years the order stood, and finally it was revealed that Annenberg was angry because the 76ers management had tried to lure popular television sportscaster Les Keiter into the Sixers' front office. Keiter was employed at a television station owned by Annenberg. Dolson concludes that the early 76ers "knew more than their fair share of hard times in Philadelphia."

Wilt Ushers in New Era

In their debut season, the 76ers earned a 34-46 record--some fourteen more losses than the previous year at Syracuse--and qualified for the semifinal playoff round against the Cincinnati Royals. The Royals won the best-of-five series and went on to meet the Boston Celtic juggernaut of Red Auerbach and Bill Russell. During the following season, Kosloff and Richman began to play the high-stakes game of bidding for top talent.

The man they pursued most vigorously was Wilt Chamberlain. On January 13, 1965, Chamberlain returned to Philadelphia as a 76er, in a deal that moved three Sixers and $150,000 cash to the Warriors.

His immediate impact on the Philadelphia 76ers was substantial. One thing the team lacked before his arrival was a physically overwhelming center, and Chamberlain filled that bill magnificently. He joined a strong squad consisting of Hal Greer and Larry Costello on backcourt, and corner men Chet Walker and Luke Jackson. Overnight, Richman and Kosloff had created a team that could challenge the mighty Celtics.

Although Chamberlain joined the team in midseason, he was able to guide the 76ers into playoff contention in 1965. The Sixers finished the regular season with a 40-40 record but conquered Cincinnati three games to one in the semifinals. That victory set up a memorable Eastern Division showdown with Russell and the Celtics.

The best-of-seven series dragged out to seven games. Boston won games one, three, and five.

Philadelphia countered by taking games two, four, and six. The final match of the series found Boston leading 110-103 with two minutes left. Chamberlain went into overdrive and scored six straight unanswered points, cutting the margin to one with four seconds remaining.

The Celtics had possession of the ball out of bounds under their basket. Russell threw it in, and--incredibly--the ball struck a guy wire on the basket and caromed back out of bounds. That gave the 76ers possession of the ball with time enough to score. Unfortunately, when Hal Greer threw the ball back into play, his pass was deflected by John Havlicek. The Celtics won the series and went on to rout Los Angeles in the championships for a seventh straight NBA title.

"The ultimate triumph, it seemed, would elude Chamberlain forever," writes a *Sports Illustrated* essayist. Outcomes notwithstanding, the rivalry between Philadelphia and Boston was the most exciting in the NBA at the time. The 76ers strengthened their roster by adding a forward from the University of North Carolina named Billy Cunningham.

Cunningham quickly established himself as the essential sixth man, and the Sixers squad seemed stronger than ever. As the regular season progressed into 1966, the 76ers began to edge past Boston. Philadelphia swept a home-and-home series from the Celtics in March and went on to clinch the lead in the Eastern Division.

The regular season was one thing, the playoffs another. While the Sixers rested with a bye in the semifinals, Boston played a tough series against Cincinnati. Having won that, the Celtics swept over Philadelphia in five games for the Eastern Division finals and won yet another championship.

Chamberlain was bitterly disappointed. He had won the scoring title for the seventh straight year and had led the league in rebounds. Years later, in an autobiography entitled *Wilt,* Chamberlain wrote: "I wish I had won all those championships, of course, but I really think I grew more in defeat as a man than Russell did in victory.... Much as I would like to have won a few more of those

Basketball Hall of Fame

Billy Cunningham

playoff games against Boston, I wouldn't trade my self-awareness and peace of mind for all [of Russell's] world championship rings and playoff checks combined."

"Brains, Blood, Bones and Sinew"

Vindication was only a season away for Chamberlain and the 76ers. Coach Schayes was fired in 1966 and replaced by Alex Hannum, who had coached Chamberlain with the Warriors. The stage was set for a year that would make the record books, not only in Philadelphia but across the whole NBA.

The 1966-67 Philadelphia 76ers are recognized as one of the very finest teams ever fielded in professional basketball. *Philadelphia Inquirer* reporter Mike Bruton notes: "The country was consumed by a civil-rights struggle and an un-

popular war in Vietnam. But even with those things going on, the 76ers of 1966-67 couldn't be ignored and wouldn't be denied."

The team ran roughshod over the league, compiling a season record of 68-13. "A great many people--including the experts who voted in two NBA-commissioned polls on the subject in the last decade--think that the 1966-67 Sixers were the best collection of brains, blood, bones and sinew to grace the courts of the NBA," maintains Bruton. "Something set them apart, made them special."

Wilt Chamberlain, at the top of his game, dominated at center. He was flanked by Greer, Wali Jones, Larry Costello, Luke Jackson, and Chet Walker. Cunningham continued his All-Star work as sixth man, and the roster was rounded out by Dave Gambee, Bill Melchionni, and rookie Matt Guokas.

This time the Sixers proved too hot for Boston to handle. After a quick dispatch of Cincinnati in the semifinals, Philadelphia beat the Celtics in five games. In the finale, Chamberlain outscored Russell 29-4.

The 1967 NBA Finals featured the 76ers against--ironically--the San Francisco Warriors. Philadelphia took the championship four games to two, and Kosloff declared that his team would be a new dynasty. Cunningham described the victorious Sixers for the *Philadelphia Inquirer:* "Like any great team, the chemistry was absolutely perfect on and off the court," he said. "We were a pretty close group. Players are different now than they were then. Everyone had a roommate (on the road) in those days. Except Wilt. Noooo, not the big fella."

Somewhat wistfully, Cunningham added: "The shame of the whole thing is how quickly they broke the team up. I don't know what happened. Wilt, Chet Walker left. And Wali. Boom. It was all gone." Cunningham himself jumped ship, joining the American Basketball Association in 1969.

The transition was not quite that fast, but Kosloff's "dynasty" did de-materialize over the following season. The 1967-68 Sixers seemed poised to repeat as champions, taking a 62-20 record into the playoffs and dispatching the New York Knicks in a best-of-seven semifinal. The Eastern Division series brought yet another showdown between the 76ers and the Celtics.

Philadelphia had home court advantage, and Russell, at 34 a player-coach, was showing the signs of wear. Quickly the 76ers jumped to a 3-1 lead in the series. Everyone but a few die-hard Boston fans gave up on the Celtics. Miraculously, Russell rallied his forces, and Boston won the final three games. Yet again the Celtics went on to beat the Los Angeles Lakers for the NBA title.

All Good Things Come to an End

That stunning defeat shredded what little good will was left amongst the Philadelphia 76ers. Chamberlain demanded to be traded. He claimed that he had been promised part ownership of the team by Richman. The claims could not be substantiated--Richman had died of a heart attack during a 76ers-Celtics game in 1965, and Kosloff would not honor a verbal deal. Chamberlain was sent to the Lakers on July 9, 1968, for Jerry Chambers, Archie Clark and Darrall Imhoff.

In retrospect, former 76er Wali Jones offered his own theory as to why such a strong Philadelphia team unraveled so quickly. "I'll be rather candid," Jones told the *Philadelphia Inquirer.* "People didn't want to see five blacks starting, so they just broke [the team] up. I wasn't being paid what I felt I should be compensated, so I left, and I think that's why the others left. There was no other reason to break up the team like that, because we were all so young."

Walker offered a similar assessment. "It was difficult," he remembered. "We were playing right in the middle of a revolution. There was the civil-rights movement and Vietnam, and we were playing right in an establishment environment. That was the first time in history, I think, that five blacks started in professional basketball."

Whatever the cause of the breakup, it was nearly complete by 1970. After a second place finish in 1969 with a 55-27 regular season record,

the Sixers declined to 42-40 in 1970 and 47-35 in 1971. Both years the team lost in the first rounds of the playoffs. In 1972 the team did not even make the playoffs, posting a 30-52 record. That dismal season was only a prelude to 1972-73, when the 76ers broke every record in the book.

No team in the history of the NBA has ever been worse than the 1972-73 Philadelphia 76ers. The team began the year with a new coach, Roy Rubin, from Long Island University. Rubin was hopelessly adrift amongst the professionals. His team lost its first 15 games and was 4-47 at the All-Star Break. At one point the 76ers of that year lost 20 games in a row. Rubin was fired mid-year and replaced by player-coach Kevin Loughery, but the devastation continued. The Sixers finished the 1972-73 season with a 9-73 record.

Rock Bottom

Philadelphia Daily News correspondent Stan Hochman writes: "To a man, the front office folks and the ex-players ... don't expect the record to be broken, don't want the record to be broken, because they don't wish the pain and humiliation they suffered to be lugged through an NBA season by anyone else."

Don DeJardin, then the general manager, spoke of preparing for the future and building from new draft choices, but nothing could take the sting out of the situation at hand. "It was torture for me," Rubin remembered in the *Philadelphia Daily News.* "I was dying a slow death, night after night. Early, we had a lot of close games and we found every conceivable way to lose them."

Rookie Fred Boyd was pressed into service as a starter, causing hard feelings among the veterans, including Greer. "After we started the season, it became a self-fulfilling prophecy. As though guys were saying, 'We're gonna lose tonight,'" Boyd recalled in the *Philadelphia Daily News.* "There weren't too many blowouts early. But we lost games we should have won because we thought we were gonna lose those games. It was a snowball going downhill." Dolson calls the

Basketball Hall of Fame

Hal Greer

squad "an absolutely gosh-awful team that wasted no time in showing its true colors: black and blue (with red faces)."

Remarkably, one survivor of that epochal year has had a fruitful career with the Sixers. Fred Carter, the captain of the 1972-73 team, returned to Philadelphia as an assistant coach in 1987 and has outlasted several head coaches. Carter told the *Philadelphia Daily News* that he gets telephone calls every time an NBA team goes on a long losing streak. "A lot of people never get to experience the downside of things," he said. "I got a balance. And I always felt that would help me as a person. Survival skills are necessary in bad times. You don't need survival skills in good times. You have to learn how to massage yourself, to work through things."

Failure seemed to breed misery for the Sixers. All-American Marvin Barnes was drafted by Philadelphia during the period. Horrified at the prospect of joining the team, he told the press: "I'll go work in a factory first." Still, glimmers of hope began to appear on the horizon. Kosloff hired Gene Shue to coach the club, and in 1973-74 the team managed to earn 25 victories. In August of 1974, general manager Pat Williams took control of the 76ers fortunes. Williams and Sixers super-scout Jack McMahon began to seek new talent for the franchise.

Williams looked upon his duties as a mason does upon building a wall. Brick by brick he assembled components of a 76ers squad that would be able to contend for a championship again. His first move was wildly popular with the fans: he brought Billy Cunningham back to the fold.

The next step had more lasting implications for the team. George McGinnis had been a Sixers draft choice in 1973 but had decided to play for the upstart ABA league. Williams courted and won McGinnis in time for the 1975-76 season. Another key acquisition was a student fresh out of high school, Darryl Dawkins. Both McGinnis and Dawkins became favorites in Philadelphia. "Let George Do It" became the rallying cry for the team, and Dawkins thrilled fans and sportscasters alike with his flamboyant attire and rap-like rhyming chatter.

Other important "bricks" followed: center Caldwell Jones, Lloyd (later World B.) Free from Guilford College, and guard Doug Collins. The 1975-76 Sixers made it to a qualifying round for the playoffs, and McGinnis made the All-Star team. A loss in the best-of-three qualifier stung a bit, but Shue predicted better fortunes for his team the following season. This time, the fans believed him.

The "Doctor" Is In

Modest optimism was stirred into a raging fire almost immediately. In May of 1976, Kosloff announced that he had sold the 76ers to Fitz Eugene Dixon. Unlike Kosloff, Dixon had been heir to a fortune derived from transportation, oil, and public utilities. He had grown up in an exclusive Main Line suburb of Philadelphia, in a 60-room mansion complete with an indoor tennis court and incomparable greenhouses. Dixon had owned shares in other Philadelphia sports franchises but relished the opportunity to be a principal owner. Thirteen years of Sixers ownership had made Kosloff rather conservative where spending was concerned. Dixon felt otherwise, and he opened his checkbook and purchased a gem for the 76ers' crown. That gem was Julius Erving.

"Everyone, every serious hoop fan certainly, remembers the first time he saw Julius Erving play basketball," writes Mark Jacobson in *Esquire*. "Flat out, there was nothing like him. No one had ever taken off from the foul line as if on a dare, cradled the ball above his head, and not come down until he crashed it through the hoop. Not like that, anyway."

Erving had studied at the University of Massachusetts with the idea of becoming a doctor. Then he went into professional basketball, dragging his medical ambitions along as the nickname "Dr. J." For two years he labored in relative obscurity for the ABA's Virginia Squires. Then he joined the New York Nets and was a secret no longer.

Erving won the last ABA championship for the Nets in 1976. Then the ABA merged with the NBA, but the Nets were unable to retain the loyalty of their star. Erving moved to the Sixers in a deal that sent $3 million to the Nets and gave him $3 million for a five-year commitment.

The new star of the 76ers brought a whole new style of play to Philadelphia. As Jacobson put it, Dr. J "successfully transmuted the black playground game and brought that cutthroat urban staple to its most sumptuous fruition. He, once and for all, no turning back, blackified pro basketball."

The 1976-77 Sixers were quickly dubbed "the best team money can buy." The roster of marquee names now included McGinnis, Collins, Free, Dawkins, Caldwell Jones, and Erving. In a book called *We Owed You One,* Williams described the talent he had assembled: "The roster had established stars and it had young, impetuous players. And it was a team that was the media's delight because almost everyone had something

to say almost every night.... Of course, there was the continuing soap opera of Julius Erving and George McGinnis and could they co-exist? Not to mention Gene Shue, highest paid coach in the NBA, trying to harness all of this chaos and put together some semblance of a team. There must have been nights when he felt like he needed a whip and a chair."

Not surprisingly, Philadelphia finished the 1976-77 campaign atop the division with a 50-32 record. The team won a hard, seven-game semi-final series with Boston and took Houston in six for the Eastern Conference championships. On the Sixers rolled into their first NBA championship series in almost a decade, heavy favorites to beat the Portland Trail Blazers.

"For all of its talent, this team was not loved across the length and breadth of the land," Williams remembers. "Maybe it was the whole idea of cornering the market that had alienated people. At any rate, the Sixers were perceived as too good, to the point that they were never the underdogs, and, as we all know, the American public rarely roots for the overdogs. Too, the image had not been helped by the new owner, who came across publicly as cold and arrogant, all the worst attributes people routinely associate with wealth."

Those who rooted for the underdogs in the 1977 NBA Finals were rewarded handsomely. George McGinnis faltered--confirming a playoff trend that the Sixers management had noticed before. Erving was brilliant as always, and the 76ers won the first two games of the series handily. Remarkably, Portland rallied and won four straight games to take the championship, an NBA "first." Williams concludes: "For the Sixers, that season, for all of its tease and agony, had one salvation. The regular season and the playoffs had demonstrated that every adjective-splattered anthem of praise that had been written about him before was true. Julius Erving was, indeed, all that had been advertised."

Erving's talent was small compensation for such a spectacular championship loss. Williams felt that he had to rekindle fan affection for the 76ers, and he did so by mounting the "We Owe

Basketball Hall of Fame

Julius Erving

more. In the Eastern Conference semifinals, they met and dismantled the New York Knicks in four straight games.

One "Galling Gulp" After Another

"We Owe You One" seemed a canny campaign until the Sixers met the Washington Bullets for the Eastern Conference Finals. Led by Wes Unseld, the underdog Bullets brought the Sixers' advance to a halt in six games. Williams writes: "It is another numbing playoff defeat, one more galling gulp from what seems like a bottomless cup of frustration. And there is a long drive home [from Washington], which is made even longer by the knowledge of the kind of reception that waits: We Owe You *Two.*"

As usual, defeat brought changes. Free was sent to Phoenix, and McGinnis was traded for forward Bobby Jones, who would enjoy a productive career in Philadelphia known as "the White Shadow." Another key acquisition--engineered by McMahon--was guard Maurice Cheeks from West Texas State University.

The Sixers tried to put "We Owe You One" behind them quietly, but the fans did not forget. The team finished the 1978-79 season in second place and was bounced from the playoffs in the second round by the San Antonio Spurs. In 1979-80, a 59-23 regular season record was only good enough for second place, but the Sixers advanced in the playoffs through a miniseries with Washington and a semifinal with the Atlanta Hawks.

For the first time in years, Philadelphia faced an Eastern Conference title showdown with the Boston Celtics. That series featured the playoff debut of Celtic legend Larry Bird, who--fortunately for the Sixers--had not yet blossomed into the superstar he would become. The 76ers won the Eastern Conference with a commanding 10 out of 12 playoff victories.

Their opponents in the 1980 championship round were the Los Angeles Lakers, a team that hosted a rookie phenomenon--Earvin "Magic" Johnson. The series bounced back and forth

You One" campaign. "We Owe You One" became the advertising slogan for the team. Little did Williams know that his slogan--built as it was on equal parts of confidence and humility--would come back to haunt the team as a mockery of its efforts.

The first victim of the 1977 debacle was Gene Shue. Four games into the 1977-78 season he was fired and replaced by Billy Cunningham. Cunningham was volatile on the bench, but he developed a close rapport with most of his players--a product of his empathy for their status. He also recruited an able assistant, Chuck Daly, from the University of Pennsylvania.

That season, the Sixers finished with a 55-27 record and took first place in their division once through five games, and then Lakers star Kareem Abdul-Jabbar sprained his ankle. Defying the better judgment of coaches and trainers, Abdul-Jabbar finished Game Five despite his injury, taking a shot and a foul at game's end that ensured the Lakers a victory.

Still the omens seemed to be in Philadelphia's favor. By the start of Game Six, Abdul-Jabbar's ankle was so swollen that he was incapacitated. With their star player on the opposite coast, the Lakers met the 76ers in Philadelphia's home arena, the Spectrum. And Magic Johnson stepped in. He scored 42 points, snatched 15 rebounds, passed out seven assists and took three turnovers. Philadelphia lost 123-107 and fell short of the championship again.

"We Owe You One" was retired in favor of the slogan "Always a Bridesmaid, Never a Bride"--at least as far as the Philadelphia fans were concerned. Even though the Sixers continued to play division-leading basketball into 1981, the crowds at the games dwindled. The Spectrum, home to the 76ers and the Flyers hockey team, can hold more than 18,000 fans for a basketball game.

By the spring of 1981, when the 76ers had advanced to the conference semifinals, only 7,000 paid to see the team host the Milwaukee Bucks. The showing was doubly embarrassing since Erving had won league MVP award for the regular season. Even though the Sixers beat the Bucks and advanced for another conference showdown with the Celtics, Dixon let it be known that he might be interested in selling the team.

Dixon's decision was confirmed by the 1981 Eastern Conference finals. The Sixers won three of the first four games on strong performances by Erving and rookie Andrew Toney. All that stood between Philadelphia and an almost certain championship against a weak Houston franchise was a single victory. That victory never materialized.

Boston won all three of the remaining games, each time coming from behind in the final minute of play. Williams notes that the outcome of the series "is recorded as one of the more memorable collapses in sports history.... Outside of Boston, this result is portrayed not so much as an heroic comeback by the Celtics as it is Philadelphia's past anguishes that cause the recorders of history to dwell more on the Sixers' defeat than on the Celtics' triumph." Williams concludes: "The Sixers [had] plumbed new depths of frustration."

For Fitz Dixon, the 1981 campaign was the final straw. The 76ers were the next thing to a laughingstock despite their stellar efforts, fan support had dwindled, and the front office was still saddled with the "We Owe You One" fiasco. During the summer of 1981 Dixon sold the team to Harold Katz.

Katz was a self-made multi-millionaire who had given up any chance of playing college basketball to run his family's small Philadelphia grocery store. An admitted workaholic, he developed the idea of a weight-reduction program that would be run from a neighborhood-based storefront.

In 1972 he invested $20,000 in Nutri/System, opening a center in a Philadelphia suburb. Soon he had a number of Nutri/System centers in the Philadelphia area, and he moved into franchising. By 1977 he had added pre-packaged diet foods to his Nutri/System program, and by 1986--when he sold the company--Nutri/System was the largest medically supervised weight control corporation in the world. In 1984, Katz's personal fortune was estimated at $300 million.

Katz Gets Involved

Katz had loved the Philadelphia 76ers for years. He purchased the team because it presented a new challenge. He made it a personal mission to restore the Sixers' credibility with the Philadelphia fans and to present the long-suffering city with a championship. Williams writes: "Many owners of professional sports teams have them strictly as hobbies; it was plain that here was an owner with a more than passing interest in his new acquisition." Indeed, Katz became the quintessential "hands-on" owner, repeatedly demonstrating a fanatical commitment to the franchise. This is not necessarily a formula for success, but in Philadelphia it worked at first.

The 1981-82 Sixers took a 58-24 record into the playoffs, finishing second to Boston for the second year in a row. After taking two games in a miniseries with Atlanta, the team advanced to a quarterfinal with Milwaukee, winning in six games. Then it was on to Boston for another Eastern Conference showdown.

There it was *deja vu* all over again, to use the old Yogi Berra expression. The Sixers jumped to a 3-1 lead in the best-of-seven series, but Boston won Game Five and Game Six to force a final, sudden-death contest--*in Boston*. The Celtics fans dressed in sheets and wailed at Cunningham and his players--"ghosts" of previous failures. Perhaps that mockery tipped the scales in Philadelphia's favor. The Sixers won the seventh game decisively. Katz was ecstatic.

In early June of 1982 the 76ers went head-to-head with the Los Angeles Lakers for the championship. This time the series lasted six games, and the Lakers won it. "There is disappointment, of course, but it is not so deep this time," Williams recalls in his memoir. "The 76ers have fought the good fight this time; they have been carried home on their shields again, but there is no disgrace, no galling sense of unfulfillment. Los Angeles has put together one of the most impressive playoff efforts in history; they are clearly the better team, and deserving champions. And, besides, on a memorable, glittering afternoon in Boston, the Sixers had earned for themselves a measure of redemption.... This time, apologies were not necessary."

One question remained: how could Philadelphia improve just enough to take the championship? The answer came from the open wallet of Harold Katz.

Moses Leads Philly Fans to the Promised Land

A sterling player had become a free agent, and Katz was ready to bid. Moses Malone had been playing professional basketball since he left high school in 1974, first for the ABA, and more recently for the Houston Rockets. With Malone at center, the Rockets had contended in the playoffs but had never advanced to a final. The talented Malone knew he would have to shop his talents elsewhere if he wanted a championship ring, and Philadelphia seemed like the best port of call.

Katz negotiated the deal himself, offering Malone a six-year, $13.2 million contract. The only disappointing aspect of the deal was the condition Houston set: the Rockets wanted Caldwell Jones, a team player who had contributed substantially for years. In the end, Katz honored the bargain, sending Jones to Houston for the mercurial Malone.

After seven seasons in the NBA, Malone had earned three Most Valuable Player awards. At center he showed speed, hustle, and most of all, stamina. Observers would marvel at Malone's ability to pick up the pace as others flagged late in games. Unlike Erving, whose pre-76ers career was best known among NBA insiders, Malone had made headlines for the way he carried the Rockets year after year on the strength of his superior talent. His addition to the 76ers in time for the 1982-83 season made Philadelphia the team to beat.

Some observers wondered how a superstar of Malone's caliber would mesh with the ever-popular Dr. J. As if to allay any fears, Malone spoke to the issue at his first press conference in Philadelphia. "It's Doc's show, and I just want to watch the show," he said, as quoted by Williams. "In the ABA, Doc was always a great show, and now I've got a chance to play with Doc and I think it's gonna be a better show.... I know what I've got to do to help this team. I'm not gonna try to do what I can't do. I'm just gonna play my game--attack the boards, go to the offensive boards, look for the fast break, look to rebound. I came into the league right from high school, a kid just like Darryl Dawkins. They tried to put labels on me. Can't do this, can't do that. Basically, I can do anything in the world with the ball."

For the taciturn Malone, that was a major speech. He only added that the one thing he wanted in life that he didn't have was a championship. He promised to be aggressive in the chase. Then he put his money where his mouth was. He meshed splendidly with Erving and the rest of the Sixers, and he earned the love of the fans for his hard-working, blue-collar attitude. "Any lingering doubts about Moses [were] emphatically answered early in the season," notes Williams. "The hated Celtics [came in for a game], and the Sixers [prevailed] in *double overtime*. Moses [played] 56 of 58 minutes. It is clear that this is not just another overpaid superstar content to collect his check."

Between 1977 and 1983 the 76ers had compiled the best cumulative record in the NBA but had been unable to win the championship. Malone changed all that. His dogged presence on the court night after night brought a needed psychological stimulus as well as an essential physical presence.

In 1982-83, the Sixers won 50 of their first 57 games and sent four starters--Malone, Erving, Toney, and Cheeks--to represent the team at the All-Star game. Season's end found the 76ers atop the Eastern Division with a 65-17 record. Then, only a few days before the playoffs, disaster loomed: Malone developed tendonitis in both knees and could hardly walk.

He rallied in time to meet the Knicks in the opening round of the playoffs, and he even predicted that the 76ers would win in four games. They did just that.

The sweep bought the Sixers a much-needed week of rest and rehabilitation before they advanced to meet the Milwaukee Bucks. If anyone was disappointed that Philadelphia would not meet Boston in the conference final, the disappointment did not last long. The 76ers beat Milwaukee in five games and prepared to square off against the Lakers for the second year in a row.

"We have the best team in basketball," Erving said on the eve of the 1983 championship showdown. "Now all we have to do is go out and prove it." They proved it in four games straight, finally earning the championship rings they had sought so long. Erving, Malone, Toney, and Cheeks were joined in celebration by coach Cunningham, Bobby Jones, Marc Iavaroni, Mark McNamara, Clint Richardson, and a host of other supporting players, trainers, and coaches.

Happiest of all was Harold Katz, who proudly displayed the championship trophy to roaring throngs along the streets of Philadelphia and in the seats at Philly's Veterans Stadium during a victory parade. An estimated 1.7 million Philadelphians turned out to cheer the champion 76ers on Parade Day, and the team was formally honored by president Ronald Reagan in a ceremony in the White House Rose Garden.

What Goes Up Must Come Down

The 1983 title marked a pinnacle in the fortunes of the Philadelphia 76ers. Malone, who pulled in more rebounds than any other player during the entire 1980s, was traded to the Bullets in 1986. Erving retired after the 1986-87 season. The team continued to make at least the first round of the playoffs, and even reached the Eastern Conference finals in 1985, but the erosion of talent and spirit was evident everywhere.

Williams resigned in 1986 and even McMahon took his scouting talents elsewhere. Cunningham left before the 1985-86 season began and was replaced by former player Matt Guokas. Upheaval in the coaching ranks and the front office was compounded by mediocre draft picks and trades for players who arrived injured or unmotivated. The 1987-88 season found the Sixers out of the playoffs for the first time in 13 years.

Most of the blame for the team's rapid demise was heaped upon Katz. It was Katz who engineered trades for players like Jeff Ruland, who played in only 18 games between 1986 and 1992. Katz earned a reputation as not only a hands-on owner, but an interfering owner--one who made decisions best left to front office personnel and who tried to curb expenses wherever possible.

Defending himself in the *Philadelphia Daily News,* Katz said: "The perception of me running this team solely is there, and I think it's wrong. If something goes wrong with a team these days, it's fashionable to blame the owner because he's the guy with the big bucks. You're talking about an average fan who's making 30- to 40-thousand or below looking at a guy

AP/Wide World Photos

Hersey Hawkins

franchise--a mixed blessing for the team's image.

Sports Illustrated reporter Jack McCallum describes Barkley as "that rare player who can operate almost anywhere on the court--carving out position under the basket, or breaking the press with a behind-the-back dribble, or guarding a small forward, or checking a center who's eight inches taller than his own 6 feet 5 inches."

Playing with an intensity unmatched almost anywhere in sports, Barkley became "the heart and soul of the 76ers, not to mention the arms, legs, head, liver and spleen," to quote *Philadelphia Daily News* correspondent Paul Domowitch. On many occasions Barkley kept the team competitive through his stellar performance and his sheer desire to win.

Barkley's only drawback proved his undoing. Emotional and outspoken on the court and off, he could not resist complaining about Katz, the Philadelphia fans, team salaries, team spirit, and a multitude of other concerns.

"Sometimes the slightest thing makes me go crazy," he said in *Sports Illustrated.* "There are nights when I feel like hitting officials, hitting fans." Barkley let it be known that he would not let the mediocrity of his supporting players influence his own greatness. "I kill myself because I do feel some type of loyalty to the Sixers," he said in the *Philadelphia Daily News.* "But I think I'm one of the few guys who really feels loyalty. I may be the only guy other than Maurice [Cheeks] who feels loyalty to this organization."

The Sixers' "Heart and Soul"

Barkley shoved his way to the heights of the NBA and even earned a spot on the 1992 United States Olympic Team. By that time, however, the honeymoon had long been over in Philadelphia. "Barkley is, like Hawaii, volcanic and very much an island," McCallum wrote early in 1992. "The long-range forecast in Philly calls for gloomy skies. Ironically, Barkley's individual brilliance generally keeps the Sixers from sinking low enough to qualify for a lottery pick in the NBA

who's worth millions and millions of dollars and saying, 'He messed up my team.'"

Needless to say, comments like that have not endeared Katz to the average 76ers fan. The owner has become more and more unpopular with each passing year, and recent efforts to curb his input in the day-to-day activities of the franchise have met with skepticism.

The Sixers might have collapsed more profoundly had they not acquired a controversial new superstar in Charles Wade Barkley. Barkley was drafted in the first round out of Auburn University in 1984 and joined the 76ers for the 1984-85 season. By 1988 he was the undisputed star of the draft and perhaps getting another player whom Barkley would respect, and Katz frittered away the two lottery picks he had [in 1991] with bad deals. Barkley's teammates, understandably, are tired of being pincushions for his verbal darts."

Another massive upheaval rocked the 76ers prior to the 1992-93 season. Coach Jim Lynam, who had been with the team since 1988, was promoted to general manager. Lynam hired veteran coach Doug Moe, who had spent the 1980s at the helm of the Denver Nuggets.

The other changes were even more remarkable: Katz promised to excuse himself from the decision-making process for the team. And Barkley, the only Sixer to find fame outside of Philadelphia, was traded to the Phoenix Suns for guard Jeff Hornacek, forward Tim Perry, and center-forward Andrew Lang.

Moe heralded the changes as the beginning of a new era for the Sixers and confidently predicted the team would win 50 games. Barkley offered a different perspective. No longer shackled by a feeling of loyalty to the franchise, he lambasted the 76er managment in the *Philadelphia Daily News* for shopping him around "like a piece of meat." He added: "That is typical of [the Sixers'] insensitive organization. We're not slaves who go to the highest bidder. Abe Lincoln freed us a long time ago. It was almost like, 'Here's some stud. We'll give him to the highest bidder.'"

It was a last blast from Philadelphia's most controversial basketball star, but for 76er fans it was a moment of reckoning. Barkley had shone for the Sixers in seasons that had little light. His departure could herald a new era of solid mediocrity, despite the fresh insights of a new coach. With Barkley, the 76ers had finished under .500 in only two of eight seasons, 1987-88 and 1991-92. Without him, the franchise floundered in a manner not seen for a decade.

After a December, 1992 loss to the Utah Jazz, *Philadelphia Inquirer* reporter Bob Ford wrote: "Like some lead-weighted diving bell searching for the ocean floor, the 76ers just keep sinking down, down, down, down. Back at the surface, the air bubbles grow smaller. Are the Sixers still there or has the pressure crushed them like a grape? A tug on the line one of these nights would be a great relief."

The signs of life from the ocean floor may be dim, but Philadelphia 76ers fans have seen such moments of misery before. Hope springs eternal in a city that has hosted champs and chumps, Charles Barkley and Dr. J., feuds with the Lakers and the Celtics, and a team whose very existence honors the birth of a nation..

Sources

BOOKS

Chamberlain, Wilt, *Wilt,* Macmillan, 1973.
Dolson, Frank, *The Philadelphia Story,* Icarus Press, 1981.
Williams, Pat and Bill Lyon, *We Owed You One: The Uphill Struggle of the Philadelphia 76ers,* TriMark Publishing, 1983.

PERIODICALS

Esquire, February 1985.
People, June 6, 1983.
Philadelphia Daily News, June 6, 1983; November 1, 1986; April 21, 1987; November 6, 1987; April 19, 1988; April 21, 1988; March 18, 1991; May 28, 1992; June 18, 1992; November 10, 1992.
Philadelphia Inquirer, October 26, 1986; December 19, 1992.
Sports Illustrated, August 18, 1986; January 11, 1988; April 18, 1988; August 10, 1992; January 20, 1992.
TV Guide, May 21, 1988.

—*Mark Kram*

WASHINGTON BULLETS

The Washington Bullets began basketball in 1961 as the Chicago Packers and were renamed the Zephyrs in the second season with little more on-court or off-court success. The franchise was lured to Baltimore in 1963 by the opening of a new mid-town arena.

Ten years later, the Bullets moved to Washington, DC, and the new, larger Capital Centre where they were known as the Capital Bullets for the 1973-74 season before becoming the Washington Bullets in 1974-75. They've kept that name ever since and played 20 years in the Capital Centre. The Bullets have also retained a Baltimore tie by playing games in that city since 1988-89—beginning with three games a year and expanding to four starting in 1991-92.

For an 11-year period—1968-69 through 1978-79, the Bullets were a prominent NBA franchise claiming 10 winning seasons and the 1977-78 NBA Championship with Wes Unseld and Elvin Hayes leading the charge. But the next 10 years found the Bullets in the middle of the pack, annually finishing with 35 to 43 wins, never good enough to contend for a title and never bad enough to get a high draft position.

Since 1989, however, Washington has tailed off to less than 30 victories per year and sagged lower in the standings, but not always higher in the draft, even with the lottery.

During the team's glory years, ex-Bullets guard Gene Shue was the first in a succession of winning coaches followed by ex-Celtics great K.C. Jones who took the team to the 1975 Finals, and Dick Motta who arrived from Chicago and led 1978 Championship and 1979 rematch in the Finals with Seattle.

Four years later, when Motta left for the expansion Dallas Mavericks, the Bullets reached back into its ex-player ranks for Shue, Kevin Loughery and finally Wes Unseld, to try and regain their past glory—without success. Recently the team has committed to youth in a rebuilding campaign (with some attendance success) by catching the coattails of overall NBA success. Patient fans await a return to the great days of the past which have been very slow in coming.

Launched Near Chicago's Stockyards

The Bullets forerunners, the Packers, opened play in 1961-62 as the first expansion team since the 1950 merger. The NBA had shrunk from 17 to 8 teams before the Packers were added, so named because they played at the Chicago Amphitheatre near the stockyards. The two teams vied for attention, not only with the established National Hockey League Blackhawks, but also with a rival in the American Basketball League, which played just one season. Walt Bellamy, the first player taken in the 1961 draft, was second in NBA scoring with 2,495 points (31.6) as Wilt Chamberlain scored a phenomenal 4,029 points (50.4) to dominate the league.

Bellamy was voted Rookie of the Year and led in field goal percentage (.519). Later, Bullets coach Bob Leonard, more famous as the Indiana Pacers coach, scored 16.1 and was eighth in league assists (378, 5.4). Dave Trager owned the team which opened with a 120-103 loss to New York. They went from a 2-3 start to 2-12 and later went 1-14 in a December 27 through January 22 stretch during which they played eight straight days, going 1-7. Jim Pollard, a former stalwart of five Minneapolis Lakers championship teams, was head coach.

The Packers had 15 draft picks, five added selections at the end of the second round. Fifth-rounder Howie Carl, from local DePaul University, was the only draft choice to last the season. Second-rounder York Larese was traded to the Warriors after eight games. The expansion list was long lost, but a look at final scoring figures gives some insight to the cast of discards from the other eight teams.

A month into the season, the Packers acquired Si Green, Joe Graboski and Woody Sauldsberry from St. Louis for Barney Cable and Archie Dees. Graboski was then dealt to Syracuse and Vern Hatton went to the Hawks in a separate deal. The Packers played 28 home games, 23 road games and 29 neutral-site games. Bellamy was the West's starting center in the All-Star Game and posted 23 points and 17 rebounds.

February of 1963 was significant for two reasons. The renamed Chicago Zephyrs were winding up their season at the Amphitheatre with the NBA's second-worst record. Still unable to get a contract to play at the Chicago Stadium, they struggled in the smaller 7,100-seat Coliseum and were preparing to move operations to Baltimore where a new arena was available. That team would be renamed the Bullets. On February 17, 1963, Michael Jordan was born in Brooklyn, New York. Years later he would make professional basketball a mainstay of the Windy City.

The Zephyrs finished their two-year Chicago stay with a 25-55 record for a 2-year mark of 43-117. Walt Bellamy finished fifth in league scoring with 2,233 points (27.9) while Rookie-of-the-Year Terry Dischinger, also a Big Ten product (Purdue), had 1,452 points (25.5) in 57 games to rank 14th in the league. Bellamy also ranked third with 1,309 rebounds (16.4) and was second in field goal percentage (.527) by .001 to Wilt Chamberlain with Dischinger (.512) fifth.

After a 16-26 start, new coach Jack McMahon was replaced by guard Bob Leonard who retired as a player. The Zephyrs played 34 home games, 26 road games and 20 (5-15) neutral-site games. Bellamy started at forward in the All-Star Game with Chamberlain now in the West. Dischinger was also on the team.

Now It's the Bullets

The Packers became the Baltimore Bullets in the summer of 1963, playing in the brand new mid-town arena with Bob Leonard as coach. Near the end of the second week of the season, the Bullets made deals on successive days (October 28 and 29) to acquire players from New York and

TEAM INFORMATION AT A GLANCE

Founded in 1961 as the Chicago Packers; renamed Chicago Zephyrs, 1962;
moved to Baltimore and renamed Baltimore Bullets, 1963;
moved to Washington, D.C., and renamed Capital Bullets, 1973;
renamed Washington Bullets, 1974

Home court: Capital Centre
1 Harry S Truman Dr.
Landover, MD 20785
Telephone: (301) 622-3865 (Ticket Info)

Seating capacity: 18,756

Team nickname: Bullets
Team colors: Red, white, and blue

Team record, 1961-93

	Won	Lost	Pct.
Regular season:	1,250	1,363	.478
Playoffs:	69	94	.423

NBA Champions, 1978

Detroit—players who would become future team coaches: Gene Shue and Kevin Loughery. Sold to the Lakers in September was reserve forward Don Nelson, a 6.8 scorer as a rookie.

The Bullets were still in the Western Division and went 31-49 to finish fourth as Bellamy scored 2,159 points (27.0) to rank fourth in team scoring. He was also third in field goal pct. (.513) and fourth in rebounds (1,361, 17.0).

In their new home, the Bullets played 39 home games (20-19), 27 road dates and just 14 (3-11) neutral-site games. Bellamy started at center over Chamberlain and also played some forward while Dischinger again was voted in as a spare.

Buddy Jeannette, player-coach of the 1947-48 Baltimore Bullets team which won the NBA's

second championship, replaced Bob Leonard as Bullets coach in 1964-65. The team improved six wins to 37-43 and made the playoffs for the first time, topping St. Louis 3-1 in the first round before falling to the L.A. Lakers in six games in the Western Finals.

In June of 1964, the Bullets swung a big trade, sending All-Star Terry Dischinger, Rod Thorn and Don Kojis to the Pistons for All-Stars Bailey Howell and Don Ohl plus Bob Ferry, the team's later long-time general manager, and the draft rights to Wally Jones and Les Hunter.

A week into the season, an ownership group including Abe Pollin, still the franchise's owner, bought the team for a then-record $1.1 million. Walt Bellamy was sixth in NBA scoring (1,981 points, 24.8) and Howell was eighth (1,534 points, 19.2). The pair placed 2-5 in field goal shooting. Bellamy, Ohl and second-year forward Gus Johnson played in the All-Star Game in St. Louis for the West. The Bullets were 24-14 at home.

The Bullets turned to Paul Seymour in 1965-66 with Jeannette becoming general manager. Johnny Kerr came from the Philadelphia 76ers who, before the season, had acquired Wilt Chamberlain from the Warriors for Wally Jones. A little more than two weeks into the season, Walt Bellamy was sent to the Knicks for Jim Barnes, Johnny Green, Johnny Egan and cash. The team improved one win and made the playoffs again. St. Louis ousted them in a 3-game sweep.

The lone rookie to survive the season was second round choice Jerry Sloan, later an All-Star in Chicago and coach of the Bulls and Jazz. Don Ohl (20.6), Kevin Loughery (18.2) and Bailey Howell (17.5) led the veteran Bullets in scoring. Howell started the All-Star Game and Ohl scored 16 off the bench in the same game.

Four weeks after the 1965-66 season ended, Mike Farmer replaced Paul Seymour as coach. Farmer was gone after a 1-8 start in 1966-67. GM Buddy Jeannette took over for 16 games (3-13) before Gene Shue, who had retired after the 1963-64 season, was called in to finish up (16-40). The 20-61 mark was the franchise's worst since the founding year in Chicago and there were no playoffs.

Jerry Sloan and John Kerr were lost in the expansion draft to the Chicago Bulls, with Kerr becoming coach. In September deals, Bailey Howell was sent to Boston for Mel Counts, and Leroy Ellis came from the Lakers for Jim Barnes. Gus Johnson, emerging as a premier power forward, led the Bullets in scoring (1,511 points, 20.7) with Kevin Loughery next (1,380 points, 18.2), and Don Ohl adding 20.2 in just 58 games. The Bullets were now in the East, with Chicago in the West. Ohl scored 17 in the All-Star Game.

Back-to-Back Rookies of the Year

In 1967-68, Shue brought the Bullets home

Retired Bullets Numbers

11 Elvin Hayes
25 Gus Johnson
41 Wes Unseld

36-46. That wasn't good enough to make the playoffs which had expanded to eight teams the year before. Expansion brought San Diego and Seattle into the NBA, and the Bullets lost John Barnhill, Johnny Green and Ben Warley in the draft to help the new teams. The Bullets lost the coin flip for the first pick in the college draft, but wound up with Earl (The Pearl) Monroe of Winston-Salem State as Detroit opted for another guard in Jimmy Walker.

In the eighth round, the Bullets found Ed Manning (father of the current Los Angeles Clippers' Danny, and now a San Antonio Spurs scout). Monroe led the Bullets in scoring (1,991 points, 24.3), was NBA Rookie of the Year and ranked fourth in NBA scoring. Gus Johnson was the team's All-Star Game representative. Don Ohl went to St. Louis in January for Tom Workman. Baltimore had a franchise-best 13 road wins. Monroe capped his brilliant rookie season with a franchise-record 56 points versus Los Angeles on February 13.

In 1968-69, the Bullets lost the pre-draft coin flip for the second straight time. San Diego took Elvin Hayes who would later be a Bullets great. The Bullets selected Wes Unseld who went on to become the second player to ever be NBA Rookie of the Year and Most Valuable Player. The Bullets lost John Egan, Stan McKenzie and Roland West to new expansion teams Milwaukee and Phoenix.

But on the floor, the team didn't miss a beat with a 21-win improvement to 57-25, then a franchise best, in the NBA's second 82-game season. Earl Monroe was second in NBA scoring (25.8) to Hayes (28.4) and Loughery was 11th (22.6). Unseld was second in rebounding (18.2) to Wilt Chamberlain.

In the playoffs, the East Champion Bullets were swept in four games by the third-place Knicks as No. 1 played No. 3 and No. 2 met No. 4, a format which would not change until four divisions were adopted in 1970-71. Abe Pollin had become the franchise's sole owner in the 1968 off-season. Gene Shue was voted 1968-69 Coach of the Year. The Bullets drew a Baltimore record 7,635 per game.

The Bullets posted a 50-32 season in 1969-70 with Earl Monroe 8th in scoring (23.4). Kevin Loughery scored 21.9, but missed 27 games. Wes Unseld (16.7) was a narrow second to Elvin Hayes (16.9) in NBA rebounds. Monroe was sixth in free-throw shooting (.830) and Unseld was eighth in field goal pct. (.518). Gus Johnson, fifth in NBA rebounding (13.9) was the team's lone All-Star Game pick and scored 10 points.

In the playoffs, the Bullets, third in the Eastern Division, were bounced in a 7-game series by eventual NBA Champion New York. For the second straight year, Baltimore was .500 or better in home, road and neutral-site games. Home attendance fell more than 1,500.

NBA Expands to Four Divisions

In 1970-71, the NBA expanded by three more teams as the Buffalo Braves, Cleveland Cavaliers and Portland Trailblazers entered the league bringing membership to 17 teams. As a result, the NBA adopted a 4-division setup—Atlantic, Central, Midwest, and Pacific.

The Bullets were sent to the Central Division along with Atlanta, Cleveland, and Cincinnati. Boston, Buffalo, New York, and Philadelphia made up the Atlantic Division and the second part of realignment created the Eastern and Western Conference.

The first round of playoffs, the conference semifinals, set the first-place team in one division against the second-place team in the other division in the conference. The division winners would have home-court advantage, even if the second-place team from the other division had a better record.

Baltimore won the Central Division with a 42-40 record, the first of five consecutive division titles and second in their history. Baltimore drew Philly (who'd won five more regular-season games), in the first round and advanced with a 4-3 series victory.

In the Conference Finals, the Bullets eliminated defending champion New York in seven games after falling behind, 2-0, then getting even with 26 and 21-point wins. Washington won Game 6 by 17 to set up a 93-91 verdict in Game 7. With their energy expended, the Bullets were swept in the Finals by Milwaukee and second-year center Lew Alcindor (later Kareem Abdul-Jabbar) in four games.

The Bullets were helped by an early-season deal which brought John Tresvant from the Lakers for a future pick. Earl Monroe was 14th in NBA scoring at 21.4. Wes Unseld was second in rebounding (16.9) while missing eight games, and eighth in field goal accuracy (.501). George Johnson (1st round) and Gary Zeller (5th) were the two draft choices to make the team. Lost to expansion were Leroy Ellis and Ray Scott, a pair of forward-centers.

In a bid to repeat as division champions, the Bullets made two key trades early in the season. The first brought Archie Clark from Philadelphia for Kevin Loughery and Fred Carter. The second fetched Mike Riordan and Dave Stallworth from the Knicks for All-Star Earl Monroe. Washington won the Central with a 38-44, the 9th-best mark in the NBA, poorer than every second place team in the other divisions and behind both Western Conference third-place divisional teams.

In the 1972 playoffs, the Bullets drew the 48-win Knicks and bowed in six games after leading, 2-1, thanks to an overtime win in Game 1 at home. When Washington lost Game 5 at home by 24 points, they were done.

Stan Love and "hardship" choice Phil Chenier proved to be key contributors as rookies. Clark (25.2) and southpaw forward Jack Marin (22.3) were 9th and 16th in NBA scoring respectively. Marin led the NBA in free-throw shooting (.894). Wes Unseld was again second in rebounds (17.6) and Clark ranked fourth in assists (8.0). Attendance rose for the second straight year to an average 6,643.

The Bullets rebounded nicely in 1972-73 to a 52-30 record and another Central Division title. New York was again the first-round playoff foe after logging a 57-25 second-place Atlantic finish. The Knicks took a giant step to their second NBA title in four years with a 4-1 series win.

The Bullets got a boost from Elvin Hayes who was acquired from Houston in June of 1972 for Jack Marin and future considerations. Hayes finished 15th in NBA scoring (21.2) with Phil Chenier at 19.7. Wes Unseld (15.9) and Elvin Hayes (14.5) were 5-7 in rebounding, the NBA's top 1-2 punch. Mike Riordan (.510) and Archie Clark (.507) were 7-8 in field goal percentage. With the team about to leave, attendance dipped by 211 to 6,431 per game.

Bullets Move to Capital Centre; Renamed

Owner Abe Pollin moved the team to Washington (actually Landover, Maryland) and his new Capital Centre—an $18-million facility completed in 15 months and boasting the first set of luxury "skyboxes" in an arena. For the 1973-74 season, the team was renamed the Capital Bullets. K.C. Jones was named the new coach after Gene Shue left. Bob Ferry, retired as a player since the end of the 1968-69 season, became General Manager,

---

Bullets in Naismith Memorial Basketball Hall of Fame

Wes Unseld, 1988
Dave Bing, 1990
Elvin Hayes, 1990
Earl Monroe, 1990

---

and former GM Jerry Sachs became Capital Centre president. In a pair of deals, Stan Love went to L.A. for a 1974 second-rounder, Len (Truck) Robinson, and cash, while Walt Wesley was obtained from the Suns for a pair of future draft picks. The Cap Centre finally opened December 2 for the team's 10th home game, and a crowd of 19,035 celebrated a 98-96 win over Seattle.

The 1973 draft picks Nick Weatherspoon (1st), Tom Kozelko (2nd) and, Louis Nelson (3rd) along with 1972 pick Kevin Porter (3rd round) made the team. The Bullets attendance leapt to over 10,000 per game as the team finished 47-35, but the division titlists fell again to New York in the first round in seven games in a see-saw series.

Phil Chenier (21.9) and Elvin Hayes (21.4) were 13-16 in NBA scoring. Hayes led in rebounding (18.1) as Unseld missed 26 games to injury and was fifth in a new category, blocked shots (2.96). Chenier was 8th in another new department, steals (2.04), and rookie Porter was 10th in assists (5.8).

On April 20, eight days after being eliminated from the 1974 playoffs, the team was renamed the Washington Bullets. Archie Clark was shipped to Seattle for Dick Gibbs and a draft pick, and Clem Haskins came from the Suns for Dave Stallworth and a pick; 1967 draft pick Jimmy Jones signed after six ABA seasons. Truck Robinson and Dennis Duval came in the draft, but Len Elmore was lost to the ABA Pacers. Washington won the Central Division and matched Boston with a 60-22 season, the franchise's all time best.

In the playoffs, now at five teams per conference, Washington ousted Buffalo in seven games after a first round bye and then eliminated the Celtics in six games. Golden State upset the Bullets in game one, 101-95, went home for one- and eight-point wins and completed the sweep with a 96-95 win in the Cap Centre behind Rick Barry.

Wes Unseld won the rebounding title (14.8) and the first J. Walter Kennedy Citizenship Award for community service. All-NBA choice Elvin Hayes was 7th in scoring (23) and 8th in rebounding (12.2), while Second Team All-NBA Phil Chenier was 11th in scoring (21.8). Kevin Porter (8.0) led in assists. Chenier (2.29) was 6th and

Naismith Memorial Basketball Hall of Fame

Elvin Hayes

Hayes (1.93) was 10th in steals and Hayes was also was 4th in blocked shots (2.28). Amazingly, attendance fell to 9,360 per game.

In 1975-76, Washington was edged out of the Central Division title by one game by Cleveland, despite a 48-34 record, the NBA's fourth-best mark. First-rounder Kevin Grevey and third-rounder Tom Kropp made the team. Dick Gibbs went to Buffalo for a 1976 first-rounder. Dave Bing came from Detroit, where he had worn out his welcome with ownership, for Kevin Porter and the Bullets got a first rounder as well.

Cleveland ousted the Bullets from the play-offs in seven games. Phil Chenier was 16th (19.9) and Elvin Hayes, 2nd Team All-NBA, was 18th (19.8) in scoring. Wes Unseld won the field goal accuracy title (.56085) by a narrow margin. Bing was 6th in assists (6.0) and Chenier 7th in steals (1.98) while Unseld was 3rd (13.3) and Hayes 10th (11.0) in rebounds. Attendance climbed almost 1,400 to 10,752. Bing was the All-Star Game MVP in Philadelphia and K.C. Jones left as coach after the playoffs.

Enter Dick Motta as Coach

Dick Motta came from the Bulls after his contract was up. He was 356-300 in eight years, but 24-58 in 1975-76. In the 1976 draft, the Bullets picked Mitch Kupchak, who would make the All-Rookie Team, and Larry Wright 13-14. Tom Kropp was traded to Chicago in the summer. In December, Bob Weiss signed as a free agent and Leonard Gray came from Seattle for Nick Weatherspoon, and in January Len Robinson went to Atlanta for Tom Henderson.

The Bullets matched their 48-34 record of 1975-76, a game behind Houston in the Central. With the playoffs expanded to 12 teams, six per conference, after four ABA teams were merged into the NBA, the Bullets avenged 1976 by beating the Cavs in three games. Houston won the Conference Semifinal in six games, taking the last three in a row.

Dave Bing won the J. Walter Kennedy Citizenship Award. Hayes was 8th in NBA scoring (23.7), third in blocks (2.68) and 6th in rebounds (12.5). Kupchak was second in field goal percentage (.572) and Henderson 5th in assists (6.9).

The Bullets fulfilled their destiny in 1977-78. Greg Ballard was acquired in the draft. Bob Dandridge was signed as a free agent from Milwaukee in August and Charles Johnson was signed as a free agent after his January Golden State release. The Bullets slid to a 44-38 record, second in the Central to San Antonio.

The team suffered a series of injuries in midseason, the most serious to Phil Chenier who played just 36 games. Johnson had been acquired so that the team could dress eight players. Veterans Wes Unseld (who eventually became the Finals MVP), Elvin Hayes, Dandridge and Johnson were key factors.

There were no Bullets among the top 20 scorers, but Hayes (13.3) and Unseld (11.9) were 4-10 in rebounding, and Hayes (1.96) was 10th in blocks. In the playoffs, the Washington march began with a 2-0 sweep of Atlanta. A 4-2 series victory over San Antonio set up a 4-2 win over Philadelphia in the East Finals.

"The man is a god in Louisville," says Bullets center Pervis Ellison. "When you come into the Capital Centre and see that jersey hanging from the rafters, you respect that.... We want to play like Wes did."

A first round Bullets pick out of Louisville, Unseld became the second player to be voted Rookie of the Year and NBA MVP in the same season. The Lousiville native was the second pick in 1968— and behind future teammate Elvin Hayes— spurned an ABA offer. He made the All-Rookie Team and the All-NBA First Team, his only time, in 1969.

An undersized (6-foot-7), but bulky (245 pounds) center, Unseld was famed for his outlet pass and was a rugged rebounder. He led the NBA in rebounding in 1975 (14.8) when the Bullets won 60 games, but lost in the Finals in four straight to the Warriors. When the Bullets made their third trip to the NBA Finals in 1978, Unseld was voted MVP as Washington won over Seattle in seven games.

He retired after the 1980-81 season, when injuries held him to 63 games, with 10,624 points, and 13,769 rebounds. A long-time favorite of

owner Abe Pollin, he became a Vice-President in 1981-82. He added assistant coach to his portfolio in 1987 and became head coach after 27 games in 1987-88. He's coached five-plus years without a winning season and just one playoff trip.

Unseld was a 1988 Hall of Fame inductee, won the first J. Walter Kennedy Citizenship Award given by the PBWAA in 1975, and remains active in the community. Wes Unseld is easily the Most Visible Person in Bullets franchise's history.

Photo: *Naismith Memorial Basketball Hall of Fame*

Seattle, 47-35 in the regular season, was the NBA Finals opponent, but the Bullets triumphed in seven games for their one and only NBA Championship. Others had the awards—no member of the Bullets team was on either All-NBA Team and attendance dropped over 500 per game—but the Bullets had the trophy.

In 1978-79 Washington, now in the Atlantic Division where they have stayed, made a game bid to repeat. Their 54-28 record was the NBA's best. GM Bob Ferry was Executive of the Year. Elvin Hayes was First Team All-NBA. Dick Motta coached the East All-Stars with Hayes and Bob Dandridge on the team.

Hayes was 17th (21.8) in NBA scoring, 6th in rebounding (12.1) and blocks (2.32). Unseld was third in field-goal accuracy (.577) and Tom Henderson was 8th in assists (6.0).

After a first round playoff bye, Washington ousted Atlanta in seven games and San Antonio, also in seven, for a rematch with Seattle. This time, the Sonics triumphed in five games after Washington won the opener at home. Phil Chenier missed 55 games with injuries. The Bullets averaged a record 12,789 attendance, a mark that still stands.

The 1979-80 season would turn out to be Dick Motta's last in Washington. Kevin Porter returned to the team as a free agent from Detroit in exchange for two second-round picks. The team got no help in the draft. Phil Chenier played only 20 games and Bob Dandridge just 45. Mitch Kupchak missed 42, Porter 12 and Kevin Grevey 17. The Bullets staggered in at 39-43, tied for third in the Atlantic. They made the playoffs with a tie-breaker over New Jersey, but went out in two straight to Philadelphia.

Hayes carried much of the load, ranking eighth in scoring, fifth in blocks (2.33) and sixth in rebounds (11.1). Unseld was third in rebounds (13.3), but Porter dropped to tenth in assists (6.5) after a record 1,099 in Detroit in 1978-79. Grevey was ninth in free-throw shooting (.867) and seventh in the new category, 3-point shooting (.370). After the season, Motta resigned to take over the expansion Dallas Mavericks in 1980-81.

Gene Shue Returns as Coach

Owner Abe Pollin and GM Bob Ferry called on Gene Shue (released from Philadelphia after coaching six games in 1977-78) to take over the aging Bullets team in 1980-81. Two-year backup Dave Corzine was sent to San Antonio for two second-round draft picks. A month into the season, Austin Carr came from Cleveland, but would play just 39 Bullet games. Mid-season pickup Don Collins (from Atlanta for Wes Matthews) helped somewhat as the Bullets matched 1979-80's 39-43 mark, fourth in the Atlantic, but missed the playoffs by five games as attendance dove 1,400 per game.

Limited to 63 games, Wes Unseld retired after the season, and in June, Elvin Hayes, tenth in rebounds (9.7) and blocks (2.11), but unranked in scoring, was traded to Houston for two second-round picks. Kevin Porter led in NBA assists (9.1). Kevin Grevey was the No. 6 triples shooter (.331).

In 1981-82 Washington reversed their record to 43-39 and made the playoffs, dispatching Atlanta in two straight in the first round before falling to Boston, 4-1, in the East Semi-finals. Mitch Kupchak had been lost as a free agent to the Lakers with the Bullets receiving Jim Chones and Brad Holland as compensation.

Frank Johnson and Charles Davis were the top draft picks. John Lucas was obtained from Golden State as Kevin Porter missed the year with an injury. Spencer Haywood's start was pushed back three weeks because of free agency. Kevin Grevey, eighth in 3-point shooting (.341) was the only ranked Bullets player. Jeff Ruland returned from a year overseas and made the All-Rookie Team. Shue was Coach of the Year and Bob Ferry won his second Executive of the Year award as attendance dipped for the third straight year.

Washington managed a 42-40 season in 1982-83, sliding to fifth in the Atlantic Division and missing the playoffs. Every Atlantic team had a winning mark, but the Bullets were seventh in the East. Attendance dropped slightly to 7,990. Jeff Ruland, who led team scoring at 19.4, was tenth in field-goal percentage (.552) and eighth in rebounds (11.0). Ricky Sobers was signed as a free agent from Chicago, who received a pair of second-round picks as compensation.

The playoffs were expanded to eight teams per conference in 1983-84, with no first round byes and the opening round boosted to five games. This gave the 35-47 Bullets, last in the Atlantic and seventh in the East, a break. But future NBA Champion Boston tripped Washington in four games, all decided by eight points or less. The Bullets' one win came in overtime.

Jeff Ruland was selected for the All-Star Game in Denver. He averaged 22.2 ppg, 15th in the NBA, and shot .579, sixth in the league with 12.3 rebounds, third-best in the NBA. Sobers was sixth in 3-point shooting (.261). Attendance again fell to what remains a Capital Centre low of 7,920—more than 1,000 below 1983-84. The team's two first rounders were Jeff Malone and Randy Wit-tman. The latter sent to Atlanta in June for future congressman Tom McMillen.

The 1984-85 season was much like the year before. Washington went 40-42 to finish fourth in the Atlantic. As the seventh playoff seed they fell to Philadelphia in four games, with no game closer than seven points.

The Bullets had made three deals on Draft Day, June 19, sending top pick Mel Turpin to Cleveland for Cliff Robinson and Tim Mc Cormick—then moving McCormick and Ricky Sobers to Seattle for old tormentor Gus Williams. Tom Sewell came from Philly for the team's 1988 first game. Williams was tenth in assists (7.7) and seventh in steals (2.25), scoring 20, with Jeff Ruland and Jeff Malone each averaging 18.9 as attendance rebounded to 9,346 per game.

Naismith Memorial Basketball Hall of Fame

Dave Bing

Shue Out, Loghery in as Coach

With the Bullets at 32-37 in 1985-86, Gene Shue was given the boot and Kevin Loughery, most recently in Chicago for Michael Jordan's rookie season, coached the last 13 games (7-6). Kenny Green, an early eligible, was the Bullets' 1985 first-round pick in the 12th spot, leaving Karl Malone for the Utah Jazz.

Manute Bol, the 7-foot-6 Sudanese center, was claimed in the second round. Before the draft, the Bullets acquired Dan Roundfield from Detroit for Rick Mahorn and the rights to Mike Gibson. Greg Ballard went to Golden State for a pair of seconds.

The Bullets wound up 39-43 and drew the 76ers in the first round, exiting in five games. Jeff Malone appeared in the 1986 All-Star Game for the winning East team in Dallas. Attendance fell back 229 per game.

Malone was 13th in NBA scoring (22.4) and 19th in free-throw accuracy (.886). Ruland was held to 30 games by injuries. Bol led the NBA in blocked shots (4.96), playing 26 minutes per game

and made the second All-Defensive Team. Kenny Green was traded to the 76ers for Leon Wood.

Before the 1986 draft, Mose Malone, Terry Catledge and firsts in 1986 and 1988 came from Philadelphia for Jeff Ruland and Cliff Robinson. John Williams, another undergraduate, and Anthony Jones were the top draft picks. Before the season started, Darwin Cook signed as a free agent, Jay Vincent came from Dallas for a 1990 first and Mike O'Koren came from the Nets for Leon Wood. O'Koren played just 15 games.

Dan Roundfield appeared in only 36 games and retired before the playoffs began. Vincent played just 51 games and Frank Johnson 18. Still, the Bullets went 42-40, 3rd in the Atlantic, and earned the sixth playoff slot. Detroit won three straight to oust Washington in the first round, but attendance nonetheless climbed more than 2,700 to 11,838, the second-best at the Cap Centre to date.

Both Malones played in the All-Star Game with Moses posting 27 points and 18 rebounds in a losing overtime effort. They also ranked 9-18 in NBA scoring with Moses averaging 24.2 and Jeff 22.0. Moses was ninth in rebounds (11.3), Jeff eighth in free-throw shooting (.885). Manute Bol finished second in blocked shots (3.68).

Wes Unseld Steps in as Coach

In 1987-88, the Bullets began a string of six straight losing seasons with a 38-44 mark, but still made the playoffs as the 7th seed, losing to Detroit. After an 8-19 start, Kevin Loughery was replaced as head coach by the man he'd lured from the vice-presidency to become assistant coach, all-time Bullets great, Wes Unseld.

Unseld went 30-25 the rest of the way and got the team to the playoffs, winning a tie-breaker with the Knicks for the 7th seed. 5-foot-3 Muggsy Bogues was the first-round draft pick and Bernard King signed as a free agent in August. Four days before the November 6 opener, Mark Alarie and Darrell Walker came from Denver for Michael Adams and Jay Vincent.

Moses Malone was in the All-Star Game again. Jeff Malone (20.5) and Moses (20.3) were 17-19 in NBA scoring. Jeff was eighth in free-throw accuracy (.882) and Moses was eighth in rebounds (11.2). Manute Bol ranked fifth in blocks (2.70). Attendance sagged more than 1,260. On the day between Playoff Games 3 and 4, Unseld was inducted into the Naismith Memorial Basketball Hall of Fame. The Bullets haven't been in the playoffs since.

Despite improving two wins to 40-42, the Bullets finished fourth in the Atlantic, ninth overall in the East, and missed the playoffs. In June, before the draft, the popular Bol was dealt to Golden State for Dave Feitl and a draft pick. In the draft, Harvey Grant and Ledell Eackles were the top picks. Free agent Moses Malone left for Atlanta and Muggsy Bogues was lost to Charlotte in the expansion draft to stock the Hornets and the Miami Heat.

Jeff Malone was 17th in NBA scoring (21.7), and tenth in free-throw shooting (.871). Crowds

dipped again by 750 to 9,814. Eackles became the team's third guard, but Grant, whose brother Horace broke in with the Bulls in 1987, was the tenth man.

In the 1989 draft, front court players Tom Hammonds, Ed Horton and Doug Roth were selected and all three made the team. Mel Turpin was signed as a free agent. Terry Catledge went to Orlando in the expansion draft to stock the Magic and Minnesota. The team sank to 31-51 in 1989-90, 11 games out of a possible playoff slot.

Jeff Malone led the scoring (24.3) and was 12th in the NBA. Charles Jones was seventh in blocks (2.43) and Darrell Walker tenth in assists (8.0). At 18 games into the season, John Williams injured his knee and was lost for the year. Susan O'Malley, 27 years old, was named Executive Vice-President during the 1989 summer.

In June of 1990, Bob Ferry resigned after 17 years as general manager and John Nash was hired away from Philadelphia six days later. The next week, 1989's No. 1 pick in the draft, Pervis Ellison came from Sacramento with a second-round pick. Jeff Malone woundup in Utah in the 3-way deal. The draft brought second-rounders Greg Foster and A.J. English.

The Bullets made some minor pickups, but still slipped to 30-52, fourth in the Atlantic, nine games out of the playoffs. Bernard King completed his comeback from 1985 knee surgery by being voted an East starter in the 1991 All-Star Game in Charlotte. He finished third in NBA scoring (28.4). Ellison who was tenth in blocked shots (2.07) climbed again to 11,880.

In 1991-92, the Bullets fell five more victories to 25-57, 6th in the Atlantic Division and fifth-worst in the NBA. However, Pervis Ellison was voted the NBA's Most Improved Player and Bernard King missed the entire season with another knee surgery. In June of 1991, Michael Adams was reacquired from Denver with the first round's 19th pick (LaBradford Smith) for the eighth pick in 1991.

Darrell Walker was dealt to Detroit in September for a pair of second-round picks. Ellison finished eighth in blocked shots (2.68) and ninth

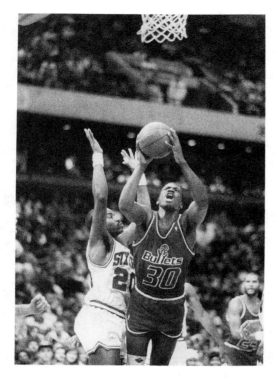

AP/Wide World Photos

Bernard King (30)

in field-goal accuracy (.539) while improving his scoring to 20.0, the team's best, and his rebounding to 11.2. Adams scored 18.1 and was ninth in NBA assists (7.6) while Harvey Grant scored 18.0. At the trade deadline, Rex Chapman was acquired from Charlotte for Tom Hammonds. Attendance was 12,341, the best since 1978-79.

In 1991, Susan O'Malley was named the first woman NBA team president.

Washington added Tom Gugliotta (sixth pick overall) and second-rounder Brent Price (brother of Cavs All-Star point guard Mark) in the 1992 draft. Don MacLean, a Detroit pick sent to the Clippers, was acquired with William Bedford for John (Hot Plate) Williams, who had played just 51 games in 1989-90 and 1990-91. Williams was suspended for the 1991-92 season and had ballooned to more than 300 pounds, despite his offi-

cially listed roster weight of 235.

Bernard King showed up unannounced at a practice one day saying he was ready to play. He physically and verbally threatened Coach Unseld and forced his release. The Nets later signed him as a spot player and he retired at a 1993 summer All-Star Game in Madison Square Garden. On the floor, the Bullets sank to 22-60, last in the Atlantic Division and third-worst in the NBA. It was the team's worst mark in the Capital Centre and the poorest since 1966-67's 20-61 record.

Gugliotta made the All-Rookie Team by scoring 14.7 ppg. Injuries continued to haunt the Bullets, with Pervis Ellison missing 33 games and having post-season surgery on both knees in May. Michael Adams missed twelve games, Harvey Grant missed ten, Rex Chapman and LaBradford Smith each missed 22. In all, 19 men played for the team in 1992-93, as attendance held close toeven with 1991-92 figures. Gugliotta was 17th in NBA rebounds, Ellison ranked 17th in field-goal accuracy (.521) and seventh in blocks (2.20). Adams was 13th in assists (7.5) and 17th in free throw-shooting (.856).

After the season, the Bullets picked sixth in the Lottery taking Indiana swing-man Calbert Cheaney. They also traded Harvey Grant (who had an option to leave after 1993-94) to Portland for 7-foot, 285-pound center Kevin Duckworth. They gained the playoff potential in 1993-94 to play big with Duckworth-Ellison-Gugliotta or with the smaller, faster combination of Ellison-Gugliotta-Cheaney. However, the team lacked consistency at guard. Unseld decided to come back and try to stop the six-season losing string that has given him a 178-287 record despite a reputation as a fine and patient teacher of the game.

SOURCES

BOOKS

Carter, Craig and Alex Sachare, *The Sporting News NBA Guide,* 1992-93 edition, the Sporting News, 1992.

Hollander, Zander, editor, *The Pro Basketball Encyclopedia,* Corwin Books, 1977.

Hollander, Zander, editor, *The NBA's Official Encyclopedia of Pro Basketball,* North American Library, 1981.

Hollander, Zander and Alex Sachare, editors, *The Official NBA Basketball Encyclopedia,* Villard Books, 1989.

Jares, Joe, *The American Game,* A Rutledge Book, Follett Publishing Co., 1971.

Nadel, Eric, *The Night Wilt Scored 100,* Taylor Publishing, 1990.

Williams, Matt, Maureen Lewis, Jim Delaney, editors, *Washington Bullets 1992-93 Media Guide,* Washington Bullets, 1992.

OTHER

NBA Editorial Staff, *All-Star Weekend Guide,* NBA Publications, 1993.

NBA Editorial Staff, *NBA News,* Vol. 47, Nos. 27 and 34, NBA Publications, 1993.

EASTERN CONFERENCE

CENTRAL DIVISION

ATLANTA HAWKS

The Atlanta Hawks' Media Guide indicates that the team began as the Tri-City Blackhawks of the old National Basketball League, but in fact they were the Buffalo Bisons before that. Added to the struggling NBL in 1946 along with four other franchises, the club accumulated a 5-8, .385 record in Buffalo until it moved to the Tri-Cities on December 27, 1946.

And what are the Tri-Cities? Moline and Rock Island, Illinois, and Davenport, Iowa, just across the Mississippi. The team played at Wharton Field House, which, when filled to capacity, seated 6,000 fans on wooden benches. Their coach was Nat Hickey; their star was Don Otten, a 7-foot center who averaged almost 13 points per game that first year.

Pop Gates, a 6'2" forward, was their other "name" player, and he averaged 7.6 points at forward. The team finished at 19-25 in that first season at the new locale, a .432 clip, for fifth place in the six-team Eastern Division.

The Blackhawks were shifted into the Western Division the following season and improved their fortunes to second place, 13 games behind the Minneapolis Lakers. After Nat Hickey started the team off to a 9-12 mark, guard Billy Hassett coached them for one game--a win--and then 5'11" backcourt partner Bobby McDermott, renowned for starting fistfights with taller men, took over as player-coach for a 20-18 record.

The steadily productive Otten had been joined by a new supporting cast: forward Whitey Von Nieda and McDermott each scored 12.1 points per game, supplemented by Hassett's 10.7 average. In the playoffs, the team knocked off the fourth-place Indianapolis Kautskys before falling to the Lakers in a 2-0 sweep.

The NBL was then on its last legs, with four teams jumping to the Basketball Association of America between seasons and four new teams taking their places. Otten led the NBL in scoring that year with a 14.0 average. McDermott's coaching record was 25-20, but he was sent to the Hammond Calumet Buccaneers in midseason as a player. Roger Potter became the Blackhawks' new coach. The team's 36-28 record put it in second place once again, and after downing the Sheboygan Redskins in the playoff openers, the squad lost the division finals to the first-place Oshkosh All-Stars.

Joining the NBA

In 1949 the NBL and BAA merged into the National Basketball Association, with the Tri-City club slotted for the Western Division. (The team name was changed from Tri-City to Tri-Cities shortly after its entrance into the NBA.) The Potter-coached team won their opener against the Denver Nuggets, 93-85, but lost the next six contests, after which owner Ben Kerner gave the helm to former Washington Capitols coach Arnold "Red" Auerbach, later to be immortalized by his leadership of the Boston Celtics.

Young center Jack Nichols came over from Washington as well in a swap for the still-productive Otten and led the team in scoring, averaging 13.1 points per game. Nichols was backed up by two forwards, Dike Eddleman and Mike Todorovich, who each averaged over 12 points a game.

Coming in third in the division in that inaugural season, at 29-35, the Blackhawks lost their playoff series to the second-place Anderson Duffy Packers. For Auerbach it was goodbye, Tri-Cities, hello, Boston.

The combined coaching efforts of Dave McMillan (9-14), guard Johnny Logan (2-1) and Todorovich (14-28) steered the Blackhawks into the cellar of the division for 1950-51, for although the team attempted a league-leading 6,041 field goals, they only made 33 percent of them. Reserve forward Cal Christensen led the league by fouling out of 19 games. Guard Frankie Brian's 16.8 points per game, supported by Eddleman's 15.3, led the team.

This was not enough to preserve the Blackhawks' existence in the Tri-Cities area. Next season found them in Milwaukee, where they were to endure four terrible years. Don Otten was back at center for 1951-52, his point-per-game average still 12.0 at age 30, but his minutes down.

The team's big rebounder was 6'6" forward-center Mel Hutchins, who led the league that season with 880 rebounds, a 13.3 average. Under coach Doxie Moore, the Hawks, as they were now known, won 17 games and lost 49 in their first season in Brewtown, a .258 winning percentage that speaks for itself.

The following year, under Fuzzy Levane, the team improved to 27-44 (.380), but remained in last place among the five western teams. In 1953-54, the division was down to four teams, and Milwaukee brought up the rear again, at 21-51. Fuzzy Levane, after going 11-35, was replaced in midseason by a second "Red"--William Holzman.

Like Red Auerbach, Holzman was a Brooklyn native who would win NBA titles in the future with another team, in his case the New York Knicks. Holzman had also played on a title team, the 1946 Rochester Royals of the NBL, after starring for City College of New York in the early 1940s. In his first full season of coaching the Hawks, the future Hall of Fame coach went 26-46, or .361. In four years in Milwaukee, the team never climbed out of the cellar and never won more than 27 games.

Out of the Depths: The Pettit Era in St. Louis

Owner Kerner moved them to St. Louis for 1955-56. The city on the Mississippi had no baseball team at the time, the hapless Browns having become the Batlimore Orioles in 1954, and thus the local fans were ready to embrace a newcomer in any sport. Kerner's move turned out to be profitable both on the court and in the ticket office.

Their first year in St. Louis, the Hawks achieved a tie for second place in the West, matching the Lakers' 33-39 record in a division where even the leader only had a .514 winning percent-

TEAM INFORMATION AT A GLANCE

Founding date: 1946; charter member of the NBA in 1949.
Team originally called the Tri-City Blackhawks; moved to Milwaukee and shortened name to Hawks, 1951; moved to St. Louis, 1955; moved to Atlanta, 1969.

Home court:
The Omni
One CNN Center
Suite 405, South Tower
Atlanta, GA 30303
Phone: (404) 827-3800
FAX: (404) 827-3880

Seating capacity: 16,510

Team colors: Red, white, and yellow
Team nickname: Hawks
Logo: Hawk profile superimposed on a white circle outlined in red

Franchise record	Won	Lost	Pct.
(1949-92)	1739	1729	.502

League championships (1): 1957-58
Division/conference first-place finishes (9): 1956-57, 1957-58, 1958-59, 1959-60, 1960-61, 1967-68, 1969-70, 1979-80, 1986-87
Last-place finishes (6): 1950-51, 1951-52, 1952-53, 1953-54, 1954-55, 1976-77

age. The major reason for the Hawks' ascent was the quick emergence of 6'9" forward Bob Pettit, out of Lousiana State University, as a star. Pettit had served his rookie season during 1954-55, the first year of the 24-second clock, and had been the club's bright spot, averaging 20 points per game.

In 1955-56 he truly blossomed, leading the NBA in both scoring average (25.7) and total rebounds (1,164, a second-ranking 16.2 average), and landing a spot on the all-NBA first team. Pettit's individual star performance was aided by double-digit scoring averages from forward Jack Coleman, center Chuck Share, guard Jack Stephens, and guard Frank Selvy, who because of military service only played in 17 games. In the first round of the playoffs, the Hawks beat the aging,

Mikan-less Lakers 2-1, winning two 116-115 squeakers with a 133-75 blowout loss sandwiched between. In the exciting Game 3, Pettit scored 41 and rookie Al Ferrari sank two foul shots to win it. For the divisional championship, the Hawks took the Ft. Wayne Pistons to the five-game limit, losing the final 102-97.

The following year was marked by a crucial trade between the Hawks and the Boston Celtics, for the Hawks traded their draft rights to Bill Russell in exchange for veteran forward Ed Macauley and talented newcomer Cliff Hagan, a 6'4" forward who had been an All-American at Kentucky. The steady Hagan, a good ballhandler and shooter, was to be Pettit's capable sidekick over a ten-year NBA career before going to the

Fans in the 1990s, discussing the greatest basketball players of the past, are likely to mention superstars such as Chamberlain, West, Abdul-Jabbar, Russell, Bird, Magic Johnson, and Julius Erving. Memories have faded, and they are less likely to include the name of Bob Pettit— but he belongs there.

In eleven years in the NBA, all with the Hawks, Pettit was named to the all-league first team ten times, the second team only in his final year. He was Rookie of the Year, twice NBA MVP (1955-56 and 1958-59), and a three-time MVP of the All-Star game (1956, 1958, and 1959).

A completely dominant forward, he was at or near the top of the league list in both scoring and rebounding every season. He averaged more than 20 points per game every season, including six 50-plus point games.

Born December 12, 1932, in Baton Rouge, Louisiana, Pettit was a product of Louisiana State University. As a high school player he had not been considered promising, but he grew to be 6-foot-9, and he worked very hard. Lacking the flashy moves of an Elgin Baylor—his major competitor at the time for best forward in the NBA—Pettit's straight-up style might be compared to that of Larry Bird in recent times.

Slim and balding, he may have lacked personal charisma, but very few players have ever been more solely responsible for a team's success. His consistency throughout a decade was one of his most remarkable traits. Former teammate Lenny Wilkins, in his autobiography, said that Pettit "worked unceasingly to develop into one of the game's true greats. He was a real southern gentleman, polite and meticulous.... If Pettit had a bad game, he would practice the very next day on that phase of his repertoire which seemed weak to him."

Pettit retired in 1965 with a career scoring average of 26.4, fourth on the all-time NBA list, and a playoff scoring average of 25.5. His number 9 was the first uniform number ever to be retired by the Hawks. He was elected to the Hall of Fame in 1970.

Photo: *Naismith Memorial Basketball Hall of Fame*

ABA as a player and coach; he was elected to the Hall of Fame in 1977. The trade of Russell seemed fair at first, given Russell's relative lack of shooting skills, but in hindsight it is clear that Boston got by far the better of the deal.

Veteran point guard Slater Martin, a future Hall of Famer who had starred for the Lakers in their glory days, also joined the Hawk roster, and yet the Hawks got off to a dismal start. Holzman was replaced by player-coach Martin after 33 games, and after eight more games, during which the team went 5-3, Martin decided he would rather play full-time. Reserve forward Alex Hannum, who had lately come from the Pistons on waivers, was named as the club's new coach. With Share's playing time and effectiveness reduced, the Hawks lacked a legitimate center and Pettit was forced to start in that position on occasion. Playing with a broken wrist at times, he averaged 24.7 points and 14.6 rebounds for the season. He also led the league in field goals attempted and made.

The 1956-67 Western Division season ended with a logjam at the top, as three teams tied for the division lead with 34-38 records. A three-way elimination was held for first place, with St. Louis winning it. The Hawks then took the playoff openers from the Lakers, winning the conclusive third game 143-135 in double overtime in Minneapolis.

The Classic Hawks-Celtics Matchups

The Hawks entered the finals as underdogs to the Celtics, who, like the Hawks, were looking for their first NBA title. The first game of this classic series went to the Hawks 125-123 in overtime at Boston Garden, with Slater Martin handcuffing Bob Cousy. In Game 2, which went to the Celtics 119-99, Cousy starred while Pettit was held to 11 points.

Game 3 began with a shoving match between Ben Kerner and Red Auerbach, and went on to a rough-and-tumble game in which the score was tied 18 times; the Hawks came out on top, 100-98, with Pettit outplaying Russell in the rebound department.

Cliff Hagan starred in Game 4, scoring eight points in the last two minutes, but the Celtics won on Cousy's quarterbacking, 123-118. Game 5 went to Boston despite Pettit's 33 points, but in the see-saw Game 6 (23 lead changes), Hagan's tap-in with two seconds remaining lifted the Hawks to a 96-94 victory. Game 7, fittingly, was the most exciting of all. In the last few minutes, alternating scoring surges led to a Celtics lead, a Hawks lead, then another Celtics lead.

Russell blocked a Hawk's shot with the score 103-101 Boston, but then fouled Pettit with three seconds left. Pettit calmly tied the game with two

Naismith Memorial Basketball Hall of Fame

Slater Martin

free throws. The game went to two overtimes, with the out-of-practice Hannum inserting himself in the lineup after four Hawks fouled out. With three seconds left and the score 125-123 Celtics, Hannum tried a full-court alley-oop to Pettit. Pettit amazingly reached the ball for the tap-in; the ball circled the rim of the basket--then bounced out.

More experienced in 1957-58, the Hawks eased into first place with a 41-31, .569 record. The frontcourt of Pettit and Hagan was an offensive powerhouse, with Share and Macauley serving as capable reserves and guards Slater Martin and Jack McMahon concentrating on running the offense and dishing assists.

The Hawks trounced the Pistons 4-1 for the divisional banner. Again, as so many had predicted, the team faced the Celtics for the top prize. This time, luck was on the Hawks' side. With the series tied after two games, Bill Russell injured his ankle in Game 3 and had to sit on the sidelines; Russell's replacement, veteran Arnie Risen, had

Naismith Memorial Basketball Hall of Fame

Cliff Hagen

a sore leg. Game 3 went to the Hawks, 111-108. The Celtics recouped for Game 4, 109-98, with Auerbach putting the 6'1" Cousy in at center, despite an injured instep tendon that was a constant hindrance to the star playmaker.

In Game 5 Celtic guard Bill Sharman injured a knee and the Hawks made adjustments to Auerbach's improvised, slowed-down new strategy; still, the Hawks only won by two points, 102-100. In Game 6, in St. Louis, Bill Russell tried to play but could only manage 20 minutes; Pettit, meanwhile, tore up the court for 50 points, 19 of them in the fourth quarter, for a 110-109 triumph and the championship.

The Hawks enjoyed a superb regular season in 1958-59, going 49-23, but didn't make the finals. Pettit and Hagan were first and fifth in the league in scoring, and Pettit finished second only to Russell in rebounding. Future Hall of Famer Clyde Lovellette had joined the team at center, freeing Pettit to specialize at forward. Despite Ben Kerner's frequent changes of head coach--from Hannum to Andy Phillip to Ed Macauley--the players remained focused.

Everything seemed set for a third consecutive Hawks-Celtics series, but on the way, Elgin Baylor's Lakers upset the Hawks in the western division playoffs. Slater Martin was out with a dislocated leg, and Pettit got involved in a fistfight with Laker Jim Krebs in Game 1, a 127-97 Hawks laugher. The Hawks looked in good shape until Game 5, an overtime loss in St. Louis that broke the Hawks' 18-game home winning streak, 98-97. The sixth game went to the Lakers in Minneapolis, 106-104, eliminating the Hawks.

The Hawks took first place again in 1959-60, their 46-29 record giving them a 16-game edge over the Pistons. The Hawks frontcourt of Hagan, Pettit, and Lovellette scored a combined 71.7 points per game, as all three men averaged over 20. In the era of Chamberlain and Baylor, Pettit was down to fourth in the league in scoring, with 26.1, and Hagan was next at 24.8; Pettit was third to Chamberlain and Russell in rebounds. The opening round of the playoffs, against the Lakers, went against expectations, for the Minnesotans took their stronger rival to seven games before succumbing. Then, for the third time in four years, the Hawks and Celtics confronted one another for the NBA crown.

Game 1 was an offensive spree or a defensive disaster, depending on one's point of view. In the 140-122 Boston win, a record was set for most total points in a finals game. St. Louis fought back for a Game 2 win, but the next four games were a low-energy seesaw. In Game 7, the Celtics, led by the assists of Cousy and rebounds of

PROFILE	Lenny Wilkens

Leonard Randolph Wilkens was born October 28, 1937, in New York City, and was raised in an integrated area of the Bedford-Stuyvesant section of Brooklyn by his Irish-American mother, Henrietta Cross Wilkens. The child's father died when Leonard was less than three years old. "Mother worked in a candy factory, did housecleaning and collected Aid For Dependent Children, yet we still were just barely able to survive," Wilkens recalls in *The Lenny Wilkens Story*.

Wilkens was intelligent and gifted, however, and was taken in hand by Father Thomas Mannion of the Holy Cross Church. He had a passion for basketball, and through determination he overcame the disappointment of not being picked for schoolboy teams—or, at Boys High School, being picked fifteenth of fifteen and quitting. Support from an understanding welfare investigator allowed him to go to college instead of to work after graduating from high school. At Providence College, he starred in an NIT tournament and was called a "defensive genius" by Gene Roswell of the New York Post.

Oddly, however, public recognition came slowly during Wilken's pro career. His relatively small size, at 6-foot-1 and 185 pounds, and quiet demeanor allowed him to be overlooked next to larger, more aggressive players. Fellow players, coaches, and true fans knew, however, that he had two of the surest hands and one of the keenest minds in basketball.

The latter quality has led to his becoming one of the most successful head coaches in the NBA. With twenty years of coaching behind him, he ranks fifth on the all-time list of winningest NBA coaches, first among active coaches; he is sixth, and climbing, in games coached. He guided the Seattle Supersonics to the championship in 1978-79. As a coach he is quiet, treating his players as adults and expecting them to produce.

Although Wilkens played only a bit more than half of his career with the Hawks, he is on their list of all-time leaders in games played, minutes played, and total points. He is third on their assists list with 3,048, out of a career total 7,211. Nine times an All-Star, league MVP in 1971, he was elected to the Hall of Fame in 1988.

Russell, took a 41-23 lead and never looked back.

The following season, impatient owner Kerner again tried to shake things up by hiring a new coach, this time former Syracuse Nationals star Paul Seymour. A rookie guard from Providence College, playmaking ace Lenny Wilkens, joined the Hawks for the start of a great NBA career as player and coach.

Pettit's scoring average for the year was up to 27.9, fourth in the league, with Hagan at 22.0. Pettit also maintained his stature as one of the game's premier rebounders, ranking third in the league in rebounds per game with 20.3. The Hawks' .646, 51-victory finish was 15 games ahead of the Lakers. The divisional finals against the Lakers--that team's first after their relocation to Los Angeles--were surprisingly close and dramatic, with none of the seven games won by a margin of more than six points, and Pettit and Baylor vying for scoring honors.

Game 6 was an overtime win for the Lakers at home, 114-113, after Pettit tied it with twelve seconds left; but the Hawks took the clincher, 105-103 in St. Louis, as Pettit scored the winning field goal.

The finals were totally anticlimactic from the Hawks' perspective, as the annual meeting with the Celtics turned into a disappointing 4-1 rout. Boston assumed command of the series from the outset with a 129-95 win in Game 1. Bob Cousy's ballhandling clinic in Game 2 enabled the Celtics to overcome a combined 70-point performance by

Pettit and Hagan for a 116-110 Boston win. St. Louis won Game 3, 124-120, but Games 4 and 5 were one-sided Celtic victories. The five-year sequence of classic finals matchups between Hawks and Celtics had straggled to its end.

The Mighty Are Fallen

In 1961-62 the Hawks collapsed from first place to fifth, with a 29-51 record that put them ahead only of the short-lived Chicago Packers. This fall was due primarily to Lenny Wilkins' departure for military service during the period of the Berlin Wall crisis; additionally, Lovellette missed the second half of the season with a heel injury.

For Pettit it was a sensational year: his 31.1 points per game remain a Hawks single-season record (he was fourth in the league), and he pulled down 18.7 rebounds per contest, also fourth in the standings. Hagan scored 22.9 points per game in support of Pettit.

But the heroics of the frontcourt couldn't make up for the lack of backcourt strength, and once again owner Kerner got into the act by firing and hiring coaches. Seymour was out after 14 games and Fuzzy Levane was back--until the last six games of the regular season, when Pettit filled in as player-coach and went 4-2.

The full-time replacement at the helm for 1962-63 was Harry "The Horse" Gallatin, formerly a seven-time All-Star with the Knicks and a future Hall of Famer. Gallatin took the Hawks back up to second place with a 48-32 record and into the Western Divison finals, thereby earning Coach of the Year honors.

Roster changes, however, were also important in the team's recovery. Wilkens was back to lead the offense, the aging Lovellette was sold to the Celtics, and rookie center Zelmo Beaty took his place. Beaty, a graduate of obscure Prairie View College, was a first-round draft choice for the Hawks who stood 6'9" and weighed 235 pounds.

Playing with the Hawks until he joined the Utah Stars of the ABA in 1970, this talented shooter and defensive pivotman remains on the all-time Hawks' leaders list in games played, minutes played, total points (8,717 with the Hawks), scoring average (17.4, tenth in team history), and rebounds and rebounding average (fourth in both categories).

His understudy on the bench was Knick veteran Phil Jordan; guards Chico Vaughan and John Barnhill, forwards Woody Sauldsberry, Bill Bridges, and Mike Farmer, and center Gene Tormohlen also joined the club in its whollesale revamping.

Pettit put in yet another stellar year, finishing fourth in scoring (28.4) and rebounds (15.1), while Hagan, now an excellent reserve, contributed 15.2 points per contest. The 1962-63 Hawks bested the Pistons 3-1 in the playoffs and then lost a seven-game series to the Lakers.

The Hawks cemented their second-place position in the west in 1963-64, coming in two games behind the Warriors at a .575 clip of 46-34. After the addition of ex-Knick star Richie Guerin at guard, their roster had stabilized, with all five starters scoring in double figures.

Wilkens scored 12 points per game while passing out 4.6 assists a game, and Beaty, although he led the league in fouls, scored 13.1 a game to go with a 10.7 rebounding average. Hagan was again in the starting rotation and tallied 18.4 points per game, while Pettit's 27.4 average was third in the league to Wilt Chamberlain and Elgin Baylor.

The club's first playoff opponent was the Lakers, whom they beat 3-2 before once again losing a seven-game divisional championship series, this time to the Warriors.

Goodbye, Bob

Bob Pettit had been a first-team all-NBA selection for ten consecutive years; in 1964-65, he was relegated to the second team, displaced by Rookie of the Year Jerry Lucas. Pettit played in only 50 of the 80 games because of a knee injury and scored 22.5 points per outing. He retired at season's end, concluding one of the greatest, and perhaps most underrated, careers in NBA history.

Meanwhile, Lenny Wilkens stepped up his offensive contribution with 16.5 points per game and 5.5 assists; Beaty posted 16.9 and 12.1 averages in scoring and rebounding, respectively; Bridges, Hagan, Vaughan, and Guerin all averaged double figures in scoring.

The team's season started slowly. When the club's reached 17-16, Kerner brought in Richie Guerin as player-coach to replace Hasrry Gallatin. Guerin's playing time was limited by a leg injury that season anyway, and under his high-decibel guidance the Hawks made a late-season run of 28 victories in their last 47 games. They lost their playoff round, however, to the third-place Baltimore Bullets, 3-1.

The following season the Hawks finished in third place in the division with a .450 winning percentage, with Guerin still in the pilothouse and Wilkens, Beaty, Hagan, Guerin, and Bridges the starting five. Wilkens and Beaty fueled the team's offense with 18.0 and 20.7 points per game, respectively; once again, Beaty was a champion fouler of opposing players, thus making up for his relative lack of height at center.

In the postseason, the team took revenge on Baltimore with a 3-0 sweep, but then lost the divisional title to the talent-rich Lakers in seven games. Cliff Hagan, after 746 games as a Hawk (still fourth on their all-time list) and five All-Star games, moved to the ABA, becoming an All-Star for the Dallas Chaparrals.

Hagan's spot was more than capably filled by rookie Lou Hudson, a hot shooter who would amass 17,940 points for a 20.2 average in 11 seasons with the Hawks and two with the Lakers. At 6'5", "Super Lou" played some guard as well as bringing down the boards at forward.

In his rookie year, he scored 18.4 points per game as the team's sixth man. His 1966-67 team finished at .481 with a 39-42, third-place record, swept the expansion Chicago Bulls in the playoffs, then fell to the Warriors in six games.

Good Times in the Late Sixties

The Hawks surged to the top of the Western Division in 1967-68, going 56-26. Wilkens was on fire and averaged 20.0 points per game, while Beaty scored a point per game more than that. Hudson missed almost half the season, not only for military service but also becuase of a threatened jump to the ABA; Paul Silas and hot-rebounding Bill Bridges made up for his absence with fine years. Guerin was named Coach of the Year after the best regular-season record in Hawks history to that point.

The team was physically strong, defensively skilled, and offensively potent; they were favored to win the divisional crown, but were upset by the no-name Warriors in six games.

Off-court disputes soured the season, for team captain Lenny Wilkens had running feuds with Guerin and Bridges and contractual and personal differences with management; although the team held a Lenny Wilkens Night on March 16, 1968, they chafed at his demand for a $75,000 salary and traded him to the Seattle Supersonics for star guard Walt Hazzard, later to be known as Mahdi Abdul-Rahmad.

Gone (From St. Louis) with the Wind

The 1968-69 season was the beginning of the contemporary Hawks era, for it marked Ben Kerner's sale of the club to former Georgia governor Carl E. Sanders and businessman Thomas G. Cousins, who moved the team to Atlanta and helped spur that city's renaissance. For their first five years in Georgia, the Hawks played in Alexander Memorial Coliseum, the Georgia Tech fieldhouse, while the Omni Arena was under construction. Their first two years in their new home were successful ones.

Benefitting from a 15.8-point-per-game year from veteran defensive ace Joe Caldwell, the Hawks finished second in the division, beat the

San Diego Rockets in the playoffs, and fell to the Lakers in five games. The 1969-70 season was a triumphant one as the Hawks finished first in the West at 48-34. Hudson paced the team with 25.4 points per game while Bridges led the club in rebounding with a 14.4 average. Beaty's leap to the ABA hurt, but replacement Jim Davis filled the void with a 13.6-point, 9.7-rebound year, and 6'11" veteran Walt Bellamy arrived from the Pistons in a trade after 56 games to further solidify the club. The Hawks easily handled the Bulls in the playoffs, but were swept in turn by the Lakers, led by Chamberlain, Baylor, and Jerry West.

The new decade brought a new gate attraction to Atlanta: Pete Maravich, the Louisiana State University superstar who was the flashiest shooter and passer in the game. Maravich's addition to the squad did not mean better all-around performance, however, since his teammates had trouble adjusting to the demands of his passing style. In both 1970-71 and 1971-72 the Hawks posted 36-46 records and finished second to the Bullets in the weak Central Division; they were whisked away in the playoff openers by the Knicks and Celtics, respectively.

In came Cotton Fitzsimmons as coach, and the team finally moved to its permanent home in the Omni. Lou Hudson lit up the league, averaging 27.1 points a game in 1972-73, with Maravich contributing 26.1 points a game, and the Hawks surged to a 46-36 record. Alas, there was still only one playoff round for the team, a 4-2 bow to the Celtics.

Skidding in the Seventies ... Toward A Fountain of Youth

The following season the Hawks skidded to a 35-47 record, still in second place to the Bullets. Lou Hudson was injured, as was guard Herm Gilliam. Maravich's 27.7 point average, second in the NBA, couldn't carry a team that barely had one double-digit rebounder, Jim Washington at 10.1. The following year, 1974-75, was even worse, as their 31-51 record allowed the Houston

Rockets and Cleveland Cavaliers to finish ahead of the Hawks, with only the expansion New Orleans Jazz protecting them from a finish in the cellar. The Hawks traded Maravich to the Jazz for two players plus several draft choices, but lost two prime draft choices to the ABA.

In 1975-76 the Hawks hit bottom: 29-53, a .354 winning percentage, their worst performance since their Milwaukee years. The remedy was to bring in Hubie Brown as coach and to bring in young players. The club traded Lou Hudson, the 11-year Hawk veteran, for Hudson had a bad back and missed much of 1976-77, another cellar year. In January 1977 media mogul Ted Turner, who already owned baseball's Braves, bought the Hawks.

The youth movement issued a moderate payoff in 1977-78 as the team hit .500, posting a 41-41 record with a starting squad of Charlie Criss and Armand Hill at guard, John Drew and John Brown at forward, and Steve Hawes in the center, backed up by 7'1" Tree Rollins. The Hawks' roster contained no player more than 28 years of age. Coach Brown was named NBA Coach of the Year, but his team was swept by the Bullets in its sole playoff round.

Yet things were definitely improving. The following season, Rollins started at center and blocked 254 shots. Eddie Johnson, a 6'2" guard out of Auburn, joined the team for his 16-points-per-game rookie season, and veteran Dan Roundfield, after serving his apprenticeship with Indiana, came over as a free agent.

The third-place Hawks went 46-36 in 1978-79, and at last won their opening playoff round, sweeping the Rockets 2-0. They took the archrival Bullets to seven games before falling in the Eastern Conference semifinals.

The Hawks were on a roll. Armed with the same starting five and same coach in 1979-80, the club grabbed first place in the Central Division of the Eastern Conference with a 50-32 record. Drew, Roundfield, and Johnson contributed 54.5 points per game among them, and Rollins plugged up the middle expertly, blocking 244 shots and leading the league in fouling out. Both statistics served as indications of Brown's emphasis on tough defense. Indeed, Brown's physical defense led to a total of 1,429 personal fouls for the starting unit. Drew, Johnson, and Roundfield all represented the Hawks in the All-Star game. The Hawks, however, were manhandled by Julius Erving, Maurice Cheeks, Darryl Dawkins, and the other Philadelphia 76ers in the playoff openers, falling 4 games to 1.

New Coaches, for a Change

What happened in 1980-81? For a club that only the year before had harbored legitimate championship aspirations, the plummet to a 31-51 record and fourth-place finish was a particularly dismaying turn of events. Brown was replaced near the end of the season by assistant coach Michael Fratello, who went 0-3 but would return in glory after an interlude.

In 1981-82, however, Kevin Loughery, former backcourt star for St. John's, Boston College, and the Bullets, and a man with previous head coaching experience with the New Jersey Nets, became the Hawks' guru. He took them to 42-40 in his first year, second to the Milwaukee Bucks.

Aside from the addition of Loughery, the Hawks traded John Drew, reserve guard Freeman Williams, and cash to the Utah Jazz in exchange for a draft choice: Dominique Wilkins, who was to become indisputably the most valuable player in Hawks history after Pettit. In 1982-83 Wilkins started at forward and, with a scoring average of 17.5 points per game, was a unanimous All-Rookie selection.

Roundfield and Rollins made the all-defense first and second teams, respectively. Rollins also led the league's shot-blockers with 343, while Roundfield contributed 19 points a game to the offense. The Hawks again made the playoffs but were beaten in the first round.

The Mike Fratello coaching era, one of hope and disappointment, began in 1983-84 with a relatively inauspicious 40-42, third-place finish. Wilkins scored 21.6 points per game, and Roundfield 18.9, but rebounding, which is a more reliable indicator of team defense than shot-blocking, was still a weakness. Another youth movement began, designed as a three-year process.

Rookie 6'4" guard Glenn "Doc" Rivers, out of Marquette, known for his canny, versatile, physically courageous play, became a starter for the playoffs and turned in almost 14 points per

---

FRONT OFFICE The Owner of Almost Everything

R. E. "Ted" Turner was born November 19, 1938, in Cincinnati, Ohio. At Brown University, he was Commodore of the Yacht Club and Vice-President of the Debating Union. Starting out as the owner of a small Atlanta UHF television station, Turner saw the future and acted on it: he beamed his signal by satellite to nationwide cable systems, creating the first superstation.

He purchase the Atlana Braves on January 14, 1976, and the Hawks on January 3, 1977, and made both teams increasingly popular across the nation through his TBS cablecasts. A keen sportsman who successfully defended yachting's America's Cup in 1977, Turner has played a major role in making Atlanta's teams successful and thus in helping his city. In 1986 he organized the Goodwill Games, which are held internationally every four years. In 1990 he innovated SportSouth, a regional network.

Turner Broadcasting System, or TBS, is the umbrella corporation for, among other things, Turner Network Television (TNT), Cable News Network (CNN), Headline News, Turner Home Entertainment, World Championship Wrestling, Hanna-Barbera, Inc., and the Cartoon Network. Turner, the husband of actress Jane Fonda, is active in civic and environmental organizations and was selected *Time* magazine's Man of the Year in 1991.

It is said of this future Hall of Famer—according to Spud Webb, in his book *Flying High*—that "he never met a shot he didn't like." Fortunately, Wilkins makes a great many of those shots, including hitting free throws at an over-.800 clip and making some of the most spectacular dunks in basketball. His "360," a spinning-in-the-air dunk, won him the Slam Dunk championship in the past.

Born in Sorbonne, France, near Paris, Wilkins—whose first name is Jacques, Dominique being his middle name—grew to be 6-foot-8 and a two-time All-American at the University of Georgia. Drafted by the Jazz in the third spot, he went to the Hawks when the Jazz sold the rights to him. He began to star in his rookie year and, except for injuries, hasn't stopped since.

He is one of the most prolific offensive forwards in the NBA and a leading rebounder as well. Half a page in the Hawks' media guide is devoted to Wilkins' "assault on the record book."

When he retires he will be at or near the top of the Hawks' all-time list in numerous categories relating to scoring, rebounding, and longevity. The older brother (by three years) of NBA player Gerald Wilkins, Dominique is also considered one of the nicest people in the league.

Photo: *AP/Wide World Photos*

postseason game. The Hawks traded 30-year-old Roundfield to Detroit for Cliff Levingston, Antoine Carr, and two draft choices. The trade eventually paid dividends for the Hawks despite Roundfield's three All-Star seasons, but during 1984-85, Carr was a bench player and Levingston represented an offensive decline compared to Roundfield.

Levingston did lead the team in rebounding. He did so, however, with an average of only 7.6 rebounds a game, further evidence of Atlanta's weakness in this phase of the game. At 34-48, the team finished fifth in the division. More size and strength was needed, and the team added it in agile forward-center Kevin Willis, 6'6" guard Randy Wittman, and seven-foot draft choice Jon Koncak.

The 1985-86 Hawks were the NBA's most improved team, finishing second to the Bucks in the division with a 50-32 record. Wilkins blossomed into a genuine superstar, earning the league's scoring championship with a 30.3 average. (His Slam Dunk championship, however, fell to rookie teammate Anthony "Spud" Webb, a 5'7" marvel out of North Carolina State who excited crowds and, although a reserve, contributed 4.3 assists per game.)

The Hawks were 34-7 at home, tying a franchise record, and Fratello was named Coach of the Year. They defeated the Pistons in the first round of the playoffs, 3-1. Atlanta won the first two games at home with mammoth offensive outputs of 144 and 137 points, and clinched the series via a 114-113 overtime victory in Detroit. However, their next opponent, the Celtics, had Larry Bird, Kevin McHale, Robert Parish, Danny Ainge, and Dennis Johnson, with a sixth man named Bill Walton; the result was a 4-1 demolition of the Hawks.

Almost a Peak

Confident of their youthful talent, the Hawks returned in 1986-87 for a franchise-record 57 wins and 25 losses, a .695 pace. Rivers' 10 assists per game were fourth in the league and his total of 823 were a new Hawks high in that department; Webb, with 5.1 assists per game, spelled him effectively for a while but underwent knee surgery in December.

Wilkins was down a point to 29.0 per game, but Willis, Rivers, Wittman, and three-point-shooting reserve guard Mike McGee all scored in double figures. The result was the leadership of the Central Division.

The Hawks' playoffs began well, as they disposed of the Indiana Pacers 3-1. The Pistons, however, who had finished behind the Hawks in the regular season, defeated them in the second round.

The Pistons, on the upswing, ousted the Hawks for first place in the Central Division in 1987-88, although the Hawks turned in a solid 50-32 regular season record. Wilkins (30.7 points per game) and Rivers (14.2 points, 9.3 assists) had All-Star years and Fratello was the All-Star coach.

The Hawks defeated the Bucks in the first round of playoffs and fought a tense seven-game series against the Celtics. Atlanta lost the final game 118-116, with Larry Bird hitting for 20 clutch points in the fourth quarter for the victors.

For 1988-89, the club tried to boost its position by adding superstar center Moses Malone and 6'7'" shooting guard Reggie Theus. These additions, though, were outweighed by the loss of Willis, who missed the entire season with a broken left foot.

Although the team set a new Omni attendance mark of 644,291 (a 15,714 average) in the regular season, and finished with a 52-30 record, they placed only third in the strong Central Division. To add to the pain, the fourth-place Bucks, whom the Hawks had beaten 6-0 in their regular-season series, beat them 3-2 in the opening round of play-offs.

Injuries reduced the Hawks to 41-41 in the disappointing 1989-90 season, a sixth-place finish. Mike Fratello resigned as coach, taking a broadcasting job with NBC, where booth-mate Marv Albert made him known to millions as "The Czar of the Telestrator."

Ex-San Antonio head coach Bob Weiss, who had served with six NBA teams in 12 years as a player, became the new Hawks leader; Kevin Loughery returned as one of his assistants. Weiss' Hawks went 43-39 for a fourth-place finish in 1990-91, as the club chugged through a 22-game home winning streak, the longest in its history. Weiss was named NBA Coach of the Month in December.

Wilkins had an outstanding year, leading the Hawks in scoring for the eighth consecutive time and ascending to the team lead in rebounds as well. Unfortunately, midway through the following season Wilkins injured his right achilles tendon and missed the second half of the season.

Also injured that year, for virtually the entire season, was Travis Mays, who had been obtained from the Sacramento Kings in a trade for Spud Webb. Fortunately, Kevin Willis stepped into the vacuum left by Wilkins' absence, setting a new club rebounding record (1,258 for the season, including 33 in one game), placing second in the league in rebounding average with 15.5, and leading the Hawks in points with 18.3 per game.

Looking Toward the Future

Small guard Rumeal Robinson, a graduate of Michigan's NCAA championship team, joined the club as a promising first-round draft pick in 1990-91. The following season, 6'8" Stacey Augmon, a defensive whiz from UNLV, added still more potential depth. Augmon played in all 82 games, the only NBA rookie to do so in 1991-92, and led the Hawks in steals, but the team's performance fell to a dismal, fifth-place 38-44. In 1992-93, the Hawks were back up to fourth place, with 43 wins and 39 defeats.

A highlight of the season was Wilkins' entry into the NBA's exclusive 20,000-point club, the 17th player ever to do so. His season total of 2,121 gave him a career output of 22,096, topping Pettit on the Hawks' all-time list; he was second to Michael Jordan in scoring average for the season, with 29.9.

Willis led the team in rebounds per game with 12.9, fifth in the league; new acquisition Mookie Blaylock, a versatile, 6'1" former Net, was the top Hawk in both assists and steals. However, the Hawks had the misfortune to encounter the Chicago Bulls in the first round of playoffs. Atlanta was unceremoniously dumped out of the playoffs in a sweep.

At the end of the 1992-93 season, coach Weiss stepped down and a new, but very familiar, face took the head coach's place on the Hawks bench. It was Len Wilkens, who had spent many successful years coaching the Cleveland Cavaliers and other teams. Atlanta fans hoped that this Hall-of-Fame Hawk would help boost their team to new levels of achievement.

SOURCES

Carter, Craig, and Sachare, Alex, eds., *The Sporting News Official NBA Guide, 1992-93*, Sporting News Publishing Co., 1992.

Dickey, Glenn, *The History of Professional Basketball Since 1896*, Stein and Day, 1982.

Hirshberg, Al, *Basketball's Greatest Teams*, G. P. Putnam's Sons, 1965.

Hollander, Zander, *The Complete Handbook of Pro Basketball, 1993*, Signet, 1992.

Hollander, Zander, and Sachare, Alex, *The Official NBA Basketball Encyclopedia*, Villard Books, 1989.

Lazenby, Ronald, *The NBA Finals: The Official Illustrated History*, Taylor Publishing Co., 1990.

Liss, Howard, *The Winners*, Delacorte Press, 1968.

Maravich, Pete, and Campbell, Darrel, with Frank Schroeder, *Pistol Pete: Heir To a Dream*, Thomas Nelson, Inc., 1987.

Neft, David S., and Cohen, Richard M., *The Sports Encyclopedia: Pro Basketball*, 2d ed. St. Martin's Press, 1989.

Taragano, Martin, *Basketball Biographies*, McFarland & Co., Inc., 1991.

Webb, Spud, with Reid Slaughter, *Flying High*, Harper & Row, 1988.

Wilkens, Lenny, *The Lenny Wilkens Story*, Paul S. Eriksson, Inc., 1974.

—Richard Cohen for Book Builders, Inc.

CHICAGO BULLS

In the early 1990s, the Chicago Bulls reigned as world champions of professional basketball, with adoring fans all over the globe. Their incredible superstar Michael Jordan is regarded by many as the greatest player in the game, and the club's young coach, Phil Jackson, boasts the best winning percentage among active coaches in the National Basketball Association (NBA). Overflow crowds regularly pack the house at Chicago Stadium, wildly cheering their team on to greater and greater heights. The franchise, understandably, is as solid as the Rock of Gibraltar. But it was not always so.

Professional basketball in the country's third largest city has had a sporadic history. Until recent years the teams that held the public eye in Chicago were the Cubs and White Sox in spring and summer, the Bears and Black Hawks in fall and winter. Pro basketball was something played somewhere else for somebody else.

Few people in Chicago today remember the difficulty that pro basketball had getting started in the city; or that the Bulls were not the first professional basketball team to call the city home, or even the second or third. In reality, they're the eighth. One of those teams only lasted for two years, and in each year played under a different name; one group went on to become the best known basketball team in the entire world, more so than even the modern-day Bulls.

There are other long-forgotten chapters in Chicago's professional basketball annals that are equally fascinating. Take, for example, the fact that the famed George Mikan, who was once voted as the greatest basketball player of the first half of the century, started his pro career as a member of a Chicago team, and would in all likelihood have continued playing in the Windy City had that particular team not folded; that on another occasion, Bob Cousy, one of the most exciting guards in the history of the sport, would have started his professional playing days in a Chicago uniform if his team too had not disbanded; that Chicago Bear pro football immortal George Halas owned and operated pro basketball teams in Chicago on two separate occasions; that the first racially integrated team in pro basketball was a Chicago club; and finally, that pro basketball in Chicago has been around, off and on, since 1925.

Although pro basketball had existed in the United States since before the turn of the century, it was primarily an eastern seaboard game through its early years, played for the most part in the states of New York and Pennsylvania.

With World War I long finished and the "Roaring Twenties" in full bloom, a group of investors headed by National Football League Commissioner Joe Carr decided the rest of the country might also be interested in the sport. They called their new enterprise the American Basketball League (ABL).

Chicago was one of nine franchises, along with Boston, Brooklyn, Washington, Rochester, Buffalo, Fort Wayne, Cleveland and Detroit. The Chicago club, which was called the Bruins, was owned and run by Halas.

The first pro basketball season in 1925-26 was played as a split season, with Chicago far down in the pack in both halves, finishing 6-10 for the first, 3-11 for the second. Some of the names of the teams were noteworthy, as were some of the owners.

Among the ABL clubs were the Cleveland Rosenblums, named after their owner, department store tycoon Max Rosenblum; the Washington Palace Five, bankrolled by laundry millionaire and future National Football League kingpin George Preston Marshall; and the Pulaski Post Five from Detroit. The league managed to stay afloat for six years before financial woes—the Great Depression had hit—forced it out of existence.

The Bruins had records of 7-14 and 6-15 in 1926-27; 13-36 (no split season) in 1927-28; 15-12 and 4-10 in 1928-29; 12-12 and 17-13 in 1929-30; and 7-14 and 11-5 in the ABL's final season in 1930-31. In that last year Chicago had the league's top scorer in Benny Bergmann, who averaged 8.8 points per game (ppg), considered quite high in those days. The Bruins' overall record during those six years was 101-152, hardly an auspicious beginning for professional basketball in Chicago.

During this same period another remarkable team got its start in Chicago. It was in 1926 that a Chicago promoter, Abe Saperstein, originated what eventually would become the most famed professional basketball team of all time. Saperstein started his club as a local attraction only, playing all of their games at a large skating rink. But when the rink closed down, he was forced to take his show on the road.

Because all of his players were black, and because he wanted a name that would identify the team as a touring club, he came up with the moniker Harlem Globetrotters. In the decades that followed, the Globetrotters would gain international fame behind such players as Curly Neal and Meadowlark Lemon.

After the ABL disbanded in the spring of 1931, pro basketball disappeared from the scene in Chicago, except for occasional visits by touring teams. In 1937 a loosely knit organization called the National Basketball League was formed. Although the majority of the teams in the league were from small Midwestern towns such as Oshkosh, Wisconsin, Waterloo, Iowa, and Hammond, Indiana, a few of the franchises were in larger metropolitan areas—Detroit, Denver, and Minneapolis.

A team from Chicago joined the league in 1939, again under the ownership of Halas, and retained the Bruins nickname. In its first year of competition the new Bruin club fought to a 14-14 record, and one of its players, Mike Novak, had the top scoring average for the league, 10.5 ppg.

Halas ran the club through two more seasons, earning an 11-13 record and a fifth place finish in 1940-41 and an 8-15 sixth place effort in 1941-42. With the advent of World War II, however, he gave up his interest in the franchise.

Sponsorship of a team in the league then was taken up by the United Auto Workers' union at a Chicago auto factory, and the club was named, appropriately, the Chicago Studebaker Flyers. The

```
Team Information At a Glance

Founding date: 1966

Home court:
Chicago Stadium
1 Magnificent Mile
980 North Michigan Ave., Ste. 1600
Chicago, IL  60611
Phone: (312) 943-5800
FAX: (312) 943-6739

Seating capacity: 18,676


Team nickname: Bulls
Logo: Words "Chicago Bulls" over drawing of angry-looking bull.
Team colors: Red, white, and black

Franchise record        Won        Lost
(1966-92)               1,085      1,046

NBA Championships (3): 1991, 1992, 1993
```

factory had a number of Globetrotter players on its assembly line, and a few of them joined the Flyer squad, making it the first racially integrated team in pro basketball.

At first everything seemed to go well, and the team was one of the best in the league. But after several games discord developed between the white and black players, and the club dropped to an 8-15 record, losing its last ten games. At the end of the season the situation had worsened to the point that the union dropped its sponsorship and the franchise folded.

Two years later another Chicago industrial organization, the American Gear Company, agreed to sponsor a team in the ABL, and naturally the name of the club became the Chicago American

Gears. The team finished 14-16 in the 1945-46 campaign and 17-17 in 1946-47, then grabbed sport page headlines the nation over by signing All-American George Mikan of DePaul University to a contract. Big George agreed to a five-year package at $60,000, or $12,000 a year, less than what some of today's players make for a single quarter of action. Mikan played in some of the team's postseason games, attracting huge crowds.

The next year started out well until Mikan abruptly quit the team, saying he was not getting his full salary. He sat out a number of games until he and the club ironed out the problem, returning in time to post a league-leading 16.5 ppg.

The Gears record, 26-18, was good for third place in the league's Western Division. But paced by the six-foot-ten-inch Mikan the club caught fire in the playoffs to capture the league championship. After the season, however, the Gears quit the league, and Mikan left the team.

During this same season, another professional basketball league, the Basketball Association of American (BAA), was formed. In the summer of 1946, owners of some of the biggest sports arenas in the United States and Canada gathered to discuss the possibility of forming a top-quality league to bring pro basketball to major population centers.

The group, led by Walter Brown, president of the Boston Garden, and Al Sutphin, owner of the Cleveland Arena, had been successful in promoting events such as ice shows, boxing, and rodeos, and felt that a good potential for pro basketball existed.

On June 16, 1946, in New York City, they met to organize the new league, choosing Maurice Podoloff, then president of the American Hockey League, as their first president. The league began with 11 teams from 11 cities—Boston, New York, Philadelphia, Providence, Toronto, Washington, St. Louis, Cleveland, Detroit, Pittsburgh, and Chicago.

The Chicago team, called the Stags, was one of the surprises of the new league, winning the championship of the Western Division with a 39-22 record before losing to the Philadelphia Warriors in the playoff finals.

During that 1946-47 season, Chicago had two professional basketball clubs, the Gears in the ABL and the Stags in the new BAA. The two leagues then embarked on a struggle for supremacy, vying for the services of the nation's top college players. Minneapolis of the ABL got the older league out front initially by signing former Chicago Gear George Mikan, basketball's greatest drawing card. But then a year later the BAA dealt the ABL a crushing blow by absorbing four of its best franchises, including Minneapolis. Within months the war was over as the two leagues merged to form the NBA.

The Stags were to play for only four years in the new NBA, up through the 1949-50 season, but they always had winning marks. The records of their two coaches, Harold Olsen, 95-63 for a .601 winning percentage, and Phil Brownstein, 50-29 and .633, were the best that any Chicago pro basketball coach would attain up to the arrival of Phil Jackson in 1989. After that first season, the team was 28-20, 38-20, and 40-28.

Had the Stags not folded in 1950, one of the rookies they would have had for the next season was the young Bob Cousy, fresh out of Holy Cross. When the league was assigning Stag players to other teams, no one showed much interest in him, primarily because of his size. He was awarded to the Boston Celtics and became a perennial All-Star.

Chicago was not to have another representative in the NBA until the 1961-62 season, when the Chicago Packers entered the league. It was actually the first new franchise in the NBA's 12-year history. Coached by ex-Laker star Jim Pollard and paced by huge rookie center Walt Bellamy, who averaged 31.6 ppg in his first year as a pro, the Packers nevertheless could not get untracked and finished with a miserable 18-62 record, 36 games behind the Lakers. Bellamy's average would probably have won the league scoring crown in any other year; however 1961-62 was the season when Wilt Chamberlain averaged 50.4 ppg, still an NBA high.

The next year the club changed its name to the Zephyrs, and added the services of another high scorer, rookie Terry Dischinger, but again finished last with a 35-55 mark. Dischinger was voted the league's Rookie of the Year and averaged 25.5 ppg. Following the 1962-63 season the club moved to Baltimore and became the Bullets. Within six years they would win the Eastern Division championship.

In 1966, after an absence of four years, professional basketball returned to Chicago when a group of business leaders headed by Dick Klein put together a $1.6 million league entrance fee, and the Chicago Bulls were born. The team would play in the Chicago Amphitheater. Here's a year-by-year look at how the franchise has fared since that time.

1966-67

Under coach Johnny "Red" Kerr, the newly-created Chicago Bulls became one of the most exciting teams in the league, scoring at an average of more than 113 points per game and winning more games than any expansion club in NBA history. The team's fourth place finish and 33-48 record earned them a playoff birth, though they were eliminated in the first round. For his efforts, Kerr was voted the NBA's Coach of the Year.

With an opening day lineup of Lenny Chappell at center, Bob Boozer and Don Kojis at forward, and Guy Rodgers and Jerry Sloan at guard, the Bulls got off to a fast start, winning their inaugural game, 104-97, over the Hawks in St. Louis.

Back home for their own curtain-raiser at the Amphitheater on October 18, the Bulls outfought San Francisco 119-116. The new club then ran all over the Los Angeles Lakers 134-124. The Bulls were able to stay over .500 through the first three weeks of the season, topping St. Louis again, 134-102, on November 3 for a 7-6 mark.

As happens to most expansion teams, the Bulls struggled through the rest of the schedule, playing well below .500 for the remainder of the season. A big win for the club occurred on March 1, when they took a 129-122 decision over the eventual champion Philadelphia 76ers, who lost only 13 times that season. The Bulls also finished well, winning their final three games of the season against Detroit, 96-91, San Francisco, 120-117, and Los Angeles, 122-109.

The scoring pace in that first campaign was hectic, to say the least. The Bulls' average of 113.2 ppg was the second highest they have attained, but they gave up 116.9, the most that has ever been scored on a Chicago team. In 17 of the contests more than 250 combined points were scored, topped by the 284 in the 154-130 loss to Los Angeles on November 23 and the 283 in the 142-141 overtime loss to San Francisco on February 5.

As an indication of the pace of the play, the 1966-67 team had 8,505 field goal attempts and 2,205 personal fouls, both still club records after more than a quarter of a century. The club also pulled down 4,546 rebounds, the second highest total they have attained. On March 10, 1967, they shot a one-game record 131 field goals, still a club high.

Rodgers led the team in scoring with 1,459 points for an 18.1 ppg average and led the league in assists with a 11.2 mark. His highpoint came on December 21 against the New York Knicks when he dished out 24 assists. Boozer was a close second in scoring with an even 18 ppg. During the year Boozer set a single game scoring mark for the team with 40 against New York on Christmas Day.

The record was soon eclipsed by Kojis, who pumped home 42 against the Los Angeles Lakers on February 12. Sloan, who would go on to play more games for the Bulls—696—than anyone in history and who would become the team's head coach in 1979, was third with a 17.4 ppg average. Erwin Mueller, the team's best rookie, was next with 12.9 ppg, followed by Don Kojis with 10.2 ppg.

The Bulls' number one draft choice, Dave Schellhase of Purdue, never could duplicate his college scoring levels and averaged only three points a game. Chappell, who began the season as the club's starting center, was traded to Cincinnati after only 19 games. Other players on that first-ever Bulls team included Nate Bowman, Keith Erickson, McCoy McLemore, Gerry Ward, and Jim Washington. Both Rodgers and Sloan were named to the NBA's Western Conference All-Star team.

1967-68

What a difference a year makes. In the Bulls' first season in the league, Kerr led the club to the most wins ever for an expansion club, earning NBA Coach of the Year honors in the process. The bloom left the rose in the team's second year, however, as the Bulls got off to a terrible start, losing their first nine games and 15 of their first 16. An eight-game losing streak later in the year added to the woes and a 29-53 record, 27 games behind the leading St. Louis Hawks. The Bulls' win total was enough, however, for another fourth place finish and a playoff berth. Again though, they lost in the first round.

This was a different Bulls team than the year before. Starting forward Kojis as well as Ward and George Wilson were lost in the expansion draft to stockpile new clubs in Seattle and San Diego. Clem Haskins was the Bulls' first-round draft choice. The Bulls also traded All-Star guard Guy Rodgers to Cincinnati for hot-shooting Flynn Robinson and two draft choices. Later in the season Robinson set a playoff mark for the Bulls, scoring 41 in the team's only postseason win, 104-98, over the Los Angeles Lakers.

Opening Day saw Boozer and Barry Clemens at forward, Erwin Mueller at center and Rodgers and Jerry Sloan at guard. Rodgers' spot was taken over by Robinson after the trade, and during the season Clemens lost his starting role to Jim Washington and Mueller gave way to McCoy McLemore.

Boozer, the team's only representative at the mid-season All-Star game, led the team in scoring with 21.5 ppg and tied a club regular season scoring mark with 42 points against the Lakers on October 27, while Washington pulled down 10.1 rebounds per game (rpg) to pace that category. Robinson was second in scoring at 16 ppg, while Sloan again had a solid year, averaging 13.3 ppg. McLemore at 12.9 ppg, Washington at 12.5 ppg, and swingman Keith Erickson at 12.2 ppg were close behind.

Kerr was fired at the end of the season and replaced by Dick Motta. Motta had been one of the nation's most successful college coaches, compiling an astounding 120-33 record and .784 winning percentage at Weber State College in Utah. The year also saw the inauguration of the new American Basketball Association (ABA) and their controversial red, white, and blue ball.

1968-69

For the second year in a row the NBA added two expansion clubs, one of them only 90 miles to the north in Milwaukee, the other in Phoenix.

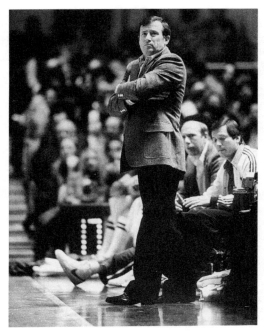

AP/Wide World Photo

Dick Motta

And again the Bulls were forced to give up a key player; this time it was forward-center McCoy McLemore, along with Craig Spitzer and Dave Schellhase. A revolving door scenario developed with Erwin Mueller and Jim Barnes of the Los Angeles club.

The Bulls traded Mueller for Barnes early in the season, then got Mueller back later in the year in a trade for Keith Erickson, then finally sold Mueller to Seattle and Barnes to Boston. In a key move that would pay off in upcoming years, the Bulls sent Flynn Robinson to the Milwaukee Bucks for forward Bob Love and guard Bob Weiss. During the year Pat Williams was named as the team's new general manager.

Opening day saw Bob Boozer and Jim Washington at the forward posts, first-round draft choice Tom Boerwinkle at center and Jerry Sloan and Robinson at guard. When Robinson was dealt to the Bucks, second-year guard Clem Haskins took over his spot on the starting five. Boozer again led the club in scoring, with 21.7 ppg, while the seven-foot, 275-pound Boerwinkle bulled his way to a club leading 11.1 rpg and also scored at a 9.8 ppg clip. Haskins surprised with a 17.2 ppg mark, and Sloan, at 16.8 ppg, dumped in 43 against the Milwaukee Bucks on March 5 to set a new Bulls' one-game scoring record. Sloan was the only Bull on the All-Star lineup, and he also made the NBA All-Defensive team.

Under new head coach Dick Motta, the club reversed its slide, showing a slight improvement by going 33-49. Despite the added wins, the club dropped a notch to fifth place, which left them out of the playoffs for the first time.

While Boston again won the league crown, their 11th title in 13 years, former Bulls Coach Red Kerr, who had taken the head coaching job in Phoenix, was having his troubles. After the team lost the coin flip to the Bucks for the right to draft UCLA's Lew Alcindor, they could only manage a 16-66 record, the worst in the league. Back in Chicago, fans were looking forward to next year, for the Bulls were finally going to play in a major league quality facility, the Chicago Stadium.

1969-70

The front office's wheeling and dealing on the trade market prior to, during, and after the season resulted in almost a complete lineup turnover. Before the season opener the club traded starting forward Jim Washington to Philadelphia for Chet Walker and Shalir Halimon; traded the other starting forward Bob Boozer and Barry Clemens to Seattle for center Bob Kauffman and a future draft choice (this one raised a few eyebrows); then gave Mike Lynn to the Lakers for another draft choice. During the season the Bulls obtained center Walt Wesley from Cincinnati for guards Norm Van Lier and Dave Newmark, and then traded Al Tucker to Baltimore for Ed Manning.

In April they sent Clem Haskins, who had been starting at guard, to the Phoenix Suns for center Jim Fox, apparently to add more scoring punch at the pivot. First-round draft choice Larry

Cannon of La Salle did not make the club.

The opening day lineup saw Bob Kauffman and Chet Walker at forwards, Tom Boerwinkle at center, and Clem Haskins and Jerry Sloan at guards. Sloan was the only one of the five that was with the team in its first season. The team continued to improve under Coach Dick Motta's physical style of play, moving up to a 39-43 record, but more importantly, to third place in the division, their highest finish ever. They finished only nine games out of first place after ending the year 22 out in 1968-1969 and 27 out the year before.

Highlights of the year included a record breaking 37 rebounds for Boerwinkle on January 8 against Phoenix, still a Bulls' record, and during the same game the team set a new record in total points in a 152-123 win. The Bulls' overall team scoring average for the year was 114.9 ppg, the highest they have ever attained. The team scored 100 or more points 75 times, a mark which held up until the 1991-1992 season.

Another high for the year was Bob Love's 47 points against Milwaukee on March 15, the most ever for a Bull to that point. In a 126-119 win over San Diego on November 16, a total of 16,282 fans filled the Stadium, the Bulls' high for the season. Another new record was the average attendance, 10,050, triple the old mark.

Walker was the only Bull on the All-Star squad, and Sloan again was voted to the league's All-Defensive team. Walker and Love became one of the top one-two scoring punches in the league, with Walker at 21.5 ppg and Love at 21. Sloan, in limited duty because of injuries, still managed to score at a 15.6 ppg pace, while Bob Weiss added 11.5 ppg. Boerwinkle again led the club in rebounds, with 12.5 per game. In the playoffs the Bulls again lost in the first round, this time to Atlanta.

1970-71

The Bulls made several more changes to their lineup entering this season. Jimmy Collins of New Mexico State was the club's first-round draft choice. The Bulls also picked up guard Matty Goukas from Philadelphia for a future draft choice, then received the draft choice back from Portland for Shaler Halimon.

The NBA's Silver Anniversary season saw the addition of three franchises: Buffalo, Cleveland, and Portland. Stockpiling those clubs necessitated three losses from the Bulls' roster: Walt Wesley, Loy Peterson, and Ed Manning.

The season was the finest in the five-year history of the Bulls, with the club topping the 50-win mark for the first time, finishing 51-31 as Motta walked off with NBA Coach of the Year honors.

With the expanded NBA now consisting of four divisions, the Bulls record was actually the third best in the entire league, better even than the records of two division champions.

Unfortunately for Chicago, however, they were playing in the Midwest Division, where eventual NBA Champion Milwaukee was having a banner year, sweeping to a 66-16 regular season mark behind Most Valuable Player (MVP) Lew Alcindor.

As for their own playoff efforts, the Bulls were eliminated in the first round, but this time they fought all the way to the seventh game before bowing to the Los Angeles Lakers.

The Bulls' scoring duo of Bob Love and Chet Walker topped their previous season's performance, Love finishing with a 25.2 ppg average, the sixth best in the league, and Walker not far behind at an even 22 ppg. Both were selected to the NBA All-Star team.

Walker's .853 free throw percentage was the best in the entire league. In addition to Love's 47-point effort, Walker hit 44 on two separate occasions.

Jerry Sloan chipped in with a solid 18.3 ppg, while Boerwinkle muscled his way to an average of 10.8 rpg, the best on the club. In his best game of the season, Boerwinkle pulled down 33 boards in a 110-103 win over the Bucks on March 9, stopping Milwaukee's club record 20-game winning streak.

1971-72

For the first time in club history four rookies made the team: first-round pick Kennedy McIntosh of Eastern Michigan, third-round choice Howard Porter of Villanova, fourth-round pick Clifford Ray of Oklahoma, and even ninth-round selection Jackie Dinkus of little Vorhees State. Ray, who eventually would share the pivot duties for the year with Boerwinkle, pulled down 10.8 rpg and was named to the NBA's All-Rookie team.

The club obtained forward Charlie Paulk from Cincinnati for Matt Goukas and a draft pick, then later traded Paulk to New York for a replacement draft choice. In October the team picked up free agent Jim King, then in November traded reserve center Jim Fox to Cincinnati for guard Norm Van Lier, who'd been with them three years earlier. With guard Bob Weiss hurt, the opening day lineup had Bob Love and Chet Walker at forward, Boerwinkle at center, and Jerry Sloan and Jim King at guard.

Although the Bulls excellent 57-25 won-loss mark might have been good enough to win a division title in most years, it again was good for only another second place finish in the Midwest Division, six games behind their neighbors to the north, the Milwaukee Bucks.

In the playoffs the Bulls were swept by the powerful Los Angeles Lakers, a club that won 33 straight on its way to a regular season record of 69-13 and the NBA Championship. A scoring high point took place on February 6 when Walker slammed in 56 to lead the Bulls to a 119-94 win over Cincinnati. The total broke the old team high by nine points and held up for 15 years until topped by Michael Jordan in 1987.

Love again led all Bulls in scoring with 25.8 ppg, the highest ever for a Bull, while Walker tallied 22 ppg and Sloan added 16.2 ppg. Boerwinkle repeated as rebounding king with a 11.2 average. Attendance for the year moved up a tad, to 10,616 per game, and the 19,500 at the Milwaukee game in November set a new Bulls' high.

1972-73

Prior to the 1972-73 season the club was sold to a group which included Lamar Hunt, George Steinbrenner, Jonathan Kovler, Phil Klutznick, Les Crown, and Art Wirtz. Also prior to the season, the club obtained center Dennis Awtrey from Philadelphia for cash and a draft choice, and forward Garfield Heard from Seattle for Kennedy McIntosh. The club's first-round draft pick, Ralph Simpson of Michigan State, did not make the team, but the second round pick, Frank Russell of Detroit, did.

Second year man Clifford Ray took over at center as incumbent Boerwinkle was out for nearly the entire season with a knee injury. Other opening day starters included Bob Love, Chet Walker, Jerry Sloan and Norm Van Lier. Love and Walker again paced the scorers, with 23.1 ppg and 19.9 ppg averages, respectively, while Sloan and Van Lier each chipped in with 13.9 ppg.

Ray led in rebounding, with a 10.9 average, and Van Lier was the assist leader, averaging 7.1 per game. Love scored 49 in back-to-back games against Milwaukee and Kansas City.

Chicago sent three representatives to the All-Star game, Love, Walker, and Van Lier. The Bulls' 51-31 mark qualified them for postseason play for the sixth time in seven years. In the playoffs the Bulls lost to the Lakers in the first round.

1973-74

The Bulls looked to strengthen themselves in the off-season. In the college draft the Bulls first choice was Kevin Kunnert of Iowa, whom they immediately traded to Buffalo along with Garfield Heard for forward John Hummer and a draft choice. Hummer apparently disappointed, for he was later traded to Seattle for another selection. In September the team obtained guard Rick Adelman from Portland for a draft choice.

The personnel moves seemed to help as the Bulls got off to their best start in history at 13-2 (including 12 straight wins) and fought to a 54-28 finish, their fourth 50-plus win season under Dick Motta. The club's second place finish, five games back of the Milwaukee Bucks, gave them their seventh playoff appearance in eight years. The team was especially strong at home, compiling a 32-9 record.

Bull top scorers were—who else?—Bob Love and Chet Walker, who averaged 21.8 and 19.5 ppg, respectively. Norm Van Lier combined a 14.3 ppg scoring average with a 6.8 assists per game (apg) average, the latter high for the team. Jerry Sloan scored at a 13.2 ppg clip and finished second on the squad in rebounds. With Boerwinkle out for all but a few games with a knee injury, Clifford Ray and Dennis Awtrey shared the pivot duties, Ray leading the team with 12.2 rpg. In personal honors, both Walker and Van Lier were named to the NBA West All-Star squad, and Van Lier and Sloan were voted to the league's All-Defensive Team.

In the playoffs, despite an injury to Sloan in the sixth game, the Chicago club topped the Detroit Pistons in seven games to win their first playoff series ever. In the next round, however, the Milwaukee Bucks and Lew Alcindor, now known as Kareem Abdul-Jabbar, eliminated the Bulls in four straight.

1974-75

In 1974-75 the Milwaukee Bucks' stranglehold in the Central Division ended with a bang, in more ways than one. Hall of Famer Oscar Robertson retired, Abdul-Jabbar broke his hand in anger against a backboard early in the season, and the Milwaukee club fell to last place. The Bulls won-loss record dipped under the magic 50-win mark for the first time in five years, but the club finally won a division championship with a 47-35 effort.

A primary reason for the Bulls' success during the season was its emphasis on defense. The club held their opponents to an average of only 95 ppg, the best in the league and the best that Chicago has ever attained. The team pulled down

2,786 rebounds for the season, also a Bulls' record. Opponents were held under 100 points 56 times, still a Bulls' record. Jerry Sloan was named to the All-Defensive Team again, but strangely, in the year that they were to win their first Division crown, no Bulls made the All-Star team.

The team also benefited from a series of moves by the front office. Before the season the Bulls lost center Awtrey in the expansion draft and traded Howard Porter to New York for a future pick. The club looked north to Milwaukee for their first round draft pick, selecting power forward Maurice Lucas of Marquette University.

With the pivot spot still a problem, the Bulls obtained veteran center Nate Thurmond from Golden State prior to the start of the season for Cliff Ray and cash. The team returned Matt Goukas to the roster and picked up two draft choices from Buffalo for Bob Weiss, then got forward Mickey Johnson from Portland for a draft pick and forward John Block from New Orleans for guard Rick Adelman.

Bob Love, at 22 ppg, Chet Walker at 19.2 ppg, and Norm Van Lier at 15 ppg topped individual scoring, while Thurmond led in rebounding with a 11.3 mark; his scoring average of only 7.9 ppg, however, was a disappointment. Van Lier dished out 5.7 apg to pace the club.

In the playoffs, Chicago topped Kansas City-Omaha in six games before bowing to Golden State, the eventual champions, in seven games. Good news came from the box office, however; attendance for the season jumped back up to an average of 10,704, a team record. Attendance at four home games during the year, against Boston, Golden State, Milwaukee, and Golden State again, topped 19,000.

1975-76

The 1975-76 season was one of the low points in the club's history. After winning the Midwest Division Championship the previous year, the Bulls sunk to a 24-58 mark, their worst record ever, falling to fourth place, 14 games behind the Milwaukee Bucks. Not that the Bucks were world beaters, for the Milwaukee club won the division title with only a 38-44 record, meaning that all clubs in the division played under .500. For only the second time in their nine year history, the Bulls failed to make the playoffs, where the Boston Celtics again won it all.

The plunge by the Bulls had a number of consequences, one of which was the resignation of the popular Motta. In his eight years at the helm in Chicago, Motta had guided the club to their first division championship, four second place finishes, and one third, for an overall record of 356-300. After his resignation he accepted the head coaching post of the Washington Bullets. Another result of the Bulls' decline was a corresponding drop in attendance, to an average of 6,303 per game, the team's lowest since beginning play in Chicago Stadium.

The few new faces that joined the team had little effect. The Bulls obtained forward Eric Fernstern from Cleveland for center Steve Patterson and forward Rowland Garrett for center Nate Thurmond. The team was able to let the two go when Boerwinkle was able to mount a comeback after two years of injuries. Also acquired during the year was veteran forward Jack Marin. On the draft scene, first-round pick Steve Green of Indiana didn't make the club, but his college teammate and Bulls' second-round pick John Laskowski did.

Despite their lowly finish, the Bulls again led the league in defense, holding opponents to 98.8 ppg. And on the other side of the coin, the club set a team record on February 20, topping Portland by 56 points in a 130-74 win. Bob Love led the team in scoring for the sixth straight year, with a 19.1 ppg average, but the other half of the Chicago one-two scoring attack, Chet Walker, retired prior to the season.

His replacement at the forward post, Mickey Johnson, contributed a 15.3 ppg average, while guard Norm Van Lier, who was selected to both the NBA West All-Star squad and the league's All-Defensive Team, chipped in with a 12.6 ppg mark. Van Lier also led the club in assists and steals.

Following the season Jerry Sloan, the Bulls all-time leader in games played, announced his retirement. The year also marked the demise of the rival ABA, with four of their teams, Denver, New York, San Antonio and Indiana, being absorbed into the NBA.

1976-77

With new head coach Ed Badger at the controls and with the addition at long last of a center who could score, the Bulls were the most improved NBA club of the year, almost doubling their win output of the previous season. The team's 44-38 record moved them up to second place in the division and back into postseason play.

Key to the Bulls' resurgence was the acquisition of center Artis Gilmore in the ABA dispersal draft. The seven-foot two-inch Gilmore led the team in scoring with an 18.6 ppg mark, in rebounding with an average of 13 per game, and in blocked shots with 203. It was the first time anyone had ever led the team in scoring and rebounding in the same season. Another factor in the club's success was their number one draft pick, Scott May of Indiana, who after a brief early season bout with mononucleosis moved into the starting lineup and scored at a 14.6 ppg pace.

Attendance for the season was an average of 11,625 per game, a new club record. The Bulls topped the Los Angeles Lakers 102-86 at the Stadium on March 22, the first time the team had ever drawn more than 20,000 at home. A few weeks later on April 8 they played before 21,652 in a win over Houston, a record that still stands.

All of this did not come after some initial adversity. Early in the season the club said good-bye to one of its all-time favorites when forward Bob Love was traded to the New York Knicks. Love led the Bulls in scoring for six straight years. During his tenure with the Bulls, Love scored 12,623 points, a club record that stood for over a decade until it was broken by Michael Jordan.

In addition, the Bulls started off the season by losing 14 of their first 17, including 13 games in a row, a team record. But a late season spurt, during which they won 20 of 24 games, brought the Bulls closer to the top and earned them the nickname "The Miracle on Madison Street." Despite their torrid finish, the Bulls were eliminated in the playoffs by the Portland Trailblazers, who would go on to win the NBA championship.

For the year, forward Mickey Johnson was second on the club in scoring, with a 17.3 ppg effort, while guard Wilbur Holland added 14.9 ppg and led the team in steals. Norm Van Lier was the only Bull selected for the All-Star game. He also led the team in assists again. As a team the Bulls again led the NBA in defense, holding opponents to an average of 98 ppg. It was the third year in a row that they had led the league, and the fourth consecutive year that they had held opponents under 100 ppg.

1977-78

After the remarkable turnaround in the 1976-1977 season, fans' expectations were at a peak, as evidenced by the Bulls' opening day crowd of 14,082 at the Stadium, the largest opening day attendance in club history. The Bulls won the game, beating Indiana 122-119. And though fan support continued through the year, setting a new high in average attendance at 13,386, the team never could put together a winning streak of any length and fell to a third place, 40-42 record, eight games behind division-leading Denver. A knee injury to forward Scott May and a dropoff in scoring by veteran guard Norm Van Lier contributed to the Bulls' problems. Coach Ed Badger's contract was not renewed.

Big center Artis Gilmore afforded one of the few bright spots, again leading in scoring at 22.9 ppg, rebounding at 13.1 rpg, and in blocked shots with a total of 181. Forward Mickey Johnson averaged 18.3 ppg and guard Wilbur Holland added 16.6 ppg, while May, playing in only 55 games, was at 13.4 ppg. Van Lier, who managed only 7.3 ppg, again led the team in assists, and Holland led in steals.

Three draft choices added to the roster were Tate Armstrong of Duke, the number one pick, as well as Mark Landsberger of Arizona State and Steve Sheppard of Maryland. Former coach Motta, unsuccessful in winning a title during his eight years as the Bulls' leader, did just that in only his second year at Washington, as the Bullets were the surprise NBA champions.

1978-79

To replace departed coach Badger, the Bulls hired their old nemesis, former Milwaukee Bucks Coach Larry Costello. But Costello, unfortunately, couldn't work his magic on the Chicago squad, and he was fired two-thirds of the way through the season after compiling a 20-36 record. His replacement, Scotty Robertson, hired on an interim basis, didn't fare much better, winning only 11 of 26 games. The Bulls' 31-51 finish landed them in fifth place in the division, 17 games behind the leader, Kansas City, and out of the playoffs.

Opening day's lineup had Mickey Johnson and second-year man Mark Landsberger at forward, Artis Gilmore at center, and Wilbur Holland and first-round pick Reggie Theus at guard. Theus had won All-America honors at the University of Nevada, Las Vegas.

Gilmore again topped the club in scoring with a 23.7 ppg average and in rebounding with a 12.7 rpg mark, as well as in blocked shots with 156. Rookie Theus had a good first year with a 16.3 ppg average, while Johnson followed with a 15.4 ppg effort.

Out for most of the year with a severe knee injury was Scott May, who was ineffective once he did return. Boerwinkle tried another comeback, but this time it wasn't to be, and the big center called it quits.

Following the season, Bulls' management selected a former Bulls' player, long-time Chicago favorite Jerry Sloan, to take over the head coaching duties. Sloan was well prepared for the job, serving as an assistant under Badger, Costello, and Robertson.

1979-80

Jerry Sloan's debut as the Bulls' head coach was anything but auspicious. After an opening day 102-96 win over Golden State, the Bulls went into a nosedive, losing 16 of their first 21 games. The club never recovered from the poor start, finishing with a 30-52 record, tied for third place 19 games behind the Milwaukee Bucks. For the third straight year the club failed to make the playoffs.

Prior to the start of the season, guard Wilbur Holland was traded to Utah for Ricky Williams, forward Mickey Johnson became a free agent and signed with Indiana, with the Bulls receiving guard Ricky Sobers as compensation, and the club signed free agent Coby Dietrick of San Antonio, giving up Tate Armstrong in compensation.

The lineup on opening day saw the return of Scott May and the debut of first-round draft choice David Greenwood of UCLA. Greenwood went on to lead the team with 9.4 rpg and in blocked shots, was second on the club in scoring at 16.3 ppg, and was named to the league's All-Rookie Team.

Theus, in his second year, led the Bulls in scoring with a 20.2 ppg mark and in assists with a total of 515. Sobers chipped in with 14.2 ppg and led in steals with 136. After playing in 670 consecutive games, Gilmore was injured and missed 34 games, with his scoring pace dropping to 17.8 ppg. Both Gilmore and Theus were named to the NBA All-Star Team.

During the year the league instituted the three-point field goal. The Bulls were successful in only 70 of 275 attempts for a .255 percentage; Theus made 28 of 105 for a .267 mark.

1980-81

With the league's first expansion in six years—Dallas was added to the NBA's lineup—realignment moved Chicago and Milwaukee from the Western to the Eastern Conference and into the Central Division. Coach Jerry Sloan's Bulls enjoyed their best season since 1974, winning 45 games and moving into second place in the division. The improvement earned them a playoff spot after an absence of four years. Attendance also made a turnaround, with the 9,505 average the first rise in three seasons.

In offseason personnel moves, the Bulls sent their first round draft selection, Kelvin Ransey, to Portland for Ronnie Lester; backup center Dennis Awtrey became a free agent and signed with Seattle; and the club signed free agent Larry Kenon of San Antonio, giving up two future draft choice.

Second-round pick Sam Worthen of Marquette and James Wilkes of UCLA both made the squad. The Bulls' opening day lineup included one free agent, forward Kenon, and one rookie, guard Worthen, along with David Greenwood, Artis Gilmore, and Reggie Theus. Worthen was moved into the starting role when Sobers was injured.

Theus again topped the team in scoring with a 18.9 ppg average, followed in close order by Gilmore, at 17.9 ppg, Greenwood at 14.4 ppg, Kenon at 14.1 ppg, and Sobers at 13.5 ppg. Gilmore's field goal percentage of .670 was the best in the entire league, and Sober's .935 mark at the free throw stripe was the league's second best in that category. Sobers had 49 straight free throws during the year. As a team the Bulls also set a record of 514 blocked shots, a mark that still stands.

In the playoffs the Bulls swept the New York Knicks in two games in the first round before being blanked in four games by the Boston Celtics, the eventual NBA champs. It was the 14th league crown for Boston.

1981-82

The Bulls again shuffled their players during the offseason, hoping to find a winning combination. Scott May and Sam Worthen were waived, their spots on the roster taken by the Bulls' first two draft choices, Orlando Woolridge of Notre Dame and Ray Blume of Oregon. The team also purchased the services of Tracy Jackson from the Boston Celtics. On opening day the Bulls forwards

were David Greenwood and Dwight Jones, Artis Gilmore manned the pivot, and the guards were Ronnie Lester and Reggie Theus.

Gilmore turned in another sparkling performance, leading the team in scoring with an 18.5 ppg average, in rebounding with a 10.7 rpg pace, and in blocked shots with 221. His field goal percentage of .652 was the best in the league, and he was the only Bull named to the All-Star squad. Theus was a close second in scoring at 18.4 ppg and also led the team with 476 assists and 87 steals. Ricky Sobers and Lester chipped in with 11.8 ppg and 11.6 ppg, respectively.

Despite Gilmore's sparkling season, the Bulls' road to recovery took a sharp detour as the club fell to fifth place and a 34-48 record, 21 games behind the division champion Milwaukee Bucks. The team's record was 19-33 when Sloan was fired. Bulls' general manager Rod Thorn took over on an interim basis, splitting even over the last 30 games, but the Bulls were only onlookers in the playoffs. As the Bulls' head coach Sloan never experienced the success he had enjoyed as a player; in his tenure as the Bulls' leader the team won only 94 of 216 games.

1982-83

Things did not go well for the team in 1982-83. Fan disenchantment with the club began even before the season began when the Bulls traded their popular center, Artis Gilmore, to San Antonio for Dave Corzine and Mark Olberding.

In addition to the loss of Gilmore, the Bulls suffered a major blow when Ricky Sobers opted for free agency and signed with Washington. To compensate for his loss, the team picked up free agent guard Dudley Bradley of Phoenix. Five players were waived during the season: Tom Burleson, Rickey Frazier, James Wilkes, Mark Davis, and Larry Kenon.

New head coach Paul Westhead had even less luck with the club than his predecessors as the Bulls slipped even further, managing only a 28-54 record. The performance was reflected at the gate, with an average attendance of only 7,343. The Bulls' fourth-place finish, 23 games behind Milwaukee, assured them of their third straight year out of the playoffs. Westhead was fired in May. Less than a month later Kevin Loughery signed on as the Bulls' ninth head coach and their fourth in the past two years.

The club's draft picks afforded hope for the future, however, as two of them, Quintin Dailey of San Francisco and Rod Higgins of Fresno State, made the league's All-Rookie team.

Another bright spot was the all-around play of guard Reggie Theus, who turned in his finest performance in the NBA to date. He led the Bulls with a 23.8 ppg average, as well as in assists with 484 and steals with 143. He was the only Bull named to the All-Star team. Other offensive leaders were Orlando Woolridge, with a 16.5 ppg mark, Dailey, at 15.1 ppg, and Corzine, at 14 ppg.

1983-84

The dark ages continued for Bulls fans as the club, under Kevin Loughery, dropped even further into the second division, managing only a 27-55 record, the second worst in the team's history. The year started off well enough, as newcomer Mitchell Wiggins scored 26 points in his first NBA game and the Bulls topped New Jersey, 104-97, in the season opener.

Early in the season the club put together a modest seven-game winning streak. But the horses simply were not there. The Bulls finished in fifth place, out of the playoffs and 23 games behind the Bucks. Attendance plummeted to an average of only 6,365 fans per game, less than a third of capacity and the lowest the Bulls ever drew in Chicago Stadium.

The club added three rookies to the roster following the annual college draft: Sid Green of UNLV, Ennis Whatley of Alabama, and Wiggins of Florida State. Whatley was in the starting lineup on opening day along with David Greenwood, Orlando Woolridge, Dave Corzine, and Quintin Dailey.

Woolridge led the club in scoring percentage with 19.3 ppg and Dailey added 18.2 ppg. Wiggins finished the year with a 12.4 ppg average, and both Greenwood and Corzine had averages of 12.2 ppg. Greenwood led the team with 10.1 rpg, while Whatley, the youngest player in the NBA that year, was the leader in assists with 662 and in steals with 119. Another popular veteran said goodbye to the Chicago scene when Reggie Theus was traded to Kansas City for Steve Johnson and three draft choices.

1984-85

Whatever will be said or written about the Bulls' 1984-1985 season, it will always be noted as the year the club drafted the incomparable Michael Jordan. Chicago fans quickly realized the treasure the team had acquired, for despite being well out of contention with a 38-44 record, attendance at the Stadium jumped by more than 5,000 to an average of 11,887 per game. The team made postseason play for the first time since 1981 but was eliminated in the first round by the Milwaukee Bucks.

The exciting Jordan teamed with veteran forward Orlando Woolridge to form one of the most potent one-two scoring punches in the league, with a combined total of more than 50 ppg (Jordan 28.2, Woolridge 22.9). Jordan's emergence on the scene was overwhelming.

In his first year in the NBA, he not only set an all-time Bulls' record for total points, 2,313, and scoring average, he also led the team in rebounding with 534, assists with 481, and steals with 196. No one had ever done that before in the history of the league.

His high scoring game for the year was 49 in a 139-126 win over Detroit on February 12. In addition to being named as the league's Rookie of the Year he was also chosen to the All-Star Team, the All-League Team, and the All-Rookie Team. Other than Jordan and Woolridge, the only other Bulls' player to finish in double figures for the year was swingman Quintin Dailey, at 16 ppg.

Jerry Reinsdorf took over as the team's new owner on March 13. Two weeks later Rod Thorn was released as the team's general manager, and Jerry Krause was named as vice president of basketball operations. Following the playoffs coach Kevin Loughery and assistants Bill Blair and Fred Carter were released.

1985-86

After Stan Albeck took over as the Bulls' new head coach on June 17, Bulls' fans had high hopes for the coming year. They recalled that with the addition of high-flying Michael Jordan to the team, the 1984-85 Bulls had improved by 11 wins over the previous season. A similar increase in 1985-86 would give the Bulls their first winning season in several years.

Prior to the season the club traded Steve Johnson to San Antonio for Gene Banks; swapped number-one draft pick Keith Lee and Ennis Whatley to Cleveland for Charles Oakley; traded forward David Greenwood to San Antonio for one of the league's all-time scoring giants, George Gervin; and signed free agents Kyle Macy of Phoenix and John Paxson of San Antonio.

Despite an 0-8 preseason record, the only time in their history that the Bulls had failed to win any of their exhibition games, the club got off to a good regular season start, winning their first three games against Cleveland, Detroit, and Golden State.

In the Golden State game, however, Jordan broke his foot and was out of the lineup for 64 games. Without him the Bulls lost eight of its next nine games and 43 of the 64. For the entire season, the Bulls won nine and lost nine with Jordan in the lineup for a .500 mark and were 21-43, a .328 percentage, without him.

The team's final record, 30-52, was a total of 27 games behind the Milwaukee Bucks. Their fourth place finish, however, earned them a spot in the playoffs, where they were eliminated in three games by the eventual champion Boston Celtics. The three losses did not diminish Jordan's almost unbelievable performance: 63 points in one game to set a new NBA playoff scoring record, and an average of 43.7 points in the three games.

Despite being out most of the year with the broken foot, Jordan was again named to the NBA's All-Star Team. In his 18 games Jordan averaged 22.7 ppg; Orlando Woolridge topped the team in total points and had a 20.7 ppg average. Other Bulls in double figures were Quintin Dailey, at 16.3 ppg in 35 games; Gervin at 16.2 ppg in his final year in the league; and Sid Green at 13.5 ppg.

Oakley led the club in rebounding with an average of 8.6 a game, and Macy led in assists with a total of 446. Oakley went on to make the league's All-Rookie Team, and Macy became one of the NBA's top three-point threats, hitting 58 of 141 for a .411 percentage.

1986-87

After the playoffs in early 1987, Albeck was fired after only a year at the helm and was replaced by new head coach Doug Collins. At the same time Gene Littles and John Bach were signed on as assistant coaches. The club also acquired Earl Cureton and Sacramento's second-round draft pick for Sid Green; in September traded Kyle Macy to Indiana for two draft choices and picked up Granville Waiters from Houston for future considerations; in October signed first round draft choice Brad Sellers and gave up Orlando Woolridge to New Jersey for a first-round and two second-round picks; and in December acquired Sedale Threatt from Philadelphia for Steve Colter and a future draft choice. The club also traded away the rights to second round pick Larry Krystkowiak.

With Michael Jordan back and healthy and under a new head coach, Doug Collins, the Bulls improved their won-loss total by 10 games, to 40-42. Attendance at the Stadium hit a new high, more than two thousand a game over the old mark, averaging 15,871.

In the playoffs, the Bulls were eliminated in three straight by the Boston Celtics, who in turn were eliminated by the Los Angeles Lakers in the finals in six games.

In his third year in the NBA Jordan became only the second player—Wilt Chamberlain was the first—to score more than 3,000 points in a single season. He finished with 3,041 and an eye-popping 37.1 ppg average, scored 40 or more in seven straight games and had season highs of 61 twice. Jordan's total points and average, as well as making 26 of 27 free throws in the 128-113 win over New Jersey on February 20, and his 236 steals during the season, were new Bulls' highs. He was a unanimous pick for the league's All-Star Game and for its All-League Team. Jordan was not the only Bull to garner NBA honors; Charles Oakley won the league's rebounding crown, hauling down 1,074 boards for a 13.1 rpg average.

1987-88

Prior to the season the team reacquired the services of Artis Gilmore, picked up from San Antonio for a second-round draft choice. The big center was over the hill, however, and was waived after only 24 games. With two first round draft picks, the Bulls selected Olden Polynice of Virginia, then traded him to Seattle for Scottie Pippen. They held on to their other first round selection, Horace Grant of Clemson. The addition of Pippen and Grant would pave the way for future Bulls' success.

For the first time since 1974 the Bulls reached the 50-win mark; it was also the club's first winning season in seven years. Led by Michael Jordan's fantastic one-man show, the Bulls moved into second place in the division, only four games behind the Detroit Pistons. The Bulls topped Cleveland in the first round of the playoffs three games to two before being eliminated by Detroit in the second round. Attendance reached a new high, averaging 18,061 per game, an increase of more than two thousand a game over the old record. And the main attraction was Jordan.

All the incredible one did was lead the Bulls in scoring in 81 of the team's 82 regular season games, totaling 2,868 points and averaging 35 ppg, again tops in the league. He set a new team record in steals with 259, and led the club in assists with 485 and blocked shots with 131. He was named as the league's MVP, the first time the honor ever had been won by a Chicago Bull, was named to the league's annual All-Star squad and was selected as the game's MVP, was voted to the NBA's All-League Team and All-Defensive Teams, and was picked as the NBA's Defensive Player of the Year.

About the only major award not captured by Jordan was the league rebounding title, won by teammate Charles Oakley for the second year in a row. The burly forward pulled down 1,066 boards for an average of 13 rpg and was second on the team in scoring, averaging 12.4 ppg. Another major factor in the club's success was its overall defensive effort, holding opponents to 101.6 ppg, the lowest in the league.

In another move, former New York Knick forward Phil Jackson was hired to replace Gene Littles as an assistant coach, and Bill McKinney was promoted to Assistant Vice President of Basketball Operations. A second major honor came the Bulls' way when Jerry Krause was voted as the NBA's Executive of the Year.

1988-89

Hoping to improve on the success of the previous year, the Bulls tinkered with their lineup during the offseason. They acquired Sam Vincent from Seattle for Sedale Threatt, traded Charles Oakley to New York for center Bill Cartwright and Ed Nealy to Phoenix for Craig Hodges, and signed their first-round pick, Will Perdue of Vanderbilt. The Bulls' opening day lineup featured Scottie Pippen and Horace Grant at forward, Cartwright at center, and Jordan and John Paxson at guard.

Throughout most of the season it appeared as if the Bulls would better their 50-win total of the previous year, but a slump at the end of the campaign, in which the club lost eight of its last ten games, gave the team a 47-35 mark. But whereas

Never in the history of professional sports did one man mean more to a franchise than Michael Jordan meant to the Chicago Bulls. Players such as Scottie Pippen, Horace Grant, and John Paxson are all fine athletes, to be sure, but without Jordan the Bulls would have been only an average club at best.

Many consider Jordan to have been the greatest basketball player in the history of the game. On offense he was virtually unstoppable. His lifetime average of 32.3 points a game is the highest in the history of the NBA. In fact, only a handful of players have ever attained that high an average for a single season.

Jordan was named as the NBA's Most Valuable Player three times, in 1987-88, 1990-91, and 1991-92, and he was the league's Rookie of the Year in his first season. Jordan was named to the All-NBA First Team for six years in a row and served as a member of the All-Defensive Team for five seasons. He was voted to the Eastern All-Star Team every year that he has been in the league.

Jordan tops the Bulls in most major offensive and defensive categories. His career point total, 19,000 through the 1991-92 season, was more than 6,000 above Bob Love's second-place total, and his steals total of 1,594 is more than double the second-highest amount. Jordan led the Bulls in scoring in eight of the nine years he was with the club; the only season he did not lead was the 1985-86 season when he was out for most of the year with a broken foot. Despite playing from the guard spot, Jordan has led the club in offensive and defensive rebounds and in blocked shots. He also led in steals, assists, field goal percentage, and minutes played, and has led the team in free throw percentage in almost every year.

Jordan is only the second player in history to win six consecutive scoring titles—Wilt Chamberlain won seven in a row in the 1960s. Jordan's 69 points in a game against Cleveland in 1990 was the ninth highest in NBA history. The 3,041 points he amassed in 1986-87 was the third highest total ever, and he and Chamberlain are the only two players ever to reach 3,000 points in a single season. His 23 consecutive points against Atlanta in 1987 is the longest string ever for an NBA player.

As much of an offensive powerhouse as he was, Jordan was also one of the finest defensive players ever to don a uniform. During the 1986-87 season he became the only player in the history of the league ever to record more than 200 steals and 100 blocked shots in the same season. Jordan was also known as one of the best clutch players in the league. In the playoffs he scored 50 or more points in five games, the only player ever to do so, and is the only player ever to win three consecutive Most Valuable Player honors in the NBA Finals.

Photo: *AP/Wide World Photos*

50 wins in 1987-88 gave them a second place finish only four games out of the lead, 47 wins in 1988-89 were good only for a fifth place finish, 16 games out. Having made the playoffs for the fifth straight year, the Bulls topped Cleveland in five games and defeated New York in six, but lost to the Detroit Pistons in the conference finals in six games.

Jordan again won the league scoring crown with a 32.5 ppg average and topped the Bulls with 650 assists, 234 steals, and 101 blocked shots. Grant pulled down 681 rebounds to pace the club in that category. Newcomer Craig Hodges was a deadeye from the three-point line, hitting 71 of 168 for a .423 average, a new Bulls' record. Jordan was picked to play in the All-Star Game for the fifth year in a row and was also chosen to the NBA's All-Defensive Team and All-League Team.

Following the season Collins' contract was terminated. In his three years as the Bulls' chief, Collins won-loss record was 137-109, good for a .557 winning percentage, the highest of any coach in Bulls' history up to that time. He also guided the Bulls to nine wins in the playoffs, more than any other coach before him.

1989-90

For several years Chicago had the greatest basketball player in the history of the game, but only an average team. Then in the mid-1980s under coach Doug Collins, the Bulls had begun to jell and grow into one of the top clubs in the NBA. Now, in the 1989-90 season under new head coach Phil Jackson's guidance, it was becoming a champion.

They didn't win it all that year—or even their division crown—but it was clear to everyone that the Bulls were a club on the rise. Behind superstar Michael Jordan's second MVP performance, the Bulls soared to a 55-27 mark, the second highest win total in their 25-year history. At home the Bulls were the terrors of the league, posting a 36-5 record, the best they had ever attained. The 55 wins earned the team a second place finish, four

AP/Wide World Photos

Scottie Pippen (33)

games behind the leading Detroit Pistons. In the playoffs, the Bulls defeated Milwaukee three games to one and Philadelphia four games to one before bowing to the eventual NBA champion Pistons in seven games.

The ten wins by the Bulls in the playoffs were the most they had ever won. Correspondingly, attendance totals at the Stadium rose to new highs: the total of 754,564 was good for an average of 18,404 fans a game. Every single game the Bulls played during the season, at home and away, was a sellout.

Jordan won his fourth straight league scoring crown with a 33.6 ppg average and scored 69 points in a 117-113 overtime win over Cleveland on March 28, the most points ever scored by a Chicago Bull in a single game. In the same game, he pulled down 18 rebounds, a personal high. He also led the league in steals with 227 and had a team-high 519 assists. Jordan again garnered the most votes for an All-Star Game berth, and was voted to the league's All-Defensive Team as well as the All-League Team.

Forward Scottie Pippen, who averaged 16.5 ppg and led the team in blocked shots with 101, was also named to the All-Star Game. The Bulls' other forward, Horace Grant, led the team in rebounding with 629. As a team, the Bulls had a .374 percentage in three-point efforts, led by guard Craig Hodges, who made 87 of 181 for a .481 mark. Both the team's and Hodge's averages were new Bulls' records. During the All-Star Game weekend, Hodges won the league's Three-Point Shootout.

1990-91

It took a quarter of a century, but the Bulls finally made it to the top. Not only did they win their first NBA Championship, they dominated the league, winning 61 games, 11 ahead of the Detroit Pistons in their division, and swept to a 15-2 mark in the playoffs.

Michael Jordan was again the catalyst, winning his third NBA Most Valuable Player Award, his fifth league scoring championship, and a host of other awards. But for a change the supporting cast made significant contributions. Forward Scottie Pippen had quietly become one of the league's top forwards; in addition to his 17.8 ppg average, he led the club with 511 assists and 93 blocked shots.

Horace Grant added 12.8 ppg and led the club with 659 rebounds, and John Paxson dropped in 42 of 96 three-point shots for a team-leading .438 average. Craig Hodges again won the annual Three-Point Shootout at the All-Star Game break. Attendance hit an average of 18,482 a game, a new high for the team, and on December 14 passed the ten million mark in all-time attendance.

It was Jordan, of course, who was the star of the show with his 31.5 ppg average and stellar all-around play. For the fifth straight year he led the All-Star Game balloting, was named to the NBA All-Defensive Team—he again led the team in steals with 223—was named to the All-League

Team and was voted as the MVP in the playoff finals.

All of this success did not come easily, as the team lost its first three games, two of which were at home. The Bulls actually did not move into first place until after the first of the year. A team-record spurt in February pulled them away from the pack.

During the year two significant marks were set: a new one-game scoring high was set in the 155-127 win over Phoenix on December 4, then two weeks later the club achieved a defensive milestone, holding Cleveland to five points in a single quarter.

In the playoffs the Bulls demolished the New York Knicks in three straight games, topped Philadelphia four games to one, swept Detroit in four games, and then blew out the Los Angeles Lakers four games to one.

1991-92

Repeat! In winning their second consecutive NBA Championship, the Chicago Bulls: finished 67-15, the best record in team history and the third best ever in the NBA; posted a 31-10 record on the road, the highest ever for the club; equaled their best home won-loss record with a 36-5 mark; set a new home attendance record with a total of 759,969 fans, an average of 18,536 a game; and led the league in road game average attendance with 18,287.

The Bulls became only the fifth team in NBA history to win back-to-back championships; scored 100 or more points in 75 of the 82 regular season games, a new club high; and saw their overall 26-year NBA record move up over .500 for the first time ever.

There were even more firsts and new records set during the whirlwind campaign. During the season the Bulls put together a 14-game winning streak and an eight-game road winning streak, both new team records, led the NBA during the year in field goal percentage with a .508 mark, and won the most games ever for a Central Division team.

Although Michael Jordan was the heart of the Chicago Bulls and the primary reason for the club's winning ways, there are other significant factors in the saga. Start at the top with the club's chairman, Jerry Reinsdorf. Long a respected administrator in sports and business, Reinsdorf headed the partnership that had purchased baseball's Chicago White Sox in 1981 and became that organization's chairman of the board.

In March of 1985 he led another group that purchased controlling interest in the Chicago Bulls. In both baseball and basketball he has been deeply active in league activities; in the former as a member of baseball's Executive Council and the Player Relations Committee and as Chairman of the Ownership Committee; in the latter as a member of the Planning and Collective Bargaining Committee. He has also served as chairman of the board for one of the nation's largest real estate investment firms, and he was the founder of the Real Estate Securities and Syndications Institute.

Running the show for Reinsdorf are a troika of vice presidents: Jerry Krause, who heads Basketball Operations; Irwin Mandel, Financial and Legal Affairs; and Steve Schanwald, Marketing and Broadcasting. Krause, who was named as the National Basketball Association (NBA)'s Executive of the Year in 1988, has been described as the architect of the Bulls' world championship team.

With the exception of Jordan, who was drafted the year before Krause arrived on the scene, he has been responsible for the addition of every coach and player on the team. With more than 25 years of service in the NBA and 16 in major league baseball, he is the only person ever to hold upper level front office jobs in both pro sports.

Finally, the master tactician who has melded the talents of Jordan with those of Scottie Pippen, Horace Grant, John Paxson, and the rest of the Bulls into a cohesive, smooth working basketball powerhouse is coach Phil Jackson. A second-round draft pick of the New York Knicks in 1967, Jackson spent 13 years in the NBA, 11 with the Knicks, before entering the coaching field. He served as head coach of the Albany Patroons of the Continental Basketball Association (CBA), leading that club to its first-ever championship in 1984. The next season he was named the league's Coach of the Year.

In 1986 Jackson joined the Bulls' staff as an assistant coach, then was named head coach in 1988. His three-year regular season record of 183-63 (55-27, 61-21, and 67-15), good for a winning percentage of .744, and his playoff record of 40-15 (10-6, 15-2, and 15-7) for a .727 mark are in fact the best three-year performances by any coach in the history of the league.

Jackson is the only person to have coached championship teams in both the NBA and the CBA, and is one of only nine men ever to be involved in a NBA Championship as both a player and as a coach. When he and his staff coached the Eastern Conference All-Star Team in 1992, it was the first time a Bulls coach had ever been head coach in the mid-season classic.

One final note of interest: both the radio and television analysts for the Bulls games have strong ties to the club. Tom Boerwinkle, now in his third season as a broadcaster for WMAQ radio, spent 10 years as the Bulls center and still holds the club record for rebounds in a single game, 37. He works the microphone with play-by-play announcer Neil Funk. John Kerr, the Bulls' first head coach and NBA Coach of the Year for the 1966-67 season, teams with Wayne Larrivee and Tom Dore for all television broadcasts.

AP/Wide World Photos

Phil Jackson

Michael Jordan continued to be pro basketball's version of Superman, winning his third NBA Most Valuable Player Award. Jordan also captured his sixth consecutive league scoring crown; his 30.1 ppg average was the sixth time he had hit 30 points or better for an entire season. At the conclusion of the season Jordan's NBA career point total stood at an even 19,000.

He was again a unanimous choice for the annual All-Star game and was selected to the All-League Team and the All-Defensive Team. Jordan also found success off the NBA courts; professional basketball players were allowed to compete in the Olympics for the first time, and he was one of twelve players named to the "Dream Team" that won a gold medal in Barcelona, Spain.

Teammate Scottie Pippen scored better than 20 ppg for the first time in his five-year pro ca-

reer, led the club in assists with 572, and was named to the All-Star team, the All-League Team, and the Olympic "Dream Team." Forward Horace Grant added to his 14.2 ppg mark with a team-leading 807 rebounds and 131 blocked shots. His field goal percentage of .578 was the best in the NBA. B. J. Armstrong topped the team in three-point average, hitting 35 of 87 for a .402 mark.

Craig Hodges, playing his last year in a Chicago uniform, was close behind with 36 of 96 for a .375 percentage. Hodges also won the league's Three-Point Shootout during the All-Star Game break for the third year in a row.

Coach Phil Jackson was awarded with a new three-year contract extension. His three-year total of 183 wins and only 63 losses was good for a .744 winning percentage, the best in Bulls history. The same can be said for his 40-15 mark in the playoffs.

In postseason play the Bulls found the going tougher than the year before, but still swept Milwaukee in three games, edged the New York Knicks in a great battle four games to three, then outfought Cleveland in six games before topping Portland in the finals four games to two.

1992-93

Entering the 1992-93 season, the talk surrounding the Bulls centered on their ability to "threepeat," to become only the third team in NBA history, along with the Minneapolis Lakers and the Boston Celtics, to win three consecutive championships.

With the nucleus of the team returning, the Bulls' chances seemed good. But questions and controversy dogged the club during the offseason. Would "Dream Teamers" Jordan and Pippen be rested enough from their Olympic experience to perform at championship level over the course of the rigorous NBA season? Could the coaching staff keep the team motivated for a run at a third title, or would the players, having grown satisfied after winning two championships, rest on their laurels? And would the addition of Danny Ainge and superstar Charles Barkley to the Phoenix Suns and solid veterans Rolando Blackman and Glenn Rivers to the New York Knicks make those clubs too strong for the Bulls?

Difficult questions, to be sure, but they were nothing compared to the tempest created when Jordan admitted that he had recently paid $57,000 in gambling debts to James (Slim) Bouler, a convicted drug trafficker. Jordan's gambling habits would remain an issue throughout the year.

Once play began, the team's performance only raised more questions. The Bulls, though clearly one of the better teams in the league, did not dominate the regular season as they had done in the previous two years. Even with Jordan winning his seventh straight scoring title, and Grant, Pippen, and Armstrong continuing to shine, the Bulls seemed to coast through a good part of the schedule, hoping to stay fresh for the playoffs.

The strategy appeared to backfire, however, for after winning a spirited, season-long battle with the Cleveland Cavaliers for the Central Division crown, the Bulls found themselves with only the second-best record in the Eastern Conference (57-25), giving up the home-court advantage in the playoffs to the Knicks. In fact, several experts were picking the Bulls as only the third-best team heading into the playoffs, behind not only New York but Phoenix, which finished with the top record in the Western Conference.

The Bulls disposed of Central Division rival Atlanta in the first round of the playoffs, then met Cleveland in the conference semifinals. The Cavaliers, who had been playing second fiddle to the Bulls for several years, were confident that they finally had the talent and attitude necessary to overcome their nemesis. But with Jordan and Pippen leading the way, Chicago took the series in four games, the last win coming in Cleveland on a buzzer-beating jumper by Jordan.

The four-game sweep of the Cavaliers set up an Eastern Conference finals showdown with the Knicks. Powered by All-Star center Patrick Ewing and the athletic but temperamental John Starks, whose suffocating defense frustrated Jordan, New York raced to a two games to none lead. The Bulls were in trouble not only on the court but off it as well; a furor arose when it was discovered that Jordan had stayed out late gambling in Atlantic City the night before Game Two. Around the country, sportswriters and fans alike debated whether Jordan's activity had hurt his—and the team's—performance and questioned whether he had a serious gambling problem.

Back in Chicago, Jordan answered his critics with two strong performances, including a 54-point outburst in Game Four, to help the Bulls even up the series. With their tenacious, trapping defense now in high gear, the Bulls took a dramatic 97-94 Game Five victory in New York, swatting away four close-range shots put up by the Knicks' Charles Smith in the game's final seconds.

And despite further allegations about Jordan's gambling—a book by Richard Esquinas entitled *Michael and Me: Our Gambling Addiction... My Cry for Help!* was released before Game Six—the Bulls maintained their focus, coming away with a series-clinching 96-88 win behind Pippen's 24 points, seven assists, and six rebounds, and earning the right to meet Phoenix in the NBA Finals.

The series promised a contrast in styles, matching the Sun's explosive offense against Chicago's swarming defense. The Bulls took control early, winning the first two games on the Suns' homecourt.

At Chicago Stadium, Phoenix bounced back with a thrilling 129-121 triple overtime victory in Game Three, and after losing Game Four to fall behind three games to one, the Suns took Game Five 108-98 to send the series back to Phoenix.

Game Six was a tense defensive struggle, and at the end of the third quarter the Bulls led 87-79. With Jordan resting on the bench, the Suns crept back and took control of the game, forcing Jackson to put Jordan back in.

Over the next eight minutes he was the only Bull to score, and his layup after a length-of-the-floor drive with 38.1 seconds left closed the Bulls to within two at 98-96. Phoenix missed its next shot, and after a timeout with 14.1 seconds left, the ball was inbounded to Jordan. He passed to Pippen, whose drive to the basket was blocked, forcing him to dump the ball under the basket to Grant.

Grant spun and dished back to sharp-shooting John Paxson, who nailed a three-pointer to put the Bulls ahead 99-98. When Grant blocked a last-second jumper by the Suns' Kevin Johnson, the Bulls' "threepeat" was complete, securing the team a place in the NBA record books. Jordan, who was magnificent during the series—averaging 41 ppg (a Finals record), 8.5 rpg, and 6.3 apg—was named the Finals MVP for the third straight year.

Jordan's presence on the team seemed to assure that the Bulls would be a championship contender for years to come. But a tragic turn of events following the playoffs cast a shadow over the team's championship. During the summer of 1993 Michael Jordan's father, James Jordan, was robbed and murdered. Then, on the eve of the 1993-94 season, Michael stunned the world with his announcement that he was retiring.

Jordan, 30 years old and still at the peak of his game, had grown weary of his celebrity and its attendant loss of privacy. In view of the recent loss of his father, Jordan cited his need to return to a semblance of a normal life. He did not, however, rule out the possibility of his returning to the game, sparking hope among his many fans that he would one day grace the court again.

Since winning championship number three, the Bulls continued to look for ways to improve their club, including signing Croatia's 6-foot-11 Toni Kukoc, considered the best player in Europe. The question remains if the addition of Kukoc and the continued excellence of the returning cast will be enough to offset the loss of Jordan.

—Jack Pearson

CLEVELAND CAVALIERS

The people of Cleveland know what it's like to come back from hard times, so they've always supported their sports teams during the bad times as well as the good. Like the Browns and the Indians, the Cavaliers have struggled through some awful seasons since their entry into the NBA in 1970, but their class, grit, and constant determination to improve has made them Cleveland's most popular and, in the early 1990s, its most successful sports franchise.

From the early teams featuring Jim Cleamons, Austin Carr, and Campy Russell to the resurgence brought by Brad Daugherty, Mark Price, and Ron Harper in the late 1980s, the Cavaliers have almost always looked towards tomorrow and gone with youth. Win or lose, the young legs and big hearts of the Cavs have meant exciting basketball in Cleveland for nearly a quarter of a century.

Though the Cavaliers are not among the founding franchises of the NBA, Cleveland has a long history of pro basketball. The Cleveland Rosenblums, named after department store magnate and owner Max Rosenblum, were the showcase team of the American Basketball League during the late 1920s, winning titles in 1926, 1929, and 1930. The Rebels, though they lasted only a single season, were one of the original franchises of the BAA in 1946.

Clearly Cavs' owner Nick Mileti didn't have to introduce Cleveland to the game of basketball in 1970 when the NBA came to town, but he did have to show that he intended to build a good team. He started by hiring heralded University of Minnesota coach Bill Fitch to his first pro coaching job and selecting Walt Wesley, Bobby "Bingo" Smith and Butch Beard in the expansion draft.

The leadership that would guide the young Cavaliers to respectability was mostly in place. At their first game, Mileti gave every customer a cocktail glass for the "largest wine toast in the world," but with no wine; the gesture paralleled the Cavs debut season--a good idea, but something was missing. With Beard in the army for the year, the Cavs reeled through 15 straight losses before they finally beat Portland, another expansion team, 105-103 on November 12.

Twelve more losses followed and it didn't get much better. The Cavs wound up 15-67, worst in the league, and last in offense despite center Wesley's 17.7 points a game and 8.7 boards and Bingo's long-range shooting.

Before the draft lottery was instituted in 1985, the team that finished last got the first pick and in 1971 the Cavs picked guard Austin Carr, maybe the greatest college player ever, out of Notre Dame. Alongside the returning Butch Beard for only 43 games due to a broken foot, Carr still shone with 21.2 points a game and selection to the All-Rookie team.

With a solid backcourt, two new big men in Steve Patterson and Rick Roberson--whose 12.7 boards a game that year remained the Cavs' record into the 1990s--and eight more wins than the year before, the Cavs were obviously changing for the better, and the changes had only begun.

Opting for more maturity in the backcourt, the Cavs dealt Butch Beard to the Seattle Supersonics for Barry Clemens and future Hall of Fame guard Lenny Wilkens during the off-season and also traded a draft choice to the Lakers for another young guard, Jim Cleamons.

Wilkens had been a player-coach in Seattle and his knowledge and leadership, along with 20.5 points and 8.4 assists a game, played a large part in the Cavs' improvement in 1972-73 to 32-50. Carr matched Wilkens's 20.5 average, both tying for sixteenth in the league, and Roberson led the team in rebounds for the second year. Forward Dwight Davis added strength on the boards and made the All-Rookie team. The Cavs were again last in team offense, but Wilkens helped them on defense and Cleveland was no longer an easy win on anybody's schedule.

Mileti and Fitch kept working on the team, adding and subtracting to find the right mix of talent, youth, and experience. They traded starters Roberson and forward John Johnson to Portland for the right to draft Jim Brewer, a 6'8" forward out of Minnesota, which let Bingo Smith emerge in the 1973-74 campaign with 14.8 points a game.

Wilkens and Carr also picked up the pace now that the Cavs had no first-rate center. In his last full season, Wilkens averaged 16.4 points a game and his 522 assists were third in the league. Carr, whose pro years never equaled his dominant play in college, had the best season of his career with 21.9 points per contest and an appearance in the All-Star game. Davis was left to take care of the boards and led the team with 8.5. The Cavs slipped a notch, back to 29-53.

The Cavs Soon Won Cleveland Fans' Hearts

Mileti and Fitch went back to work. Wilkens went to Portland for the 1974-75 season, but some crafty trading brought four new players to Cleveland, players who would make the Cavs' new home, the Richfield Coliseum, rock with excitement. Jim Chones took over the center spot, veteran Dick Snyder stepped into the hole Wilkens had left at guard, and rookies Campy Russell and Foots Walker gave the Cavs new depth on the bench.

The problem in 1974-75 was that the Cavs had to use that bench more than they would have liked to. Carr injured his knee and played only 41 games. Chones missed time too with a broken foot. The Cavs were 32-29 when Jimmy Cleamons went down with a shoulder separation in February. Cleamons ran the team from the point and his importance became clear as the Cavs dropped seven of the eight games he missed and slipped to 33-36.

Still, the Cavs were battling New York and Houston for a playoff spot in late March and on April 3, the Knicks came to Cleveland needing only to beat the Cavs to make the tourney and keep the Cavs out. Fans numbering 20,239 packed into the Coliseum and saw the Cavs pull out a 100-95 win. It all came down to one game with the Kan-

Team Information At a Glance

Founding date: 1970

Home court:
The Coliseum
2923 Streetsboro Rd.,
Richfield, OH 44286
Phone: (216) 659-9100
FAX: (216) 659-2101

Capacity: 20,273

Team colors: Royal blue, burnt orange, white
Team Nickname: Cleveland Cavaliers
Logo: Name Cavs, with letter "V" forming a basketball net

Franchise Record	Won	Lost
(1970-1993)	816	1,070

Division First-Place Finishes (1): 1975-76
Division Last-Place Finishes (6): 1970-71, 1971-72, 1972-73,
1973-74, 1981-82, 1986-87

sas City-Omaha Kings for the last berth. If the Cavs won or Knicks lost that Sunday, the Cavs were in. Buffalo let down against the Knicks in their game earlier that day and lost, so it was all up to the Cavs.

The Kings controlled the game early, but then it swung back and forth. With four minutes to go, the Kings were up by 14. Snyder, Brewer, and Chones wouldn't quit. The Cavs fought back to within one, 95-94, with three seconds to go. Fred Foster's final shot was blocked and with it the Cavs' first entry to the playoffs. Their 40-42 record and third place finish in the Central Division were the Cavs' best ever, though, and their balanced offense and tough defense, third in the league, along with the gripping finale to the season, once and for all put the Cavaliers into the hearts of Clevelanders.

Without any superstars, Bill Fitch had assembled a tough, half-court team. With Austin Carr back from knee surgery and the addition of Nate Thurmond to spell Chones, the Cavs looked to challenge for the Central Division crown in 1975-76. They started slowly, but led by Chones's 15.8 points a game and Brewer's rebounding, the Cavs won seven in a row in December to get over .500 for good.

By February they were 27-22. A club record eight straight wins put them into first place at the end of the month by a game and a half over the Washington Bullets, who had won the Central every year since the Cavs had come into the league.

March was a race between the Cavs and the Bullets, but Washington lost eight of their last twelve and on April 10 the Cavs beat the Knicks

99-94 at the Coliseum to win the Central Division and the team's first playoff spot. They finished the regular season 49-33 and boasted the number-two defense in the league. That was the good news. The bad news was that their first opponents in the play-offs were the Bullets, and they wanted revenge.

The Team Engineered a Miracle Win

The series was a classic. The Bullets jumped out to a lead by winning at Richfield 100-95 in game one. Game two in Washington was decided with two seconds to go. Down by one, Bingo Smith, the last original Cav, hit a 30-footer to win it 80-79 and even the series at one apiece.

The Cavs took game three 88-76 and the Bullets won the next 109-98. Game five was another thriller. The Bullets led 91-90 with seven seconds to go when Bingo let loose another prayer. This time he came up short, but Jim Brewer, facing Smith, snagged the air ball and in mid-leap dunked it back over his head for a 92-91 win at the buzzer.

Washington fought back in overtime and won game six 102-98. It all came down to the game seven in Richfield. It was tied at 85 with nine seconds to go. Cleamons inbounded to Snyder, who was covered by center Wes Unseld. Snyder drove past the big man and popped it in with four seconds to go. Bullet Phil Chenier's final shot missed and 21,564 fans mobbed the court to celebrate the 87-85 miracle win.

The Boston Celtics were next, but Chones broke his foot in practice prior to the series. Without their leading scorer, the Cavs couldn't compete with the eventual NBA champs. The Celtics took the Eastern Conference finals four games to two, but Bill Fitch won Coach of the Year and Jim Cleamons made second team All-Defensive. The Cavs wouldn't get this close to an NBA championship for another 16 years.

Everybody expected another great season out of the 1976-77 Cavs, but injuries held them back from repeating their 1975-76 heroics. Chones was not at full strength, dropping to a 12.9 scoring average, and Campy Russell, Cleamons, and Foots Walker all missed a substantial number of games. Center Elmore Smith came in a deal with Milwaukee to shore up the pivot, but the aging Nate Thurmond injured his knee in February and the Cavs were lucky to finish 43-39, fourth in the Central Division.

Russell and Carr led in scoring with 16.5 and 16.2, respectively, and Brewer's 762 boards and 94 steals earned him a place on the second squad All-Defensive team. The Cavs made the playoffs, but the Bullets were too strong this year and the Cavs too weakened by injuries. The Bullets won the short series two games to one.

Injuries had kept the Cavs from going as far as they could have in 1975-76 and 1976-77, and hope still remained that it wasn't too late for this talented, hard-working unit to go all the way in 1977-78. Floor-leader Jim Cleamons played out his option and went to the New York Knicks during the off-season, which allowed the Cavs to pick up Hall of Famer Walt Frazier as compensation.

At first it appeared that Frazier's experience and talent would put the Cavs among the league's best teams. They won 13 of their first 18 games, including seven in a row in November, but again injuries held them back. The Cavs dropped 16 of their next 22 games, forcing Fitch to make some changes—Smith became the starting center and Chones went to power forward.

The shift seemed to work, as the Cavs edged back over .500 to 29-27. Then Frazier injured his foot. His season was over and so were the Cavs' hopes for competing in the play-offs. Foots Walker stepped in to run the team and did well, finishing sixth in the league with 5.6 assists a game, but he couldn't do it all. The Cavs faltered badly and only a six-game winning streak at the end of the regular schedule put them over .500 and let them squeak into the play-offs.

The Knicks invaded Richfield for game one of their three-game set and shredded the Cavs, 132-114. Game two at the Garden was a heartbreaker in many ways. The Cavs led most of the way, but Spencer Haywood hit a jumper with one second to go, giving the Knicks a 109-107 win. The Cavs were done for the season, and so, essentially, was this Cavs team. Play-off action didn't return to Cleveland until 1985.

Injuries Marred Another Season

1978-79 was the last year of the memorable Cavaliers squad Fitch had put together. Dick Snyder had already gone to Seattle as a free agent, but Chones, Russell, Carr, Frazier, and Elmore Smith still made for a tough team. Unfortunately, injuries destroyed this season as they had so many others. Frazier's foot problems returned; he played in only 12 games. Bingo Smith was out the first ten. Elmore Smith had knee surgery just prior to the start of the season and missed 56.

In all, Cavs missed 176 games in the '78-79 season. Campy Russell picked up as much slack as he could, leading the team with 21.9 points a game, 348 assists, and 2859 minutes of play, and was second in rebounds and steals. Even with his own injuries, Walker finished fourth in the league with 130 steals and Chones had a respectable 842 boards.

Still, all these individual heroics could not lift the Cavs beyond a 30-52 record and a tie with Detroit for fourth in the Central Division. On May 21, 1979, Bill Fitch resigned from the troubled Cavaliers and moved on to guide the Boston Celtics back from their own 32-50 season. Two months later Stan Albeck left his post as an assistant coach with the Los Angeles Lakers to become the Cavs' second head coach.

More things changed about the Cavs than just the head coach. Jim Brewer had been traded in February and the first of many debatable Cavalier trades involving draft picks brought guard Randy Smith over from the San Diego Clippers for cash and the Cavs' first-round pick in 1980. Chones was sent to the Lakers in October for Dave Robisch and a draft pick. That same month Frazier was waived, Bingo Smith was sent to San Diego, and Kenny Carr came from the Lakers for second-round picks in 1980 and 1981. Injuries played their

role in October, too, when Elmore Smith had a knee operation that basically ended his years as a Cavalier. The new faces seemed to make a difference, though.

Second-year man Mike Mitchell led the way on offense with 22.2 points a game and the Cavs flirted with the .500 mark halfway through the season. The playoffs looked like a possibility, but Campy Russell only played in 41 games due to injuries; Mitchell's athleticism, Randy Smith's 17.6 points a contest, and Foots Walker's 607 assists weren't enough. Even with an eight-game winning streak in March, the Cavs finished in fifth place in the Central with a 37-45 record.

The biggest change of all for the Cavs followed the 1979-80 season, when Nick Mileti sold his majority interest in the team and Ted Stepien took over as the team's owner. It was a new start for the Cavs, but they only went downward during the three years under his management.

With Stepien at the helm, the Cavs traded away all their first round picks from 1980 to 1986, which allowed other teams to sign players like James Worthy, Detlef Schrempf, Roy Tarpley, Sam Perkins, Derek Harper, and Rodney McCray.

Stepien introduced a new mascot to Richfield as well--a man called "Fat Guy Eating Beer Cans," who stood at mid-court during time outs and bit a hole into a beer can. "Fat Guy" also ate eggs and glass. Such displays did little to hide the fact that good basketball had left Richfield with Fitch and Mileti.

Stepien moved immediately in 1980 to put his mark on the Cavs. Albeck was replaced by Bill Musselman, who dealt Campy Russell to the Knicks for Bill Robinzine. Musselman then sent Robinzine and two first round picks to Dallas for Richard Washington and Jerome Whitehead. Washington spent two years on the bench and one year on injured reserve, while Whitehead played in all of three games for the Cavs.

Another first-round pick went to Dallas for three-point expert Mike Bratz, who was gone before the start of the next season. Dallas struck another blow by choosing Austin Carr in the expansion draft. The one good deal the front office made was to trade guard Chad Kinch and a draft pick for playmaker Geoff Huston. The gutted Cavs roster could only manage 28 wins. Mike Mitchell provided the season's few highlights, posting 2012 points, a 24.5 average, and 3194 minutes played--all Cavalier records. He also lit up the All-Star game, played in Richfield that year, with 14 points in 15 minutes.

A rookie named Bill Laimbeer showed promise with 693 boards and almost ten points a game. With 11 games to go, Musselman was moved aside as coach and Cavs' general manager Don Delaney stepped in to finish this dismal season.

A Record Set for Consecutive Losses

The Cavs tried to solve their problems by signing free-agents Scott Wedman, James Edwards, and Bobby Wilkerson prior to the 1981-82 season. Nothing helped, however; in fact, the Cavs got even worse. Delaney was gone after their 4-13 start. Bob Kloppenburg led the team to one more loss until December 4, when the Cavs hired Chuck Daly as their new head coach.

Daly shook things up. He traded Mitchell and Roger Phegley to San Antonio for Reggie Johnson and Ron Brewer, and then dealt Johnson to Kansas City for Cliff Robinson, and Laimbeer and Kenny Carr to Detroit for future Cavs' stalwart Phil Hubbard, Paul Mokeski, and a couple draft choices. Brewer and Robinson charged what little offense the Cavs had with their 18.8 and 18.5 averages, and Huston chipped in with 590 assists, including 27 against Golden State on January 27.

Daly's Cavs went 9 and 32 before Stepien brought back Bill Musselman for the last 23 games. The Cavs did set a record that season--for consecutive losses. They dropped their last 19 games and wound up 15-67, matching their worst record from their debut season. The Cavs had hit bottom.

With one of the few draft picks the Cavs had held on to, they chose John Bagley in the 1982 draft. Bagley only played 990 minutes in his rookie year, but he was to develop into a team leader down the line. Just before the start of the season Bill Musselman resigned and Tom Nissalke became the Cavs' head coach.

Trading Ron Brewer to Golden State for World B. Free on December 15 soon made Cavs fans forget their 3-20 start. Free was Cleveland's first real superstar, a free-wheeling hot shooter with playground instincts. The fans loved him. Though the Cavs slipped back down to last in the league on offense, Free's 23.9 points a game, good for seventh in the NBA, and Robinson's 18 points and 856 rebounds made them a much more dangerous--and popular--team.

Huston continued his solid play at the point and while trading Scott Wedman and James Edwards for more benchwarmers didn't help the situation, the Cavs ended the season 23-59 and out of the cellar in the Central Division. On May 9, the owners of the Coliseum, George and Gordon Gund, bought the Cavaliers and began the slow process of rebuilding the franchise.

The Gunds made a few moves, drafting Roy Hinson and Stewart Granger, trading for Lonnie Shelton and buying Ben Poquette from the Jazz, but the 1983-84 campaign showed just how long the rebuilding process would take.

Nissalke and the front office brought stability to the Cavaliers and along with a 23-18 home record and the electric World B. Free, they reestablished the Cavs as a team to watch in Cleveland. Free averaged 22.3 points a game, third best in Cavs' history, Robinson finished eighth in the league with 10.3 rebounds a game, and rookie Hinson's 1.81 blocks a game were sixth.

Unfortunately, the Cavs' inability to win on the road washed out most of their improvements. They went 5-36 away from Richfield for a 28-54 overall record--an improvement, but not enough for the Gunds. Nissalke was out and 33-year-old George Karl, director of player acquisition, was in as coach.

An ill-conceived trade on draft day of 1984 sent Cliff Robinson and Tim McCormick to Washington for Mel Turpin. While Robinson went on to stardom over the next few years,

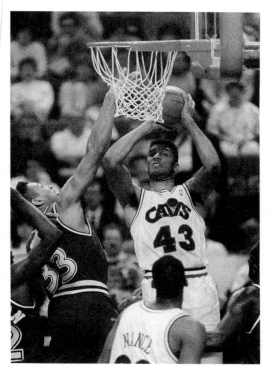

AP/Wide World Photos

Brad Daugherty

Turpin's only great talent proved to be eating. The Cavs and Turpin lumbered off to a 2-19 start in 1984-85 before hard-nosed George Karl ignited the team. Hubbard took on a starting role and, in an unpopular move, Karl began to use World B. Free off the bench because he felt Free lacked defensive intensity and was selfish on offense.

Karl wanted a more balanced attack and the Cavs turned around once John Bagley had a chance to distribute the ball more. His 697 assists were fifth in the league. Coming off the bench also seemed to heighten Free's efforts. He was Player of the Week for the week ending January 13 and had the third best scoring game by a Cav with 45 against the Rockets on February 16. Free also led the team again with 22.5 points a game.

On April 9, the Cavs clinched their first play-off spot since 1978 by beating the Nets 114-100

at Richfield. Their 36-46 final tally earned them fourth in the Central Division and the chance to be smacked down by the Celtics three games to one in the first round of the play-offs. Faces weren't too long around Cleveland, though, and the next year promised to be great.

1985-86 started with another draft day mistake. The Cavs selected Charles Oakley and Calvin Duncan, and then packed them off to Chicago for Keith Lee and guard Ennis Whatley. Lee missed 23 games due to injuries and never became more than a bench player, while Whatley's Cavalier career amounted to 66 minutes.

The Cavs did show courage by drafting John "Hot Rod" Williams in the second round. Williams at the time was awaiting the outcome of a point shaving case and was forced to sit out the season. Despite their improved showing the year before, the Cavs never got off the ground in 1985-86.

Phil Hubbard went out for the season with a wrist injury in January and the rift between Free and Karl grew. Rumors of Karl's ouster spread and by March he began discussions with the University of Pittsburgh about taking over their basketball program. The Cavs' management wasn't happy with Karl's job hunt, or with the team's performance, so on March 16, during a 12-hour lunch meeting, George Karl was fired. Assistant coach Gene Littles assumed the role of head coach and the Cavs wound up this very disappointing season 29-53.

Thing Begin to Look Up

In just one week, in June of 1986, everything changed for the better. Wayne Embry, former vice-president of the Indiana Pacers, became the Cavs' vice-president and general manager. His emphasis on youth led the Cavs to personnel shifts that enabled them to pick up center Brad Daugherty, Ron Harper, and guard Mark Price on draft day. That same week, Hot Rod Williams was cleared of all charges in his point shaving case.

Suddenly the Cavs had the core, albeit a very

young one, of a winning team. The last piece fell into place when Lenny Wilkens returned to Cleveland a few weeks later as head coach, replacing Gene Littles. Wilkens shared Embry's belief in youth and the 1986-87 Cavaliers started the youngest squad since the 1955-56 Rochester Royals.

These new Cavs immediately gave notice that they were a team to watch, as four Cavs scored 20 or more points in an opening-game win over the Bullets, 113-106. Another clear sign that this was a new team was the decision to not come to terms with World B. Free. An era was over.

A youthful enthusiasm now energized the team, but their erratic play throughout the season showed their youth as well, and injuries to Bagley and Price allowed the team to make only a token improvement over the previous year's mark at 31-51. Ron Harper had the greatest single season ever for a Cavalier--he led the team in points, assists, steals, minutes, and games played and made the NBA All-Rookie team along with Daugherty and Williams. Harper's 209 steals were the second most ever by a rookie.

Like Fitch and Mileti in the 1970s, Wilkens and Embry stood fast in their commitment to youth, but, also like Fitch and Mileti, they were not afraid to make moves that they felt would help. When Ron Harper went down with an ankle injury early in the 1987-88 season, Mark Price made the transition from sixth man to quarterback of the team. This allowed the Cavs to trade their other promising point guard, number-one pick Kevin Johnson, along with Mark West, Tyrone Corbin, and two draft picks to the Phoenix Suns for Larry Nance and Mike Sanders.

Nance brought more size to the front line and played a crucial role in bringing the Cavs up from eleventh in defense in '86-87, to second in 1987-88. Poor road play prevented the Cavs from doing more than breaking the .500 mark with their 42-40 record, but considering that this was the team's first winning season since 1977-78, Cleveland was charged up for the Cavs' opening play-off series against the Chicago Bulls.

In only two years the Cavs had become a contender, but no amount of talent or enthusiasm could stop Bulls superstar Michael Jordan in this series. In game one, Jordan scored 50 to lead the Bulls to a 104-93 win and then followed it up with 55 in the Bulls' 106-101 win in game two.

The Cavs pulled back with a win in game three, 110-102, behind Price's 31 and Williams' 20; Ron Harper, back since December, took charge with 30 in game four, leading the Cavs to a 97-91 win and a tie in the series. The fifth game went back to Chicago and Jordan was not to be denied. He tallied 39 points to average a play-off record 45.2 for the series. The Bulls won 107-101 and moved on to face the Detroit Pistons, while the Cavs came back to Cleveland and prepared for their breakout season.

1988-89 was the year this young Cavaliers squad grew up. With Price and Daugherty each averaging 18.9 points a game, Price's 8.4 assists and Harper's 2.26 steals a game both eighth in the league, and Nance and Williams teaming up for 340 blocks, the Cavs roared off to a 30-8 start.

They set a team record with 11 straight wins in December and January and never lost more than two games in a row all season. The Cavs dominated on both sides of the court. On January 7, they tied an NBA record with 21 blocks against the Knicks and then 16 days later established a new team scoring record in a 142-109 victory over the Warriors. Daugherty, Nance, and Price were chosen for the All-Star team, coached this year by Lenny Wilkens, and Nance made it to the first team of the NBA All-Defensive team.

The Cavs clinched a play-off spot on March 22, but a little slump at end of the year let the Pistons slip by them for the Central Division title despite their 57-25 record, best ever by a Cavs team. The Cavs finished ten games above the Bulls in the Central, but it didn't help them in their first-round series against Chicago. Though Jordan didn't roll up record-setting numbers, he was all the difference.

After the teams split the first four games, the series came to Richfield for game five. Long-range specialist Craig Ehlo, who topped the Cavs with 24 points, gave Cleveland a one-point lead with a

AP/Wide World Photos

Mark Price

Charles Barkley and the 76ers won the Atlantic and the Cavs did well to compete against them. Game one went to the Sixers with a 111-106 victory in Philadelphia. Barkley posted Jordan-like numbers with 38 points, but added another dimension with his 21 rebounds. Mark Price's 27 didn't help much in game two; the Sixers still won 107-101. But the Cavs wouldn't quit. They set a team playoff scoring record in their 112-95 win in game three and tied the series with a 108-96 win in game four behind Daugherty's 34 points and Price's 18 assists. Like the last two years, though, the Cavs couldn't take game five. The Sixers won it 113-97.

Another Heartbreaking Season

The 1990-91 season is one the Cavs would like to forget. In November, Hot Rod Williams sprained his foot and then Mark Price tore a knee ligament, an injury that can end a career. Nance and Daugherty tried to make up the lost offense. Daugherty scored 21.6 a game and snatched 830 rebounds and Nance hit 19.2 a game, but without Price and Williams, the Cavs were just not a winning team. They lost 11 games in a row during December and January and wound up 33-49, fifth in the Central Division.

The biggest drama of the season involved Price's knee surgery. He went under the knife in December and began the long road back. The fortunes of the Cavaliers depended on whether or not Mark Price could come back from an injury that would prevent some from ever walking again, let alone playing professional basketball.

The 1991-92 Cavs started poorly, going 1-4 on a road swing through the West. On November 11, Mark Price was activated and all of Cleveland held its breath. Questions were answered quickly though, as the Cavs ran off eight of their next nine games and Price went on to average 17.3 points a game, dish 535 assists, and play 2138 minutes.

With their starting lineup intact, the Cavs began to dominate the league. Their 148-80 blowout of the Miami Heat on December 17 was the

lay-up with three seconds to go. But then Jordan stepped in. Jordan hit the last of his 44 points by sinking a 16-footer at the buzzer, winning it 101-100. For the second year in a row, the Cavs fell in the first round of the play-offs.

The next two seasons recalled memories of the great Cavs teams of Bill Fitch: teams, ruined by injuries, that never fully realized their potential. Daugherty, Nance, and Price all missed enough games at the start of the 1989-90 season to keep the Cavs from hitting .500 until an April 18 win over the Nets.

With Ron Harper gone, traded to the Clippers for Danny Ferry and Reggie Williams, Craig Ehlo provided the excitement with his three-point shooting. Ehlo led the league by hitting .507 of his long-range shots. Still, after games like that of March 28, when Jordan racked up 69 against them, the Cavs were lucky to make the play-offs. This year's first-round opponent was no easier than Jordan's Bulls.

biggest point differential in NBA history and the most points ever scored by a Cavalier team. Eleven wins in a row in December and January left them 29-13 halfway through the season.

With his 21.5 points a game and 760 rebounds, which pushed him past Jim Chones as the Cavs' all-time rebounder, Daugherty, along with Price, appeared in the All-Star Game again. In March and April, the Cavs settled down to finish strong at 57-25. This time the Cavs were not going to fold.

In the first round, the Cavs took on the Nets, a young team just happy to be in the playoffs. After taking the first two at the Coliseum, the Cavs dropped game three at the Meadowlands. Nightmares of choking were quickly dispelled with a 98-89 win and the Cavs moved on to meet the Celtics.

Memories of the classic Bullets-Cavs series in 1975-76 were rekindled with this seven-game set. The Cavs jumped out to a lead, winning the first game 101-76, but the Celtics could not be counted out. They took the next two and the Cavs faced a deep hole if they dropped game four at the Boston Garden. This time it was Larry Nance's turn to make Cavalier history. His 32 points led the Cavs to a 114-112 overtime win and a tied series.

The momentum shifted to Cleveland. Daugherty paced the Cavs with 28 in game five and Cleveland took the lead in the series with a 114-98 victory. Boston fought back for a 112-91 win in Boston to set up the deciding seventh game. Motivated by their drubbing in game six, the Cavs went on a 21-8 run in the first quarter. The Cavs had delivered the knock-out blow. The Celtics never got within ten and the Cavs won 122-104. For the first time, Cleveland would be playing in the Eastern Conference Finals.

Throughout the season, the Cavs' great play was overshadowed by the dominance of the World Champion Chicago Bulls but, weakened by a tough series with the Knicks, the Bulls were vulnerable. The Cavs split the first four games, with strong play by Daugherty and Price. Game five went to the Bulls 112-89.

The series came back to Richfield and the Cavs gave it their all. After three quarters the game was tied at 72. A Mark Price three-pointer evened the game again with 47 seconds to go, but Michael Jordan drained one of his own on the opposite end and the Bulls went on to win game six 99-94. The Cavaliers were forced to the sidelines once again, but with their young players just beginning to peak, the club was already thinking about a championship banner in 1992-93.

The Cavaliers enjoyed a fine regular season campaign in 1992-93, although the team again was forced to settle for second place in the division behind the two-time champion Chicago Bulls. Cleveland knocked off New Jersey in the first round, but was foiled in the second round, relegated to musings on the elusive championship crown. During the off-season prior to the 1993-94 season, Lenny Wilkens moved on to coach elsewhere. The Cavaliers quickly signed the animated Mike Fratello, former head coach of the Atlanta Hawks, to coach the club. Cavalier followers hope that Fratello can guide the talent-rich club to a championship and end the frustration they've endured over the past couple of seasons.

Sources

BOOKS

Carter, Craig and Alex Sachare, editors, *NBA Guide 1992-93,* The Sporting News, 1992.

George, Nelson, *Elevating the Game,* Harper-Collins, 1992.

Hollander, Zander and Alex Sachare, editors, *The Official NBA Basketball Encyclopedia,* Villard Books, 1989.

Neft, David S., and Richard M. Cohn, editors, *The Sports Encyclopedia: Pro Basketball,* 3rd edition, revised and updated by John Hogrosian and Bob Gill, St. Martin's Press, 1990.

Price, Bob, editor, *1992-93 Cleveland Cavaliers Media Guide,* Cleveland Cavaliers, 1992.

Ryan, Bob and Terry Pluto, *Forty-Eight Minutes,* Collier Books, 1989.

Taragano, Martin, *Basketball Biographies,* McFarland, 1991.

PERIODICALS

Cleveland Plain-Dealer, October 29, 1970; April 5, 1975; April 7, 1975; April 11-May 20, 1976; April 10-April 26, 1985; March 17, 1986; June 16-June 20, 1986; May 3-May 29, 1992.

DETROIT PISTONS

Fort Wayne is the industrial hub of northeast Indiana, about halfway between Indianapolis and Detroit. Though a small market by television standards, it was a sensible location for a basketball team in the 1940s, when the pro leagues, with teams like the Akron Goodyear Wingfoots and the Oshkosh All-Stars, grew up around the bus stops of the not-yet-rusted Midwest and Northeast.

Earlier, Fort Wayne had had a pro team for a season, for the General Electrics were one of the founding franchises of the NBL in 1937. That team was only a memory, however, when local piston manufacturer Fred Zollner, a sports enthusiast who already owned a top-ranked softball team, decided to create a basketball team. And so, in 1940, the Fort Wayne Zollner Pistons were born. After one sporadically scheduled season as an independent venture, they joined the NBL in 1941.

They quickly established themselves as the "class" team of the NBL, finishing second to Oshkosh in 1941-42 and first in the next four regu-

lar seasons. Zollner deserved much of the credit, for he cared enough to acquire top players and put them comfortably on the Zollner Machine Company payroll. In those years, the Pistons played in the Fort Wayne North Side High School gym, which players called "The Pit."

The team was known for its roughhouse style—and so were its fans, who sat close enough, according to ex-NBL player Bruce Hale, to smack an opponent on the head. The Pistons' ongoing strategy was to rough up each opposing player once during the early part of each game, to see whether he could be intimidated.

Like the later "Bad Boys" of the NBA, however, those earlier Pistons matched their physical strength with solid court skills. Their star, and at times player-coach, was Bobby McDermott, a feisty New York high school dropout and former Celtic. This six-foot guard was the best long-range, two-handed set shooter of the era and a capable floor leader, consistently leading the team in points with about 13 per game. His backcourt partner was rookie Herm Schaefer of Indiana University.

Five-foot eleven-inch Curly Armstrong had also graduated from Indiana in the same year, and switched off between forward and guard, while 6-foot-1 veteran forward Paul Birch, who had starred for the NBL Pittsburgh Pirates in earlier years, joined to help the team later in the season. Holding down the center was the towering Blackie Towery, at 6-foot-4. These Pistons were good enough to beat the Akron Goodyears in the playoffs, though they lost to Oshkosh in the finals.

The war years were uncertain ones for the NBL, and by the 1942-43 season the league had shrunk from seven teams to four. In other words, if a team was in the league, it made the playoffs. The Pistons added three good players to their roster, including veteran 6-foot-6 center Jake Pelkington, and motored to the best record in the league before losing to Sheboygan in the postseason.

The Pistons lost Schaefer, Armstrong, and forward Gus Doerner to military service, but acquired star guard Buddy Jeannette from Sheboygan and five-eleven guard-forward Chick Rieser from the ABL's Brooklyn team. The Pistons now had height and bulk, with forward Jerry Bush at 6-foot-3, 210 pounds complementing Towery and Pelkington, and their big men played competent defense.

The team achieved its first league title by sweeping Sheboygan in an exciting three-game series, with McDermott scoring a long tiebreaker in the closing seconds of the first game. They went on to beat the Dayton Aviators, the New York Rens, and the Brooklyn Eagles for the World Tournament championship.

The following year, the Pistons solidified their perch despite the loss of Towery to the military, and the league expanded to six teams. McDermott led the NBL in field goals, and led his team in points per game with 20.1. The Pistons were 16-1 in their first seventeen games, including a 14-game streak. For the playoffs, they added veteran center "Big Ed" Sadowski, a 6-foot-5 former Detroit Eagle who helped them to another finals sweep against the Sheboygan Redskins and

a second World Tournament championship, this time against the Dayton Acmes.

Postwar basketball crowds were growing. More than 15,000 had attended the World Tournament final game, and a record 23,912 watched the Pistons beat the College All-Stars in Chicago in November of 1945. Former Pistons Schaefer and Armstrong were back from the service, and center Bob Kinney and guard Bob Tough were part of a more dependable bench.

However, the overall strengthening of the league meant more competition for the Pistons. Though they edged the Rochester Royals for first place in the regular season, they lost to that same team 3-1 in the playoffs before the Royals went on to the league title. The Pistons won their third straight World Tournament, however, beating Oshkosh in the finals.

Into the NBA

The Fort Wayners faltered through two more seasons in the NBL, then jumped to the BAA for 1948-49, finishing fifth in the Western Division and not making the playoffs. The following season saw the BAA and NBL merge into the NBA. The Pistons, coached by Murray Mendenhall, now had two 6-foot-5 forwards in Fred Schaus and Bob Carpenter and two 5-foot-11 guards in Curly Armstrong and Boag Johnson, with 6-foot-6 Schultz starting at center.

They were good enough not only to come in third in the Central Division to the mighty Lakers and Royals, but to sweep the Royals 2-0 in the playoff openers, including a 79-78 overtime clincher, before succumbing to George Mikan's Laker dynasty in the 2-0 division semifinals.

First-round draft pick Larry Foust, a 6-foot-9 center from LaSalle, gave a boost to the team for 1950-51 and for the rest of their tenure in Fort Wayne. Twice an All-Star, he would lead the league in rebounds in 1952 and field goal percentage in 1955, before retiring with almost 12,000 points, an average of 13.7 per game over a 12-year career with four teams. It was Foust's job to guard

TEAM INFORMATION AT A GLANCE

Founding Date: 1941, as Ft. Wayne (IN) Pistons;
moved to Detroit, 1957

Home Court:
The Palace of Auburn Hills
Two Championship Drive
Auburn Hills, MI 48326
Phone: (313) 377-0100

Seating Capacity (for basketball): 21,454

Team uniforms: Home—base color white, with red and blue trim
Road—base color blue, with red and white trim
Team nickname: Pistons
Logo: "DETROIT PISTONS" in white block letters on a
red stylized basketball in a blue frame

Franchise Record	Won	Lost	Pct.
(1948-92)	1649	1799	.478
Playoff Record			
(1948-92)	111	105	.514

NBL Championships (Fort Wayne): 1943-44; 1944-45
NBA Championships (Detroit): 1988-89; 1989-90
NBA Western Division Championships (Fort Wayne): 1954-55; 1955-56
NBA Eastern Conference Championship (Detroit): 1987-88

the Lakes' Mikan and the Royals' Arnie Risen, among others, and though he did it capably, and was aided by Schaus' 15 points per game, the 1950-51 Pistons again lost to Rochester in the postseason.

The Mikan era was not a happy one for the Pistons. Under head coach Paul Birch they sank to fourth place, behind the Indianapolis Olympians, the following year, again falling to Rochester in the playoff openers. The next year the team rose to third, partly because the scandal-plagued

Olympians had been tossed out of the league, but also because they had added jump-shooting forward George Yardley and veteran guard Max Zaslofsky.

Yardley, the first NBA player ever to score 2,000 points in a season, was one of the most consistent scorers of the mid-1950s. A bald, stringy 6-foot-5 former engineering student who was nicknamed "The Bird" for his hang-time ability, he steadily improved his play by working on his moves against defenders, and in 1957-58 his 27.8

points per game was the NBA highest average in history. His hook shot supplementing his jumper, he recorded two 50-point games and was twice an All-Star during his career.

Zaslofsky, nicknamed "The Touch," had been a prime scorer in the 1940s for the Chicago Stags and the early 1950s for the Knicks, and was still capable of helping a team with his long-distance set-shot. However, the most memorable Piston events of 1953-54 may have been the banning of rookie forward Jack Molinas for betting, and the 19-18 Thanksgiving victory over the Lakers, the lowest-scoring game in history.

Eckman's Surprises

The 24-second rule took care of that situation the following year, and with Mikan retired and the Royals fading, the Pistons were destined to move up in the standings. For 1954-55, owner Zollner made an eccentric, much-criticized personnel move that turned out surprisingly well: he hired Charlie Eckman, a 32-year-old former NBA referee with no coaching experience, to pilot the team. Eckman, a great talker with a comic flair, was always eager to embellish his own legend.

According to writer Roland Lazenby, Eckman won his job after a Fort Wayne loss to Minneapolis, when he approached George Mikan in a restaurant and said, "If I was coaching the Pistons, I'd beat you big clowns." Zollner overheard the boast and, after the season ended, flew Eckman to Miami for a job interview. If anyone was likely to pass an interview for any job whatsoever, it was probably Eckman.

Whatever the new coach's skills, he did not make the mistake of overcoaching. "We had only two plays and when we ran them I didn't even know where the ball was," he told Lazenby. "We had no blackboards ... or X's or O's or assistant coaches. We had no strategies.... I was a cheerleader, and I kept everybody happy." He openly admitted that he preferred coaching to officiating because of the higher pay, better working conditions, and lower fan hostility; and he lifted the

morale of sportswriters, fans, and players with his chatter.

This master plan worked. To give him all due credit, Eckman did make a couple of important, beneficial coaching moves. He made Yardley, who had not gotten along with coach Birch, a starter. And because of his experience observing the entire league as a ref, he was expert at gauging individual matchups. Perhaps this was all the guidance the solid Piston lineup needed. They now had veteran defensive forward Mel Hutchins and guard Andy Phillip rounding out the starting five, and bench depth with Frankie Brian averaging 9.7 points per game and rebounding forward-guard Dick Rosenthal averaging 7.8 points.

Finishing first in the West, they faced the Syracuse Nationals for a memorable seven-game finals series that was marked by a fan's chair-throwing in game five and a fistfight between Piston Don "Monk" Meineke and the Nats' Wally Osterkorn in game six. The Pistons' home games in this series had to be played in Indianapolis, because the North Side High administration, not expecting that the team would make the finals, had booked a bowling tournament for those dates. This prompted Zollner to threaten to move the team to Detroit.

On the court, the action was every bit as dramatic, with stars Dolph Schayes and Red Rocha battling for Syracuse to come back from early deficits. In game seven, the Pistons were in front by 17 points early in the second quarter, but the Nats' bench brought them back to a six-point deficit at halftime. With Syracuse leading 92-91 in the final seconds, each team in turn was called for traveling. Then, at the buzzer, the Nats' Paul Seymour nudged Andy Phillip on the inbound pass, but the foul was not called and the Nats won their only NBA championship.

The Pistons returned to the top of the Western Division standings the following year with only a 37-35 record. Rookie guards Chuck Noble and Corky Devlin had joined the team, the former as a starter and the latter an often-used reserve, while Zaslofsky was released early in the season. Coach Eckman made another good strategic move by innovating a four-man front, with forward Mel Hutchins sometimes playing in the guard position.

This Pistons team had height in its two-guard alignment, as well, with Noble at 6-foot-4, Phillip 6-foot-3, and Devlin 6-foot-5. It was a good offensive team, with Yardley and Foust the ninth and tenth leading scorers in the league respectively. It was also considered the best defensive team in the circuit. However, there were off-court problems—for example, owner Zollner, afraid of further gambling scandals, hired a private detective to follow the team throughout the season.

And ultimately, there was one team in the league that was even better than the Pistons—the Philadelphia Warriors. The Pistons were able to squeeze by the St. Louis Hawks in the five-game playoff series despite losing the two opening contests, and despite the presence on the Hawks of star scorer Bob Pettit.

When it came to playing the Philadelphia Warriors in the finals, however, the difference in sheer talent showed. The Warriors had the league's top scoring combination in Neil Johnston and Paul Arizin. They also had a top-flight rookie in former LaSalle star Tom Gola—like Arizin, a future Hall-of-Famer. With the 6-foot-6 Gola at guard, the Warriors' backcourt surpassed the Pistons' for height, and had led the league in assists.

The 1955-56 finals had some exciting moments, but were not as close as fans and sportswriters had expected. In game one, the Pistons' defense effectively stymied the Warrior offense in the first half, but hot-shooting reserve Ernie Beck brought the Warriors back to within nine at halftime. Beck's 11 points in the third quarter, and Gola's leadership and defense, gave Philadelphia a 98-94 victory.

The Pistons evened the series with an 84-83 win in Fort Wayne, the margin coming from last-minute free throws by Yardley and a crucial interception by Devlin, who was normally anything but a defensive star. The Warriors won game three in Philadelphia, in front of a then-record 11,698 fans. Game four was the Warriors' first victory in Fort Wayne in four years, as the Pistons fought back from a six-point to a one-point deficit in the

last two minutes. After a Philadelphia free throw made it 107-105, Devlin's last-second, desperate longshot would have made it an overtime game, but it went in a fraction of a second after the buzzer. From that point it was an easy clincher for the Warriors at home, 98-88.

Few people at that time suspected that a new basketball epoch was about to begin. The Boston Celtics were on the threshold of their dynasty, about to put a virtual lock on NBA championships for years to come—much to the chagrin of teams such as the Lakers, Warriors, and Hawks. In the Western division, 1956-57 saw a three-way tie for first place between the Hawks, Lakers, and Pistons, at the exalted plateau of 34-38, or a .472 percentage.

This was worse than the last-place finish in the East. All three teams had problems of personnel transition. The Lakers were floundering between the era of Mikan and that of Baylor and West. The Hawks had traded away their number-two draft pick—who turned out to be a fellow named Bill Russell—and went through three coaches in the season.

The Pistons' problems may not have been any worse than their rivals', but the club was on a slide. Foust and Noble suffered injuries and Phillip had been sent to Boston. The starting guards were now Billy Kenville and future pro coach Gene Shue, whose field goal percentages were 34 and 38 respectively. Fortunately, Yardley was better than ever, moving up to fifth place among league scorers with 21.5 points per game. But the Pistons lost a one-game tiebreaker to the Hawks, 115-103, in St. Louis. Their season was over, as was their tenure in Fort Wayne.

Motown

Zollner had talked of moving to Detroit in the past, and now he did it, contributing importantly to the NBA's development into a big-city league. (The Rochester Royals moved to Cincinnati the same year.) Playing at Olympia Stadium and sometimes at the University of Detroit fieldhouse, the Pistons were able to capitalize on the expanded attendance and television opportunities of a major urban market.

Along with their change of locale, the Pistons made manic roster changes for 1957-58. Harry "The Horse" Gallatin, the long-time Knicks star, arrived as a starting forward and went on to complete not only his playing career but a 746-consecutive-game streak. Sweetwater Clifton, Dick McGuire, and Dick Atha came from New York. Devlin and Foust were traded to Minneapolis for Ed Kalafat and seven-foot center Walter Dukes. And coach Eckman was gone after 25 games, with Red Rocha replacing him.

The trades and coaching change accomplished a moderate turnaround in midseason, enabling the Pistons to finish second in their division with a 33-39, .458 record. The more stable elements of the Pistons lineup were at least as important, for Yardley had a career year, leading the league in points and scoring with 2,001, or 27.8 per game.

It is still the highest single-season point-per-game average ever by a Piston. It was also the first time an NBA player had ever scored 2,000 points in a season, though the arrival of Wilt Chamberlain the following year would make Yardley's achievement seem small by comparison.

Nevertheless, he made the All-NBA first team for the only time in his career. Shue and McGuire joined Yardley in the All-Star game, as they would the following season too—though by that time, Yardley would be playing for another team.

The Pistons swept the Royals 2-0 in the playoffs, with a 100-93 home win and an even more impressive 124-104 road triumph. But they fell to the Hawks in the next round, 4-1, winning only the third game. This was the year that the Hawks were to go all the way, defeating the Celtics for their first world title—a brief hiatus in the Celtics' dynasty.

Why did the Pistons trade Yardley to Syracuse for another 6-foot-5 forward? Whatever the reason, they did so after 46 games, obtaining in return Ed Conlin. True, Yardley's point production was down to 19.8, tenth in the league. The younger Conlin, however, scored only 11.9 per game and was to spend but a single season with the Pistons before going on to Philadelphia.

Yardley, meanwhile, helped the Syracuse Nationals, the only remaining small-city team in the league, become a major postseason factor. The Pistons finished the regular season at 28-44, or .389. They lost to the Lakers—that is, to Elgin Baylor—2-1 in the playoffs.

New superstars were coming into the league, people like Wilt Chamberlain and Jerry West, and the Pistons didn't have any. They hadn't even had a winning season since moving to Detroit. The first thing to do in a case like that is, of course, fire the coach. Midway through 1959-60, Piston guard Dick McGuire replaced Rocha at the helm. A bright spot in the Piston backcourt was Shue, who led the Pistons in scoring with 22.8 points per game and the entire league in minutes played, making the All-NBA first team.

A very bright spot up front was 6-foot-7, 220-pound forward Bailey Howell, in his rookie year out of Mississippi State. In his five seasons with Detroit, Howell was to average 21.1 points per game—still on the team's leader list. Howell and Dukes contributed scoring and an imposing physical presence—they were first and second in the league in disqualifications, with 20 for Dukes and 13 for Howell. Their rebounding, however, was far from the Chamberlain-Russell level.

The Pistons rose to a 30-45 regular-season record for second place in the West. However, the Lakers brushed them off in two games in the playoffs: a 113-112 squeaker in Detroit, followed by a 114-99 runaway in Minneapolis.

The Grim 1960s

The Pistons were thin enough in talent that Howell, in his second year, was considered a veteran. With Dick McGuire as coach for the entire season, the 1960-61 club finished third in the West, 34-45, or one game ahead of the cellar-dwelling Royals. Howell and Shue were ninth and tenth in

PROFILES | DeBusschere, Bing, and Lanier

In the hard times of the 1960s and 1970s, the spirits of Detroit basketball fans were lifted by the spectacular performances of three future Hall of Famers: forward Dave DeBusschere, guard Dave Bing, and center Bob Lanier.

DeBusschere was a hometown boy, born in Detroit on October 16, 1940. At the University of Detroit he was an All-American three times, averaging 24.8 points and 19.4 rebounds per college game. A superb all-around athlete, he was given a $60,000 bonus by the Chicago White Sox and pitched for them during the 1962 and 1963 seasons, but quit baseball when he decided his curveball couldn't get big-league players out.

As a basketball player, in contrast, he was unsurpassed at stopping opponents. A defensive star, he used physical toughness to deny the ball to swifter and taller players, crowding and shoving them until they were virtually removed from the play. For six of his twelve years in the NBA, he was selected to the all-league defensive team. Offensively, too, he was a threat, finishing his career with an average of 16.1 points per game.

Equally important, DeBusschere was a natural leader. This was the primary reason for his being selected as Pistons player-coach at the age of 24, the youngest head coach in NBA history. His trade to the Knicks in 1969 was a key element in that team's rise to the championship. After retiring as a player, he became the New York Nets' general manager, then in 1975 served as the ABA's last commissioner. In 1982 he was appointed Executive Vice President of the Knicks, and inducted into the Hall of Fame.

Next of the threesome to arrive in Detroit was Dave Bing, whose rookie season was 1966-67. Born November 24, 1943, Bing grew up in the nation's capital and was a Syracuse University college star. (Coincidentally, his college scoring average of 24.8 per game exactly equals DeBusschere's.) Coming to the Pistons, he had a Rookie of the Year season, and went on to be a seven-time All-Star. In 1968 he was the league scoring champion, and in 1976, the All-Star Game MVP.

In an era dominated by big men, Bing, with his smooth, fluid driving and shooting style, was one of the few guards who consistently ranked among the league's top scorers. His .775 career free-throw shooting, which improved markedly after his first three years in the pros, contributed to 18,327 total points, an average of 20.3 per game. A well-rounded player, he racked up 5,397 career assists.

After spending 1975-76 and 1976-77 in Washington and 1977-78 with the Celtics, Bing retired and returned to Michigan, where, as a successful businessman in the steel industry, he numbers some former teammates among his employees. He was elected to the Hall of Fame in 1989.

Bob Lanier is the most recent Piston inductee, entering the Hall in 1991. Not as famous or overpowering as Chamberlain, Russell, or Abdul-Jabbar, he was nevertheless one of the premier centers of his time. Born September 10, 1948 and a graduate of St. Bonaventure, the 6-foot-11, 265-pound Lanier was the first pick of the 1970 draft.

Possessed of a midrange jumper and a hook shot, he averaged over 15 points per game in his first year as a Piston, and beat that average by more than ten points in his sophomore season, when he came into his own, playing more than 3,000 minutes for the first of three consecutive years. In those three years, he also grabbed more than 1,000 rebounds per campaign.

Remarkably consistent, Lanier averaged over 20 points per game in eight seasons. He was eight times an All-Star, and finished his career with a .514 field goal percentage, .767 free-throw percentage, and 19,248 total points, or 20.1 per game.

the league in scoring—23.6 and 22.6 respectively. These two mainstays also amassed solid statistics in free throws and assists for Shue and rebounds for Howell. Walter Dukes joined those two teammates at the All-Star Game. However, the league as a whole was experiencing an offensive burst.

Chamberlain, Baylor, and Robertson all finished with scoring averages over 30. In a season marked by the dominance of the Celtics and Hawks and the migration of the Lakers to Los Angeles, the Pistons clung to their usual playoff spot, and for their efforts they were knocked off by the Lakers in five games.

Through the remainder of the 1960s and halfway through the 1970s, the Pistons were not to rise above third place in their division. Playing in Cobo Arena from 1961-62 through 1977-78, their average per-game attendance stabilized in the mid-four-figure range, dipping to a low of 3,346 in 1963-64 and never rising above 7,492.

In 1961-62, the Pistons defeated the Royals, who had finished ahead of them, in the Western Division semifinals, but lost the division finals to the Lakers, 4-2. This was to be their best showing for the remainder of the decade.

The Pistons of this era were a physically strong team without much finesse or depth, whose games were made interesting by the presence of some memorable individual stars. One who arrived as a rookie in 1962 was Dave DeBusschere, a local favorite from his days at the University of Detroit.

At 6-foot-6 and 220 pounds, DeBusschere was built to be a forward, and would work over the years to become the best defensive player in the NBA at that position. In his rookie season, however, he was the smallest forward on the team, after Howell, Ray Scott, and Jackie Moreland. So DeBusschere switched between forward and guard, coming off the bench to sub for starting guard Willie Jones. He finished the season with 12.7 points and 8.7 rebounds per game.

Charlie Wolf was to become the new head coach for 1963-64, coming over from Cincinnati. The Pistons plummeted to the Western Division basement with a 23-57, .288 record, though

Howell played in his third straight All-Star game and shooting guard Don Ohl his second straight. DeBusschere, with a broken leg and military commitments, played only 15 games.

Perhaps desperately, the Pistons made DeBusschere player-coach after eleven games of the following season. At 24 he was the youngest in league history to command a team. It helped to the extent that the Detroiters finished in next-to-last place with a won-lost percentage exactly a hundred points higher than the previous year.

Hot-scoring Terry Dischinger (18.2 points per game) joined the team in a multi-player trade with Baltimore that sent Bailey Howell away. The Pistons now had a seven-foot center in Reggie Harding and solid forwards in DeBusschere and Scott. But they fell back into the cellar in 1965-66, though DeBusschere, whose playing ability was essential, remained as coach.

Basketball was expanding—not only had the NBA grown to ten teams, but the ABA was competing for talent. Fortunately, the Pistons obtained a prize rookie in 1966: Dave Bing, the 6-foot-3, 185-pound guard whose shooting was to spark the team for almost a decade. In his rookie year, Bing ranked tenth among league scorers with 20 points per game, also leading the team in assists. (The fact that he led them with 4.1 per game says something about the team play of the 1960s Pistons.)

New center Joe Strawder led the league in personal fouls and foul-outs—indeed the starting five led the league by far in disqualifications. DeBusschere the player continued to be productive off the boards and in scoring, but DeBusschere the coach was replaced by Donnie Butcher for the last eight games.

League expansion made the Pistons' lot happier the next season. The team moved into the Eastern Division when Seattle and San Diego joined the West. Dischinger, who had been on extended military service, was back in a Pistons uniform as sixth man. Starting forward Happy Hairston and quality reserve Len Chappell had arrived from Cincinnati in a trade.

Bing was, however, the team standout, leading the league in scoring with 27.1 points per game, and boosting his assists to 6.2 for fourth place in the league. He was the first guard to lead the NBA in scoring, Max Zaslofsky having done it for Chicago of the BAA in 1947-48. His performance led the Pistons to their best record in several years, a 40-42 fourth-place finish.

Unfortunately they drew the Celtics in the playoffs, and were eliminated 4-2. But the series did include a Piston victory in Boston Garden, 109-98 in the third game. At the time, it gave the Pistons a 2-1 edge in the series, but any dreams of glory were shattered when Bill Russell and companions pulled themselves together on the way to yet another championship.

More personnel moves occurred during the postseason, notably the trade in which DeBusschere went to the New York Knicks—helping solidify that future championship team—in exchange for veteran center Walt Bellamy and guard Howard Komives. A new head coach, Paul Seymour, was named in midseason, though his 1968-69 record turned out to be worse than his predecessor's.

Bellamy, in the middle of a distinguished career that took him to several teams, was a consistent scorer and rebounder, a powerful physical presence, and a likable person, but was sometimes criticized for a lack of fierce determination. The trade unquestionably helped New York more than Detroit, as the Pistons finished out of playoff contention again. A season later, with Butch van Breda Kolff as the new coach and Bing injured, they slumped to last place.

A Winning Season at Last

Divisional realignment in 1970-71 put the Pistons in the Midwest Division. This was rather unfortunate for their standings, for despite improvement to a .549 record they were again in last place. Detroit fans had to be pleased, however, for it was the team's first winning season since moving to the Motor City. Bing had a superb season, averaging 27 points per game and leading the league in free throws made and attempted.

And importantly for the future, the Pistons had gained a dominating center in rookie Bob Lanier, a 6-foot-11, 265-pound all-American from St. Bonaventure. In this first season he averaged 15.6 points per game and led the team in rebounds. Lanier would be one of the gate attractions for the Pistons for years to come.

Van Breda Kolff was gone after winning six games and losing six the next season. He was replaced by Earl Lloyd, who would win only 20 of the remaining 70 games. With three starters averaging over 20 points per game (the third was All-Star guard Jimmy Walker), the Pistons on paper ought to have had a respectable season.

Indeed, they got off to a nine-game winning streak at the beginning. But they were doing it with Dave Bing on the sidelines because of a detached retina, which forced him to sit out the first two months of the season. And despite guard Komives as a productive sixth man, the Pistons roster had very little in reserve. In Bing's absence, Lanier stepped up to play more of a scoring role, finishing the season with a 25.7 per-game average. He capped that with 14.2 rebounds per game. The team as a whole, however, went 26-56.

The pattern of replacing the head coach in the early season continued for 1972-73, as former Piston guard Ray Scott came in after seven games. The Pistons now had two perennial All-Stars in Bing and Lanier, with the rest of the lineup in flux. Rookie forward Curtis Rowe, a UCLA graduate who stood 6-foot-7, was a happy acquisition—he grabbed almost ten rebounds per game and was the only starter whose field goal percentage (52) exceeded 50.

The Pistons, with a late-season surge, improved to a 40-42 record and third place, but were still out of the playoffs.

The Pistons lineup solidified the next year. Second-year man Chris Ford was promoted to a starting guard berth, filling out a top-flight backcourt with Bing, who in his later years was taking on more of a playmaking and less of a scoring role. Forward Don Adams, who had been acquired from Atlanta a year earlier, averaged over ten points per game along with Rowe.

Fitting into Piston tradition, this playoff team was built around physical strength and ball control. The combination clicked for the best Piston record in Detroit to that point: 52-30. Though this was only good enough for third in the Midwest Division, it was also good enough for third best in the entire NBA.

In this tough division, where Kareem Abdul-Jabbar kept the Milwaukee Bucks comfortably on top, the battle for second place between the Pistons and the Chicago Bulls was a dramatic high spot at the heart of the continent. The two teams were similar in style, with the Bulls stronger at forward and more consistent at guard, but the Pistons having the two most impressive individual talents in Lanier and Bing. Team play outdid talent in this case, for the Bulls won two more games than the Pistons in the regular season and beat them 4-3 in the playoff openers.

It was a physically tough, tense playoff series in which the home team lost the first two games before settling into the more usual win-at-home, lose-on-the-road pattern; and it came down to a victory by one basket for the Bulls, 96-94 in the seventh contest. The Pistons had the satisfaction of knowing that they had taken so much out of their rivals that the Bulls were swept by Milwaukee in the conference finals. And Ray Scott was named NBA Coach of the Year—the only Piston pilot ever to be so honored.

The Davidson Era Begins

Longtime owner Fred Zollner sold the Pistons at this relative high point, on July 29, 1974, to a group of investors headed by Bill Davidson. The NBA now had 18 teams, and the 1974-75 Pistons had high hopes. With Jabbar injured and asking to be traded, the Bucks were no longer formidable in the Midwest Division.

The Pistons seemed to be in place for a surge to the top, but their momentum collapsed in midseason after forward Don Adams was released—a move that caused consternation among the players. Adams ended up with St. Louis of the

ABA. Howard Porter, who was acquired from the Knicks in exchange for a first-round draft choice, filled in capably at forward, but Chris Ford had an off year, falling out of the regular-season starting rotation, to be replaced by veteran John Mengelt. The Pistons lost their playoff openers to Seattle, 2-1.

A major trade occurred in the off-season: Dave Bing was sent to the Washington Bullets in exchange for Kevin Porter and a first-round draft choice. Bing, a Washington native, made the move willingly, and it seemed to make sense for the Pistons as well, because the 6-foot-1, 175-pound Porter was a younger, if somewhat less gifted, version of Bing.

But as with so many previous Piston trades, it didn't achieve the desired results. Porter suffered a knee injury when the season was a month old, and had to sit out the rest of the campaign, while Bing contributed solidly to the Bullets.

The Midwest Division was abysmal that year: all four teams had losing records. The Pistons might have made it to first place but for the Bucks' late-season surge. Another coaching change, with Herb Brown coming in at the halfway point, helped only slightly.

Curtis Rowe had an All-Star year with 16 points and almost nine rebounds per game. But lacking their starting point guard, the Pistons were off-balance. they managed to squeak by the Bucks in the opening playoff round, with a 107-104 victory in the third game; but they were taken care of by the Portland Trail Blazers with relative ease in a six-game series.

The 1976-77 team received two quality forwards from the St. Louis ABA team, when the junior league folded. M. L. Carr was a 6-foot-6 forward who could score and rebound, while the 6-foot-9 Marvin Barnes could switch to center when needed. Unfortunately, Barnes was hampered not only by an ankle injury but by a parole violation—a weapons charge. Equally damaging was Bob Lanier's broken hand, which reduced his season to 64 games.

Former reserve Howard Porter became a starting forward in Barnes's absence and had a good year. Shooting guard Ford and playmaker Kevin Porter, though not compiling impressive statistics, helped carry the team to a 44-38 record, tying the Bulls for second place in the Midwest. It was an indication of the entire division's weakness, however, that the top finisher was an ex-ABA team, the Denver Nuggets.

In the playoffs, the Pistons started off well with a 95-90 road win over the Golden State Warriors; but the Warriors paid them back in Detroit with a 138-108 blowout. That is not an overtime score.

The relatively good years, the playoff years of the mid-1970s, were over. Lanier had another injury, this time to the knee, in 1977-78, again limiting his season to 60-plus games. Though he made the All-Star team in both those years and compiled impressive scoring stats, he was missed for too much of the season. Reserves—center Leon Douglas and guard Eric Money—took over much of the Pistons' everyday burden. Rebuilding was in order, and it proceeded—or at least, sputtered forward.

A flurry of player changes were made, with both Porters going to the New Jersey Nets in exchange for reserve Al Skinner and a first-round draft choice. (The Pistons would change their minds in 1978, however, and get Kevin Porter back in exchange for guard Money.) Marvin Barnes was banished to Milwaukee in a complex deal involving two players and two draft choices. A new coach, too, was acquired, in Bob Kauffman. It made for an unsettled year in which the Pistons, at 38-44, came in third in the Midwest and out of playoff contention.

Hitting Bottom

A divisional realignment and another coaching change did not help the next year. The 1978-79 Pistons were in the Central Division of the Eastern Conference and were steered by one of their former assistant coaches, the excessively demonstrative future sportscaster Dick Vitale. A change of stadium did not help the team's record either—they were now housed in the Pontiac Silverdome, a friendly, boisterous place in a working-class suburb. Lanier's bad knees further reduced his effectiveness, and forward John Shumate missed the entire season with a blood clot in his lung.

The Pistons had added two home-town rookies: 6-foot-7 shot-blocking forward Terry Tyler and 6-foot-5 guard John Long, both graduates of the University of Detroit, and both capable shooters. Leading the team was the returned Kevin Porter, who broke the single-season assists-per-game record with 13.4, for a total of 1099. But the Pistons could do no better than fifth in a deep division paced by the San Antonio Spurs (George Gervin) and the Houston Rockets (Rick Barry, Rudy Tomjanovich, Moses Malone).

As had so often happened in Piston history, a brief ascent was followed by a downslide. The 1979-80 season marked an all-time team low and one of the most horrendous season in NBA history, as the Pistons faltered their way to a 16-66 record. They were still a team that could score, and had in fact added one of the great shooters of all time when Vitale obtained Bob McAdoo in a trade.

But Lanier resented McAdoo's intrusion, and personal friction augmented the Pistons' on-court weaknesses. McAdoo would finish the following season in New Jersey. The Lanier years in Detroit were over, too—the aging star was to be traded to Milwaukee for 6-foot-10 Kent Benson in February of 1980.

McCloskey Starts the Long Climb

More than cosmetic changes were needed. The team had to be rebuilt from scratch. And although the 1980-81 season saw only a marginal improvement—to 21-62 under new coach Scotty Robertson—the rebuilding was already underway, beneath the surface. Two first-rate rookies had been drafted: 6-foot-6 forward Kelly Tripucka of Notre Dame and 6-foot-1 guard Isiah Thomas of Indiana.

A front-office executive played a major role in the Pistons' turnaround of the 1980s. After the infamous 16-66 year, McCloskey was brought in as GM in the middle of the 1979-80 season. Two months after taking over, he traded Bob Lanier; shortly afterward, he released Bob McAdoo. Both moves stunned and angered many in Detroit, for both players were undeniably stars. But McCloskey's style had made its mark, and was to be proven right when Isiah Thomas joined the team the following year. For the rest of the decade, in a series of shrewd deals and through expert scouting, McCloskey built a championship squad piece by piece.

His father had been a coal miner in Jackson's Patch, Pennsylvania, and young Jack had seen sports as a way out. Growing to 6-foot-2, he was a good all-around athlete and, more importantly, extremely competitive. He won a scholarship to Penn, and played the big three sports before joining the Navy in World War II as the nineteen-year-old captain of a landing craft. He took part in the invasion of Okinawa.

After the war and college graduation, he was a minor-league pitcher in the Philadelphia A's organization until he ruined his arm trying to pitch some soreness out of it. Then he turned to basketball, and played guard for the Sunbury Mercuries of the rough-and-tumble Eastern League, winning an MVP award and progressing to coaching. He established a pattern of taking losing high-school teams and making them winners by emphasizing hard practice.

A few years later, as head coach at Penn, he took that school to the Ivy League championship. He then moved to Wake Forest, turning it into an ACC contender. Given a chance to pilot the expansion Portland Trail Blazers in 1972, he had a personality clash with temperamental star Sidney Wicks, and was inevitably fired. He settled for an assistant coaching job with the Lakers, then, after a staff shakeup, descended to an assistantship with the Indiana Pacers. At that point, the Piston general managership became available, and McCloskey, a dark horse, was given the job.

McCloskey is the focus of Cameron Stauth's excellent study of the Pistons, *The Franchise*. A quotation from McCloskey serves as the book's epigraph, and could serve as the team's motto: "Winners are losers who just won't quit!"

A front-office change of equal magnitude had been the catalyst for these acquisitions: Jack McCloskey, a tough former player who had knocked around the basketball world for years, was made general manager. McCloskey's acumen at making trades and drafting prospects was perhaps the key ingredient in the Pistons' 1980s turnaround.

This was to be the Pistons' time of growth, until by decade's end they were repeat world champions, notorious as the "Bad Boys" of basketball. When Isiah Thomas first arrived on the scene, however, he was dismayed by the absence of any team tradition, any discernable image at all.

In his book, *Bad Boys,* Thomas writes, "Back then, the Pistons had no particular style of play. We were just another NBA team with a bunch of average guys playing the same 82-game schedule as everyone else.... So, for the first six to eight years, we wanted to build a winning tradition. We wanted to make the people in the community aware of our playing style, of our determination to play a specific brand of basketball, and of our commitment to being successful. We wanted to make the community understand what it is like to be a Detroit Piston, and to show them what sets a Detroit Piston apart from everyone else."

This kind of thinking exemplifies the character of Isiah Thomas, of Jack McCloskey, and of others who would be drawn into the Pistons' orbit in the coming years. It shows a kind of indomitable competitiveness that had been lacking not only in the team but in their fans—for the Pistons, with attendance figures falling toward 5,000 per game, had still not developed a loyal following equal to those of the three long-time Detroit teams, the Tigers, Lions, and Red Wings. The small core of loyal fans—led by Leon "The Barber" Bradley, the most visible and audible fan in the NBA— deserved better, and they deserved more company.

The 1981-82 season marked the first visible signs of the climb toward the championship. Tripucka and Thomas, both starters in their rookie year, made the All-Star team. A crucial midseason acquisition was center—and central Bad Boy— Bill Laimbeer, who came from Cleveland in a trade.

With these three additions, the Pistons had a talented, promising foundation for years to come. Tripucka averaged 21.6 points per game, Thomas 17 point per game and 7.8 assists. The team rose to a 39-43, .476 record, third in the Central Division, and though they didn't make the playoffs, a winning attitude had been instilled.

A slight decline in the won-lost record was the 1982-83 harvest, for despite a stellar year by Tripucka (third in the league in scoring with 267.5 per game) and All-Star years by Thomas and Laimbeer, with respectable numbers amassed by forward Terry Tyler and guard Vinnie Johnson, the team's best players were still inexperienced and the supporting cast not strong.

Chuck Daly—Professor of Winning

It was then that Chuck Daly arrived as head coach, replacing the popular Scotty Robertson. It

AP/Wide World Photos

Chuck Daly

Bad Boy, Good Man

Magic Johnson, in television broadcasts, has called his buddy Isiah Thomas the best ballhandler in the history of basketball. Magic was including himself among the competition. True, Magic probably never saw Bob Cousy play, but then Thomas's career stats are higher than Cooz's.

And although he was the driving force behind the Bad Boy championship teams, Isiah Lord Thomas III is a likable, supremely responsible human being who puts team success ahead of personal glory. Like his former bosses, Jack McCloskey and Chuck Daly, he is known for incredible competitive drive. It's a truism that good athletes want to win, but Thomas, according to his autobiography, stays up nights thinking about how to do it. Teammates and opponents alike have often expressed wonder at where Thomas' fund of supercompetitiveness comes from.

Undoubtedly it had something to do with growing up the youngest of nine children in a Chicago ghetto. Born April 30, 1961, he was a college star for coach Bobby Knight on the 1981 NCAA champion Indiana team, and was MVP of that year's tournament.

AP/Wide World Photos

He was a star of the 1980 U.S. Olympic team which defeated NBA All-Star squads 5-1. Drafted by McCloskey in the first round (the only player taken ahead of him was future Bay Boy Mark Aguirre), Thomas proceeded to make the All-Star team in all of his first eleven seasons. (Due to injury, he did not play in the 1991 game.) Twice he was All-Star MVP.

Throughout the 1980s, his versatile shooting and flashy passing and dribbling made him a favorite with NBA fans. Capable of sinking jumpers or driving for layups, he added an accurate three-point shot late in his career to further stymie defenders. He is now the all-time Pistons leader in points, steals, and assists, and is third on the all-time NBA assists list behind Magic Johnson and Oscar Robertson. He also holds the Pistons record for consecutive field goals made (13) and most points scored in a quarter (24, tied by Joe Dumars).

Many people questioned his exclusion from the 1992 U.S. Olympic team. Some traced it back to the 1985 NBA All-Star game, when point guard Thomas did not give Michael Jordan the ball enough for M.J.'s liking. Be that as it may, Isiah Thomas has established his personal credentials well enough to serve as president of the NBA Player's Association.

He holds a degree in criminal justice and is known for his staunch opposition to drug use, and for his 1990 Summer Classic All-Star Game, which benefitted the homeless. In October 1988 he signed a contract which keeps him in Detroit for the remainder of his playing career.

caused some protest among fans and sportswriters at the time, but history blessed the transaction. Daly, a flashy dresser who had grown up in small-town western Pennsylvania, was a self-proclaimed "basketball lifer" who had coached high school for years in Punxsutawney, Pennsylvania, then had replaced Bob Cousy as head coach of Boston College, then returned to his home state for a successful tenure at Penn before going to the NBA as an assistant coach for the Philadelphia 76ers.

He was a defensive-minded coach who, despite his own consummate understanding of the game, was willing to learn from his veterans and to let them handle much of the motivating of new players. Like McCloskey, he was willing to work on a respectful, person-to-person basis with players who had been labeled as problems on other teams; and part of his gift for working with individuals was that, without diminishing their self-respect, he made them believe in the greater importance of the team. Isiah Thomas has described Daly as "the perfect coach for us."

Daly's efforts during his first season were aided by the acquisition of 6-foot-8 starting forward Cliff Levingston, a first-round draftee from Wichita State.

With Thomas, Laimbeer, and Tripucka all going to the All-Star Game, the 1983-84 Pistons finished in second place in their division with a 49-33, .598 record, a drastic improvement which was to be consolidated over the next several seasons. This first playoff year of many, they lost to the Knicks in a 3-2 series.

They were now a steady, playoff-quality team, and sometimes an exciting one, too. On December 13, 1983, for instance, at Denver, the Pistons won the highest-scoring game in NBA history, a triple-overtime 186-184 nail-biter, with Thomas, Long, and Tripucka scoring 47, 41, and 35 points respectively.

Back home, average attendance rose to almost 16,000 per game, to lead the NBA, and was to climb still higher for four consecutive seasons, peaking at 26,120 in 1987-88, the last year in the big Dome. From the personnel standpoint, management's task was now to iron out the kinks,

eliminate weak spots, and thus take Detroit to the next level of basketball accomplishment.

How to Build a Champion

Defense at the forward position was a continuing problem. Over the next couple of seasons, McCloskey would tinker with the pieces, sending Levingston to the Hawks for Dan Roundfield, Antoine Carr, and two draft picks, then sending Roundfield to the Bullets for key Bad Boy Rick Mahorn. The next step was to send Tripucka, who was purely an offensive player, and Kent Benson to the Utah Jazz for star forward Adrian Dantley.

Meanwhile, the Pistons remained at the playoff level, in large part because of Thomas's, Laimbeer's, and Tripucka's offensive contributions. Thomas led the league in assists in 1984-85 with 13.6 per game, while scoring 21.2. He really stepped up in the playoffs, scoring at a 24.3 clip per game as the team swept the New Jersey Nets. The series against Boston opened with two lopsided road losses, followed by two close home wins, and concluded with the Celtics triumphing, 4-2.

The time was near. Rookie guard Joe Dumars, a 6-foot-3 first-round draftee from little McNeese State, spent 1985-86 as the sixth man, and the mighty Mahorn, at 6-foot-10, 245 pounds, provided strength and intimidation from the bench. Laimbeer's 13.1 rebounds per game led the league, while Thomas, second in assists to his pal Magic Johnson, was named to the postseason All-NBA first team for the fourth straight year.

After a third-place regular-season finish, the Pistons lost 3-1 to Atlanta in the playoffs, with the concluding game a 114-113, double-overtime heartbreaker. The 1985-86 season, incidentally, was memorable for the collapse of the Silverdome roof, which forced the Pistons to play their last 15 games at the Joe Louis Arena and, for one game, at Cobo Hall.

Between seasons, McCloskey made the trade for Adrian Dantley. It surprised the public, for Tripucka was a local favorite and Dantley had a reputation as a difficult player to handle. In addition, Dantley, at 6-foot-5, 210 pounds was an inch and 15 pounds smaller than the forward he replaced. But Dantley was a shot-blocker and a tough post-up player; Daly liked the fact that he could drive to the basket and get fouled for a three-point play. In his book, *Daly Life,* the coach writes of Dantley, "he elevated our entire team."

It wasn't just Dantley's presence, however important that might have been. The Pistons now had two fine draftees, Dennis Rodman and John Salley, whose shot-blocking and rebounding added to the defense, and who could score. Laimbeer, meanwhile, was working as hard as ever and improved his free-throw shooting to the point where, at .894, he was third in the league.

Given the Pistons' rough style of play, free-throw shooting was an invaluable asset; aside from Laimbeer, Dantley, Thomas, Dumars, Mahorn, and Vinnie Johnson were all capable-to-excellent in that area.

The 1986-87 record was 52-30, or .634, and the playoffs were well played. Thomas and Dantley led the scoring for the Pistons, and Thomas led the postseason in steals with 39. The Pistons took care of the Bullets with little difficulty in three straight, the only close game being the 97-96 clincher in Washington.

Then they surprised the basketball world by taking a five-game series from the Hawks, who had beaten them for first place in the Central Division. Indeed the Pistons were a good choice to take the Eastern Conference championship from the Celtics, who had overextended themselves physically in a seven-game series against the Bucks.

The Pistons lost two games in the Boston Garden, but then blasted the Celtics out of the Silverdome with victories of 122-104 and 145-119. The fifth game was crucial and with five seconds left the Pistons had a one-point lead and possession. Then Larry Bird stole an Isiah Thomas pass, and passed to Dennis Johnson, who scored for a 108-107 win. The Pistons came back for a home victory in the sixth game, but lost the clincher in Boston, 117-114, paving the way for a

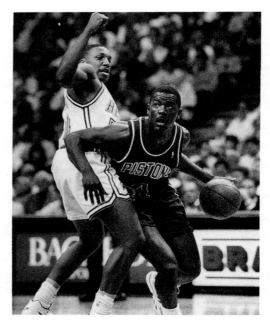

AP/Wide World Photos

Joe Dumars

classic Celtic-Laker finals confrontation.
The Finals

The Pistons were skilled enough, tough enough, mature enough but still young enough, to feel that they deserved to be in the finals too, and 1987-88 was their year to cross that threshold. By now they were known throughout the basketball world as the Bad Boys, a name that evoked comparison with the Oakland Raider championship football teams.

Some of the Pistons consciously modeled themselves in the Raider image, seeing themselves as a collection of hard-working, hard-knocks individualists who overcame personal differences and defeated finesse-oriented teams. Raider owner Al Davis helped cultivate the image by sending the Pistons Raider jackets and caps.

Image, however, needs substance to back it up, and the new Pistons had plenty of that: a first-rate bench, a basic but highly effective defense coached by Ron Rothstein, and scoring punch. In midseason, seven-foot center James Edwards, a reserve capable of brilliance in the clutch, was acquired from Phoenix, and charismatic backboard smasher Darryl Dawkins was added to the roster as well. Though the team's individual statistics were down a bit—Dantley led the club in scoring with 20 points per game—teamwork was up. A 54-29, first-place finish was the result.

The Pistons were thoroughly pumped for postseason. Thomas, who for years had been obsessed with winning a championship, was to lead the postseason in steals and, more importantly, in drive. With Dantley scoring, Laimbeer rebounding, Salley blocking shots, and Joe Dumars supporting Thomas in the backcourt, the Pistons defeated the Atlantic Division champion Bullets 4-2 in the playoff openers, then sent Michael Jordan, Scottie Pippen, and the rest of the Bulls down to defeat 4-1. Old rivals the Celtics were next on the list.

As in the previous year, the aging Celtics were already tired by the time they faced the Pistons, and were roughed up by the Bad Boy style. After dismissing the Celtics and their mystique, 4-2, the Pistons went on to a classic finals series.

The Lakers had won the championship the year before, and coach Pat Riley had guaranteed a repeat. The series was also notable for the rivalry of two close friends, Magic Johnson and Isiah Thomas, who consulted often during the year and who startled fans with a pregame, fraternal kiss on the cheek.

The first game, however, was Dantley's, as the star forward sank 14 of 16 field goal attempts in a 105-93 win that caught the Lakers napping. The west coast team was tired, and Magic Johnson played with the flu for game two, but the Lakers evened it with a 108-96 score.

Huge, enthusiastic crowds awaited the Pistons back in Detroit, but the Lakers played at top form on the road and in the course of the 99-86 loss, Thomas sustained a back bruise. In game four, Dennis Rodman's defensive pressure frustrated Johnson, who, in the fourth quarter, elbowed Thomas to the floor. The Piston offense pressured

Johnson into foul trouble, and the two-front get-Magic strategy resulted in a 111-86 Detroit win.

Game five was the team's last ever in the Silverdome, where, for the first time in NBA history, one million customers had gone through the gate in a season. (This figure included the all-time high of 61,983 for a regular-season game, on January 29 against the Celtics.)

The farewell performance saw the Lakers trying to match the Pistons physically and getting into foul trouble, for a 104-94 Piston win. The Pistons now had to win only one of two games in Los Angeles. But Thomas, playing a great game—43 points, 8 assists, 6 steals—sprained his ankle severely in the third quarter. With a minute left in the game, the Pistons led 102-99. But Laker Byron Scott scored a jumper, Thomas missed a shot, and Laimbeer fouled Abdul-Jabbar, who scored the winning two points on free throws.

In game seven, the Pistons rallied from a fifteen-point deficit in the fourth quarter, making it 102-100 with a minute to go; but Rodman missed an ill-chosen jumper with 39 seconds left, and Laimbeer's three-pointer could not overtake the Lakers' final scoring burst. With a 108-105 victory, the Lakers had repeated as champions. And the Pistons had been without a title longer than any other NBA team.

The Champs of Auburn Hills

The Palace of Auburn Hills welcomed the Pistons for the new season. The new stadium's sedate, middle-class atmosphere worried McCloskey, but all seats had been sold as season tickets, and as long as the team won, the fans were jubilant enough. And the team was winning—a 54-28 first-place finish. There was dissension on the club, however, as Dantley was disgruntled at having been benched in game seven of the Lakers series, and Daly wanting to pick up the team's offensive pace.

The solution, in midseason, was to trade Dantley for Mark Aguirre, a childhood friend of Isiah Thomas who was considered to have an attitude problem among the Dallas Mavericks. It was a trade of equivalent players, but people wondered whether Aguirre would be able to adjust to the unselfish style of the Pistons. To the surprise of many, he toned down his act with great success, sharing his playing time with Dennis Rodman and enabling the Pistons to move the ball around more on offense. Dumars, who had been Dantley's best friend, had a fine year despite his grief over the trade.

Detroit knocked the Celtics over in a 3-0 playoff sweep, then swept the Bucks 4-0. The Bulls managed to win two games against the Pistons before bowing out of the Eastern Conference finals. Then it was the Lakers' turn. The Pistons won the first game in Auburn Hills, behind the backcourt's scoring and Mahorn's coverage of James Worthy.

In game two, Magic Johnson pulled a hamstring, putting him on the bench alongside injured Byron Scott, and the Pistons took a two-game edge after a contest that was decided by free throws in the last seconds. In game three, Dennis "The Worm" Rodman grabbed 19 rebounds despite back spasms that sent him to courtside for periodic rubdowns. Vinnie Johnson, "The Microwave (he heats up in a hurry)," scored 13 of his 17 points in the fourth quarter, and Dumars had 31 in the game, to Thomas's 26 points and 8 assists.

The most spectacular play of the game came with nine seconds left, when Dumars, not normally a shot-blocker, made a terrific lunge to deflect Laker rookie Dave Rivers' shot. Game four was Abdul-Jabbar's final pro game, but for the Pistons it was their first title clincher in Detroit, and a sweep of a dominant team. Dumars, a quiet man who had spent years hidden behind his more flamboyant teammates, won the Finals MVP award.

Delirious celebrations, including a street parade, greeted the champions, but the team sustained an emotional blow almost immediately. It was an expansion year, and four players had to be left unprotected in the draft. To his own deep regret, general manager McCloskey saw no way out of leaving Rick Mahorn unprotected.

AP/Wide World Photos

Dennis Rodman

Mahorn was very popular with fans, teammates, and coaches, and was respected for the weight-loss campaign that had improved his recent play. Affectionately called "The Worst Boy," he typified the Pistons' style. "We feel like we're being penalized for having depth," McCloskey said. Debate raged in Detroit.

Adjustments were made, with Rodman and Edwards becoming starters and Aguirre moving to sixth man. The Pistons had a rough first two months of the season, partly because other teams were gunning for them physically. But the Pistons were confident and resilient. They scored less than in the previous year, but allowed fewer points. After a shocking, physically rough loss to the Lakers in Michigan in January, they had a 25-1 winning streak. Dumars broke his left hand in late March. The team faltered, seemingly out of gas, to a 59-23 first-place finish.

| PROFILES | Classic Bad Boys . . . |

Though the nickname has been generalized to all the recent Pistons teams, Isiah Thomas believes it should only be used for the 1988-89 championship team that contained Rick Mahorn. "In the long run, the image was going to hurt us," Thomas writes in *Bad Boys*. "Most of us were fined more extensively, or even suspended, because of this image." Here are the key members of that classic team:

Mark Aguirre: Born December 10, 1959, in Chicago. Acquired in midseason in the Adrian Dantley trade, his presence was a surprise addition that clicked everything into place. After an All-American career at DePaul, averaged double-digit scoring for his first eleven years in the NBA. Holds many Dallas Maverick all-time records from earlier in his career. A talented offensive player, a moody but likable person, he showed great willingness to learn the Pistons team style. Formed a tight offcourt threesome with Isiah Thomas and Magic Johnson. Didn't make his elementary school team on the first try: a lesson to all young people.

Joe Dumars: Born May 23, 1963 in Nachtioches, Louisiana. Made the NBA all-defense first team in 1988-89, 1989-90, and 1991-92, and the second team in 1990-91. Led the Pistons in scoring for two straight years. Made three consecutive All-Star teams from 1990-92. Used to be considered underrated, but has come into his own. Hit 62 consecutive free throws in 1990-91, a team record.

James Edwards: Born November 22, 1955. A solid reserve center, competitive but not mean, and a nice guy offcourt. Was acquired from the drug-plagued Phoenix Suns in order to add bench depth. In 1,254 minutes in the championship season, he was charged with 226 personal fouls.

Vinnie Johnson: Born September 1, 1956, grew up in Brooklyn where he learned one-on-one schoolyard ball. A 6-foot-2, 200-pound shooting guard out of Baylor. His playing style is more selfish than is typical of the Pistons, but it fit in perfectly when quick scoring was needed from the bench. Danny Ainge nicknamed him "The Microwave" because he heats up so quickly from the bench. Popular with teammates, a close friend of Bill Laimbeer.

Dennis Rodman: Born May 13, 1961 in Dallas. Had two older sisters who were high school All-Americans. Did not play basketball in high school: he was 5-foot-11 in senior year and grew seven inches after graduation. A second-round draft pick out of Southeastern Oklahoma State, the Pistons discovered him at a summer All-Star game for "lesser" prospects.

Was NBA defensive player of the year in 1989-90 and 1990-91, and second in the two years bracketing those. A perpetual all-defense team member, he also led the NBA in field-goal percentage in 1988-89 with .595. Holds the Pistons single-season records for offensive, defensive, and total rebounds, plus the team single-game rebounding record (34). An outspoken person and a pinball wizard.

John Salley: Born May 16, 1964. A seven-footer out of Georgia Tech. Another Piston defensive specialist and bench star, he elevated his game in the 1989 postseason to help the team to the title. Popular with the press, funny, media-conscious.

Repeating, Minus Mahorn

Things picked up for the playoffs, as the Pistons downed the Indiana Pacers 3-0 and the Knicks 4-1. Then came the Chicago Bulls. In a series in which the home team won every game, the Pistons had the homecourt advantage, thus advancing to the finals with a 4-3 margin. Their opponents would be the Portland Trail Blazers, who had surprised the Lakers. The fast-breaking Portland team had Clyde Drexler, Terry Porter, Kevin Duckworth, Buck Williams, and Jerome Kersey—a lineup that would serve as finals also-rans for the

Bill Laimbeer: Born May 15, 1957 in Boston. Often called "the most hated man in the NBA," though not by his teammates. Some feel he used violent tactics to overcome a lack of physical talent, while others feel his unorthodox moves, the result of learning basketball in relative isolation, called extra attention to his fouls. Seems to thrive on abuse from opponents' fans. Took a lot of physical pounding early in his career, and apparently decided to retaliate.

Raised in an affluent family, Laimbeer was an overweight kid who was taunted by playmates. A graduate of Notre Dame, where he languished in the shadow of teammate Kelly Tripucka. Considered the clumsiest player at the 1980 U.S. Olympic trials. Went to Europe to play, and was not considered a good prospect to make it in the NBA. Became a star through sheer effort, always active without the ball, and developed a good outside shot to compensate for not being a dominant-type center. A four-time All-Star in the mid-1980s, he holds Piston record for career rebounds, ahead of Bob Lanier and (so far) Rodman. Offcourt, an energetic contributor to muscular dystrophy charities, and a scratch golfer who dreams of joining the pro tour.

Rick Mahorn: Often called "the Worst Boy." Full name, Derrick Allen Mahorn; born September 21, 1958; a 6-foot-10, 240-pound graduate of the Hampton Institute. In five years with the Bullets he developed a reputation as a physical player, and was particularly hated by the Pistons, but became loved by them when he was on their side. Also extremely popular with Detroit fans and sportswriters. Had a weight problem, which he overcame through strict discipline. Also had a bad back.

Mahorn blocked shots, rebounded, and most importantly, intimidated opposing players during the 1988-89 season. Disqualifications decreased markedly after he left the Bullets, but a bad reputation with officials led to numerous fines, which became a nagging problem for the Pistons. Piston players and front-office personnel universally remember the moment of his release, amidst the victory celebration, as a devastating trauma. Was exiled to the Minnesota Timberwolves.

next three years. Detroit was hurting, but had a deeper bench than Portland. In game one, the Blazers took an early lead and held it most of the way.

Then Portland's stars began making mistakes, and Thomas turned up the juice, hitting jumpers, free throws, and a new shot he had been perfecting in practice: the three-pointer. He led the team to a 105-99 win in the final minutes. Game two, marred by turnovers and fouls, was a 106-105 overtime loss despite a 19-point scoring burst by Laimbeer in the last 17 minutes of the fourth quarter.

It was then on to Portland, where the Pistons hadn't won a game in 17 years. Sadly, Joe Dumars's father, a trucker who was a strong role model for his son, died of heart failure before the tipoff, but Dumars had asked not to be informed of his ailing father's condition, and played the game, which Detroit won 121-106. Game four, a tight contest dominated by Vinnie Johnson's shooting, was almost pulled out by a Portland basket at the buzzer, but the officials—confirmed later by videotape—ruled the shot late and the Pistons won, 112-109.

No NBA team had ever returned from a 3-1 deficit in the finals, and the Blazers didn't blaze any new trails in that category. Again led by Vinnie Johnson's scoring, the Pistons came from behind to capture the lead twice in the last seven minutes.

But in the last two minutes, Johnson scored seven points, including an amazing tie-breaker with seven-tenths of a second left. The Pistons had taken three straight in Portland for their second world championship in a row. Isiah Thomas, fittingly, was voted Finals MVP.

Looking Ahead—Again

The Pistons had achieved a place among the memorable winning basketball teams of the modern era. But a "three-peat" had never been accomplished, and it wasn't to be for the Pistons, for the Chicago Bulls (who were to accomplish the feat by winning their third consecutive title in 1992) were in the ascendancy.

Meanwhile, Isiah Thomas and his teammates were growing older. Thomas, Dumars, and Rodman still played All-Star-caliber ball, especially on defense, and Laimbeer still battled, though for fewer minutes.

But the Pistons' role during the early 1990s seemed to be that of testing the physical mettle of younger, rising teams. In 1990-91, the Pistons outlasted the Hawks and the Celtics in long, tough playoff series, but were swept by the Bulls for the Eastern title. The following year, the Pistons were knocked off, 3-2, in a hard-fought, low-scoring series against the Knicks, who were no wimps themselves.

Chuck Daly moved to the head coach position with the New Jersey Nets, who needed his skill in dealing with difficult players. He achieved greater glory by coaching the 1992 U.S. Olympic team—which, however, did not include any Pistons, allegedly because of Michael Jordan's vetoing of Isiah Thomas—to a gold medal.

McCloskey left the scene, and the general managership was abolished by owner Davidson in favor of a new structure, with Tom Wilson as president and former NBA player Billy McKinney as Director of Player Personnel.

Ron Rothstein, who had spent time coaching the Miami Heat and doing Pistons broadcasting since his days as defensive assistant to Daly, entered as head coach for the 1992-93 season, instituting an off-season conditioning program. The team's focus was on developing young players.

(McKinney, a scout for the Bulls, had been credited with discovering Scottie Pippen and Horace Grant). Unfortunately, as often happens during rebuilding periods, the team played unevenly, and failed to make the playoffs.

Increasingly sullen and uncommunicative, Dennis Rodman missed portions of the season due to personal problems and asked to be traded. To complicate matters, Rodman missed the stabilizing presence of his friend and mentor, Daly, and openly suggested he be traded to the Nets. His teammates grew increasingly critical of Rodman's apathetic attitude and play and, combined with a dismal season, team morale suffered.

Prior to the 1993-94 season Rothstein was replaced by former Houston Rockets coach Don Cheney and Rodman was traded away to the San Antonio Spurs.

SOURCES

BOOKS

1992-93 Detroit Pistons Media Guide.

Carter, Craig, and Alex Sachare, editors, *The Sporting News Official NBA Guide,* 1992-93 edition, Sporting News Publishing, 1992.

Daly, Chuck, with Joe Falls, *Daly Life,* Masters Press, 1990.

Dickey, Glenn, *The History of Professional Basketball Since 1896,* Stein and Day, 1982.

Fox, Larry, *Illustrated History of Basketball,* Grosset & Dunlap, 1974.

Hollander, Zander, *The Complete Handbook of Pro Basketball,* 1993 edition, Signet Books, 1992.

Hollander and Sachare, *The Official NBA Basketball Encyclopedia,* Villard Books, 1989.

Lazenby, Roland, *The NBA Finals,* Taylor Publishing, 1990.

Liss, Howard, *The Winners,* Delacorte, 1968.

Neft, David S., and Richard M. Cohen, *The Sports Encyclopedia: Pro Basketball,* St. Martin's Press, 1989.

Stauth, Cameron, *The Franchise,* Morrow, 1990.

Taragano, Martin, *Basketball Biographies,* McFarland & Company, 1991.

Thomas, Isiah, with Matt Dobek, *Bad Boys,* Masters Press, 1989.

PERIODICALS

New York Times Magazine, January 8, 1989.

Rolling Stone, May 8, 1988.

INDIANA PACERS

The Indiana Pacers have spent their 17-year NBA existence striving to approach the success they enjoyed as a preeminent ABA franchise. A charter member of the ABA, founded in the spring of 1967, the Pacers won three NBA championships, more than any other franchise, and reached the finals two other times. They were one of only two ABA franchises to play all nine ABA seasons in the same city under the same name—Kentucky's Colonels were the other.

The Pacers were the most successful of the four survivors of the ABA who merged with the NBA in 1976, although non–survivor Kentucky had a better record. However, the Pacers had the ABA's best playoff record.

The Pacers had succeeded in Indianapolis where two NBA teams, the 1948–49 Indianapolis Jets and 1949–53 Indianapolis Olympians, had failed. Also distinguishing the Pacers in basketball history is the fact that they were the first NBA team to sign a woman player to a men's professional basketball contract in the late summer of 1979.

In 17 NBA seasons, the Pacers, who never missed an ABA playoff trip in nine campaigns, have gone on to postseason play just five times, including a three–year run. They've managed just four playoff wins in those five appearances, but have made the play–offs four times in a 5–year span ending in 1992–93. The Pacers, who won three ABA division titles, but twice won championships after finishing second in their division, have never finished above third in their division in the NBA.

Still, the Pacers have enjoyed far superior fan attendance in the NBA, beating the best ABA average of 8,604 (1974–75) in every season but two (1981-82, 7,758; 1982–83, 4,814). Hoosiers love their basketball and the state's only major professional team for many years enjoys a stable, fervent fan base in "Nap-town."

ABA teams began acquiring players in whatever fashion they could to stock their teams for the

1967–68 season. They held a five–round draft and then allowed teams to draft more players. The names of the players were released in alphabetical order, a grand ploy to reduce bargaining power with no player knowing if he was the first player taken in the league or by his team or the 55th in the first five–round phase.

Indiana got a real keeper in the five–round phase when Bob Netolicky of Iowa's Drake University was selected. Of the 12 players taken, only three ever played for the team. "Neto" played eight years and took part in six play–offs and the first four ABA All–Star Games. Illinois guard Jim Dawson took part in 21 games in the inaugural season after being taken in the five–round phase, while Northwestern forward Ron Kozlicki, a later choice, played in 37 games that first year.

Little did the Pacers know that they had drafted a future team public relations director in the NBA era in a late round when they chose 6'8" forward Ed McKee from tiny Rockhurst College in Kansas City. Their acknowledged top pick, Providence, Rhode Island's Jimmy Walker, signed as Detroit's top NBA choice.

The Pacers set to gathering players however and wherever and for whatever. It should have been expected in a league where a protest was upheld because a court was too short, a coach was demoted or promoted to PR man and Les Selvage of the Anaheim Amigos tried 26 three–pointers and made 10 in a single game. The Pacers did their part by finding their best player working in a General Motors factory in his Dayton, Ohio, hometown.

When Mike Storen, business manager of the NBA Cincinnati Royals and former front office staffer of the Baltimore Bullets, was signed as Pacers general manager for $15,000, he asked for a $500 check to go out and sign a reluctant player.

Roger Brown wasn't sure he wanted to sign with a new basketball league and give up five years seniority at GM, where he was making $114 a week while his wife, a nurse, was not anxious to move to Indianapolis. Brown had been implicated in a point–shaving scandal with teammate Connie Hawkins at the University of Iowa as a freshman

several years before. He was playing Amateur Athletic Union (AAU) ball after work and in summers and was leery of the ABA since the American Basketball League, which had ignored Indianapolis in the early 1960s, had lasted just two years. Finally, Brown signed for $17,000 and a $2,000 bonus saying, "I was convinced the ABA would at least make it through the first season and I figured this might be my last chance [at age 25] to play pro ball, so I took it."

The Pacers now had a player, but no front office or coach. The team rented a jewelry store, but the store had two months left on its lease and stayed in business. The "office" for two months was Storen's desk and phone. On strong recommendations, he hired former Cincinnati Royal–turned–Notre Dame assistant Larry Staverman for $15,000 and a new station wagon.

The Pacers then went to work signing the free–spirited Netolicky, son of a surgeon and already 25 years old. On this deal they had to go head–to–head with the expansion San Diego (now Houston) of the NBA. Indiana offered Netolicky $16,500, agreed to pay his attorney fees, and acceded to his request for a car. (Storen didn't know then what a Corvette was—"some kind of Chevy, I guess.") The Pacers also lost All–American wide receiver Gene Washington of Michigan State, listed in the Pacers Media Guide as the team's 7th–round pick, to an All–Pro career with the NFL Vikings.

Pacers Hit the Court

Finally, the team was ready to play. The Pacers went 38–40 to finish third in the East. To differentiate itself from the NBA, the ABA not only adopted the famed red–white–and–blue basketball (which it never trademarked), but also for the first several years pitted the first place team vs. the third and the second vs. the fourth in the first play–off rounds. Pittsburgh swept the Pacers, 3–0, in the best–of–five series by margins of 19, 13, and 19 points, respectively. Freddie Lewis, an original signee who would play the team's first seven sea-

TEAM INFORMATION AT A GLANCE

Founding date: 1967 (ABA); 1976 (NBA)

Home court:
Market Square Arena
300 East Market St.
Indianapolis, IN 46204
Phone: (317) 263-2100
FAX: (317) 263-2127

Seating capacity: 16,912

Team colors: Blue and yellow.
Team nickname: Pacers
Logo: Capital "P" with basketball filling empty space,
name "Pacers" written below.

Franchise record	Won	Lost
(1976-1993)	932	1,002

sons before being traded and then return for the first NBA season, was 10th in ABA scoring at 20.6 to lead the team. Netolicky was third (.504) in field goal shooting, Jimmy Rayl was fourth in three–point shooting (.326), and Brown was fifth in assists (4.3). Brown, Lewis, and Netolicky played for the winning East team in the first ABA All–Star Game at sold–out Hinkle Fieldhouse on the Butler University campus.

After a 2–7 start in 1968–69, Coach Larry Staverman was fired and the Pacers hired Bob ("Slick") Leonard, a Hoosier hero at Indiana University and a seven–year NBA guard before retiring to coach during the 1962–63 season. Two months into Leonard's first season with the Pacers, team president John DeVoe died while watching the Indiana battle Houston on December 14, 1968.

The major off–season move was to acquire the league's best center (and second–best player of the first season), Mel Daniels, for $75,000 plus Jim Dawson and Ron Kozlicki from the cash–strapped Minnesota team. Leonard whipped the team, whose members had been poorly conditioned, into shape and Indiana won the East at 44–34 by a game over Miami. Then the Pacers ousted Kentucky in seven games in the first round, and crushed Miami, 127–105, in the last game of the 4–1 East Finals.

In the ABA Finals, Rick Barry led the Oakland Oaks to the title, 4–1. The Pacers' lone win was by a 150–122 count in Game 2. Two losses, including the decisive game, were in overtime. Pacer attendance increased (to 5,864) as it would for each of the next three seasons and the Pacers were ready to roll. Daniels led the ABA in rebounds (16.5) again and was also sixth in scoring (24.0) again.

Pacers Claim Three of Next Four Titles

The 1969–70 season marked the first of three Pacers ABA titles. With Bob Leonard around from the start and running a brutal training camp, the Pacers raced out of the gate, 14–2, to the ABA's best record at 59–25 and eased through the play-offs with a 4–0 sweep of Carolina, a 4–1 blasting of Kentucky, and besting the Los Angeles Stars in six games—four of them decided by four points or less.

The ABA All–Star Game returned to Denver when CBS wanted the game played on a day the Carolina Coliseum was unavailable. It drew more than 11,000 fans and a nationwide audience saw Spencer Haywood, the 1968 Olympic hero and should–have–been college junior, excel. He was the All–Star and regular–season MVP, but the Pacers had the big trophy.

Stars coach Bill Sharman claimed the Pacers could beat half of the NBA teams. "In fact, if games could be arranged, I'd bet my salary on that." Mel Daniels was second (17.5) to Haywood in rebounding and Roger Brown was ninth (23.0) in scoring, making them the team's only ABA leaders.

In 1970–71, the Pacers' bid to repeat as champions ended in the seventh game of the Western Finals vs. Utah, 108–101. The Pacers had an ABA–best 5824 record, but just one game better than the Los Angeles Stars. Indiana swept Memphis, 4–0, in the first round, but the bitter fight with the Stars went the limit. Utah then went on to beat Kentucky in seven games for the ABA title.

Mel Daniels had a career–best 18.0 rebounds to lead the league and ranked 3–4 in field goal percentage with Bob Netolicky, while Billy Keller was third in free–throw shooting (.867). Pacer fan attendance jumped to 7,787 per game, leading the ABA. Daniels's All–Star Game effort of 29 points and 13 rebounds gained him the MVP nod. He was the season MVP too. The 8,187 average attendance led the ABA.

During the 1971–72 season, forward Roger Brown was elected to the Indianapolis City Coun-

cil. He also became the first ABA player to have a car phone so he could conduct business while driving to and from Pacer practices. He was also a key as the Pacers won their second ABA title in three years, defeating New York in six games. Indiana's 47–37 was second in the West, 13 games behind the Stars, who were now in Utah.

But Slick Leonard's team caught fire in the play–offs. They swept Dallas, 4–0, upset Utah, 4–3, and claimed the title with a 4–2 series victory over the New York Nets, the East's third–best regular–season team at 44–40. For the first time, every ABA team was in the same place as the season before. Mel Daniels was second in rebounding (16.4) to first–ranked Rookie of the Year Artis Gilmore, while Freddie Lewis was fourth in free–throw shooting (.861). The Pacers averaged 8,476 in attendance.

The next year the Pacers did what no other team could do in pro basketball in the 1970s—repeat as champions—by besting their closest rival Kentucky in seven games. After ousting San Diego in four games in the first round and rebounding from an opening loss to upset Utah in six games in the West Finals, Indiana had to win the title the hard way.

After falling behind, 2–1, and surging ahead, 3–2, the Pacers scored an 88–81 win at Louisville's Freedom Hall before a crowd of 16,597 as George McGinnis scored 27. McGinnis, who averaged 27 points per game in the Finals, and Mel Daniels were named to the All–ABA Second Team. McGinnis was second in scoring (27.6) to Julius Erving, and Daniels was second in rebounding (15.4), again to Artis Gilmore. Billy Keller won the foul–shooting title (.870), and Roger Brown was second in three–point shooting (.356), with Freddie Lewis fifth (.345).

Regular–season attendance dipped for the first time to an 8,281 average, but the play–offs were played to packed houses. Utah had finished four games in front of Indiana's 51–33 record in the West before the Pacers caught fire.

In 1973–74 the Pacers made a bid for a trifecta, but the Utah Stars were waiting in the Western Finals and prevailed 4–3. The Stars were

PROFILES	The Big 4: Brown, Daniels, Leonard, and McGinnis

The Pacers' most memorable players/personalities are still those from ABA days. Players Roger Brown, Mel Daniels, and George McGinniss all had their uniform numbers retired, and are the only ones in Pacers team history to be honored as such. Coach Bob Leonard returned as TV announcer after his coach-general manager career ended. Daniels has been a staff member since 1984—except for a 1989-91 lapse—as an assistant coach and/or scout. And all four, along with several other former Pacers, have continued to live in the Indianapolis area.

Roger Brown spent eight years as a Pacer and made the All-ABA first or second teams three times. He was THE original Pacer, and is the franchise's number-two all-time scorer (10,058 points) in 559 games. He had a career-high 53 points in 1970—third-best in Pacers history—and once sank all 14 field goal tries in a game.

Mel Daniels, the first solid ABA big man, came to the team for its second season. In six seasons Daniels averaged 19.5 points and 15.9 rebounds while making the first or second All-ABA teams four times. Had 7,622 Pacer rebounds, set a season mark (1,475—an ABA record) and at one time held the single-game record (31).

George McGinnis played seven seasons (1971-75; 1979-82), was the ABA co-MVP with Julius Erving in 1975 and All-ABA three times. He's the Pacers' career number-three scorer, with a record 58 in ABA play. He also holds the team one-game rebounds mark (37). McGinnis scored 2,353 points in last ABA year.

Bob Leonard was the franchise's most successful coach with three titles, two other Finals trips, and an overall winning record in 12 seasons. He also was general manager for four years after the ABA/NBA merger.

51–33 in the regular season, to Indiana's 46–38. Indiana had to battle back from 1–0 and 2–1 disadvantages to oust San Antonio in seven games in the first round. Then, Utah jumped ahead 3–0 in the West Finals before the Pacers 11, 9, and 2–point wins before being routed 109–87 in game seven.

George McGinnis was again second (25.9) to Julius Erving in ABA scoring and was voted to the All–ABA First Team. McGinnis (15.0) and Mel Daniels (11.6) rated 2–5 in rebounding. Billy Keller (.382) and Roger Brown (.361) rated 2–3 in three–point shooting.

During the season, Coach Leonard was fined $1,000 and suspended for two games for throwing a rack of 12 multicolored basketballs at a referee, drawing three technical fouls in the process. McGinnis had 33 rebounds in a game vs. the Nets and a monster night of 52 points and 37 rebounds as Indiana beat Carolina, 124–105, on January 12. It was still quite a year.

The Move to Market Square Arena

In 1974–75 the Pacers moved to Market Square Arena, a downtown arena that today has a capacity of 16,530, but has held as many as 17,096. It was also the Pacers' last winning season under Bob Leonard at 45–39, a drop in wins for the second straight year. The team had to be sold in mid–season as the original owners, Indiana Professional Sports Inc., bought the Indiana Racers of the World Hockey Association and ran short of money.

Arena Sports Inc. bought the team and ownership was transferred to Indiana Pacers L.P. in 1976 when the ABA–NBA merger occurred. Still, the team was more than competitive and reached the ABA Finals, where Kentucky avenged the 1973 meeting with a 4–1 win. Indiana built a 3–0 lead before downing San Antonio in a six–game first round.

Scoring champion George McGinnis (29.8) and Julius Erving shared the MVP and McGinnis, fifth in rebounding (14.2), second in steals (2.61), and fourth in three–point shooting (.354) was on the All–ABA Team. He also averaged 5.1 assists.

As future Pacers vice–president of basketball operations George Irvine, then an Erving team-mate in Virginia that season has said, "As great as Julius was, George had a better year. I still don't think there was ever a player his size [6–foot-8, 235 pounds] and that quick. When he got every-thing together, he was totally dominating. He became a monster and that's when the McGinnis–Erving comparisons heated up."

In what turned out to be the ABA's final sea-son, the Pacers dropped to a 39–45 record, the first losing season since ABA Year One. With three teams gone—Baltimore in training camp, San Diego after 11 games, and Utah after 16 games—the ABA played without divisions. The Pacers finished fifth and bowed 2–1 to Kentucky in the first round of the play–offs. George McGinnis left for the NBA's Philadelphia 76ers.

Roger Brown had also retired. Mel Daniels and Freddie Lewis were traded away, along with Johnny Neumann. Bob Netolicky played only four games in 1975–76. The Pacers still had players in veterans Don Buse and Billy Keller in the back-court, number–two ABA scorer Billy Knight (28.1), and Darnell Hillman, Len Elmore, and Dave Robisch.

The rookies included future NBA All–Star Game pick Dan Roundfield, plus Mike Flynn and a Jordan—Charles. Buse led in assists (8.2) and steals (4.12) and Keller was tops in free– throw shooting (.896). Keller (.352) and Buse (.348) were 4–5 in three–point shooting, and Elmore was fourth (2.34) in blocked shots.

Attendance tum-bled to 7,739 per game. The rumors of an ABA–NBA merger continued to swirl. Before the season, the financially strapped

Pacers were sold to Arena Sports Inc. By the next season, they would be operating as Indiana Pac-ers, L.P.

Finally, the Merger

June 17, 1976: The ABA and the NBA finally merged. The NBA came to Indianapolis, and the Pacers entered the NBA along with Denver, New Jersey, and San Antonio. Kentucky and St. Louis didn't make it, but were compensated. Virginia had folded a month earlier. The Pacers and the other three teams paid $3.2–million to the NBA by mid–September, but were barred from partici-pating in the NBA draft. They received no rev-enues generated from television until 1979–80.

The Pacers did take part in the Dispersal Draft of the other three ABA teams and selected 8th–choice Wil Jones for $50,000. The eldest of the four Jones brothers from Georgia's Albany State played one year for the Pacers, finishing his ca-reer in 1977–78 in Buffalo.

In a season of streaks, the Pacers lost their first three games, won the next four, lost six straight, and put together another four–game winning streak. Six straight wins between December 30 and January 12 had the Pacers 21–20 at the half-way point. They limped in at the end of the sea-son 36–46 by winning four of their last five games. Billy Knight was second in NBA scoring at 26.6, the highest finish ever by a Pacer.

Don Buse led the NBA in assists (8.5) and steals (3.47), the second straight player to turn the trick and one of only four ever. Original signee Freddie Lewis returned and played 32 games to call it a career. The team drew a franchise record 10,551 fans per game in the inaugural NBA sea-son.

In the 1977 off–season the Pacers dealt Darnell Hillman to the Nets, completing the in–season deal for John Williamson. They sent Billy Knight to Buffalo for Rookie of the Year Adrian Dantley and Mike Bantom, and peddled Don Buse to Phoenix for Ricky Sobers. The day before the October 19 opener vs. the Lakers, Indiana sent a

1968 •

The ABA's first All-Star game was played on January 9 in Indianapolis and the East scored a 126-120 win with game MVP Larry Brown, who would be coach of the Pacers come 1993-94. The 5-foot-9 Brown of New Orleans dazzled 10,862 fans at Butler Fieldhouse. He had 17 points and five assists, playing tough defense in 22 reserve minutes for the losing West.

Mel Daniels of the Pacers had game bests of 22 points, 15 rebounds for the winners. Roger Brown and Bob Netolicky of Indiana each added 12 and "Neto" had 11 rebounds. In the ABA's 8th and 9th seasons, Brown would be coaching in the All-Star games as his West team lost to the East, 151-124, in 1975 and his Denver team whipped the ABA All-Stars, 144-138, in Denver in 1976.

1970 •

The third ABA All-Star game was played on January 24 in Indianapolis before a then-record All-Star game crowd of 11,932 and televised to a nationwide CBS audience as the Pacers excelled. (The game had been set for Charlotte on a Tuesday, but CBS wanted it on a Sunday and the Charlotte Coliseum was booked.) The West gained its second straight win, 128-98, and set a ABA All-Star victory margin mark.

Spencer Haywood, who would jump to the NBA Seattle SuperSonics the next season, was the All-Star game MVP and later was voted the ABA's MVP. Haywood had 23 points, a game-high 19 rebounds, and seven blocked shots. Denver teammate Larry Jones scored 30 for the West. Mel Daniels netted 13 points and 12 rebounds for the East and Pacers Roger Brown and Bob Netolicky divided 30 points. The game almost wasn't played, due to a planned player's strike. A compromise wasn't reached until just before tipoff time.

1985 •

Indiana and the Hoosierdome hosted the game on a snowy February 10. An All-Star record crowd of 43,146 (later broken in 1989, when 44,735 filled the Houston Astrodome) saw Ralph Sampson score a game-high 24 points and collar ten rebounds in 29 minutes at forward to win the MVP Award. The game had only been played in a domed facility once before, in 1979 at the Pontiac (Michigan) Silverdome. More dome games would follow in 1987 (Seattle) and 1989 (Houston). The Slam-Dunk Contest and Legends Game, inaugurated the year before in Denver, were continued with Dominique Wilkins scoring two perfect 50 dunks in the finals to beat rookie Michael Jordan 147-136, while Bob Leonard's West team lost 63-53. Ex-Pacers Roger Brown (ten points) and Mel Daniels (eight points, seven rebounds) led the West.

pick, and cash, to Buffalo for Johnny Neumann and later moved Dantley and Dave Robisch to the Lakers for 7–foot center James Edwards and Earl Tatum.

The season started with a quartet of streaks, giving the Pacers a 6–8 record. A 4–17 stretch from January 4 through February 10 left them with a 19–34 slate. A 12–17 finish with an end–of–March six–game loss streak doomed the team to a 31–51 mark. Still, the fans kept coming: the second Pacers NBA season was even better at the gate with an average 12,238—a mark which stood until

1986–87—paying to watch the team.

In 1978–79, the Pacers came in at 38–44, a seven–win improvement over 1977–78, thanks to a 12–4 finish in the last four–and–a–half weeks of the season. In the off–season, Johnny Davis came from Portland along with Buffalo's first, Rick Robey, for the Pacers' own pick, Mychal Thompson, the top choice in the draft.

The Pacers also signed Milwaukee free agent Alex English. Indiana traded Earl Tatum to Boston and Dan Roundfield to Atlanta and picked up Corky Calhoun in a trade as well as Kevin Stacom via free agency. The starting unit of Davis, Ricky Sobers, James Edwards, English, and Mike Bantom was good for 83.0 points per game of the team's 108.8. Billy Knight was added in mid–season in a swap with Boston for Robey, and Stacom was sent back to Boston at the trade deadline. Attendance that season fell nearly 3,300 and there were no sellouts.

Sign In, Ann Meyers

New Pacers owner Sam Nassi, who had made his fortune as the nation's "Master Liquidator" by liquidating the E.J. Korvette and W.T. Grant chains, unsold DeLorean automobiles, and others, was from Beverly Hills and had many Hollywood pals. He decided to make a big splash by signing the NBA's first woman player. The player he had in mind played as a collegiate near his home at UCLA in Westwood, California. Had he known that one day she would be inducted into the Naismith Memorial Basketball Hall of Fame, he might have prevailed on Coach Leonard to keep her.

The Pacers signed UCLA Bruin four–time All–American Ann Meyers, one of 11 children. (Her older brother Dave had also been Bruin All–American and was returning that year for his fourth and final pro season; he had taken a year off in 1978–79 and would retire after the 1979–80 campaign to pursue his religious path.)

At 5-foot-9 and 135 pounds, Ann Meyers was taller only than 5-foot-8 Charlie Criss of the Atlanta Hawks and just a tad smaller than 5-foot-10 Calvin Murphy, an All–Star Game pick the previous February for the Houston Rockets. Meyers weighed 30 to 50 pounds less than these players, but was still given a guaranteed contract for $50,000. She would be paid if she made the Pacers team. If she didn't, it would fall to Pacers broadcaster Bob Lamey to teach her the tricks of his trade.

This wasn't the first time an NBA team had fancied a woman player. The New Orleans Jazz in 1977 drafted Lucy Harris from Delta State,

Mississippi, in the seventh round, but never signed her—she joined the team at their rookie free agent camp, but a physical exam showed she was pregnant and she didn't participate.

Around the NBA, opinions ran negative over the signing of Meyers. Celtics legend Red Auerbach, known for his opinionated comments, said, "Annie's a nice girl, but this is reminiscent of [the late White Sox owner] Bill Veeck signing that midget." Nassi insisted that it was no publicity stunt, but it was widely agreed that he had some "show biz" in him. After all, the average NBA player that season was about 6-foot-6 and 205 pounds. Leonard, also the team's general manager, had not been consulted on the controversial signing, but in training camp insisted, "She's just another athlete to me."

Meyers stuck until the end of rookie camp when it fell to new Pacers assistant coach Jack McCloskey, later the general manager who rebuilt the Detroit Pistons into two–time NBA champions, to deliver the news. "She gave me a kiss on the cheek and a hug. It meant a lot to me. I've never gotten a kiss from a player who got cut," said McCloskey. Meyers said of her tryout, "It's something I'll cherish for the rest of my life. It was the chance of a lifetime, to be the first at something."

After nearly three months as a Pacers TV commentator, Meyers joined the Women's Basketball League New Jersey Gems, and became a two–time league MVP. In the 1980s she married Baseball Hall of Fame pitcher and later major league broadcaster Don Drysdale. They became sports' first husband–and–wife Hall of Fame team when she was inducted into the Basketball Hall in May of 1993. Less than two months later, Don died of a heart attack in his Montreal hotel room before a L.A. Dodger game.

On the 1979–80 court, the Pacers limped in at 37–45. It was the team's fifth consecutive losing season under Leonard, who then left as coach and general manager. Not even trading Alex English, who would become a scoring machine, and Boston's 1980 first–round pick to Denver for George McGinnis on February 1 could save the Pacers. The Pacers were 26–28 at this point, but went only 11–17 the rest of the way in their first season in the NBA's Eastern Conference Central Division after playing their first three NBA years in the Midwest Division of the Western Conference.

Jack McKinney Takes Over

A year before, Jack McKinney had moved from assisting Jack Ramsay in Portland to succeed Jerry West as coach of the Lakers. After a 10–4 start, he fell while riding a bicycle and suffered serious head injuries, sidelining him for the rest of the season. Paul Westhead took over and led the Lakers to the title in Earvin "Magic" Johnson's rookie season. McKinney was informed during the playoffs that he would not get his job back. After turning down an offer to coach the Pistons, McKinney became the third head coach in Pacers history, one–year general manager Dick Vertlieb's choice.

The Pacers responded in 1980–81 with the team's first winning season (44–38) since 1974–75. The franchise earned its first NBA playoff berth and McKinney was voted Coach of the Year. The Pacers traded away Mickey Johnson the day before training camp began and came out of the blocks 8–3 through November 1.

Standing at 12–10 on November 25, the Pacers brought Don Buse back from Phoenix. A seven–game winning streak to start 1981 sent the team to 28–18. Three wins in the final four games assured a berth vs. Philadelphia in the play–offs. The 76ers won, 124–108 at home, and two nights later in Indiana, 96–85, to end the Pacer year.

Still, seven players on the team averaged double–figure points. Among them was second–round pick Louis Orr (10.5), the team's top choice in the 1980 draft. Johnny Davis was 9th in NBA assists (6.3) and Dudley Bradley was 6th in steals (2.27). Bill Knight scored a Pacers NBA–record 52 points at San Antonio on November 10, bettering his own record of 44, set a season earlier.

Herb Williams was the Pacers' 1981 first round choice, 14th over–all. Tom Owens came

from Portland for Indiana's 1984 first, a pick that became Sam Bowie when the Blazers lost the coin flip to Houston, who took Hakeem Olajuwon, while Portland passed on Michael Jordan, who went third to Chicago. Dudley Bradley was sent to Phoenix for a pair of second–round choices and James Edwards signed with Cleveland; the Pacers got two more second picks in 1981 and 1982.

They also averaged 5.4 points per game less and gave up 2.2 fewer points than the year before, but a 2–7 finish cemented a 35–47 record. The Pacers could only put together five streaks of two or more wins with a best of five, between February 21 and March 2. Billy Knight tumbled from 17.5 to 12.3 in scoring; Williams was 7th in blocked shots (2.17); and Don Buse rated 5th in three–point shooting (.386 and 10th in steals [2.00]) as attendance slid more than 2,200 to 7,758—19th in the NBA. Bob Salyers, an attorney, had arrived before the 1981–82 season as president and general manager.

Clark Kellogg, Herb Williams's Ohio State teammate, was 1982's first–round pick, the 8th overall. Tom Owens was sent to Detroit for a second–round pick, and Louis Orr was signed by the New York Knicks as a free agent, with the Pacers getting a second–round pick and other considerations as the final year of Sam Nassi's team ownership began.

For the fourth time in five years, attendance dropped, sagging to an all–time low of 4,814—21st of the 23 NBA teams, with no sellouts for the second straight season. The season also paralleled an all–time franchise worst record of 20–62 and the first of four straight 6th–place (i.e., last) finishes in the Central Division.

In the off–season, Coach McKinney explored his career options in the NBA. He interviewed in Detroit, where Scotty Robertson's contract was not renewed (Robertson became the Pacers' assistant during the summer.) It's believed he turned down a Detroit offer; Chuck Daly then set about to build a winner with the Pistons.

The Pacers went into their own rebuilding mode. Missouri center Steve Stipanovich was their first–round choice (second overall) after losing a

| **PACERS** | Honored Members |

Retired Uniform Numbers: 30—George McGinnis, forward; 34—Mel Daniels, center; 35—Roger Brown, forward.

ABA Most Valuable Player: Mel Daniels, 1968-69, 1970-71; George McGinnis, 1974-75 (tie).

ABA All-Star Games: Roger Brown, Freddie Lewis, Bob Netolicky (East), 1968; Netolicky, Mel Daniels (East), 1969; Netolicky, Daniels, Lewis, Brown, Coach Bob Leonard (East), 1970; Brown, Netolicky, Daniels (West), 1971; Brown, Daniels, Lewis (West), 1972; George McGinnis, Daniels (West), 1973; McGinnis, Daniels (West), 1974; McGinnis (West), 1975; Billy Knight, Don Buse (ABA), 1976.

All-ABA First Team: Mel Daniels, 1968-69, 1969-70, 1970-71; Roger Brown, 1970-71; George McGinnis, 1973-74, 1974-75.

ABA All-Rookie First Team: Bob Netolicky, 1967-68; George McGinnis, 1971-72; Billy Knight, 1974-75.

ABA All-Defensive First Team: Don Buse, 1974-75.

NBA Coach of the Year: Jack McKinney, 1980-81.

NBA Rookie of the Year: Chuck Person, 1986-87.

NBA Sixth Man of the Year: Detlef Schrempf, 1990-91, 1991-92.

NBA All-Star Game: Don Buse, Billy Knight (West), 1977; Reggie Miller (East), 1990; Detlef Schrempf (East), 1993.

NBA All-Defensive First Team: Don Buse, 1976-77.

NBA All Rookie First Team: Clark Kellogg, 1982-83; Steve Stipanovich, 1983-84; Chuck Person, 1986-87; Rik Smits, 1988-89.

coin flip with Houston, which grabbed three–time College Player of the Year Ralph Sampson. A second first–round pick, Mitchell Wiggins (23rd overall), was dealt to Chicago for Sidney Lowe, later to become Minnesota's coach, and cash. Second–rounders Leroy Combs and Jim Thomas made the team and rookies Granville Waiters and Brooke Steppe were acquired in trades.

The latter deal sent Billy Knight away again. Only five players—Williams, Kellogg, Butch Carter, George Johnson, and Jerry Sichting—remained from 1982–83. And things began looking up: the Pacers improved by six wins to 26–56 and attendance more than doubled to 10,273. It was the first of four straight years of gains. The Pacers operated without a general manager in the first year of ownership by shopping center magnates Melvin and Herbert Simon.

At season's end in 1984, McKinney left as coach and three–year Pacers assistant and six–year

ABA player George Irvine moved from basketball operations vice–president to become coach. He brought in as assistant coach Donnie Walsh, Larry Brown's backcourt mate at North Carolina. (Walsh followed Brown for two years at Denver before being fired 20 games into the 1980–81 season and spending two–plus years in business.)

Olympic point guard Vern Fleming was the team's 1984 first–round choice. Second–rounders Devin Durrant and Stuart Gray made the team. Later picks Ralph Jackson (4th) and Kenton Edelin (7th) played one and 10 games, respectively. Dallas first–rounder Terence Stansbury and former Mavericks first–rounder Bill Garnett were acquired in exchange for a 1990 Pacer first.

1983 seventh–rounder Tony Brown made the team and, with Stipanovich, played in all 82 games. The nucleus of the Pacers became Kellogg and Williams, and Stipanovich with Fleming, joined by Thomas as a starter. The Pacers had a four–game sag to 22 wins. The highlight of the 1984–85 season was the Pacers hosting the NBA All–Star Weekend; the Saturday Legends Game and Slam–Dunk Contest at Market Square; and Sunday's All–Star Game at the Hoosierdome.

In 1985–86, Indiana improved four wins to 26–56 but came in last in the Central Division. Average attendance rose to 11,243 as the Pacers were still in play–off contention after a mid–March three–game winning streak. But 11 losses in 12 games in the season's last 25 days doomed them.

In the first year of the lottery, the Pacers again got second prize, Wayman Tisdale, while the Knicks got Patrick Ewing. Tisdale was a factor, since Clark Kellogg played just 19 games due to injury. Second–rounders Bill Martin and Dwayne McClain also made the team and contributed. No Pacers, however, appeared among the NBA stats leaders. Herb Williams was Indiana's top scorer (19.9) and rebounder (9.1).

Another Coaching Change

Irvine stepped down as coach after the 1985–86 season and returned to vice–president of basketball operations; Donnie Walsh became general manager. Jack Ramsay, who had been forced out at Portland, was quickly hired as head coach. Dick Harter came from Detroit and Dave Twardzik moved from Portland to join holdover Mel Daniels as assistants. The Pacers took Chuck Person with the fourth pick in the first round and Greg Dreiling in the second round. Clark Kellogg played only four games in his final season, but the Pacers improved with 15 wins to 41–41, finishing fourth in the Central Division.

They made the playoffs, but Atlanta trounced the Pacers in four games. Attendance again grew, to 12,683 per game, and Person led the scoring (18.8) and rebounding (8.3) to take the NBA Rookie of the Year Award and an All–Rookie Team berth. John Long, acquired from Seattle (Detroit had sent him to Detroit just a few days before) was the only officially ranked Pacer, sixth in free–throw percentage (.890).

In 1987 the Pacers selected UCLA's Reggie Miller at number 11 in the last seven–round NBA draft. Indiana also sent a second–rounder to the Milwaukee Bucks for point guard Scott Skiles, a Hoosier native.

Clark Kellogg's player career ended and he turned his full attention to working as a TV analyst. The starting Pacers crew was Chuck Person, Wayman Tisdale, Steve ("Stipo") Stipanovich, Vern Fleming, and John Long, with rookie Miller and Herb Williams as the first subs. Person led in scoring (17.0) and Stipo was the best board man (8.3). Long came in third (.907) in NBA foul shooting, with Williams eighth in blocked shots (1.95). Indiana slipped that season to 38–44 and attendance slid to 12,252.

1988–89 was a shambles although Donnie Walsh had become team president. After an 0–7 start, future Hall–of–Fame coach Jack Ramsay retired on a road trip. Mel Daniels finished the trip 0–2 and George Irvine took over on an interim basis when the team returned home. He was 6–21 before Dick Versace arrived from Detroit to go 22–31 as the team finished 28–54, last in the Central Division once.

Attendance dropped to 11,437 per game. The Pacers came up second in the lottery to start the year and got 7'4" Rik Smits, who Smits made the All–Rookie Team in the absence of Steve Stipanovich, who had played five solid seasons, but injured his knee in the off–season and never played again. Before the season, swing–man Ron Anderson was dealt to Philadelphia. As the trade deadline approached, the Pacers sent Wayman Tisdale and draft pick to the Kings for LaSalle Thompson and Randy Wittman, and Herb Williams to Dallas for Detlef Schrempf and a pick.

Person paced the scoring (21.6) and came in 18th in the NBA. Scott Skiles was third in free–throw accuracy (.903); Smits was 10th in blocked shots (1.84); and Reggie Miller 9th in three–point shooting (.402). Dick Versace drove the Pacers to a 42–40 mark, the team's first winning record since 1980–81, with 1989–90 his only full season as coach. The Pacers were fifth in the expanded Central Division and received the eighth playoff slot on a tie–breaker with Cleveland. Detroit bounced the Pacers in three straight by 12, 13, and 12 points.

Reggie Miller played in the 1990 All–Star Game, the Pacers' first selection since the merger season. Scott Skiles was lost to Orlando via expansion and Stuart Gray was traded to Charlotte. Miller soared to a career–high 24.6 points per game, 8th in the NBA. Detlef Schrempf began to develop as a "sixth man," or the fourth front–court player. George McCloud was the seventh player drafted in 1989 and played less than 10 minutes per game in 44 contests, trying to find a position.

Indiana got no help in the 1990 draft and made no trades. Many felt that the maturity of the players already on hand would be the key. With the team at 9–16, Dick Versace was fired and assistant Bob Hill as stand–in went 32–25 the rest of the way. The Pacers hit the 41–41 mark to stand fifth in the Central, gaining the 7th play–off seed; Indiana lost, 3–2, in a 124–121 fifth game in the Boston Garden with Chuck Person at his trash–talkingest vs. Larry Bird.

Reggie Miller was again the top scorer (22.6) and led the NBA in foul shooting (.918) over Jeff Malone (.917). Detlef Schrempf won his first of two straight Sixth Man of the Year awards, leading the Pacers in rebounding (8.0) and ranking second in minutes and field goal pct. The Pacers gained more than 1,000 in attendance to 12,618.

A final–day–of–the–season loss to Cleveland at home dropped the 1991–92 Pacers to 40–42 and tied with New Jersey for the East's sixth–best record, but the Nets won the tie–breaker. Boston then swept the Pacers 3–0 in 11, 7, and 4–point victories.

Schrempf repeated as Sixth Man of the Year, and was the team's top rebounder (9.6) and top field goal shooter (.536). Reggie Miller again led the team scoring (20.7), and Micheal Williams emerged as a top–rank point guard, finishing second in NBA steals (2.95) and eighth in assists (8.2). And, to top things off, Schrempf and Miller each turned in triple–doubles.

The Pacers had been 15–28 on January 25 and finished 25–14, similar to 1990–91's 24–16

AP/Wide World Photos

Reggie Miller

sprint to the finish. The 12,618 average attendance was the franchise's third best to date. First–round pick Dale Davis, a 6–10 forward, was a part of the top–eight rotation, but second–rounder Sean Green played only in spots.

General manager Donnie Walsh took a bold step a month before the opening of 1992–93's training camp when he dealt Chuck Person and Micheal Williams to the Timberwolves for Sam

Mitchell and Pooh Richardson, Reggie Miller's former UCLA backcourt partner. The Pacers had already drafted Malik Sealy at number 14 in the first round. Detlef Schrempf became a starter and appeared in the 1993 All–Star Game, the first European–born player to do so.

The Pacers, at 22–28 on February 15, used a 19–13 surge to finish 41–41 and tie for the East's 8th–best mark, but won a tie–breaker with Shaquille O'Neal's Orlando Magic. Once again the Pacers went out in the first round, this time to the Knicks, 3–1.

Coach Bob Hill received a contract extension early in the season with the Pacers winning, but was dumped after the season. (General manager Donnie Walsh's former North Carolina guard partner Larry Brown, who got his playing and coaching start in ABA cities, is set to take over in 1993–94 and completes the cycle of coaching each of the four ABA teams merged into the NBA in 1976.)

In 1992–93, Reggie Miller was 14th in NBA scoring (21.2) with a career–best 31.5 in the playoffs. He also was 7th in free throws (.880) and 13th in three–pointers (.399). Schrempf was 18th in NBA rebounding (9.5) while Dale Davis was third in field goal percentage (568) and 14th in blocks (1.80). Richardson ranked 11th in assists. Indiana set an all–time average attendance mark of more than 12,930. The next building block will be 6–10 center Scott Haskin, the Pacers' top pick in 1993's college draft..

SOURCES

BOOKS

Carter, Craig and Alex Sachare, *The Sporting News NBA Guide,* 1992–93 edition, The Sporting News, 1992.

Hollander, Zander, editor, *The Pro Basketball Encyclopedia,* Corwin Books, 1997.

Hollander, Zander, editor, *The NBA's Official Encyclopedia of Pro Basketball,* North American Library, 1981.

Hollander, Zander, and Alex Sachare, *The Official NBA Basketball Encyclopedia,* Villard Books, 1989.

Jares, Joe, *The American Game: A Rutledge Book,* Follett Publishing Co., 1971.

Nadel, Eric, *The Night Wilt Scored 100,* Taylor Publishing Co., 1990.

NBA Editorial Staff, *All–Star Weekend Guide,* NBA Publications, 1993.

Pluto, Terry, *Loose Balls: The Short, Wild Life of the American Basketball Association,* Simon & Schuster, 1990.

Pluto, Terry, *Tall Tales: The Glory Years of the NBA in the Words of the Men Who Played, Coached and Built Pro Basketball,* Simon & Schuster, 1992.

Ratermann, Dale, *Indiana Pacers 1992–93 Media Guide,* Indiana Pacers, 1992.

—Jack Pearson

MILWAUKEE BUCKS

Professional basketball and even the National Basketball Association (NBA) itself had existed in Milwaukee prior to the advent of the Milwaukee Bucks. As early as 1951, the vagabond Tri-City Blackhawks deserted their original locale (Moline and Rock Island, Illinois, and Davenport, Iowa—three adjacent cities along the Mississippi) and moved to the Wisconsin city, at which time they changed their name to "the Hawks."

They stayed in Milwaukee for four years, but the club was a perennial cellar-dweller, and attendance was correspondingly poor, so they moved again, this time to St. Louis. After calling this city home for a little more than a decade, they moved for the third time, to Atlanta, where they now reside.

During this period throughout the United States, pro basketball was catching fire in the public eye, and the city of Milwaukee was still among the have-nots.

In the late 1960s, a group headed by young entrepreneurial whiz Wesley Pavalon and Milwaukee businessman Marvin Fishman fought for and eventually won another NBA franchise. The franchise was awarded on January 22, 1968.

The group, which called itself Milwaukee Professional Sports and Services, Inc., named Pavalon its president and Fishman as its executive vice-president. Three months later Pavalon's title was upgraded to chairman of the board, making way for former University of Wisconsin basketball star Ray Patterson to become the team's new president.

Fishman became vice-chairman of the board, and at the same time, John Erickson, former head basketball coach for the University of Wisconsin, was named vice-president and general manager, and former NBA guard Larry Costello became the new head coach for the Milwaukee team. Tom Nissalke, an assistant coach at Tulane University in Louisiana, was named the club's assistant coach and chief scout.

Although the Milwaukee Bucks did not become a member of the NBA until 1968, the state of Wisconsin and the city of Milwaukee did have representation in professional basketball and the NBA long before that. During the 1930s, an organization called the American Basketball League (ABL) operated for a number of years. One of its key teams was a club from Oshkosh, Wisconsin, called the All-Stars. The league folded and was succeeded by another—the National Basketball League (NBL). This latter league was formed by Lonnie Darling, who had operated the Oshkosh team in the ABL. Oshkosh then became a member of the NBL.

In the years following, the majority of the teams in the NBL were from small, Midwestern communities. In addition to Oshkosh, they included Anderson, Flint, Youngstown, Toledo, the Tri-Cities, Fort Wayne, Dayton, and Waterloo, and larger cities such as Chicago, Detroit, Minneapolis, Denver, and Syracuse. But the NBL also went bankrupt.

With the end of World War II and the creation of the National Basketball Association (NBA) in 1946, a number of Midwestern cities had franchises for short periods, including Sheboygan, Wisconsin, in the 1949-50 season, and Milwaukee, for four years beginning with the 1951-52 campaign. The Tri-City Blackhawks changed their name to the Hawks when they moved to Milwaukee. Unfortunately, the Hawks finished last in their division in each of their four years there before dwindling interest and low attendance precipitated the club's move to St. Louis in 1955.

Had the Hawks managed to stick it out for just one more year in Milwaukee, the entire future of the NBA may well have been quite different: Although the Hawks did finish last in their final year in Milwaukee, the club had a number of good, young players who would form the nucleus of the powerful St. Louis Hawks in years to come. On their roster that last year in Wisconsin was Bob Pettit, who was named the Rookie of the Year that season, and Frank Selvy. In the '54-'55 season, the two were among the league's top five scorers. After the '67-'68 season, the Hawks packed their bags in St. Louis and moved to Atlanta, Georgia. But if the Hawks had stayed in Milwaukee and been as successful as they would become in St. Louis, the creation of the Bucks franchise 14 years later might never have come to pass.

Bucks Joined the NBA in '68 Expansion

Prior to 1968, only 12 teams—Baltimore, Boston, Cincinnati, Detroit, New York, and Philadelphia in the Eastern Division, and Atlanta, Chicago, Los Angeles, San Diego, San Francisco, and Seattle in the West—were members of the NBA. The addition of Milwaukee and another expansion team, Phoenix, brought the total to 14. By the early 1990s, the NBA would become a 27-team league.

In April of 1968, the as-yet-unnamed Milwaukee team made Charlie Paulk of Northeastern State College in Oklahoma its first draft choice. The 6'8" Paulk had been an alternate on the 1968 U.S. Olympic team. Milwaukee next participated in the league's expansion draft, selecting 18 players from a pool supplied by the loop's 12 existing teams. The other expansion franchise—Phoenix—also took part in the draft. Among Milwaukee's selections were four players who were to contribute significantly to the first year team—forward Lenny Chappell, center Wayne Embry, and guards Jon McGlocklin and Guy Rodgers. Two days later, the college draft was conducted, and in addition to Paulk, Milwaukee picked two more players who were also to play a role in the coming season—Greg Smith and Sam Williams.

On May 22, the team finally got its name, the Milwaukee Bucks, after a community-wide name

TEAM INFORMATION AT A GLANCE

Founding date: 1968.

Home court:
The Bradley Center
1001 North Fourth St.
Milwaukee, WI 53203-1312
Phone: (414) 227-0500

Seating capacity: 20,000
Team colors: Green and white
Team nickname: Bucks

Franchise record	Won	Lost	Pct.
(1968-93)	1192	858	.581

League championships (1): 1970-71
Conference first-place finishes (2): 1970-71 and 1973-74
Division first-place finishes (12): 1970-71, 1971-72, 1972-73, 1973-74, 1975-76,
and 1979-80 (in the Midwest Division); 1980-81, 1981-82, 1982-83, 1983-84, 1984-85,
and 1985-86 (in the Central Division)

selection contest. More than 14,000 fans participated in the process, with R.D. Trebeleax of Whitefish Bay, one of 45 people who had put forth the name "Bucks," chosen as the winner. He was selected over the other 44 because of the reason for his choice: "Bucks are spirited, good jumpers, fast and agile." His prize was a new automobile.

On October 16, before a crowd of 8,467 at the Milwaukee Arena—a crowd that included NBA Commissioner Walter Kennedy—the Bucks played their first regular season game. Unfortunately, it was an 84-89 loss to the Chicago Bulls. Milwaukee's first win came in their 6th game, 134-118 over the Detroit Pistons, on October 31. The Bucks went on to win 27 games and averaged 7,246 for 34 Arena games. (The price of a courtside ticket at the Arena back in 1968 was only $7.)

Prior to the season opener, Milwaukee acquired rookie center Dick Cunningham from Phoenix, and then during the year traded for Flynn Robinson, Don Smith, and Rich Niemann. Robinson averaged 20.3 points a game as a Buck and was voted the outstanding Milwaukee player by local fans. McGlocklin actually scored the most points for the team, 1,570, on a 19.6 average, and was the only Buck to be chosen to play in the NBA All-Star game in January of 1969.

Besides Robinson and McGlocklin, other Bucks who played major roles in that initial campaign included forward Fred Hetzel, who averaged 15.9 points per game in 53 contests before being traded to Cincinnati for strong rebounder Don Smith in January; forward Len Chappell, who muscled in 14.6 a game for his new club; center Wayne Embry, who jammed home 13.1 points per game; swingman Dave Gambee, who added an average 12.1 points in 34 games before being traded in January to Detroit for Rich Niemann;

guard Guy Rodgers, who led the team in assists; and forward Greg Smith, also known as "Captain Marvel," who at only 6'5" was the team's top rebounder. Paulk, the club's top college draft choice, played in only 17 games before leaving for U.S. military duty on December 13.

Included in the 27 Buck wins in 1968-69 were six victories in eight games against co-expansion club Phoenix; four wins in six games against the established Detroit Pistons; six wins in a row in February against Los Angeles, Atlanta, Detroit, Phoenix, San Diego, and Baltimore; a hard fought 114-110 win over NBA champion Boston at the Milwaukee Arena on January 12; and then three wins in their last four games, all on the road.

Oscar Robertson

Milwaukee Gets Abdul-Jabbar

The Bucks finished last in their division, as did Phoenix in theirs. Those last place finishes, however, made the Bucks and the Suns the two teams that would participate in what became the most famous coin flip in sports history. The toss was for the rights to superstar Lew Alcindor of the powerful UCLA Bruins. (Alcindor later changed his name to Kareem Abdul-Jabbar).

On Wednesday, March 19, 1969, Commissioner Kennedy himself handled the flip. Phoenix chose heads, and the coin came up tails. Milwaukee had won the rights to the greatest basketball player of the era. Big Lew made his debut in a Milwaukee uniform on June 22 in an intersquad game before a packed house—10,482—at the Arena.

He became an instant star, teaming with McGlocklin, Robinson, Bobby Dandridge and the rest to lead the club from the cellar up to a runner-up spot in the East. Alcindor's 28.8 scoring average was second in the league, and he led the Bucks in rebounding and blocked shots. Robinson was tops in assists.

The Bucks won 56 and lost 26, then defeated Philadelphia in the first round of the play-offs before bowing out in five games against a strong New York Knicks team in the next round. Alcin-

dor was named Rookie of the Year and made the NBA All-Star squad, the latter honor also accorded to Robinson.

1970-71 World Champions

Following the season, Milwaukee was involved in a blockbuster of a trade, obtaining the services of perennial All-Star guard Oscar Robertson from Cincinnati for Flynn Robinson and Charlie Paulk. A few months later, just prior to the opening of the '70-'71 season, sparkplug Lucius Allen and Bob Boozer were acquired from Seattle for reserve center Don Smith.

With Abdul-Jabbar as center, Greg Smith and Bobby Dandridge as forwards, and Oscar Robertson and Jon McGlocklin as guards, the third year Bucks completely outclassed the competition in their own division, winning 66 while losing only 16. In so doing they set six NBA marks: home wins, 34; road wins, 28; winning streak, 20; field goal percentage, .509; total field goals, 3,972; and total assists, 2,749. Abdul-Jabbar led the league in

| KAREEM | The Inimitable |

Few teams—perhaps only the Celtics and the Lakers—can boast of as many superstars in their history as the Milwaukee Bucks. But the biggest of these was the incomparable center Kareem Abdul-Jabbar.

Abdul-Jabbar went by his birth name, Lew Alcindor, until 1971. At UCLA, he became one of the most acclaimed college basketball players of all time, not only winning All-American honors in each of his three years with the Bruins, but also leading the California school to three NCAA Championships in a row, an achievement never before accomplished.

Alcindor won Rookie of the Year honors when he became a Buck, scoring a phenomenal 28.8 points per game for Milwaukee—the best a rookie in the NBA could boast. In the process, he turned the 27-55 expansion club Bucks into a 56-26 powerhouse in just one year.

Big Lew changed his name to Kareem Abdul-Jabbar soon after that and put in a total of six magnificent years with Milwaukee before asking to be traded to Los Angeles following the '74-'75 season. In those six years, Abdul-Jabbar scored a total of 14,211 points, averaging 30.4 points a game, and pulling down 7,161 rebounds—all still Bucks records. He was chosen to the NBA All-star team every year and was selected the Most Valuable Player in the league three times.

Abdul-Jabbar went on to play 14 more seasons in the NBA—all with the Lakers—winning three more league MVP awards, leading the Lakers to five NBA Championships. For his entire career, he scored a total of 38,387 regular season points for a 24.6 average, adding 5,762 more in the play-offs and 251 more in NBA All-Star game action.

scoring with 31.7 average and was named the NBA's Most Valuable Player.

In the ensuing play-offs, the Bucks swept by San Francisco and Los Angeles, and then overwhelmed Baltimore in four straight for the World Championship. During the 1970-71 season, the Milwaukee team had climbed farther and faster than any other expansion club in the history of professional sports.

The next year saw the Bucks again dominating the Midwest Division, winning 63 and dropping 19. It was the third straight division championship for the young Bucks. Abdul-Jabbar repeated as MVP and scoring champ, this time with a 34.8 average. During the same year attorney William Alverson was named the new president of the Bucks, and former NBA standout Wayne Embry became the club's general manager.

Injuries, however, played a factor in the Bucks attempt to repeat as champs, with Robertson out for several games. Milwaukee topped Golden State (SF) in five games before bowing to a powerful Los Angeles Laker squad in six. During the year, Abdul-Jabbar set a single game scoring mark, pumping in 55 against the Boston Celtics on December 10. He and Robertson were again named to the NBA All-Star team.

Throughout the '72-'73 season, the Bucks continued their torrid pace, winning 60 games. It was the first time an NBA team had ever won 60 or more for three consecutive years. The club stumbled in the first play-off series, however, losing to the Golden State club in six games.

The Bucks just missed making it four in a row the next year, posting a 59-23 record, but again winning their division. Abdul-Jabbar was responsible for a number of unforgettable accomplishments, among them that famous 15-foot hook shot with only seconds remaining to beat the Celtics in the sixth game of the NBA championships. It became known in the world of sports as "the shot heard 'round the world." Unfortunately, the Bucks couldn't follow up on that effort and lost in the finals to the Celtics.

In all of those early years, the "Voice of the Bucks" was the irrepressible little dynamo Eddie Doucette. Whenever Abdul-Jabbar would score, especially on one of his long hook shots, Doucette would scream into the mike, "Kareem-ABDUL—JABBAR!" in a rising, gleeful crescendo. And since Abdul-Jabbar was doing a considerable bit of scoring in those days, there was a good deal of screaming as well.

Losses in the Mid-1970s and the Departure of Abdul-Jabbar

During '74-'75, the Bucks endured a frustrating season. A pre-season broken hand kept Abdul-Jabbar sidelined for the first 16 games of the season, during which the rest of the squad fell flat and managed only three wins, putting them far behind their Midwest Division rivals. With Robertson retired, the Bucks had traded Lucius Allen to Los Angeles for sharpshooter Jim Price, but Price too fell victim to the injury bug and missed the last half of the season.

Milwaukee finished with a losing 38-44 record, their first since their opening season. The Bucks had lost 18 of those games by five points or fewer, 11 by three points or fewer. Abdul-Jabbar again topped 30 points per game and made both the NBA All-Star team and the All-Defensive team. Price and Dandridge also made the All-Star squad.

An even bigger problem than those injuries and the close losses faced the Milwaukee club, however. Abdul-Jabbar, who had two years remaining on his contract, nevertheless wanted out. He wanted to play in either New York or Los Angeles, and by virtue of his status as the premier player in the league, managed to get his way.

On June 16, 1975, the Bucks executed the best trade that they could put together for their superstar, sending him and reserve center Walt Wesley to the Los Angeles Lakers for center Elmore Smith, guard Brian Winters, and two All-American rookies, forward Dave Meyers and swingman Junior Bridgeman.

Naismith Memorial Basketball Hall of Fame

Bob Lanier

Winters, Meyers, and Smith became starters almost at once, and Bridgeman developed into one of the league's best "Sixth Man" players, but the club continued to founder, repeating that 38-44 record in '75-'76 and falling to 30-52 in '76-'77. During that second season, the Bucks underwent a major shakeup within the organization. After only 18 games, Costello resigned as head coach and assistant Don Nelson, a former Boston Celtic, took over the reins.

Other changes in the team's management structure came about when a group headed by James Fitzgerald, William Blake, and J. P. Cullen purchased 361,000 shares of Milwaukee Sports and Services (the organization that owned the Bucks) common stock. Fitzgerald became chairman of the board and president of the new corporation; Wayne Embry, formerly the general manager, became a consultant; and John Steinmiller, formerly the team's public relations director, was promoted to director of business operations.

HALL OF FAME	Oscar Robertson and Bob Lanier

Kareem Abdul-Jabbar is not in the NBA Hall of Fame yet; a player must be retired for five years before he can become eligible, so the big guy still has to wait. But the Bucks do have representation in the Hall: Oscar Robertson, elected in 1979; Bob Lanier, named in the spring of '92; as well as "Little" Nate Archibald, who played for the Bucks for one season ('83-'84), and Dave Cowens, who also played for Milwaukee for only one year ('82-'83), both of whom were elected in 1991.

Oscar Robertson compiled the bulk of his playing time before his years as a Milwaukee Buck. Nonetheless, "the Big O" contributed four outstanding seasons to Milwaukee that were most significant. His acquisition by the Bucks in a momentous April 21, 1970 trade sent Flynn Robinson and Charlie Paulk to Cincinnati and made Milwaukee's one and only NBA Championship possible.

During the four years that the Big O wore the Milwaukee green, the Bucks averaged 62 wins a year, totaling 248 victories and only 80 losses for an incredible .768 winning percentage. Robertson's scoring production with the Bucks was not on the level of his earlier years with Cincinnati but was still a respectable 19.4 for the '70-'71 season—and 17.4, 15.5, and 12.7 in the next three years before he announced his retirement.

For his entire NBA career—both in Cincinnati and Milwaukee—Robertson amassed 26,710 points for a 25.7 average and handed out 9,887 assists. When he called it quits as a player in '74, only one player, Wilt Chamberlain, had scored more points, and no one had come close to his assist total. Even today, only three NBA greats, Kareem Abdul-Jabbar, Chamberlain, and Elvin Hayes, have higher scoring totals, and only Magic Johnson has made more assists.

Robertson's total number of assists—668 in '70-'71 season alone—remains a Bucks record. The Big O was chosen to the NBA All-Star team as well as the All-NBA team at the end of Milwaukee's World Championship year. In his entire career, he was an All-Star 11 times. Today Robertson operates a construction company in Cincinnati.

The "Dobber," as Bob Lanier used to be called, spends more time these days on the golf course than he ever did on the basketball floor. (A tremendous belter, he smacks a golf ball farther than most pro golfers do.) When he retired from basketball at the end of the '83-'84 season, he had amassed a total of 19,249 points in regular season NBA play. At that time, there were less than a dozen players in the history of the league who had scored more. In addition, the Dobber was the only Milwaukee Buck to make the NBA All-Star team for the '81- '82 season.

During the nine years he was with Detroit, Lanier scored better than 21 points per game for eight straight years: 25.7, 23.8, 22.5, 24, 21.3, 25.3, 24.5, and 23.6. For his entire 14 years in the NBA, his overall average was 20.3.

Lanier is now the National Chairman of the NBA Stay in School Program for youngsters. He is also the primary color analyst for NBA Radio. An eight time NBA All-Star, today he operates Bob Lanier Enterprises, a promotional marketing firm in Milwaukee.

At the end of the year, the Bucks had obtained Cleveland's top draft choice, Marques Johnson, and with two first round draft choices of their own picked up Indiana center Kent Benson and Tennessee forward Ernie Grunfeld. John Killilea, once a scout for the Bucks and more recently an assistant coach with the Boston Celtics, joined Nelson's staff as an assistant coach and director of player personnel.

Attendance figures proved that the team's popularity with the fans was continuing. For example, in the '78-'79 season, Coach Nelson's third, the team had another of those 38-44 records but set a club attendance mark of 443,926—including 32 sellouts—for an overall 99 percent of capacity mark.

But Nelson's start with the Bucks was anything but auspicious. After succeeding Costello early in the '76-'77 season, Nellie's contribution to that forgettable season was a 27-37 mark. With the help of new draft choices Marques Johnson, Kent Benson, and Ernie Grunfeld, however, Nelson brought the team back to winning ways in '77-'78 with a 44-38 record, but then sank back to 38-44 the following season, the third time in their short history the Bucks were to post that win-loss total. In the play-offs that year, they topped Phoenix in the first round before bowing in seven games to Denver.

In '79-'80, with the mid-year acquisition of NBA scoring great Bob Lanier and rookie guard Sidney Moncrief, the Nelson-led Bucks rebounded to a 49-33 winning mark. It was to be the first of eight consecutive winning seasons for the Bucks and Coach Nelson, a span in which the club averaged nearly 54 wins a season and won seven Midwest Division crowns in a row.

Although the Bucks won 60 games in '80-'81—the fourth time they had reached that plateau and only the 19th time that it had been done in the league—the team lost to Philadelphia in the first round of the play-offs. The scenario was virtually repeated in '81-'82, as Milwaukee posted a 55-27 record, and then again lost to Philly in the first round of post-season play.

Problems in the Play-Offs

During the late 1970s and early 1980s, the Bucks were always one of the top three or four clubs in the NBA—but always faltered in the early rounds of play-off competition. Pacing the Milwaukee club on the court in all of those years were Marques Johnson and Sidney Moncrief, All-Star and All-NBA team selections virtually every year.

Milwaukee's regular season win-loss effort dropped slightly in '82-'83 to 51-31, but Nellie's

squad did manage to sweep the Boston Celtics in four games in the first round of the play-offs before falling to Philadelphia again, 4-1, in the second round. In '83-'84 after a 50-32 regular season effort, the Bucks beat Atlanta and New Jersey in the first two rounds before losing to the Celtics in the Conference Finals.

In a major trade in September of 1984, the Bucks sent the popular Marques Johnson, Junior Bridgeman, and Harvey Catchings to the L.A. Clippers for Terry Cummings, Craig Hodges, and Ricky Pierce. The Bucks improved to 59-23 during the '84-'85 season, finishing more than a dozen games ahead of the second-place Pistons in the Midwest Division.

At home, Milwaukee set a club record with a stellar 36-5 mark. After beating Chicago in the first round, the Bucks were swept in four by Philadelphia in the second round.

Johnson was plagued with back problems in the latter years of his career, spending three seasons with the Clippers and the part of a fourth with the San Francisco Warriors before retiring in 1990. Terry Cummings, Johnson's replacement as the Bucks' premier forward, put in five productive years with Milwaukee from the '84-'85 season through '88-'89, averaging an overall 21.7, a pace topped only by Abdul-Jabbar in Buck history.

Ricky Pierce, another Clipper who came to Milwaukee in the Johnson-Cummings trade in '84 became one of the game's most feared Sixth Men. Playing in a total of 421 games for the Bucks in seven seasons from '84-'85 through '90-'91, he started in only 42 of them, none in his last two years with the team.

Despite this, Pierce led Milwaukee in scoring over those last two seasons. His .866 free throw average has been topped by only two other Bucks, Jack Sikma and Flynn Robinson, and he is also fifth in the Bucks all-time field goal average totals. Pierce won the NBA's coveted Sixth Man Award in '87 and '90. He was traded to Seattle for Dale Ellis prior to the '91-'92 season and became the Supersonics' top scorer.

Overall, throughout the early to mid-1980s, the Bucks were winning more than all except three

PROFILES	More NBA Greats Who Played for Milwaukee

Six-foot-six Bobby Dandridge, who toiled for the Bucks for nine years from '69-'70 through '81-'82, averaged 18.6 points per game as a Buck, and in three seasons topped 20. On the all-time Milwaukee statistics lists in just about all categories, Bobby D. is third in total points scored, second in rebounds, third in games played, and first in total minutes played at 22,094. No Buck has ever been on the court more.

Two other NBA greats who will surely be in the league's Hall of Fame someday are Jack Sikma and Moses Malone. Sikma spent the last five years of his career with Milwaukee, from '86-'87 through '90-'91, averaging 13.4 points and developing into one of the league's top free-throwers at better than .900 two years in a row. He also became one of the league's top three-point scorers, hitting 82 of 216 attempts in '88-'89 and 68 of 199 the following year. Sikma has the highest Buck free throw career average at .884, and the third-highest three-point career average, both highly unusual achievements for a center.

Among the all-time top scorers for the NBA, Moses Malone stands behind only Abdul-Jabbar and Wilt Chamberlain. Big Mo played for a number of teams before coming to Milwaukee for the '91-'92 season: Houston for six years, followed by four more with Philadelphia, two with Washington, and three with Atlanta.

A couple of other prolific NBA scorers also played briefly with Milwaukee. Adrian Dantley, ninth on the all-time league scoring list, played his final year with the Bucks in '90-'91; and Alex English, seventh on the list, was drafted second by the team in 1976 and played for them for two years as a reserve before becoming a free agent in 1978. He later signed with Indiana, then was traded by that team to Denver, where he became one of the league's top scorers for more than 10 years. He was one the Bucks let get away.

NBA Hall of Famers "Little" Nate Archibald and Dave Cowens each played one season with the Bucks during their career. And lanky Paul Pressey, who was drafted by the Bucks in the first round in '82 and was with them for eight years, still holds the Bucks' lifetime record for assists, with 3,272.

One final name: Mike Dunleavy, the team's current coach, concluded an 11-year NBA playing career with Milwaukee, playing for the Bucks in a spot role during the '83-'84 to '89-'90 seasons, when he was an assistant coach. Although he appeared in only 43 games during those four seasons, scrappy Mike demonstrated an uncanny shooting eye, putting in exactly half of his field goal attempts and coming up with a .831 free throw percentage. In the '83-'84 season, he also pumped in 19 of 45 three pointers for a terrific .402 average.

or four teams in the league and were playing before enthusiastic crowds at home games in the Arena. But, in the hectic world of modern day sports, fortunes and situations can change quickly. The success of professional franchises in all sports had become more and more measured not by wins, losses, and championships, but by profit and loss statements.

Here they were, on the one hand playing before packed houses—some of the most faithful, adoring fans anywhere—and on the other fighting a losing battle to stay afloat financially, being located in one of the smallest television markets of all NBA cities and playing in one of the smallest and oldest arenas.

And so the financial picture, coupled with the significant number of cities across the land seeking NBA franchises, made the possibility of the Bucks leaving Milwaukee for greener pastures much closer than anyone realized.

A Change in Ownership

On March 1, 1985, influential Milwaukee businessman Herb Kohl stepped forward and purchased the team. A long-time Milwaukee sports booster and close friend of Milwaukee Brewers baseball team owner Bud Selig, Kohl had political as well as business pull in the area. His savvy and status (he later became a state senator) helped to save the team and keep it in Milwaukee. Former Milwaukee mayor Henry Maier noted: "Mr. Kohl is a local man with deep roots in the Milwaukee community. His purchase has alleviated our fears that we would lose the Bucks. We can rest assured now that the team will remain in the city."

At about the same time that the purchase of the Milwaukee franchise by Kohl was taking place, two other Milwaukeeans, Jane and Lloyd Pettit, announced their intention to pay for the creation of a magnificent new sports arena, the total cost of which eventually reached $71 million.

The new facility, which was to be called the Bradley Center, in honor of Mrs. Pettit's late father, Milwaukee industrialist Harry Bradley. Today the Bradley Center is considered one of the most beautiful and functional arenas in the entire NBA.

The '85-'86 and '86-'87 seasons, in which the Bucks were to finish 57-25 and 50-32, respectively, were Coach Nelson's last with the team. After completion of the '86-'87 campaign, the popular Nelson resigned and was replaced by assistant coach Del Harris. That year the club made it all the way to the conference finals before bowing out in four straight against Boston.

Under Del Harris in '87-'88, Milwaukee recorded its ninth straight winning season, albeit barely, posting a 42-40 mark. In the play-offs, the Bucks lost to Atlanta in a five-game series in the first round.

In '88-'89, Harris's second season at the helm, the club improved its regular season performance, taking 49 wins and 32 losses. During the season Milwaukee became the top free throw shooting team in league history, posting a team .8207 average.

First Draft Choice: Overrated?

Every spring during the annual NBA College Draft, a great deal of hoopla is invariably made over each club's number one pick. To be selected for such an honor today virtually guarantees a player instant millionaire status. Historically, however, a surprisingly small percentage of each club's primary selections actually fulfill expectations. Most quickly fall by the wayside and are forgotten.

The Bucks' success—or lack of success—in their own 24 drafts between 1968 and 1991 bears this out. Gary Freeman, Collis Jones, Russell Lee, Gary Brokaw, Clyde Mayes, and George Johnson were all Bucks number one picks prior to 1980. And in the '80s, Milwaukee's top choices included such players as Alton Lister, Randy Breuer, Kenny Fields, Jerry Reynolds, and Scott Skiles. A few of them developed into journeymen performers, but none became truly outstanding.

Several Bucks number one picks who did achieve stardom, however, include Lew Alcindor (who became Kareem Abdul-Jabbar), Quinn Buckner, Sidney Moncrief, and Paul Pressey.

With a much larger attendance area in the Bradley Center, the Bucks set a new attendance record with an average home crowd of 17,097, including 20 sellouts. In the play-offs, Milwaukee topped Atlanta in the first round, then lost to a strong Detroit Piston squad.

As the decade closed with the '89-'90 season, the Bucks were decimated by injuries, losing an alarming total of 235 player games to injury. The team finished third in their division with a 44-38 record.

In both the '88-'89 and '89-'90 seasons, the club was eliminated from play-off competition in the first round, which was a factor in Harris's resignation 17 games into the '91-'92 campaign.

But Harris's replacement, Frank Hamblen, had little luck with the Milwaukee club. It came as little surprise when he was relieved as head coach at the end of the season.

AP/Wide World Photo

Sidney Moncrief (4)

Mike Dunleavy Revamps the Team

Bucks owner Herb Kohl favored Mike Dunleavy, a former Bucks assistant, as his new head coach. Dunleavy had been the head coach for the Los Angeles Lakers for two years, and few felt Milwaukee had much of a chance of luring him away from the California club. The offer of a multi-million dollar, eight-year contract did the trick. It also helped that Dunleavy had greatly admired the Bucks organization and the city of Milwaukee.

Dunleavy inherited an aging, slow team that was doing little more than growing older and slower. It was expected that the new coach would make changes, but no one could have envisioned the extent of those changes. As of the first of July, the Bucks' drafting, trading, and cutting of players had resulted in the biggest single season turnover in the history of the team.

Of the 12 players on the Milwaukee roster at the end of the '91-'92 season, six were gone—Dale Ellis, via a trade to San Antonio; guards Jay Humphries and Larry Krystkowiak, swapped to the Utah Jazz; and Jeff Grayer, Brad Lohaus, and Steve Henson, all released. Still on the roster were aging veterans Moses Malone, at 37, and Dan Shayes, at 33, forwards Frank Brickowski and Fred Roberts, and guards Alvin Robertson and Lester Conner.

The new players included forward Anthony Avent, who played in Italy in 1991; current Buck draft picks Todd Day and Lee Mayberry, both guards from the University of Arkansas; Alaa Aldelnaby, a third year forward-center obtained from Portland in a three-way transaction between Milwaukee, San Antonio, and Portland; and guards Blue Edwards and Eric Murdock, both from Utah.

—Jack Pearson

ORLANDO MAGIC

The Orlando Magic has introduced Central Florida to a form of entertainment that does not wear big ears or dive through colored hoops. The Magic, one of four National Basketball Association teams introduced in 1987, has targeted as its audience not the legions of tourists that flock to Disney World and Sea World, but the permanent residents of this well-known Florida vacation destination. Indeed, despite the team's expected slow start after its debut in 1989, the Magic has reaped fan support from throughout most of Florida and—since 1992—has won a national audience on the strength of the on-court exploits of young Orlando star Shaquille O'Neal.

The Magic team's financial success has been most strongly influenced by president and general manager Pat Williams. An executive in professional basketball most of his life, Williams was a founder and former part-owner of the Magic. Today he charts the team's course and is known throughout the NBA as the engineer of numerous creative promotional gimmicks hatched to lure fans to the fledgling franchise. At a time when the Magic was losing three games to every one it won—in classic expansion franchise fashion—Williams filled Orlando Arena for every home game with a philosophy he inherited from former big-league baseball owner Bill Veeck. "When the crowd goes out to get in their cars and fight the traffic, all they're taking with them other than a program or maybe a cap or a T-shirt is a memory," Williams told *Florida Trend* magazine. "It's either a good memory or a bad memory. If it's an unpleasant memory, they're probably not going back. If it's a good memory, they'll be back. We are in the memory business."

Business has never been better. Just a year after the franchise was purchased for some $40 million, it was said to be worth more than $50 million—and climbing. The Magic has a cable and local television deal for broadcasting games that ranks among the very best in the NBA, and season ticket sales reach 10,000 annually, accounting for two out of every three seats in Orlando Arena.

The quest for an NBA franchise for Orlando began in 1985. Local real estate developer Jim Hewitt decided to try to bring big-league sports to central Florida, a region with an ever-growing population of wealthy retirees and support staff for the massive tourist industry. Hewitt approached Williams, who was at that time the respected general manager of the Philadelphia 76ers. Although Williams could have stayed in Philadelphia—he had helped to engineer the 76ers' 1983 national championship—he chose to accept the challenge offered in Florida. He and Hewitt began to assemble a package of financing that would meet the approval of the NBA Expansion Committee.

Together Williams and Hewitt put together a 32-investor syndicate of people willing to help buy a team. Such methods of team acquisition are not terribly rare, but the NBA prefers a strong commitment from at least one investor. In due course, those interested in bringing basketball to Orlando were able to secure that one major investor—William duPont III, a Florida real estate magnate. William duPont agreed to head a limited partnership and contributed $9 million in cash toward the $32 million purchase price of the team.

The NBA Expansion Committee had stipulated that cities interested in purchasing a franchise should provide a state-of-the-art sports arena, preferably new, as well as advance season ticket sales of 10,000. By October 3, 1986—some six months before the franchise was even awarded to Orlando—the region had sold its 10,000 season tickets. Plans were also under way for the construction of the $100 million Orlando Arena. The name "Orlando Magic" was chosen as winner in a "name that team" contest that drew more than 4,000 entries.

Orlando was one of four cities awarded an NBA franchise on April 22, 1987. Two of the four new teams—the Charlotte Hornets and the Miami Heat—began regular season play in 1988. Orlando and the Minnesota Timberwolves, based in Minneapolis, entered the league in 1989 after an ex-

AP/Wide World Photos

Shaquille O'Neal

pansion draft in the summer of that year. Pat Williams became the team president and general manager when he sold his ownership interest in the club. He was joined in the front office by Marlin Ferrell, John Gabriel, and the Magic's first head coach, Matt Guokas.

On expansion draft day, June 12, 1989, the Magic won the coin toss. Orlando chose to pick before Minnesota in the expansion draft and after them in the college draft. The Magic's draft selections included forward Sidney Green, guard Reggie Theus, forward Terry Catledge, guard Sam Vincent, guard/forward Otis Smith, guard Scott Skiles, and guard/forward Jerry Reynolds. The team's first pick in the college draft a week later was 6'6" forward Nick Anderson from the University of Illinois. Anderson was joined some time later by forward Michael Ansley from the University of Alabama.

The Magic made its regular season debut on November 4, 1989, in an extravagant home opener against the New Jersey Nets. Catledge scored 25 points in the game, but the Magic lost, 111-106. Orlando went on to post an 18-64 record for the

TEAM INFORMATION AT A GLANCE

Founding date: April 22, 1987

Home court:
Orlando Arena
One Magic Place
Orlando, FL 32801
Phone: (407) 649-3200
FAX: (407) 839-3479

Seating capacity: 15,077 for basketball

Team colors: White, blue, black and silver
Team nickname: Magic
Logo: Silver star with white-and-black border

Franchise record (1989-93)	Won	Lost
	111	217

1989-90 regular season. If the team failed to win consistently, it did not lack for home attendance. All but one game in the inaugural season sold out, and the trend continued into 1990-91 despite Orlando's 31-51 record. While other struggling expansion franchises made coaching changes, the Magic retained Guokas through the team's first four seasons—and Orlando showed gradual improvement throughout the period. In June of 1993, Guokas was promoted to vice president of basketball development for the Magic, and former assistant coach Brian Hill took over the head coaching duties.

The spark that ignited Magic fever throughout America was kindled in November of 1992 when rookie sensation Shaquille O'Neal joined the Magic. The seven-foot, 300-pound O'Neal literally achieved superstardom before he even took the court in the NBA. Merchandisers loved his on-court aggression and off-court gentleness. Before his rookie season was over, O'Neal could be seen on television endorsing the usual round of athletic footwear, soft drinks, and apparel. His presence on the Magic helped the team to achieve the NBA's most improved won-loss record in 1992-93.

Williams continues to promote the Magic tirelessly, but now that the "honeymoon" is over in Central Florida his emphasis has changed. Where once local fans had been satisfied to experience NBA basketball—win or lose—they are now expressing a desire for a championship contender. Williams has made moves to bring that level of play to Orlando. In 1993 he stirred controversy by trading top draft pick Chris Webber to the Golden State Warriors for future first-round draft picks in 1996, 1998, and 2000, as well as highly-touted rookie guard Anfernee Hardaway. The Magic also stand to reap two first-round picks from the Los Angeles Clippers in upcoming years.

Williams hopes to combine those draft picks with current talented players on the squad such as Anderson, Scott Skiles, and Dennis Scott to surround O'Neal with the supporting cast he needs as he moves into his prime.

In 1990, owner duPont told *Florida Trend* that his management staff would build a successful team, one that made regular playoff appearances. "We wouldn't have the franchise if it was going to be anything other than wildly successful, because the NBA wasn't going to allow any weak-sister expansion franchises," he said.

In 1991 duPont turned the principal team ownership over to the DeVos family—better known as the owners of Amway. Orlando Magic chairman Rich DeVos and his children plan to take the same philosophy of rapid growth by excellence into their period of team ownership. The Magic has its sights set on bringing a big gold trophy to the town of Disney delights..

SOURCES

PERIODICALS

Florida Trend, May 1990.
New York Times Magazine, November 15, 1992.

—*Anne Janette Johnson*

Western Conference

Midwest Division

CHARLOTTE HORNETS

Few areas of the country can boast more avid basketball fans than North Carolina, home state of Michael Jordan, the Duke Blue Devils, the ubiquitous Tar Heels, and now the Charlotte Hornets of the National Basketball Association. Charlotte, a city with less than a half million in population, won an expansion franchise in the NBA in 1988 and quickly set league attendance records for home games at spacious Charlotte Coliseum. Hornets fans come to games from a wide region that encompasses both Carolinas and southern Virginia, a populous area long addicted to competitive basketball.

The announcement by the NBA Board of Governors on April 22, 1987, awarding Charlotte a franchise was the dream come true of local millionaire businessman George Shinn. A man of impoverished background who had made a fortune from a chain of proprietary schools, real estate development, auto sales, writing, and consulting, Shinn had ties to other minor league professional sports franchises but longed for a major league team for his city. After attempts to lure a United States Football League club failed in the mid-1980s, he turned to basketball. By May of 1985 Shinn was committed to bringing an NBA team to North Carolina.

The enthusiastic young owner-to-be had little trouble convincing NBA executives that the region could support a franchise. College basketball is a huge business in the state, as students, alumni, and local supporters fill the arenas for Atlantic Coast Conference contests between such powerhouses as Duke, North Carolina, Wake Forest, and North Carolina State. Shinn was also able to sweeten his sales pitch with an attractive home arena proposal.

On August 12, 1985, ground was broken for a state-of-the-art coliseum six miles outside of Charlotte, a facility financed by voter-approved bonds. Months later Shinn negotiated an agreement that his team could rent the new arena for the token fee of one dollar per game for five years—

a leasing arrangement that would save the fledgling franchise a hefty sum of money during its infancy. All of these circumstances helped advance Shinn's case for a Charlotte-based team.

In order to pay for the franchise, Shinn enlisted the aid of three partners. Rick Hendrick and Felix Sabates each invested more than a million dollars on October 3, 1986, and Charlotte television station owner Cy Bahakel added some $6 million a month later. Shinn remained the majority partner and the principal negotiator for the city's interests.

Season ticket sales were brisk even before the NBA officially chose Charlotte as a site: by mid-October of 1986 more than 8,000 seats had been sold; when the NBA Expansion Committee recommended Charlotte for a franchise in April of 1987, another 5,000 were sold in a month.

The Charlotte Hornets became part of the NBA on April 22, 1987. Originally known as The Spirit, the team name was changed to Hornets in June of that year after a "name that team" contest. The name stems all the way back to colonial times, when North Carolina militia men were compared to hornets during a Revolutionary War campaign. Other Charlotte teams had borne the Hornet name over the years, including a World Football League club and a minor league baseball franchise.

The new NBA Hornets made headlines in the summer of 1987 when the club hired fashion designer Alexander Julian to determine team colors and design uniforms. Julian's uniforms followed traditional lines, but his colors—teal and purple—were a new combination in the NBA. A teal-and-purple hornet, designed by Cheryl Henson of Muppet fame, became the mascot.

The Hornets' first vice president and general manager was Carl Scheer. Scheer and associate Gene Littles were given the task of evaluating talent in preparation for the June 1988 expansion draft and the annual college draft. The expansion draft came first, on June 23. In a conference call held between Charlotte, Miami (the other expansion team that year), and the NBA offices in New York City, the Hornets chose Tyrone Bogues, Michael Brooks, Mike Brown, Dell Curry, Ricky

AP/Wide World Photos

Larry Johnson

Green, Michael Holton, Dave Hoppen, Ralph Lewis, Bernard Thompson, Sedric Toney, and Clinton Wheeler. The same day, Mike Brown was sent to Utah for veteran Kelly Tripucka. Of those Hornets pioneers, only Bogues and Curry remained with the team through 1993.

For head coach, the Hornets chose Dick Harter, an assistant at Indiana under Hoosier Coach Bobby Knight. In the college draft held on June 28, 1988, the Hornets selected Rex Chapman from Kentucky in the first round. Later selections brought the services of Tom Tolbert and Jeff Moore.

The Hornets made their home debut before a packed Charlotte Coliseum on November 4, 1988. They lost that game 133-93 to the Cleveland Cavaliers. Charlotte's first-ever regular season victory came four days later in a 117-105 win over the Los

TEAM INFORMATION AT A GLANCE

Founding date: April 22, 1987

Home court:
Charlotte Coliseum
c/o Charlotte Hornets
Hive Drive
Charlotte, NC 28217
Phone: (704) 357-0252

Seating capacity: 23,901 for basketball

Team colors: White and teal
Team nickname: Hornets
Logo: Cartoonish teal-and-purple hornet clad in
tennis shoes and bouncing a basketball

Franchise record	Won	Lost	Pct.
(1988-93)	140	260	.350

Angeles Clippers. In that first season, it mattered little whether the Hornets won or lost. Crowds flocked to the Coliseum, owner Shinn was a local hero, and the players—some of whom had community service clauses written into their contracts—were mobbed wherever they went.

As is customary with first-year expansion franchises, the team did not perform particularly well in 1988-89, finishing 20-62.

The Hornets' honeymoon with Charlotte ended in 1989 when negative publicity about Shinn began to circulate. The team had generated an estimated $8.5 million in positive cash flow during its first season, and Shinn decided he wanted to enforce a buyout agreement that his partners had signed.

Hendrick, Sabates, and Bahakel were surprised—they had assumed the buyout clause was a mere formality. Instead, Shinn was adamant. Hendrick and Sabates agreed to sell their shares. Bahakel refused and took the matter to court. When the court decided in Shinn's favor, Bahakel appealed. The resulting headlines eroded Shinn's popularity, but the ownership quarrels did little to stifle "Hornet Hysteria" among the Charlotte faithful.

In 1989-90 the Hornets finished 19-63 in a season marked by the franchise's first head coaching change. On January 31, 1990, Harter was replaced by Gene Littles, but the personnel change did little to improve the team's fortunes. Littles was able to effect a slight improvement in 1990-91.

That season Charlotte compiled a 26-56 record on the strength of players like Bogues, Curry, Mike Gminski, and Tripucka. At the end of the 1990-91 season, Littles became vice president and special assistant to the president of the Hornets, making way for new head coach Allan Bristow.

It was Bristow, a former assistant coach at San Antonio and Denver, who would lead the Hornets to their first postseason games in 1993. Bristow made ample use of Tyrone "Muggsy" Bogues, the scrappy five-foot-three-inch point guard to push the ball up the floor.

It was the talented young triumvirate of Larry Johnson, Kendall Gill, and rookie Alonzo Mourning, however, that enabled Charlotte to advance into the 1993 playoffs against the Boston Celtics. A thrilled Shinn and his legions of Hornets fans watched proudly as the team from North Carolina beat the mighty Celtics in the first round—a rare accomplishment for an expansion club only five years old.

The Hornets were eliminated from the 1993 playoffs by the New York Knicks, but Shinn and the fans viewed the season as a glimpse of greater future glory. The team continued to set NBA attendance records, continued to remain among the league-leaders in season ticket sales, and continued its pattern of fan allegiance in the southern mid-Atlantic region.

Charlotte remained busy during the off-season in preparation for the 1993 season. The club signed popular forward Larry Johnson to a record-setting long-term contract (a reported $84 million over 12 years) and shipped disgruntled guard Kendall Gill to Seattle. To fill the spot vacated by Gill, Charlotte traded for long-range sharpshooter Hersey Hawkins of the 76ers. Owner George Shinn has reason to smile: he turned a dream into a team that has brought new excitement to the heart of Dixie.

SOURCES

PERIODICALS

Business-North Carolina, January, 1990.
Sporting News, May 17, 1993.
Sports Illustrated, November 25, 1991; April 12, 1993.

DALLAS MAVERICKS

Like the blue-collar Chicago Bears and the "Showtime" Lakers of Los Angeles, a successful team often embodies the aspect of its hometown that its residents take most pride in. True to their own Texas home, the Dallas Mavericks have always done everything on a grand scale—and with drama to boot. In their short history, the Mavericks have hit all the gushing highs and bone-dry lows of a Texas oil field.

Like any other expansion team, the Mavs were not immediately competitive, but coach Dick Motta and his squad of talented young players, including Mark Aguirre and Rolando Blackman, quickly grew into one of the best organizations in the league. They made their mark off the court, too, with fiery personality conflicts and tragedies that would have played as well on the TV show *Dallas* as they did in the headlines of the Dallas papers.

Despite feuds among players, coaches, and the media, the Mavs challenged for the NBA title in the mid-1980s. Then the drug problems of star Roy Tarpley drove the team down to depths they hadn't seen since their first season, depths from which the Mavs have yet to emerge. Given the colorful history of the team, though, it's only a matter of time before Dallas is back among the NBA elite.

The creation of the Mavs took two long years. Norm Sonju, the GM of the Buffalo Braves, wanted to move his team to Dallas in 1978, but instead the Braves became the San Diego Clippers. Once the Braves relocated, Sonju teamed up with businessman Donald Carter to pursue an NBA franchise for Dallas.

After much negotiating and financial wrangling, the league finally notified Carter and Sonju on April 28, 1980, that Dallas had a team. With Sonju as GM and Carter as owner, the Mavericks formed their organization. They hired former Bulls and Bullets coach Dick Motta, who had actively campaigned for the job, as head coach and drafted their first players. But not everyone was as excited about Dallas as Norm Sonju and Dick Motta. The Mavs' first pick in the college draft, Kiki Vandeweghe, refused to play in Dallas and was traded to Denver that December for a first-round draft pick in 1981.

Even with the disappointment of losing a promising player like Vandeweghe, the Mavericks were game from the start, and Motta's hard-driving, unpredictable coaching style allowed for no excuses. In their first game ever, the Mavs shocked the San Antonio Spurs 103-92 at Reunion Arena. Afterwards, Spurs coach Stan Albeck said, "They are not like other expansion teams."

This may have been true about their coaching and their overall composure on the court, but the Mavs still lacked real talent. This opening night win was the highlight of the season, as Dallas went 15 and 67, including a 15-game losing streak, and finished last in the Midwest Division. Guard Jim Spanarkal led in scoring with 14.4 points a game, and former Supersonics center Tom LaGarde hauled in an average of 8.1 rebounds a night.

The best move the Mavs made on or off the court all season was to sign Brad Davis out of the CBA. Davis had shuttled around the NBA and the CBA as a guard and was ready to call it quits when Mavs Assistant Coach Bob Weiss convinced him to come to Dallas. For much of the next 11 years, Brad Davis ran the Mavs' offense from the point until Derek Harper took over the job; injuries eventually forced Davis to retire.

The Mavs made the most out of their two first-round picks in the 1981 draft by choosing College Player of the Year Mark Aguirre as number one overall, Rolando Blackman out of Kansas State ninth, and Jay Vincent in the second round. Dallas now had some explosive offensive strength—along with the seeds of some problems.

Aguirre was a brilliant forward, but many criticized him for being immature. He and Motta, notoriously tough on rookies, didn't hit it off. Aguirre also suffered the first of the many injuries that would dog him in Dallas when he broke his foot in December and missed 31 games. The Mavs got off to a 1-13 start and never fully recovered, though they did show signs of the kind of play that would make them contenders down the line. After Aguirre went down, Vincent stepped in at forward and scored over 30 points 15 times.

He led the Mavs in scoring with 21.4 a game and made the first team of the NBA All-Rookie squad. Aguirre added 18.7 in his 51 games, including a three-pointer on March 23 that gave the Mavs their first victory over the powerhouse Lakers, 118-116. The team's final record was 28 and 54, a 13-game improvement that proved the Mavs were on their way.

Finished Third Season 38-44

Their improvement carried into 1982-83. The questionable choice of Bill Garnett in the draft over Fat Lever, John Bagley, and Ricky Pierce, while adding only a role player, allowed Motta to concentrate on developing the considerable talent he already had. The Mavs started well, over .500 in December at 11-9, then dropped 12 of their next 14. Now the toughness and intensity Motta was instilling in his young players came out.

The Mavs fought back to 25-24, and by February they were in second place in the Midwest Division. They were still chasing a winning record and a play-off spot in March when a seven-game losing streak pushed both goals out of reach. Though only a three-year-old expansion team, the Mavs finished 38-44.

Brad Davis was among the league leaders in field goals and free throws, yet his 7.2 assists a game—tenth in the league—showed that his real value lay in his ability to get the ball to Aguirre, Blackman, and Vincent. Aguirre's 24.4 points a game put him sixth in the league and the Mavs' offense was fifth overall. Motta was riding his men hard, and it was beginning to turn them into winners.

Derek Harper and Dale Ellis, two more rookies with great potential, joined the Mavs after they were drafted in the summer of 1983, but the player with the most potential still hadn't realized his full abilities. Mark Aguirre had always been a special

TEAM INFORMATION AT A GLANCE

Founding date: 1970

Home Court:
Reunion Arena
777 Sports St.
Dallas, TX 75207
(214) 748-1808

Seating: 17,502; opened April 28, 1980

Team Colors: Blue and Green
Team Nickname: Dallas Mavericks

Franchise Record	Won	Lost
(1980-93)	466	600

Division First-Place Finishes: 1986-87
Division Last-Place Finishes: 1980-81

project for the Mavs, and as they entered the 1983-84 with no true center, his ability to use his large frame in the low post became crucial to their chances.

When Jay Vincent went down with a muscle pull in the second game of the season, Aguirre's role became even more pivotal. Vincent missed only five games, but Motta cut his minutes way down once he came back for not staying in prime shape and asking to be traded. Aguirre stepped it up as Vincent sat, and the former had the best season of his career; he led the Mavs to a 13-4 start into December and never let up through the regular season, averaging 29.5 points a game, second only to Adrian Dantley of the Denver Nuggets.

By the All-Star break the Mavs were 25-19, and Mark Aguirre played the first minutes in an All-Star game by a Dallas Maverick. The November surge proved necessary, as the team played just under .500 ball in the second half. Aguirre continued his dominating work on offense, aided by Blackman's 22.4 points a game and rebounding by Pat Cummings and Kurt Nimphius. On April 1, 1984, the Mavs made the play-offs for the first time when the Lakers beat Golden State and two weeks later wrapped up their first winning season at 43-39, second in the Midwest Division behind Utah.

As usual with the Mavericks, their first-round series, against Seattle, was full of drama. In their first-ever play-off game, the Mavs fell victim early to nerves and Seattle's Gus Williams. The Sonics shot out to a 21-6 lead and seemed in control until Brad Davis began to cover Williams in the third quarter. Davis shut him down and the Mavs roared back. With 6:48 to go they led 83-78 but then went cold, and Seattle edged ahead. With only 11 seconds left, Blackman hit a jumper off his own rebound that gave the Mavs the lead for good at 87-86 and added a final free throw with one second on the clock to ice an 88-86 win.

In Game Two the Mavs again fell behind early and pulled back. Cummings tied the score with 46 seconds to go, but at the buzzer Gus Williams sank a three-pointer that won it for the Sonics 95-92 and took the series back to Seattle tied. The two teams split the pair in Seattle. Back in Dallas, tennis had moved into Reunion Arena and the series was to be decided at Moody Coliseum on the Southern Methodist University campus.

Rolando Blackman was the difference in Game Five. With 47 seconds to go and Seattle's star center, Jack Sikma, out of the game after fouling out, Pat Cummings hit two free throws to bring the Mavs within four. Then Blackman stole the ball and dunked. Seattle couldn't get the inbounds pass in, so Dallas got the ball again and Blackman hit a jumper with 15 seconds to go to tie the game and send it into overtime.

The Mavs controlled the overtime until the Sonics went on a 7-2 run. With only one second to go the Mavs led 105-104, and Jay Vincent tried to inbound off of Tom Chambers of the Sonics to kill the clock. Chambers bobbled the ball and his final shot was waived off by the ref. But one second still remained on the clock. The controversy took 14 minutes to work out. Seattle was finally awarded the ball, but Chambers couldn't get to the lob pass under the net. The hustling, scrapping Mavericks had won their first play-off series and went on to Los Angeles to meet the Lakers.

Trounced by Lakers After Winning First Play-off Series

The Mavs had beaten the Lakers 3-2 in their regular season series and thus had the homecourt advantage, but they didn't have the advantage in play-off experience. The Lakers trounced the Mavs in Games One and Two and while the Mavs managed a 125-115 victory in Game Three, their youth showed in Game Four. Derek Harper, with the score tied and 12 seconds remaining, ran out the clock, believing that the Mavs were ahead.

Instead, the game went into overtime, and the Lakers won to build a 3-1 edge in the series. Trouble loomed on the Dallas bench as well. Aguirre, whose play-off performance did not match his regular season play, came down hard on his hip during Game Four and sat himself out during some crucial minutes.

Motta didn't believe the injury was severe enough to keep an All-Star out of a do-or-die game and left him out of the starting lineup in Game Five as punishment. Dale Ellis, though he would later become a star, was not up to the task of filling in for Aguirre, and the Lakers rolled over the Mavs 115-99 to take the series. Still, the Mavericks were just beginning to make headlines—on the court and off.

The Mavs managed to up their record in 1984-85 to 44-38, one game better than the year before. It looked good on paper, but the Mavs really weren't going anywhere. There were no winning or losing streaks longer than four games, and they were healthy, but Mark Aguirre's erratic play was starting to have its effect on the team.

On December 18, Dick Motta pulled Aguirre out of a game against Milwaukee for not hustling. Their public confrontation cost Aguirre a spot on the All-Star squad, and the steady Rolando Blackman represented Dallas instead. Blackman scored 19.7 points per game, second on the team to Aguirre's 25.7, but Blackman's elegant style, good defense, and team attitude put him up next to Brad Davis in the estimation of fans and his fellow players.

They became the reliable core of a club that often threatened to explode. There were other positive developments, though. Jay Vincent came out of Motta's doghouse to reassume his starting role, and newcomer Perkins earned a spot on the NBA All-Rookie team. Combined, Vincent and Perkins pulled down 1309 rebounds.

Also, as proof of Motta's coaching effectiveness, the Mavs led the league with the least turnovers for the third straight year. On the nights that

Aguirre was on, the Mavs were very hard to beat. They finished the season in third place and faced the Portland Trailblazers in the first round of the play-offs.

The Mavericks' short appearance in post-season play in 1984-85 mirrored their season—big numbers from Blackman and Aguirre and a never-say-die attitude but not enough consistency to fully exploit the team's talent.

Game One in Dallas was a double-overtime thriller sparked by Blackman's heroics. His short-jumper with four second left sent the game into overtime, and then his 13-footer with six seconds to go brought the second overtime. Blackman then scored seven of his 43 points in the second extra session to lead the Mavs to a 139-131 win.

Blackman tried to do it on his own again in Game Two, but his 41 points couldn't stave off a late Portland run that sent this one into overtime too. Portland wouldn't be denied this night, and their command of the boards had much to do with their finally winning 124-121.

Both Blackman and Aguirre scored 30 points in Game Three, but the Mavs old nemesis, Kiki Vandeweghe, the man who wouldn't play in Dallas, killed them by keying a late 22-9 run that won the game. The Blazers took the advantage two games to one and finished the job two nights later with a 115-113 win in Game Four on a last-second bucket. Aguirre's 39 points couldn't make up for Blackman's off-night, and Vincent's cold play in post-season forced Motta to sit him down in favor of Ellis. The Mavs' had taken one step forward in the regular season, but had fallen back when it counted.

Drafted for Height

Dallas was still treading water through the 1985-86 season. The team tried to solve its problems at center by drafting for height—6'10" Detlef Schrempf and seven-footers Bill Wennington and Uwe Blab—and in November they traded Kurt Nimphius to the Clippers for 7'2" James Donaldson. The added inches, both Aguirre and second-

time All-Star Rolando Blackman averaging over 20 points a game, and the league's best three-point shooting, pushed the Mavs to second in the league on offense.

Unfortunately, the emphasis on offense took away from the team's concentration on defense and the Mavs slipped to 21st. Dallas played around the .500 mark all year and, like the season before, didn't run up any streaks in either the win or the loss column. In another repeat from the prior season, Mark Aguirre and Dick Motta clashed heads.

Aguirre's sometimes lackadaisical play had forced a situation where he had to make an agreement with Motta that if his concentration lapsed during a game, he would be benched. On December 19, in Atlanta, Aguirre didn't get back on defense on a play in the second quarter and Motta pulled him.

Confronted by the coach between halves, Aguirre chose not to play the rest of the game. The Mavs suspended Aguirre for two games, and all the accusations about his soft defense, bad shot selection, and excessive ball-handling rolled out. On his side, Aguirre felt that Motta applied a much tougher set of rules to him than he did to the rest of the team. Despite all the controversy, the Mavs finished at 44-38, a record identical to that of 1984-85, and third in the Midwest Division.

In their six years in the league, the Mavs had developed a rivalry with the Utah Jazz, and this first-round series would be the first time the two teams would meet in the play-offs. Utah came into Dallas without their star, Adrian Dantley, and the Mavs took advantage of his absence, winning Games One and Two easily.

Karl Malone sank a jumper in the last minute to win Game Three for Utah, but Brad Davis locked the door in Game Four. His five-for-five three-point shooting and 15 points in the fourth quarter pushed the Mavs over the top. Dallas won 117-113 and took the series three games to one.

The Western Conference Semifinals opened at the Forum in Los Angeles. The Lakers won 62 games during the regular season and led the league in offense. The Mavs hoped that Donaldson and Perkins could match up against the Lakers' powerful front line, but Games One and Two showed the Mavs' big men just how hard a job that was.

Kareem Abdul-Jabbar scored 26 in Game One and 28 in Game Two, and James Worthy went to town on Perkins. The Lakers won both games and walked into Reunion Arena looking to sweep. The Mavs may have been weak on defense, erratic and sometimes immature, but, like all of Dick Motta's teams, they were tough.

Game Three was a test of pride for the young Dallas team. Rolando Blackman brought the Mavs to within one at 108-107. Twenty-four seconds were left. Blackman then fouled Michael Cooper, who missed both free throws. Aguirre missed his shot on the other end, and Worthy flipped the rebound over his shoulder as he was going out of bounds. The ball went right to Derek Harper.

Two years earlier, to the date, Derek Harper had run out the clock with a chance to beat the Lakers in Game Four of the 1984 Western Conference Semis. For two years, Harper was dogged by the mistake. On this night he knocked down a three-pointer to win the game 110-108.

Aguirre was the hero of Game Four, hitting a jumper at the end to win it 120-118. The series was tied and Brad Davis closed the Lakers' lead to two in Game Five with a basket with seconds to go, but Worthy sank a free throw for a Los Angeles win. The Lakers polished off the Mavs in Game Six 120-107, a win made easier by an ankle injury late in the third quarter to Mark Aguirre. Aguirre played a few minutes in the fourth, then sustained a further injury to his already ailing reputation by sitting himself down for the rest of the game.

The Mavs were well stocked with talent, but the final pieces hadn't fallen into place yet. Something had to change. 1986-87 turned out to be a pivotal year for the franchise. In the short term, the Mavs became contenders, but some of their choices had a direct effect on the team's downward slide a few years later.

To start, they drafted forward Roy Tarpley of Michigan as their number-one pick despite rumors of his drug use while in Ann Arbor. Then they traded future All-Star Mark Price, who they had

AP/Wide World Photos

Dick Motta

drafted in the second round, to Cleveland for a draft choice. Feeling that the team was too deep at small forward, the Mavs sent Dale Ellis to Seattle for Al Wood and Jay Vincent to the Bullets.

When the season started, the roster changes made Sonju, Carter, and Motta look like geniuses. With Vincent gone, Schrempf got more time and added some much needed-defense to the lineup. The Mavs climbed from near the bottom of the league defensively to 14th as they moved out to a 21-9 record in January. Aguirre and Blackman both made the All-Star team with their 25.7- and 21-points-a-game averages.

Tarpley came off the bench well in the second half and began to show dominance on the boards. Strong play at Reunion Arena, matched with a 20-21 mark on the road, totaled up to a 55-27 record and first place in the Midwest Division when the season ended. The Mavs couldn't escape controversy though; on April 4th the NBA suspended Dick Motta for one game after the coach accused the Houston Rockets of not playing to win in a 117-104 loss to the Suns, a loss that helped set up a situation in which the Rockets would not have to face the Lakers in an early round of the play-offs. It wasn't the end of headlines regarding Motta that season.

Game One of the first round against the Sonics made most Mavs fans believe this was their year. Dallas crushed Seattle 151-129, setting 11 team records. Ten Mavs hit double figures, and Dallas began thinking about the next round. Dale Ellis wasn't, though. Having scored 24.9 points a game during the season, Ellis was ready to give his former team a jolt.

He scored 32 points in Game Two, including two free throws with two seconds left that won it for the Sonics 112-110. The surprise loss seemed to stun the Mavs in Game Three in Seattle. Dale Ellis tallied 43 points and pulled down 14 rebounds to lead a 117-107 Seattle win.

James Donaldson missed Game Four with a leg injury and Blackman and Tarpley did their best to make up for his absence, but it was too late. The Sonics flew off to a 12-point lead and won the game 124-98. The season that the Mavericks were supposed to challenge for the NBA title ended instead with them exiting early.

Departure of Tough Guy Motta

Late in the 1986-87 season, rumors circulated that Motta, tired of wrangling with his players, was soliciting offers from other teams to leave Dallas. The Mavs management did not react to the talk until the team collapsed in the first round against Seattle. Motta came in to discuss his plans with the organization on May 20th, but instead of delivering the expected statement of devotion to the Mavericks and his desire to take them all the way, Motta resigned.

Players, management, and fans expressed anger and surprise at Motta's leaving. Somehow the dream had existed that this upstart basketball team could win it all with essentially the same crew that brought it to life seven years before. The

Mavericks were closer than ever to the top, but it wouldn't be the same without Motta.

On June 4th, the Mavs announced that John MacLeod would be the new head coach. Formerly with the Suns, MacLeod was one of the few men in the league with the personality and track record to lead this high-strung and talented team.

An indication that he would need all the experience he could summon came prior to the 1987-88 season, when Roy Tarpley admitted in August that he had a substance abuse problem. According to NBA rules, this was Tarpley's first strike. If he was caught or admitted to breaking the league's anti-drug agreement two more times, he would be banned from the NBA. In order to help the 23-year-old Tarpley stay clean, the Mavs instituted a complex support system of chaperons.

Whether or not Tarpley could abide by the rules off the court was still to be seen, but on the court he became the team's catalyst as the sixth man. The Mavs rolled out to a 17-8 record by year's end behind Tarpley's dominating board play. His 11.8 rebounds a game, seventh in the league, added to their league-leading 46.8 a contest and bolstered the team's defense. With the ability to both pull down rebounds and score, Tarpley was the element for which the Mavs had been looking. By the All-Star break, the Mavs were 28-15.

As usual, Aguirre led the team in scoring in 1987-88 with 25.1 points a game and represented Dallas, along with James Donaldson, in the All-Star Game. Derek Harper firmly took over the job of point guard from Brad Davis, who now came in off the bench. Charged by Tarpley's 20 points/20 rebounds capability, the Mavs won 11 in a row in February and ended the season at 53-29.

Though it was the first time the Mavs had not equalled or bettered their previous season's record, it was also the first time a team that had won 50 under one coach won 50 the next season under a new one. Roy Tarpley, the man responsible for much of their success, received the NBA Sixth Man Award.

After the previous season's embarrassment against the Sonics, the Mavs went into their first-round series versus Houston determined to get the job done quickly. They took Game One, despite sub-par performances from Aguirre and Blackman, but 42 from Sleepy Floyd and 41 from Hakeem Olajuwon in Game Two were too much for Dallas. Houston won 119-108, tying the series. Games Three and Four showed why Tarpley's addition was so vital.

Aguirre had been off his game in the first two contests and was still off in Game Three, so Tarpley led the way by hitting clutch shots and pulling out a 93-92 Dallas victory. In Game Four, Aguirre found his touch again. He scored 38, including 27 in the third quarter, and the Mavs won going away, 107-97. The additional threat of Tarpley somewhat lifted the burden from Aguirre, making the team less reliant on the mercurial star.

The second-round series against Denver started out tough. The Nuggets took the first two out of three, but when they lost Fat Lever and Jay Vincent, the advantage swayed decidedly to Dallas. Aguirre scored 34 in Dallas' 124-103 win in Game Four and 25 more in their Game Five victory. Blackman, Perkins, and Tarpley did the job in Game Six, balancing Nugget Alex English's 34 points, and the Mavs won 108-95. The Mavs had made it to the conference finals to face the Lakers.

Faced Lakers in 1988 Conference Finals

Dallas had not forgotten the way the Lakers handled them on the boards back in their 1986 play-off series. In 1988 the Mavs outrebounded L.A. throughout the series, but the Lakers had more weapons. Los Angeles won the first two games easily, 113-98 and 123-101. The series moved to Dallas.

Roy Tarpley's 21 points and 20 rebounds were the difference in a 106-94 Game Three victory, and Derek Harper's 35 points in Game Four helped the Mavs even things at two games apiece. It was now a two-out-of-three series. Game Five at the Forum was another blow-out by the Lak-

ers, 119-102, and the Mavs were on the ropes for Game Six. The entire city of Dallas had been preparing for this night with rallies and parties, and the Mavs did not disappoint.

In one of the team's most memorable games, Donaldson rejected a last-second James Worthy shot, preserving a two-point lead with three seconds to go. The Mavs won 105-103 and forced a seventh game. The deciding game was tight until the third, when the Lakers stretched out to a ten-point lead.

The Mavs hustled back in the fourth, cutting it to 100-94, but their chances were fatally damaged when Aguirre bent back two fingers on his non-shooting hand. Aguirre sat out three minutes, claiming a "knuckle injury." The Mavs lost 117-102, and Aguirre's decision to sit during a seventh game was loudly criticized. Still, the Mavs vowed to be back next season.

Roy Tarpley's brilliant play was responsible for the Mavs' surge forward since 1986—and Tarpley's problems were largely responsible for the Mavs' ensuing decline. Since his arrival the team had focused on this player, often considered the best to ever play in a Mavs' uniform.

As Aguirre and Blackman were already peaking and the Mavs hadn't done well in the 1987 and 1988 drafts, Tarpley was asked to both provide what the team needed now and to create its future. It was a management decision that placed enormous emphasis on one player and a position that demanded great maturity from a young man not known for that quality. Whether or not Tarpley's off-court troubles would have surfaced if he had stayed healthy can't be guessed, but when he tore cartilage in his knee in November, the Mavs began to come apart as well.

Dallas was 4-3 when Tarpley underwent knee surgery on November 16. Their 11-7 record on his return reminded everyone that Dallas had hovered around the .500 mark for a few years before Tarpley came along. Their 17-9 record a few weeks later with him in the lineup only further stressed the point—without Tarpley, the Mavs simply weren't contenders. On January 5, the NBA suspended Tarpley indefinitely without pay

| PROFILE | Rolando Blackman |

Born in Panama City, Panama, Rolando Blackman came to the United States when he was eight and grew up in Brooklyn, New York. As a boy, his heroes were New York Knicks guards Earl Monroe and Walt Frazier, and Blackman began to show their kind of smoothness and scoring touch as he played for Kansas State University. Blackman was first-team All-American in 1981, and the Mavs selected him ninth overall in the 1981 draft. During his 11 years in Dallas, Rolando rarely got involved in turmoil off the court. His consistency and maturity provided emotional support for the other players, as did his reliable outside shot, to which they could go in the clutch.

He averaged just over 19 points a game as a Maverick and represented Dallas four times in the NBA All-Star game. 1983-84 was his best season, when he scored 22.4 points a game, finishing 13th in the league in that category. He leads the Mavs all-time in points and is second only to Brad Davis in games played as a Mav. Rolando entered the 1992-93 season as 41st on the league's all-time scoring list. Dallas traded Blackman to the Knicks in 1992 for New York's first-round draft pick in 1995.

for violating the terms of the aftercare program constructed for him. Tarpley now had two strikes on him, and the Mavs had some difficult decisions to make.

At this point in the season the team was still winning, but by mid-February the Mavs had skidded to 25-21. With Tarpley out, the pressure fell back onto Mark Aguirre, and he was either unwilling or unable to handle it. Team morale plummeted as Aguirre would play hard one game and barely make an effort the next. Though Donald Carter and Aguirre had become close friends over the years, the Mavs made the choice to trade the forward to Detroit for Adrian Dantley and a draft pick.

Dantley, too, had been accused of attitude problems during his career, but no one ever said he didn't hustle or keep in shape, two major issues between Aguirre and Dallas. Days later the team sent Detlef Schrempf to the Pacers for center Herb Williams to shore up their play on the boards. The addition of Dantley gave the team a fresh start, and for a short time hope rose.

Then James Donaldson went down with a knee injury. Despite Tarpley's return to action in mid-April and Dantley's 20.3 a game for Dallas, a 12-game losing streak buried them. The Mavs

could only manage a 38-44 record and fourth place in the Midwest Division. It was the first time in six years that the Mavericks missed the play-offs.

1989-90 started with more bad news from Roy Tarpley. Though management showed confidence in him by extending his contract for three years in August, Tarpley was arrested November 15th for drunk driving and resisting arrest. The next day he was suspended again, but while the league did not ban him, the Mavs took a harder stance and did away with his support program.

All of this controversy did not help the Mavs play. They were 5-6, including a 47-point loss to Seattle at home, when John MacLeod was fired on November 29. Assistant Coach Richie Adubato stepped in and kept the team near .500 until Tarpley's return to action on January 23. By this point the Mavs were showing some life again. From January 19th through February 25th, Dallas won 14 out of 17. Unfortunately, Dantley broke his right leg on February 3rd, ending his year and his time with the Mavs; he would be waived after the season.

Blackman provided the offense, leading the team in scoring with 19.4 points a game, and Harper dished 609 assists. Tarpley was suspended for two more games for missing practice in early

TEAM RECORDS

Total Games: Brad Davis—883

Total Minutes: Rolando Blackman—29,684

Field Goals Attempted: Rolando Blackman—13,061

Field Goals Made: Rolando Blackman—6,487

Blocked Shots: James Donaldson—615

Free Throw Attempts: Rolando Blackman—4,166

Free Throws Made: Rolando Blackman—3,501

Free Throw Percentage: Jim Spanarkel—857

Rebounds: James Donaldson—4,589

Assists: Brad Davis—4,524

Three Pointers Made: Derek Harper—507

Personal Fouls: Brad Davis—2,040

Steals: Derek Harper—1,334

Points Scored: Rolando Blackman—16,643

Scoring Average: Mark Aguirre—24.6

April, but the Mavs finished strong and wound up with a 47-35 record. Defense had a lot to do with it. Without the overwhelming offense of a Dantley or Aguirre, the Mavs had to rely more on stopping the other team. For the second year in a row, they finished fourth in the league in that department.

Given the troubles the team had with injuries and other personnel issues, their third-place spot in the Division was a pleasant surprise. The Blazers' three-game sweep of the Mavs in their first-round play-off series, though, was thoroughly unpleasant. The Mavs had never been so outplayed in the playoffs before.

The front office made some major changes after the Mavs' prompt departure from the play-offs. Over the summer they acquired Fat Lever, Rodney McCray, and Alex English through trades and free agency. All three were proven stars, and the season began 4-1. On November 9th, the season ended. Both Tarpley and Lever went down for the year with knee injuries. Herb Williams joined them for a month in December when his knee went out too.

Blackman and Harper were once again re-

sponsible for what offense the Mavs could muster, as each averaged over 19 points a game and Harper provided 548 assists. By February the team was 15-26 and going down. If the poor showing on the court wasn't enough, Roy Tarpley was again arrested by police for suspicion of driving while intoxicated on March 30th. The NBA treatment program again suspended him indefinitely.

By now, the Mavs were ready to lose Tarpley. The team was paying him millions of dollars not to play, and having that much money tied up with one problematic player was hampering any efforts the front office tried to make towards rebuilding. The Mavs had not drafted an impact player since they chose Tarpley in 1986, and now the lack of promising young talent was showing on the court. It was hard to find anything positive in the Mavs' 28-54 record.

Terminated Troubled Tarpley

When the NBA finally dismissed Roy Tarpley from the league on October 16, 1991, the Mavs tore up their contract with him and tried to rebuild. It would not be easy. Tarpley had left a cloud over the team, and it was unlikely that Dallas would be interested in talking to him if he successfully petitioned the NBA and the players' association for reinstatement in October of 1993, as provided by the anti-drug agreement.

The Mavericks decided to go with youth in 1991-92 as their way back to contention. The problem was that the youth they had on the team was not top caliber. San Antonio's 140-99 opening-night demolition of the Mavs sadly seemed to mirror the Mavs' debut victory 11 years earlier; stalwarts Blackman, Harper, and Donaldson started much of the way, other older players such as Herb Williams and Fat Lever contributing what they could.

Longtime fan favorite Brad Davis finally retired, 11 years after he first considered it, when a back injury took him out in January. As the season went on, Adubato began to fold in young players like Mike Iuzzolino, Don Hodge, and Doug

Smith. The Mavs' increasingly untested lineup fared poorly, running up losing streaks of 11, 8, and 15 games, and finished with the team's worst record since the franchise was started at 22-60.

The Mavs moved during the off-season to focus entirely on youth for 1992-93. They traded the team's all-time leading scorer, Rolando Blackman, to the Knicks for New York's 1995 first-round pick and not long after, sent Herb Williams to New York as well.

In the draft, Dallas chose Ohio State All-American Jim Jackson as their first selection. Jackson could not come to terms with the Mavericks before the season started and even expressed doubts about wanting to play in Dallas. The Mavericks thus entered the 1992-93 season with trepidation that proved well-warranted.

Early in the campaign it became clear to observers that the Dallas squad might well qualify as the worst club in NBA history. Adabuto was fired early in the season, a move that a number of Maverick players publicly denounced.

As the season wore on and the losses piled up, speculation increased as to whether or not the Mavericks would be able to match the nine victory-season posted by the 76ers in 1972-73, the worst record in NBA history. To the credit of the players on the Maverick squad, however, no one faulted the team's effort; the club was simply outmanned.

Late in the season, however, with the club's record standing at four wins and 50 losses, Dallas held a press conference in which they announced that Quinn Buckner would take the helm as head coach for the 1993-94 season. Team officials then stunned all in attendance by introducing Jimmy Jackson and announcing that they had signed him to a long-term contract.

Jackson quickly joined the club and his impact was immediately felt. The club finished out the season by winning seven of their last 21 games to finish 11-71 for the season, two games better than the record posted by Philadelphia 20 years before.

The outlook for the Mavericks heading into the 1993-94 season is brighter than it has been for quite some time. Buckner has promised a new era for the club, and Jackson and top draft pick Jamal Mashburn look like potential stars. Long-suffering Dallas fans are hopeful that the infusion of new blood can return the club to new levels of glory.

SOURCES

BOOKS

Carter, Craig, and Alex Sachare, editors, *The NBA Guide 1992-93,* The Sporting News, 1992.

Cirillo, John, *New York Knicks 1992-93 Media Guide,* New York Knicks, 1992.

Hollander, Zander, and Alex Sachare, editors, *The Official NBA Basketball Encyclopedia,* Villard, 1989.

Neft, David S., and Richard M. Cohn, editors, *The Sports Encyclopedia: Pro Basketball,* third edition, revised and updated by John Hogorosian and Bob Gill, St. Martin's, 1990.

Sullivan, Kevin, and Tony Fay, *Dallas Mavericks 1992-93 Media Guide,* Dallas Mavericks, 1992.

Taragano, Martin, *Basketball Biographies,* McFarland & Co., 1991.

PERIODICALS

Dallas Morning News, March 15, 1980; October 11, 1980; March 23, 1982; April 17, 1984; May 8, 1984; December 19, 1984; December 21, 1985; April 27, 1986; May 8, 1986; September 9, 1986; April 3, 1987; May 20, 1987; May 23, 198, 1988; June 4, 1988; January 5, 1989; February 15, 1989; January 5, 1989; February 15, 1989; November 15, 1989; November 29, 1989; April 5, 1991; October 10, 1991; January 14, 1992.

—*Richard Cohen* for Book Builders, Inc.

DENVER NUGGETS

The Denver Nuggets were born in 1967 as the Denver Rockets, a member of the renegade American Basketball Association (ABA), which sprang up in markets ignored by the National Basketball Association to challenge the established league. Nine years later, the Nuggets were one of just four ABA teams to gain admission to the NBA as the two leagues merged.

The Denver franchise was one of the most aggressive in the ABA and had a good deal to do with the war that eventually brought about the merger. The team made sports history by signing a star college underclassman, Spencer Haywood, for the fledgling ABA and later by signing the nation's most coveted player, David Thompson.

The ABA's acquisition of Thompson, the North Carolina State star known as "Skywalker," was perhaps more responsible than any other single act for bringing the NBA to the bargaining table to talk merger. Carl Scheer, general manager of the Nuggets for a decade, was at the table where

the merger was negotiated with then-NBA commissioner Larry O'Brien.

Many of Scheer's marketing schemes for the ABA were ultimately adopted by the NBA, including the slam-dunk contest he devised to highlight the last ABA All-Star Game in Denver in 1976. Upon taking over the team in 1974, Scheer changed its name from the Rockets to the Nuggets to give it more local identity. More recently, the Nuggets made history by becoming the first minority-owned major league franchise in American sport. Beset by weak financing and a lack of control, the minority owners lasted only three years.

Along the way, the Nuggets have been home to the talents of Thompson, Byron Beck, Dan Issel, and Alex English, whose retired uniform numbers hang from the scaffolding high above the basketball floor at McNichols Sports Arena, where the team plays. The franchise helped launch two coaching careers, those of nomad Larry Brown and iconoclast Doug Moe.

The team has enjoyed considerable success, winning 65 and 60 games in its last two seasons in the ABA and going to the NBA playoffs every year from 1982 to 1990 under Moe. But the Nuggets have never won a championship in either league. And recently, after Moe was fired in 1990, they sank to their lowest depths as a franchise, winning just 20 and 24 games in two disastrous seasons under coach Paul Westhead.

In a town where the competition ranges from football's Broncos to Rocky Mountain skiing 90 minutes away, the Nuggets have never taken themselves too seriously. The most identifiable personality in their history was that of Moe, their coach throughout the 1980s.

He won more games than any coach in franchise history, as well as leading the Nuggets to the playoffs in nine consecutive seasons. As he approached his milestone 600th career coaching victory near the end of his tenure in Denver, Moe was asked what he would like written on his gravestone when he died. He hesitated only a moment. "I'm decayed," he suggested.

Team Origins with the ABA

The Denver Rockets made their debut October 15, 1967. A referee tossed up a red, white, and blue ball to begin their first game. The tri-color ball would become the trademark of the ABA. There were 2,748 fans on hand at the downtown Denver Auditorium Arena for that game between the Rockets and Anaheim Amigos. The Rockets won, 110-105.

Though many ABA franchises ran into financial trouble quickly as a result of small crowds and shallow pockets, the Rockets had one of the league's strongest owners. Trucking magnate J. W. Ringsby, whose Ringsby System trucking line was worth $40 million in 1967, kept the franchise alive through the ABA's lean, early years.

On the floor, the Rockets proved to be one of the new league's better teams in the inaugural season. They finished with a record of 45-33 (the first ABA season was 78 games), good for third place

in the ABA's Western Division, three games back of the division champion New Orleans. The Rockets' top player was guard Larry Jones, who averaged a team-high 22.9 points per game and was named to the all-ABA first team.

Also on the club was Byron Beck, a local favorite as an AAU all-American from the University of Denver. He was the first draft choice the franchise signed to a contract. Beck and Louis Dampier of Kentucky would become the only players to play all nine ABA seasons with a single team. The Rockets' coach was Bob Bass, who would go on to a long NBA career as a coach and, ultimately, as a general manager.

The Rockets lost to the Buccaneers in the playoffs that first season. The New Orleans team featured two top players who would return to Denver when their playing careers were finished: guard Larry Brown, the most valuable player of the inaugural ABA All-Star Game, and forward Doug Moe, the league's No. 2 scorer.

The second season was much like the first, with much of the same cast. The Rockets finished 44-34, third again in the West. In the first round of the playoffs they faced the Oakland Oaks, who had coaxed NBA star Rick Barry to jump to the ABA. The Oaks also had Brown and Moe by that time. The Oaks won the series in seven games.

Bass moved on to Texas Tech following the 1968-69 season, and John McClendon was named the club's second head coach. After a 9-19 start to the 1969-70 season, McClendon was replaced by Joe Belmont, who would lead the team to its first real success in the ABA.

Aggressiveness Breeds Success

In the escalating battle with the NBA for players, the Rockets set a new tone of aggressiveness by plundering the University of Detroit for 6-foot-9, 225-pound forward Spencer Haywood, who had completed just two years of school. The 20-year-old Haywood, an all-American and hero of the 1968 gold medal U.S. Olympic team, made an immediate impact, averaging 29.9 points and 19.4

TEAM INFORMATION AT A GLANCE

Founding date: 1967 as the Denver Rockets of the American Basketball Association (ABA);
team changed its name to Nuggets, 1974; became part of the NBA, 1976

Home court:
McNichols Sports Arena
1635 Clay St.
Denver, CO 80204
Phone: (303) 893-6700

Capacity: 17,022

Team colors: White, blue, green, yellow, red, purple, and orange
Team nickname: Nuggets
Logo: City skyline with peaked mountains in background

Franchise record	Won	Lost	Pct.
(1967-92)	1,073	981	.522

rebounds per game in his rookie season of 1969-70 and leading the Rockets to the ABA Western Division title. Denver won its first playoff series that year, defeating Washington in the opening round before falling to the Los Angeles Stars in the second round.

The team's promise crumbled during the off-season. In a dispute with ownership, Haywood took the Rockets to court and had his contract terminated, then jumped to the NBA. Jones, the team's other star, went to Florida for cash. Without its two best players, the club floundered, finishing the 1970-71 season with a record of 30-54 (the ABA had expanded to 84 regular-season games for the 1969-70 season).

Belmont was replaced during the season by Stan Albeck, the team's fourth head coach. The only bright spot of the 1970-71 campaign was the arrival of Ralph Simpson, who left Michigan State after two years. Simpson would become one of the stars of the ABA.

The team's performance in 1970-71 convinced the Ringsby ownership that it needed an experienced hand at the head of the team's basketball operation. Ringsby hired colorful Alex Hannum and turned the franchise over to him, naming him president, general manager, and head coach. At the time, Hannum was the only coach ever to win championships in the NBA (with St. Louis in 1957-58 and Philadelphia in 1966-67), the ABA (with Oakland in 1968-69), and the Amateur Athletic Union (with the Wichita Vickers in 1958-59).

In his second year, Simpson established himself as one of the ABA's best offensive players, averaging 27.4 points per game, fifth best in the league. The 1971-72 season also saw the emergence of a little-known Virginia Squires rookie named Julius Erving.

On December 14, 1972, the Ringsbys sold the Denver franchise to a pair of San Diego businessmen, Frank M. Goldberg and A. G. (Bud) Fischer. Despite Simpson's efforts, the club finished the 1971-72 season with a record of 34-50.

Hannum's influence began to show in his second season, when Simpson, Beck, and newly acquired Warren Jabali led the Rockets to a 47-37 record. For the second straight year, the Rockets were eliminated from the ABA playoffs by the Indiana Pacers, who went on to win their second consecutive ABA title.

The 1973-74 season saw a return to the struggles of the '71-72 campaign. The Rockets finished 37-47 and failed to qualify for the playoffs. It was the end of Hannum's tenure in charge.

New Identity

When the Carolina Cougars were bought and moved by a group from St. Louis, the men running the Cougars went in search of work. It wasn't long before they found it. The Denver franchise hired Scheer to run the front office and Brown and Moe to coach the team. The first thing Scheer did was change the club's identity. On August 7, 1974, the Denver Rockets became the Denver Nuggets.

Scheer rapidly remade the roster that summer, acquiring veteran point guard Mack Calvin and North Carolina star Bobby Jones. The roster Scheer assembled, which still included Simpson and Beck, was one of the best in the ABA. Under Brown's wide-open style of coaching, the Nuggets raced to a 65-19 record, still a franchise record. But once more the playoffs proved disappointing. Paced by George McGinnis, the Pacers upset the Nuggets in the second round of the post-season tournament.

During the off-season of 1975, it was clear that North Carolina State's David Thompson was the most coveted rookie in the country. Atlanta made him the first pick of the NBA draft. The Virginia Squires made him the first pick of the ABA draft. The Squires, however, did not have the

Naismith Memorial Basketball Hall of Fame

Dan Issel (25)

financial resources to sign him. Denver's Carolina connection of Scheer, Brown, and Moe knew how much Thompson could mean to the Nuggets and the ABA.

The Nuggets cut a deal with Virginia for Thompson's draft rights, sending Calvin and forwards Mike Green and George Irvine to the Squires. On July 25, 1975, Thompson signed a contract with Denver, completing the ABA's single greatest victory over the NBA.

Riding their 65-win season and the signing of Thompson, the Nuggets moved out of the cramped Auditorium Arena into the new, 17,000-seat McNichols Sports Arena at the beginning of the 1975-76 season, which would be the ABA's last. Thompson was astonishing as a rookie, winning ABA rookie-of-the-year honors and the ABA All-Star Game most valuable player award, and leading the Nuggets in six offensive categories, including scoring, averaging 26.0 points per game.

Despite a league-best record of 60-24 and Thompson's superstar performance, the Nuggets could not manage to win the ABA crown. Behind Erving, who would come to be known as "Dr. J" and would be inducted into the Pro Basketball Hall of Fame in 1993, the New York Nets defeated the Nuggets four games to two in the final ABA championship series.

End of the ABA

After nine years, 28 teams, and some $50 million in losses, the ABA closed its doors. Along with the Nuggets, New York, Indiana, and San Antonio were admitted to the NBA as part of the 1976 merger agreement. The Nuggets quickly disproved claims of a great disparity in talent between the two leagues. They ran to an 8-0 start in their first NBA campaign and won the Midwest Division with a 50-32 record.

Thompson, Dan Issel, and Bobby Jones all earned starting berths on the Western Conference All-Star team in 1977. In their first NBA playoff series, the Nuggets lost to Bill Walton and the Portland Trail Blazers, who went on to beat the Philadelphia 76ers for the NBA championship.

The following year, the Nuggets won their second straight Midwest Division title, posting a 48-34 record. Thompson and San Antonio's George Gervin put on a thrilling race for the scoring title. On the final day of the season, in Detroit on April 9, 1978, Thompson scored 73 points, the third-highest single-game total in the history of the NBA. Gervin came back later that night to score 63 points to win the title. Gervin averaged 27.22 points per game; Thompson averaged 27.15. In the playoffs, Denver got past Milwaukee in the first round, then fell to Seattle in six games in the Western Conference finals.

Frustrated by their inability to win a championship, the Nuggets engineered a major trade prior to the start of the 1978-79 season. They dealt popular forward Bobby Jones to Philadelphia for big George McGinnis. It did not have the intended effect. The team went sideways, finishing at 47-35, and was ousted by the Los Angeles Lakers in the first round of the playoffs.

Larry Brown began his nomadic wanderings that season, stepping down when the team was 28-25 and handing the reins to assistant coach Donnie Walsh. Walsh guided the Nuggets to a 19-10 finish.

From 1975 to 1979, the Nuggets won 203 regular season games, 15 playoff games, and three division championships, the most successful stretch in club history. But they did not win a championship, and it would be a long time before they would come as close.

Though they still had Thompson, Issel, and McGinnis, the Nuggets began to unravel in the 1979-80 season. They lost their first seven games. Thompson, bothered by a succession of injuries and ailments, saw action in only 39 games. The Nuggets limped to a 30-52 record and missed the playoffs. In mid-season, they shipped McGinnis to Indiana in exchange for a reserve forward named Alex English. English would become a fixture at forward for the Nuggets throughout the 1980s, developing into one of the best offensive players in NBA history.

Because of their dreadful performance the previous season, the Nuggets had the fifth overall pick of the 1980 NBA draft. They used it to select James Ray from Jacksonville, the 1980 Sun Belt Conference Player of the Year. It was perhaps the worst draft choice in club history. Knee problems prevented Ray from making a contribution. He appeared in just 18 games during his rookie year, averaging just 2.1 points per game.

Lacking Resources

In the aftermath, the poor selection was blamed on the team's lack of resources. The San Diego owners had sold their interest in 1976 to a consortium of Denver investors assembled by Scheer. But there was no deep-pockets investor in the group, and the team struggled to keep its head above water. Scheer could not afford scouts, and he scouted the available college players by watching them on TV. The Ray selection proved the system inadequate.

After an 11-20 start to the 1980-81 season, Walsh was relieved as head coach, and assistant Doug Moe was named to take his place. Moe guided the team to a 26-25 finish. He would coach the Nuggets for the next nine seasons and take them to the playoffs after each one.

Scheer made up for the Ray selection by dealing two future first-round draft choices to Dallas for the rights to unsigned draft choice Kiki Vandeweghe and a future draft choice. Vandeweghe would team with Issel and English to form one of the most explosive offensive frontcourts in NBA history.

By the 1981-82 season, injuries and a substance-abuse problem had robbed Thompson of much of his magic. The Nuggets dealt him to Seattle following that season, receiving defensive ace Bill Hanzlik in exchange. Powered by the "Big Three," the Nuggets won 46 games in the 1981-82 season, good for second place in the Midwest Division. They lost to Phoenix in the first round of the playoffs.

The 1982-83 season was much the same. English became the only member of the Nuggets ever to win the NBA scoring title, averaging 28.4 points per game. Vandeweghe was the runner-up, averaging 26.7 points per game. Issel was 18th in the league, averaging 21.6. The Nuggets won 45 games, finishing second in the Midwest again. Denver defeated Phoenix in a first-round playoff rematch, then was dispatched by San Antonio in the second round.

Throughout this period, Moe was refining the motion offense he and Brown had installed in the 1970s. An instinctive coach, Moe removed almost all the structured plays from the Nuggets' offense, leaving a fast-paced, free-lance, playground game that left it to players to make the right decisions in the flow of the game. It produced the league's highest-scoring team throughout the 1980s.

In 1982, desperately in need of cash, the Scheer syndicate sold the team to B. J. "Red" McCombs, a Texas oilman and investor. After a decade in Denver, Scheer departed in 1983 for a short-lived stint running the Los Angeles Clippers. After a disappointing 38-44 record in 1983-84,

McCombs hired Vince Boryla as president and chief operating officer.

In his first month on the job, Boryla pulled off the biggest trade in club history, shipping Vandeweghe to Portland for Wayne Cooper, Lafayette Lever, Calvin Natt, and two future draft choices. The deal paid off immediately. Natt proved to be the most relentless inside player the franchise had ever had. Lever excelled in every phase of the game from the backcourt.

Midwest Division Title

In their first year, they ran away with the Midwest Division title, earning a 52-30 record, the first time in eight years the franchise had won 50 games. Boryla was named NBA executive of the year. The Nuggets squeezed past San Antonio in the first round of the playoffs, three games to two, then breezed by Utah, four games to one, to make it to the Western Conference finals against the Los Angeles Lakers.

The two teams split the first two games of the best-of-seven series, but Game 3 spelled disaster for the Nuggets. Lever, hobbled by a sore knee, was unable to play. English broke the thumb on his shooting hand during the game. The Nuggets did not win another game in the series. To this day, Denver fans debate whether the team might have made the NBA Finals for the first time in its history had Lever and English been healthy for the rest of that series with the Lakers.

The end of that season marked the end of Issel's sensational playing career in Denver. "The Horse" closed out a 15-year pro career that included six years in the ABA. Counting his production in both leagues, Issel retired with 27,482 pro points. Today, that total is exceeded by only four players: Kareem Abdul-Jabbar, Wilt Chamberlain, Julius Erving, and Moses Malone. In his entire career, Issel missed only 24 games because of injury, hence, his nickname.

After the 1984-85 season, McCombs sold the club to fellow Texan and businessman Sidney Shlenker. Although favored to repeat as Midwest

Division champs, the Nuggets slipped to 47 victories and finished second in the division. English averaged a career-best 29.8 points per game, tied for second in the league scoring race. The Nuggets eased past Portland in the first round of the playoffs before falling to Houston, four games to two, in the conference semi-finals.

The following season would prove a disappointment. Natt, the team's toughest player and inspirational leader, ended his season in the third quarter of the first game, tearing his Achilles' tendon. The Nuggets struggled the rest of the way, compiling a 37-45 record, one of only two sub-.500 records in Moe's nine full seasons as head coach. They did qualify for the playoffs, but were blitzed three games to none in the first round by the Lakers, who went on to win the NBA title.

Downhill Slide

Though the cast would remain largely unchanged for three more seasons, the Nuggets teams of the 1980s had seen their greatest glory. As the players aged, they grew more brittle. But they had one last hurrah in them, and it would come in the 1987-88 season.

One week before the start of the season, Boryla resigned as president and general manager and was replaced by Pete Babcock, the team's vice president of player personnel. Three days before the start of the season, Babcock made his first trade, dealing forward Mark Alarie and guard Darrell Walker to the Washington Bullets for forward Jay Vincent and guard Michael Adams.

The team took a while to gel. On March 18, 1988, the Nuggets trailed Dallas by five and a half games in the Midwest Division. But led by the diminutive and speedy Adams at point guard, the Nuggets won 17 of their last 19 games, including one streak of 10 straight victories. The spurt gave them 54 wins for the season, their highest total since joining the NBA, and shot them past Dallas to their fourth Midwest Division crown. Moe was named coach of the year. English and Lever were starters on the Western Conference All-Star team.

The Nuggets edged Seattle in the opening round of the playoffs, then met Dallas in the second round. In a finish reminiscent of the 1985 heartache, the Nuggets led the series two games to one but lost Vincent and Lever to injuries. Without them, the Nuggets lost three straight to the Mavericks and were ousted.

The team was noticeably older in 1988-89. Though it dominated at home, winning 35 of 41 games at McNichols, it was helpless on the road, winning just 9 of 41. The Nuggets finished 44-38. Vincent and Natt, no longer contributing, were shipped off to San Antonio. The team was third in the Midwest. Phoenix wiped out the Nuggets, three games to none, in the first round of the playoffs.

Team Sold to Minority Owners

That summer, Shlenker announced he was selling the team to a group of African-American investors headed by Bertram M. Lee of Boston and Peter C. B. Bynoe of Chicago. NBA commissioner David Stern acknowledged he had helped bring the parties together and congratulated the Nuggets on making history by welcoming the first minority owners of a major league franchise.

As summer dragged into fall and the deal still hadn't closed, it became apparent that Lee and Bynoe were having difficulty securing adequate financing for the purchase. Former Utah Jazz president David Checketts was brought in to run the Nuggets under the new owners. But he quickly backed out, suggesting the new owners did not have sufficient capital to run a competitive franchise.

In a last-ditch effort to save the purchase, Stern brought in his old friend Robert Wussler, a former television executive who had just taken over Comsat Video Enterprises, a subsidiary of huge Washington-based Comsat Corp. The deal finally closed in November with Comsat providing most of the cash and owning a controling interest. Conflicts among the owners would bring disaster to the franchise. In less than two years, the team would fire or lose four top executives: Checketts, Babcock, Jon Spoelstra, and Scheer, who returned for a second stint as club president, but lasted less than a year.

Following a 43-39 record in the 1989-90 season and another first-round exit in the playoffs, Moe was fired. Bernie Bickerstaff was hired as general manager, and he hired Paul Westhead as the new head coach. Westhead promised to "blow your socks off" with the space-age, up-tempo game he had made famous at Loyola Marymount University. But the system and the Nuggets' dearth of talent spelled catastrophe.

Before he was fired, Moe engineered the beginning of the Nuggets' rebuilding phase, trading Lever to Dallas for a pair of first-round draft choices, then dealing the picks to Miami for the third pick overall. With it, he took Louisiana State University phenom Chris Jackson.

Worst Season Ever

The team went 20-62 under Westhead in 1990-91, the worst record in its history. It was the first time the Nuggets had missed the playoffs since 1981. Westhead's system produced a slew of records, but not the sort he had promised. The 1990-91 edition of the Nuggets was the worst defensive team in NBA history by a number of measures.

The franchise was a disaster off the court as well. Wussler reported it had lost $10 million in the 1990-91 season. Rumors flew that the franchise would be sold and moved to Toronto or Anaheim or Memphis, Shlenker's new base of operations. When Scheer became the fourth front-office executive to leave or be dismissed under the new owners, Tim Leiweke was hired from the expansion Minnesota Timberwolves in the spring of 1991 to stanch the flow of red ink.

Bickerstaff drafted 7-foot-2 center Dikembe Mutombo and guard Mark Macon with the fourth and eighth choices of the 1991 draft, adding them to Jackson as the foundation of the rebuilding project. Results were slow to show. The team was

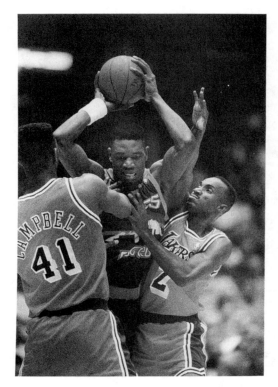

AP/Wide World Photos

Dikembe Mutombo

only slightly better in 1991-92, finishing 24-58. Westhead radically changed his system to a slow-down, low-post game centered around Mutombo, but the team remained woefully talent-poor.

Westhead was fired after the two worst seasons the franchise had ever seen. Issel, one of the most popular athletes in Denver history, had been doing color commentary on Nuggets' telecasts for several years.

In the spring of 1992, he announced his intention to leave Denver and accept a position as secretary of tourism for the Commonwealth of Kentucky, where he had been a hero for the University of Kentucky and the ABA's Kentucky Colonels. Before he left, Bickerstaff called him and asked him to coach the Nuggets. Issel canceled the moving vans. Without a day's experience in coaching, Issel was named head coach on May 20, 1992.

Bickerstaff added two more pieces to the growing stable of young talent, drafting forward LaPhonso Ellis and guard Bryant Stith with the 5th and 13th choices of the 1992 draft. Under Issel, the team returned to a modified version of the motion offense pioneered by Brown in the 1970s and refined by Moe in the 1980s. With a young team that lacked the instincts to make good decisions on the fly, however, Issel installed a series of set plays as well.

The complicated ownership situation was finally resolved in 1992. Lee had been ousted from the partnership the previous year after his finances grew so shaky he was evicted from his Denver apartment and his possessions deposited in the street. In June of 1992 Comsat bought out Bynoe, ending the period of minority ownership and giving the Nuggets a single, deep-pockets corporate owner.

Headed for Improvement

Relying heavily on their young talent, the Nuggets improved to 36-46 in 1992-93, Issel's first year as coach. Ellis had an outstanding season, becoming the first player in franchise history to start every game of his rookie season. Mutombo had another excellent year at center, setting a new franchise record for blocked shots in a season, with 287. The big surprise of the season was Jackson, the little point guard from LSU, who shook off two poor years under Westhead to become the team's leading scorer, averaging 19.2 points per game.

Though the Nuggets missed the playoffs for the third consecutive year, attendance improved, and the club's financial picture brightened with the help of Leiweke's aggressive salesmanship in the front office.

With what they hoped would be their last lottery draft choice of the 1990s, the Nuggets selected forward Rodney Rogers from Wake Forest with the ninth pick of the 1983 draft. Bicker-

staff also acquired Brian Williams, a former lottery pick, from the Orlando Magic during the off-season. Williams joined Reggie Williams and Tommy Hammonds as former blue-chip draft choices scooped up by the Nuggets after their original teams gave up on them.

Between the reclamation projects and the Nuggets' own premium draft picks of the previous four years, the roster was now stocked with more young, elite athletic talent than the franchise had ever accumulated before. Jackson, who had become a Muslim in 1991, took a pilgrimage to Mecca in May of 1993 and returned having adopted his Muslim name, Mahmoud Abdul-Rauf.

With the ownership and front-office problems behind them and a young, talented cast from which to mold a team, the Nuggets entered training camp in October of 1993 with high hopes of returning to the playoffs and building a consistent contender for the balance of the 1990s..

SOURCES

BOOKS

Carter, Craig, and Alex Sachare, *The Sporting News NBA Guide,* 1993-94.

Clark, Jay L., and Brian Bain, *Denver Nuggets Media Guide,* Denver, CO, 1993-94.

Hollander, Zander, and Alex Sachare, *The Official NBA Basketball Encyclopedia,* Villard Books, 1989.

Sachare, Alex, and Mark Shimabukuro, *The Sporting News NBA Register,* 1993-94.

PERIODICALS

Articles on Nuggets' history by Jay L. Clark and Brian Bain in *The Nugget,* a magazine published by the Denver Nuggets, 1991-92.

—*Dave Krieger*

HOUSTON ROCKETS

As they venture through their second quarter-century, the Houston Rockets rank as one of the more intriguing franchises in professional sports. This is a franchise which has gone from expansion woes to the brink of two world championships to the quicksand of mediocrity. There are rollercoaster rides and then there are "Rocket-coaster" rides. With these zany Rockets, anything's possible. "Looking back on it all, I'm sure there's not a franchise in the NBA which had as unpretentious of a beginning," said Ray Patterson, who presided over the Rockets as general manager for 18 years.

The odyssey began on January 11, 1967 when the San Diego Rockets were admitted as the 12th team in the National Basketball Association. The original owner was Bob Breitbard, who suffered through four uninspired seasons despite having drafted a kid named Elvin Hayes in 1968.

The expansion Rockets are a trivia question today because of their original No. 1 pick in 1967.

They drafted a forward from Kentucky named Pat Riley. As it turned out, Riley didn't exactly set the league on fire as a player, but he went on from there to eventually become one of the league's great coaches.

Hayes, Tomjanovich, and Murphy

The original Rockets of 1967-68 had the expected growing pains, turning in a 15-67 record. Center John Block averaged 20.2 points and forward Don Kojis added 19.7. But the defense was porous, as evidenced by the opponents' 121.0 scoring average. The last place finish enabled the Rockets to draft Hayes, the celebrated forward who had bested Lew Alcindor and UCLA in the now-legendary Astrodome game in 1968. Hayes would shoot just .447 as a rookie, but averaged 28.4 points and 17.2 rebounds. Thanks to Hayes' robust play, the Rockets had a 22-win improvement to 37-45 and made the playoffs, losing 4-2 to Atlanta in the first round.

But the enthusiasm for pro basketball in San Diego would not last long. In 1969-70, the Rockets experienced a 10-game disintegration to 27-55. Hayes was again a feared scorer and rebounder, but the team lacked focus and never recovered from a 1-9 start.

Following their third season, the Rockets enjoyed a draft which brought them two individuals who would withstand the test of time. First-round pick Rudy Tomjanovich and second-round pick Calvin Murphy would go on to have banner careers. Both men have had their playing numbers retired and both still work for the Rockets' franchise, with Tomjanovich serving as head coach. Tomjanovich and Murphy helped the Rockets get back on track in 1970-71. The club finished 40-42, third in the Pacific Division. But while there was some success on the court, there was anger and frustration off the court.

The Rockets Blast Off to Houston

Breitbard had become disenchanted with San Diego city officials over what he considered an exorbitantly high contract for use of the team's arena. Finally, an exasperated Breitbard decided to sell the franchise to a group of 17 Houston businessman. Presto. The San Diego Rockets had been transformed into the Houston Rockets. "I think the transfer of the club could be tied into the impulsiveness of the Houston business community in 1971," Patterson said. "There was an impulsiveness to buy everything from real estate to basketball franchises. Because of the appreciation, most things turned out all right."

But the original group of Houston owners had a hard sell in a football-crazy state. The main premise for buying the team was that the beloved Hayes, who had put the University of Houston on the basketball map, would pack the Astrodome whenever the Rockets played there.

Wrong, wrong, wrong. "The owners remembered Elvin, packing 50,000 into the Astrodome

for the UCLA game in 1968," Patterson said. "They were thinking, 'let's see 50,000 people at $10 a head, that's a $500,000 gate every night." Truth was, the Rockets didn't even have a legitimate home arena when they moved to Houston. In their first Houston season, they played "home games" in Waco, San Antonio and El Paso, as well as the Astrodome, AstroHall and Hofheinz Pavilion in Houston.

Patterson Steers the Team

With Coach Tex Winter at the helm, the vagabond Rockets weren't able to win friends and influence people. They finished 34-48 in '71-72 while struggling to win acceptance at the gate. It was then that the organization called on Patterson to become a Texas pioneer. Patterson had been the general manager of a Milwaukee team which won the world championship in 1971. But sensing that there was great long-term potential for pro basketball in the Southwest, Patterson gave up his Bucks' position to lead the Rockets into basketball prominence.

Patterson, who retired in 1990, remembers those early years from 1972 to 1975 as a time when only a wildcatter's spirit could keep the Rockets afloat. Patterson recalls a Thanksgiving Day game which was being nationally televised, but brought in only about 400 people to Hofheinz Pavilion. The fans were encouraged to come down to the choice seats so the camera could focus on the "crowd." Patterson's wife Ruth surveyed the scene and gently asked her husband: "Honey, should we invite everyone over to the house for Thanksgiving dinner?"

Former Rockets' assistant publicity director Harry Barrett relishes telling the story of what happened when the '72 Rockets played a designated home game in Waco, which is about 130 miles from Houston. The game was scheduled on a Wednesday night—church night—and legend has it that each church in town drew more than the Rockets. According to Barrett, the Rockets sold only one box seat. It was purchased by an elderly gentleman who fell asleep during the game and

TEAM INFORMATION AT A GLANCE

Founded in 1967 as the San Diego Rockets;
moved to Houston, 1971

Home court:
The Summit
Ten Greenway Plaza
Houston, TX 77046
Phone: (713) 627-0600

Seating capacity: 16,279

Team nickname: Rockets
Team colors: red, gold
Team logo: Team name superimposed on a stylized basketball

didn't stop snoring until somebody woke him well after the final buzzer.

A big part of the identity problem was that the Rockets simply couldn't win. They were 33-49 in 1972-73 and 32-50 in 1973-74. Few victories meant few fans. How bad was it? There was one occasion when the Rockets were hoping for a big draw against headliner Pete Maravich and the Atlanta Hawks.

Patterson began driving toward Hofheinz Pavilion and was encouraged when he got stuck in a traffic jam. "But then we got up there and everybody turned off to go to a nearby stadium for high school football," Patterson said. "The high school game drew about 20,000. We had about 200."

The futility of the early Houston years was not lost on the players. Tomjanovich remembers the arena being so quiet that the few fans actually became privy to bench conversations. "One night we were on the bench at Hofheinz, talking about where we wanted to go after the game," Tomjanovich said. "It was so quiet that a guy way up in the stands yells out 'no, no, don't go there.

That's not a good place to eat.'"

Houston ownership changed three times in the first four seasons and it required sleight of hand to balance the books. "Deferred salaries was the only way we stayed in business," Patterson said. The breakthrough came in 1974-75 when Houston finally achieved its first .500 season. After finishing second in the Central Division with a 41-41 mark, the Rockets knocked off the New York Knicks 2-1 in an Eastern Conference mini-series. It was during that season that Houston achieved its first sellout (10,518) at Hofheinz.

Financial Stability Yields Wins

During the Knicks' playoff series, Patterson invited Houston real estate tycoon Kenneth Schnitzer to attend a game. Schnitzer must have been impressed. He wound up buying the Rockets and constructing The Summit, where Houston still plays. According to Patterson, Schnitzer's involvement was the single most important development in Rockets' history. "From then on, we were le-

Calvin Murphy stands only 5-foot-9, but he always ranked as the Rocket with the biggest heart. In a 13-year career that culminated with the retirement of his No. 23 jersey, Murphy defied the odds and confounded the critics. A 5-foot-9 guy simply wasn't supposed to flourish in the land of giants. "They said I was too small and I always thrived on proving people wrong," Murphy said.

Murphy, who is now a Rockets' telecaster, scored 17,949 points in his 13-year career. He is best known for his NBA-record 78 consecutive free throws during a span from December 27, 1980 to February 28, 1981. "There has never been a more competitive person than Calvin Murphy," said former Rockets' General Manager Ray Patterson. "His lack of height simply wasn't going to stop him."

Murphy, who had a legendary college career at Niagara University, has been nominated three times for the Basketball Hall of Fame.

He made up for his lack of size with a brilliant shooting touch and amazing speed and quickness. All things considered, Murphy's greatest professional game had to be Game 7 of the 1981 Western Conference semifinals against rival San Antonio.

Naismith Memorial Basketball Hall of Fame

The Spurs had rallied to win Game 6 in Houston and star center Moses Malone got sick to his stomach shortly before Game 7 in San Antonio. Murphy had been a Sixth Man most of the year, but Coach Del Harris made an instinctive decision to start Murphy in the biggest game of the season. Murphy responded with a 42-point explosion to propel Houston to a 105-100 victory.

The Rockets would go on to reach their first-ever NBA Finals. "That game in San Antonio, I was not going to be denied," Murphy said. "I was in a zone where I felt like every shot I put up was a cinch basket."

Murphy led the NBA in free throw percentage twice (1981, 1983) and finished among the Top Five nine other times—including second on eight occasions. Murphy and Rick Barry are the only players in league history to have shot .500 or better from the line in five or more seasons.

Some have argued that Murphy ranks as the best sub 6-footer in NBA history. Rockets' officials would second that notion. "Calvin was so determined that size would not prevent him from becoming a great professional player," said Rudy Tomjanovich, the Rockets' coach and a former Murphy teammate. "He's a great inspiration to kids everywhere. It just proves that if you are talented enough and work hard enough, little guys can make it big in basketball."

gitimate," Patterson said. After eight struggling years, the Rockets finally had a financial foundation. The success would follow. With first-year Coach Tom Nissalke leading the way, the Rockets won the Central Division championship with a 49-33 record in 1976-77 and narrowly missed advancing to the world championship series.

Nissalke had convinced Houston management to trade two No. 1 draft picks to Buffalo for a talented but unproven center, Moses Malone. It turned out to be the greatest deal in club history. With Malone establishing himself as a great player and Tomjanovich, Murphy and point guard John Lucas making significant contributions, Houston made it to the Eastern Conference Finals against Philadelphia.

Trailing 3-1 in that series, the Rockets staged a heroic comeback in Game 5 at Philadelphia to force Game 6 at The Summit. The sixth game was close, but in the end Lucas was called for a controversial charging violation against Doug Collins. Fifteen years later, there is still debate among Rockets' fans about whether Collins flopped on the play. Despite the heartbreaking finish, Rockets' basketball had arrived to challenge the baseball Astros and football Oilers for the sports entertainment dollar in Houston.

But disaster struck 23 games into the 1977-78 season when Tomjanovich was felled by a Kermit Washington punch in one of the uglier scenes in NBA history. During a Rockets-Lakers game at The Forum, a scuffle broke out and Tomjanovich tried to intervene. He never saw Washington's punch, which forced Tomjanovich to have massive reconstructive surgery and miss the remainder of the season. Although Tomjanovich would come back the following season and play until 1981, many long-time Rockets' observers think Tomjanovich was never the same after the Washington punch.

Barry Fires Houston Up

Without their All-Star forward, the Rockets sank to a 28-54 record in '78, forcing club management to make a bold move in the off-season.

With Schnitzer looking to sell the club, Houston management felt it needed a marquee name to enhance the club's marketability.

Enter free-agent Rick Barry. Although Barry was in the twilight of his marvelous career, he brought along the credibility which helped persuade New Mexico businessman George Maloof to purchase the club. With Malone, Murphy, Tomjanovich, Barry, Robert Reid and Mike Newlin, Houston had plenty of offensive firepower in '79. The club shot a sizzling .497 from the floor and averaged 113.4 points while posting a 47-35 record. Malone was particularly adept as a scorer and rebounder and wound up being honored as the league's Most Valuable Player.

For much of the season, it appeared Houston would win its second divisional title. But the Rockets finished in second place, one game behind San Antonio. That meant the Rockets had to meet Atlanta in the playoffs.

"Atlanta had John Drew, who was a top scorer, and we weren't able to guard him," Nissalke would say. "The Hawks were probably the toughest matchup in the league for us. Had we won the division, we wouldn't have had to worry about them."

The Hawks sprang an upset at The Summit in Game 1 and wound up sweeping the mini-series 2-0. The new ownership then decided a coaching change was in order, promoting assistant Del Harris. Under Harris, the Rockets got off to a 2-7 start in 1979-80, but pulled together to finish 41-41 and earn a homecourt playoff advantage against Interstate 10 rival San Antonio.

The Rockets won the mini-series in three games and Maloof was so excited that he told reporters: "We're going to beat Boston. You can quote me." That quote wound up on the Celtics' bulletin board and rookie Larry Bird and Co. had all the motivation they needed for the second-round series. Houston fell 4-0, with Boston winning the last two games convincingly on the Rockets' homecourt.

Houston's 1980-81 season appeared for the longest time to be another ho-hum march toward mediocrity. The Rockets, in fact, needed to win

Moses Malone has had a long and distinguished reign as a center in the National Basketball Association. Houston fans will note with pride that six of Malone's prime years came during his tenure with the Houston Rockets. From 1977 through 1982, Malone displayed a relentless work ethic that helped take the Rockets' franchise to a new level. While with Houston, Malone was the league's Most Valuable Player in 1979 and 1982. His bullish work in the trenches catapulted the Cinderella Rockets into the 1981 NBA Finals against Boston. "Every time a shot went into the air, Moses thought the ball belonged to him," former Rockets Coach Del Harris said. "The key to his rebounding success was that he went after everything with 100 percent effort."

Malone was not a media darling, often declining interview requests in a gruff manner. But one quote of Malone's has withstood the test of time. With Houston locked in a 2-2 tie against Boston in the '81 Finals, Malone said: "I could take four guys off the streets of Petersburg [Va., Malone's hometown] and beat the Celtics." Inspired by that comment, Boston won the next two games to close out the season. Asked why he made the inflammatory remark, Malone said: "I was just trying to give my team some extra pep."

In February of 1982, Malone enjoyed a month which will long be remembered among NBA observers. He averaged 38 points and 17 rebounds while leading Houston to an 11-3 record. That month was an illustration of the 6-foot-10 Malone at the peak of his career.

The Rockets decided to trade Malone after the 1981-82 season because they had a financial gun pointed at their heads. Malone had been extended an offer sheet by Philadelphia for $13.2 million. Had they matched the bid, the Rockets felt it would be tantamount to financial suicide. Malone was torn between making the best business deal for himself and remaining with the organization he deeply cared for. He told close friends during the offer-sheet waiting period that he didn't want to go and hoped Houston would match the bid.

Malone would wind up with the Sixers, teaming with Julius Erving to lead Philadelphia to the 1983 title. But he continued to have a soft spot for Houston and still makes his off-season home there. "It's hard to imagine a better center than what I saw when Moses was with the Rockets," former Houston swingman Robert Reid said. "He was extraordinary. Most of the time, we just climbed on the big guy's shoulders and rode him to victory."

four of their last six games just to qualify for the final Western Conference playoff spot. But what happened in the playoffs was pure Cinderella theater. In a classic rags-to-riches turnaround, the Rockets stunned the Lakers 2-1 in a first-round mini-series. Malone was dominant throughout the series and Earvin "Magic" Johnson wasn't his usual sharp self after having missed much of the season because of a knee injury.

In the decisive Game 3, Houston trailed by a point in the waning seconds when unheralded guard Mike Dunleavy hit a 17-foot jumper to give the Rockets the biggest win in the 14-year history of the franchise. From there, the Rockets would go on to whip San Antonio 4-3, winning Game 7 on the road when Murphy responded with an incredible 42-point explosion. The Cinderella march continued with Houston's 4-1 win over Kansas City, leaving the Rockets as Houston's first established pro sports franchise (NBA, NFL, or major-league baseball) to reach the world championship round.

Houston played tough in The Finals, but lost 4-2 to Bird and the Celtics. Alas, Cinderella finally lost its glass slipper. But the '81 Rockets are still the example most cited by underdog playoff

Hakeem Olajuwon has truly lived the American dream since coming to the United States from his Nigeria homeland in 1978. Olajuwon was merely in pursuit of an American college education when he arrived in Houston in 1979. He wound up mastering the sport of basketball and has become one of the NBA's brightest stars in his eight-year pro career. "Everybody knows that America is the land of opportunity," Olajuwon said. "It certainly was for me."

The 6-foot-11 Olajuwon was a soccer goalie as a youngster in Nigeria, but a coach there evaluated his athletic talent and decided he could play basketball at the college level. Once in America, Olajuwon improved his game tremendously under Coach Guy Lewis at the University of Houston.

He was an instant sensation with the Houston Rockets in his rookie season and now ranks with David Robinson and Patrick Ewing as the finest centers in the game. There's no question he is earmarked for the Hall of Fame when his career ends.

Olajuwon's rare blend of size, quickness and shot-blocking instincts have made him a world-wide figure and a multi-millionaire. "I just want to win and be respected by the players and the management," Olajuwon said. "If management tells me after the season that I did an excellent job, I say, 'Thank you, I'm satisfied.' I don't care about the individual glory. Considering where I come from, I've already gone way beyond expectations."

Through his first eight seasons, Olajuwon was an offensive force, consistently averaging more than 20 points per game. But it was his dominating defensive presence that most impressed the masses and prompted comparisons to Bill Russell and Wilt Chamberlain. "Hakeem is a great player who changes the entire complexion of a game with his intimidation," Rockets Coach Rudy Tomjanovich said.

Heading into the 1992-93, season, Olajuwon figured his American dream story would have several more exciting chapters. "I feel like I've only completed the first half of my basketball career," said Olajuwon. "I'm really looking forward to bigger and better things in the second half." Olajuwon narrowly missed wining an NCAA championship. His University of Houston teams were beaten in the title games in 1983 and 1984. Olajuwon led the Rockets to the NBA Finals in 1986, but Houston lost the title series to the Boston Celtics. "Winning a championship is the ultimate goal," Olajuwon said. It would put the exclamation point on Olajuwon's Hall of Fame career.

Photo: *AP/Wide World Photos*

teams. "That team showed there is always hope, even if you're a low-seeded playoff club," Harris said. In an effort to maintain the impromptu play-off momentum of 1981, Houston brought back Hayes in time for the 1981-82 season. Hayes had enjoyed his best years with the Washington Bullets, but yearned to finish his career at home. With Malone and Hayes anchoring the front line, the Rockets went 46-36. But there was no playoff magic this time. Houston lost a first-round series to Seattle, paving the way for a monumental decision.

Houston car dealer Charlie Thomas had purchased the club from the Maloof family in June of 1982. When the Philadelphia 76ers presented Malone with a staggering (at the time) $13.2 million, six-year offer sheet, Thomas chose to trade Malone because the numbers didn't add up. Houston was drawing about 11,000 per game and projected to win from 42 to 46 games. "From a salesmanship standpoint, when all the factors were in, it made sense to let Moses go," Patterson said.

The Rockets got a draft pick from Philadelphia which turned out to be Rodney McCray. They finished last the next two years and won coin flips, netting them Ralph Sampson and Hakeem Olajuwon. With these quality attractions, the Rockets were on their way to new heights on and off the court. With hard-driving Coach Bill Fitch in charge, the Rockets enjoyed their greatest season in 1985-86, winning the Midwest Division title at 51-31 and advancing to the NBA Finals against Boston.

The Rockets became the hottest ticket in town. The young front line acquired through the draft was augmented by guards Lucas, Lewis Lloyd and Mitchell Wiggins. Perhaps the greatest moment in Rockets' history came in Game 5 of the Western Finals at Los Angeles when Sampson hit a desperation shot at the buzzer to complete a 4-1 series victory. Had the 1986 Celtics not been one of the great teams of all time, the Rockets might have gotten the world championship. Boston—with Bird, Kevin McHale and Robert Parish at their peak—prevailed 4-2.

Drugs and Injuries Take Their Toll

The young Rockets figured at that point they would rule the league for many years. But the club started slowly in 1986-87 and then heard the devastating news in January that Wiggins and Lloyd were receiving two-year bars because of drug violations. Lucas had also been released at the end of the previous year because of a drug relapse. "We've been on our way [to a title] a couple of times," Patterson said. "After going to the conference Finals in 1977, everybody got hurt the next year. After 1986, we lost our guards [to drugs]."

The losses of Lucas, Lloyd and Wiggins tore apart the Rockets' rotation and a knee injury to Sampson in 1987 compounded the problems. The Rockets' empire had begun to crumble and Houston has yet to adequately put the pieces back together.

The club tried to shore up the depleted backcourt with a blockbuster trade in December 1987. Sampson and Steve Harris were sent to Golden State for Sleepy Floyd and Joe Barry Carroll. That deal, however, turned out be Much Ado About Nothing. Sampson's injury-plagued career went straight downhill and Floyd and Carroll failed to live up to advance billing, although Floyd has remained a Rocket for the last five years.

The Rockets won a first-round playoff series in 1986-87, but haven't prevailed in the playoffs since. Olajuwon has continued to be a dynamic center who regularly ranks among the league leaders in blocked shots and rebounding. But the cast around him has been suspect since the '86 Western Conference championship club was broken up.

The Rockets won 46 and 45 games in 1988 and 1989, respectively, but simply didn't have enough ammunition in the playoffs. Houston had a temporary rejuvenation in 1990-91 under Coach Don Chaney, using a blistering 23-5 surge in the second half of the season to build a club-record 52-36 record. However, the Rockets were derailed by the Lakers in the first round of the playoffs and then slumped to 42-46 in 1991-92, missing the playoffs for the first time in Olajuwon's eight-year career.

In hopes of getting back on track in the rugged Western Conference, the Rockets have turned to their most loyal company man for guidance in the '90s. Tomjanovich, 43, has been with the Rockets' organization for 22 years as a player, scout, assistant coach and now head coach. "I'm going to expend all my energies toward turning this thing around," Tomjanovich said. "I guess you could say I love this franchise. I love the Rockets."

And for more than a quarter-century, there has been a lot to love. There has also been a lot of frustration for Houstonians who crave a world championship in any pro sport. But love them or loathe them you have to admit the Rockets have always been interesting. Literally and figuratively, they've come a long way since San Diego.

—Robert Falkoff

MINNESOTA TIMBERWOLVES

With the advent of the Timberwolves in 1989, the state of Minnesota once again enjoyed National Basketball Association (NBA) play after a 29-year hiatus from the league. The former home of the Lakers, the Twin Cities had languished without an NBA team for nearly three decades until an expansion provided a new franchise for the region. The scrappy young Timberwolves today play in their own arena—generally to packed houses—and are engaged in the standard fight for respectability that attends the arrival of any expansion team.

The Timberwolves began NBA play in 1989, but attempts to win the franchise date to 1984. On January 12, 1984, Minnesota governor Rudy Perpich appointed a 30-member task force to lobby for a new Minnesota team. Heading that task force was ex-Laker great George Mikan, one of the early superstars of NBA basketball. Joining Mikan in the quest as early as 1986 were a pair of multimillionaire Minneapolis businessmen, Har-

vey Ratner and Marv Wolfenson. "Harv and Marv" had worked as partners for decades, becoming wealthy men with a string of health clubs and numerous apartment complexes in the Twin Cities area.

Ratner and Wolfenson were the principal investors for the $32 million franchise, and they also secured financing for one of the few privately funded arenas in the nation, the luxurious Target Center in downtown Minneapolis.

Ratner and Wolfenson faced one dilemma: both were well into their sixties and therefore unwilling to run another major business themselves. They therefore recruited Wolfenson's son-in-law Robert Stein as future president of the potential ball club. Stein, a former professional football player and an attorney, took over the day-to-day business of putting together the franchise and running it once it was secured.

Once the NBA Expansion Committee expressed a willingness to front four more teams, it set certain standards for competing cities to fill. One was the sale of 10,000 season tickets by the time the committee made its decision. Another was the provision of a modern, state-of-the-art facility for home games.

Ratner and Wolfenson were able to solicit promises for almost 9,000 season tickets in a single month in the autumn of 1986. Preparations were also being made for ground breaking on Target Center, with an expected opening in 1990. A contest was held to determine the team name, and "Timberwolves" beat out "Polars" by a narrow margin.

On April 3, 1987, the NBA Expansion Committee recommended that Minneapolis be the site of one of four new franchises slated to begin play by 1989. The NBA Board of Governors approved the recommendation on April 22, and the Timberwolves were officially launched. Bill Musselman, a former University of Minnesota coach with years of NBA experience, was hired as the first Timberwolves head coach on August 23, 1988. He helped the front office to prepare for the June, 1989 expansion draft that would provide the Wolves with the bulk of their player personnel for the inaugural season.

The Timberwolves joined the NBA at the same time as the Orlando Magic. Both teams participated in an expansion draft on June 15, 1989. Minnesota's first pick in that draft was power forward Rick Mahorn from the then-World Champion Detroit Pistons. Mahorn heard the news less than an hour after a rally celebrating his Pistons' world championship victory, and he was furious.

In the end he never played for the Timberwolves but was traded to the Philadelphia 76ers for several high-round draft picks. Other players selected by Minnesota in the expansion draft included Tyrone Corbin, Steve Johnson, Brad Lohaus, David Rivers, Mark Davis, and Scott Roth.

In the college draft a week later, the Timberwolves added point guard Jerome "Pooh" Richardson of UCLA to the roster, as well as center Gary Leonard and guard Doug West.

The Timberwolves made their NBA debut on

AP/Wide World Photos

Christian Laettner

November 3, 1989, losing to the SuperSonics in Seattle. Five days later they were welcomed home to their temporary arena, the Metrodome.

More than 35,000 fans watched the Wolves lose to the Chicago Bulls that night in a game marked by Michael Jordan's scoring 45 points for the opposition. The spacious Metrodome provided excellent temporary housing for the rookie Timberwolves. So ample was the seating that at season's end in 1990, Minnesota had set a new all-time NBA attendance record with well over a million paying customers.

Expansion teams are notorious for slow starts and growing pains. The Timberwolves have experienced more than their share of difficulties while still providing a surprisingly competitive team. In the first four years of play, three head coaches came and went—Musselman was fired in

TEAM INFORMATION AT A GLANCE

Founding date: April 22, 1987

Home court:
Target Center
600 First Avenue North
Minneapolis, MN 55403
Phone: (612) 337-3865

Seating capacity: 19,006 for basketball
Team colors: Blue, green, silver, and white
Team nickname: Timberwolves
Logo: Timberwolf in front of a basketball

Franchise record	Won	Lost
(1989-1993)	85	243

May of 1991; his successor, Jimmy Rodgers, lasted just one season.

In April of 1993 Rodgers was unseated in favor of Sidney Lowe. The Timberwolves' best season in the early years was 1990-91, when the sophomore franchise compiled a 29-53 record.

Now comfortably settled in Target Center—and engaged in the process of building a team around experienced players obtained in trades and potential stars such as former Olympic "Dream Team" member Christian Laettner—the Timberwolves hope to become an imposing presence in the NBA.

The club's 1992 Media Guide published the team "philosophy" as articulated by owners Ratner and Wolfenson. Minnesota's "mission statement" is simple and reflects the highest aspirations of the entire NBA: "To profitably provide the highest quality sports and entertainment experience.... To earn the respect and support of Minnesota and make a positive impact on the Upper Midwest's quality of life."

SOURCES

PERIODICALS

Corporate Report Minnesota, November 1991; June 1993.

Minneapolis-St. Paul CityBusiness, September 18, 1992.

Sports Illustrated, June 26, 1989; November 6, 1989; February 25, 1991; May 6, 1991.

SAN ANTONIO SPURS

As a charter member of the American Basketball Association, the team known as the Dallas Chaparrals in 1967-68 has survived name and location changes, but is still seeking its first league title, and has never made the trip to the finals in either the ABA or the NBA. San Antonio fans have been fervent supporters since the ABA team moved to the Alamo City in 1973-74 in its seventh season of existence.

Having only one professional team in the city (except for two years of World League of American Football, a spring sport in 1991 and 1992), San Antonians have always revered their players. From George Gervin and James Silas, the only players to have their uniform numbers retired, to modern-day hero David Robinson, the celebrated "Admiral" whose NBA debut was delayed two years by U.S. naval duty after his top choice selection in 1987, Spurs players have been raised to the hero-level of Jim Bowie and Davy Crockett.

The Spurs were merged into the NBA (the NBA called them expansion teams) on June 17, 1976, along with the Denver Nuggets, Indiana Pacers and New Jersey Nets. The Pacers won three ABA titles and the Nets two. The Pacers also played in two other ABA Finals, while the Nets and Nuggets each played one.

But the Spurs never got to an ABA Final despite having an overall winning ABA record (378-366) and posting the best NBA record (689-623) of the four teams. Only the Spurs and Nuggets have posted winning NBA marks since the merger. Like the other three teams, the Spurs are still looking for their first trip to an NBA Final as well as an NBA Championship. The Spurs have missed the playoffs just four times in 26 ABA-NBA years and have 16 winning seasons, three break-even campaigns and seven losing years. In 1992-93, the Spurs went over the 1,100 mark (1,116) in all-time wins and passed Denver (1,111).

Off the court, the Spurs have been a success as well. They immediately improved on a dreary

Dallas existence in the first San Antonio season of 1973-74 and posted attendance increases each year through 1979-80 before attendance declined for seven straight years through 1986-87. Since the 1987 drafting of Robinson, fan attendance has been on an upswing. The last four seasons, through 1992-93, have seen the Spurs set records each year and in 1993-94 a new era begins when the team moves to the $177-million Alamodome which will seat up to 32,500 for basketball.

Whether Robinson will ever achieve the popularity of Gervin is a moot point, but more people will see him play than saw the fabled Iceman, and it falls to Robinson and his supporting cast of players to finally bring the San Antonio Spurs its first championship.

It's the Dallas Chaparrals!

The San Antonio Spurs were born in 1967 as the Dallas Chaparrals, a charter member of the ABA. The franchise played its first six seasons in Dallas before moving to San Antonio, changing the team name and achieving its finest moments. In that first season, the Chaps forged a 46-32 record, second best in the 6-team West. In the playoffs, they swept fourth-place Houston (matchups, for some reason, were 1-3 and 2-4) in three games, but fell to first-place New Orleans, 4-1, in the West Finals.

Player-coach Cliff Hagan, the University of Kentucky great who won an NBA title as a player with the 1958 St.Louis Hawks, was second in ABA assists (4.9). Charley Beasley led the league in free-throw percentage (.872) and was fifth in field-goal percentage (.493). Beasley was also third in rebounding (12.8) and free-throw shooting (.842).

The team nickname was conceived at a meeting held in a private club at the Dallas Sheraton, the Chaparral Room. One of the team's 30 investors noticed a club napkin imprinted with the chaparral (roadrunner) and suggested it would be a good name for the team. The first players were picked because a secretive former club official took general manager Max Williams' alphabetical list of players, thought it was a priority list, and selected the first five names.

Some 3,800 fans saw Dallas win its ABA home-opener, 129-124, over Anaheim while its mascot, Miss Tall Texan, who was 6-foot-7 ("give or take a few inches for my hairdo") watched from the sidelines.

The Chaps slipped to 41-37 in 1968-69, again under Cliff Hagan, and were beaten by New Orleans, 4-3, in the first round of the playoffs. Three-point shooter Glen Combs was second in the ABA at .361. Like the first year, attendance records for the team were lost. John Beasley scored 19 for the winning West Team in the All-Star Game at Louisville as the team's only representative.

In year three, 1969-70, Cliff Hagan departed with a team record of 22-21 and Max Williams took over. The Chaparrals went 23-18 the rest of the way and their 45-39 mark was second in the West. In the playoffs, the L.A. Stars ousted Dallas in six games—a mild upset since the Stars were 43-41 in the regular-season. Glen Combs was tenth in ABA scoring (22.2), fourth in 3-point shooting (.351) and third in free-throw percentage (.832). Dallas attendance averaged 3,687, just under the league average of 3,900.

This Year It's the Texas Chaparrals

In 1970-71, the team was renamed the Texas Chaparrals, but that only lasted for the team's first losing season. Max Williams came back, but after a 5-14 start was bounced. Bill Blakely, a recent college coach, took over. He went 25-40 and the team ended with a record of 30-54. Though the Chaps secured a playoff berth, they were put out by eventual champion Utah in four straight with no game closer than the ten-point opener.

John Beasley was the only player ranked on the team, finishing fifth in field-goal percentage at .497. Attendance sagged to 3,426. Donnie Freeman, the team's lone representative, scored 17 for the West in the 126-122 loss in Greensboro, North Carolina. The Chaps' largest crowd (9,247) was

TEAM INFORMATION AT A GLANCE

Formed in 1967 as the Dallas Chaparrals (ABA);
became the Texas Chaparrals, 1970;
reverted to Dallas Chaparrals, 1971;
moved to San Antonio, 1973; joined the NBA, 1976

Home court:
HemisFair Arena
600 E. Market St.
Suite 102
San Antonio, TX 78205
Phone: (512) 224-4611

Seating capacity: 15,910

Team nickname: Spurs
Team colors: Metallic silver and black
Team logo: Team name featuring a stylized riding spur for the letter "U"

on Kids Night, but Memphis' Steve Jones ruined it for Chaps' fans of all ages with a 35-footer at the buzzer for a 113-112 victory. In the off-season, Jones was acquired by the Chaps. Donnie Freeman was on the All-ABA Team.

The team was renamed the Dallas Chaparrals for 1971-72 and Tom Nissalke, assistant coach of the 1970-71 NBA Champion Milwaukee Bucks, was brought in as head coach. The Chaps went 42-42, but were again eliminated in four straight in the playoffs, and again by Utah. The games were closer this time with none more one-sided than the ten-point opener.

Guard Donnie Freeman became the ABA's ninth-best scorer (23.8). Tiny, second-year guard Joe Hamilton was fifth in three-point shooting (.348) and Steve Jones (current analyst for the Blazers and NBC-TV), was third in free-throw shooting (.870). All eleven ABA franchises were in the same place as the previous season for the first time as Year 5 opened. Attendance declined to 3,106. Freeman repeated on the All-ABA Team, and along with Freeman and Jones played in the All-Star Game for the losing West.

In 1972-73, Babe McCarthy left Memphis to coach Dallas as Tom Nissalke took the NBA Seattle position. But in March, with the Chaps at 24-48, McCarthy quit to coach at the University of Georgia. Dave Brown went 4-8 as the team finished with its worst ABA mark of 28-56. It was the only ABA year the team missed the playoffs.

Steve Jones, the team's top scorer, was dealt to Carolina in mid-season. Goo Kennedy was second in field-goal shooting (.550) and Joe Hamilton fourth (.346) in three-point accuracy. James Silas (Captain Late) was fifth in free-throw shooting (.833). Jones appeared in the All-Star Game in Utah for the winning West.

Things got ugly after the season when black players charged that management was trading blacks for whites. Bringing the issue to a head was the trading of 24-point scorer Donnie Freeman to Indiana for Bob Netolicky. There was even talk about the team moving to New Jersey, but the deal fell through. In five years the Chaps went through six coaches, five in the last two and a half years.

San Antonio, Here We Come

The team made its move to San Antonio for the 1973-74 season and brought back Tom Nissalke as head coach. Nissalke had gone to the NBA's Seattle Supersonics in 1972-73, but was let out after 45 games (13-32). Actually, the team was being loaned to an ownership group which included future sole owner Angelo Drossos and current owner Red McCombs. They were to have $800,000 in working capital for two years after which, if they still wanted the team, they could buy it for $800,000.

The working capital was gone in 90 days with $200,000 going to buy the concession rights to all events at the HemisFair Arena. The team started slowly on the court and attendance fell to 1,700 in October, but in early November Drossos bought backup center Swen Nater from Virginia. On November 11, the Spurs beat Kentucky before a crowd of 10,146.

As crowds consistently reached 9,000, management dealt for 21-year old George Gervin, a second-year pro. Nater went on to play in the ABA All-Star Game along with teammate Rich Jones. Nater was selected Rookie of the Year and made the All-ABA Second Team. Jack Ankerson was the ABA Executive of the Year as attendance averaged 6,303 after an 11,240 high.

Before season's end, Drossos negotiated an outright purchase of the team from the Dallas Group. In the playoffs, they lost to second-place Indiana, 4-3. With the Spurs at 17-10 in 1974-75, Coach Tom Nissalke was fired December 13 and GM Bob Bass took over. The Spurs went 34-23 the rest of the way for a then-franchise record 51 wins and finished second in the West.

They were upset by Indiana, 4-2, in the first round of the playoffs, despite the emergenmce of George Gervin and James Silas as All-Star players. Gervin, Silas and Nater were in the All-Star Game hosted by San Antonio January 28 in the city's first national sports exposure. John Begzos was brought in as GM and attendance climbed to 7,853 per game with a high of 11,146.

Gervin, Nater and Silas were All-ABA Second Team choices. Nater led the ABA in rebounds (16.4), Gervin was seventh in scoring (23.4) while Silas was second in free-throw shooting (.885).

After a series of off-season deals, only Gervin, Silas, Coby Dietrick and current Seattle coach George Karl returned for what would turn out to be the final year of the ABA. Larry (Mr. K) Kenon came from the Nets for Nater and Mike Gale was purchased in a related deal. Billy (Whopper) Paultz was acquired from New Jersey for four players. The Spurs finished 50-34 in 1975-76, third in the ABA which had been consolidated into a single group.

They went out in the Semi-finals, after a bye, to the Nets, 4-3, when Silas broke his ankle in the first game and Gervin played the series with a broken right wrist. Gervin, Kenon, Paultz and Silas all played in the All-Star Game.

Silas was All-ABA First team and Gervin was on the second unit. Silas (23.8) and Gervin (21.8) were 6-9 in league scoring, Silas was fourth in field-goal shooting (.519) and free-throw shooting (.872) and fifth in assists (5.4). Paultz led in blocked shots (3.05) and Kenon was fourth in rebounding (11.1). The team averaged 8,003 fans per game with a high of 11,717.

Hello, NBA

On June 17, the long-awaited merger with the NBA occurred and San Antonio along with Denver, Indiana and New Jersey were admitted. Left out were Kentucky and St. Louis with Virginia folding before the merger. The four newcomers each paid $3.2-million to get in. They also had to pay St. Louis $3-million for not getting in and St. Louis $2.2-million for not getting in. St. Louis also received 1/7 of each of the four survivors' TV share (when it began in 1979-80) in perpetuity.

In the Dispersal Draft, the Spurs took all-time ABA top scorer and assists leader Louie Dampier for $20,000 as the tenth pick. At one time, he held the ABA single-game (54) scoring record and the All-Pro consecutive free-throw (57) mark. The Spurs went to a 12-bank consortium to get $5-million to stay alive. The investment paid immediate dividends as they went 44-38 to finish third in the Central Division and played a half-dozen times on CBS-TV. However, they went out in two games in the playoff first round.

Gervin was one of ten ABA products among the 24 All-Star Game players and was ninth (23.1) in scoring while making the All-NBA Second Team. They were the NBA's top scoring team at 115 per game and set club attendance marks of 9,174 per game with a best of 12,594. On Dec. 26, 1976, Larry Kenon set an NBA record which still stands—11 steals vs. Kansas City.

In 1977-78, the Spurs began a run of five division titles in six years (including a 1980-81 switch to the Midwest Division) with a 52-30 record including 32-9 at home. With a first round bye, they had the misfortune to meet future champion Washington in the Eastern Semifinals and fell in six games. Attendance held virtually the same with a slight dip to 9,115. The HemisFair Arena roof was raised 33 feet and 6,000 seats were added.

The team took part in its first NBA draft (no ABA team drafted in 1976), but got no help. Some 100 players took part in a summer walk-on camp. The title march was fueled by an 18-4 spurt begun in late December. George Gervin, who won his first of three straight scoring titles (four in five years) and Larry Kenon were All-Star Game starters.

Two days later, the first South Texas game (vs. the Nets) was snowed out. Gervin had to score 63 points on the last night of the season in New Orleans to win the closest-ever title (27.22) over David Thompson (27.15), who had 73 that afternoon in Detroit. Gervin was an All-NBA First Team choice, his first.

If 1977-78 was a good Spurs year, 1978-79 might have been even better. The team won four fewer games (48-34), but repeated as Central Division Champs. Gervin won his second straight scoring title, averaging 29.6, his best so far. Gervin made the All-NBA First Team, won the Seagram Seven Crowns of Sports Award and, along with Larry Kenon, played in the Atlanta All-Star Game.

In the playoffs, after drawing a bye, the Spurs downed Philadelphia in the second round, 4-3, then bowed to eventual Champion Washington, 4-3, in the Eastern Finals after leading 3-1. The Spurs drew a record 11,907 per game, a mark which stood until 1989-90. They drew a record 15,764 vs. Houston in regular-season play and 16,709 vs. the 76ers in the playoffs. The Spurs averaged a franchise record 119.3 ppg to lead the NBA.

In 1979-80, the Spurs sank to 41-41 and tied for second in the Central Division with Houston, nine games behind Atlanta. The Spurs faced the Rockets in the first round and were knocked out in three games. The Rocket wins were by 10 and 21; San Anotonio's by five. The Iceman, George Gervin, won his third straight NBA scoring title with a career-best 33.1 ppg, was the All-Star Game MVP in Washington with 34 points and also made the All-NBA First Team.

Coach Doug Moe was fired March 1 and Bob Bass again took over and went 8-8 for the final 16 games. Larry Kenon was 20th in NBA scoring (20.1) and James Silas fourth in free-throw accuracy (.887). Attendance dropped for the first of eight straight years.

Albeck In as Coach; Bass as GM

Stan Albeck, a veteran ABA coach who had just gone 37-45 in his one Cleveland year, was hired as head coach in June and Bob Bass became General Manager in August. Owner Angelo Drossos instituted the "incentive plan." Bonuses for all players kicked in at 36 wins and ended at 56. It was designed to satisfy George Gervin's contract demands. He went on to gain another All-Star Game berth and First Team All-NBA selection while finishing third (27.1) in scoring to

Adrian Dantley and Moses Malone.

George (Swat) Johnson won the blocked shots title (3.39). The "Bruise Brothers" were born and the Spurs, despite having no player average double figure rebounds or rank among NBA leaders, led the league in boards in addition to blocked shots. San Antonio went 52-30, tying the franchise record, and set a mark with 17 straight home wins. Still, Houston, 12 games back, ousted the Spurs, who had drawn a bye, in seven games.

With expansion Dallas in the league (Wiley Peck was lost in the draft), the Spurs moved to the Midwest Division where they still reside. Attendance sagged to 10,747, but had a record 16,114 single-game crowd. Kenon left in summer of 1980 as a free agent.

The Spurs repeated as Midwest Division Champs in 1981-82 with a 48-34 record, two games better than Denver. George Gervin won his fourth and final scoring title (32.3) and started his fifth straight All-Star Game. He also made the All-NBA First Team again. He was out for three games with an injury and Ron Brewer, later traded to Cleveland with Reggie Johnson for Mike Mitchell (18th in NBA points at 20.5) and Roger Phegley, scored 39-40-44 as a starter. Gervin healed quickly and scored 47 in his first game back.

James Silas was dealt to Cleveland before the season. Mike Bratz was picked up in a trade. Johnny Moore won the assists title (9.6) and George Johnson repeated as blocked-shots champion. In the playoffs, after a bye, the Spurs crushed Seattle in five games, but were swept in four by soon-to-be-champion Lakers in the West Finals. Attendance fell to 10,591 per game.

Coach Stan Albeck started 1982-83 with a new contract and the Spurs won a franchise-record 53 games (it stood until David Robinson's 1989-90 arrival). They also claimed another Midwest Division title and defeated Denver, 4-1, in the second playoff round after an opening bye. However, the Lakers were waiting in the West Finals and prevailed again, 4-2. Attendance slid to 9,734.

George Johnson was traded in August after Artis Gilmore was acquired in July from Chicago

for Mark Olberding and Dave Corzine. Gervin and Gilmore went to the All-Star Game and Gervin was First Team All-NBA for the sixth and last time while finishing fourth (26.2) in NBA scoring. Gilmore led the NBA in field-goal percentage (.626), was fourth (12.0) in rebounds and fifth in blocks (2.34). Johnny Moore was second in assists (9.8) and third in steals (2.52). Mike Dunleavy won the three-point shooting title (.345) as a backup shooting specialist.

Albeck, whose three-year 153-93 (.622) is still the Spurs' best career won-lost percentage, moved to New Jersey as coach after a court case and the Spurs received compensation. Assistant Morris McHone was promoted with ex-Spur Allan Bristow as assistant. With the team 11-20 on December 28, McHone was fired and Bob Bass coached the rest of the way (26-25) for a 37-45 and 1983-84 fifth-place Midwest Division mark.

The team missed the playoffs for the first time in the NBA and second time in franchise history. Attendance fell to 9,168. George Gervin, sixth in NBA scoring (25.9), became the tenth all-time scorer in history and was voted to the All-Star Game in Denver. Mike Mitchell was 8th (23.3) in scoring, Artis Gilmore led in field-goal accuracy (.631) and was fifth in blocks (2.06). Johnny Moore was third in three-point shooting (.322). Moore (10.7) and John Lucas (9.6), now the Spurs coach, were 4-5 in assists.

The Spurs had their own "Dr. G" as Gilmore received an honorary degree from Jacksonville University. His consecutive game string ended at 314 and the Iceman's streak of 406 games scoring in double figures was stopped December 7 in Atlanta with 8 points. The franchise retired James Silas' number 13 on February 28, the first Spur so honored. Denver beat San Antonio, 163-155, for an NBA non-overtime record.

Cotton-Ball Comes to San Antonio

Well-travelled Cotton Fitzsimmons, one of three NBA coaches ever to pilot teams in all four divisions since the NBA went to a 4-division alignment, came on in 1984-85 with "Cotton-Ball". The team improved to 41-41, fourth in the division, and lost in the playoffs (which in 1983-84 had been enlarged to eight teams) to Denver, 3-2 in the first round. No more best-of-three series.

Mike Mitchell was 17th (22.2) in NBA scoring. At 21.2, George Gervin was not among the top 20, but still made the NBA All-Star Game for the ninth straight time. It was his 11th straight All-Star Game overall. He also rose to ninth on the all-time points list.

Alvin Robertson was the team's best first-round pick thus far in the NBA (three times the team didn't have a first) after being on the 1984 Gold Medal USA Olympic Team. He scored 9.2 as a reserve and missed the playoffs with a broken foot. The team made five player moves in ten days in December and attendance slipped to 8,888.

The 1985-86 season began a string of four straight losing seasons. This one was 35-47, sixth in the division. The Spurs still gained a playoff berth, but were crushed in three straight by the Lakers. Gene Banks was traded before the draft for Steve John and Alfredrick Hughes was picked 14th, one pick behind Karl Malone.

A week before the season, George Gervin was traded to Chicago for David Greenwood and the team said his number 44 would be retired when he stopped playing. Johnny Moore held out until after the season-opener. In December he came down with Desert Fever, a form of meningitis, and was lost for the season. John Paxson signed with Chicago as a free agent.

With room having been made for him, Alvin Robertson grabbed all the honors. He started in the All-Star Game, was the first Most Improved Player Award-winner, was voted Defensive Player of the Year, but only made the Second All-Defensive Team. He was 2nd Team All-NBA. Mike Mitchell was ninth in scoring (23.4). Johnson (.632) and Gilmore (.618) were 1-2 in field-goal percentage.

Robertson set an NBA steals record (301, 3.67) that still stands. In February, he posted the NBA's second-ever quadruple-double with 20 points, 11 assists, 10 rebounds and 10 steals. The team lost 21 of the last 25, and attendance skidded to 8,205. In May Cotton Fitzsimmons was fired and Bob Weiss hired.

In 1986-87, just when the Spurs thought things couldn't get worse, they did. On the floor, the record fell again to an all-time low of 28-54 (21-20 at home) for sixth and last place in the Midwest Division. It was the NBA's fourth-worst mark. In the stands, attendance fell for the eighth straight year to 8,010 despite the boom underway in the NBA.

Alvin Roberston made his second straight All-Star Game Trip, repeated as Defensive Player of the Year and made the NBA's All-Defensive First Team. He also repeated as NBA steals champion (3.21); Gilmore was second in field-goal percentage (.597); Johnny Dawkins came as the team's first-round draft pick and second-rounder Kevin Duckworth was swapped near mid-year for Portland's Walter Berry, the 1986 College Player of the Year. Johnny Moore came back from Desert Fever.

In January, the Spurs had a seven-game winning streak, but a late-season ten-game loss assured there would be no playoffs. In May, the Spurs won the NBA's Lottery and the chance to draft David Robinson.

Robinson Drafted; the Wait Begins

In 1987 the Spurs did indeed draft David Robinson, the 7-foot Navy center. Season ticket sales began to climb, even though Robinson would have to put in two years of naval duty. He was the tallest U.S. Navy grade ever. Attendance started a climb (8,426) that has continued, even if the record improved only slightly to 31-51, fifth in the Midwest, but good enough for a playoff date with the NBA-best L.A. Lakers. The Lakers swept the first round in three games.

The team's second first-round choice brought Greg (Cadillac) Anderson who made the All-Rookie Team. Robinson ended speculation that his rights might be traded by signing a contract in November. The Spurs played at a .500 pace until January 1 when they lost 26 of the next 35 games.

Johnny Moore's comeback ended November 19. Mike Mitchell had knee surgery in November but still played 68 games. In December, George Gervin's number 44 was retired. Alvin Robertson played in the All-Star Game and made the 2nd All-Defensive Team while ranking second (2.96) in NBA steals. Walter Berry was fifth in field-goal percentage (.563) and Johnny Dawkins was fifth in free-throw accuracy (.896). Gilmore was traded to Chicago in June 1987.

The Spurs began 1988-89 under new ownership as two months of bargaining between board member Red McCombs (once Angelo Drossos' employer at a McCombs car dealership) and Drossos produced the sale of the team to McCombs for $47 million. McCombs then released Bob Weiss from his coaching contract and brought in Larry Brown who had just won the NCAA Championship at Kansas. It is Brown's third of five NBA jobs as he's on his way to being the third man to coach in all four NBA divisions and becoming the only man to coach all four of the ex-ABA teams merged into the NBA.

Brown hoped that David Robinson would be released early from the navy, but he wasn't. The team has a franchise-worst 21-61 record, the team's first losing home record (18-23) in 15 years and Brown's only losing season as coach.

In 1988 Olympian Willie Anderson was the team's first-round pick and made the Olympic Team while being runner-up for the Rookie of the Year Award. Johnny Dawkins, leading the NBA in free-throw percentage, was lost after 32 games with a peroneal nerve injury.

The team had a 1-12 February and 2-9 April while losing a team-record 20 straight road games. Attendance leapt to 11,208 with four 15,861 sell-outs. Robertson (3.03) was again second in NBA steals. John Sundvold was lost to Miami in the 1988 Expansion Draft and Scott Roth went to Minnesota in 1989.

David Robinson was released from the navy and the 1989-90 Spurs, with the much-honored rookie, improved 35 victories—the largest-ever NBA turnaround. They went 56-26, won the Midwest Division, improved 3,515 to 14,723 in atten-

AP/Wide World Photos

David Robinson

dance and had the best record in franchise history before or since.

Robinson played in the 1990 All-Star Game in Miami, was voted Rookie of the Year, won the Schick Pivotal Player award, made the All-Rookie Team, the All-Defensive Second Team and Third NBA All-Star Team. He was a three-time NBA Player of the Week in the last two months-plus of the season.

Sean Elliott, the 1989 first-rounder (third overall), was on the Second All-Rookie Team. Alvin Robertson was traded to Milwaukee for All-Star power forward Terry Cummings. In the playoffs, San Antonio swept Denver in three games in the first round, then fell in seven games to Portland who were on their way to the Finals. Robinson, in a superlative year, was tenth in scoring (24.3), second in rebounds (12.0) and third in blocks (3.89). Bob Bass, assistant to the president, was voted NBA Executive of the Year.

The 1990-91 season was almost a duplicate of the year before. The Spurs' 55-27 record won the Midwest Division again, but Don Nelson outfoxed the Spurs as Golden State won the first-round playoff matchup in four games after the Spurs won the opener. The team sold out 40 of 41 home games (15,901) to set a franchise attendance record.

David Robinson went to the All-Star Game, was voted All-NBA First Team, repeated as Schick Award winner, and made the All-Defensive First Team and the All-Interview Second Team. Robinson was ninth in scoring (25.6), led in rebounds (13.), was second in blocks (3.90) and was ninth in field-goal percentage (.552). Guard Rod Strickland, obtained from the Knicks, missed 21 games with a hand injury, but Sean Elliott continued to improve. Draft picks Dwayne Schintzius, Tony Massenburg and Sean Higgins each gave bench help.

Goodbye, Larry Brown

The 1991-92 season was a strange one for the Spurs. With a 21-17 record, Larry Brown was released from his contract after returning from a road trip in January. For the fourth time, Bob Bass took over as coach and once again logged a .500-or-better record (26-18). However, the team finished second in the Midwest to Utah by eight games. In the playoffs, minus an injured David Robinson, Phoenix bounced the Spurs in three straight games.

The franchise sold out all 41 games at 16,057 each, with seating capacity up 149. Robinson repeated as NBA Defensive Player of the Year and made the All-Defensive and All-NBA First Teams. He missed the last 14 games (5-9) with a torn ligament in his left hand but played three games after being injured. The team was 40-24 going into the game where he was injured, 19-7 under Bass.

Still, Robinson won the NBA blocks title (4.49), was fourth in rebounds (12.2), and seventh in both scoring (23.2) and field-goal percentage (.552). Rod Strickland, who missed 22 games as

an unsigned free agent and three more with injury, ranked fifth in assists (8.6). Willie Anderson missed 25 games with a broken left tibia and his April 17 surgeries kept him from the playoffs.

The era of Jerry Tarkanian as head coach in San Antonio lasted just 20 games (9-11). He was fired December 15 and John Lucas, hired earlier in the day, debuted December 18 with a 122-101 at-home win over Dallas. The team wound up 49-33, two wins better than 1991-92, and second in the Midwest Division.

In the playoffs, the Spurs ousted Portland in four games and took Phoenix to six games before exiting. David Robinson and Sean Elliott both appeared in the All-Star Game in Salt Lake City. Robinson ranked ninth in both scoring (23.4) and rebounding (11.7) and fifth in blocks. Antoine Carr, playing major minutes with Terry Cummings out for the first 74 games after a summer 1992 knee injury, was tenth in field-goal percentage (.538). Avery Johnson was 14th in assists (7.5) after Rod Strickland went to Portland as a free agent. Willie Anderson missed 44 games after surgeries on both tibias at the end of the 1991-92 season.

Robinson made the Second All-Defensive Team and Third All-NBA Team. Elliott improved again to 17.2 ppg, but missed 12 games after the All-Star Break. Dale Ellis came from the Bucks (12th in three-point shooting, .401) and top pick Tracy Murray was traded to Portland.

For 1993-94, the Spurs' only draft pick was second-rounder Chris Whitney, a 6-foot point guard from Clemson. Improvement will have to come from maturity and a reduction of team injuries.

SOURCES

Carter, Craig and Alex Sachare (eds.), *The Sporting News NBA Guide,* 1992-93 edition, The Sporting News, 1992.

Hollander, Zander, *The NBA's Official Encyclopedia of Pro Basketball,* Corwin Books, 1977.

Hollander, Zander and Alex Sachare (eds.), *The Official NBA Basketball Encyclopedia,* Villard

Books, 1989.

Jares, Joe, *The American Game,* Follett Publishing Co., 1971.

Nadel, Eric, *The Night Wilt scored 100,* Taylor Publishing, 1990.

NBA Editorial Staff, *NBA News,* Vol. 47, Nos. 30-35, 1992-93.

Pluto, Terry, *Loose Balls,* Simon & Schuster, 1990.

San Antonio Spurs 1992-93 Media Guide, San Antonio Spurs, 1992.

UTAH JAZZ

Basketball was late arriving in the Mississippi delta region: it was solidly football country. LSU had rabid football fans and few basketball rooters—until the fall of 1966, when people began to talk about something special happening during the freshman squad games that preceded the varsity games. There was a new kid, a stringbean, 6-foot-4 and only 175 pounds, a magician with a roundball: his name was Pete Maravich, and his father, Press Maravich, was the new head coach.

Pete Maravich put on a display of fancy shooting, passing, and dribbling in each freshman home game; and when it was over and the varsity game began, the customers left for their cars. He was already called "Pistol Pete," a name created in his high school days by a newsman in recognition of the slightly built player's from-the-hip shooting style.

Fans couldn't wait till Pete joined the varsity team, and for three amazing years, from 1967 to 1970, they got their wish. The two Maraviches led

LSU to the finals of the 1970 NIT tournament against Marquette—but Pete, hung over from celebrating in the unfamiliar New York atmosphere the night before, performed limply in the final, and Marquette walked over his team, 101-79.

Still, Maravich finished his amateur career as the second-highest-scoring player in college history, with 3,667 points, or 44.2 per game. In 28 of those games, he scored 50 points or better, including games of 69 and 66 points apiece.

During the late 1960s the new American Basketball Association brought professional basketball to Louisiana. The New Orleans Buccaneers finished first in the Western Division in 1967-68, but sank to second place the next season, and fourth the next, and then became the Memphis Pros in 1970-71, and soon folded altogether.

So there was an open marketing niche in the early 1970s, a new audience for basketball but no professional basketball team. The situation was rectified in 1974 when a group of businessmen won permission from the NBA to inaugurate a franchise in New Orleans: the Jazz, named in recognition of the city's glorious musical tradition.

Realizing that their expansion team was not likely to post a strong record at the outset, the Jazz owners opted for a gate attraction—and the obvious one was Pistol Pete Maravich. In four years with the Atlanta Hawks (who had drafted him in the first round, third overall in the NBA, and signed him for an unprecedented million-dollar contract), Maravich had put on an impressive individual performance, averaging 24.3 points and 5.6 assists per game with an .809 free-throw percentage.

Maravich had experienced conflicts with teammates, however, because of his star status, and the Hawks, after four straight second-place finishes, needed a kick-start. So the Hawks traded Maravich to New Orleans for the Jazz's first draft picks in 1974 and 1975, their second picks in 1975 and 1976, their first and third picks in the next expansion draft, and the option to trade first-round picks in 1976 and 1977. It was a deal that many observers, including the *New Orleans Times-Picayune,* questioned. For a single player, who had yet to give his team a championship, the Jazz had traded away a big chunk of their future development. Maravich himself, although fond of New Orleans, resented being traded and was unhappy to leave his Atlanta home.

The trade made business sense, however. Louisiana fans, for whom Pete Maravich *was* basketball (from his days at LSU), packed the old Municipal Auditorium at the beginning of the first season. Later that year, the Jazz would play home games at the field house of Loyola University. The New Orleans Superdome, primarily a football facility, was still under construction, and when it was completed in the 1970-71 season, its basketball games drew football-type crowds.

Maravich, in his autobiography, *Heir To A Dream,* recalled a night when the city of New Orleans was drenched in a foot of rain; he expected the game to be cancelled—his own front lawn was flooded—but the game was played, and 39,000 people showed up.

Losing Seasons

Maravich's starting teammates that season were two 6-foot-8 forwards, Aaron James and E. C. Coleman, guard Louie Nelson, and center Otto Moore, a veteran ex-Piston. Veteran 7-foot center Mel Counts came off the bench for more playing time than Moore, and forward Bud Stallworth was a much-used sixth man. The team was a kaleidoscope of players, with 22 names appearing on the roster during the year. Maravich, with 21.5 points and 6.2 assists per game, was the only standout, the only starter scoring more than 12 points per game. He was fifth in the league in assists. Rebounding was spotty: nobody on the team was in double digits, the leader was Moore at 8.2.

Under coach Scotty Robertson, the Jazz went 1-14 in their first 15 games. All-time great Elgin Baylor stepped in to coach one game, which the team lost. Then Butch Van Breda Kolff, former Knick player and Princeton (Bill Bradley era), Lakers (where he was much-maligned by Wilt Chamberlain), Pistons, and Suns coach, took over the Jazz pilothouse for the bulk of the season, going 22-44. The team's overall performance in hits rookie season was 23-59, a .280 percentage that landed it solidly in the basement of the Central Division.

It was the beginning of a pattern. Throughout the 1970s—their entire period of residence in New Orleans—the Jazz never made the playoffs. In 1975-76 they climbed one step to fourth place as Maravich's scoring average rose to 25.9, third in the NBA behind Bob McAdoo and Kareem Abdul-Jabbar. He was on the first-team All-NBA squad, but played only 62 games because of a shoulder separation, and starters Coleman and Ron Behagen also accumulated injury time.

Center Moore turned in an improved performance with 9.8 rebounds per game, and seven-foot Rich Kelley backed him up capably. Sixth man Nate Williams contributed 12.8 points per game, and some rebounds, at forward and guard. Satisfyingly for Maravich, his new team, at 38-44, outpaced his old one as the Hawks replaced the Jazz in the cellar.

TEAM INFORMATION AT A GLANCE

Founding date: 1974, as the New Orleans Jazz;
moved to Salt Lake City, Utah, in 1979.

Home court:
Delta Center
3011 West South Temple
Salt Lake City, UT 84101
Phone: 801-325-2500
FAX: 801-325-2578

Seating Capacity: 19,911

Team nickname: The Jazz
Team uniform colors: Home—base color white, trim purple, green and gold
Road—base color purple, trim green, gold, and white
Team logo: "JAZZ" in team colors with "UTAH" nesting above it; the letter J in the shape of a
musical note with its head in the form of a basketball

Franchise record:	Wins	Losses	Pct.
(Regular season)	749	809	.481
(Playoffs)	33	41	.446

Divisional first-place finishes: 3 (1983-84; 1988-89; 1991-92)
Divisional last-place finishes: 4 (1974-75; 1978-79; 1979-80; 1981-82)

Maravich's personal career as a pro reached its height in 1976-77, when he took the scoring championship with a 31.1 average, including a 68-point game against the New York Knicks. In 13 games, he scored 40 points or more. He also led the league in minutes per game, with 42, and hit his free-throws 84 percent of the time. He led the Jazz in assists with 5.4 per game, and led Jazz guards in rebounding with 5.1. Again he was on the all-league first team.

The Jazz were still weak defensively and on the boards, however. Moore's 7.9 rebounds per game led the team in that department. Maravich's new partner in the backcourt, the smooth-shooting veteran Gail Goodrich, had a leg injury and

only played in 27 games, his 12.6 scoring average in those games taking second place on the team.

Jim McElroy, a 6-foot-3, 190-pound guard, came off the bench for over 2,000 minutes at a 10.6-point scoring clip. Overall, the team's performance was down from the previous season, and though still one notch ahead of the Hawks (in a division that now contained six teams), their record slipped to 35-47, a .457 percentage.

Elgin Baylor returned to coach the entire 1977-78 season. It was a time of soul-searching for Maravich, who sat out 32 games with a knee injury. His scoring was still a highly repsectable 27.0 per game and his foul-shooting was a fifth-

The story of Pete Maravich and his father-coach, Press Maravich, is a classic study of American father-son relationships in sports: the heights they can achieve and the tensions they can share. The two men were so close that they must be considered a unit: Press Maravich created his son's basketball greatness as an act of will. Press Maravich's official first name was Peter; the nickname Press was given to him by friends because of his habit of acting like an expert in conversations. He named his second son Peter, giving him the official middle name Press. In Pete Maravich's autobiography, the first six chapters are devoted to Press Maravich's early life; Pete is born on page 55.

Press Maravich was an excellent college basketball coach, known for his psychological astuteness with players as well as his knowledge of strategy and tactics. From the earliest moment, he selected his son Pete as the subject of his training, the heir who would achieve his dream of championship professional play. According to Pistol Pete's book, "When Dad first laid eyes on me, he swore then and there that I had the potential to be a great basketball player. `Look at those hands! Look at his feet! The kid's got it, I tell you!" he said, as he grabbed nearby hospital personnel." It was June 22, 1947, in Aliquippa, PA. Press coached at Aliquippa High. Later he became a highly successsful head coach at Clemson, LSU, and was even offered a chance at an NBA coaching job, which he declined.

As a child and even an adolescent, Pete was small and frail-looking: when he started for his high school basketball team as a freshman, he was only 5-foot-2 and ninety pounds, a head shorter than his teammates. But he was already a superb and stylish ballhandler due to the daily practice his father had instilled in him for years. Skillfully the elder Maravich reinforced his son's love of the game and made sure that the practices were enjoyable as well as useful: he would sometimes, for instance, have Pete dribble out the window of a slowly moving car, at changing speeds. It was no exaggeration to say that the youngster spent all his free time dribbling and shooting.

Fortunately he grew tall enough, at 6-foot-4, to play against serious competition; and though he was at first skinny and plagued by such ailments as mononucleosis, he eventually filled out to 200 pounds as a pro. At LSU, where Press coached Pistol Pete, they made national headlines together and brought an entire basketball program to life. Pete's pro exploits were perhaps not as glorious as his years at LSU, but they were enough to make him a five-time All-Star and ensure his election to the Hall of Fame in 1986.

Press Maravich died on April 15, 1987, of cancer. According to the account in his 1987 book, Pete, who had recently become a devout Christian, leaned over his dying father and whispered, "Someday I'll be with you." Pete Maravich died suddenly on January 5, 1988, less than eight months after his father. He collapsed during a pickup basketball game with friends in Pasadena, CA. Examination showed that the collapse was due to congenital heart abnormalities, including the absence of a left coronary artery.

in-league .870, but the accusations of being a ball-hound, and the lack of a championship-caliber team, had gotten to him over the years.

One night, according to his autobiography, he decided to change his approach and only took four shots in the first half. The Jazz were leading by twelve at halftime, but the home crowd was boo-ing. "What do you think you're doing out there?" coach Baylor demanded, grabbing Maravich.

When Maravich explained that he was playing to win, Baylor told him, "Then you need to be shooting the ball." The Pistol stepped up his shooting during the second half, and the Jazz lost the game.

The Presence of Truck Robinson

For the first time, however, the Jazz of 1977-78 had a serious supporting cast. Goodrich, though 34 years old, stayed healthy and shot for 16.1 points per game. The really big addition was 6-foot-7, 225-pound forward Leonard "Truck" Robinson. The nickname suited him to a T.

He was a dominating physical presence under the back-board and a good short-range shooter and low-post player; in an 11-year NBA career, which started with the Washington Bullets in 1975 and traveled through Phoenix and New York as well as New Orleans, this Tennesee State graduate scored 11,988 points for a 15.5 average, and hauled down 7,267 rebounds, or 9.4 per contest.

The 1977-78 Truck, a durable model, led the NBA in minutes played with 3,638, or 44 per game, and in total rebounds (1,288) and rebounding average (15.7). He also scored 22.7 points per game, second on the team. Indeed, all five Jazz starters averaged in double digits in scoring for the first time in team history. Aaron James at 12.2 and center Rick Kelley at 10.2 (with 9.3 rebounds) were the others. It was Truck Robinson who represented the Jazz on the all-league first team that year, as Maravich was selected to the second team; it was the first time the Jazz had two players on the All-Star squad (though Maravich was injured and could not play).

Nevertheless, the team's overall record for the year was almost exactly where it had been: next-to-last place win 39 wins and 43 defeats, a .476 percentage. The rival Hawks had leapfrogged into fourth place, but the Houston Rockets, who finished first the previous season, had plummeted to last.

The 1978-79 season was the last in New Orleans for the Jazz, and it marked a downturn in their on-the-court fortunes as well. The team sank to sixth and last place in the Central Division with a 26-56, .317 record. The factors in the decline included a knee injury to Maravich which forced him to miss 33 games late in the season, and caused him to be ineffective during many of the games he did play.

The Jazz traded Truck Robinson to Phoenix for a couple of bench players, creating a gaping hole under the boards. To fill it, they acquired star forward Spencer Haywood from the Knicks. Haywood, at 29, was a veteran of the University of Detroit's varsity squad, the U. S. Olympic Team, the ABA Denver Nuggets and the NBA Seattle Supersonics. At 6-foot-9 and 225 pounds he was taller and the same weight as Robinson, and he led the Jazz in scoring with 24 points per game; however, he was not the rebounder or the defensive presence Robinson was.

Haywood would spend only part of the 1978-79 season with the Jazz and, for 1979-80, play on the Laker's championship team. Jazz center Rich Kelley was a bright spot, becoming the league's second most productive rebounder at 12.8 per game and toting up 15.7 points per contest, and the aging Goodrich contributed 12.7 points per game as sixth man. However, there was just not enough defense, not enough bench strength, and not enough Maravich.

Go West—and Get Dantley!

Big changes happened in 1979-80, the most dramatic of which was the team's move to Salt Lake City, a locale whose public image was virtually the opposite of New Orleans's. The team had a new owner in Larry H. Miller and a new head coach in Tom Nissalke, who had never played in the NBA. They were also in a different division, the Midwest Division of the Western Conference.

Their conference rivals now were the Kansas City Kings, Denver Nuggets, and Chicago Bulls, all of whom, in that order, finished ahead of the Jazz in 1979-80, for it was another cellar year. The team's record was 24-58, a .293 performance. Maravich, still hurting at the knee, and plagued by personal problems as well, was released on January 18, 1980 and picked up by the Celtics as a reserve; however, his personal pride did not allow him to serve as a substitute, and he quit training camp of the 1980-81 season, thus missing his only chance to play on a championship team.

The Jazz, meanwhile had traded Haywood to the Lakers for Adrian Dantley in a star-forward-for-star-forward deal. It turned out well for the Jazz in the long run. Dantley, 6-foot-5 and 210, had bounced from Buffalo to Indiana to Los Angeles during the early part of his pro career; he would play seven strong seasons for the Jazz before joining the Detroit Pistons for another couple of seasons. His 28 points per game were third in the NBA in 1979-80; he also grabbed 7.6 rebounds per outing, a mark which—unfortunately for the Jazz—led the team in that department.

The Jazz had an all-new starting lineup. Guard Terry Furlow had arrived from Atlanta, and 33-year-old guard Ron Boone, with his .893 free-throw percentage, from the Lakers. The starting center, at only 6-foot-9, was Ben Poquette, who also played some forward (he was backed up by the 6-foot-8 Ben Hardy). Kelley had been traded to the Nets for veteran Bernard King, but King was a disappointment, limited to 19 games by a foot injury and alcohol-related problems.

Dantley's frontcourt partner was 6-foot-7 Allan Bristow, a veteran who would last two seasons on the Jazz before finishing his NBA career with the Dallas Mavericks. In short, Dantley was the centerpiece of the team. It was not enough.

The following season, some new strength was added to the lineup, and former starters went to the bench. Wayne Cooper, at 6-foot-10, became the starting center but was not the answer to the team's long-term problem in that area; Poquette, at forward, led the Jazz in blocked shots by a wide margin, with 174, and in rebounds, with 7.7.

At starting point guard, with 5 assists and 9 points per game, the team now had Rickey Green, the former all-American for the University of Michigan. Green, a 6-foot-1, 170-pound speedster, had played one season apiece for Golden State and Detroit and would spend eight seasons at guard for the Jazz, specializing in steals and assists. (He is second to John Stockton in both departments on the Jazz all-time lists.)

Equally important was a rookie backcourt

acquisition, Darrell Griffith. At 6-foot-4 and 190, Griffith, a Louisville grad, entered the league with a blistering 20.6 scoring average, earning Rookie of the Year honors as well as boosting his team. It was the beginning of a distinguished decade-long career: in 765 games from 1981 to 1991, Griffith would score 12,391 points, just above Cazzie Russell and just below Joe Barry Carroll on the all-time NBA list, an average of 16.2 points per game.

The unmistakable star of the team, however, was Dantley, and in 1980-81 he had one of his finest years, leading the NBA in scoring average at 30.7, as well as in total points (2,452) and minutes played (3,417). He was on the all-league second team as well. The Jazz's offensive production had picked up, but they lacked lack the size, defense, and depth to make them a winning franchise.

The problems would continue in 1981-82 despite some tinkering with the lineup. Cooper went to the Mavericks; Poquette became sixth man; the Jazz's center was now 6-foot-11, 240-pound Jeff Wilkins, an Illinois State grad, in his second year with the team, and their power forward was 6-foot-8, 220-pound James Hardy. Neither player was a major threat to score, rebound, or block shots, however; Wilkins's 7.5 boards per game led the team in that area, as did his total of 77 blocks.

Dantley had another fine scoring season with 30.3 points per game, third in the NBA behind George Gervin and Moses Malone; Griffith contributed 19.8 points per game, and Green brought up the ball to the tune of 14.8 points and 7.8 assists.

The Jazz also had a new head coach in Frank Layden, who was installed after Nissalke had led the club to an 8-12 record in their first 20 games. Layden would serve six full sseasons and two partial seasons as the Jazz head coach, winning a total of 277 games and losing 294 for a respectable .485 percentage, in addition to an 18-23 playoff record. Layden's record that first season, however, was a dismal 17-45, and the team overall went 25-57, a last-place .305.

Although better things were on the horizon,

<table>
<tr><td>**PROFILE**</td><td>Adrian Dantley</td></tr>
</table>

His full name is Adrian Delano Dantley and he was born on February 26, 1956 in Washington, D.C. He grew to 6-foot-5 and almost 210 pounds and graduated from Notre Dame, where he was all-American, averaging 25.8 points and 9.8 rebounds per game. Though only as tall as many guards, he played forward and made a success of it with his inimitable fakes. Relying on his accurate outside shooting and free-throws, he amassed 23,177 points in his 15 NBA years, an average of 24.3 per game.

His total points are ninth on the all-time list as of 1992-93, just ahead of Elgin Baylor and just behind Jerry West. At .540, his field-goal percentage is among the highest for all forwards, and exactly the equal of Wilt Chamberlain's. His free-throw percentage is .818; his total rebounds, 5,455. He had several 50-plus points games as a pro, including two 57-pointers. He was NBA Rookie of the Year for the Buffalo Braves in 1976-77, and won the league scoring title twice with Utah—in 1980-81 and 1983-84.

On the Jazz career list, Dantley is ninth in games played, sixth in minutes played, second in points scored, third in field goals made and fields goals attempted, second in free throws made and free throws attempted, fifth in rebounds, fifth in assists, and fifth in steals.

troubles continued in 1982-83. The teram's poor financial shape, which of course was a direct result of its losing record, deepened its problems in the short run. The Jazz had drafted Dominique Wilkins in the Number 3 overall position, but could not come up with enough money to sign him, and so on September 3, 1982, he was traded to the Atlanta Hawks for two veterans, forward John Drew and guard Freeman Williams, plus cash.

The result is well-known to basketball fans: Wilkins became a superstar for the Hawks, a scoring sensation second only to Michael Jordan during the late 1980s and early 1990s. Meanwhile, Drew spent two months of the season in drug rehabilitation, and Williams, having played only 210 minutes, was released in midseason. An injury to Dantley deepened the Jazz's woes: a wrist injury limited him to only 22 games (during which, tantalizingly, he averaged 30.7 points). Reserve center Dan Schayes played 50 games as a starter for the Jazz, then was traded for a familiar face, Rich Kelley.

Neither Schayes nor Kelley was much needed, for the Jazz had at last filled up the hole in center: Mark Eaton had come to town. The 7'4", 280-pound colossus came off the bench that first

season to block 275 shots. Given the fact that Poquette blocked 116 and that Green led the league in steals with 220, this meant that the Jazz were now taking the ball away from their opponents regularly and rapidly; something they had never managed to do before. Griffith's flashy dunking and outside shooting—he was 38 for 132 in three-point attempts and scored 14.3 points per game—aided the team as well.

If Dantley had been healthy, it might have been a good year despite the fumbling of the Wilkins draft. As things stood, it was an improvement over the previous season as the Jazz won 30 games and lost 52, for fifth place.

A New Height

The 1983-84 season was a giant step. Eaton was the starting center; he played in all 82 games and constituted a truly formidable defensive presence in the lane, even though he did not have the speed or leaping ability to be a first-rate rebounder (at 7.3 boards per game, he led the team).

His league-leading 351 blocked shots were supplemented by the 122 of rookie power forward Thurl Bailey, a 6-foot-11 graduate of North Caro-

They are, of course, John Stockton (12) and Karl Malone (32). Stockton, born March 26, 1962, went to Gonzaga Prep in his native Spokane, Washington and Gonzaga University, graduating in 1984. He was Utah's first-round draft pick and has played his entire pro career for the Jazz.

He won six con-secutive assists titles between 1987-88 and 1992-93 and is the only man in NBA history to record more than 1,000 assists more than twice. (He has done it five times so far). Through 1992-93 he recorded 32 20-plus-assists games for the Jazz. His single-season assists mark of 1,164 set in 1990-91, is an NBA record.

He has also been durable, missing only four games in the first nine years of his pro career. He is fourth on the all-time NBA assists list, second to Isiah Thomas among active players, and third on the steals list.

On the Jazz lists, he is third in games played and minutes played, fifth in points scored and field goals made, sixth in field goals attempted, third in free throws made and free throws attempted, second in three-point field goals, tenth in rebounds, and of course, first by a wide margin in assists and steals.

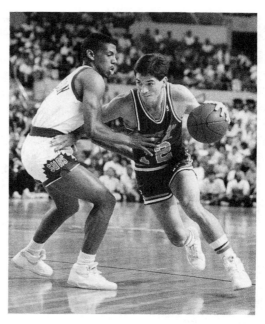

AP Wide World Photos

lina State. The Jazz now had huge size under the basket, complementing the healthy Dantley's league-leading 30.6 points per game. (Dantley's 813 free throws made and 946 attempts also led the league.)

Griffith's scoring average was an even 20 points, his three-point percentage rising to .361. Playmaker Green had a hot year, leading the league in steals for the second straight time, with 215, and dishing out 9.2 assists per game to go with his 13.2 points. All five starters were healthy: they all played more than 2,000 minutes and at least 79 games. Drew was back in form as a productive sixth man, scoring 22.2 points per game in 81 contests. Jeff Wilkins and Rich Kelley contributed some rebounds off the bench.

All in all, it was a well-balanced team, and its 45-37 finish led the Midwest Division. It was the first winning season and first playoff season in Jazz history. A landmark had been reached—a plateau on which the team would remain for several years—and Layden was voted NBA Coach of the Year, another franchise first.

The playoffs started successfully as the Jazz got the third-place Denver Nuggets out of the way in a five-game series. After winning the first game in the Delta Center, 123-121, the Jazz faltered for two games—a rare home loss, 132-116, then a 121-117 road loss—then pulled themselves together to defeat the Nuggets in Denver, 129-124, and take the series in Salt Lake City, 127-111.

Their next opponent was the Phoenix Suns,

. . . AND 32 | PROFILE

AP/Wide World Photos

Karl Malone was born July 24, 1963 in Summerfield, Louisiana and after Summerfield High, went to Louisiana Tech, graduating in 1986. Drafted in the first round by the Jazz, 13th overall, he went on to the all-rookie team and to become one of the most reliable scorers and rebounders in basketball, averaging more than 20 points per game in every season except his rookie year, and 31 points per game in 1989-90.

He has played in six All-Star Games through 1992-93, missing one because of injury but being voted MVP in two of them. Starting out as a sub-.500 free-throw shooter, he has worked to improve consistently and his career average in 1993 was .722, with a high of .778 in 1991-92. He is known for muttering a mysterious message to himself before each free-throw.

He is also known for appearances in the broadcast and print media, for his ownership of a fleet of trucks, and for his nickname, "The Mailman," which a Louisiana sportswriter gave him because he always delivers. Malone, a real family man and outdoorsman, likes to hunt and fish, and owns a ranch with his wife Kay, a former Miss Idaho, and a home in Salt Lake City. They have two daughters.

who, at 41-41, had only finished fourth in the Pacific Division. The Suns had had to upset the Portland Trail Blazers just to reach this point; and against the Jazz, they lost the first game decisively, 105-95 at the Delta Center.

Again, however, the Jazz lost the second home game and the first road game. Down by two games to one, they took Game 4 to overtime for a heartbreaking 111-110 loss. A scrappy, 118-106 victory back in Utah gave them hope, but they lost Game 6 and the series, in Denver, by a whopping 102-82.

It was the Jazz's turn to be 41-41 the next season. John Drew succumbed to drug problems again in 1984-85, and though he averaged 16.2 points per game, he only played in 19 games.

Adrian Dantley was a holdout at the beginning of the season; his playing time was limited to 55 games, or 1,971 minutes, and his production was down to 26.6.

Eaton's 456 blocked shots not only led the league but made him the first-team all-NBA selection and the league's Defensive Player of the Year. The 456 was an NBA season record, as was his per-game average of 5.56.

Bailey, Griffith and Green once again had solid years, with point averages of 15.2, 22.6, and 13.0 respectively, and 7.8 assists per game for Green. A new acquisition, 6-foot-1, 175-pound guard John Stockton, would be little noticed in his rookie season, but he played in all 82 games at an average of 18 minutes per game, contributing 5.6

points and 5.1 assists per contest. His role in the future would be gigantic.

The problems outweighed the gains in 1984-85, and the team subsided back to fifth place. They made the playoffs, and in the opening round, upset the second-place Houston Rockets in a 3-2 series, in which they came from a 2-0 deficit to win two home games and a road clincher. In a high-scoring series against the division-leading Denver Nuggets, however, who had shooting ace Alex English and ex-Jazz Wayne Cooper, they could only win one game, the third of five, by a score of 131-123.

Stockton became a starter in 1985-86, as did former Jazz reserve guard Bobby Hansen. Griffith missed the entire season with a broken foot—thus Hansen's presence in the starting lineup. Bailey and Green's contributions were still major, however, as their played as many or more total minutes coming off the bench than Stockton and Hansen did.

Most importantly, the Jazz had a great rookie power forward, Karl Malone. The 6-foot-9, 250-pounder was one of the nicest guys in the NBA off the court and one of the strongest, most physically intimidating competitors on it.

His 8.9 rebounds per game led the team (Eaton was seond with 8.4, and blocked 369 shots), and also scored 14.9 per game. He was selected to the NBA All-Rookie team. Malone, at that point, did not go to the free-throw line nearly as often as he would when he became better-known, and his percentage was only 48. Dantley, Stockton, Bailey, and Green, however, gave the Jazz strength in that department with percentages of 79, 84, 83, and 85 respectively. Hansen was a good outside shooter, going 17-for-50 in three-pointers.

At 42-40 in the regular season, the Jazz had inched back up above .500 and from fifth to fourth place. Unfortunately, Dantley did not play in the postseason and his replacement, 6-foot-9 veteran Marc Iavaroni, averaged only 3.3 points per playoff game. The Jazz lost their opening round to the third-place Mavericks, 3-1, winning only Game 3, their first home game, 100-98.

Dantley was traded to Detroit the following season for Kelly Tripucka: a trade of one veteran Notre Dame-educated forward for another. Tripucka was three years younger than Dantley and, while not the same scoring powerhouse (he only averaged 10 per game), was not prone to holdouts. Griffith was healthy once again and scored at a 15-point clip; Green and Stockton shared the starting point-guard role, with Green getting slightly more minutes. Green's assists were 6.7 per game, Stockton's 8.2. Tripucka and Hansen shot effectively for three-pointers.

Bailey, at sixth man, was a solid backup, averaging almost 14 points per game with 5.3 rebounds. Eaton, though reduced to the all-defenisve second team after two straight seasons as the first team's center, again led the NBA in shot-blocking with 321. It was Malone's year, however, as the Mailman led the Jazz in scoring average, at 21.7, and rebounding average, at 10.4. With the playmaking of Green and Stockton, the inside scoring of Malone, the outside shooting of Griffith, and the physical presence of Eaton and Malone on defense, this was a team to reckon with.

Their major drawback now was not in the failure to fill any specific role, but in the fact that, because of the players' individual sizes and styles, all the roles were so clearcut. Eaton did his few things and Griffith his and Stockton and Malone did their things. What was lacking—what a championship required—was a complete player, a small forward or tall shooting guard who could work both ends of the court, and a center who was an offensive as well as defensive power.

They climbed another double-step in 1986-87, rising to second place in the division with a 44-38 record. The Golden State Warriors, in a stronger division, had finished third at 42-40. These two teams met in the opening round of playoffs, and for the first four game, the decision went to the home team.

Utah won the opener, 99-85, on 15 rebounds by Eaton and 20 points apiece by Bailey and Malone; Griffith was the scoring star in Game 2, with 25 points in a 103-100 victory, as Malone grabbed 13 rebounds. After the series was tied, the teams returned to the Delta Center for Game 5, where the Jazz fell five points short, 118-113.

The Stockton-Malone Era

The 1987-88 season was when Stockton became a star. More accurately, perhaps, it was the year when he and Karl Malone meshed perfectly to form the best point-guard-to-power-forward tandem in basketball. Stockton's 1,128 assists, a 13.8-per-game average, set new NBA records; he scored 14.7 points per game as well. Most of those assists went to Malone. Game after game, quarter after quarter, it was Malone running full steam down the court to a spot where he knew Stockton would get him the ball, just a step short of charging the defender; or it was Stockton, slashing and penetrating and dishing off a pass in midair to Malone or one of the other players.

It was superb, exciting basketball, though predictable. Malone's 27.7 points per game put him fifth in the league; his 12.0 rebounds per game were fourth best; Stockton was third in the league in steals, fourth in field-goal percentage with .574. Tripucka's .419 three-pointer percentage put him fifth among the league's longball aces. Stockton won the Good Hands Award and was on the all-league second team, while Malone and Eaton were on the second team for defense.

Once again, Eaton led the league in shot-blocking, with 304, an average of 3.71 per game. The Jazz placed third in their division during the regular season, going 47-35 for a .573 percentage. In the playoffs, they defeated the Trail Blazers 3-1 in the first round, losing only Game 1, on the road. Bailey's performance was particularly strong as he scored 31 points in Game 1 and 39 in Game 3; Malone had 37 points in Game 2 and 38 in Game 4, and was the team's high rebounder in the first three games.

Then, for the Western Conference Semifinals, the Jazz faced the Lakers. It was Stockton against Magic Johnson at point guard, Eaton versus Abdul-Jabbar in the middle, Malone and Bailey against James Worthy and A. C. Green. The Jazz took the Lakers to seven games, but lost the finale in Los Angeles, 109-98. For the postseason, Malone averaged 29.7 points and 11.8 rebounds per game, Stockton 19.5 points and 14.8 assists.

The Jazz returned even stronger in 1988-89 as they paced the Midwest Division with a 51-31, .622 record. Layden was replaced as head coach, after going 11-6, by former Chicago Bulls star Jerry Sloan. The starting five of Bailey, Malone, Eaton, Griffith and Stockton was so solid that of the team's substitutes, only Mike Brown, a 6'10", 280-pound center-forward, played more than 1,000 minutes.

Stockton led the league in steals as well as assists and assists average (13.6), scored 17.1 points per game, and won a second straight Good Hands Award. Malone scored at a 29.1 point per game clip and brought down 10.7 rebounds; he was also voted MVP of the All-Star Game. Eaton's 315 blocked shots, second in the league, were seconded by Griffith's 141, the most of any NBA guard.

Eaton made the all-league first team for defense and won his second Defensive Player of the Year Award; Stockton made the second team both defensively and overall, along with his second straight Good Hands Award. Bailey won the NBA's J. Walter Kennedy Citizenship Award.

The Jazz were the stingiest defensive team in the league: at 99.7, the only NBA team to hold their opponents to under 100 points per game. The postseason, however, was a disappointment, as the Jazz were swept by the Warriors 3-0 in the first round.

Utah's regular-season record was even better in 1989-90 as the team won 55 games, its highest total ever, losing only 27; but its .671 percentage was one game behind the division-leading San Antonio Spurs. Again Stockton led the league in assists, with a sizzling 14.5 per game, and was second in steals to Michael Jordan.

Stockton now showed up among the league's three-point leaders with a .416 conversion rate, while Malone, with his 31.0 points and 11.1 rebounds per game, was second and fourth in the league in those departments, as well as fourth in field-goal percentage with .562. On defense, the team was the third stingiest in the league.

Again, in 1989-90, the Jazz lasted only one round in the playoffs, falling to the Trail Blazers 3-2, and losing the last game 104-102 in the Delta Center.

In 1990-91, the Jazz obtained a valuable veteran in Jeff Malone, the 6-foot-4 guard who had spent seven years with the Bullets, and who now became the team's starting two-guard for most games, averaging 18.6 points per game with a team-leading high game of 43. His free-throw percentage of .917 was second in the NBA. With Karl Malone at his remarkably consistent level—29.0 points per game—Stockton at 17.2 points and 14.2 assists, and Bailey contributing on the boards as well as in the bucket, the team was 54-28—again, just one game behind the division-leading Spurs.

The Jazz met the Suns in the first round of playoffs—a rematch of the previous year—and this time they prevailed, winning the best-of-seven series in only four games. Game 1 was a blowout in Phoenix, 129-90, with the Mailman scoring for 27 and pulling down 10 rebounds.

In the Jazz's other two wins in that series, Karl Malone had 32 and 38 points. Then the Jazz faced another old playoff rival, the Trail Blazers, in the Western Conference Semi-Finals. They lost the first two games in Portland, went home to take Game 3, 107-101, but dropped Game 4, 104-101, and returned to the west coast to finish off the process, 103-96, to lose the series 4-1.

In 1991-92, the Jazz equalled their best regular-season record, going 55-27 to lead the Midwest. The team's home record, 37-4, was the best in the NBA. Karl Malone's 28.0 points per game put him second to Jordan in the NBA; he was ninth among the league's rebounders.

Jeff Malone's free-throw level was .898, fifth best in the league. Stockton was first in the NBA in both steals (2.98 per game) and assists (1,126 total, a 13.7 average). Karl Malone was the power forward on the all-league first team, with Stockton placing on the second team both defensively and overall.

Karl Malone was NBA Player of the Week during two weeks of the regular season—including the final week—with Stockton and Jeff Malone taking one week apiece. Notable newcomers to the Jazz were 6-foot-10 reserve center Isaac Austin, an off-court leader of the team, and 6-foot-8 forward David Benoit, an Alabama graduate who had been Spain's Rookie of the Year.

The 1991-92 Jazz went to the Western Conference Finals for the first time in their history, after overcoming the L.A. Clippers 32 in the opening playoff round and the Supersonics 4-1 in the semifinals. Their opponent was the Trail Blazers, powered by Clyde Drexler, Terry Porter, and Jerome Kersey.

Unfortunately for the Jazz, the first two games were in Portland and the home team won, 113-88 and 119-102. The Jazz resurged for two wins in Utah, 97-89 and 121-112, but came a hair's-breadth short of a win on the road in Game 5, losing in overtime, 127-121. Back in Portland for Game 6, the Jazz succumbed 105-97. Their problem was to win on the road—and to win when they were down.

After the Olympics

The 1992-93 season saw fatigue and age begin to take their toll on the veteran stars of the Jazz. Karl Malone and Stockton had extended themselves in the offseason to play on the U. S. Olympic team, and Stockton had incurred a stress fracture of the fibula. For the first time in 6 seasons, Stockton totaled fewer than 1,100 assists—indeed, fewer than 1,000.

His 987, and 12.0 average, were still the top marks in the NBA, however, showing how clear-cut Stockton's dominance had become in those areas of the game. He was the fourth player in NBA history to achieve 8,000 assists, after Magic Johnson, Oscar Robertson, and Isiah Thomas, and on his way to becoming the all-time leader.

Stockton was third in the league in steals for the season, and the third player in league history to achieve 1,800 thefts. Karl Malone was third in the league in scoring, at 27.0 (he reached the 15,000 career point level in November; Jeff Malone did so in March), and tied for tenth in rebounding average at 11.2.

The previously durable Eaton, the franchise leader in career games played, had knee problems, participating in only 64 games, during which his minutes were strictly limited—only 1,104 minutes altogether, or 17.5 minutes per excursion. Second on the all-time shot-blocking list behind Abdul-Jabbar, he hoped to last long enough to get the 126 blocks necessary for first place.

Mike Brown, playing in all 82 games for the fourth straight year, started in 21 of them, and the Jazz added a veteran center, James Donaldson, near the end of the regular season. At the beginning of the season, they had traded two young players, Blue Edwards and Eric Murdock, to the Milwaukee Bucks for two veteran guards, Larry Krystowiak and Jay Humphries. Humphries saw considerable playing time—2,034 minutes in 78 games, 20 of them, late in the season, as a starter—and was second on the team in assists and steals.

Krystowiak missed the final 11 games of the regular season with a foot injury, but averaged almost 20 minutes per game off the bench before that.

Jeff Malone had back problems, and his free-throw shooting declined from .898 to .852—still among the league's all-time elite. Playing in his tenth pro season, he averaged 18.1 points per game, below his career average; he was a starter in 59 of the Jazz's matches, but was moved to the bench later in the year. During the All-Star weekend, held at the Delta Center, Jeff Malone won the Shooting Stars showdown; the greatest glory of the All-Star game was reserved, however, for Karl Malone and Stockton, who shared co-MVP honors in the winning effort they put on at their home coliseum.

The Jazz were now an established NBA franchise, having played their 1,500th game on December 26th. They had been in the playoffs for ten consecutive years, a level reached only by the Celtics, Trail Blazers, and Lakers. Their regular-season record of 47-35 for 1992-93 was somewhat disappointing—the first time coach Jerry Sloan had failed to achieve 50 victories—and their home record slipped to 28-13, something short of dominance.

Their playoff season again fizzled, as the Jazz fell to the Supersonics in their first round. There was no doubt, however, that they were among the class acts of the NBA both on and off the court.

SOURCES

BOOKS

Carter, Craig, and Sachare, Alex, editors, *The Sporting News NBA Guide,* 1992-93 edition, Sporting News Publishing Co., 1992.

Hollander, Zander, *The Complete Handbook of Pro Basketball 1993,* Signet, 1992.

Hollander, Zander, and Sachare, Alex, editors, *The Official NBA Basketball Encyclopedia,* Villard Books, 1989.

Maravich, Pete, and Campbell, Darrel, with Frank Schroeder, *Heir to a Dream,* Thomas Nelson Publishers, 1987.

Neft, David S., and Cohen, Richard M., *The Sports Encyclopedia: Pro Basketball,* St. Martin's Press, 1989.

Taragano, Martin, *Basketball Biographies,* McFarland, 1991.

PERIODICALS

Facts on File, January 1-8, 1988; January 25, 1993.

Sports Illustrated, October 28, 1974; February 17, 1975; November 10, 1975; October 15, 1979; December 24, 1979; October 20, 1980.

OTHER

UTAH JAZZ 1993 PLAYOFF MEDIA GUIDE.

—*Richard Cohen* for Book Builders Inc.

Western Conference

Pacific Division

GOLDEN STATE WARRIORS

In 1946 a new basketball league, the Basketball Association of America, was formed to compete with the National Basketball League; among its eleven charter franchises, all big-city teams, were the Philadelphia Warriors. The Warriors were owned and coached by Eddie Gottlieb, the go-getting, colorful former coach of the Philadelphia Sphas, the legendary team of the South Philadelphia Hebrew Association that had been the premiere American Basketball League team throughout the 1930s.

Philadelphia, with its sidewalk-and-playground culture, its mix of ethnic groups, was rich ground for basketball. The Warriors' starting five were Howie Dalmar and Joe Fulks at forward, 6-foot-7 Art Hillhouse at center, and guards George Senesky and 5-foot-9 Angelo Musi.

Fulks was the star not only of the Warriors but of the entire BAA. At 6-foot-5 and 190 pounds, the 29-year-old rookie had not been a standout in college basketball at Murray State, and had missed basketball entirely durng his wartime Marine hitch, but exploded as one of the sport's early offensive superstars when he hit the pros.

His great innovation was the jump shot—at the time, it was considered unstoppable. He contributed single-game scoring efforts that, in those days, could equal the outputs of entire teams: 63 points in one game in 1949, a record that stood until Elgin Baylor beat it by one point in 1960, an entirely different era.

In an eight-season Warriors career that spanned the BAA and NBA, Fulks scored 8,003 points, an average of 16.4 per game; his first three seasons, with averages of 23.2, 22.1 and 26.0, were league-leaders. As a foul shooter he was outstanding, with averages of .855 in 1950-51 and .825 in 1951-52. Fulks, born in 1926 in Birmingham, Kentucky, died in 1976 and was elected to the Hall of Fame the following year.

Supported by the fine work of Dallmar and Musi, Fulks led the Warriors to second place in

---

the Eastern Division with a 35-25 record that was far behind Red Auerbach's Washington Capitols. They beat the St. Louis Bombers in the playoffs, then beat the New York Knicks in the second best-of-three series, then faced the Chicago Stags, who

Naismith Memorial Basketball Hall of Fame

Joe Fulks

had upset the Capitols, for the championship. In the first game, in Philly, Fulks scored 37 for an 84-71 victory. Art Hillhouse starred in the second game, 85-74, Warriors. Back in Chicago, Game 3 also went to the Warriors.

The Stags were granted one victory on their home court, and then, in Philadelphia, with Game 5 tied at 80 in the final minute, Dallmar sank a basket to win it. The final score was 83-80. Fulks had contributed 34 points to the Warriors' first league championship.

Center Chick Halbert, 6-foot-9 and 225 pounds, joined the Warriors from the Stags for 1947-48, giving the team a truly impressive frontcourt. The season was a battle for first place between the Warriors and Knicks, the Capitols having been moved into the Western Division in order to plug up holes left by failed franchises.

The Warriors emerged on top by one game in the regular season, going 27-21, and in a seven-game opening playoff round, beat the Bombers 85-46 in a humiliating final game. They then faced the Baltimore Bullets, whom they beat 71-60 in the opening game, in Philadelphia. Alas, the Bullets won the next three games by scores of 66-63, 72-70, and 78-75. An intervening Warrior win, 91-82, only postponed the outcome, and the Bullets took the title away with an 88-73 score in the sixth contest.

The BAA looked vastly different in 1948-49, adding four NBL teams and reshuffling its divisions. The East now had the Capitols in first place, Knicks second, Bullets third, and Warriors finishing a mere fourth, with a .467, 28-32 record, in a season when Dallmar was not only injured, but he had to miss games because of college coaching duties. The 15.3 points per game average of Ed Sadowski, the tough Boston Celtics center acquired in a trade for Halbert, only partly offset the loss of Dallmar.

The Warriors fell to the Bullets in the opening round of playoffs, with scoring-champ Fulks only playing one of the two games and not taking a single shot.

TEAM INFORMATION AT A GLANCE

Team founded in 1946 as the Philadelphia Warriors;
relocated to San Francisco, as San Francisco Warriors, 1962;
moved to Oakland, CA, and renamed Golden State Warriors, 1971

Home court:
Oakland Coliseum Arena
7000 Coliseum Way
Oakland, CA 94621
Seating capacity: 15,025
Telephone: (501) 638-6300
FAX: (501) 638-6017

Uniform colors: Home—base color white, trim blue and gold
Road—base color blue, trim white and gold
Team logo: Gold basketball with map of California superimposed in gold,
with blue star representing Oakland area

Franchise record:	Won	Lost	Pct.
Regular season	1,766	1,870	.486
Postseason	99	112	.469

League Championships: 3 (1946-47, 1955-56, 1974-75)
First-Place Finishes: 7 (1947-48, 1950-51, 1955-56, 1963-64, 1966-67, 1974-75, 1975-76)
Last-Place Finishes: 8 (1952-53, 1958-59, 1964-65, 1977-78, 1978-79, 1979-80, 1984-85, 1985-86)

Entering the NBA

1949-50 marked the birth of the NBA. The Warriors were in the Eastern Division, competing with the Syracuse Nationals, the Knicks, the Capitols, the Bullets, and the Celtics. Sadowski was sent to the Bullets after 17 games, but rookie Vern Gardner, a 6-foot-5 player from the Universities of Utah and Wyoming, contributed 13.5 points per game. However, Fulks was down to the same level, at 14.2, and the team sank to fourth place, the lowest playoff spot.

A strong bounceback occurred in 1950-51, as not only did Fulks break out of his slump, but two stellar new arrival joined the Warriors. Guard Andy Phillip, a 6-foot-2 playmaking whiz from the Stags and a future NBA coach, led the league in assists with 6.3 per game, as well as sinking 11.2 points. It was the first of two All-Star seasons for this future Hall-of-Famer before he went to the Ft. Wayne Pistons.

Meanwhile, joining the Warriors as a rookie was 6-foot-4 forward Paul Arizin, one of the major offensive threats of the era, thus giving the team two superb jump-shooters in the corners. Arizin, a Philadelphia home product and the Warriors' first-round draft choice, had once scored 85 points in a college game for Villanova.

He suffered from an asthmatic condition that made him wheeze audibly as he ran up and down the court, but it did not affect his play. In 11 of his 12 seasons with the Warriors, he averaged over 20 points per game. One of the flashiest offensive players of his era, he was known for his strong leaping ability and accurate jumper.

Arizin averaged 17.2 points per game in his rookie year, second on the team to Fulks's 18.7. Bill Closs was the center-of-the-season for the Warriors. The team steamed through the regular season to win 40 games and lose 26, a .606 percentage, but in the opening round of playoffs they were upset by the fourth-place Nationals, first 91-89 in overtime, then 90-78.

In 1951-52, the Warriors finished 33-33, with Arizin leading the NBA in scoring (25.4 points per game) and Phillip leading it in assists (8.2 per game). A notable rookie, 6-foot-8 center Neil Johnston, served on the bench for the start of a brilliant career.

In fourth place, the Warriors barely sneaked into the payoffs, and lost them to Syracuse, 2-1. The 1952-53 team suffered an abysmal plunge to 12-57, a .174 record. It was Fulks's last season, and Arizin was away on military service during this Korean War year. Johnston joined the starting five as pivot man, and led the lead not only in total scoring and average, with 1,564 points or 22.3 per game, but in minutes played (3,166), field goal percentage (45) and free throws attempted and made.

Johnston was the only member of the starting five to return for 1953-54. He led the league in most of the same categories—his scoring average had risen to 23.4—and led his team up to fourth place with a 29-43, .403 record. Arizin's return for 1954-55 gave the Warriors two twenty-point-per-game shooters, with Johnston again leading the league (22.7) and Arizin taking over the first spot in minute splayed (2,953) and field goals made and attempted. Johnston also led the league in rebounding with 15.1 per game.

Gottlieb Steps Down

It was the following season, 1955-56, that marked a turning point as the Warriors made massive personnel changes on and off court. Perhaps the most important change was the stepping down of Gottlieb as coach, to be replaced by former Warrior guard George Senesky. As a player, Senesky had specialized in dishing out the ball for assists; his team-oriented, defense-conscious attitude proved invaluable when he became a coach. In comparison with Gottlieb, however, Senesky also had better material to work with.

Guard-forward Tom Gola, a great college star at La Salle and a Philadelphia native, had arrived as a rookie. Though his professional statistics would not match his college heroics, he had a long and distinguished career as a Warrior and Knick, returning thereafter to La Salle as its coach and

Naismith Memorial Basketball Hall of Fame

Neil Johnston (6)

Naismith Memorial Basketball Hall of Fame

Tom Gola

being inducted into the Hall of Fame. With the Warrior forward positions filled by Arizin and capable veteran Joe Graboski, Gola switched to the backcourt and became the tallest guard in the NBA at 6-foot-6.

His backcourt partner, point guard Jack George, had a productive year in his third season with a league-leading 39 minutes per game and a team-leading 6.3 assists. (George is currently tenth on the team's all-time assists list.) All five Warrior starters scored in double figures, led by Arizin's 24.2 and Johnston's 22.1, which were second and third in the league. The team's scoring average jumped from 93 points per game to 103. Their balanced offense and upgraded defense gave the Warriors a first-place, 45-27 finish.

In the opening round of playoffs, they disposed of the rival Nationals, 3-2. Their opponents for the NBA championship were the Ft. Wayne Pistons. In Game 1, Johnston was held to 10 points by the defense of Bob Houbregs, but Warrior reserve forward Ernie Beck took over the scoring for 23 points, also making key rebounds. The result was a 98-94 Warrior win. Game 2 went to

the Pistons, 84-83. In Game 3, four Warriors scored in double figures for a 100-96 victory. Game 4 was 107-105, Warriors, with the Pistons' tying shot forestalled by the buzzer, and Game 5 clinched it with a 99-88 walkway.

Although Johnston had slumped throughout the finals, scoring 20 points only once, his teammates had filled in the gap for a world championship. Arizin, in particular, scored 289 points in ten postseason games, the best playoff average to that point by anyone except George Mikan.

The Warriors' rise to the top lasted only one season, as Gola missed 1956-57 for military service and as the Boston Celtics began the Bill Russell dynasty. The Warriors slid back to third place, 37-35, although Arizin led the league's scorers with 25.6 points per game, and Johnson was still up there with 22.8 points and 12.4 rebounds. The Warriors' postseason was nothing to write home about, as the Nationals swept them in two games, 103-96 and 91-80.

The Warriors posted an identical regular-season record the folowing year. Gola was back, with almost 14 points per game, 10.8 rebounds and a team-leading 5.5 assists, but Arizin's scoring was down to 20.7 and Johnston's to 19.5. Graboski and George had become substitutes; Beck, at guard, and Rookie of the Year Woody Sauldsberry, at forward, both had productive years.

The team had three double-digit rebounders in Sauldsberry, Johnston and Gola, but once again finished behind the Celtics and Nationals. This time they ousted the Nats from the playoff openers, 2-1 but were outclassed by the Celtics for the Eastern championship, 4-1, winning only Game 4, in which Gola and Arizin combined for 62 points.

The 1958-59 Warriors had a new coach in future Hall of Famer Al Cervi, formerly a great guard for the Nationals, who had led the old NBL in scoring in 1947. They also had a fine rookie prospect in Guy Rodgers, a 6-foot point guard who, unfortunately, could only play 45 games because of a military commitment. Rodgers, a great playmaker and a tough little guy, was to collect more than 7,000 assists in his twelve-year

Born March 28, 1944 in Elizabeth, New Jersey, Barry describes himself, in his autobiography *Confessions of a Basketball Gypsy,* as a skinny, tough kid who often got into fights. As a player, he was known for for his emotionalism, often complaining about referees' calls and getting into arguments with fans and players, but was not the kind of player who dished out physical punishment to opponents. "I squawk more than most guys because I get fouled more than most guys," he wrote, and also asserted that complaining paid off in his being sent to the free-throw line more.

He was all-American at the University of Miami, leading the NCAA in scoring in 1964-65 with a 37.4 average. Rookie of the Year the next season, he became the only player ever to lead both the ABA and the NBA in scoring. Possessed of flashy moves but lacking jumping ability, he was known for his superb fakes and outside shooting.

He was a great passer and perhaps the best free-throw shooter of all time, with an individualistic underhand style and a .900 career average in the NBA, .893 overall as a pro. He is eleventh on the all-time combined NBA-ABA total points list, with 25,279, a 24.8 average. He has been a broadcast announcer since his retirement, and was elected to the Hall of Fame in 1986.

Naismith Memorial Basketball Hall of Fame

Rick Barry

NBA career, finishing second to Oscar Robertson five times in six years and leading the league twice; he is still the Warriors' all-time career assists leader with 4,855, fifth on their minutes-played list and eighth in games played, as well as eighth all-time in assists in the NBA.

Neil Johnston, nearing the end of his playing career, missed most of the 1958-59 season with a knee injury. Center was a temporary weakness, with 6-foot-8 Graboski enlisted to fill that spot. The Cervi-led Warriors finished in the cellar, 32-40.

The Man on Stilts

Why was center only a temporary weakness? The answer contains three words: Wilton Norman Chamberlain. A new era not only for the Warriors but for the entire sport of basketball began when Wilt the Stilt joined his home-town Warriors as a rookie in 1959-60, after a college career at Kansas during which he had astounded fans, opponents, coaches, scouts and sportswriters, and a year's hiatus touring Europe and America with the Harlem Globetrotters. At 7-foot-1 and 250, Cham-

Naismith Memorial Basketball Hall of Fame

Paul Arizin

berlain was far from the only big center ever to play in the NBA: George Mikan, in a previous era, had been cut from similar cloth, as were Clyde Lovellette and, of course, the 6-foot-10 Bill Russell.

Chamberlain, however, was simply the most overpowering presence on the court of any player up to that point—and perhaps any player since that point. Although he did not invent the slam dunk, he made it his personal weapon in a way no player had before, along with the finger-roll, the hook shot, and a fine outside jumper.

Amazingly strong, he could bench-press five hundred pounds and had been a national shot-put champion in college. His physical gifts were such that, during his playing career, he came within a hair's breadth of signing a contract to fight his friend Muhammad Ali for the heavyweight boxing crown—a fight which, in many observers' opinion, he might have won. His powers of intimidation on the basketball court were such that in his entire fourteen-year playing career he never fouled

out of a game—he didn't have to actually *touch* the opposing players to alter their paths.

Chamberlain's rookie year was sensational. He was not only Rookie of the Year but league MVP and All-Star starting center. He had six 50-point games and led the league in both scoring (37.6 points per game) and rebounds (27.0 per game). Both those averages were well above anything that had been achieved to that point, as was his 2,707 point total. He played 46 minutes per game for a league-leading 3,338 total minutes.

Chamberlain had personal conflicts with his new head coach, Neil Johnston, but they did not prevent his leading the Warriors into second place with a 49-26, .653 record. Arizin scored 22.3 points per game to suport him, and Gola and Rodgers were also double-digit scorers. One statistic is highly indicative of Chamberlain's importance to the Warriors as a franchise: between 1958-59 and 1959-60, their average attendance per home game more than doubled, from 4,206 to 9,211.

The Warriors beat the Nats in the opening playoffs, 2-1, winning their two games by 23 and 20 points and losing the middle contest by only six. Then they faced the real challenge: the Boston Celtics in the Eastern finals. Chamberlain scored 42 points in Game 1, but his team lost, 111-105. In Game 2, a shoving fight occurred between Chamberlain and 6-foot-7 Boston forward Tom Heinsohn. The Warriors took the game, 115-110.

Playing Game 3 with a bruised hand (which may have been caused by smacking the rim, not by hitting Heinsohn), Chamberlain was ineffective and the Celtics won, 120-90. With the famous hand still hurting in Game 4, the Warriors lost 112-104. In Game 5, Chamberlain, under attack by sportswriters, responded with a 50-point performance, a total no other rookie has matched in a playoff game, before or since. By the way, he also grabbed 35 rebounds. He contributed 55 points to Game 6, but the Celtics won it, and the championship, by a score of 119-117.

The 1960-61 regular season was a repeat performance for Chamberlain and the rest of the Warriors. The big man led the league with 38.4

It may be the most memorable individual performance in NBA history. It took place in Hersehy, PA, where the Philadelphia Warriors played a fraction of their homes games. The crowd contained 4,124 lucky fans. The opposing center for the Knicks was Darrall Imhoff, a 6-foot-11 reserve and a tough defender. Chamberlain, who, according to his autobiography, *Wilt*, had gone without sleep the night before and had spent much of the day accumulating records at a rifle-shooting arcade, started off the game by hitting six outside shots.

Chamberlain's 23 points in the first quarter got Imhoff into foul trouble, so 6-foot-9 forward Cleveland Buckner joined the job of defending the big man, allowing him "only" 18 points in the second quarter. Wilt came back with 28 points in the third quarter, and got Imhoff to foul out in the fourth, which left Buckner and 6-foot-7 forward Willie Naulls to contend with him. Chamberlain's previous scoring record in one game had been 78, achieved in a triple-overtime contest; he passed that mark at 40 minutes into the Hershey game.

At that point, the Warriors were comfortably ahead and consciously decided to feed the ball to Wilt so that he could break the record. The Knicks, on the other hand, tried to freeze the ball and to foul the Warrior passers early, to prevent Chamberlain's scoring. The Knick strategy did result in a two-minute scoring drought for Chamberlain late in the fourth period, but he charged back in the final minutes. His hundredth points, on a stuff, were scored with 46 seconds remaining.

The unheralded key to Chamberlain's performance that night was his foul shooting. Normally converting foul shots at little more than a 50 percent rate, he went 28 for 32, a .875 clip, on the crucial night. Credit must also be given to Guy Rodgers, who made 20 assists, most of them to Chamberlain.

Al Attles had a great game that night, but few noticed: he went eight for eight in field goals and sank a free throw for a total of 17 points, with 6 assists. Paul Arizin and Tom Meschery had 16 points apiece. Among the Knicks on that 169-147 occasion, three had 30-point games: Richie Guerin with 39, Buckner with 33, and Naulls with 31.

Recalling his feat in his autobiography, Chamberlain claimed it was not the most exciting moment of his NBA career, because he felt that field-goal percentage and rebounding were more mportant than total points. His greatest satisfaction, he wrote, came from averaging 50.4 points per game; however, he admitted that the feat created excessive expectations among fans and press.

points and 27.2 rebounds per game. Sauldsberry having been sent to the St. Louis Hawks, the Warriors now had Andy Johnson along with Arizin in the frontcourt. The team's 46-33 finish again placed it second to the Celtics. However, the postseason was a significant comedown, as the third-place Nationals upset the Warriors in three straight games.

The 1961-62 season took scoring to new heights in the NBA. Elgin Baylor, Jerry West, Bob Pettit, Walt Bellamy, and Oscar Robertson all averaged over 30 points per game. The average team score per game was 118.9, a new high. Leaping above all others was Chamberlain, who averaged 50.4 points per game, or 4,029 total points, and an incredible 48.5 minutes per game.

Chamberlain also led the league in rebounds per game with 25.7. Under new Warriors coach Frank McGuire, the team strategy was to feed the ball to Wilt as often as possible. It worked to the extent of giving the Warriors a 49-31 (.613) record—but they were still second to the Celtics.

The most famous scoring performance of the season—and perhaps of all time—was Chamberlain's 100-point night on March 2, 1962, against the Knicks in Hershey, PA. However, in that same season he had games of 78, 73, and 65 points, two games of 67, and, within a single eight-game stretch, three of 62.

In the postseason, the Warriors bested the Nationals in five games. Arizin scored 40 points in Game 1 and starred again in Game 2, both wins for Philadelphia. Syracuse returned to form to tie the series with wins in Games 3 and 4. In Game 5, Chamberlain, who had slumped a bit, resurged with a 56-point performance to give his team the series. In the Eastern finals against the Celtics, the latter team won the first game, and then the series became a matter of alternating victories.

Game 5 was marred by fistfights—at one point Boston's Sam Jones picked up a stool and approached Chamberlain theateningly, before being restrained. Game 7 was the basketball, as opposed to pugilistic, thriller of the series, with Chamberlain playing an all-around game and the injured Gola scoring 16 points. Chamberlain tied the game in the final seconds on a three-point play, then Jones' jump shot put the Celtics up 109-107 with two seconds remaining. Then Jones intercepted the Warriors' last-chance pass, and the Celtics had again come out on top.

The City on the Bay

The year 1962 was one of enormous transition. Eddie Gottlieb sold the Warriors to a group of San Francisco businessmen, and the team moved to the city on the Bay. Coach McGuire, not wishing to move from the East Coast, stepped down to return to college coaching and was replaced by Bob Feerick. The Warriors also traded Gola to the Knicks for forwards Willie Naulls and Ken Sears.

Placed in the Western Division, the Warriors finished fourth with a 31-49 record. Rodgers led the league in assists with a 10.6 average; Chamberlain again paced the NBA in scoring average,

at 44.8, and rebounding, at 24.3. Guard Al Attles, one of the few Warriors who made the westward move with the team, had a fine year with 10.4 points per game. It was the third season in a distinguished 11-year playing career which then led to 12 years of coaching and then to a front-office position as vice-president and assistant general manager of the Warriors; on February 10, 1977, Attles' Number 16 was retired.

The 1963-64 season was Franklin Mieuli's first as owner of the Warriors, and Alex Hannum's first as their head coach. Hannum, a former NBA star, had been Coach of the Year for the Hawks in 1958 and would repeat in 1963-64 with the Warriors. Eventually would rack up that honor and the league title in both the NBA and ABA. Perhaps his key strategic move was to have Chamberlain concentrate more on shot-blocking, defense, and passing. As a result, the great center's scoring average fell to 36.9 without his having to give up the league lead; his assists rose to five per game to supplement Rodgers' seven.

The Warriors were now the stingiest team in the league, giving opponents only 102.6 points per game. Having sold Naulls to Boston, they had 6-foot-11 rookie forward-center Nate Thurmond backing up Chamberlain and starting forwards Tom Meschery and Wayne Hightower. (Later, when the played on different teams, Chamberlain was to name Thurmond as the toughest defensive center he had to play against.) The Warriors' 48-32, .600 record led the West, but after defeating the Hawks in the playoffs, they lost to the Celtics, 4-1.

Goodbye Wilt, Hello Rick

Somehow, Hannum's strategies didn't work as well the next season, and the Warriors were 5-16 after their first 21 games. The solution, the team felt, was to trade the high-priced Chamberlain (who had not proven to be the popular favorite in San Francisco that he had been in Philly) and install Thurmond as the starting center. The idea of Thurmond as a starter was extremely sound—his

18.5 rebounds were third in the league, and included a 37-rebound game—but in exchange for Chamberlain the Warriors got only a backup center, Connie Dierking, a guard, Paul Neumann, a third player, who never set foot on an NBA court again, and some money. With their highest scorer, Rodgers, at 16 points per game, the Warriors plummeted to last place with an appalling 17-63, .213 record.

Rick Barry, the skinny, 6-foot-7 rookie forward out of the University of Miami, came to the rescue in 1965-66, drawing Rookie of the Year honors and being selected to the all-NBA first team. Scoring 25.7 points per game, Barry was fourth in the league; he was second in free-throw percentage with .862. Rodgers was second in assists with 10.7 per match. Thurmond's 18.0 rebounds per game, including 42 in a game against the Pistons on November 9, were fourth in the league. This newly balanced Warriors team rose to fourth place at 35-45, or .438.

The squad really jelled for 1966-67, going 44-37 in the regular season and wining the Western Division championship. Their new head coach was Bill Sharman, longtime backcourt partner of Bob Cousy on the Celtics and often called the best pure shooter in the history of the sport.

Barry soared to the top, leading the NBA in scoring with 35.6 points per game and having an MVP, 38-point All-Star game. Thurmond, despite a broken hand that caused him to miss 16 games, was the league's fourth rebounder with 21.3 per game, and scored at an 18.7 clip. The Warriors' three other starters, plus three reserves, all had double-digit scoring averages.

After sweeping the third-place Lakers in the playoffs, the team beat the second-place Hawks in a surprisingly tight series in which the Hawks, with Lenny Wilkins, Zelmo Beaty, Lou Hudson, and player-coach Richie Guerin, won Games 3 and 4 in St. Louis. The Warriors' finals opponent was none other than the Philadelphia 76ers—Wilt Chamberlain's team and Alex Hannum's as well, one of the greatest assemblages in basketball history, who had won 68 games and lost only 13 in the regular season.

The first game went to overtime, but the Sixers pulled ahead by six points, 141-135, although Thurmond outrebounded Chamberlain. Game 2 went to the Sixers as well, with Chamberlain expertly defending Thurmond and holding him to seven points.

Barry's 55 points in Game 3 helped win that one, 130-124 in San Francisco, but the Sixers returned to take Game 4, when Chamberlain blocked Barry's path toward a last-gasp layup and forced him to take an off-balance shot that missed. The series went anticlimactically to six games, with the Warriors' road victory in Game 5 not altering the ultimate result.

Barry Jumps Leagues—Team Slumps

In 1967-68 Barry jumped leagues to the ABA and Thurmond missed 31 games with a late-season hand injury. The Warriors slumped to third place, winning 43 games and losing 39. Veteran forward Rudy LaRusso, bought from the Pistons, helped the team with 21.8 points per game.

George Lee was the new coach in 1968-69, and his record was a third-place 41-41. The healthy Thurmond was the league's second-best rebounder at 19.3 per game, and scored 21.5. Guard Jeff Mullins was the Warriors' hot shooter with 22.8 points per game, and Al Attles was the playmaker with 6 assists per contest.

After winning the first two playoff games against the Lakers, 99-94 and 107-101, both in Los Angleles, the Warriors collapsed and lost the next four.

In 1969-70, Thurmond again missed much of the season with an injury, this time 39 games' worth. Needing a big man, the Warriors got Jerry Lucas from the Royals for two players; his 15.4 points and 14.3 rebounds per game would help, but he too had an injury—a broken hand. Mullins' 22.1 points per game, twelfth in the league, were among the season's few bright spots. Attles took over as player-coach for the last 30 games, but only won eight of them; the team fell to sixth place at 30-52.

In 1970-71, the Warriors were in the Pacific Division of the expanded NBA and, with Attles coaching for the entire season (and playing in 34 games with limited minutes), finished second to the Lakers at 41-41. Thurmond, Lucas, and Mullins were all healthy and productive. Thurmond was named the league's All-Defensive center, and played in all 82 games. In the opening round of playoffs, however, the Warriors could not get past Lew Alcindor's and Oscar Robertson's Milwaukee Bucks; they salvaged only Game 4, by a 106-104 margin, and were blown away in the decisive Game 5, 136-86.

Just Across the Bay

The 1971-72 season was another of transition as the Warriors moved across the Bay from San Francisco to Oakland, changing their name to the Golden State Warriors. Though they played some games in San Diego, which had recently been vacated by the Rockets, they played most of their games in the Oakland Coliseum Arena, their present home. The Warriors traded Jerry Lucas to the Knicks for ex-Michigan forward Cazzie Russell, an exchange of star for star.

Russell was one of three Warrior starters that season who averaged 21.4 or 21.5 points, the others being Thurmond and Mullins; Russell's frontcourt partner, Clyde Lee, handled the rebounds, with 14.5 per game to Thurmond's 16.1. The Warriors reached a 51-31, .622 level but were way behind the Lakers, who set an all-time record of 69-13. The Warriors lost their playoff round to Abdul-Jabbar's (formerly Alcindor's) Bucks, 4-1, winning only the opening game.

The Warriors took revenge in 1972-73 as they upset the Bucks in the playofs, 4-2. The season marked the return of Rick Barry from the ABA. Barry's 22.3 points per game did not place him among the leader's in point production, but his .902 free throw average led the NBA, and he was named a second-team all-league member. Also second in the league — in rebounds — was Thurmond, with 17.1. And again second in the

Pacific Division standings, the Warriors were 47-35. After going through the Bucks in the playoffs, they received their second consecutive 4-1 drubbing by the Lakers.

Barry was second in the league in free throws (.899) in 1973-74, fifth in scoring average (25.1), fifth in steals (2.11) and eighth in assists (6.1). Thurmond and Lee missed 20 and 28 games respectively with injuries, however, and the Warriors' 44-38 record, despite being second in the division, was not good enough to earn them a playoff spot in a league where other divisions had more depth.

That Championship Season

Thurmond was gone the next season—gone to the Chicago Bulls for 6-foot-9 center Clifford Ray, money, and a draft choice. Lee was off to the Hawks, and Cazzie Russell signed with the Lakers. These were significant losses, but the team more than made up for them. Ballhandler Butch Beard and shooting guard Charlie Johnson had good years, center Ray controlled the boards for the team, and 190-pound UCLA grad Keith (later Jamaal) Wilkes, a smooth shooter and tough defender, had a Rookie of the Year season at forward. with 14.2 points and 8.2 boards per game.

It was one of Barry's best seasons, too, as he averaged 30.6 points a game, second in the NBA, with 6.2 assists and a league-leading .904 free-throw average. The Warriors finally returned to the top of the division, winning 48 and losing 34. Much of the credit for molding this young team into champions belonged to coach Attles, who stressed finding the open man, pressing on defense, and sharing playing time.

Indicative of the Warriors' defensive style was the fact that they led the NBA in team rebounds although their individual leader, Ray, only grabbed 10.6 per game. Underrated by opponents and the press, the Warriors came from behind repeatedly to win their games.

This occurred dramatically in their playoffs against the Bulls, a low-scoring series in which the two teams traded victories until the Warriors took Game 7, 83-79, in Oakland, for the Western championship. Ironically, Attles benched the slumping Barry for much of Game 7, beforing sendng him back in to hit some crucial shots. (Their previous playoff round, against the Seattle Supersonics, had been a relatively easy 4-2 affair except for a fistfight with fans on the way to the locker room after the final victory.)

They were heavy underdogs to the Washington Bullets in the NBA finals, as the Bullets included Wes Unseld, Elvin Hayes, Kevin Porter, Nick Weatherspoon, and Phil Chenier, but the Warriors' defense brought them the crown in a 4-0 sweep, holding the Washingtonians to 95 points per game. The Warrior guards took Porter out of contention, and Wilkes held off the threat of Hayes. Rick Barry's 28.2 points per game, with a .918 average from the foul line, gave the Californians their scoring impetus.

"I don't think there's ever been a team so looked-down upon that wound up winning the championship," Barry told sportswriter Roland Lazenby in a 1990 interview. Both Barry and Attles gave full credit to center Ray for his defensive presence; Barry also mentioned backup center George Johnson for his shot-blocking. Wilkes offered another view of Ray's value, citing his offcourt leadership and teaching ability.

No Repeat

Unfortunately, the Warriors' tenure at the top was not to last. An early sign was the trading of Butch Beard to Cleveland, a move that happened immediately after the championship and that has been seen in retorspect as a mistake. The Warriors now had young Phil Smith—who blossomed with 20 points per game—and rookie Gus Williams at guard, and it was enough to give them the highest wining percentage in the NBA, .720, with 59 wins. Barry was named to the all-NBA first team, his free-throw percentage soaring to .923; Smith was on the second team defensively as well as all-NBA.

Naismith Memorial Basketball Hall of Fame

Al Cervi

The Pacific Division Champion Warriors defeated the Pistons, 4-2, in the opening playoffs, but had to get past the Phoenix Suns for the Western Championship, and couldn't. In Game 7 of that upset series, Barry went scoreless for 30 minutes; the score was 94-86.

Barry's free-throw shooting reached new heights in 1976-77 as he sank 60 consecutively, a record at the time. (His average of .916 was second in the league.) Wilkes, Smith, and Ray had fine seasons, as did reserve center Robert Parish (9.1 points, 7.1 rebounds per game), who would later become an all-time star for the Celtics. However, with the NBA and ABA having merged, the all-around bench strength of NBA teams was greater than in the past, so that the Warriors' advantage in that department was diminished. Their 46-36 record was third to the Lakers and Trail Blazers in the regular season. After winning against the Pistons in the playoffs, they lost to the Lakers in seven games, each of which was won by the home team.

The 1978-79 season was an off-year as the team sank to fifth and last place, 43-39. Barry's .924 free-throw average became a team record that has endured. The loss of Wilkes and Williams to free agency, and of Ray to a knee injury was damaging. The following year, Barry went to Houston as a free agent; on the plus side, the Warriors acquired young guard John Lucas, with his 9.3 assists (second in the league) and 16.1 points per game. Parish was the starting center, leading the team with 12.1 rebounds per game, and established a club record for blocked shots with 217. However, the team was the youngest and least experienced in the league. With a 38-44 record, they again settled in the basement, which now meant sixth place.

They dug deeper in 1979-80, going 24-58, or .293. Phil Smith and starting forward Purvis Short were injured, as was coach Attles, who tore an achilles tendon in practice and missed the last 21 games. (Assistant coach John Bach, taking over, went 6-15.) The team's 0-8 mark in overtime games was a new NBA record.

Climbing Back

So far down were they that despite being the league's most improved team in 1980-81 they still missed the playoffs. The Warriors now had 6-foot-7 forward Bernard King to help them, having arrived from Utah after recovering from alcohol problems. He was the first Comeback Player of the Year in NBA history, Player of the Month in January, and shot a club-record .588 from the field. Joe Barry Carroll, a seven-footer, and power forward Larry Smith were elected to the league's all-rookie team. Smith's 12.1 rebounds per game were third in the league. World B. Free suffered a finger injury but averaged 24.1 points in his 65 games, ninth in the league, and 3-point specialist Joe Hassett made a valuable contribution. The Warriors ascended to fourth place with a 39-43, .476 record.

Again in 1981-82, the Warriors finished one game shy of a playoff spot, their record 45-37.

Their squad had coalesced around Carroll, King, Smith, and Free, with King and Free ending up eighth and ninth in the league in scoring, the first time the Warriors had had two players on the leaders' list since the days of Chamberlain and Arizin. Coach Attles logged in his 500th career win on January 2, against Dallas. The team was hot-shooting from the field, with a franchise record percentage of .496, but from the line they only went .711, tied for last in the NBA.

The 1982-83 season was the end of the Attles era as far as on-court activities were concerned, for the longtime coach resigned shortly before seaso's end. It was a year of tumultuous personnel moves. King, a free agent, tried to sign with the Knicks, but the Warriors matched the New Yorkers' offer, signed the star, then traded him to — yes, the Knicks — for the troubled Micheal Ray Richardson and a draft choice. When Richardson failed to report, the Warriors suspended him, activating him shortly afterward, then trading him to Atlanta three months later for a second round draft choice. They traded Free to the Cavs for Ron Brewer. In addition, injuried plagued the team: their 238 missed games was an NBA record at the time. Altogether, 19 players passed through the Warriors' roster, a club record. Carroll had an outstanding year, averaging 24.1, as did Purvis Short with 21.4, but these bright spots could not fully illuminate the Warriors' clouded landscape. Finishing fifth, they were 30-52.

Attles stepped down as coach after the season, to be replaced by his assistant, John Bach, who at age 58 became the youngest rookie head coach in league history. It was a Purvis Short year, as the forward led the team with 22.8 points per game. His 57 points on January 7, 1984, against the San Antonio Spurs, were a league high for the year and contributed to a 154-point total, a single-game record for the Warriors on the West Coast. It was also a Joe Barry Carroll year, as the veteran center scored 20.5 points per game with 8.0 rebounds. The Warriors finished fifth in their division, one game out of the playoffs with a 37-45 record.

Things got worse the following season as the

Warriors only won 22 games against 60 defeats, tying the Indiana Pacers for the worst record in the NBA, and ensconcing themselves in the cellar of the Pacific Division by 110 percentage points over the Seattle Supersonics.

With 28.0 points per game, Short soared to fourth place among the league's scorers; guard Eric "Sleepy" Floyd had 19.5 with 5.0 assists. However, Carroll was missing from the pivot, having signed with an Italian team as a free agent. Things looked up for the future as the Warriors' first pick in the draft lottery—seventh pick overall—was Chris Mullin, the 6-foot-7 forward from the playgrounds of Brooklyn and St. John's University.

The Warriors remained in the cellar for 1985-86, but at least the gap between them and the Sonics was only one game, as the Warriors went 30-52. Mullin, in his rookie year, hit free throws at an .896 rate, second best in the league. Carroll was back after a complex transaction involving his acceptance of a Milwaukee Bucks offer which was then matched by the Warriors; he scored 21.2 points per game with 8.5 boards, and led the NBA in fouling out, with 13 disqualifications. The Warriors once again had a presence at center.

Smith led the team in rebounds with 11.1 per game, sixth in the NBA, including 16 offensive boards in one game against the Denver Nuggets. Floyd's 9.1 assists per game were sixth in the league. Three-point shooting by Short, Floyd, and reserve forward Greg Ballard gave the team an offensive lift.

Hiring George Karl as the new head coach paid off for 1986-87. The Warriors broke .500 with a 42-40, third-place regular season, and Karl came in second for Coach of the Year honors. With Short, Smith, and Carroll in front and Mullin and Floyd in the backcourt, the team had a talented starting unit, and although Short was injured and only played in 34 games, Greg Ballard and guard Terry Teagle came off the bench to play in all 82. Floyd and Carroll made the All-Star team, with Floyd's 10.3 assists per game, and 73 three-point goals, setting club records.

For the first time in ten years, the Warriors were in the playoffs, and they made much of it, coming back from a 2-0 deficit to defeat the Utah Jazz in the first round. They fell to the Lakers, however, in five games, winning only Game 4, a home contest. Floyd was the star of that one, scoring 51 points, 29 of them in the fourth quarter.

Attendance was up the folowing season—the 11,350 mark was the Warriors' best in a decade—but performance was way down, largely due to injuries and other assorted traumas. After missing practice, Chris Mullin voluntarily entered an alcohol rehabilitation program at Centinela Hospital in Inglewood, California, missing 22 games but greatly improving himself for the long haul.

It was another season of player-shuffling for the Warriors as 21 players passed through the roster and 204 games were missed due to injury. The most notable trade was that of Carroll and Floyd to the Houston Rockets for veteran 7-foot-4 center Ralph Sampson and reserve guard Steve Harris.

Sampson had a good year for the club, with 15.4 points and 10.0 rebounds per game. Point guard Winston Garland was solid in 67 games, working around the difficulties of being placed on waivers, picked up by no other club, and then being resigned by the Warriors as a free agent.

That 1987-88 team was particularly ineffective on the road, their 4-37 road record being the worst in the history of the franchise. Coach Karl resigned in March and was temporarily replaced by assistant coach Ed Gregory, but neither coach could work miracles with the troubled team. Their 20-62, .244 percentage was not in the cellar but in fifth place, by grace of the Los Angeles Clippers, who went 17-65.

The Don Nelson Era

Fortunately, Don Nelson, a former NBA player and longtime head coach of the Milwaukee Bucks, had joined the Warriors' organization as Executive Vice President in July, 1987. During the season he became General Manager, and after the seasons' close it was announced that

| PROFILE | Chris Mullin |

Born July 30, 1963 in Brooklyn, NY ... 6'7", 215 pounds ... graduated from Xavieran High School, Brooklyn, and St. John's University, where he led the Redmen to the NCAA final four and was named Big East Conference Co-Player with Patrick Ewing and won the John Wooden Award as the nation's top college player in 1985 ... first-round, Number 7 draft choice, held out through training camp and the first six games of 1985-86 before signing with the War-riors, and missed the last 20 games with a sore heel ... Played all 82 games in 1986-87, but missed much of the following season owing to alcohol rehabilitation ... Joined Chamberlain, Barry, and Purvis Short in the Warriors' 2,000-point club in 1988-89, also totaling more than 400 in the rebound and assists columns that year ... In 1991, became first Warrior since Rick Barry to start in an All-Star game ... He wears Number 17 because he was a childhood fan of Celtic John Havlicek ... Is a close friend of Manute Bol, who roomed with Mullin's brother John at University of Bridgeport and who named his son Chris ... Supports Chris Mullin's Fund for Families, Children and Youth, a United Way charity ... is married to Liz and has a son, Sean ... Signed a nine-year contract on September 29, 1989.

AP/Wide World Photos

Nelson would become head coach for 1988-89. Nelson had accumulated a 540-344 record as pilot of the Bucks and was working on numerous records for coaching longevity. By 1992, his 2,524 games as player and/or coach were the most of any individual in NBA history.

His experience paid off, as did increased stability on the roster. Mullin was back full-time and was NBA Player of the Month in January and an All-Star. It was to be the first of four consecutive All-Star games for Mullin. His scoring average (26.5) and free-throw percentage (.892) were both third in the league.

When guard Mitch Richmond's 22.0 points per game were added, the Warriors had the highest-scoring duo in the league. Richmond, a 6-foot-5, 215-pound graduate of Kansas State, was Rookie of the Year, adding 4.2 assists and 5.9 rebounds per game to his scoring.

Another addition was 7-foot-6 center Manute Bol, the shot-blocking specialist whose 345 total, 4.31 per game, led the league in that department. Although Bol was not a complete performer at center, his presence made up significantly for the month-long absence of Sampson due to arthroscopic surgery on his left knee. Bol played 1,769 minutes at center, in 80 games, compared to Sampson's 1,086 minutes in 61.

Versatile sixth man Rod Higgins, playing some center as well as forward and guard, contributed 10.6 points and 4.6 rebounds per effort. The 1988-89 team went 43-39 in Nelson's first year at the helm, fourth in the division. Emphasis on free throws helped: the Warriors' .799 percentage was the best in their history.

Entering the playoffs against the Midwest Division leaders, the Jazz, they swept the Utah team, 3-0, winning Games 1 and 2 in the fabled Delta Center, where the Jazz were supposedly unbeatable. However, the next round, against the Phoenix Suns, was a different story. The Warriors only won Game 2 of that best-of-seven series.

A great rookie joined the Warriors in 1989-90: Tim Hardaway, the solidly built six-foot point guard out of Texas-El Paso. His presence on the team made an immediate difference both on and off the court, as he was awarded the first ever Jack McMahon Award as the Warriors' most inspira-

tional player. A unanimous All-Rookie first team selection, he came in second to David Robinson in the Rookie of the Year voting. He was ninth in the league in assists, tenth in steals, and scored 14.5 points per game.

A second fine rookie, Lithuanian guard Sarnuas Marciulionis, joined the team as a non-draft selection, playing 1,695 minutes in 75 games as a reserve and averaging 12.1 points per game. Marciulionis was the first player from the Soviet Union to join the NBA.

A real powerhouse at 6-foot-5, 215 pounds, ambidextrous and a student of martial arts, with huge hands and a supercompetitive nature, Marciulionis throws fear into the opposition and admiration into his teammates. Hardaway has said of him, in a quote for the Warriors' Media Guide, "If Sarunas and I were on opposite teams, and we were running toward a loose ball, I wouldn't go for it. Not against Sarunas. Let him have it."

Meanwhile, All-Star Mullin's name in 1989-90 was among the list of league-leaders in scoring (25.1) and free throw percentage (.889). Along with those two stars, Teagle was a third Warrior who won the Player of the Week Award that season, doing it for the week ending January 7.

The team's free-throw percentage went up to .806 and its per-game scoring average of 116.3 led the NBA, the first time the Warriors had paced the league in that department in 14 years. (In both seasons flanking 1989-90, they averaged 116.6 points per contest but did not lead the NBA.)

Despite these encouraging gains, however—and despite selling out all their home games for the first time in their history—the Warriors only won 37 games in 1989-90, losing 45. Once again they dipped below playoff level.

The team was resurrected for the 1990-91 season, as their 44-38 record was their best in nine years. Mullin, Richmond and Hardaway combined as the league's top scoring threesome, placing eighth, tenth, and eleventh in the league respectively with averages of 25.7, 23.9, and 22.9. Manute Bol was sent to the 76ers for a first-round draft pick, and Terry Teagle went to the Lakers for similar compensation. Marciulionis had knee prob-

AP/Wide World Photos

Chris Webber

lems, and Richmond broke the tip of his left thumb.

The first playoff opponent was the Spurs, and after coming up short, 130-121 in San Antonio, the Warriors charged through the next three games to upset the Texas team. Going against the Lakers in the next round, they lost the first game, 126-116, then bounced back for a 125-124 squeaker, their first postseason win in Los Angeles since 1969. However, the Lakers won the following two games, in Oakland, clinching the series in Los Angeles is overtime, 124-119.

Mitch Richmond was no longer a Warrior in 1991-92, having been shipped to Sacramento along with another player and a draft pick in exchange for 6-foot-9 forward-guard Billy Owens, the third player chosen in the 1991 draft.

Though lacking an effective jump-shot, the Syracuse graduate averaged 14.3 points in his entry year, leading the team in rebounds with 8.0 per game and blocked shots with a total of 65. He was third in the Rookie of the Year voting, and

with a seven-year contract signed in November, 1991, he looked to be a big part of the Warriors' future.

Coach Nelson, in the team's Media Guide, called Owens "probably as perfect a rookie as I've ever had. Not only is he gifted, he's just a really nice young man that you want to be around. He listens. He tries to do what you say. He's sensitive. He's polite. And besides that, he's this wonderful 6-foot-9 basketball player."

With that kind of boost, the Warriors, were off to a 55-27 regular season, the second-best in the history of the franchise. Mullin was voted a first Team all-NBA player and Hardaway was named to the second team; it was Mullin's fourth straight season on the honor squad. Nelson was voted Coach of the Year for the third time—something no other NBA coach had ever achieved. The team's scoring average, 118.7 per game, led the league, and their field-goal percentage, at .507, was a franchise record. Mullin, Hardaway, and Marciulionis combined to be the league's top scoring trio.

Another key statistic was that the Warriors led the NBA in forcing turnovers by opponents, with 18.4 per game. (They gave up 16.5 per game.) The Warriors were weak at center, with 7-foot Alton Lister injured much of the year and 6-foot-9 forwards Victor Alexander and Tyrone Hill filling in; however, overall it was a strong season's performance. In the postseason, they faced the underdog Supersonics, who upset them 3-1 despite being outscored by the Warriors.

Chris Mullin achieved worldwide recognition between the 1991-92 and 1992-93 seasons by participating on the U.S. Olympic team in Barcelona, where his contribution was crucial. Unfortunately, the 1992-93 season was a downer for the Warriors as injuries plagued three stars: Mullin, Hardaway, and Marciulionis. Rarely were all three on the court at the same time during the season.

Hardaway managed enough playing time (66 games) to qualify for second place among the league's assists leaders, with 10.6 per game to John Stockton's 12.0. Mullin was second in three-point field-goal percentage, with .451, two percentage points behind Chicago's B. J. Armstrong. Hill's 10.2 rebounds per game, tied for fifteenth in the league, led the team. Finishing in sixth place at 34-48, the Warriors had to be disappointed—yet they had to be optimistic, too, for their key players were likely to return healthy for 1993-94.

In addition, their low finish had enabled them to snatch a prized draft pick. Picking third overall, they chose Anfernee Hardaway, then traded him plus future draft choices to the Orlando Magic to get the overall first pick in the draft, Michigan's super-sophomore, Chris Webber. A proven rebounding ace with potential for tremendous improvement, Webber was one of the key pieces in the puzzle which, the Warriors hoped, might make them one of the NBA's dominant teams in the mid-90s.

SOURCES

BOOKS

1993 NBA Playoffs Media Guide.

Barry, Rick, with Bill Libby, *Confessions of a Basketball Gypsy: The Rick Barry Story,* Prentice-Hall, 1972.

Carter, Craig, and Sachare, Alex, *The Sporting News NBA Guide,* 1992-93 edition, Sporting News Publishing Co., 1992.

Chamberlain, Wilt, *A View from Above,* Villard Books, 1991.

Chamberlain, Wilt, and Shaw, David, *Wilt,* Macmillan, 1973.

Dickey, Glenn, *The History of Profesional Basketball Since 1896,* Stein and Day, 1982.

Golden State Warriors 1992-93 Media Guide.

Hollander, Zander, *The Complete Handbook of Pro Basketball 1993,* Signet, 1992.

Hollander, Zander, and Sachare, Alex, *The Official NBA Pro Basketball Encyclopedia,* Villard Books, 1989.

Lazenby, Roland, *The NBA Finals,* Taylor Publishing, 1990.

Libby, Bill, *Goliath: The Wilt Chamberlain Story,* Dodd, Mead & Co, 1997.

Liss, Howard, *The Winners,* Delacorte Press, 1968.

Nadel, Eric, *The Night Wilt Scored 100,* Taylor Publishing, 1990.

Neft, David S., and Cohen, Richard M., *The Sports Encyclopedia 1891-1989: Pro Basketball,* second edition, St. Martin's Press, 1989.

Taragano, Martin, *Basketball Biographies,* McFarland & Company, 1991.

—*Richard Cohen* for Book Builders, Inc.

LOS ANGELES CLIPPERS

The Los Angeles Clippers have had a storied existence in the 23 years since they were born as the Buffalo Braves. The greatest success came in the eight Buffalo seasons with a 3-year run of play-off trips. The team moved to San Diego in the summer of 1978 and was renamed the Clippers, but a lack of on-court and in-stands success caused the team's new owner to defy the NBA and take the team to Los Angeles and the Sports Arena which the Lakers had departed. It was much closer to his Beverly Hills home than the more logical choice of Anaheim in Orange County and not in the Los Angeles Lakers' backyard.

Through the years, rumors have circulated about the Clippers/Braves being moved to another city. In the case of the Buffalo Braves, a sale/trade of franchise and subsequent move proved true. With the Clippers in San Diego, it also proved true, even if it was in defiance of NBA rules. However, owner Donald Sterling is a friend and admirer of the Los Angeles Raiders' Al Davis who moved his team from Oakland to L.A. The Clips have also been rumored or reported to be doing something: having a new arena built for the team or moving to a new facility in Orange County (Anaheim or Santa Ana), neither of which has happened.

But Sterling watches Davis and sees how Davis plays landlord against other cities and thinks he can pull off a better deal where he is in the Sports Arena, which actually is in as good or better shape than the newer Forum, with better sightlines but fewer seats and is in only a slightly worse part of Los Angeles County than is the Inglewood's Forum.

From their three-year playoff run as the Braves in 1973-74 through 1975-76 until finally making the playoffs in 1991-92, the Braves/Clippers set an NBA record for futility with 15 consecutive non-playoff seasons. From the time the Braves had three playoff years under Jack Ramsay, until Larry Brown finally got the team to post-season play in 1991-92 and 1992-93, the franchise went through twelve coaches and enough staff and players to make up a regiment, 149 in all.

True to the Clippers tradition, when success came, Brown phoned in his resignation while vacationing in Hawaii in May, 1993. More than two months later, after the team flirted with some other high-profile candidates (and no doubt some low-profile ones as well), recently-released Atlanta Coach Bob Weiss was hired.

During their 15 years as the Clippers, the team has become known for producing All-Stars for other teams and acquiring other team's All-Stars after their best years. They've had only a few All-Stars of their own and team chemistry has usually been found lacking. Hopes for success in the early 1990s were dashed when free agency, potential free agency and an urge to overhaul threatened any real run of success.

Buffalo is One of Three New Teams

In 1970-71 the NBA continued a five-year run of expansion which took the nine-team league to 17 teams--one added in 1966-67, two each in 1967-68 and 1968-69 and three franchises in 1970-71. As the NBA went from two divisions (Eastern and Western) to four in two conferences (Eastern and Western), the Buffalo Braves were admitted to the Atlantic Division, Cleveland's Cavaliers were placed in the Central Division and the Portland Trailblazers became the fifth team in the Pacific Division in 1970-71. All finished last in their division the first year.

Buffalo's 22-60 record was second-best of the three to Portland's 29-53 while the Cavs were 15-67, the worst-ever expansion record (tied by Dallas in 1980-81). The Braves were allowed twelve players in the expansion draft. The three new teams drafted after the six non-playoff teams (Cavs, Blazers, Braves odd rounds; Braves, Blazers, Cavs even rounds). Ten of the expanded players were among the 15 who played for the Braves that first year under long-time NBA great, player-coach Dolph Schayes. One was traded and another jumped to the ABA. Bob Kauffman was Buffalo's

top scorer (20.4) and rebounder (10.7) and the team's All-Star Game rep in San Diego.

The team's second season saw the draft bring shot-blocking center Elmore Smith in the first round and second-rounder Fred Hilton. A key, long-shot pick was 7th-rounder Randy Smith from local college-division school Buffalo State where he was better known as an All-American triple-jumper and outstanding soccer player who also played basketball forward. The 6-foot-3 guard would go on to play an NBA record 910 games with the Braves, Cavs and Braves.

Dolph Schayes was fired after the team lost the opener and John McCarthy, a 6-year pro guard from local Canisius, went 22-59 the rest of the way. The team was last in the Atlantic again, four wins better than Portland, the worst team in the NBA. Bob Kauffman was again the team's All-Star Game player and the top scorer (18.9) while Elmore Smith was No. 6 in rebounds (15.2) and on the All-Rookie Team. Newly-acquired Walt Hazzard was tenth in assists (5.6). Randy Smith, scoring 13.4, was a starter by years end.

Braves Draft Mac, Hire Jack

Despite losing the coin flip for the first pick, The Braves got a break in the 1972 draft. Portland took Loyola's LaRue Martin even though new Coach Jack McCloskey wanted Bob McAdoo who had been on his ACC Wake Forest team at North Carolina. He was overruled. The Braves took Big Mac, but insisted he was too small at 6-foot-9, 210 pounds to play center.

McAdoo scored 18.0 with 9.1 rebounds and was Rookie of the Year (the first of three Braves in five years to be so honored) and he led the All-Rookie Team.

Bob Kauffman made his third straight All-Star appearance in the last season every team had to be represented in the game. He was ninth in field goal percentage (.505). Elmore Smith led the scoring (18.3) and rebounding (12.4). But the team slipped back to 21 wins, tying Portland and ahead of only 9-73 Philadelphia, the all-time worst.

TEAM INFORMATION AT A GLANCE

Founded in 1970 as the Buffalo Braves;
moved to San Diego and renamed the Clippers, 1978;
moved to Los Angeles, 1984

Home court:
Los Angeles Memorial Sports Arena
3939 S. Figueroa St.
Los Angeles, CA 90037
Phone: (213) 748-8000

Seating capicity: 15,350

Team nickname: Braves, 1970-78; Clippers, 1978—
Teasm logo: Team name superimposed on a stylized basketball
Team colors: Home: White, with red and blue trim
Road: Red, with white and blue trim

Franchise record:	Won	Lost	Pct.
(1970-93)	619	1103	.359

In 1973-74, the Braves became the first of the three newest teams to post a winning season (42-40) and make the playoffs. In the first round, the Braves drew the future champion Celtics who prevailed in six games by winning the last two including Game 6 in Buffalo, 106-104.

Bob McAdoo, playing primarily at center with Elmore Smith who had been traded to the Lakers, won his first of three straight scoring championships at 30.6. He also led in field goal percentage (.547) and was third in blocked shots (3.32) during the first season the category was kept. Randy Smith was third (2.48) in steals, another new statistic.

Ernie DiGregorio, the third pick in the first round in 1973, made good on his boast that he would lead the NBA in assists (8.2) and free-throw shooting (.902) and was the team's second straight Rookie of the Year. McAdoo made his first All-

Star Game appearance and was Second Team All-NBA. Jim McMillian came for Elmore Smith and scored 18.6, for the NBA's top-scoring team (111.6).General Manager Eddie Donovan was voted NBA Executive of the Year.

Bob McAdoo cleaned up in 1974-75 as the Braves won what is still a franchise-best 49 games. They finished second in the Atlantic Division in the Eastern Semifinal, but went out in seven games to eventual NBA finalist Washington after a first round bye. McAdoo repeated as scoring champion (34.6), was the starting East All-Star Game center, was an All-NBA First Team pick and the NBA's Most Valuable Player. He was also fifth in field-goal shooting (.512), fourth in rebounding (14.1) and sixth in blocked shots (2.12).

With Ernie D limited to 31 games due to a disabling injury, Randy Smith stepped in and finished fourth (6.5) in assists. Jack Marin, acquired from Houston, was seventh in free-throw shooting (.869). The Braves had the NBA's third-best record. Future congressman Tom McMillan was the team's top pick.

Buffalo came back in 1975-76 with a 46-36 record, second-best again in the Atlantic Division (tied with Philadelphia) and fifth-best in the NBA. In the first round, the Braves downed Philly in three games as each team won on the other's court. In the East Semifinals, eventual champion Boston ousted the Braves in six games.

Bob McAdoo became the fourth player to win three straight scoring titles (31.1) and played in the All-Star Game with Randy Smith. Big Mac was sixth in blocks (2.05) and seventh in rebounding (12.4). Smith was seventh in NBA assists (5.9) and made the All-NBA Second Team. John Shumate, who had missed the 1974-75 season with a heart ailment, was acquired in mid-season and was on the All-Rookie Team while ranking second in league field-goal percentage (.56081 to Wes Unseld's .56085) in the closest race ever. Jim McMillian (.536) was third.

The team got no help in the draft, having traded its first two choices away. Ernie DiGregorio came back, but was a 20-minutes a game backup. After the season, Coach Jack Ramsay resigned to go to Portland where he would coach the Blazers to the 1977 NBA Championship.

The Beginning of the Braves' End

Buffalo tumbled to a 30-52 record and fourth place in the Atlantic Division. The NBA had been enlarged by four teams in a merger with the ABA. Denver, Indiana, New Jersey and San Antonio came over and the New Jersey Nets were in the Atlantic, the only team below the Braves. Guard Bird Averitt was selected seventh in the ABA Dispersal Draft for $125,000, but was little help as a 15 minutes a game backup.

The worst move came when Moses Malone, acquired from Portland for what would become the third pick in the 1978 draft, was used in just two games for six minutes with no points and one rebound, was sent away by new coach Tates Locke who didn't want him. Malone went to Houston for 1977 and 1978 firsts which the Braves also traded away.

Owner Paul Snyder was at work selling off players for cash and lesser talent in preparation for an eventual sale of the team. Bob McAdoo was the first to go, along with Tom McMillen, to New York. Jim Price came from Milwaukee and went to Denver in a deal for Gus Gerard. George (Swat) Johnson came from Golden State to rank 6th in blocks (2.27). Randy Smith was 20th in NBA scoring (20.7) and 10th in steals (2.15). Ernie D led in free-throw shooting (.945), but had only 4.7 assists in 28 minutes per game.

Adrian Dantley scored 20.3 and was the Rookie of the Year as Buffalo used 19 players. Locke was gone after 46 games (16-30). Assistant Bob MacKinnon went 3-4 until Joe Mullaney, out of work after the ABA folded, arrived to go 11-18 in the last 29 games.

As the 1977-78 season began, the Braves were at work moving players again. Former scout, Cotton Fitzsimmons, came in to coach the team for one season. The Braves used 18 players. Adrian Dantley and Mike Bantom went to Indiana before the season for Billy Knight and Ernie D went to the Lakers. Marvin Barnes, Larry McNeill, Bird Averitt and Scott Lloyd were acquired in-season. Swen Nater came in pre-season while John Shumate went to Detroit along with Gus Gerard.

Paul Snyder finally sold the team to John Y. Brown who had owned the ABA Kentucky Colonels. The Braves staggered in at 27-55, fourth in the Atlantic, the second-worst record in the NBA. The season's highlight was Randy Smith's MVP performance when he scored a game-high 27 points with seven rebounds and six assists off the bench in 29 minutes.

The NBA iron-man was 7th in NBA scoring (24.6), second in minutes played (3,314) and eighth in assists (5.6) and steals (2.10). Knight missed 29 games and 18 players in all were in uniform. Players and staff stayed at motels and checked out with their belongings before road

TEAM RECORDS	Honored Braves/Clippers

NBA ROOKIE OF THE YEAR

1973 Bob McAdoo, F
1974 Ernie DiGregorio, G
1977 Adrian Dantley, F
1983 Terry Cummings, F

ALL-ROOKIE TEAM MEMBERS

1972 Elmore Smith, C
1973 Bob McAdoo, F
1974 Ernie DiGregorio, G
1976 John Shumate, F
1977 Adrian Dantley, F
1983 Terry Cummings, F
1989 Charles Smith, F

NBA MOST VALUABLE PLAYER

1975 Bob McAdoo

ALL-NBA SELECTIONS

1974 Bob McAdoo, 2nd
1975 Bob McAdoo, 1st
1976 Randy Smith, 2nd
1979 World Free, 2nd

ALL-STAR GAME PLAYERS

1971 Bob Kauffman
1972 Bob Kauffman
1973 Bob Kauffman
1974 Bob McAdoo
1975 Bob McAdoo
1976 Bob McAdoo, Randy Smith (Tie)
1978 Randy Smith
1980 World Free
1985 Norm Nixon
1986 Marques Johnson
1993 Danny Manning

trips, not knowing if they would be back.

It's the Clippers Out West

After the season, John Y. Brown traded teams with Celtics owner Irv Levin who moved his new team to San Diego for the 1978-79 season and renamed them the Clippers after the old sailing ships of the Pacific coast area. Gene Shue was brought in to coach. Among new acquisitions were Nick Weatherspoon (from Chicago), Kermit Washington (Boston), Sidney Wicks (Boston), Kevin Kunnert (Houston) and draft picks Jerome Whitehead, John Olive and Bob Bigelow. The real deal was getting Lloyd (World B.) Free from Philadelphia for a 1984 first rounder named Charles Barkley.

The Clippers went 43-39, their only winning season on the West Coast until 1991-92, and missed the playoffs by two games. Free was an All-NBA Second Team pick, second in scoring at 28.8. Swen Nater (.569) and Washington (.562) were 5-6 in field-goal percentage and Randy Smith was sixth in steals (2.16).

The Clippers sagged to 35-47 in 1979-80 with World Free again second (30.2) in scoring and selected for the NBA All-Star Game in Cleveland. Philadelphia dealt the Clippers Joe (Jellybean) Bryant for a 1986 first-round pick which turned out to be Brad Daugherty, the No. 1 pick in that draft. Randy Smith was dealt to Cleveland. Bill Walton was signed from Portland as a free agent with Kevin Kunnert, Kermit Washington, the 1980 first-round pick (Mike Gminski), and cash.

Gene Shue took advantage of the NBA's adoption of the ABA's 3-point field goal to turn his final Clippers team into the "Mad Bombers". Brian Taylor (90-239) and Freeman Williams (42-128) were 4-10 in percentage and had more makes and attempts than most teams. However, the 177-543 Clippers would only have ranked eighth in makes and sixth in attempts in 1992-93. Swen Nater led the NBA in rebounds (15.0) and was seventh in field-goal percentage.

Paul Silas, who won three NBA rings with Boston and Seattle, signed with the Clippers as a free agent in 1980 and the team gave up a second round pick. He never played again, but as coach guided the Clippers to a 36-46 record, fifth in the Pacific Division and two games better than Seattle. Free Williams (19.3) led the team scoring. Randy Smith was signed as a free agent on opening day to keep his soon-to-be record-setting consecutive game string alive. World Free was shipped to Cleveland. Another Philadelphia player, Henry Bibby, found his way to the Clippers.

Bill Walton missed this and the next season, the second and third full seasons he had missed since being the number one pick in 1974. Brian Taylor (.383), Williams (.340) and Bibby (.337) ranked 1-2-5 in 3-point shooting. Swen Nater was ninth in field-goal percentage (.553) and second in rebounds (12.4). First rounder Michael Brooks showed well.

The Donald Sterling Era Begins

On June 16, 1981, Beverly Hills real estate owner Donald Sterling bought the team from Irv Levin, also a Beverly Hills resident. When the team won its opener over Houston, he raced across the floor and jumped into arms of surprised coach Paul Silas. The team would win just 16 more all year, going 17-65, last in the Western Conference, but better than 15-67 Cleveland.

Rookie Tom Chambers topped the scoring (17.3). Michael Brooks (15.6) was next. Freeman Williams and Phil Smith were traded and Charley Criss, Al Wood and Armond Hill acquired. Bill Walton missed the whole season, Swen Nater was limited to 21 games and Brian Taylor played just 41 as injuries struck. Criss was second in NBA free-throw shooting (.887).

In 1982-83, the Clippers improved to 25-57, but were still last in the Pacific. Terry Cummings was the Rookie of the Year and tenth in NBA scoring (23.6), though limited to 70 games by a heart condition which required a defibrillator and medication. He was also tenth (10.6) in rebounds and along with Tom Chambers (17.6) gave the Clips a starting forward pair capable of more than 41 points per night.

Bill Walton returned to play a limited schedule (no back-to-back games) and was second in NBA blocked shots (3.61) with 14.1 points. Michael Brooks gave the team a solid third forward. Randy Smith was signed opening day with the team short of guards and kept his soon-to-be NBA consecutive games streak alive. After 65 games, he was waived at his own request to catch on with a playoff contender. The team played before he was picked up by Atlanta and the streak ended at 906 games. Again, the Clippers used 18 players.

When Paul Silas was let go after his contract ran out, Portland assistant Jim Lynam was hired and the team improved to 30-52 in 1983-84, but was still last in the division. In a big pre-season deal, Norm Nixon was acquired from the Lakers for the rights to first-round pick Byron Scott. In a second deal, Tom Chambers and Al Wood went to Seattle for 7-2 James Donaldson and Greg Kelser.

Terry Cummings averaged 22.9, ninth in the NBA. Nixon was second to ex-teammate Magic Johnson in assists (11.1) and scored 17.0. Ricky Pierce, acquired from Detroit, was fifth in free-throw shooting (.861). Bill Walton played 55 games (12.1 points, 8.7 rebs.), his most since 1977-78.

Los Angeles, Here We Come

When the season ended, the Clippers defied the NBA and moved to Los Angeles, setting up shop in the Sports Arena. Many felt, and still feel, that the location should have been Anaheim, the home of Disneyland, but owner Donald Sterling felt his real and imagined Hollywood friends

PROFILE	Randy Smith, NBA Ironman

Randy Smith was just about the unlikeliest player to make the 1971-72 Buffalo Braves team. He was a seventh-round pick from a local school (College Division Buffalo State) which today is the equivalent of a Division II or III school. While he was a fine forward at 6-foot-3, he was better known as an All-American triple-jumper and excellent high-jumper and long-jumper as well as an All-American soccer player.

Most dismissed him as a public relations ploy by General Manager Eddie Donovan who had come to the Braves from nearby St. Bonaventure University where he had been head coach and athletic director. But, Smith surprised everyone, not only did he make the team, but by season's end he was the number four scorer at 13.4.

It was also during that first season that he began a string of 906 consecutive games to break the existing record of 844 set by John Kerr. Kerr in 1965 had shattered the mark of 706 by Hall-of-Famer Dolph Schayes in 1961. Smith's string of games began February 18, 1972, and continued through March 13, 1983, when he asked to be waived by the San Diego Clippers in hopes of catching on with a team that had a chance to win a title.

Between the time he was waived and his acquisition by Atlanta, his string was broken at 906. He played in 80 games that year, but the Hawks were eliminated in three games by Boston and his career was over with his record secure. Smith never played another NBA game. He gave up his private goal of 1,000 consecutive games for chance at a ring.

Smith almost missed the record. He had been traded after seven Braves and one Clippers season to Cleveland in 1979. After three years, he was sent to New York and then released at the end of the 1981-82 season. He was without a team as the season neared. The Clippers found themselves short of guards and Smith, now a San Diego resident, was tracked down by Paul Silas and signed on opening day. He played that night, scored 13 points and had a job until he asked to be set loose.

The other close call came in 1980 when his wife was having a baby and he wanted to leave the team to be with her. "You take care of the streak, I'll take care of the baby," she said. He had other close calls with a hip injury and a case of the flu that he beat to score a career-high 41 points.

Smith is currently NBA Player Programs Manager under former Celtic Tom (Satch) Sanders and the VP for Player Programs, located in the NBA Offices in the Olympic Tower Building. He goes largely ignored by the Clippers since "He never played for us in L.A.," sniffed one official several years ago. The team is the only one other than the four latest expansion teams—Charlotte, Miami, Minnesota and Orlando—which has never retired a number. But Smith's number 9 has not been used since he left.

would only come to see the team in Los Angeles, less than 10 miles from Inglewood and the successful Lakers. The legalities of the move eventually wound up in court to be settled during the 1988-89 season when the Clippers agreed to forego their share of expansion fees ($5.65-million) in exchange for the suit being dropped.

On the eve of the 84-85 season-opener, a blockbuster trade sent Terry Cummings, Ricky Pierce and Craig Hodges to Milwaukee for Junior Bridgeman, Harvey Catchings and Marques Johnson. Third-year man Derek Smith was 18th in NBA scoring (22.1) with a strong finish. Norm Nixon was fourth (9.8) in assists and played in the 1985 All-Star Game at Indiana. Bill Walton played 67 games with 10.1 points and 9.0 rebounds.

James Donaldson led in NBA field-goal percentage (.637) and Bridgeman was eighth in free-throw percentage (.879). Jim Lynam was fired with the team at 22-39 and ex-Celtic Don Chaney finished out 9-12. The 31-51 mark was one win better than the year before.

Lancaster Gordon (8) and Michael Cage (14) were the team's first-rounders. With Don Chaney in charge for all of 1985-86, the Clippers improved one more win to 32-50 and climbed from fourth to third in the Lakers-dominated (62-20) Pacific.

Bill Walton was traded to Boston for Cedric (Cornbread) Maxwell and a 1986 first-rounder whom the Clips sent to Portland for Darnell Valentine. Derek Smith was limited to 11 games by a devastating knee injury. Marques Johnson was 20th in NBA scoring (20.3) and made the 1986 All-Star Game in Dallas. Franklin Edwards (.874) and Johnson (.871) were 6-7 in free-throw accuracy. Norm Nixon was eighth in assists (8.6) and rookie Benoit Benjamin, the team's first-rounder (3rd), was fifth in blocks (2.61) after getting in shape for the last 30 games. James Donaldson was dealt to Dallas after 14 games for Kurt Nimphius.

At the end of the season, Laker legend Elgin Baylor was hired as general manager and arrived to find the cupboard bare. He had no pick in the draft until the third round (Dwayne Polee, 53rd). Norm Nixon was lost for the season after playing in a summer softball game to help aid wife Debbie Allen's charity. He ruptured a quadriceps tendon above the left knee. After ten games, Marques Johnson ruptured a cervical disc when he tripped and ran into Benoit Benjamin. He never played for L.A. again, but did try a 1989-90 comeback at Golden State.

Mike Woodson and Larry Drew came from Sacramento for Derek Smith and Franklin Edwards. Cedric Maxwell played just 35 games. The team hit bottom at 12-70 and Don Chaney somehow finished the 1986-87 season before he was mercifully discharged. Michael Cage was sixth in rebounds (11.5) and Benoit Benjamin (2.60) was fourth in blocked shots.

In 1987-88, Gene Shue returned as head coach. He had been released by Washington late in the 1985-86 season and had not coached since. The Clippers improved just five wins to 17-65, two wins behind New Jersey. Norm Nixon tore an achilles tendon and missed the entire season. Mike Woodson (18.0) again led the L.A. scoring. The team had three firsts through Elgin Baylor's deals and tookie Reggie Williams (4th), Joe Wolf (13th) and Ken Norman (19th), but 25-year second-rounder Norris Coleman was an early starter waived after playing 29 games.

Cage led the NBA in rebounds (13.03) over Charles Oakley (13.0), the closest finish ever, with 30 grabs in the season-ending game at home. Benoit Benjamin, a factor again late in the season, was second in blocks (3.41). Across town, the Lakers became the first team to repeat since the 1968-69 Celtics.

Clippers Win the Lottery, Take Manning

In May of 1988, the Clippers, coming off the NBA's worst record, won the lottery's first pick. Elgin Baylor immediately held up a No. 25 jersey with the name Danny Manning. Manning was NCAA Champion Kansas' College Player of the Year. Baylor staged this display despite the fact that Earl Cureton had worn the number 25 for the last two seasons and was still on the roster. When Cureton went to Charlotte as a free agent the identity crisis was solved.

Baylor's other draft-day deals brought Charles Smith (3rd) and Gary Grant (15th) in the first round as a pick. Hersey Hawkins and Michael Cage were dealt to Philadelphia and Seattle. Manning held out for the first week of the season as his agent, Ron Grinker, took shots at owner Donald Sterling.

In January, with the team at 10-19, Manning tore his anterior cruciate ligament in Milwaukee, was lost for the rest of the season and missed the first 11 games of the next. Charles Smith picked up much of the slack and led team scoring (20.0) to make the NBA All-Rookie Team. Norm Nixon's contract was bought out after 53 games and he retired to open the way for the flamboyant Grant at point guard.

Once again, Benoit Benjamin finished strong to rank sixth in blocks (2.80) and eighth in field-goal shooting (.541). Still, the team could do no better than 21-61, a four-win improvement. Shue was fired with the team at 10-28. Assistant Don Casey was promoted and went 11-33.

AP/Wide Word Photos

Danny Manning

Don Casey's status dangled for three months until he was finally given a one-year contract for 1989-90. The Clips were second in the lottery and took Danny Ferry as the "best player"in the draft. Ferry stunned the Clippers by leaving August 2 for Il Messagero Roma and a 4-year deal with escape clauses after every season.

Taking heat in the media, the Clippers finally struck gold November 16 dealing Ferry to Cleveland for first-round picks in 1990 (Loy Vaught) and 1992 (Elmore Spencer) and shooting-guard Ron Harper. They persuaded the Cavs to take disappointing swing-man Reggie Williams. On the move, the team was at 15-19 after a rugged (5-3) Eastern trip when Harper tore his anterior cruciate ligament in the first game back against Charlotte on January 16.

The Lakers won that game and the next two

reaching 18-19, but ended at 13-32. The 31-51 mark was a one-win improvement despite Benoit Bejamin's early-season holdout and persistant player injuries. Nevertheless, Don Casey was given the boot one day after the season finale.

Five weeks after Casey left, former Coach of the Year Mike Schuler was hired over Mike Fratello and given a long-term contract—3 years plus an option. Other personnel changes followed in the front office and a new trainer hired on along with new assistants for Schuler.

In the draft, the Clips avoided demolition of the Sports Arena by taking Bo Kimble from nearby Loyola Marymount (8th) and Loy Vaught (13th). Harper was able to play 39 games, Charles Smith led the scoring again (20.0) and Ken Norman and Danny Manning had strong years while Vaught was an early presence.

In mid-season Benjamin was traded to Seattle for Olden Polynice who ranked sixth in field-goal accuracy (.560). Still, the Clippers could only match the 31-51 mark of 1989-90 in 1990-91. Gary Grant, Winston Garland and Tom Garrick shared point guard.

Hello, Playoffs

In the 1991 draft, the Clippers took LeRon Ellis, son of Elgin Baylor's former Laker teammate Leroy Ellis, but LeRon was a disappointment and played only the 1991-92 season. With the team at 21-24, Mike Schuler was ousted. Assistant Mack Calvin split his two games as interim coach and Larry Brown, who brought Schuler into the NBA as a Nets assistant in 1981, was hired just weeks after leaving San Antonio.

The team responded by winning its first five games and going 23-12 under Brown for a 45-37 mark. It was their first winning season since 1978-79 in San Diego and the first playoff berth since 1975-76 in Buffalo. Such was the state of Los Angeles-area sports that the .540 overall and .740 home marks (regular-season and playoffs combined) was the best of the seven major teams.

In the playoffs, the Clippers took Midwest

LOS ANGELES CLIPPERS

Professional Sports Team Histories • Basketball   319

Champion Utah to five games in a series interrupted by the riots. Game 4, delayed three days, was moved to Orange County. Danny Manning led the scoring (19.3) and played all 82 games as did Ron Harper (18.2). Charles Smith missed 49 games in the last year of his contract. Doc Rivers was acquired from Atlanta for the Clippers own 1991 first and two future seconds. James Edwards came from Detroit. Manning was eighth in NBA field-goal shooting (.542) and hopes were high for 1992-93.

In 1992-93 the Clippers won four of the last seven games to finish 41-41, two games ahead of the Lakers. Once again, Coach Larry Brown's charges drew the Midwest Division Champ, this time Houston. Again, the Lakers exited in five games with the Rockets winning all of the odd-numbered games.

Charles Smith had signed a one-year qualifying offer in the summer and traded with Doc Rivers and Bo Kimble to the Knicks in a 3-way deal which brought Mark Jackson from the Knicks and Stanley Roberts from Orlando. John (Hot Plate) Williams came from the Bullets for Don MacLean and William Bedford (both obtained from Detroit).

Kiki Vandeweghe and Jarren Jackson were signed as free agents while James Edwards went to the Lakers as a free agent and Elmore Spencer was selected in the draft. Danny Manning ranked tenth in NBA scoring (22.8). Jackson was fourth in assists (8.8) and 19th in steals (1.66) to Ron Harper's (2.21) sixth. Roberts was 13th in blocks (1.83) and 14th in field-goal percentage (.527). Los Angeles had the heaviest front line in the game with Roberts and Williams in camp at 325 each and Spencer at 270.

With the Clippers missing the Lottery for the second straight year, Larry Brown, vacationing in Hawaii, livened up proceedings that Sunday by phoning in his resignation, via his agent. A few weeks later, to no one's surprise, he turned up as coach of the Indiana Pacers leaving the Clippers coachless. After a typical two-month-plus delay, Bob Weiss was hired.

Weiss got his coaching start as a Clipper as-sistant during Gene Shue's San Diego tenure and filled in as a Clippers TV analyst in the playoffs of 1992. In the summer of 1993 Danny Manning signed a one-year qualifying offer, the intent being to become an unrestricted free agent after the 1993-94 season.

Ken Norman signed a 6-year free agent pact with Milwaukee and Gary Grant was not tendered an offer. Still to be signed in summer 1993 was veteran guard Ron Harper. In the college draft, L.A. took Terry Dehere with the 13th pick in the first round and Leonard White in the second (53rd overall).

Most importantly perhaps, the Clippers need to get overcome the Lakers' curse. During their nine years in Los Angeles, the Clippers have developed a well-founded inferiority complex to the Lakers. In their nine years in Los Angeles, the Clippers have barely won more games (260) than the Lakers have lost (227). The Lakers have 521 wins in that time—twice as many.

SOURCES

Carter, Craig and Alex Sachare, *The Sporting News NBA Guide,* 1992-93 edition, The Sporting News, 1992.

Hamamoto, Lori, *Los Angeles Clippers 1991-92 Media Guide,* Los Angeles Clippers, 1991.

Hamamoto, Lori, and Cary Collins, *Los Angeles Clippers 1992-93 Media Guide,* Los Angeles Clippers, 1992.

Hollander, Zander, editor, *The NBA Official Encyclopedia of Pro Basketball,* North American Library, 1981.

Hollander, Zander, and Alex Sachare, editors, *The Official NBA Basketball Encyclopedia,* Villard Books, 1989.

Nadel, Eric, *The Night Wilt Scored 100,* Taylor Publishing Co., 1990.

NBA Editorial Staff, *All-Star Weekend Guide,* NBA Publications, 1993.

NBA Editorial Staff, *NBA News,* Vol. 46, No. 30, 1991-92; Vol. 47, Nos. 27, 28, 29, 30, 32, 35, 1992-93.

LOS ANGELES LAKERS

Since 1960 the team has sunbathed in southern California, but its name harks back to its origins in the land of ten thousand frozen lakes. The Minneapolis Lakers originated in 1947, during the post-World War II boom when professional basketball was a growth industry but not yet a major sport. Several teams had jumped from the National Basketball League (NBL) to the fledgling Professional Basketball League of America (PBLA), and a group of Minneapolis businessmen pooled their resources to create a new team to replace the Detroit Falcons.

But the PBLA folded almost before anyone could even remember its name, and its players were returned to the NBL in a draft. In a historic move, the Lakers picked up the contract of the league's superstar, bespectacled 6'10" center George Mikan. Instantly they became the dominant team in the league—indeed, its first dynasty. In their first six years of existence, they won five championships.

Mikan wasn't the first big center in pro basketball, but he was the first whose athletic skills matched his size. His accurate hook shot, arcing over the outstretched arms of defenders, made him a constant scoring threat from inside. As a shot blocker and rebounder he was unmatched in his time. Lack of speed was his weakness, but coach John Kundla tailored the Lakers' style to their star's limitations. "We didn't run much," Kundla told Bill Libby, author of *We Love You Lakers*. "We had a lot of set plays.... We dominated the boards at both ends. We were tremendously strong and wore teams out."

The Lakers were by no means a one-man team. Small forward Jim Pollard, at 6'3", was a graceful shooter and passer, respected for his unselfish, consistent play, and even beating Mikan in a 1952 players' poll for best player of the era. Forward Arnie Ferrin had been the leader of the National Collegiate Athletic Association (NCAA) champion University of Utah team in the mid-for-ties, and guards Swede Carlson and Herm Schaefer skillfully set the table for the front men.

In the general public's mind, however, the Lakers were synonymous with George Mikan. One slow winter night during the 1948-49 season, the Maidson Square Garden management tried to boost attendance with this marquee sign:

Tonight:
George Mikan
vs.
Knicks

Is this the origin of modern superstar hype?

The Lakers' rivals in those days were the Rochester Royals, ancestors of the Cincinnati Royals and Kansas City-Omaha-Sacramento Kings. From 1947 to 1949, the two teams jumped in unison from the NBL to the Basketball Association of America (BAA) and finally to the newly formed National Basketball Association (NBA), playing dramatic championship series wherever they landed.

In the 1947-48 finals, the Royals were weakened by injuries: center Arnie Risen had had his jaw broken in the Eastern Division championships, guard (and future coaching great) Red Holzman had a bad leg, backcourt partner Al Cervi a bad knee and the flu, and sixth man Fuzzy Levane a bad foot. The Royals toughed out a home game victory in a game where Mikan scored 32 for the Lakers, but the tide was against them and the Lakers were champions in their first year of existence.

The 1948-49 season found both rivals switching leagues in response to the siren song of BAA president Maurice Podoloff. The BAA featured a solid lineup of big-city clubs, bringing Mikan and crew to larger markets.

The Lakers finished one game behind the Royals in the Western Division regular season, at 44-16, but swept the Rochester club in the division playoffs and proceeded to beat the Washington Capitols for the crown in six. Mikan broke his wrist in the fourth game of the Washington series, but played with a cast in the fifth game and scored 22 points.

The 1949-50 season was a watershed for basketball. The NBL and BAA merged into the NBA under the guiding hand of commissioner Podoloff. For the Lakers it marked a shift to the Central Division and a rise to new heights of achievement. Two talented rookies joined the starting five: 6'7" rebounding forward Vern Mikkelsen and 5'10" point guard Slater "Dugie" Martin. Ironman Mikkelsen, a Minnesota native and a schoolteacher, belied his offseason gentleness by setting forth toward a career record 127 disqualifications.

He was to serve as team captain for six years, missing only one game in an equal span of time. Martin, a great shooter who had set a school career scoring record at the University of Texas, willingly changed his style to blend in with the Lakers, becoming a playmaker and defensive whiz. The Celtics' legendary Bob Cousy called Martin the toughest defender he ever played against. For sophisticated fans, the matchup of these two brilliant ball handlers was one of the great thrills in early NBL history.

The Lakers now had a balanced starting team with some bench depth. They tied the Royals for the 1949-50 Central Division pennant and won it in a 78-76 playoff game in Rochester, Mikan scoring 35. Then on to Syracuse for the playoff series, where reserve guard Bob Harrison won the first game by sinking a 40-foot set shot at the last second. The Lakers took the best-of-seven series in six, including a fight-filled final in which Mikan scored 40 points.

1950-51 was the inaugural season for the NBA All-Star game, and Minneapolis had four members on the Western team: the entire starting front line plus Martin. More importantly, it was the year when "fixing" scandals rocked the college basketball scene.

Disillusioned fans began to turn to the pro game in greater numbers. Responding well to the spotlight, the Lakers beat the Royals by three games in the regular season, winning 44, including a 29-game undefeated streak at home. Unfortunately, the Royals upset the Lakers 3-1 in the Western Division finals, going on to beat the Knicks for the league trophy.

Team Information At a Glance

Founding date: 1947 as Minneapolis Lakers (NBL);
franchise moved to Los Angeles in 1960

Home court:
Great Western Forum
3900 West Manchester Blvd.
Inglewood, CA 90301
Phone: (213) 419-3100

Seating Capacity (for basketball): 17,505

Team colors: Royal purple and gold
Team nickname: Lakers
Logo: LOS ANGELES LAKERS in gold, superimposed on a royal purple basketball

Franchise Record	Won	Lost	Pct.
(1947-1993)	2,207	1,379	.615

West Championships: 1958-59, 1961-62, 1962-63, 1964-65, 1965-66, 1967-68,
1968-69, 1969-70, 1972-73, 1982-83, 1983-84, 1988-89, 1990-91
NBA Championships: 1948-49, 1949-50, 1951-52, 1952-53, 1953-54,
1971-72, 1981-82, 1984-85, 1986-87, 1987-88
NBL Championship: 1947-48

The rest of the league had long wondered what to do about Mikan. Between seasons, the foul lane was widened from six to twelve feet as a direct response to his powerful inside presence; but it didn't hinder him. Mikan averaged almost 24 points per game, including a career-high 61-point game on January 20 in Rochester, where a home-team fan threw an open pocket-knife at the great center. The Lakers lost the division title to the Royals by one game, but beat them 3-1 in the playoffs and went on to overcome the Knicks 4-3 for the championship.

The Lakers had an easier time the following year. The rival Royals were upset by the Fort Wayne Pistons in the playoffs, and though they gave the Lakers a run in the Western Division finals, the Lakers came back in the deciding fifth game with a 74-58 romp. Once again the Lakers faced the Knicks in the finals—and this time they prevailed in five games, including three consecutive close ones in New York.

By 1953-54, Mikan's bad knees were slowing him down. The action on NBA courts was slowing down too, to the chagrin of club owners and fans. In those early days of television, it was vitally important to convince the public that pro basketball was a fast, exciting, high-scoring game. But just the reverse was occurring, as that 19-18 yawnfest had showed.

The league's style of play had become a cornucopia of stalling tactics. The final minutes of games were often excruciating exercises in the

---

refusal to shoot, punctuated by deliberate, rough-house fouls and endless trips to the freethrow line.

To relieve Mikan, the Lakers added 6'9", 250-pound hook-shooting center Clyde Lovellette. He kept up the Lakers' tradition of strength in front, but he was awkward and even slower than Mikan. Mikan still had enough in him to have the league's fourth best scoring average, at 18.1, and to lead in rebounds with 17.1. Once again he led the team to a division title against the Royals, the last burst of fireworks in this great rivalry. The Lakers went on to defeat Syracuse for the league championship in seven low-scoring games, making it three straight titles.

But the glory days were over for Minnesota NBA fans and their heroes. After the championships, George Mikan announced his retirement. He was 29, and the Lakers were headed for hard times.

Hard Times in the North Country

Minnesotans can take hard winters, but the chill that froze the Lakers lasted half a decade. In 1954 not only was Mikan off the court—he had become general manager—but the 24-second rule had been introduced. This was good for basketball, but bad for teams that relied on strength rather than speed. Future Hall-of-Famer Lovellette, though scoring well, couldn't fill Mikan's rebounding shoes at center, and Pollard would retire after failing to keep pace with the new clock.

The Lakers managed a 40-32 second-place finish in the West, partly because the Royals were even slower than they, but after beating their rivals in the opening playoff round, they were swept by the Pistons in four games.

The slide continued. The 1955-56 season saw a 33-39 record, tied with Red Holzman's St. Louis Hawks for second in the West. In midseason the Lakers, under .500 for the first time in their history, had brought back the overweight Mikan for a 37-game comeback; but though he helped the team, his time was past, his points per game average down to 10.5. In the playoffs, the Hawks, led

by Bob Pettit, twice beat the Lakers 116-115; the 133-75 Lakers blowout in between was a wasted effort.

The next season followed a similar pattern: 34-38 in the regular season for a three-way first-place tie; a sweep of the Pistons in the first playoff round; but a sweep by the Hawks in the next round. The Hawks, who now had Slater Martin on their roster, had become the Lakers' main division rival, but without the sparks of the earlier Rochester rivalry.

The Lakers were in trouble not only as a team but as a business. At their Mikan-era peak, attendance had averaged about 6,000. Now it was down to half that. In 1957, Bob Short, a local businessman in the trucking and hotel industries, bought the franchise for $50,000. He made Mikan coach and promoted John Kundla to general manager. As a box-office attraction, he signed the Royal's top draft pick, the University of West Virginia's charismatic 6'4", 185-pound guard Rod "Hot Rod" Hundley, giving up Lovellette in exchange. But Hundley was what would one day be called a "party animal," and the Lakers became a party team, staying out late and carousing to forget their on-court embarrassments. Mikan was, to understate the case, not a good coach. He only knew how to play the old-style game, but he didn't have George Mikan at center to dominate the opposition, and he didn't win the respect of his frolicsome players. After amassing a 9-30 record, he switched jobs with Kundla, but this move could not strengthen the Lakers' roster. The team finished the season deep in the league's basement with a 19-53 record.

Saved by Elgin Baylor—and on to California

But cellar teams get prize rookies, and 1958 marked the debut of one of the all-time greats, Elgin Baylor. The 6'5", 225-pound forward from the University of Seattle brought a distinctively individual brand of basketball to the league, and was the first player known for such magic tricks

PROFILE	George Mikan: Basketball's First Star

In the late 1940's, the most a famous basketball player in America could hope to make was $12,000 dollars a year. Those were the terms of the contract George Mikan signed with the Chicago Gears of the National Basketball League (NBL): a $60,000 five-year package. It was considered a phenomenal sum, partly because no one was sure the NBL, or its rival league, the Basketball Association of America (BAA), would last five years. And indeed the Gears were out of existence after Mikan's first season. Who would take the risk of picking up the remaining four years of his contract? Several teams turned the opportunity down, but the Minneapolis Lakers signed him—and that made all the difference.

Mikan's name is less familiar to young basketball fans than it once was, but without him, there might not be an National Basketball Association (NBA) today. He was professional basketball's first drawing card at a time when the college game had higher prestige. He changed the style of the game, not just by dominating play with his size and strength—there had been earlier, less gifted bruisers at center and, if anything, they gave the pro game a thuggish reputation—but by combining size with athleticism. As a three-time all-American at De Paul, he had twice been named Player of the Year. He led the league in scoring in his first year in the NBA and in two later years, and was voted the Associated Press' player of the Half-Century.

This was a young man who had been declared "hopelessly clumsy" by the coach at his first-choice college, Notre Dame. Mikan had grown up in Joliet, Illinois, and was a talented young pianist whose life was often made miserable by taunts from other children about his height. He reached six feet at age 11, and later admitted that he had often stooped to try to appear shorter. Fortunately, he found a profession in which his height could be a source of self-esteem.

He *was* clumsy as a youth, 6'10", 245 pounds, and seriously nearsighted, but he worked hard in gyms to become more graceful. Whether he achieved a level of play comparable to today's big men is doubtful, but if he were a youngster today, Mikan would benefit from training methods far superior to those of his time. The question, "Could Mikan have gone one-on-one against Jabbar or Ewing?" can never fairly be answered. George Mikan retired with 11,764 career points, a 22.6 per-game average. He became a lawyer and, in 1967, the first commissioner of the NBA.

Photo: *Naismith Memorial Basketball Hall of Fame*

as changing directions in midair and sinking impossible off-balance shots. He was also an exceptional rebounder who habitually followed up his missed shots with scoring tap-ins. It was Baylor, not Hundley, who became the star attraction throughout the basketball world. In his rookie year, he was fourth in scoring with 24.9 points per game, third in rebounds per game, and second in minutes played. Largely because of him, the Lakers, after collecting a 33-39 record in the regular season, upset Detroit in the playoff openers, 2-1, and St. Louis in the conference finals, 4-2. The good things came to an end there, however. The Boston Celtics swept the finals in four games, beginning a dynasty that would frustrate the Lakers for more than a decade.

A new coach was in order, and owner Short tried John Castellani, who had been Baylor's coach at Seattle; but when the team was 11-25, Short had seen enough. He replaced Castellani with ex-Laker Jim Pollard and embarked on a rebuilding spree. New forward Rudy LaRusso, at 6'7", was to help the club for the next several years, as was 6'3" guard Frank "Pops" Selvy, who was acquired from Syracuse.

But too many of the Lakers were still, in John Kundla's words, "selfish individuals more interested in playing cards than playing games." Pollard's regular-season record that first half-year was 14-25. The Lakers defeated the Pistons 2-0 in the playoff openers, then took a 3-2 lead over the Hawks in the Western finals before losing the decisive two games by wide margins.

It had been a grueling, flukey season. Owner Short had fined Hundley $1,000—ten percent of his yearly salary—for missing a plane. Another airborne incident was more harrowing still. In January 1960, the Lakers were flying home from St. Louis when their DC-3 lost power in a snowstorm. The pilots, who had to point flashlights through the cockpit window in order to see, made a safe crash landing in a cornfield near Cornell, Iowa.

Were these omens of the role airplanes would play in the Lakers' future? For they now became a transcontinental team. Bob Short asked for permission to move to Los Angeles, and received it, after the owners first voted the request down and then reconsidered. The team had lost $300,000 in 1959-60; its stadium rent was overdue; its airline credit card had been cancelled. It wasn't just a matter of shuffling rosters anymore. The Lakers had no future in Minneapolis.

Looking back, the small scale of NBA operations in that era is startling. Short sent his general manager, Lou Mohs, to the coast with only $5,000 and orders not to ask for any more. The team's viability depended totally on Mohs' ability to sell season tickets—which he did, at least to the extent of $150,000 that enabled the team to meet its payroll.

The new Lakers' head coach was now Fred Schaus, whom Short lured away from the University of West Virginia. At 6'5" and 250 pounds, Schaus had the responsibility of changing the Laker players' attitudes as well as sharpening their skills. He was the kind of coach who was always well-prepared and, though emotional at courtside, did not draw emotionally close to his players. He had coached Hundley at West Virginia, where one of his younger stars had been a hardworking 6'3", 175-pounder named Jerry West.

West signed with the Lakers for $15,000, a very respectable sum for a rookie in 1960, but his pro career started off shakily. He was used as a substitute for the first half of the season, and resented it—but then he was selected for the All-Star team despite his junior role. With this added stature, his playing time and prominence increased in the second half of the season and for the duration of a glorious career.

The Lakers now had two young, developing talents of the first rank. Interestingly, in the cases of both Baylor and West, club owner Bob Short, who claimed to know little about basketball, had pursued and signed the rookies over the objections of supposedly more knowledgeable advisors. If he hadn't followed his instincts, it might have meant extinction for a team that had just moved to an untried location after several dismal years in Minneapolis.

The Great Two-Man Team of the Early 1960s

Baylor and West played together beautifully. Off the court, they showed mutual respect but were never close, never "buddies." Neither was there any noticeable friction between them. They shared top billing unselfishly, and as a result they led their team to the finals year after year. Winning the championship was another matter, however. During the 1960's the Lakers were to come so close, so often, and be beaten so regularly by the same team—the dreaded Boston Celtics—that it became a public agony for these two proud athletes and their city.

Two stars just weren't enough. The rest of the Laker team wasn't weak, but wasn't championship caliber either. There was a gaping hole at center, which wouldn't be filled till the Chamberlain era. Filling out the starting five were tough, consistent veterans Frank Selvy at guard and Rudy LaRusso at forward.

It wasn't enough to boost attendance, either. The average home game was played in front of fewer than 4,000 filled seats; even playoff games struggled to sell 5,000 that first year on the coast. Total attendance was 150,000. This despite the fact that the Lakers were putting the ball through the hoop with flair. Baylor set a single-game record for scoring on November 15, with 71 points. True, the team's record was only 36-43, but they got into the playoffs and beat Detroit in the first round, and stretched their semifinal series against St. Louis to a dramatic seventh game, in which, with three seconds to go, Baylor missed an off-balance shot for a 105-103 loss.

The following season might have been a career year for Baylor if he hadn't missed 32 games for Army duty. He scored a career-high 38 points per game. When he was out, LaRusso stepped up to fill the gap admirably, including a 50-point game. West, too, made up for the absence of Baylor, in an early indication of his classic role as "Mr. Clutch."

On January 17, 1962, West, suffering a bad cold, scored 63 points—a record for guards which would stand until the days of Michael Jordan. He accomplished this feat in front of 2,766 paid customers.

Scoring was not the 1960s Lakers' problem, and eventually, fans got the message that at Laker games they would see as many flashy two-pointers and bulls-eye free throws as their hearts desired. In a triple-overtime game in Philadelphia, Baylor scored 63 to the Warriors' Chamberlain's 78, with West coming in at 32. Angelenos began to respond. The finals against Boston marked a breakthrough in attendance: an average of 11,000 per game. The Celtics were trying to match the

1949-54 Laker's championship record of five titles in six seasons.

The third game, with the series tied 1-1, was the high point in the rivalry to that date. The score was tied with three seconds left, and Boston had the ball. West intercepted Sam Jones' inbound pass to Cousy and laid the ball up at the buzzer for a 117-115 win, and 15,000 home fans were delirious.

In Game 5, Baylor's 61 points led the team to a 126-121 victory in Boston. Game 6, however, was given away in an atrocious third quarter. The concluding game marked a return to good form. The score was tied at 100 with 18 seconds left. Selvy, wide open for a Hundley pass, missed the crucial shot, and the game went into overtime— which turned out to be an anticlimax. Baylor fouled out, and the tired Bill Russell was brilliant for the Celtics. The fast-breaking Bostonians won the game and the title, 110-107.

In retrospect, the loss of that 1962 title game seemed to mark a turn in the Lakers' fortunes. The pattern would take years to emerge, but when it did, it was heartbreakingly clear: the Lakers getting almost all the way and missing by inches.

Long afterward, Coach Schaus would tell sportswriter Bill Libby, "If we'd won that one, that first one in Boston, I think maybe we'd have won others that we lost in the years that were to come." Wishful thinking, or an example of what scientists call "the butterfly effect"—a small, early difference creating massively different results later on?

Still, the Lakers had solidified their position at the gate and in their new city, at a time when television was making the NBA a permanent fixture in American living rooms. In the locker room, the Lakers were a happy team.

They still had a reputation as party goers— which would grow to outrageous proportions in the 1980's, when they were called the "La La Lakers"—but unlike in the 50's, partying celebrated their optimism rather than being a sour attempt to forget incompetence. For 1962-63, the team acquired a good sixth man in Dick Barnett, a streaky shooter with a deadly fallback jump shot, and an all-league clotheshorse. The team entered the season anticipating a rematch with Boston, and that's what they got, despite West's missing 24 late-season games with a hamstring injury. They carried a 53-27 record into the playoffs and beat St. Louis in seven games for the Western division title. But like a recurring bad dream, Boston beat them in six.

The Lakers' financial condition was now good enough so that Short turned down a $3,000,000 purchase offer from Angels owner Gene Autry in the off-season. The team was playing full-time at the Los Angeles Sports Arena, having journeyed from site to site in previous years, and average attendance was up to 8,000. The 1963-64 season was an off-year on the court, though, as Baylor suffered bad knees and West a broken thumb. The Lakers came in third in their division, after San Francisco and St. Louis, and were eliminated by the latter 3-2 in the opening playoff round.

The team nucleus was improving, however, and the downturn was temporary. Next season, University of California, Los Angeles (UCLA), star Walt Hazzard joined as a rookie. The 6'2", 190-pound guard would help the Lakers over three seasons, shuttling between the starting lineup and the bench before going to Seattle in the expansion draft.

In 1964-65, a healthy Jerry West averaged 31 points per game, while Baylor turned in 27 per game despite calcium deposits on his knees. The team rose again to the top of the division. Unfortunately, Baylor tore his left kneecap in the first quarter of the first semifinal game against Baltimore, collapsing in pain.

Fortunately, however, West stepped in with one of the classic performances that would eventually make him synonymous with clutch play. He scored 49 points in that first game and 52 in the next, excelling on the freethrow line, on the boards, and in steals.

Game 3 was even more impressive, since West scored 44 with a newly broken and cotton-stuffed nose (an appendage he would break nine times in his career). Game 4 posed a double challenge: Barnett was out with a pulled groin. West

Naismith Memorial Basketball Hall of Fame

Elgin Baylor

made it up with 48 points—but his 49th and 50th, which would have tied the final score at 114, were whistled invalid when teammate LaRusso was called for an offensive foul.

Exhausted, hurting physically and mentally, West led the team to a 117-115 victory in the series clincher. But he had little left for Boston, making 6 out of 27 shots in the conclusive Game 5 of that series. Boston won that game, 129-96. Few players ever had more cause for pride than Jerry West, who set a league record 40.6 points per game in the postseason, but the lost title meant far more than individual numbers to this magnificent competitor.

In September, 1965, Short sold the Lakers for five million dollars to Canadian communications tycoon and self-described "supersalesman" Jack Kent Cooke, whose further goal, realized a year later, was to win an National Hockey League (NHL) franchise for Los Angeles. Cooke spent another $16,500,000 building the Great Western

Forum, the Laker's present home, in Inglewood. Reputed to be hard to work with, there was no doubt of Cooke's commitment to his teams. He exerted close control over his coaches, was quick to fire, and willing to pay top dollar to his stars while underpaying lower-level players and personnel.

Baylor's knees confined him to spotty performance in 1965-66, and he was out for a month with a secondary injury to his right knee ligaments. Barnett had been traded for 6'8" Bob Boozer, who played almost as many minutes at forward as Baylor and helped with rebounding and scoring.

Reserve center-forward Leroy Ellis stepped up to 12.2 points and 9.2 rebounds per game. Hazzard and 6'2" Jim King turned in good performances at guard, and Gail Goodrich joined the now guard-rich team. Goodrich had been Hazzard's roommate on the championship UCLA team, but many considered him, at 6'1" and 170 pounds, too slight for the NBA. He was sparingly used—in contrast to what his role would be a few years down the road.

The Lakers won their division by 7 games with a 45-35 record, ousted the St. Louis Hawks from the playoffs in seven games, and—yet, again—lost to the Celtics in seven. After a 133-129 overtime victory in which West scored nine points in the extra period, Boston took three straight. Then the Lakers came back for a 121-117 thriller, which was tied with 35 seconds to go.

Back in Los Angeles, Goodrich starred in Game 6, earning 28 points for a 123-115 victory. Game 7 was marked by poor shooting on both teams, except for Bill Russell, who gave 25 points and 32 rebounds to Boston. With 40 seconds left, the Celtics led 95-85. The Boston Garden crowd, jumping to conclusions, had already begun to pour onto the court.

Then the Lakers made a valiant comeback when Boston lost the ball, West hit a long jumper, and K. C. Jones was called for charging. The referees cleared the fans. Ellis passed to King for an L. A. basket, and it was 95-91 with nine seconds on the clock. West deflected the Celtics' inbound pass, which was knocked out of bounds by Bos-

ton, and Ellis sank the next shot to bring the Lakers within a field goal of a tie. The Celts' next inbounds pass got loose—but steady John Havlicek recovered it, and the Celtics held on. It was the Lakers' fourth finals loss in six years to the same team.

Postseason expansion led to depletion of many clubs' rosters, and the Lakers general manager was ailing, which led to some questionable decisions. Boozer and King went in the draft, and Ellis was traded to Baltimore for Jim Barnes. Center-forward Mel Counts also arrived from Baltimore, to help after Gene Wiley's retirement, but did not play much.

Darrell Imhoff had a good year at center, leading the team in rebounds with 13.3, and Baylor was strong, but West was out for 21 games with assorted injuries. The team finished with a losing record, and West broke his hand in the first minute of the first playoff game.

Another year of changes followed. A second expansion draft deprived the team of Hazzard and other reserves. Mohs was dead, and coach Schaus became general manager. The new head coach was ex-Marine Bill "Butch" van Breda Kolff, who had recently coached Bill Bradley at Princeton. As befit his military experience, van Bred Kolff was known to be tough in practice but loose in off-hours, friendly to his players, understanding of their need for recreation.

He was likely to blow up in anger at games and unleash a stream of profanities. In short, he was a players' coach, prized for his winning attitude, and he took his team to another finals against the Celtics, compiling a 52-30 regular-season record. The Boston series was tied after 4 games. In the fifth, West sprained his left ankle but managed to tie the game with twelve seconds left. But Baylor missed a last shot, and Boston won in overtime and breezed through Game 6.

Goliath Arrives

Something had to be done, and in the off-season, Cooke did it. He traded center Imhoff and two other players, plus $250,000 for Wilt Chamberlain. If that didn't get the team a title, what would?

The Lakers now had three certified superstars—quite possibly, three of the starting five in most fans' all-time lineup. But Chamberlain, or at least the media's portrayal of him, brought controversy. He earned a total of a million dollars over five years, a colossal sum then, but he was reputed not to be a team player, and like West and Baylor, he had not taken his previous teams all the way to the championship.

He and the other Lakers, especially off-court leader Baylor, got bogged down in locker-room squabbles. Chamerblain and his coach argued about his attitude toward practice and about his role on offense and defense, and van Breda Kolff quietly arranged to go to Detroit at season's end.

Nevertheless, the team's record was 55-27, with Chamberlain averaging an impressive 20 points and 21 rebounds. Total season attendance surpassed 600,000, averaging 12,000 in the regular season and 16,000 in postseason.

For once, the Celtics were the underdogs in the finals, having finished fourth in the East. Bill Russell was now a player-coach, finishing his last season. Game 1 was sensational, a 120-118 Laker victory with West scoring 53 points. In Game 2, Baylor rallied to score the team's last 12 points for a victory. But the Celts came back for two wins in their Garden, before Chamberlain outscored and outrebounded Russell in the Game 5. Game 6 went the other way, 99-90, with the Laker's new center scoring only one field goal.

Nightmarishly, it was down to Game 7 again. A large Celtic lead—then a Laker rally near the end of the first half—then a Laker cold spell after halftime—then a pullback to 103-102 on a Counts basket. Counts, pumped up, sank the tie-breaking shot—but was called back for traveling. It was Boston, 108-106, and a postseason field day for second-guessers.

The new coach for 1969-70, Joe Mullaney, couldn't have been more of a contrast with van Breda Kolff. A quiet man, he got along well with Chamberlain. However, the big man tore his right knee tendons in the ninth game of the season for

Naismith Memorial Basketball Hall of Fame

Wilt Chamberlain

the first serious injury of his career—which shows his amazing physical condition.

It was a year of injuries and trades, with rookies and substitutes filling in for ailing starters. Happy Hairston, a 6'7" forward out of New York University (NYU), came over from Detroit to average over 20 points and 12 rebounds per game. Thankfully, West led the league in scoring average with 31.2 and led the Lakers in assists. The team finished 46-36, second to the Hawks.

The playoffs were when Chamberlain won the respect of his teammates. He came back against doctors' advice, and led the team back to a playoff victory against the Phoenix Suns (who now included Gail Goodrich in a starring role) after a 3-1 deficit.

The Lakers then swept Atlanta in a series marked by threats of roughness from Hawks' coach Richie Guerin. And who was the Lakers' finals opponent? None other than ... the New York Knicks. Their classic 1969-70 team included Willis Reed, Walt Frazier, Dave DeBusschere,

Dave Stallworth, Bill Bradley, Cazzie Russell, and Dick Barnett. After two games, the series was even.

In Game 3, West's 55-foot jumper tied it at the buzzer, but the Knicks won in overtime. Game 5 sent the series into the realms of melodrama when the Knick captain went down before half-time with a torn thigh muscle. Improvising, Knick coach Red Holzman assigned forwards DeBusschere and Stallworth to cover Chamberlain, and it worked — he took only three shots in the second half. Indeed, Baylor was the only Laker to score in the fourth quarter of that 107-100 loss.

Chamberlain slammed in 45 points in Game 6, which Reed sat out, but as Game 7 loomed, the Lakers feared fate was against them. They had been here too often before. An inspiring comeback by crippled captain Reed gave the Knicks an emotional boost, as did Frazier's 36 points, and the crown was lost in a 113-99 runaway.

What new piece of bad luck could happen in 1970-71? Baylor was out for the season with a torn Achilles tendon, and West missed the postseason with a torn knee. But in an important trade, the Lakers reacquired Gail Goodrich. He had proved his mettle at Phoenix and was ready to score 17.5 per game for his hometown team. Jim McMillian, who like Hairston had grown up in North Carolina and gone to college in New York, filled in at forward, while Pat Riley was picked up on waivers from Portland. He played only 500 minutes.

Propelled by Chamberlain's 18.2 rebounds per game, this aging Laker team won its division by seven games over San Francisco, but were wiped out in the Western Conference championships by Kareem Abdul-Jabbar and the Bucks.

At Last, A Title

Mullaney was not enough of a disciplinarian for the tastes of the front office, and Bill Sharman was in as head coach. Sharman had been the sharpshooting partner of Bob Cousy in the best backcourt duo of the 1950's. He brought K. C. Jones with him as assistant coach. If the Lakers couldn't beat the Celtics, they could hire ex-Celtics to join them.

Sharman, conservative in his personal style, polite, tough, thorough, stressed conditioning, practice, meetings, movies, and team play as opposed to individual spotlight-hogging. He pioneered the contemporary mode of the high-tech basketball coach who uses every sophisticated technique to gain every millimeter of advantage. A four-time All-Star and champion, he was used to winning. His task was, in mental terms, to erase the Lakers' expectation of loss, and in physical terms, to convert an aging team into a running one.

He had to do it without captain Elgin Baylor, whose knees forced him to retire after nine games. Sharman appointed Chamberlain team captain, and it was exactly the right move. The Lakers embarked on a 33-game winning streak, the longest in NBA history, including triumphs in 10 of their last 11. They coasted into the division lead at 69-13.

It was a balanced team. Chamberlain and Hairston were the first NBA teammates ever to total more than 1000 rebounds apiece in a season, with Wilt grabbing 19.2 per game. Hairston supplemented his 13.1 rebounds per game with exactly 13.1 points. West and Goodrich were each responsible for almost 26 points per game — Goodrich nosing out West by a tenth of a point for the team lead — while McMillian came in at almost 19.

Attendance was booming: more than 16,000 per regular-season game, more than 800,000 total. The team scored more than 100 points in 81 games. It was their twelfth playoff season in twelve years — the best record in the league, with the second-best won-lost record during that span. What could go wrong? For once, nothing did.

The Lakers swept the Bulls in the first-round playoff, then took the Bucks, who were missing the injured Oscar Robertson, in six. Highlights were Game 2, in which McMillian outscored Jabbar 42-40, and which the Lakers won 135-134 after an official helped them by getting in the way of a loose ball; and the 102-97 Game 3, in which Chamberlain shut out Jabbar for the last ten minutes and a sizzling Goodrich scored the winning three-pointer.

The finals were against the Knicks, who now had Jerry Lucas at center. The Knicks were a great outside shooting team but couldn't match the Lakers on defense or near the boards. The Lakers lost the first game at home, but won the second and pulled ahead in the third. Game 5 was crucial.

Chamberlain had a sore right hand, exacerbated by a fall on the court. West, toward game's end, was uncharacteristically off the mark. The Knicks tied at the last moment, when Frazier leaped above Chamberlain to take away the rebound from Lucas' missed shot; but the Lakers prevailed in overtime, 116-111.

In Game 6, Chamberlain set an example by playing despite his hand injury: he got 24 points and 29 rebounds, and blocked 10 shots. Four Lakers each scored 20 or more points that game. With a 114-100 win, the Lakers ended their tradition of lost finals and ascended to their first title in Los Angeles.

As a sidelight, Sharman became the only coach ever to guide championship teams in the NBA, American Basketball Association (ABA), and American Basketball League (ABL).

Next year's record was 60-22, with Chamberlain leading the league in rebounds, but the Knicks beat the Lakers for the championship, 4-1, winning the last four games with less than 100 points each. The following year, Chamberlain left to become head coach of the San Diego Conquistadors of the ABA, and West, in his last season, was injured and played only 31 games. Goodrich stepped into the vacuum to lead the club in scoring, with 25 points per game, and the league in free throws made. But it wasn't enough. They lost the playoffs to the Bucks, 4-1.

Jabbar to the Rescue

The following year, the slide became an avalanche. With a 30-52 record, the 1974-75 Lakers were in last place in their division, with the second worst average in the league, and denied a playoff berth.

Naismith Memorial Basketball Hall of Fame

Jerry West

The solution? Trading players, including young center Elmore Smith, and then three others for Kareem Abdul-Jabbar. It stopped the downslide—Jabbar was league Most Valuable Player (MVP)—but not dramatically enough to return the team to playoff stature. Incidentally, Pat Riley was sent to Phoenix. He'd be back.

In 1976, the year the NBA and ABA merged, Jabbar played at his personal peak. For the fifth time in his career he was voted MVP, leading the league in field goals and rebounds. Jerry West was in as coach, Sharman having moved to the front office, and the Lakers had a fine season, their 53-

29 record the best in the league. However, it was Bill Walton's greatest season for the Portland Trail Blazers, who swept the Lakers in the conference final.

The Pacific Division of the Western Conference was emerging as the strongest in the NBA. In 1977-78, every team in the division finished over .500, the Lakers coming in fourth at .549. The team was strengthened by the arrival of 6'5" forward Adrian Dantley from Indianapolis, who produced an average of 19.4 points and 7.2 rebounds per contest. However, Jabbar's broken hand and forward Jamaal Wilkes' broken finger offset the gain. The Lakers lost the opening playoff round to Seattle, 2-1.

A year later, Jabbar was healthy—he blocked an astonishing 316 shots—but Dantley was injured. Though the Lakers defeated Denver in the playoff opener, they lost the semifinals to Seattle, 4-1, including two overtime games.

Magic

The 1979-80 season was not the most remarkable for being the league's first season of the three-point shot. It was most remarkable for the arrival of Earvin "Magic" Johnson along with Celtic rookie Larry Bird. Johnson had been on the cover of *Sports Illustrated* as a sophomore for Michigan State and had led that team to an NCAA championship before being picked first by the Lakers in the pro draft.

Now the 6'8" guard-forward, who could play any position and either end of the court, proceeded to dazzle NBA audiences with a style of play that featured intelligent decision-making, unselfish distribution of the ball to teammates, and unprecedented passing flamboyance. The Lakers also had a new owner in Jerry Buss, a Ph.D. chemist turned real estate developer who had bought the Lakers, the hockey Kings, and the Forum for a total $67.5 million, and a new head coach in Jack McKinney.

Bizarrely, McKinney suffered a brain injury in a bicycle accident when the team was 10-4. (He would recover later in the season and move to the coaching position at Indianapolis the following year.) Paul Westhead took over. Not that the Lakers needed much coaching at this point. It was one of Jabbar's best years, and one of the most dramatic in Laker history. The great center averaged almost 25 points per game and was superb on the boards, winning his sixth MVP award.

A healthy, productive supporting cast featured Jamaal Wilkes and Jim Chones up front, guard Norm Nixon, and reserves Michael Cooper and Spencer Haywood. The team defeated the Suns and Supersonics handily in the early playoff rounds, then faced the Philadelphia 76ers, who now included ex-ABA drawing card Julius Erving. The opponents split the first two games in Los Angeles, then split the next two in Philadelphia, and Dr. J. was in spectacular form.

In Game 5, Jabbar injured his ankle in the third quarter, but came back to complete a 40-point performance in a 108-103 win. Jabbar had to sit out Game 6, and the versatile Magic Johnson played center for the Lakers, scoring 42 points and bringing down 15 rebounds. The Lakers had won another title, and Johnson was voted finals MVP, with Jabbar coming in second. Strangely, however — and a sign of how far pro basketball still had to go — the final game was not telecast live on any national network.

After a rookie year like that, Johnson was offered a 25-year, $25-million contract, the longest and most lucrative in sports history to that point. As luck had it, he suffered an early-season knee injury, and though he led the team in steals per game with 3.43, he played only 37 games. Norm Nixon took over the playmaking role, finishing second in the league in total assists and assists per game. The Lakers finished second in the division to Phoenix, but lost their opening playoff round to Houston, 2-1, with both losses occurring in the Forum.

The mercurial season of 1981-82 began with a clubhouse rebellion led by Johnson who, along with several teammates, wanted coach Westhead banished. Jerry Buss and Jerry West had already privately decided to axe the coach when Johnson, exasperated after a game, complained to the press that he wanted to be traded. The sticking point was that Westhead had instituted a slowed-down, half-court offense which did not take advantage of the Lakers' flair for the fast break.

The home fans booed Johnson for this quasi-mutiny, but he was right, for when Westhead was replaced by his assistant coach, dapper ex-Laker Pat Riley, the team clicked. Riley favored a free-spirited offense in which Johnson blossomed, and a close, trapping defense. Johnson responded by leading the league in steals and coming in second in assists and assist average.

A notable addition to the club was 30-year-old, 6'9" center-forward Bob McAdoo, acquired from the Nets. Often called the best pure shooter in the NBA, McAdoo had led the league in scoring for three consecutive years when he played for Buffalo early in his career. Now he provided the Lakers with valuable points off the bench.

After a 57-25 regular season, the postseason was a brisk and happy one for the Lakers. They swept San Francisco for the Western Conference championship, then took the finals 4-2 from Philadelphia. In the final game, Johnson scored 13 points with 13 rebounds and 13 assists. Again he was named finals MVP.

AP/Wide World Photos

Magic Johnson

Improving in the Eighties

The Lakers' regular-season record was even better the next year, at 58-24. The team nucleus was healthy, and the aptly named James Worthy, a 6'9" forward out of North Carolina, had been added as a rookie. Johnson led the league in total assists and assists average — a pattern that would hold true through most of his career.

The Lakers took care of San Francisco in the conference championship, 4-2, but when the finals against Philadelphia came around, Worthy broke a leg and McAdoo and Nixon suffered lesser injuries. Philadelphia center Moses Malone outscored Jabbar 103-94 during the series and outrebounded him 72-30. It was a 76ers sweep.

Jabbar was still one of the greatest centers of all time, however, and in April 1984 he beat Chamberlain's record of 31,419 career points, with several seasons still to go. James Worthy and defensive ace Michael Cooper were now starters, and McAdoo had a plum year off the bench, averaging 13.1 points per game. Rookie guard Byron Scott was the sixth man. This crew amassed a 54-28 record and stormed through Kansas City, Dallas, and Phoenix in the postseason, until coming up against a too-familiar roadblock in the finals.

It was the Celtics' sixteenth finals, the Lakers' nineteenth. Like Ali and Frazier, they stepped into the fight with the ghosts of past battles urging them on from ringside.

There was something new this time, however: the first professional confrontation between Magic Johnson and Larry Bird. (They had faced one another in the 1979 NCAA championship.) The Lakers got a lift by winning the first game in Boston, 115-109. In Game 2, they had a 2-point lead and possession of the ball with 15 seconds remaining, when Boston guard Gerald Henderson intercepted Worthy's cross-court pass and scored an uncontested basket. The Celtics went on to a 124-121 overtime win.

Back on the west coast, the Lakers eased through a 137-104 Game 3 victory, with Johnson scoring 12, rebounding 11, and getting 21 assists. The rest of the series, however, was marked by missed opportunities on the Lakers' side and clutch play on the Celtics'. Game 4 was another overtime loss, 129-125, and the occasion of a bench-clearing dispute when Celtic power forward Kevin McHale committed a flagrant foul again hustling Laker guard Kurt Rambis on the way to a clear shot at the basket. Magic Johnson later wrote, "McHale's move ... was the turning point of the series."

Game 5, played in the un-air-conditioned Boston Garden on a 97-degree day, was a 121-103 shellacking by the Celtics. The Lakers rallied in Game 6 for a 119-108 home victory, which set the stage for a decisive game in Boston. In front of the largest TV audience in NBA history up to that point, the Celtics scrapped their way past their rivals. Johnson's playoff-leading assists and James Worthy's 60 percent postseason field-goal shooting could not overcome the physically strong, verbally intimidating, resourceful Celtics team which popular coach K. C. Jones had molded. After it was over, Larry Bird, the finals MVP said humiliatingly of the Lakers, "They should have swept."

The following year was the Lakers' chance to get back at the Celtics, not only for their victory but for their comments in the media. The Lakers had choked, the Celtics claimed; they were intimidated by physical play. For 1984-85, coach Riley borrowed a leaf from the Celtics' book. No longer relying solely on finesse, he fostered a tougher physical approach by his team. "We're playing Celtic basketball," he said.

Whether it was physical toughness, mental motivation, or both, it improved the team. All five starters had field-goal percentages of at least 54 percent for the regular season, with Jabbar at 60

AP/Wide World Photos

Pat Riley

percent. The Lakers rose to a 62-20 record, whisked aside Phoenix, Denver, and Portland in the playoffs, and got their revenge against the Celtics in a six-game finals series.

After a shocking 148-114 loss in the opener, the Lakers took themselves in hand. The key, and the finals MVP, was Jabbar. In the Laker's four victories, he averaged over 30 points per game with more than 11 rebounds; in their two losses, only 16.5 points and 4.5 boards.

The Lakers arrived at the 1985-86 season with great expectations. Early on, they were 29-5. *Sports Illustrated* speculated that this assemblage might be the greatest team in NBA history. (Immediately after the article appeared, they lost three straight.) Despite some faltering, they finished at 62-20. Then came postseason series against three Texas teams: the San Antonio Spurs, Dallas Mavericks, and Houston Rockets. Things went well until Houston.

The Rockets had the Twin Towers at center—

Relatively few sports stars have transcended the realm of game-playing and become part of American history. Occasionally, a Bill Bradley or Jack Kemp enters elective politics; and Byron "Whizzer" White became a U.S. Supreme Court Justice. Magic Johnson's impact on American society has possibly been as great as any of those men's. It came about not through choice, but through the way he responded to misfortune.

Earvin Johnson, Jr., was born on August 14, 1959, in Lansing, Michigan, where his father worked night shifts at General Motors' Fisher Body plant. The neighborhood was working-class and predominantly black. The family was strongly religious, though divided between his father's Baptist beliefs and his mother Christine's conversion to Seventh-Day Adventism. As Johnson describes it in his autobiography, his upbringing combined ideal proportions of parental strictness and love. Though his father worked two jobs and had little free time, he watched National Basketball Association (NBA) games on television on Sundays with Earvin, Jr., and, more importantly, taught him how to play all aspects of the game, from offense to defense, from the physical to the mental.

The youngster developed a fierce love of the sport and was constantly seen dribbling and shooting on the streets and playgrounds of his neighborhood. Reaching six feet in seventh grade and six-five in ninth, Johnson became a local basketball figure in junior high. His childhood nickname was June Bug because of his nonstop energy, but when he was fifteen, a reporter for the Lansing *State Journal,* Fred Stabley, Jr., decided Earvin needed a better nickname, and thought up "Magic," after a game in which Johnson had 36 points, 18 rebounds, and 16 assists.

Closely attached to his birthplace, Johnson was torn between the University of Michigan in Ann Arbor and Michigan State University in East Lansing. Partly because of an affectionate pressure campaign in his home town, he chose the latter college, though it had the weaker basketball record, and he led it to an National Collegiate Athletic Association (NCAA) championship in 1979, in a finals confrontation against Larry Bird's Indiana State team. Johnson's entrance into the NBA that fall, along with Bird's, marked a new era of popularity for the league. After a period of declining television ratings, the new superstars added excitement and charm.

Their passes and outside shots were as glamorous as the dunks of seven-footers. Johnson was clearly a thinking person's ballplayer, and his upbeat personality made him a natural for commercial endorsements. Though Bird beat him out for Most Valuable Player (MVP) honors on three earlier occasions, Johnson got the votes

Ralph Sampson and Hakeem Olajuwan—and they had youth and hunger. The Lakers took the first finals game easily, but coach Riley sensed that his players were getting complacent. Horrifyingly, the Lakers saw it all go down the drain in the next four games. Game 3 was particularly scary, not because of Olajuwan's 40 points but because of a collision between Worthy and Houston reserve center Jim Petersen. For several minutes it was feared that Worthy had broken his neck, till finally the team

doctor decided it was safe to carry him from the floor. Although Worthy returned to action in the second half, he did not score again.

Game 5, from which Olajuwan was ejected for fighting, seemed like a Laker victory till nearly the end; with 37 seconds left, they were ahead by three points. But the Rockets tied the score and the Lakers missed a final shot. With one second remaining, Houston called a timeout. Then Ralph Sampson made a spectacular midair catch of the in 1986-87, 1988-89, and 1989-90. He was perennially first or second in the league in assists and assists average, retiring with a total of 9,921, and averaged close to 20 points per game over his twelve-year career. In 1990, he was named *Sport* Magazine's Athlete of the Decade.

He was also known as one of the most popular bachelors in the NBA, and a desk clerk at the Grand Hyatt hotel in New York once informed Johnson that he had set the record for most incoming messages for a guest. Johnson's autobiography, *My Life,* is frank but discreet about the temptations of being a superstar on the road. It is not known exactly when Johnson contracted the Human Immunodeficiency Virus (HIV) or from which casual female partner, but the infection was discovered in late October, 1991, when he failed a routine insurance physical. After two weeks of anguished consultation with doctors, family, and friends, Johnson announced his retirement at a press conference at which he displayed the same positive personal qualities that the public had long known.

Unlike many ex-athletes, Johnson was not at a loss about what to do. He was invited to join the National Commission on AIDS (from which he later resigned because of political differences with the Bush Administration) and became a universally recognized spokesman for the fight against the disease. He wrote a book, *What You Can Do To Avoid AIDS,* as part of a three-book contract with Random House, and undertook a heavy schedule of personal commitments. He made a point of addressing himself especially to African-American youth, not only on Acquired Immune Deficiency Syndrome (AIDS) but on other educational matters. He expanded his business interests (he owned a Pepsi distributorship and aspired to buy an NBA franchise) and kept in good enough physical shape to lead the 1992 U.S. Olympic basketball team to a gold medal.

Through this difficult time, his wife Earleatha ("Cookie"), whom he married in the summer of 1991 after a long, on-and-off romance, was a support to Johnson, as was the arrival of his second son, Earvin III. The fact that both Cookie and Earvin III were HIV-negative was a wonderful relief. Support from the public and from fellow athletes was constant and virtually unanimous. Adding to the optimistic side was the fact that the infection had apparently been discovered at an early stage and that AZT treatments had begun promptly. Combined with Johnson's physical and emotional strength, this made the prognosis as hopeful as it could be under the circumstances.

inbound pass and, twisting, shot the ball before his feet hit the ground. The Rockets had won the clincher, 114-112.

The Repeat

For 1986-87, the Lakers were bringing along sophomore power forward A. C. Green. Reserve center Mychal Thompson, a 6'10" Bahamian, ar-

rived from San Antonio. The team had speed, renewed youth — including the 39-year-old Jabbar, who was embarked on a strenuous conditioning program — and depth. It had four members — Jabbar, Worthy, Johnson, and Thompson — who had been Number 1 draft picks.

And it had Magic Johnson stepping up his offense to take pressure off Jabbar, and having a career year in the process. His 23.9 points per game were a personal high; he supplemented them with 977 total assists, or 12.2 per game. He was MVP in both the regular season and the finals. The team's record was 65-17, with easy postseason wins over Denver, Golden State, and Seattle. Again the finals opponent was Boston, but this time the Lakers won, 4-2, their momentum ensured by high-scoring wins in the opening two games at Los Angeles.

The day after winning the championship, Riley made a statement which aroused surprise and criticism. He guaranteed a repeat championship for 1987-88. Throughout the postseason and the next season, asked about his prediction wherever he went, Riley constantly repeated it, for it had been a conscious tactic he had concocted a week before uttering it.

Riley, a shrewd student of motivational psychology, knew the risks that kind of prediction involved — especially after being called the greatest team in history had plunged the Lakers into a tailspin — but he also knew that a team needed extra incentive to win a second successive title. All season long, this prediction would hang over the team, providing that extra motivation. Riley had known that his players respected him enough to want to prove him right.

The Lakers had become the dominant NBA team of the decade, comparable to the Celtics of the 1960s. The images of the two teams were quite different. The Celtics, in the public mind, were a gritty, hard-working team of underdogs who came back despite pain and short-handedness, while the showtime Lakers were a team of talented, flashy, fast-living Californians who hob-nobbed with movie stars.

While it was true that Jack Nicholson and other celebrities frequented Laker games, the image of the Lakers as getting by on sheer talent was certainly not true. The coaching staff epitomized scientific record-keeping, Riley's practices were considered as grueling as real games, and the players, from Jabbar down, approached self-improvement as a serious mission.

They were on their way to their fifth title in nine years, compiling a .758 record in those five championship postseasons. It wasn't to be a cakewalk, for in the 1987-88 postseason they had to achieve the unprecedented feat of winning three successive seven-game series, from Utah, Dallas, and finally Detroit. After the first five games, Detroit led 3-2. But in Game 6, at home, the Lakers won 103-102, neutralizing a 43-point display by the injured Isiah Thomas. In Game 7, Worthy was brilliant; his numbers: 36 points, 16 rebounds, 10 assists. It won the Lakers the repeat championship, and he was voted finals MVP.

Goodbye, Kareem

The 1988-89 season was to be Jabbar's twentieth and last in the NBA. This complex, private, bookish, religious man, who had rarely smiled during his career on the court, had loosened up visibly in recent years, letting his feelings and his unpredictable, playful side show on occasion. His amazing career records, such as 787 consecutive double-figure scoring games, testified to stamina and pride as well as skill.

As he made his final appearances around the league, he was greeted with emotional farewells in each city, especially New York, where he had starred for Power Memorial High School. Another championship would have been a fitting sendoff, but after sweeping the Phoenix Suns in the conference finals, the Lakers succumbed to a sweep by Detroit, partly because of injuries to MVP Johnson and Byron Scott.

In the final game, Jabbar left the floor with nineteen seconds left, and at Riley's signal, both teams' players and fans gave an ovation. It had been a relatively weak season for the 41-year-old Jabbar — he averaged only 10.1 points per game, and sank less than half his field goals for the first and last time in his career.

Even without Jabbar, the Lakers went 69-13 the following year for the league's best regular-season record, and won their ninth straight division pennant, tying the record of the 1957-65 Celtics. Johnson was MVP in both the regular season and the All-Star game, and Riley, who had compiled a 553-194 record in nine years, was voted Coach of the Year.

There were signs of strain, however. Riley was more distant from his players than he had been in his early years, and he was beginning to exhaust his motivational bag of tricks. A possible sign of his loosening the reins was his refusal to play either Johnson or Worthy in the season's last game, a 130-88 loss to the Trail Blazers in Portland, which prompted league commissioner David Stern to fine the Lakers $25,000. The Lakers did predictably well in the playoffs, sending Houston home 3-1, but they suffered a shocking 4-1 loss to Phoenix in the conference semifinals.

Soon afterward, Riley announced his resignation. He would go to NBC as a broadcaster, and then to the only other city in the nation that could slake his thirst for stardom, to coach the Knicks. Milwaukee Bucks assistant coach Mike Dunleavy was named the new skipper of the Lakers.

In Dunleavy's freshman year, the Lakers lost the Pacific Division title for the first time since 1980-81, coming in second to Portland with a 58-24 record. Nevertheless, they ran through Houston and Golden State in the early postseason rounds, then showed up Portland by prevailing in a 6-game conference finals series, winning 91-90 when Johnson ate up the final seconds with a full-court pass.

The Lakers went on to their ninth NBA finals in twelve years. On April 15 of the regular season, Johnson had surpassed Oscar Robertson's mark for career assists, and during the postseason he was to chalk up his 29th and 30th postseason triple-doubles. The finals against the Bulls were billed as "Magic versus Michael," a confrontation from which Johnson came out ahead in assists and rebounds, Jordan in points and steals.

The Lakers took the opening game of the finals in Chicago, but in Game 2 the Bulls bounced back with the highest team field-goal percentage in finals history, 61.7 percent. The trend was downhill as the Bulls swept the rest of the series.

In Game 5, Scott and Worthy were out with shoulder and ankle injuries respectively, and although forward Elden Campbell supplied 21 points off the bench, and reserves Tony Smith and Terry Teagle bore more than their share of the load, the Laker's were crushed by John Paxson's clutch three-pointers in the concluding minutes.

The Shock of Magic's Departure

The next year marked a traumatic event in the history of sport. On November 7, 1991, Magic Johnson announced that he had contracted the Human Immunodeficiency Virus (HIV), which is responsible for Acquired Immune Deficiency Syndrome (AIDS), and that he was retiring. The story was the lead news item on the television networks that night, and for weeks afterward the entire country was preoccupied with Johnson's situation and his decision.

The outpouring of love and concern on the part of Americans, from school children to business and government leaders, was memorable for all who participated in it, and the episode did much to raise the country's awareness of the AIDS problem. Fittingly Johnson's name was still on the All-Star ballot, and though he did not play during the season, the fans voted him in.

He came out of retirement for that one game, which was marked by a series of spontaneous, dramatic one-on-one showdowns between Johnson and his great rivals and friends, such as Isiah Thomas and Michael Jordan. He scored 25 points in the game and was voted All-Star MVP.

Exactly a week later, on February 16, the Lakers retired his Number 32 uniform in a home game against the Celtics. Staying in competitive shape, he would play again for the public at the 1992 Olympic Games in Barcelona and would consider returning to the NBA, but in the end deciding against it.

The Laker's actual season was a demoralized afterthought. The team barely made it into the playoffs, finishing sixth in their division with a 43-39 record. What made it especially frustrating was that their crosstown rivals, the upstart Clippers, finished ahead of them with 45 wins.

The Lakers won the last playoff spot on the last day of the season with a 109-108 overtime win in the Forum against the Clippers. Anticlimactically, they were defeated by Portland in the first round of playoffs, 3-1.

Byron Scott and James Worthy were now co-captains of the team, with Scott starting all 82 games and excelling at three-pointers and free throws. Guard Sedale Threatt was the other Laker to start in all 82 games, and took over the team lead in assists with a resounding 593 and a 15.1 average.

A. C. Green played in his 456th consecutive game, for a club record. Eastern European Vlade Divac, the 7'1" center, missed much of the season because of back surgery, but 6'11" Elden Campbell and 6'9 1/2" Sam Perkins were capable rebounders and shot-blockers. The club looked forward to a productive future from second-round draft pick Duane Cooper, a 6'1" guard.

On May 12, 1992, coach Dunleavy resigned to move to the Milwaukee Bucks. His assistant, Randy Pfund, was promoted to take his place. The 1992-93 regular season was an inauspicious one for the club.

The Lakers could do no better than a 39-43 fifth place finish in the Pacific Division. The club nonetheless snuck into the playoffs in the last conference postseason slot to face the heavily favored Phoenix Suns.

The Lakers, led by Sedale Threatt, shocked Phoenix in the first two games to take a quick 2-0 lead in the best-of-five series, and the league was abuzz. Phoenix recovered, however, and pulled out the series by winning the final three games.

Sources

BOOKS

Abdul-Jabbar, Kareem, and Mignon McCarthy, *Kareem,* Random House, 1990.

Carter, Craig, and Alex Sachare, editors, *The Sporting News Official NBA Guide, 1992-93,* Sporting News Publishing, 1992.

Chamberlain, Wilt, *A View from Above,* Villard Books, 1991.

Chamberlain, Wilt, and Don Shaw, *Wilt,* McMillan, 1973.

Dickey, Glenn, *The History of Professional Basketball Since 1896,* Stein & Day, 1982.

Fox, Larry, *Illustrated History of Basketball,* Grosset & Dunlap, 1974.

Hirschberg, Al, *Basketball's Greatest Teams,* Putnam, 1965.

Hollander, Zander, editor, *The Complete Handbook of Pro Basketball,* 19th edition, Signet, 1992.

Hollander, Zander, and Alex Sachare, editors, *The Official NBA Basketball Encyclopedia,* Villard Books, 1989.

Johnson, Earvin, and William Novak, *My Life,* Random House, 1992.

Libby, Bill, *Goliath: The Wilt Chamberlain Story,* Dodd, Mead, 1977.

Libby, Bill, *We Love You Lakers,* Sport Magazine Press 1972.

Litsky, Frank, *Superstars,* Derbibooks, Inc., 1975.

Neft, David S., and Richard M. Cohen, *The Sports Encyclopedia: Pro Basketball,* 2nd edition, St. Martin's Press, 1989.

Riley, Patrick, *Show Time,* Warner Books, 1988.

Rust, Art, Jr. and Edna Rust, *Art Rust's Illustrated History of the Black Athlete,* Doubleday, 1985.

PERIODICALS

Ebony, April, 1992.

Esquire, February, 1992.

GQ, February, 1993.

Newsweek, June 6, 1988; June 27, 1988; July 4, 1988; May 6, 1989; August 12, 1991; November 18, 1991; November 16, 1992.

New York Times, September 16, 1991; November 8-17, 1991; November 19-21, 1991; November 26, 1991; December 1, 1991; December 7, 1991; December 10-12, 1991; December 15, 1991; December 19, 1991; December 27, 1991.

Sport, June, 1987.

Sports Illustrated, June 15, 1987; June 22, 1987;

June 29, 1987; April 18, 1988; May 23, 1988;
June 13, 1988; January 23, 1989; December
3, 1990; February 18, 1991; November 18,
1991; February 17, 1992; March 23, 1992;
November 9, 1992.

Time, July 4, 1988; February 20, 1989; November
18, 1991.

—*Richard Cohen* for Book Builders, Inc.

PHOENIX SUNS

In 1940, the city of Phoenix, Arizona, was a sleepy, mid-sized western resort community of roughly 48,000 permanent residents. By 1950, the first year of the National Basketball Association, the city had grown to slightly more than 100,000, but at that size it could hardly be considered as a possible future home for a major professional sports franchise, But then came the start of this country's mass exodus to the Sun Belt states.

By 1968, when the NBA awarded a franchise to Phoenix, the city's population had skyrocketed to 584,000 and was shooting up by nearly 2,100 a month. By 1993 the Phoenix metropolitan area had well over a million dwellers. And growing with them were the Phoenix Suns, in 1993 celebrating their 25th anniversary, winning more games than they had ever accomplished in a single season, and fighting all the way to the NBA Championship finals.

Today there are 27 teams, four divisions, and two conferences in the NBA; so many teams and so many games, pre-, regular, and post- season, that league play now runs from mid-October all the way to mid-June. An eight-month season, with 16 teams qualifying for playoff competition. Only 25 years ago, just prior to the admittance of Phoenix and Milwaukee into the league, the NBA consisted of only 12 teams and two divisions, and only eight teams qualified for the playoffs; the Championship was settled by mid-April.

When the Suns entered the league they were in the Western Division, along with Los Angeles, Atlanta, San Francisco, San Diego, Chicago and Seattle. By the 1992-93 season, after a number of realignments, they were playing in the Pacific Division, one of two divisions in the Western Conference, and the only teams that were still in the division were Los Angeles, San Francisco (which had changed its name to Golden State), and Seattle. Portland, the LA Clippers and the Sacramento Kings came along later.

Pro basketball did not catch on that strongly

with the Phoenix area fans in the early years. The city did not have any history of major professional sports, and the only basketball team of note in the area was at nearby Arizona State. And the Sun Devils in those years were primarily football oriented—attendance at Suns's games during the first year of play averaged only 4,340 a game and did not reach the 10,000 level until after nine years.

All that changed by the 1990s. During the 1989-90 campaign, sales of season tickets had climbed to 9,687, a new record; it jumped to 12,202 the next year and set another franchise high in 1991-92 with 13,068. Overall attendance continued to rise as well, reaching 14,000 for the first time in 1989-90, increasing to 14,385 the next season and rose to 14,496 in 1991-92—full capacity for the team's 24th and final season in the Arizona Veteran's Memorial Coliseum.

In the 1992-93 season, firmly entrenched in their new America West Arena, the Suns again set new attendance records, reaching a season total of 779,943 and an average of 19,023 per game. It was on January 22, 1968, that the National Basketball Association Board of Governors had granted the franchise to the Phoenix group; it was on April 25, 1968 that the name "Suns" was selected in a contest sponsored by the Arizona Republic newspapers. The winning entry had been submitted by Mrs. Selinda King of Phoenix.

Sunny Beginnings

With Jerry Colangelo heading franchise operations, Johnny Kerr, the first Head Coach, and a team name, chosen by the fans, all the club needed were players. On May 6, 1968, the NBA conducted an expansion draft to help stock Phoenix and the other newcomer to the league, the Milwaukee Bucks.

In the draft the Suns chose 18 players from among those left unprotected by existing teams. They selected three players each from Los Angeles, New York and Chicago; two each from Baltimore and Atlanta; and one each from Detroit, Philadelphia, San Diego and San Francisco. Eight

of those 18 made the team, and two of them, Dick Van Arsdale and Gail Goodrich, turned out to become an excellent backcourt scoring combo.

Van Arsdale, the first selection and thus the first player ever to become a Phoenix Sun, was formerly a New York Knick; Goodrich had been on the Los Angeles Laker team. Goodrich led the team in scoring with a 23.8 average (7th highest in the league) and 518 assists; Van Arsdale led the team in minutes played with 3,388 and was a runner up in scoring with a 21 point average and 388 assists. Goodrich had the single game high with 47 in a 146-133 win over the San Diego Rockets on March 9. Both were named to the All-Star squad.

Others from that first draft who stuck with the team were Dick Snyder (from Atlanta), and Stan McKenzie (from Baltimore), both of whom were starters, Neal Johnson (from New York), Dave Lattin (from San Francisco), McCoy McLemore (from Chicago), and George Wilson (from Seattle).

A month later, on June 4, in the annual College Draft, the Suns first round choice was forward Gary Gregor from South Carolina. Gregor, the eighth pick overall, was the only rookie to get any significant court time with the team. His 12.1 scoring average and team leading 711 rebounds earned him a spot on the NBA's All-Rookie team. Also signed were Dick Cunningham, peddled to Milwaukee prior to the season for cash and a future draft pick, and Rodney Knowles, who lasted until November 6 before being cut.

The Suns won their first regular season game, 116-107 over the Seattle Supersonics. Then, playing the majority of their early schedule at home, got off to a 4-3 start. It was a brief period of success, however, as the team went through the usual expansion club struggles, finishing with a 16-66 mark, 39 games behind the division leading Los Angeles Lakers.

Attendance during the Suns first year totalled 160,565, an average of 4,340, with 735 season tickets sold. Those figures can be compared to the total of 594,336, average of 14,496 and season tickets mark of 13,068 reached in the 1991-92 sea-

TEAM INFORMATION AT A GLANCE

Founding date: 1968

Home court:
America West Arena
2800 North Central Ave.
Phoenix, AZ 85004
Phone: (602) 222-5888
FAX: (602) 222-5737

Seating capacity: 19,000

Team colors: Purple, orange, and copper
Team nickname: Suns
Logo: Word "Phoenix" on top of a picture of a sun—with a basketball
as the sun—and the word "Suns" underneath.

Franchise record	Wins	Losses
(1968-91)	975	911

NBA finals appearances (2): 1976, 1993

---

son. In the playoffs, the Boston Celtics won it all again, the 11th time in the past 13 years. The Suns, meanwhile, had finished seventh in their division.

The following season, the fortunes of the Bucks and the Suns hinged on the flip of a coin. As the teams with the worst records, they were eligible to choose first in the college draft. Obviously, had the Suns won the celebrated coin toss and the services of Lew Alcindor (who later took on the name Kareem Abdul-Jabbar, became the NBA's all-time leading scorer, and played on several championship teams), it would have been a tremendous advantage to the team. As it was, even without him, the Suns shot up from a 16-66 mark in their first year to 39-43, a huge improvement of 23 games, and their first trip ever to the playoffs. (By way of comparison, the Milwaukee Bucks, with Alcindor, improved from 27 wins to 56, a hike of 29 games.)

The Suns had a completely new front court: rookie center Neal Walk, power forward Paul Silas, and former ABA scoring phenom Connie Hawkins. League headquarters had admitted Hawkins into the NBA earlier as part, of the out of court settlement to his damage suit, eight years after he had been barred from play in the league for not reporting a bribe while he was still in college.

Scoring an average of 24.6 per game and earning a first team All-Star berth, Hawkins became an immediate hit in the league and most definately, amongst Phoenix's faithful fan.

The team got off to a slow start, which cost Coach Johhny Kerr his job, but they came on strong late in the season to make the playoffs. Silas, obtained in a trade with the Atlanta Hawks for

Gary Gregor, gave the Suns inside strength, pulling down 916 rebounds for a 11.7 average, one of the top board performances in the league. Dick Van Arsdale, with a 21.3 average, and Gail Goodrich, at an even 20, gave the club continued scoring punch from the backcourt. Van Arsdale was also named to the All-Star game.

Kerr had a 15-23 record on January 2 when he resigned as the club's coach, just minutes before a game with San Diego. General Manager Jerry Colangelo took over the coaching duties for the rest of the year himself, posting a 24-20 record.

In the playoffs the Suns gave the powerful Los Angeles Lakers all they could handle, taking a 3-1 lead before the Lakers rallied to win the last three games. Los Angeles went on to the finals, where they were defeated by the New York Knicks. Following the season Goodrich was traded to the Lakers for center Mel Counts.

The Suns Cottoned to New Coach

Under new Head Coach Cotton Fitzsimmons, who in the college ranks the year before had led Kansas State to the Big Eight Championship, the Suns put together their first winning season. The team's 48-34 record was not only the fourth best in the league for the year, it was an improvement of nine games over their 1969-70 finish, and a whopping 32 games better than their first year total in 1968-69.

Unfortunately, because they were in the tough Midwest Division, (the NBA had split two divisions into four prior to the season) that performance did not qualify them for the playoffs. The first place team in the Midwest, the Milwaukee Bucks, featuring Abdul-Jabbar, the league's Most Valuable Player, went on to win the NBA Championship.

Guard Dick Van Arsdale, the only member of the original Sun squad still on the team, led the club in scoring with 1,771 points and a 21.9 average. He was named to the league's All-Star Team as was forward Connie Hawkins, close behind in scoring with a 20.9 mark. For Van Arsdale, it was

his third straight appearance in the annual All-Star game.

The Suns's other starting guard, Clem Haskins, had his best year with, a 17.8 average, while forward Paul Silas became the first Phoenix player to top a thousand in rebounds, pulling down 1,015 for a 12.5 average. Incidently that total, as well as the 27 he grabbed in a single game against the Cincinnati Royals, a 118-99 win for the Suns, are both still record highs for the team. At center, Neal Walk upped his rookie stats, scoring at a 12.9 clip and hauling in 674 rebounds.

No sophomore jinx for Head Coach Fitzsimmons. The Suns's skipper led the Suns to a 49-33 record, only a game improved on his first year on the job, but representing the highest win total for Phoenix to date.

But for the second year in a row a great win-loss effort did not get the Suns into the playoffs. Despite having the 6th best record in the entire league, the Suns finished behind both the Milwaukee Bucks and the Chicago Bulls in their division. In playoff action the title was grabbed by the Los Angeles Lakers.

Forward Paul Silas was named as the Suns's Most Valuable Player in a fan vote, after again leading the club in rebounding, this time with an 11.9 average. His running mate at forward, Connie Hawkins, led the team in scoring with a 21 point a game effort, and both were voted on to the All-Star Team. Dick Van Arsdale turned in another solid performance, averaging 19.7 points a game. At the other guard spot, Clem Haskins averaged 15.7 points a game, and center Neal Walk had his best year to date with a 15.7 mark.

On March 14 the team obtained the rights to guard Charlie Scott from the Boston Celtics in exchange for future considerations. Scott, a 6' 6" high scoring threat, had played with the Virginia Squires in the ABA, where he averaged 35 points a game. In his six games with the Suns he scored at an 18.8 clip.

In the season's 80th game on March 21 the Suns rolled over the Portland Trail Blazers 160-128 in the season's top scoring game and the highest in Suns's history.

Naismith Memorial Basketball Hall of Fame

Connie Hawkins

1973 Marked Start of MacLeod Era

Following the season, Coach Fitzsimmons resigned to take over the head coaching position with the Atlanta Hawks, and Paul Silas was sent to the Celtics to complete the Scott trade. Fitzsimmons was replaced as the Suns's mentor by Butch van Breda Kolff. The former Detroit Piston head coach lasted just eight games into the season before General Manager Jerry Colangelo fired him and took the job himself in a repeat of the 1970 scenarlo.

Despite the move, the Suns never could put it together and fell back into the losing side of the ledger with a 38-44 record, and were now in the Pacific Division. In another league realignment, the Central Division's Cincinnati Royals moved west, became the Kansas City-Omaha Kings and switched into the Midwest Division, taking the place of the Suns, who were bumped into the Pacific. It was a move designed to improve the geographical sturcture of the divisions.

Connie Hawkins's scoring production dropped off a bit to 16.1, but this was offset by newcomer Charlie Scott, who became the first Sun player to top 2000 points in a season, totalling 2,048 for a 25.3 average. The average was the 6th best in the league for the season and was a Suns's franchise high. Big Neal Walk had his best year in the pro ranks with a 20.2 average. He also led the team in rebounds with 1,006, only the second Phoenix player to top the thousand mark. Hawkins and Scott were named to the All-Star squad, but passed over was Dick Van Arsdale, who again was among the leaders with an 18.4 scoring pace.

In the Championship finals, the New York Knicks won in five games over the Los Angeles Lakers. The Suns came away third in the Pacific division.

Next season, Suns management again dipped into the college ranks for coaching leadership, this time signing young John MacLeod, who had coached at the University of Oklahoma for the previous six years, winning two NIT titles along the way. The Suns players, however, had difficultly adjusting to MacLeod's style and struggled early in the season, losing 10 games in a row. The club eventually finished at 30-52 and dropped a notch into 4th place in their division. It was also their lowest win total since their first year in the NBA.

After the first week of the season, forward Connie Hawkins was traded to the Los Angeles Lakers for Keith Erickson; neither player had exceptional production with their new clubs, Hawkins managing only a 12.8 mark for the Lakers, Erickson 14.6 for the Suns, but Erickson was nonetheless voted as the Suns Most Outstanding Player by the fans.

A major blow to the Suns' hopes occurred two-thirds of the way into the season when All-Star guard Charlie Scott broke his arm. Scott had been scoring at a 24.3 points per game clip, fifth highest in the league and was also leading the team in assists at the time of the mishap. With Scott out, Dick Van Arsdale's 1,389 points were high for the team, a 17.8 average. Neal Walk contributed a 16.8 scoring pace and again led the club in rebounding, with 837 for a 10.2 average.

Newcomer Mike Bantom was voted onto the league's All-Rookie team, and further distinguished himself by fouling out of 15 games during the season, the most in the league.

In the Championship finals, the Boston Celtics, with ex-Sun Paul Silas playing a key role at power forward, topped the Milwaukee Bucks to reclaim the title after an absence of five years.

The 1974-75 season was prefaced by one of the biggest trades in Phoenix Suns' history, with center Neal Walk and a second round draft pick sent to the New Orleans Jazz in exchange for forward Curtis Perry, center Dennis Awtrey, reserve guard Nate Hawthorne and a first round selection in 1976.

Injuries plagued the team all year. First round pick John Shumate of Notre Dame had to sit out the entire year for treatment for blood clots. Then, late in the season when the Suns had a shot at making the playoffs, injuries to both Dick Van Arsdale and Keith Erickson ended their hopes. Perry had his best season in the pros, averaging 13.4 points a game and 11.9 rebounds. Charlie Scott again led all Suns scorers with a total of 1,680 and an average of 24.3, and also paced the team in assists with 311; he was the Suns only All-Star representative, his third year in a row at the game. Van Arsdale averaged 16.1 points a game.

The Suns's 32-50 finish earned them another 4th place spot in the Pacific Division, 16 games behind the Golden State Warriors, who went on to win the NBA Championship. Following the season Scott was traded to the Boston Celtics for Paul Westphal and two future second round picks.

With the addition of two key players, Coach John MacLeod was able to turn the Suns back into a winner, and they made the playoffs for the first time in six years; the players were first round draft pick Alvan Adams, a slim, 6' 9" center, and guard Paul Westphal, obtained from the Boston Celtics in the Charlie Scott trade. Adams's 19 points a game average, 727 rebounds, and 450 assists earned him NBA Rookie of the Year honors and a spot on the All-Star Team, while Westphal led the Suns in scoring with 1,679 points and a 20.5 average.

Both Adams and Westphal were among the league leaders in assists, and Westphal was third in the loop in steals. (Although Adams would become a 13-year veteran starter for the Phoenix club, he would never again reach the point, rebound, and assist totals he put up in his rookie year.)

Dick Van Arsdale suffered a broken arm and played in only 58 games, with his average dropping to 12.9 points a game, and forward Curtis Perry again led the club in rebounding average, pulling down 9.6 a game. On November 3, 1975 the Suns picked up a veteran guard from the Los Angeles Lakers who was at the end of his playing days but had as yet not started on his coaching career. Pat Riley was his name, and he would later coach several championship teams centered by Kareem Abdul-Jabbar.

"The Most Thrilling Game in Suns' History"

In the playoffs the Suns surprised the Seattle Sonics, dumping them in six games, then shocked the Western Division's first place team, the Golden State Warriors, in an exciting seven-game set.

The Championship series against the Boston Celtics featured one of the greatest games in NBA history. The series was tied at two games each for the pivotal fifth game in Boston. Down by five points in regulation with less than a minute to play, the Suns miraculously tied it on a jumper by Westphal, a steal, another basket, and a free throw.

The two teams fought through the first overtime without breaking the tie. With five seconds left in the second overtime, Perry hit on a shot to put Phoenix ahead 110-109. The Celtics then went to their bread and butter man, John Havlicek, who came through with a clutch shot with two seconds left to give the lead back to Boston.

Phoenix called time-out to regroup but had no time-outs left. Boston was awarded a technical foul free throw and made it, for a two-point lead. The ball was inbounded to Garfield Heard, who tossed up a prayer from far out that swished

Gorillas in the Sun

The hairy creature seen bounding about the America West Arena during the '93 playoff games by the record number of television viewers was Arizona State University gymnast Bob Woolf in his guise, as the Suns's "gorilla" mascot. Woolf thrilled the capacity crowds with his antics of repelling from the rafters and performing trampoline powered dunks. Four other ASU gymnasts are also doing the same act for other NBA teams.

After Woolf got the Gorilla job four years ago, his ex-roommate Mike Zerrilla was hired as the Charlotte Hornets's mascot, "Hugo." Then Paul Lenne became the Indiana Pacer's popular "Boomer," Jerry Burrell became the Houston Rockets' "Booster," and, finally, John Sweeney the Seattle Sonics's "Squatch." They should have given the Suns's job to the ex-roommate. What could be better than "Zerrilla the Gorilla?"

the net and tied the game again.

In the third extra period the Celtics prevailed by two points to win the game, often called the most thrilling in Suns's history; the final 128-126. In the sixth and final game, played in Phoenix, the Celtics came out on top 87-80 to capture their record 13th NBA Championship. Even with the loss, it was a tremendous year for the Phoenix Suns, all topped off when General Manager Jerry Colangelo was voted as the NBA's Executive of the Year.

After the remarkable 1975-76 campaign, the Suns opened the season with the highest of hopes. Injuries, however, ravaged the entire Phoenix front line. Forwards Gar Heard and Curtis Perry each missed nearly half of the season, and although center Alvan Adams managed to get into 72 games, he played hurt for most of the year and was far below top form. Adams did manage to tie the Phoenix one-game scoring mark, pouring in 47 in a game against Buffalo on February 22.

The team ended the year at 34-48, dropping to 5th place in their division. Paul Westphal continued to be a bright spot, leading the team in scoring with 1,726 points and a 21.3 average as well as in assists with 459. He was voted to the starting unit for the All-Star game. Steady center Alvan Adams contributed at an 18 point clip.

Despite the disappointments, the Suns set a new home attendance mark, averaging better than 10,000 a game.

The season also saw twins Tom and Dick Van Arsdale (Tom was obtained from the Buffalo Braves in exchange for a future draft pick) on the same professional team for the first time. Unfortunately both were at the tail end of their excellent careers. In backup roles Dick averaged 7.7 points a game, Tom 5.9, both retired after the season. Pat Riley and Paul Wetzel also retired.

Prior to the season's start the old ABA folded. Four of their teams—the New York Nets, Indiana, San Antonio, and Denver—were absorbed into the NBA, Indiana and Denver into the Midwest Division, San Antonio into the Central, and the Nets into the Atlantic. Twenty-two teams now existed in the NBA.

The reorganized Pacific Division now included Phoenix, the Los Angeles Lakers, the Portland Trail Blazers, the Golden State Warriors and the Seattle Supersonics. While Phoenix found itself at the bottom of the Pacific heap, the Trail Blazers, second in the Pacific Division during the year, went on in the playoffs to win the NBA Championship.

In John MacLeod's fifth year as the Suns's Head Coach, he led Phoenix to a 49-33 record, a tie for the most wins in franchise history. Their second place finish in the division was also the best in their ten-year history.

All-Star guard Paul Westphal became only the second Suns player to top 2000 points in a season, totaling 2,014 for a 25.2 average. It was the sixth highest scoring mark in the league for the season. On November 27, 1977, against Denver he pumped in 48 points for a new club single game record. Close behind Westphal in scoring was the Suns's top draft pick Walter Davis, with a 24.2 average. Davis was named the NBA's Rookie of

In addition to celebrating their 25th season in professional basketball and putting together the greatest winning season in the history of the team during the 1992-93 season, the Phoenix club also unveiled their sparkling new home, the America West Arena.

Named for the city's hometown airlines, the facility represents an unprecedented partnership involving the Suns, the city of Phoenix, and America West Airlines.

Since they came into the league in 1968, the Suns had played all of their home games in the 14,500-seat Arizona Veteran's Memorial Coliseum. While the Coliseum was their home for nearly a quarter of a century, it was also one of the smallest and oldest of all of the arenas in the NBA.

The dream of a new arena for the Suns began to take shape in 1989 when Jerry Colangelo, now the club's President and CEO but then its General Manager, led a group of investors in the purchase of the Phoenix franchise. At that time he also began exploring possibilities with the city of Phoenix to construct the new arena.

A mutually beneficial agreement was reached in which the Suns would receive a home built specifically for basketball while featuring all modern amenities; the city would get downtown activity estimated at up to two million people annually) and a guarantee that the Suns would play in downtown Phoenix for at least 40 years. In August of 1989 America West Airlines joined the team and agreed to become the arena's naming sponsor.

the Year and was voted onto the All-Star Team. Team captain Garfield Heard grabbed 652 rebounds to pace the club in that category; Westphal dished out the most assists, 437; and guard Ron Lee led in steals with 225. Center Alvan Adams was steady, but his 15.5 points per game average was the lowest of his three-year career.

Finishing second in their division, Phoenix was eliminated from the playoffs in two games by the Milwaukee Bucks. The Washington Bullets won their first NBA Championship.

The Suns finally reached the 50-win plateau, posting a 50-32 mark, the third highest win total in the entire league, better than the winners of both the Central and Midwest divisions. The two teams with higher victory totals were Washington (54) and Seattle (52), and unfortunately for Phoenix, Seattle was in the same division as the Suns. The Suns's second place finish, only two games out of first, was the closest they had ever come to winning a divisional crown.

Phoenix was bolstered by the addition of power forward Truck Robinson, acquired from the New Orleans Jazz on January 12, 1979, for Ron Lee, Marty Byrns, cash, and first round picks over the next two years. Robinson not only scored an average of 16 points a game, he was one of the top eight rebounders in the league and led the Suns with a 11.6 rebounding average. His addition compensated for the loss of Curtis Perry, who was forced into retirement prior to the season because of injuries.

For the third year in a row Paul Westphal started in the All-Star classic, and Walter Davis made it for the second time. Westphal, serving as team captain for the year, led the Suns in scoring with 1,941 points and a 24-point average, seventh best in the league, and doled out 529 assists, fifth highest. Davis was close behind in scoring with a 23.6 pace, and center Alvan Adams improved to 17.8. Don Buse was the team leader in steals with 156. As a team, Phoenix led the entire league in steals with 915, an average of 11.2 a game.

The Suns qualified for the playoffs for the second year in a row and the fourth time in their 11-year history, and nearly won it all. In the first round Phoenix brushed past the Portland Trail Blazers 2-1, then overwhelmed Kansas City 4-1. In the Western Conference Championship finals against Seattle, the Sonics prevailed in seven hard fought games. Seattle took the first two games, but the Suns bounced back to win the next three. In the sixth game in Phoenix, the Sonics won by a point, 106-105.

The team's 55 wins, the highest ever for a Phoenix club, was topped by only four teams in the entire NBA in 1979-80, but two of them, the Los Angeles Lakers, with 60, and the Seattle Supersonics, with 56, were in the same division as the Suns. The Suns's home record for the team, an outstanding 36-5, was aided by the highest average per game attendence (11,723) and more than 8,000 season tickets sold.

In scoring, Phoenix was again led by their All-Star guard and team captain, Paul Westphal, who banged the nets for 1,792 points and a 21.9 average. Westphal also led the club in assists for the fifth year in a row and set a new single game scoring mark with 49 on February 21 against Detroit.

The team's other All-Star, Walter Davis, averaged 21.5 points per game, and Truck Rob-inson added 17.3 along with his team leading 770 rebounds. Alvan Adams, out for much of the year with injuries, contributed at a 14.9 clip.

Don Buse was the top pilferer on the club, swiping 132. The Suns were the only team in the NBA with five former All-Stars as starters— Westphal, Robinson, Davis, Adams and Buse. For the second year in a row Buse, Adams, Davis, and Westphal each had more than 300 assists; no other club in the history of the league had ever accomplished that before.

In the playoffs, the Suns defeated Kansas City 2-1, but then lost to the eventual NBA Champion Los Angeles Lakers 1-4. After the season the Suns traded Westphal to Dallas for a second round pick in 1981 and future considerations.

Season's Efforts Eclipsed

The 1980-81 season could well have been considered at the time as the greatest in the history of the Phoenix Suns ... almost. The team's win total, 57, was the highest the Suns had ever achieved or would achieve until the 1992 season; the team's Pacific Division Championship was their first; the win total was the most in the NBA's Western Conference; and it was the first time the Suns had ever put together four consecutive winning seasons.

Their 36-5 home record tied for the best they had ever managed, and their 21-20 record on the road was the first winning road record in the team's history; the 11,773 home attendance average was another Phoenix Suns high point; and, finally, Suns General Manager Jerry Colangelo was named as the NBA Executive of the Year for the second time.

These accomplishments by the Suns were eclipsed in the first round of the playoffs, however, as the Suns were upset in a disappointing seven-game set by the lowly Kansas City Kings. Not only was Kansas City coached by former Suns mentor Cotton Fitzsimmons, the Kings hadn't even won half of their games during the regular season.

In that playoff series, after winning the first game in Phoenix with comparative ease, 102-80, the Suns dropped three close battles, 88-83 in Phoenix, 93-92 and 102-95 in Kansas City, to fall behind 3-1. The club picked itself up off the ground to win 101-89 in Phoenix and 81-76 in Kansas City before heading back home for the finale. But in that seventh game the gritty Kings prevailed, taking a 95-88 win to dim the Sun's bright season.

Prior to the season Colangelo had confounded Suns fans by trading the extremely popular Paul Westphal to the Seattle Supersonics for guard Dennis Johnson; then, on November 25 he peddled the other Suns backcourt ace, Don Buse, to Indiana for cash and future draft picks. To compensate for the loss of this ball handling strength, All-Star forward Walter Davis was moved to a guard position.

The annual All-Star game in Cleveland had a definite Suns flavor, with John MacLeod and his staff running the show, Walter Davis at a starting position, and Dennis Johnson and Truck Robinson also on the team.

During the regular season both Robinson and Johnson posted 18.8 scoring averages; Robinson's was actually 18.817, Johnson's 18.810, an important difference in that Robinson pulled down 789 rebounds to lead the team. It thus was the first time in Suns' history that a player led in both scoring and rebounding in the same season. Davis, at an even 18 points a game, and Alvan Adams, at 14.7, were also in double figures for the Suns. The Suns's 57-25 win-loss mark pulled the team's overall record to 539-527 for their 13 years in the league, the first time they had been over .500 since the first two weeks of their first year in the NBA, when they had a 4-3 mark after seven games. In the playoff finals, the Boston Celtics won their 14th crown.

The team suffered a crippling blow only days before the 1981-82 season opener when All-Star Walter Davis fractured his elbow. With his top scorer out for the first two months, Coach John MacLeod was forced to improvise with different lineups, eventually switching Alvan Adams from his customary center position to forward and moving Rich Kelley into the pivot.

When Davis finally returned he was used as a sixth man, and his average dropped off to 14.4 points a game. Davis's running mate at guard, former Supersonic Dennis Johnson, paced the team with a 19.5 average and was the only Sun represented at the All-Star game. Truck Robinson led the Suns in rebounding for the third year, but was unappreciated, for he was traded after the season to the New York Knicks for another power forward, Maurice Lucas.

The Suns finished the regular season with a 46-36 mark, good for third place in the Pacific Division, and also good enough for a playoff spot. In the first round they ousted Denver 2-1, but were then swept by the eventual NBA Champion Los Angeles Lakers in four games. Number one draft pick Larry Nance was used sparingly and averaged

only 6.6 points a game.

During the next season, the Suns used a balanced scoring attack—all five starters were within five points of one another in scoring averages—to win 53 games, one of only six teams in the entire NBA to top 50 wins. Walter Davis paced that scoring fivesome with an even 19 points a game average, followed by a much improved Larry Nance (16.7), Maurice Lucas (16.5), and Alvan Adams and Dennis Johnson (both at 14.2).

Lucas pulled down 799 rebounds to lead the club. Nance also did his share on the boards, grabbing 710 rebounds as well as setting a new Suns franchise record with 217 blocked shots. Davis dished out 397 assists, closely followed by Johnson with 388 and Adams with 376.

Lucas was the only Suns player to make the annual All-Star game. During the last half of the season, the Suns were the hottest team in the league, winning 23 of 30 games. The club made the playoffs for the sixth year in a row, but was eliminated in the first round 2-1 by the Denver Nuggets. Following the season the club traded Dennis Johnson to the Boston Celtics for forward-center Rick Robey.

Am amazing series of injuries prevented the Suns from achieving any degree of consistency, and subsequently the team fell to a break even 41-41 record, their first non-winning season in seven years. Coach John MacLeod had planned to start the newly acquired James Edwards at center, but the former Cleveland Cavalier suffered a broken hand early in the season, botching that plan.

Former scoring star Paul Westphal was re-acquired and was expected to offer backcourt assistance, but he too was plagued by injuries and was of little help. Those and other problems caused the club to get off to a poor start, 5-13 by December 2, and they did not climb out of the minus side of the won-loss column until the last day of the season. To do that, they had to win their final six games, their only significant winning streak of the year.

Both Suns forwards Maurice Lucas and Larry Nance had good years, with Lucas leading in rebounding and averaging a 15.9 scoring pace while

Nance upped his scoring average to 17.7, pulled down 678 rebounds and again led the team in blocked shots with 173.

Walter Davis recovered from his injury woes to boost his scoring to a team-leading 20 points per game and also led the Suns in assists with 429. He was the only Sun player named to the All-Star game.

Despite the so-so record, the team managed to qualify for the playoffs, where they played their best ball of the year. In the first round they upset the Portland Trail Blazers 3-2, then outfought the Utah Jazz in another surprise, 4-2, before finally bowing to the Los Angeles Lakers 4-2.

Fans Remained Faithful

The game of professional basketball was definitely established in the city of Phoenix. The Suns set a new high in attendance, averaging 12,035 a game, despite the fact that the team had their first losing season in eight years.

In recent seasons it seemed as if the Suns had their share of injuries and illnesses, and it was no different in the 1984-85 campaign. Walter Davis, the club's top scoring threat, missed 59 games; Larry Nance and Maurice Lucas, the starting forwards, missed 21 and 19 games, respectively; center Jim Edwards was lost for 12 games; and guard Kyle Macy missed 17. In all, the Suns missed a total of 266 player games, an all-time high. Only Alvan Adams escaped the injury bug, and the slim pivotman played in all 82 games.

With Davis out for the majority of the year, team captain Nance took team scoring honors with a 19.9 average, and also paced the club in blocked shots again, enroute to an All-Star berth. Lucas took top spot in rebounding for the third year in a row, and Macy's 127 free throws in 140 attempts for a league-leading .907 average was an all-time Suns record. In October the team waived former All-Star guard Paul Westphal.

The Suns's 36-46 record placed third in their division, but it earned them a playoff spot for the eighth straight year. They didn't go far, however,

getting shut out 3-0 by the eventual NBA Champs, the Los Angeles Lakers.

The team's problems continued mounting in the 1985-86 season as the Suns sunk to a 32-50 mark, their worst record in more than a decade and the first time in nine years they did not make the playoffs. For the first time in their history the team also the team failed to place a player on the All-Star squad.

Prior to the season, Suns management confirmed their intention to go with more speed and youth, trading veteran Maurice Lucas to the Los Angeles Lakers and allowing free agent Kyle Macy to sign with the Chicago Bulls. The team got off to their worst start ever, losing their first nine games.

Early in the year the club signed Georgi Glouchkov, a rangy forward-center from Bulgaria. Glouchkov, the first Eastern Bloc athlete to play in the NBA, became a crowd favorite but did not significantly help the team, averaging only 4.9 points a game before being released. Walter Davis again led the Phoenix club in scoring with 1,523 points and a 21.8 average.

Team captain Larry Nance had his best scoring year to date, averaging 20.2 points per game to go along with his team leading 618 rebounds and 130 blocked shots. Center James Edwards also had his top year scoring, hitting for a 16.3 average. Despite the decline in the win column, attendance held up, averaging 11,121 per game. In the playoffs, the Boston Celtics swept to their 16th NBA Championship.

Injuries, Illnesses, Trades ... and the Return of Fitzsimmons

On February 26, 1987, after consecutive losses to the Lakers and with their record at 22-34, the Suns fired Head Coach John MacLeod. In 14 seasons MacLeod had guided the Suns to 579 regular season and 37 playoff wins. But he had not had a winner since the 1982-83 season, and little job security exists for NBA coaches. Former Suns backcourt ace Dick Van Arsdale stepped aside as the color commentator for Suns' telecasts to take over as interim coach.

Van Arsdale led the Suns to a l4-l2 mark, but the improvement was not enough to qualify the team for the playoffs. On the court, Walter Davis, at 23.6, and Larry Nance, at 22.5, again carried the brunt of the scoring load. No other Suns averaged more than 12 points a game. Third year guard Jay Humphrles led the team in assists (632) and steals (112). Nance's 599 rebounds, in only 69 games, and 148 blocked shots were team highs.

Following the season another former Suns player, John Wetzel, was named as the club's new Head Coach. Herb Brown was named assistant coach, and in a surprise move, former Head Coach Cotton Fitzsimmons was brought aboard as Director of Player Personnel.

A couple of months later, Suns General Manager Jerry Colangelo led a group of area businessmen to purchase the Suns franchise for a reported $44.5 million. In the process, his title was changed from General Manager to President. Amidst all these activities, the Los Angeles Lakers won their 11th NBA title.

If Suns fans thought the last three years of the John MacLeod era were bad, the 1987-88 season was a nightmare. With John Wetzel at the controls, the Suns won only 28 games, losing 54, their worst record since their first year in the league as an expansion club. In Wetzel's defense that old Suns's bugaboo—injuries—again decimated the team.

During the course of the year, injuries, illnesses, and trades forced Wetzel into 17 different starting lineup combinations. Larry Nance got into only 40 games and James Edwards 43, while Walter Davis missed 14; Armin Gilliam, who made the league's All-Rookie team, missed 27; and Jay Humphries was out 32.

In late February the Suns new Director of Player Personnel put together some major trades. First he peddled center Edwards to the Detroit Pistons for two draft picks and Ron Moore. A day later he dealt Nance and reserve Mike Sanders to the Cleveland Cavaliers in exchange for their first and second round picks in 1988, a second rounder

in 1989 and players Kevin Johnson, Mark West and Tyrone Corbin. Finally, he traded Humphries to the Milwaukee Bucks for Craig Hodges and another future pick.

Following the season, the club compensated somewhat for the loss of all of this talent by signing high scoring free agent Tom Chambers from the Seattle Supersonics. With Davis's scoring down to a 17.9 average, Nance took honors for the team with a 21.1 mark, while Eddie Johnson chipped in with 17.7, and Edwards 15.7. Newcomer Mark West had 523 rebounds for the season, but 281 of those came before he was picked up by the Suns, so Gilliam was the team's top rebounder with 434, the lowest leader total in club history.

After the season, to nobody's surprise, Wetzel was fired and replaced by Fitzsimmons, and assistant Herb Brown was also canned, and replaced by Paul Westphal. The season was the last for Alvan Adams, who retired after 13 years with the club, longer than anyone in the history of the franchise. Adams's stats—988 games, 27,203 minutes played, 6,937 rebounds, 4,012 assists and 1,289 steals—are still a Suns record. Also bidding goodbye to the Phoenix club was Walter Davis, who played out his contract and signed with the Denver Nuggets. Davis's 15,666 total points with the Suns is still a team record.

If Cotton Fitzsimmons had chosen to run for Mayor of the city of Phoenix following the 1988-89 NBA campaign, he probably would have won by a landslide. After four dismal losing seasons in a row, topped off by the disastrous 1987-88 season, the Suns skyrocketed under Fitzsimmons's direction to a 55-27 winning record, the third biggest turnaround in NBA history. The Suns were the league's top scoring team, averaging 118.6 points a game, and they won 18 of their last 22 games, including a record-tying nine in a row, and a franchise record six in a row on the road.

The team won nearly twice as many games as it had the year before and was the only team in the NBA to have three players averaging more than 20 points per game—Tom Chambers with 25.7, Eddie Johnson with 21.5, and Kevin Johnson with 20.4. Chambers, season total of 2,085 points and his scoring average of 25.7 were both new records for a Suns player. Chambers also led the club in rebounds, with 684. Kevin Johnson set a new club record in assists, with 991, and also set a single game assist mark with 21 against the Los Angeles Lakers on February 26.

And to top off the new record splurge, center Mark West set a new high in field goal accuracy, with a .653 average. Forward Armin Gilliam contributed at a 15.9 pace, and rookie Dan Majerle gave an indication of his future worth with an 8.6 average in a part-time role. The fans also got into the record act, setting a new Coliseum attendance mark with an average of 12,405 per game.

When Fitzsimmons took over the head coaching duties, he added three assistants, Paul Westphal, Lionell Hollins, and Truck Robinson, and the combination clicked. On the court, the Suns bore little resemblance to the teams of previous years, with only one player, Jeff Hornacek, remaining on the squad from two years earlier.

In the playoffs, the Suns faced the Denver Nuggets in the first round, their first post season appearance in four years. They responded with a vengeance, shutting out the Colorado club in three games. Then they topped a strong Golden State team 4-1. But by this point the team had used up all of their magic, and the defending champion Los Angeles Lakers shut them out 4-0.

The players and even the administration were showered with post season awards. Eddie Johnson won the league's Sixth Man Award. Kevin Johnson was named the Most Improved Player. Fitzsimmons won the coveted NBA Coach of the Year honor, and President-CEO Jerry Colangelo was named NBA Executive of the Year, for the third time.

With all of these accomplishments it seemed unusual for only one Suns player, Chambers, to be named to the All-Star squad.

Following another 50-plus win season, the Suns made it to the finals of the Western Conference playoffs in 1990. But again they advanced no further, bowing to the Portland Trail Blazers 4-2.

The club led the NBA for the second year in a row in differential between points scored and points allowed, 7.1, scoring on a 114.9 clip and allowing 107.8. Team records set during the season included 19 wins in a row at home and a total of 22 wins on the road; a new single game free throw mark with 61 against the Utah Jazz on April 9; a new average home attendance high, 14,114; and a total of 26 sellouts.

Individual records were established by forward and team captain Tom Chambers, whose 27.2 scoring average and 2,201 total points were new records for the Suns and are still highs for the team. Chambers's 56 points against the Golden State Warriors on February 18 was a new single game high for the team. It only stood for a month, however, until he poured in 60 against the Seattle Supersonics on March 24. That 60 total is still a Suns's record. Chambers also became the only Phoenix player to score more than 2,000 points twice.

Other Suns's scoring totals included a 22.5 average by Kevin Johnson, 17.6 by Jeff Hornacek, and 16.9 by Eddie Johnson, who also set a new Phoenix free throw completion percentage of .917, hitting on 188 of 205. Both Chambers and Kevin Johnson were named to the All-Star team.

In the playoffs the Suns topped the Utah Jazz 3-2 in the first round, then ran all over the Los Angeles Lakers 4-1 in the second set, their first post season series win over Los Angeles. In the finale the Suns bowed to the Portland Trail Blazers 4-2.

After two consecutive trips to the Western Conference finals and two straight 50-plus win years, expectations for the Suns were high. And the faithful were not disappointed, as Phoenix rolled to 55 wins. Following a 7-1 preseason mark, the best the Suns had ever achieved, the team journeyed across the wide Pacific to Japan to open the 1990-91 season against the Utah Jazz. It was the first time that two professional sports teams from the United States played regular season games outside of North America. The Suns won the first game handily, 119-88, but were edged 102-101 in the second game a day later.

A number of records were set on November 10 during a game between the Suns and the Denver Nuggets. To begin with, it was the 700th NBA win for Head Coach Cotton Fitzsimmons. He was only the seventh coach in league history to reach that milestone. As a team, Phoenix set a new league record for points in a half, 107, and for an entire nonovertime game, 173; for points in a quarter, 57; for total field goals, 67; and for total assists in a half, 33.

On November 27 the Suns topped the Portland Trail Blazers in Portland, 123-109, their first win in 20 tries in the Oregon city. On December 7, to toughen the club the Suns traded forward Eddie Johnson, primarily a scorer, and draft picks to Seattle for Xavier McDaniel, a rugged defender and rebounder. During March the club posted a 13-3 mark, the most wins it had ever had for one month, and also set a franchise record with eight consecutive road wins.

The Suns finished the year with a 32-9 home record and 23-18 on the road; the 23 away wins eclipsed the record of 22 set the previous year. And again the club set a new attendance mark, totalling 589,591 by selling-out all 40 home games.

Kevin Johnson, who averaged 22.2 points per game, and Tom Chambers, at 19.9, were named to the All-Star team. Jeff Hornacek added a 16.9 mark and McDaniel 15.8, while Cal Natt led in rebounds with 564 and in blocked shots with 161. Kevin Johnson also parcelled out the most assists, 781, and came up with the most steals, 163.

In the playoffs the Suns were quickly eliminated by the Utah Jazz, 3-1; the Chicago Bulls outfought the Los Angeles Lakers for the NBA crown.

The Suns topped the 50-win plateau for the fourth year in a row, completing the season with a 53-29 record. During that four year period the team's win total was toppd only by NBA powerhouses the Chicago Bulls, the Los Angeles Lakers, the Detroit Pistons, and the Portland Trail Blazers.

During the year the Suns chalked up win number 1,000, only the 12th franchise in the history of the league to achieve that total. Only the Boston Celtics, the Los Angeles Lakers, the Milwaukee Bucks, and the Philadelphia 76ers did it quicker. The team's 36-5 won-loss record at home tied their previous best, set during the 1978-79 and 1980-81 seasons.

Five Phoenix players, Jeff Hornacek (20.1), Kevin Johnson (19.7), Dan Majerle (17.3), Tom Chambers (16.3), and Tim Perry (12.3), averaged in double figures, and the team itself averaged 112.1 points per game, second highest in the league.

Perry, with 551 rebounds, and Andrew Lang, with 546, led the Suns on the boards, while Kevin Johnson again paced the team in assists, with 836. Lang blocked 201 shots to lead in that category. Phoenix All-Stars were Hornacek and Majerle, the first time for both of them.

In the playoffs the Suns were solid in the first round, eliminating San Antonio 3-0, but then were beaten by the Portland Trail Blazers 4-1. The Suns had completed their 24th and final season at Veteran's Memorial Coliseum with a new attendance mark, 14,496 per game. Starting with the 1992-93 season, all home games would be played in the newly constructed America West Arena.

The season also marked the finale for Cotton Fitzsimmons as the Suns's Head Coach. The popular Fitzsimmons moved upstairs to become the club's Senior Executive Vice President, and was replaced by Paul Westphal, whom Fitzsimmons had groomed as his successor. In major offseason roster moves, the club traded Hornacek, Perry, and Lang to the Philadelphia 76ers for power forward Charles Barkley, and then on July 29 signed free agent Danny Ainge.

Barkely and Majerley Had the Right Stuff

As the Suns moved into their 25th year in professional basketball, the club and its fans had high expectations. The team had a new coach, Paul Westphal, who had served his apprenticeship for the position as a star player with the team and then as an assistant coach. New hopes also dawned with

AP/Wide World Photos

Charles Barkley

the two exciting offseason additions of Barkley and Ainge to the team. The revamped Suns squad did not disappoint, shooting out of the blocks and winning a team record 62 games. That win total was also the highest in the NBA for the year.

During the regular season the Suns had seven players in double figures, led by Barkley, with a 25.6 average, and followed by Dan Majerle (16.9), Kevin Johnson (16.1), Richard Dumas (15.8), Cedric Ceballos (12.8), and veterans Tom Chambers (12.2) and Ainge (11.8). Ainge and Majerle were particularly effective from three-point range: Ainge and Reggie Miller of Indiana tied for the most three-pointers in the league at 167 each, and Majerle was third with 150. Rookie forward/center Oliver Miller showed promise but was limited to only 56 games because of an assortment of ailments, and scored only at a 5.6 pace. Mark West's

per game scoring average dropped off to 5.3, but the big center was second on the team in rebounds, with 458, and led in blocked shots, with 103.

Barkley not only led the team in scoring, he also was the team leader in rebounds, with 928, and in assists, with 385 (better than the 384 compile by Kevin Johnson, who missed 33 games due to injuries), the only time that rare feat has ever been accomplished by a Suns player. Barkley's scoring and all-around play earned him the coveted NBA Most Valuable Player award. The "bad," bald, and burly Barkley was a clear leader. Majerle was the surprising club leader in playing time, putting in a total of 3,199 minutes for the season. He also led in steals with 138.

The Suns's record, 62-20, was two games better than that of Eastern Conference kingpin New York, and five better than that of defending champion and Midwest Division leader Chicago. The total was also the best ever for a first year coach. Phoenix's strong home record of 35-6 was matched only by the Cleveland Cavaliers, and their road mark of 27-14 was the best in the league for the year and the best ever for the Suns.

After winning more games than any team in the league during the regular season (and thus winning home-court advantage throughout the playoffs), as well as boasting the most productive offense (the Suns 113.4 points per game was tops in the NBA), the team was the early favorite going into the playoffs. The defending champion Chicago Bulls were seemingly in decline and had struggled at times during the year.

Phoenix was an especially heavy favorite in the opening round, facing the Los Angeles Lakers, a team they had swept in five straight games during the year. The Lakers confounded the experts and the Suns, however, winning the first two games in Phoenix, 107-103 and 86-81, immediately placing the Suns on the brink of elimination right off the bat.

Because the first round of the playoffs is only a five-game set, one more loss would end the Suns's hopes. Phoenix rebounded, behind Barkley and Majerle, winning the next two games in Los Angeles 107-102 and 101-86. During the finale held in Phoenix, the Suns prevailed in overtime, 112-104.

In the second round Phoenix topped the San Antonio Spurs 4-2, and then faced a strong Seattle Supersonic team in the Conference title round. The two teams traded wins in Phoenix, with the Suns taking the first game 105-91 and dropping the second 103-99.

The scenario was replayed in Seattle as the Suns won the first game 104-97 and dropped the second 120-101. Back to Phoenix for the fifth game, won by the Suns, 120-114, but the Sonics came back to take the sixth game in Seattle, 118-102. Thus facing elimination again, the Suns rose to the occasion, winning 123-110.

That win set up the eagerly awaited clash between the Chicago Bulls and the Suns, featuring the league's most dominant and celebrated players—the Bulls's Mr. Everything, Michael Jordan, and the Suns's NBA MVP Charles Barkley.

The Bulls had roared through the East with ease, sweeping Atlanta 3-0 and Cleveland 4-0 before knocking out the New York Knicks 4-2. As they had against the Lakers, the Suns came in cold. They quickly fell 20 points behind in the opener before finally losing, 100-92,

Chicago also won the next game 111-108 and headed home with a seemingly insurmountable 2-0 series lead, with the next three games in the Windy City. Phoenix again fought back, winning a memorable triple overtime battle 129-121 in Chicago stadium, Kevin Johnson, who was below

par in the first two games, scored 25 points and set an all-time playoff record with a total of 63 minutes played in the game.

In game four, however, Jordan was virtually unstoppable, scoring 54 points and leading the Bulls to a 111-105 win and a 3-1 lead in the series. As they prepared for the fifth game in Chicago, the Suns were facing elimination for the fifth time in their long post season journey. But behind Barkley, Majerley, and Johnson, the Suns won 108- 98 to move the series back to Phoenix.

The Bulls again moved out to a significant lead in game six, one of the most memorable NBA games ever, but the Suns rallied in the third quarter and led by four points with 38 seconds left in the game. Jordan drove unmolested nearly the length of the floor to cut the lead to two. Majerle missed a three-pointer with 14.1 seconds left, and the Bulls called time out.

The ending seemed predestined—everyone watching could almost predict the ball was going to Jordan, but it eventually wound up in Jim Paxson's hands beyond the three-point line, and the Chicago reserve drilled it home to give the Bulls a one-point lead with 3.9 seconds left. After another timeout, the ball came in to Kevin Johnson, but his shot was blocked by Horace Grant and the Bulls had their third consecutive NBA Championship. For the Suns, it was close, as it had been against the Boston Celtics in 1976.

—*Jack Pearson*

PORTLAND TRAIL BLAZERS

Prior to 1970, the entire expanse of northwest America was represented by only one National Basketball Association team, the Seattle Supersonics. Residents of the sprawling mountain states of Oregon, Idaho, Montana, Wyoming, and Utah were given a new franchise to support on February 6, 1970, when Portland, Oregon, was granted an NBA team.

That team, subsequently named the Trail Blazers, would win phenomenal fan support as it charted its path through the Pacific Division in the NBA. Over the course of its first 23 years, the Blazers franchise qualified for post-season play 16 times and posted 14 winning seasons (including six with 50 wins or more). Even more impressively, in only its seventh year of existence it brought a world championship to its eager Oregon fans.

Portland's record of winning seasons has brought it unprecedented support in the region. Since the year following the Blazers' world championship in 1977, all Portland home games have been sellouts, a string of 656 games through 1993. Including playoff contests, the total is 726, an all-time NBA record and the longest streak in professional sports. In 941 regular season and 68 playoff games between 1970 and 1993, the Blazers have drawn nearly 11.8 million fans, an average of more than 11,600 a game.

Professional Basketball Comes to Oregon

Portland was granted its franchise at a February 6, 1970, meeting of the NBA Board of Governors in Los Angeles. Herman Sarkowsky, Robert Shmertz, and Lawrence Weinberg were named as the new team's principal owners, while Harry Glickman, who led the drive for a franchise, was elected Executive Vice President and General Manager.

Portland came into the league with two other newcomers, the Buffalo Braves and the Cleveland Cavaliers. It was the second expansion for the NBA in two years; the Milwaukee Bucks and the Phoenix Suns had been admitted in 1968. Prior to the second expansion, the league had been divided into only two divisions, the Eastern and Western. With the addition of Portland, Buffalo, and Cleveland, the NBA was forced to expand into four divisions, to be called the Atlantic, the Central, the Midwest and the Pacific.

Portland was placed into the Pacific Division along with the Los Angeles Lakers, the San Francisco Warriors, the Seattle Supersonics, and the Houston Rockets. Two weeks later, on February 20, Stu Inman was named as the club's first chief scout. Inman was expected to prepare for the upcoming college draft and initiate a program that would evaluate upcoming NBA-caliber talent.

The name "Trail Blazers" came into being on March 13, 1970, during an NBA regular season game between the New York Knicks and the Seattle Supersonics played in Portland's Memorial Coliseum. The title was announced at the game as the team's new name after a contest that had attracted some 10,000 entries.

Geoff Petrie of Princeton University became the team's first college draft selection on March 23, 1970. Then, on April 21, University of Nevada-Las Vegas coach Rolland Todd was named the first Trail Blazers head coach. In the NBA Expansion Draft on May 11, LeRoy Ellis of the Baltimore Bullets became the Blazers' first selection from the professional ranks.

The young Trail Blazers played their first preseason game on September 24 before 2,800 fans at Mark Morris High School in Laguna, Washington, losing 119-118 to San Francisco. Stan McKenzie and Jim Barnett led Portland with 23 points each. The opening of the team's first season was less than a month away.

The 1970 NBA season began on a high note for the Trail Blazers, as they defeated Cleveland 115-112 before 4,273 fans in Memorial Coliseum. NBA Commissioner Walter Kennedy, Oregon governor Tom McCall, and Portland mayor Terry Schrunk were honored guests at the game. The Blazers' starting lineup included 6-foot-10 LeRoy Ellis at center; 6-foot-6 McKenzie and 6-foot-6 Shaler Halimon at forward; and 6-foot-4 Geoff Petrie at one guard spot, while 6-foot-4 Jim Barnett and 6-foot-1 Rick Adelman shared the other guard spot. Adelman was elected as the team's first captain. Others on that first squad were center Dale Schlueter, center/forward Dorie Murrey, forwards Ed Manning, Gary Gregor, Ron Knight, Walt Gilmore, and Bill Stricker, and guard Claude English.

The First Season

Portland went on to post a 29-53 record in their inaugural season, fifth and last in their division. The team's record, however, was considerably better than those compiled by the other two expansion teams—Cleveland (15-67) and Buffalo (22-60). Indeed, the Trail Blazers displayed their trademark toughness at home even in their initial season, winning 18 of 39.

Geoff Petrie averaged 24.8 points a game, the seventh highest in the league, and shared Rookie of the Year honors with Boston's Dave Cowens. Petrie became only the second guard in the history of the league (Oscar Robertson was the other) to score more than 2,000 points in a year, totalling 2,031. He also became the first Trail Blazer to be named to an NBA All-Star Game. In addition to his prolific scoring he also paced the Blazers in minutes played, with 3,032, and in assists, with 390. Ellis, as expected, was the top board man, with 907 rebounds. Later the club traded Barnett to the San Francisco Warriors for three future draft picks and peddled Ellis to the Los Angeles Lakers for cash and a future draft choice.

With 29 wins under their belt in their first year in the league, the Trail Blazers and their fans had high hopes for an even better performance in 1971-72. All were disappointed. The club dropped to an 18-64 mark, the worst record in the entire league. The Blazers finished a whopping 51 games behind the division-leading Los Angeles Lakers,

TEAM INFORMATION AT A GLANCE

Founding date: February 6, 1970

Home court:
Memorial Coliseum
1401 North Weaver
Portland, OR 97227
Phone: (503) 235-8771

Seating capacity: 12,884

Team nickname: Trail Blazers
Team colors: Scarlet, black, and white

Franchise record	Won	Lost	Pct.
(1970-92)	994	892	.527

League championships (1): 1976-77
Division/conference first-place finishes (3): 1977-78, 1990-91, 1991-92

the greatest difference between a first- and last-place team in NBA history, after being only 19 games behind at the end of the previous year.

The Lakers, of course, had a record 69 wins, but Portland was also 16 games behind the fourth place Houston Rockets. The lackluster performance cost head coach Rolland Todd his job. He was dismissed three-quarters of the way through the season after leading the team to a 12-44 record. Chief scout Stu Inman took over for the last 26 games, putting together a 6-20 mark. On April 3 the Blazers dipped into the college ranks again for a new head coach, naming Jack McCloskey of Wake Forest as their new mentor.

First round draft pick Sidney Wicks from UCLA became one of the only bright spots for the 1971-72 team, scoring at a 24.5 per game pace and totalling 2,009 points. He was named to the NBA All-Rookie team as well as the annual All-Star contest. Wicks not only led the team in scoring,

he paced Portland in rebounds as well, with 943, and was second to guard Rick Adelman (who had 413) in assists with 350. A knee injury hampered Geoff Petrie for most of the year and his scoring average fell to 18.9 points a game.

McCloskey Arrives

Under new Head Coach Jack McCloskey—the team's third coach in three years—the 1972-73 Blazers managed to eke out a season that was a slight improvement over the previous year's finish. The club's 21-61 record again relegated them to last place in the Pacific Division. On the court, guard Geoff Petrie regained his scoring touch, pumping home a team record 24.9 points a game.

Second-year forward Sidney Wicks added a 23.8 points per game performance and led the club with 440 assists. The two players gave the Blazers one of the best one-two scoring punches in the league. On January 20, 1973, Petrie scored 51 points against the Houston Rockets, the first Blazer ever to reach 50 or more in a game; he then duplicated the 51 points against the same team on March 16.

Two of the club's top draft choices, forward Ollie Johnson of Temple and center Lloyd Neal of Tennessee State, made the starting lineup. Neal went on to score an average of 13.4 points a game and led the team in rebounds with 967, still a Portland record. His efforts earned him a spot on the NBA All-Rookie team.

Six more wins in 1973-74 (27-55) were not enough to get the Blazers out of the Pacific Division cellar or to save coach Jack McCloskey's job. The Blazers did move closer to the other teams in the division—only three games separated Portland from fourth-place Phoenix in the division. They were also winners at home for the first time in their four years in the league, taking 22 of 41 in Portland. On the road, however, they posted the worst record in the league, winning only five of 39 (two games were at neutral sites).

Prior to the season the Blazers acquired forward John Johnson and center Rick Roberson from the Los Angeles Lakers for future draft considerations. Both became starters. Geoff Petrie was again among the NBA's leaders in scoring, averaging 24.3 points a game, seventh highest in the league. He was supported by Larry Steele, who swiped 217 steals over the course of the season for a 2.7 per-game average, tops in the NBA. Sidney Wicks averaged 22.6 points per game, his third year in a row over the 20 mark, and again led the team in assists, with 326.

Building to a Championship

On May 4, 1974, UCLA All-American Bill Walton signed a Portland contract, turning down offers from the rival American Basketball Association to do so. The arrival of the big redhead proved to be a pivotal moment for the franchise. Two weeks later McCloskey was released as the team's coach, and then on May 24 former NBA standout Lenny Wilkins was named as the team's new head coach.

The 1974-75 season found the Blazers out of the cellar for the first time in their history, with the most wins ever for the team. Their 38-44 record moved them up into third place in the Pacific Division, six games ahead of the Phoenix Suns and eight ahead of the Los Angeles Lakers. At home in 1974-75 the Blazers won a record 28 games. Sidney Wicks (21.9 points a game) and Geoff Petrie (18.3) continued to pace the team in scoring, although both averages were down from a year earlier. Wicks was named to the annual All-Star Game.

Rookie Bill Walton averaged 12.8 points a game and was leading the club in rebounding before suffering a foot injury that caused him to miss the last 47 games of the season. Forward John Johnson chipped in with a 16.1 scoring average, while Lloyd Neal averaged 12.3 points a game in the pivot after Walton's injury. Wicks took rebounding honors for the year with 877, while Petrie led the team in assists for the first time since his rookie season, dishing out 424. On February 26 Wicks hauled down 27 rebounds in a game in Los Angeles for a team record which still stands.

Early in 1975 Larry Weinberg became the new president of the franchise, which was quickly growing in popularity throughout the region. Average attendance jumped over 10,000 a game for the first time as 441,506 fans passed through the turnstiles at Memorial Coliseum during the course of the season.

The Blazers' 1975-76 win total dropped by only one from the previous year, yet the club found itself once again in the cellar of the competitive Pacific Division, 22 games behind the division champ Golden State Warriors. At home, though, the Blazers again put on a good show for their fans, winning 26 against 15 losses.

A primary trouble spot for the Trail Blazers was the continuing series of injuries to center Bill Walton, the cornerstone of the team when he was able to play. The big redhead's broken ankle limited him to only 51 games. Prior to the mishap he

PROFILE	Bill Walton

One of the greatest players in Portland history (as well as one of the most injury-prone), center Bill Walton was in a Blazers uniform for only portions of four seasons. The most regular season games he ever managed to stay healthy for in a single campaign was 65; in the 328 games Portland played in the four years between 1974 and 1978, he played in less than two-thirds of them (209).

Nevertheless, Walton is the only player ever to wear a Portland Trail Blazers jersey to be elected to the National Basketball Association Hall of Fame (in 1993); he was the primary reason for the Blazers' one and only NBA Championship.

Walton compiled an outstanding record while an underclassman at UCLA. He was named to the *Sporting News* All-American teams for three consecutive years and garnered College Player of the Year honors. He was the NCAA Tournament's Outstanding Player in both 1972 and 1973 and was on the NCAA Championship Team in both of those years. He holds the NCAA record for having the highest field goal completion percentage over the course of one tournament— .763.

Naismith Memorial Basketball Hall of Fame

Walton was the object of a spirited bidding war between the ABA and the NBA before finally signing with Portland. His third year with the Blazers was his best; he averaged 18.6 points a game, and despite playing in only 65 games, led the team in rebounds with 934 and in blocked shots, with 211. His rebounding average that year, 14.4, is still a Blazers record. He was also a tremendous passer, and was the primary trigger for the Blazers vaunted fast break. He was also voted the Playoff Most Valuable Player and was named to the league's All-Defensive Team.

Walton left the Blazers in acrimony following the 1978-79 season, in which he sat out the entire year with a stress fracture of his foot. He charged that the Blazers management forced him to play when he was injured. Angry, the big redhead refused to play for Portland any longer. When he eventually signed on with San Diego in May of 1979 as the first veteran free agent ever in the NBA, Portland received Kevin Kunnert, Kermit Washington, a first-round draft pick, and cash in compensation. Walton played for San Diego for three years and then moved on to Boston, where he played sparingly for a couple of seasons.

He played on two NBA Championship teams, one with Portland, the other with Boston. He ended his career with a total of 6,215 points and a 13.3 scoring average as well as 4,923 rebounds; the statistics from for his Blazers days only were 3,578 points, a 17.1 scoring average, and 2,822 rebounds.

Walton was voted as the league's MVP in 1977-78; was named to the All-NBA Team in both 1976-77 and 1977-78; made the league's All-Defensive Team for the same two years; and participated in two All-Star Games. His number, 32, was retired at the Blazers' 20th Anniversary Night on November 3, 1989.

was scoring at a 16.1 clip and had the team lead in rebounds with 681.

Sidney Wicks's average dropped for the fourth straight year, to 19.1 points a game, but it was still good enough to lead the team. With Walton missing the last third of the season, Wicks pulled into the rebounding lead with 712. Geoff Petrie was close behind Wicks in scoring with a 18.9 average, and led the team in assists with 330. Another piece of the puzzle had also been solved with the addition of Lionel Hollins, who averaged 10.8 points per game on his way to being selected to the NBA All-Rookie team. Nonetheless, the absence of Walton was a blow that dashed the club's playoff hopes.

Jack Ramsay, who had led the Buffalo Braves to three straight playoff appearances, was named as the team's new head coach in 1976, replacing Lenny Wilkens. He named Jack McKinney as his assistant. In the annual college draft, the Blazers selected Wally Walker of Virginia as their first round pick.

Championship Fever

Professional basketball fans were in for a big surprise as the Trail Blazers moved into their 1976-77 season. No one expected a team that had finished in last place the year before to win the Pacific Division, let alone the world championship. The Blazers, however, clicked on all cylinders throughout the campaign, and the faithful fans in Portland have been rewarding the team ever since with record-setting attendance and enthusiasm. Under new head coach Jack Ramsay and controversial center Bill Walton, who was healthy for most of the season, the 1976-77 Trail Blazers won the National Basketball League championship. In only their seventh year in the league they were on top of the world.

The success was even more astounding because prior to the season new head coach Ramsay made a major and controversial move by trading away the team's two most popular and high scoring players, Geoff Petrie and Sidney Wicks. The trade of Wicks was made possible when the team picked up Lucas in the ABA disposal draft. Controversial though these decisions may have been, they certainly contributed to the Blazers' championship drive.

The season was in fact the first one in which the team won more games than it lost and the first in which they qualified for post-season play. Their 49-33 mark was good for second place in the Pacific Division, four games back of the resurgent Los Angeles Lakers and their MVP pivotman Kareem Abdul-Jabbar. At home, where attendance surged to an average of 12,178 a game, nearly double their first-year figure, the Blazers won a team record 35 of 41 games.

In the playoffs Portland gave little early indication of the miracle that was about to occur. In the first round they edged the Chicago Bulls 2-1, raising few eyebrows. But then they outfought a strong Denver squad 4-2 to move into the Western finals against Los Angeles. Underdogs against the powerful Laker club, the Blazers astounded everyone but themselves by sweeping the Californians 4-0, winning the last three games by a total of only 11 points.

In the finals against the Atlantic Champion Philadelphia 76ers, a squad dotted with such stars as Julius Erving and George McGinnis, the Blazers lost the first two games and appeared to have finally run out of gas. The club rebounded, though, and whipped the 76ers in the next four games, securing the crown.

The finale, a 109-107 thriller in Memorial Coliseum in Portland, ignited what was later to be called "Blazermania." The city of Portland and the entire state of Oregon enjoyed a celebratory explosion that firmly entrenched the team in the city's consciousness. From the time of that NBA finale in early 1977 on through the 1993-94 season—16 consecutive years—every Portland Trail Blazer home game has been sold out.

Bill Walton culminated a tremendous season in that championship game, scoring 20 points, pulling down 23 rebounds, blocking eight shots and even dishing out seven assists. He was a unanimous choice for the playoffs Most Valuable Player

| PROFILE | Kiki Vandeweghe |

When Portland traded for Kiki Vandeweghe on June 7, 1984, the high-scoring forward had just completed a banner (29.4 points a game) season for the Denver Nuggets. To obtain Vandeweghe, the Blazers sent Calvin Natt, Lafayette Lever, Wayne Cooper, a first-round pick in 1985, and a second round selection in 1984 to Denver.

In Portland, under coach Jack Ramsay's more controlled offensive patterns, however, Vandeweghe's output was somewhat curtailed. The 6-foot-8 forward still put together four consecutive 20-plus scoring seasons— 22.4, 24.9; 26.9, and 20.2. His 26.9 single-season scoring average and 2,122 total points in 1986-87 both set new Blazers records, since topped by Clyde Drexler.

Vandeweghe still holds the highest career scoring average in Portland history, 23.5 points a game over five seasons and 285 games. He was a tremendous marksman, as evidenced by his career averages of .526 in field goal attempts and .881 from the free throw line. His 48 points against Seattle on March 5, 1987, and 47 against Kansas City on Oct. 23, 1984, were personal highs for him in Portland and are still among the top seven individual efforts by a Blazers player in one game.

After 18 games of the 1988-89 season Portland traded him to the New York Knicks for a future draft choice. For his four and a quarter seasons with the team he totalled 6,698 points.

award. During the year, he was also the first Blazer ever honored with selection to the NBA's All-Defensive Team. Walton averaged 18.6 points a game, averaged a league-leading 14.4 rebounds per game, averaged a league-leading 3.25 blocks per game, and was a demon on defense.

Both Walton and forward Maurice Lucas, whose 11.4 rebounds per game was ninth in the league, were named to the annual All-Star Game. Lucas was also the club's top scorer, with a 20.2 average. The other starters on that Blazer championship team were guard Lionel Hollins, who had a 14.7 scoring average and led the team with 313 assists; forward Bob Gross; and guard Dave Twardzik. Key reserves include Larry Steele, Herm Gilliam, and Johnny Davis.

As champions of the professional basketball world, expectations were high for the Trail Blazers in 1977-78. The club responded with a 58-24 mark, the best record in the NBA for the season, and one that was good enough for their first divisional crown. Running over the field in the Pacific Division, easily the most competitive division in the league, the Blazers finished nine games ahead of the second-place Phoenix Suns. At home the

Blazers again posted an exceptional 36-5 mark.

The team actually was on its way to an even more glittering record, rolling off to a 50-10 start before their MVP center Bill Walton was forced out of the game. Walton, the first Portland player ever to win an NBA Most Valuable Player Award, went down with what at first seemed to be a minor foot injury. It was eventually diagnosed as a stress fracture, and the team finished at 8-14 without him. Then, to add insult to injury, Walton was able to play sparingly in only two playoff games, and the Blazers fell in their first series, the semifinals, to the Seattle Supersonics.

Walton was not the only Portland player to be felled by injuries. Forward Bob Gross missed the last ten games of the year and all playoff games with a broken ankle, and forward-center Lloyd Neal missed 21 games with a knee injury. Prior to his mishap Walton was leading the team in scoring with an 18.9 average and again was the team leader in rebounds with 766. His blocked shot total of 146 was also a team high.

During the year the club had a balanced scoring attack, with seven players in double figures. Hollins again led the team in assists with 380 and in steals with 157. Walton and Lucas were named to the All-Star team; Walton again was named to the league's All-Defensive squad; and Walton, Lucas, and Hollins were the team's representatives at the annual All-Star Game.

Bill Walton's injury that had ended Portland's hopes prior to the 1977-78 playoffs was even worse than the Blazer faithful had feared, and the great but fragile center sat out the entire 1978-79 season. Even without him the club continued to play exceptionally well at home, posting a 33-8 won-loss mark in Memorial Coliseum, one of the two best home records in the league. But on the road the Blazers could win only 12 of 41 games and dropped to an overall 45-37 record and fourth place in the Pacific Division. The Trail Blazers were eliminated by Phoenix in the playoffs.

Walton Exits

The team was then rocked by controversy. Walton publicly criticized Portland officials for forcing him to play during the 1977-78 season while he had a broken foot; he announced that he would not return to the team and demanded to be traded. Walton expressed a preference to play in warm Southern California, and eventually wound up with the San Diego Clippers, who agreed to pay Portland compensation for his services.

Center Tom Owens did a yeoman's job of filling in for Walton, however, leading the team with 1,520 points (18.5 per game average) and 740 rebounds. Forward Maurice Lucas had the top scoring average (20.4) in a season abbreviated by injuries.

Lucas was the only Portland player named to the 1979 All-Star game, which was coached by Portland mentor Jack Ramsay. It was the first time a Portland coach had ever called the shots at an All-Star contest. Steady Lionel Hollins was third on the team with a 15.3 scoring average, but was the leader in assists (325) and steals (114) for the third consecutive year.

Portland had two first-round draft picks the following year; the club selected center Mychal

Thompson and swingman Ron Brewer, both of whom played their college ball at Minnesota. Thompson responded with a 14.7 scoring mark in 1978-79, while Brewer chipped in with a 13.3 average. Both were named to the NBA All-Rookie team, the first time two Blazers had been named to that annual honorary squad. On March 24, 1979, the Blazers retired Lloyd Neal's number 36, the first player so honored by the club. Following the season assistant coach Jack McKinney resigned to become the head coach for the Los Angeles Lakers.

On September 18th Portland received Kermit Washington, Randy Smith, Kevin Kunnert, and a future draft pick from San Diego in compensation for the Clippers signing of Bill Walton. San Diego fans quickly learned what it was like having the talented but brittle Walton on their club as the redhead again injured his foot and played only 14 games for the Clippers.

The Trail Blazers jumped out to a fine start at the beginning of the 1979-80 season. The club posted a 9-2 record in October, the most wins ever for a Portland team in the first month of the season, but the Blazers sagged throughout the rest of the 1979-80 campaign and fell to a 38-44 mark, their first losing season under coach Jack Ramsay. The record dropped them to fourth place in the division, 22 games behind the Pacific Division winners, the Los Angeles Lakers. Injuries were again a key. Center-forward Mychal Thompson was lost for the entire season with a broken leg. The club did make a brief appearance in the postseason before being eliminated by the Seattle Supersonics.

Personnel Changes

The season was marked by several other key personnel changes in addition to the Walton transaction. The Blazers traded guard Lionel Hollins on February 8 to Philadelphia for a future draft pick, then traded that pick for Kelvin Ransey. On the same day Portland peddled forward Maurice Lucas to New Jersey for Calvin Natt. Thus by the

PROFILE	Maurice Lucas

As an undergraduate at Marquette University in Milwaukee, Maurice Lucas had been dubbed the "Aircraft Carrier" by his colorful coach, Al McGuire, in an attempt to describe how Lucas dominated the battle arena. He continued to solidify his menacing reputation in the professional ranks, using his 6-foot-9 height and great strength not only to become one of the league's top rebounders, but to become an excellent scorer as well.

Lucas originally played professional basketball with the old ABA Kentucky Colonels. But within two years the league folded and he was drafted by the Portland franchise in the NBA in the first round of the dispersal draft.

Lucas made an immediate impact, leading the Blazers in scoring in his first year with a 20.2 average and teaming with center Bill Walton to lead Portland to its first and only NBA championship. During the year Lucas hauled down 899 rebounds, ninth best in the league. Lucas also led the club in scoring throughout the playoffs, averaging 21.2 points per game.

Lucas's output dropped during his second year, as he averaged 16.4 points a game to go with 621 rebounds, but he bounced back in 1978-79 to a 20.4 scoring mark, again high for the team. Injuries plagued him during the next year, and he was subsequently traded midway through the season to the New Jersey Nets for Calvin Natt.

After a number of years with the Nets, the Phoenix Suns, and Seattle, he returned to the site of his most rewarding days as a pro. Lucas was reacquired in 1987 from the Supersonics for Portland's 1990 second-round draft choice. Used as a key reserve throughout the season, he retired with a total of 330 games played for Portland and a 15.6 career scoring average.

For his entire career Lucas played in 855 games and averaged 14.4 points a game for a total of 12,339 points. He still ranks seventh on the all-time Portland list in rebounds and tenth in blocked shots. Lucas made the All-Defensive Team in 1977-78, and was named to three All-Star games, in 1977, 1978 and 1979.

---

end of the season several key members of the World Championship team of just three years ago were gone.

Washington started at power forward and led the team in rebounding with a total of 842, as well as in blocked shots with 131, and scored at a 13.4 pace. Natt, playing only 25 games with the Blazers after the trade, averaged 20.4 points a game. The scoring leader for the entire year, however, was center Tom Owens, who averaged 16.4 points a game. Guard Ron Brewer was close behind at 15.9.

The Blazers returned to the winning side of the ledger for the 1980-81 season, winning 45 games and moving up a notch in Pacific Division play to third place. The improvement was over-shadowed, however, by failure of the club to advance past the first round of the playoffs for the fourth straight year. For the season the Blazers exhibited a balanced scoring attack. Second-year backcourt man Jim Paxson scored 1,354 points for a 17.1 average; center Mychal Thompson returned to tally 1,345 points and a 17-point average; guard Kelvin Ransey, who was named to the league's All-Rookie team, averaged 15.2; and reserve sharpshooter Billy Ray Bates posted a 13.8 average.

Two significant transactions took place prior to and just following the 1980-81 season; one turned out to be most fortuitous; the other became a tremendous lost opportunity for the club. On August 15, 1980, the team traded T.R. Dunn to the

Denver Nuggets for a 1983 first-round draft choice, a selection which enabled the Blazers to eventually draft Clyde Drexler. That was the fortuitous action. But then on June 5, 1981, the club traded backup center Tom Owens to the Indiana Pacers for a 1984 first-round draft choice. The Blazers used that selection in 1984 to draft center Sam Bowie, who has suffered a number of debilitating injuries during his pro career, instead of Akeem Olajuwon or Michael Jordan, both of whom were available.

Despite Mychal Thompson's improvement in the pivot for Portland—he had a team-leading 20.8 scoring average and 921 rebounds, the latter the fourth highest in the entire league for the season—the 1981-82 Blazers remained a mediocre club. The team's won-loss mark for the campaign was 42-40, a performance that dropped them into fifth place in the Pacific Division, 15 games behind the eventual NBA Champion Los Angeles Lakers. The decline dropped the Blazers out of playoff competition for the first time in six years.

On October 11, 1981, the Portland club retired three more jersey numbers, Geoff Petrie's 45, Larry Steele's 15 and Dave Twardzik's 13. On January 5, 1982, the club sold out its 200th consecutive game in Memorial Coliseum. Just two

months later, on March 18, the five millionth fan passed through the gates at the Coliseum. It was only the second time in NBA history that a total of five million had been reached within 12 years; Seattle was the first. The Pacific Northwest had indeed proven fertile ground for NBA basketball.

Other Blazer business that year included a trade of Kelvin Ransey to Dallas for Wayne Cooper and a future draft choice on June 28. That future choice turned out to be Terry Porter, who would go on to become one of the Blazers' finest talents.

The 1982-83 Blazers clawed their way to 46 wins for the year, their highest total in five years, and returned to post-season play after a one-year absence. In the playoffs the club won its first series since the championship year of 1976-77, sweeping Seattle 2-0 with 108-97 and 105-98 wins. The Blazers advanced to the second round, only to face Pacific Division kingpin Los Angeles, who eliminated them in five games, 4-1.

For the first time in three years the Blazers had a representative at the annual All-Star Game—Jim Paxson, who led the club in scoring with a 21.7 mark. Forward Calvin Natt was also over the 20-point level, hitting 20.4, while Mychal Thompson added a 15.7 average and led in rebounding with

753. First-round draft pick Lafayette Lever led the club in both assists (426) and steals (153), while backup center Wayne Cooper led in blocked shots with 136.

On January 7, 1983, the team obtained the services of guard Don Buse from the Indiana Pacers for cash and future considerations. Following the season, on June 21, former player Rick Adelman was named assistant coach; he replaced Jim Lynam, who left to take the head coaching job with the San Diego Clippers.

The 48 wins for the Blazers in 1983-84 marked their third highest win total since coming into the league. The season also marked the first for first-round draft pick Clyde Drexler, who would go on to become the greatest of all Blazer players. Portland's 48-34 record was good enough to move the team into second place in the tough Pacific Division, only six games behind leader Los Angeles. Unfortunately, the Blazers continued their annual post-season swoon, losing again in the first round to Phoenix.

Jim Paxson, the only Blazer invited to play in the All-Star Game, again led the team in scoring, with a 21.3 average. Other Blazers in double figures included forward Calvin Natt, at 16.2; center Mychal Thompson, at 15.7; and forward Kenny Carr, at 15.6. Drexler, brought along slowly by Coach Ramsay, averaged only 7.7 points a game in his first NBA season. Thompson again was the big man on the boards, grabbing 688 rebounds. Guard Darnell Valentine dished out 395 assists to pace the team in that category.

Team Milestones Reached

The 1983-84 campaign was marked by several records and milestones for the Trail Blazer team. On November 22, 1983, Portland scored 156 points in beating Denver, the most points ever scored by the team in a single game. On March 3, 1984, the team sold out its 300th consecutive game, and on March 29 a 120-113 win over Kansas City marked Coach Jack Ramsay's 700th NBA victory. Following the season Portland traded Lever and Cooper and future draft picks to the Denver Nuggets for high scoring Kiki Vandeweghe.

For the first time in 1984-85, the Pacific Division had more teams with losing than with winning records. Thus the Blazers' 42-40 won-loss record was good enough for another second-place finish. It was the team's fifth straight winning season. However, unlike the scenario in 1983-84 when their 48 wins placed them only six games behind Los Angeles, their 42 wins in 1984-85 found them a whopping 20 games back of the Lakers.

The addition of Kiki Vandeweghe (22.4 points per game) and the emergence of second-year man Clyde Drexler (17.2) as a scoring threat added punch to the Blazer attack that season. Mychal Thompson, moved to power forward to make room for first round draft pick Sam Bowie at center, scored 18.4 points per game in his new role, and guard Jim Paxson added 17.9. Bowie led the club in rebounds, with 654, and in blocked shots, with 203. Guard Darnel Valentine led in assists, with 522, while Drexler's 177 steals led the team.

In the 1985 playoffs Portland defeated Dallas 3-1, with two of the games overtime triumphs, but the club lost in the second round to the eventual NBA Champion Los Angeles Lakers 4-1.

Before the 1985 season began, the Blazers selected little-known Terry Porter of the University of Wisconsin-Stevens Point in the NBA draft. Once the season began, the Blazers performed well enough through the first three months of the season, but a 12-game losing streak in February, the second longest in team history, was more than they could overcome and the squad dropped to a 40-42 record, the team's first losing season in six years.

The normally strong Pacific Division saw five of its six teams come up with losing records, with the Blazers' 40-42 mark actually good enough for second place, although the mark was a distant 22 games behind the perennially tough Los Angeles Lakers.

Drexler and Vandeweghe again led the team;

Drexler continued his development into one of the league's top all-around talents, while Vandeweghe enjoyed another fine season, moving into the top ten in the NBA in scoring with his 24.8 average, good for sixth place in the league. Despite their best efforts, however, Portland's visit to the postseason was, once again, a brief one: the club was trounced in the first round of the playoffs by the Denver Nuggets.

Coach Ramsay Leaves

The 1985-86 season also saw Coach Jack Ramsay leave the team to take on the head coaching duties for the Indiana Pacers. In ten years Ramsay had led the Portland squad to a 453-367 record in the regular season, with eight winning records out of ten, a 29-30 mark in the playoffs and one world championship. On May 28 Mike Schu-ler was named as his replacement.

In 1986-87, new head coach Mike Schuler was named NBA Coach of the Year over several other deserving coaches around the league after leading the Blazers to 49 wins in his first season. NBA observers noted ironically that Jack Ramsay, one of the league's most highly regarded coaches, hadn't garnered Coach of the Year honors in any of his ten illustrious years at the helm of the club.

During the season Kiki Vandeweghe enjoyed his greatest year in the pro ranks, scoring 2,122 points for a 26.9 per game average, both new Blazers records. His scoring average was the fifth highest in the league and his free throw completion percentage, .886, was seventh best.

Clyde Drexler also continued to improve, moving up to a 21.7 scoring average, leading the team in steals with 204, and adding 566 assists. In the steal category his total was fifth best in the league. Drexler became only the third player in NBA history (along with Larry Bird and Magic Johnson) to average 21 points or more per game in a season while at the same time averaging at least six rebounds and six assists.

Center Sam Bowie got off to what might have been his best year, but broke his leg after only five games. Steve Johnson, obtained in a trade with San Antonio for Mychal Thompson, contributed a 16.8 scoring average, while second-year man Terry Porter stepped into a starting role at point guard, averaged 13.1 points a game, and led the club in assists with 715. That latter total was a new team record. As a team the 1986-87 Blazers averaged 117.9 points a game, high for the entire NBA for the year. On March 19, 1987, Harry Glickman, a founder of the team and most recently its Executive Vice President, was named the Blazers' president.

In the 1987 playoffs the Blazers continued reading from the same old script, losing in the first round to Houston, three games to one. The Pacific Division champion Los Angeles Lakers repeated as NBA kingpins.

The Blazers Build Up Steam

During the 1987-88 campaign, Blazers guard Clyde Drexler emerged as one of the shining stars of the NBA and finished in fifth place in the balloting for league Most Valuable Player. The silky-smooth Drexler upped his scoring output to 2,185 points and a 27-point average. Both figures were team records, besting marks set the previous year by teammate Kiki Vandeweghe. During the season he was named as Player of the Week three times and became the first player in NBA history to win the award on consecutive weeks. He was voted the team's MVP by his teammates, and scored a personal best 42 points on three separate dates.

As a team the Blazers won 53 games, the second highest in their history, but finished second again in the Pacific Division, nine games behind their seemingly eternal nemesis, the Los Angeles Lakers. The frustrating trend of first-round departures from the playoffs continued that season as the Blazers bowed to the Utah Jazz.

While the sun was rising on Drexler's game, it was on the decline for Vandeweghe, who was limited to 37 games by injuries and saw his scoring average drop to 20.2 points a game, his low-

PROFILE — Clyde Drexler

Clyde Drexler is essentially Portland's "Mr. Franchise." He is the all-time Portland Trail Blazers leader in more major categories than all other players who ever played for the team combined. Drexler leads the Trail Blazers in total points, with 15,833. No one else is even close. He is the leader in total games played, 758; in minutes played, with 25,734; and in offensive rebounds, 1,989.

He also ranks as Portland's all-time leader in field goal attempts, field goals made, free throw attempts, and free throws made, to name just a few other categories. He was also second in total rebounds, with 9,660, at the outset of the 1993-94 season and is expected to move into first place in that statistic as well. He is also second on the all-time Blazers list for three-point field goals.

AP/Wide World Photos

Drexler has been named to the annual NBA All-Star Game seven times. No other Portland player has made the classic more than four times. He has led the Blazers in scoring for six consecutive years, and his total of 2,185 points during the 1987-88 season and his 27.2 scoring average the following year are both Blazers records.

Drexler is only the second Portland player to lead in scoring, assists, and steals in the same year. His scoring totals, in addition to leading the team, were fourth in the NBA in 1988-89 and 1991-92, and sixth in 1987-88. His assist total in 1985-86 placed him tenth in the league; and his steals total in 1985-86 placed him third in the entire league.

Drexler's long list of honors includes, in addition to those seven All-Star Games, a second-place finish in the balloting for league MVP in the 1992-93 season and inclusion in 1992 on the U.S. Basketball Team, the "Dream Team," in the Summer Olympics.

---

est output in seven years. Other Blazer players came to the fore during the year. Forward Jerome Kersey also hiked his offensive performance, moving from a 12.3 average in 1986-87 to 19.2 points per game. He also led the club in rebounding with 657.

Center Kevin Duckworth had his best year as a Blazer, averaging 15.8 points a game, while guard Terry Porter dished out 831 assists, a Port-

land record which still stands, to go with a 14.9 scoring average.

In 43 games Steve Johnson averaged 15.4 points per contest, earning a berth at the 1988 All-Star game along with Drexler. The 1988 season was also marked by a change in ownership, as Larry Weinberg announced on May 31 that he had sold the team to Seattle computer magnate Paul Allen, co-founder of Microsoft.

The Portland club had high hopes going into the 1988-89 campaign; the club was both young and talented. Yet Blazers Head Coach Mike Schuler—NBA Coach of the Year in 1986-87—was fired two-thirds of the way through his third season. Theories and rumors abounded as to the reason (difficulties with Drexler was one oft-heard reason, a disappointing record was another). Professional basketball coaching history is littered with tales of similar swift falls from grace.

Schuler was relieved of his duties on February 18, 1989. At the time the team's record was 25-22. Assistant coach Rick Adelman, a player for the club in its early days, was named to replace him on an interim basis. On February 23 the team traded Kiki Vandeweghe to New York in exchange for a 1989 first-round draft pick. Vandeweghe had played 18 games at that point and was averaging 13.9 points a game. For the remainder of the season Adelman's record was 14-21. In the playoffs the tune was a familiar one, with Portland being swept by the Los Angeles Lakers, three games to none.

Clyde Drexler obliterated Portland scoring records during the season as he compiled 2,123 points and a 27.2 scoring average. The average was fourth highest in the league for the season. He also led the team in steals, with 213, a total that was fifth highest in the league. Terry Porter upped his scoring again, to 17.7 points per game, and finished fourth in the NBA in assists, with 770. Center Kevin Duckworth, who averaged 18.1 scoring, joined Drexler on the annual All-Star game squad, and Jerome Kersey scored at a 17.5 clip.

Adelman Delivers

Rick Adelman, given the permanent head coaching job on the basis of his performance at the helm the previous season, silenced his critics in 1989-90 by leading the Blazers to a 59-23 record, the most wins in a single season ever for a Portland team. There was only one other team in the entire NBA with more victories; unfortunately it was longtime division foe Los Angeles, who put together a 63-win campaign. So the Trail Blazers were held to another second-place finish, despite their lofty win total.

The season was nonetheless a fine one. Aided by newcomer Buck Williams, a power forward acquired in an off-season trade involving center Sam Bowie, the club proved particularly adept at winning on the road, a difficult feat in the NBA. The team was 24-17 away from the friendly confines of Memorial Coliseum in Portland, the second best road mark in the league. The season also featured the retirement of Bill Walton's number.

In all there were five new faces on the Blazers' roster for the 1989-90 season; in addition to Williams, Portland added another power forward in Cliff Robinson; journeyman center Wayne Cooper, back with the team after a six-year absence; forward Nate Johnson; and a young Yugoslavian player, Drazen Petrovic. The latter, despite playing only in a back-up role, led the team in three-point shooting, hitting on 34 of 74 for a .459 mark, a completion percentage that was also third highest in the entire league.

Clyde Drexler once again led the team in scoring with 1,703 points and a 23.3 average (he also became the club's all-time leading scorer); he was followed by Terry Porter at 17.6; Kevin Duckworth at 16.2; and Jerome Kersey, at 16 points a game. Williams paced the team in rebounding, pulling down an even 800, the highest total for the Blazers in eight years. Porter again led in assists, with 726, eighth best in the NBA, and in steals, with 151; while Cooper blocked 95 shots to lead in that category. Drexler—for the fourth time, and Duckworth—for the second, made the 1990 All-Star Game lineup, and Williams was named to the NBA's All-Defensive Team.

Galvanized by their 59-win season, Portland finally made some noise in the playoffs. In the initial playoff encounter the Blazers swept Dallas, then outfought a tough San Antonio club 4-3 in a series in which two of the last Portland wins were in overtime. In the Western finals the team toppled Phoenix 4-2 to qualify to vie for the championship for only the second time in its history.

The Trail Blazers faced the defending cham-

PROFILE	Terry Porter

When Portland made Terry Porter their number-one draft selection in 1985, more than one eyebrow was raised. "Who is Terry Porter? What is UW-Stevens Point?" the doubters asked. They learned soon enough that the 6-foot-3 Porter was well worth the high pick. He has gone on to put in eight outstanding years as the Blazers' playmaking guard, rewriting the Portland record book in the process.

In addition to his ball handling prowess, Porter has become one of the most consistent scorers on the club and one of the league's top three-point marksmen. Over the past five years he has consistently averaged 17 to 18 points a game. An extremely durable player as well, Porter has played in 79 or more games in every year in the league. He holds the all-time single game assist mark for the team—19—set on April 14, 1988, against Utah.

He has dished out 18 assists twice and 17 five times. Only one other player has totaled 17 even once for the Blazers—head coach Rick Adelman, back in his playing days. For his career Porter is the franchise's leader in career assists, with 4,785; is second on the team in total points scored, with 10,008, and in steals, with 1,071; is third in games played, with 645; and tenth in rebounds, with 2,316.

Porter was selected to the All-Star game in 1993, the second time he has been so honored. He was also named the second annual recipient of the J. Walter Kennedy Award given to an NBA player, coach or trainer for meritorious community service. During his years as a Blazers player, Porter has helped raise more than a million dollars for Portland area charities.

pion Detroit Pistons in the championship series. When the Blazers split the first two games of the series in Detroit, Blazer fans were ecstatic, for the Pistons had dropped 20 straight regular season games to the Trail Blazers out in Portland, where the next three games would be played. Indeed, it had been 16 years since the Pistons had won out on the Blazers home turf.

The three games in Portland took a nightmarish turn for the Blazers, however, as they dropped all three contests to the Bad Boys from Detroit. The Pistons' defense, coupled with their sharpshooting trio of guards—Isiah Thomas, Joe Dumars, and Vinnie Johnson—proved too much for the Trail Blazers to handle. Drexler led the Portland effort with a 26.4 scoring average for the season, and Kersey and Porter enjoyed fine moments during the series as well. In the end, though, the Blazers were thwarted one step short of the crown.

The 1989-90 campaign was a satisfying season, one that Portland fans have recalled with pride. One of the lasting ramifications of the year was Drexler's emergence as a national NBA star.

Never one to court the limelight, Drexler preferred to confine his public activities to the Portland area. His on-court ability could no longer be kept a secret, however, and his performance in the playoffs in 1989 signaled his emergence as one of the premier talents in the NBA.

Continued Success

The Trail Blazers uncorked another division-leading season in 1990-91. In only his second full year at the controls, Coach Rick Adelman led Portland to a 63-19 record, breaking the total win mark set just the year before. The total was also the most in the entire league for the year, and gave the Blazers the Pacific Division title, their second in 21 years. Portland got off to a roaring start, winning its first 11 games and 19 of its first 20—the latter the second best in the history of the NBA.

Newcomer Danny Ainge teamed with Drexler, Porter, Kersey, Duckworth, Williams, and Robinson to form one of the most feared teams in the league. The Blazers' 27-14 road mark was the best in the league for the year, and their 36-5 record at home tied for the best. Along the way the team put together a 16-game winning streak.

Forward Buck Williams's field goal completion percentage of .602 on 358 of 595 attempts was tops for the entire league for the year. The team's outside shooting aces, Terry Porter and Danny Ainge, were fourth and sixth in the league in three-point shooting accuracy. Drexler again led the team in overall scoring with a 21.5 average; Duckworth followed at 15.8 and Jerome Kersey at 14.8.

Milestones were plentiful over the course of the year. On November 27, 1990, fan number 10 million passed through the turnstiles of Memorial Coliseum, and on January 6, 1991, the club recorded its 600th sellout in a row. During the year, Vice President of Basketball Operations Bucky Buckwalter was named the NBA's Executive of the Year. At the 1991 All-Star game the Blazers had their best representation ever with Adelman serving as the Head Coach, and players Drexler, Duckworth, and Porter on the squad.

In the 1991 playoffs the Blazers were given an unexpected battle by the Seattle Supersonics before coming out on top 3-2 in the first round. In the second round, Portland had little trouble with the Utah Jazz, winning 4-1. In the Western finals, however, the Lakers stole the first game in Portland, 111-106, then hung on to upset the Blazers, 4-2. It was a disappointing end to a fine season.

In contrast with the 1990-91 season, the 1991-92 Blazers got off to a comparatively slow start and were only 9-6 after the first month of play. But behind their fine backcourt duo of Drexler and Porter, now recognized as one of the league's premier tandems, the team rallied to post 57 wins and secure its second consecutive Pacific Division title.

Clyde the Glide

The year was especially significant for Clyde Drexler, who led the team again with a 25-point scoring mark, which was fourth highest in the NBA. Drexler also earned an All-Star berth for the sixth time; in the All-Star Game he scored 22 points and had nine rebounds and six assists, his best All-Star marks ever. Following the season, he became a member of the famed "Dream Team," which won the Olympic Gold Medal in basketball and gained international acclaim. "Clyde the Glide" provided a refreshing counterpoint to some of his more heavily-publicized "Dream Team" cohorts such as Charles Barkley, Magic Johnson, Michael Jordan, and Larry Bird.

During the 1991-92 division title repeat, the team set a new attendance record at 528,404. For the 15th consecutive year all Blazers games were sold out, a total encompassing some 683 regular and post-season contests, an all-time NBA record and the longest such streak in any major professional sport.

The team made the playoffs for the 10th straight year and 15th in the past 16, and fought their way to the finals for the second time in three years. Along that post-season trek they eliminated their perennial rivals, the Los Angeles Lakers, 3-1; toppled the Phoenix Suns 4-1; and knocked off the Utah Jazz in the Western finals, 4-2. Once again, however, they proved unable to secure the championship; the Blazers bowed to Michael Jordan, Scottie Pippin and the rest of the Chicago Bulls, four games to two.

As Clyde Drexler goes, so go the Portland Trail Blazers. With a leg injury to their All-Star guard limiting him to a total of only 49 games, the 1992-93 Trail Blazers struggled to a 51-31 record, well below their pace in the last few years, and slipped to third place in the Pacific Division race behind the resurgent Phoenix Suns and the Seattle Supersonics. Hampered by Drexler's injury, Portland bowed out of the playoffs quickly.

Drexler's regular season average for the campaign dropped to 19.9 points a game, and the Blazers had no one among the league's top 20 scorers. Following Drexler and his 19.9 scoring average was Terry Porter, at 18.2—his highest ever; newcomer Rod Strickland, at 13.7; and Jerome Kersey, at 10.6. At the pivot Kevin Duckworth's scoring output dropped to 9.9 points a game, while Buck Williams, despite pulling down a team-high 690 rebounds, saw his scoring average drop to only 8.3

points per game. The season did feature the emergence of another Blazer player as a league star, however. Cliff Robinson notched 19 points a game off the bench and exhibited an explosive talent that bodes well for the club's future.

With Porter forced to assume more of a scoring role on the club in Drexler's absence, Strickland took over as the assist leader, dishing out 559; he also led the club in steals with 131. Robinson was second on the team in rebounds with 542, and led in blocked shots with 183. Porter was selected as the recipient of the second annual J. Walter Kennedy Award, given to an NBA player, coach or trainer for meritorious community service.

Entering the 1993-94 campaign, the Trail Blazers appear to be at something of a crossroads. Drexler and Porter are established stars, and Strickland and Robinson are young talents who should continue to improve over the course of the next couple years. The club's depth is not what it once was, however, and the competition in the Pacific Division from the Phoenix Suns, Seattle Supersonics, and Golden State Warriors, among others, is likely to be fierce. Only time will tell if the Blazers can conjure up enough magic to make yet another run for the championship crown.

—*Jack Pearson*

SACRAMENTO KINGS

Born as the Rochester (New York) Royals of the National Basketball League in 1945, the Kings have one of the longest lineages in professional basketball. The Royals' original coach was also their owner, Les Harrison, and his team had plenty of talent. The backcourt ace was tough, 5-foot-11 Al Cervi, an experienced pro who had not gone to college; Cervi's backcourt partner was 5-foot-10 ex-CCNY star Red Holzman, later to achieve glory as head coach of the New York Knicks.

The other starters had all been recent college standouts: 6-foot-8 center John Mahnken of Georgetown, forwards George Glamack of North Carolina and Bob Davies of Seton Hall. Fuzzy Levane, who had been captain of the 1943 NIT-championship St. John's Redmen, was a reserve. A couple of original Royals would later become star players in other pro sports: Del Rice as a baseball catcher and Otto Graham as a Cleveland Browns football star. Another name on the roster, Chuck Connors, was not only a baseball player but

as future television star as well.

Though military service depleted the team, it had depth. Coach Ed Malanowicz joined the team early in the regular season and stayed the course. The Royals' first season was one of their most successful, as they finished second to the Ft. Wayne Zollner Pistons in the Eastern Division, then defeated the Pistons 3-1 in the opening play-off round and swept the Sheboygan Redskins 3-0 for the league championship, on the passing of Davies, the hook shots of Glamack, and the outside scoring of Holzman and Cervi.

They finished in first place in the division the following season, with a .705, 31-13 record, having added one of the NBL's first black players, 6-foot-4 center-forward Dolly King, and 6-foot-5 frontcourtman Arnie Johnson, to compensate for Mahnken's loss to the BAA. In the playoffs, the Royals put down the Syracuse Nationals 3-1, then the Pistons 2-1, but lost the finals to George Mikan and the Chicago Gears by a 3-1 margin.

The 1947-48 Royals added Arnie Risen, a star 6-foot-9 center bought from the Indianapolis Kautskys, and six-foot guard Bobby Wanzer. With Malanowicz coaching most games and Harrison going 4-4 in the remainder, the team increased its regular-season percentage to .733, or 44-16, and defeated the Pistons and the Anderson Duffy Packers in the postseason before losing the championship to another Mikan-dominated team, this time the Minneapolis Lakers.

The Royals-Lakers rivalry would be one of the great ones of the era and would be transferred intact from the NBL to the BAA in 1948-49, then to the NBA in 1949-50. Placed in the Western Division of the BAA, the Royals finished in first place at 45-15, one game ahead of the Minnesotans. The Royals-Lakers matchup was the center of attention in the postseason, but unfortunately for the Royals, it occurred during the semifinals and the Lakers won.

Naismith Memorial Basketball Hall of Fame

Bobby Wanzer

A Champion Charter Franchise

The next year, the NBL and BAA consolidated into the NBA. The Royals, coached again by Les Harrison, tied the Lakers for the Central Division lead, with 51-17, .750 records. The Lakers were the physically stronger team, the Royals had better ballhandling. A one-game tiebreaker was held in Rochester, and the Royals lost, 78-76, after which they were swept by the Pistons, 2-0, in their playoff round.

Divisional realignment put the Royals and their chief rival in the Western Division in 1950-51, and they finished in second place to the Lakers at 41-27. It was ultimately to be the franchise's most successful year, however: its only NBA championship season. The team now had Arnie Johnson and 6-foot-7 Jack Coleman at forward, with Davies and Wanzer the guards and the other Arnie—Risen—in the middle. Veteran Holzman and young Bill Calhoun were the top subs.

As predicted, the Royals bested the Pistons in the playoff openers, 2-1, then faced the real threat in the divisional championship—and beat the Lakers 3-1, reversing the previous year's experience. They won three straight games in that series after losing the opener, 76-73, in Minneapolis. Their opponent in the finals was the New York Knicks, making travel less of a problem for both teams. The Royals took the first two games at home and then Game 3 in Madison Square Garden by a 78-77 score.

Then the Knicks turned things around and won three, forcing a climactic seventh game in Rochester. It was a tense one. With 40 seconds remaining, the score was 75-75; then Davies hit two foul shots to make it 77-75. After the jump ball which the rules then required, the Royals got possession and hit another basket for a 79-75 victory and the basketball championship not only of the NBA, but of New York State.

The stable Royals squad came out one game ahead of the Lakers for the 1951-52 leadership of the Western Division, with a 41-25 posting, as Wanzer's .904 free-throw percentage led the NBA. However, after sweeping the Pistons 2-0 in the first round of playoffs, the Royals lost the Western divisional championship to the Lakers,

TEAM INFORMATION AT A GLANCE

Founding date: 1945, as the Rochester Royals; moved and became the Cincinnati Royals, 1957; the Omaha Kings, 1972; the Kansas City Kings, 1975; and the Sacramento Kings, 1985.

Home Court: ARCO Arena
One Sports Parkway
Sacramento, CA 95834
Telephone: 916-928-0000
Fax: 916-928-6912
Seating Capacity: 17,280 (since 1988)

Team nickname: Kings
Team logo: bottom half of a blue basketball, beneath top half of a round crown,
with nickname "KINGS" in white above equator line
Team uniform colors: Home—base color white, trim blue and red
Road—base color blue, trim red and white

Franchise record:	Wins	Losses	Pct.
Regular season:	1625	1906	.460
Playoffs:	45	70	.391

NBL Championships: 1 (1945-46)
NBA Championships: 1 (1950-51)
Divisional first-place finishes: 6 (1946-47*; 1947-48*; 1948-49**; 1949-50 [tied]; 1951-52; 1978-79)
Divisional last-place finishes: 14 (1955-56; 1956-57; 1958-59; 1959-60; 1960-61; 1972-73; 1973-74; 1977-78; 1984-85; 1987-88; 1989-90; 1990-91; 1991-92; 1992-93)
* — NBL ** — BAA

3-1, aftering winning the opening game.

The following season, the story ended earlier, as the Royals took second place to the Lakers, going 44-26, then bowed to the Pistons in the playoff openers, 2-1, losing Game 3 in Rochester in a 67-65 squeaker.

By 1953-54, Arnie Johnson had retired and Davies and Wanzer were 33 and 32 years of age. The Royals still took second place with a 44-26 record, two games behind the Lakers, and swept the Pistons in the playoff openers, but lost the Western title to the Lakers 3-1.

The Maurice Stokes Tragedy

The 1954-55 season marked the beginning of the modern era with the introduction of the 24-second shot clock, and the sped-up game was not kind to the aging Royals, whose youngest starter, forward Odie Spears, was 29 years old. They fell to third place and, at 29-43, their first below-.500 finish. Managing to get into the playoffs anyway, they lost to the Lakers in the opening round, 2-1. The following season found them hitting bottom with a 31-41, last-place finish.

Maurice Stokes and Jack Twyman were both powerful, hot-shooting forwards, Stokes at 6-foot-7 and 240 pounds, Twyman an inch shorter and thirty pounds lighter. Stokes was African-American, Twyman white. They arrived in Rochester as rookies in the same season, 1955-56, and both made immediate impacts. They also become friends.

Twyman, a University of Cincinnati star and second-round draft choice, led the team in field goals made and field goal percentage, and shot at a 14.4 clip. Stokes led in playing time, field goals attempted, free throws attempted and made, rebounds, assists, points, scoring average (16.8), personal fouls, and disqualifications. Stokes was Rookie of the Year. Twyman would go on to a Hall of Fame career (elected 1982) in which he would play all eleven seasons for the Royals. He was generally recognized as one of the premier shooting forwards in the NBA.

Stokes would very likely have gone on to a Hall of Fame career. In all three of his pro seasons he was an all-star. He led the league in rebounds in his second year. In 1958 he was third in both rebounds and assists. After three seasons his scoring average, achieved with remarkable consistency, was 16.4.

Naismith Memorial Basketball Hall of Fame

Jack Twyman

However, his life and career were cut short by a fluke accident whose effects weren't even noticed at first. During the last game of the 1957-58 regular season, he hit his head on the floor. It didn't prevent him from returning to the opening game of the playoffs, but shortly afterward, he sank into a coma, which was first diagnosed as encephalitis. He emerged from the coma, but was paralyzed, requiring constant care, for the rest of his life. Twyman arranged for that care. He not only stayed close to Stokes as a friend, he became Stokes's legal guardian. During his playing days and after his retirement in 1966 to become a broadcaster, Twyman ensured that his friend received the kind of first-class treatment and moral support he deserved. Maurice Stokes was born June 17, 1933, and died April 6, 1970.

Bobby Wanzer, having retired as a player, was their head coach, young Art Spoelstra was their center; and two outstanding rookie forwards—6-foot-6 Jack Twyman and 6-foot-7 Maurice Stokes—heralded much for the future, a future that was to be tragically short in Stokes's case. Stokes, the former star of St. Francis College in Pennsylvania, was Rookie of the Year, leading the league in rebounding with 16.3 per game and leading his team in scoring with 16.8. The team repeated in last place for 1956-57 with an identical record.

With two NBA teams in upstate New York and a third in the Big Apple, and performance weakening, attendance naturally had become a problem for the Royals. Owner Harrison attempted to solve it by moving to Cincinnati.

He acquired veteran Laker center Clyde Lovellette to shore up the middle, and two new guards in 6-foot-6, 200-pound Jim Paxson, father of two future NBA players, and playmaker George King. The result was a slight improvement to 33-39, worthy of third place, and a sweep by the Pistons in the first round of playoffs.

Overshadowing the season's climax, however, was the collapse of Maurice Stokes. He had hit his head on the floor during the last game of the regular season but had appeared ready to play in Game 1 of the playoffs. The following day, however, he went into a coma, and when he came out of it, he was paralyzed for the remainder of his short life.

The loss of Stokes would haunt the Royals for years. Searching for a frontcourt partner for Twyman, they tried Dave Piontek, Hub Reed, Phil Jordan, and Mike Farmer before finally hitting on Bob Boozer in the early 1960s.

A talented rookie center, 21-year-old, 6-foot-8 Wayne Embry, joined them in 1958-59 to lead the team in rebounds with nine per game; and Twyman was second in the league in scoring at 25.8.

However, the backcourt was in flux and Wanzer led the team to a 3-15 record before its new owners replaced him with 27-year-old player-coach Tom Marshall, a reserve forward out of Western Kentucky. At 19-53, or .264, the Royals were again in last place.

Twyman had a career year in 1959-60, scoring at a 31.2 clip, second in the league to Wilt Chamberlain; however, the Royals remained in the cellar with a 19-56, .253 finish.

Three players, Hub Reed, Phil Jordan, and Wayne Embry, shared the center role, and it would be another year before talent — more accurately, genius—arrived in the backcourt.

Oscar

The genius, of course, was Oscar Robertson, whose name is forever linked with that of the Royals. The University of Cincinnati All-American was already a local hero, and in his Rookie-of-the-Year 1960-61 season he would lead the NBA in assists per game with 9.7, coming in third in scoring (to Chamberlain and Elgin Baylor) at 30.5. Robertson was chosen for the All-Star Game for the first of ten consecutive seasons with the Royals, and the only one of those ten when he did not start.

Twyman's 25.3 points per game were fifth in the league, and with both Robertson and Embry in double digits in rebounding (10.1 and 10.9 respectively), and rookie Bob Boozer, of Kansas State, coming off the bench for 8.4 points and 6.2 rebounds per contest, the Royals now had a far more balanced team than in preceding years. New coach Charlie Wolf took them to an improved, 33-46, .418 record, but it was still last place, for the third straight year.

Improvement followed in 1961-62 as the Royals ascended to second place with a 43-37 record. Robertson's 11.4 assists per game led the league, and he had 30.8 points per game (third in the standings) and 12.5 rebounds (eighth) to boot. This was—and remains—the only time in NBA history when a player averaged a triple-double (double digits in points, rebounds, and assists) for an entire season.

In his second year as a pro, Robertson had become a genuine superstar. Twyman's 22.9 points per game, Embry's 19.8 with 13.0 rebounds, Boozer's 13.7 with 10.2 rebounds, and guard Arlen Bockhom's 15.8 gave the Royals a productive starting five. In the playoffs, however, they lost to the third-place Pistons, 3-1.

Another divisional realignment put the Royals in the Eastern Divison beginning in 196263. They finished third at 42-38, well behind the Celtics and less distantly behind the Syracuse Nationals.

Robertson was down to second in the league in assists—behind Guy Rodgers—and stil third in scoring. He led the team to an upset defeat of the Nats, 3-2, then to an exciting sveen-game series in which the Royals stretched the Celtics to the limit, taking Game 1 in Boston Garden, 135-132, then alternating victories in Games 2, 3, and 4, falling behind in Game 5 in Boston, tying the series in Game 6 at home by ten points, but coming up short, 143-131, in the clincher in Boston.

The 1963-64 season marked the departure of Wolf as head coach and the arrival of former Rochester player Jack McMahon, who would become, after Les Harrison, the second-winningest coach in Royals-Kings history.

Having played 4 ½ seasons with the Hawks after his 3 ½ with the Royals, McMahon got off to a fine start, guiding the Royals to second place at 55-25, a hot .688, only four games behind the Celtics. With 11 assists per game, Robertson was back on top of the league, and its second-leading scorer with 31.4 points per game.

Having traded Boozer to the Knicks, the Royals had an outstanding replacement for him in Rookie of the Year Jerry Lucas, the 6-foot-8 forward out of Ohio State. Lucas's 17.4 rebounds per game led the team and were third in the league; his 17.7 points were second on the Royals. In the first round of playoffs, the Royals took care of the Philadelphia 76ers—who were an old rival, the Syracuse Nationals, under a new name—but then lost a five-game series to the mighty Celtics.

Still in second place in 1964-65, the Royals came in at an even .600, or 48-32, Robertson upping his assists average to 11.5 per game, which is still the team's best mark ever. His scoring was 30.4 points per game and his rebounds 9.0, while Lucas's scoring was 21.4 and rebounding 20.0. Lucas played only 66 games, however, owing to injured ribs.

In the playoffs, against the Chamberlain-enhanced 76ers, the Royals lost Game 1 at home in an overtime thriller, 119-117, then tied the series in Philly by one point, 121-120, but fell short in the next two games despite solid all-around performances.

The Royals slipped to third place in 1965-66 as the 76ers and Celtics played the role of super-teams. The Royals' recorrd was a very respectable 45-35, led by the Big O's 31.3 points and 11.1 assists, and Lucas's 21.5 points and 21.1 rebounds, per game. Guard Adrian Smith, working in the shadow of Robertson, aervaged 18.4 points per game, and sixth man Happy Hairston contributed 14.1 with 7.6 rebounds.

Twyman, 31 years old, had become a reserve, replaced on the front lines by another Royal veteran, Tom Hawkins. Hairston rather than Hawkins started at forward in the playoffs against the Celtics, which the Celtics won in five.

Goodbye to Familiar Faces

The regular-season standings repeated themselves in 1966-67, with the Royals, however, dipping below .500 with 39 wins and 42 defeats. Twyman had retired, finishing his career—which included a stretch of 609 consecutive appearances—with 15,840 regular-season points, a 19.2 average; he was elected to the Hall of Fame in 1982, and his number (27) was retired by the team. His 11 seasons with the Royals are second-most on the franchises's all-time list; he is second in games played, total points, field goals made, free throws made, and personal fouls, and fifth in rebounds.

Also leaving the Royals in 1966-67 was center Embry, who went to Boston and picked up a championship ring as Bill Russell's understudy. Thirty-year-old veteran Connie Dierking was promoted to starting center for the Royals. The Cincinnati team had the misfortune to draw the 7ers as their first playoff opponent, and although winning the first game, 120-116 in Philadelphia, succumbed, 3-1.

The 1967-68 season was a downer for the Royals, as the steadily improving Knicks and Pistons passed them in the Eastern standings. They traded Hairston for older forward John Tresvant, an exchange that helped the Pistons in the frontcourt, although the Royals also acquired a fine 6-

foot-5 guard-forward, Tom Van Ardsdale, in the muli-player deal. The Royals also had a new head coach in Ed Jucker. The key to the season, however, was a thigh injury to Robertson, which limited him to 65 games although he led the NBA in scoring average (29.2) and assists (9.7).

Robertson did not play enough that season to qualify for the official scoring title, and so, like many other all-time greats—Magic Johnson, Larry Bird, and Bill Russell among them—he never earned one during his career. Lucas had another fine year, with 21.5 points and 19.0 rebound per match.

The Royals were out of the playoffs, however, and protected from the basement only by the Baltimore Bullets. To add to their future woes, their first draft choice center Mel Daniels, opted for the ABA—the Minnesota Muskies, no less.

Fifth place again, at 41-41, was the Royals' fate for 1968-69. Van Ardsdale was now Robertson's starting backcourt partner, shooting 19.4 points per game to O's 24.7. Lucas's averages were slightly down: a bit over 18 in points and rebounds per game.

The following season, they declined to 36-46, holding fifth place under a new head coach: Bob Cousy, who, after a glorious playing career with the Celtics, had successfully turned Boston College into a winning team. Cousy was unable to do the same with the Royals.

In his memoir of his coaching days, *The Killer Instinct*, Cousy names Robertson, Lucas, and Van Ardsdale as the quality players on the Royals at that time; however, he cites Lucas as an example of a talented player who did not live up to his potential.

Lucas, suffering from knee problems, was traded at his own request to the San Francisco Warriors for young forward Bill Turner and guard Jimmy King, neither of whom worked out well. Adrian Smith was traded to the Warriors for a second-round draft choice—who turned out, a year later, to be Nate Archibald. The Royals also had a fine rookie in Norm Van Lier, a 6-foot-1, 175-pound guard from Maurice Stokes's college, St. Francis, whom Cousy began to groom to take over the playmaking role. In addition, Cousy activated himself as a sub, playing a total of 34 minutes in 7 games and scoring a total of 5 points.

The Trade

Cousy and Robertson on the same team, with one as the head coach, was a situation bound to cause comparisons in the press, and the comparisons were increasingly weighted in favor of the Big O. Cousy, in his book, claims that Robertson was "a coach's dream" and that there was no personal tension between the two; however, during the coach's first season in Cincinnati, he and general manager Joe Alexson had already talked extensively about trading Robertson, whose contract was due to come up in 1970-71, and who had missed 13 games in 1969-70 due to a groin pull.

Cousy adduces decreased attendance and the ascent of guard Van Lier as reasons why trading Robertson seemed to make sense at the time, adding that Robertson "would not [agree to] play another season in Cincinnati." The Royals sent the great superstar to the Milwaukee Bucks, thereby making that team a first-rank NBA power. In exchange they received the swift 6-foot-1 guard Flynn Robinson, who had been a Royal in 1966 and 1967, and 6-foot-8 forward-center Charlie Paulk. Neither player became a starter for Cincinnati.

Placed in the Central Division in 1970-71, the team finished in third place, one slot above the bottom, at 33-49. Van Lier showed promise of achieving Cousy's hopes for him, leading the league in assists with 10.1 per game and contributing an even 16 points, plus being named to the second-string all-defensive team.

Rookie Nate Archibald matched Van Lier's point production precisely; forward Johnny Green exceeded it by 0.7 points per game; and Van Ardsdale led the team with 22.9. The rebounder in the middle was first draft choice Sam Lacey from New Mexico State and, before that, rural Mississippi. Lacey was destined to become the franchises's all-time longevity leader, playing

Born in the Bronx on April 18, 1948, Archibald first attended Arizona Western, then transferred to the University of Texas at El Paso, where he set school scoring records in bunches. In a talent-rich draft year, he was the second player selected in the second round; the first in that round was Calvin Murphy, and players in the first round included Bob Lanier, Rudy Tomjanovich, Pete Maravich, Dave Cowens, Sam Lacey—and a host of lesser lights.

Archibald's slightness of build, in addition to his relatively short height, made him injury-prone and reduced his overall NBA statistics, but those were still first-rate: 13 seasons for five teams altogether, a total of 876 regular-season games in which he scored 16,481 points for an 18.8 average, passed for 6,476 assists, and hit free throws at an .810 clip. In seven of those seasons, he played 2,800 minutes or more; in four of those, more than 3,000 minutes; while in six seasons his contribution was diminished by injury.

His greatest season was 1972-73, when he led the NBA in both scoring and assists, a feat unique in league history. And he didn't just top the charts, he leaped high above the competition, with 34.0 points and 11.4 assists per game. Archibald was one of the most exciting players in NBA history because of his skill as both a scorer and playmaker, and because of his fancy, slashing, playground-trained style, which sent him gliding around and leaping above larger players.

Naismith Memorial Basketball Hall of Fame

Nate Archibald

twelve seasons and 888 games; his Number 44 would be retired by the team. In 1970-71, he led the Royal rebounders with 11.3 per game, adding 13.5 points to his scoring column. Fellow rookie Archibald, the sensation out of Texas-El Paso, had more than quadrupled his signing price—from $100,000 to $465,000 for three years—with scorching shooting performances in a couple of between-seasons all-star games. The Royals were now a young and talented team; but they would not play in the playoffs again while based in Cincinnati.

The Archibald Era

The best team in the Central Division in 1971-72 was the Baltimore Bullets, with a .463 record. The Royals were in third place at .366, with 30 wins and 52 losses. Van Lier was gone early in the season, sent to the Chicago Bulls for 6-foot-10 reserve Jim Fox. Van Ardsdale at forward, Lacey in the middle, and Archibald at point guard now made up the nucleus of the team. Archibald's 28.2 points per game were second in the league to Abdul-Jabbar's 34.8; his 9.2 assists were third.

Archibald was quickly emerging as one of the most exciting players in basketball, a little man (about six feet tall and only 160 pounds) whose slashing style of passing and shooting ignited the crowd. Lacey's 12 rebounds per game, and Fox's nine-plus, were the team's top efforts at controlling the boards.

The following season was Archibald's greatest as he led the league in both scoring (34.0 points per game) and assists (11.4), as well as minutes played (46 per game). It was the only time in NBA history that the same man led the league in both scoring and assists, and it was the highest point average for any guard before Michael Jordan.

He also led the league in free throws attempted and free throws made, compiling an .847 percentage. Behind him, Lacey scored 13.5 per game with 11.8 rebounds. Van Ardsdale had been traded to Philadelphia, however, and the forwards were now Ron Riley and John Block.

Royals Become Kings

The most important event in team history for the year, however, was their move to Kansas City, along with a name change from Royals to Kings. They were now the Kansas City-Omaha Kings, since they played several home games in the Nebraska capital. Cincinnati and Oscar Robertson were fading memories; Nate Archibald was the team's future in the Midwest Division. In their first year in their new home, they fell to last place with a 36-46 record, but things would improve eventually.

Before that happened, they had to endure a second consecutive last-place season, as a foot injury kept team leader Archibald out of 47 games in 1973-74. No one on the team reached 20 points per game—new acquisition Jimmy Walker was almost there, at 19.8, but Tiny was down to 17.6.

A bright new spot on the team was Ron Behagen, a slim, 6-foot-9 forward-center who was named to the all-rookie first team with 11 points and just over 7 rebounds per game. Behagen would play two seasons with the Kings before

joining the New Orleans Jazz and then traveling to seven other teams in three years, including, briefly, the Kings again.

The Kings' coaching situation was fluid as Cousy quit after 20 games, assistant Draff Young supplanted him for four losing efforts, and Phil Johnson finally arrived to lift the team with a personal 27-31 record in his first season as head coach.

Johnson did better the next season as the team rose to second place, 44-38. A big reason, of course, was the return to health of Archibald, whose 26.5 points per game were fourth in the league, and whose .872 free-throw percentage was also fourth. He was third in assists in the NBA as well, with 6.2 per game. Meanwhile, Lacey was heating up under the board, his 14.2 rebounds per game ranking third in the league, and the stalwart center was named to the All-Star Team, as was Archibald.

The Kings also had a fine rookie in 6-foot-7 forward Scott Wedman from the University of Colorado, whose 11.1 points and 6.1 rebounds per game got him named to the all-rookie first team: the second year in a row the Kings had placed a player on that hopeful squad. Wedman would play seven seasons for the Kings, moving the Cleveland in 1980 and finishing his career with several seasons as a Celtic.

The 1974-75 Kings qualified for the playoffs, the first time the team had done so in Kansas City-Omaha, but did not make the most of the opportunity, as they fell to the division—leading Bulls in six games. Phil Johnson was elected Coach of the Year, the first Kings coach to have that honor.

The 1975-76 Kings were a one-town team— the Kansas City Kings—having stopped the practice of playing home games in Omaha. Archibald had another fine year—his third starting All-Star season—scoring 24.8 points per game, fourth in the NBA, with 7.9 assists, second in the league.

Wdman was an All-Star game reserve, playing 20 minutes of that contest and scoring eight points with six rebounds. When it counted, though, the Kings as a team were disappointing, going only 31-51 in the regular season, for third place, and not making the playoffs. An oddity of the season was that reserve forward Bill Robinzine led the league in disqualifications with 19, his per-game personal fouls average 3.9.

The teams disaqualifications leader the next season was rookie Richard Washington, a 6-foot-11 starting forward from UCLA who also made his presence felt with 13 points and eight-and-a-half rebounds per outing. Making his absence felt was Nate Archibald, who had been traded to the New Jersey Nets in exchange for several players and draft choices. The deal worked out poorly for the Nets, as Tiny broke his foot—he would later serve distinguished years in Boston, including an All-Star Game MVP performance in 1981.

Veteran guard Ron Boone became the Kings' scoring leader with 22.2 points per game; back-court mate Brian Taylor had 17 points and 4.4 assists, although Lacey, with 4.7 per game, was now the team's assists leader. In third place in the Midwest Division of the Western Conference of the newly expanded NBA, the Kings had a 40-42 regular-season record and did not qualify for the playoffs.

The Birdsong Years

A team that has traded Nate Archibald must look for another floor leader. In 1977-78 the stop-gap solution was Lucius Allen, a 30-year-old veteran of the Supersonics, Bucks, and Lakers. He led the Kings in assists with 4.7 and averaged just under 12 points per game. Also joining the team, and coming off the bench for heavy playing time and a 15.8 point average, was an outstanding rookie, Otis Birdsong of the University of Houston.

At 6-foot-4 and 195 pounds, the slim guard had a magnificent shooting touch, especially from midrange, which he would consistently demonstrate through four years with the Kings before spending seven with the Nets and one with the Celtics. Relying heavily on the bench in 1977-78, the Kings also inserted forward Robinzine and 7-foot-3 center Tom Burleson at times; but they fin-

ished in the cellar at 31-51. Johnson was replaced in mideason by Larry Staverman, a move that led to a late-season improvement.

True improvement came in 1978-79 with the hiring of Cotton Fitzsimmons, former head coach of the Buffalo Braves, as pilot of the Kings. Fitzsimmons' tenure was to begin with three consecutive playoffs seasons, and in his first year with the Kings, when he helped propel them from the bottom to the top of the Midwest Division in one leap, he was named Coach of the Year.

Equally crucial to the Kings' resurgence was the arrival of Rookie of the Year Phil Ford, the 6-foot-2, 175-pound point guard who had starred for the University of North Carolina. Ford was a first-round draft pick, second overall, who was well worth it. On February 21, 1989, he tied Oscar Robertson's franchise record for assists with 22. His season's numbers were 15.9 points and 8.6 assists per game, fourth in the league in the latter department.

Birdsong led the team in scoring with 21.7 points per game, Wedman hit for 18.3, and Robinzine and Lacey provided the physical touch on the boards while both scoring in double figures. This was a team that was, according to the headline of a *Sport* magazine article, "So loose it's ridiculous."

Going 48-34, the Kings took their first divisional title in 27 years. Receiving a bye in the first round of playoffs, they unfortunately lost to the Phoenix Suns, 4-1. A between-seasons fluke was the collapse of the roof at Kemper Arena on June 4, though fortunately no one was injured.

The Kings' regular season record in 1979-80 was one game short of the preceding year's mark, at 47-35, and their place in the standings was one notch lower as they finished two games behind the Bucks.

Though Wedman missed 11 games—and the All-Star exhibition—with facial fractures incurred during a game, the team's roster was stabilized after the waiver of Lucius Allen and two other players, and the trade of Richard Washington to the Bucks.

Attendance was up, as were season-ticket sales. Amost 17,000 fans attended the rededication of Kemper Arena on February 20, 1980, and saw an exciting game against the Supersonics which the Kings won, 107-105, on a last-second jumper by Ford. The playoffs were again a loss to the Suns, but management was satisfied with Fitzsimmons' performance and signed him to a new four-year contract.

The 1980-81 season marked Birdsong's third consecutive All-Star Game selection, and another good regular season for the team as they finished second to the San Antonio Spurs in the Midwest. They fell below .500, however, at 40-42. An injury to the left orbital, caused by Lloyd Free's thumb, and a congenital kidney infection, combined to limit Ford's appearance to 66 games, but Birdsong flew high at 24.6 points per game. Reserve guards Ernie Grunfeld and Jo Jo White, both recently acquired, helped make up for Ford's absence, though the veteran White retired during the season.

Forward Reggie King, a second-year man, led the team in rebounds with 9.7 per game while scoring at a 14.9 rate. King also starred in the opening round of playoffs, with 28 points and 15 rebounds in the Kings' clinching game of a 2-1 miniseries against the Portland Trail Blazers. The team then faced its old rival, the Suns, in the semifinals, and it didn't start out well for the Kings, as the Suns blew them away in Phoenix, 102-80. Adding to their troubles, Birdsong sprained an ankle, leaving with Kings without a first-string guard.

Grunfeld and Wdman started at guard for Game 2, Leon Douglas filling in for Wedman at forward—and it was a Kings road victory, 88-83. Game 3, back in Kansas City, was a 93-92 Kings squeaker on a last-minute Wedman jumper; and Game 4 was a Grunfeld star performance—27 points—for a 3-1 series lead.

With the series victory in their grasp, the Kings stumbled during the next two games, but they won Game 7 on Easter Sunday in Phoenix, with Birdsong playing 15 minutes on his bad ankle. It was the first time since the championship season in Rochester, 1950-51, that this franchise had gone to a third playoff round. Their opponent was the Houston Rockets. The Kings had Phil Ford back in the lineup, but lost Game 1, 98-78. Game 2 evened the series as King scored 31 of his team's 88 points. Game 3 of the seesaw series went to Houston, 92-88, with the Rockets holding on to fight off a late Kings surge.

Then Houston took Games 4 and 5, bumping the Kings from a post-season in which they had played a franchise-record 15 games with a franchise-record 7 wins.

Wholesale Changes

Birdsong, Wedman and Lacey were gone the following season. Birdsong went to the Nets for versatile forward Cliff Robinson, who was soon sent to Cleveland for another 6-foot-9 forward, Reggie Johnson. Wedman was released to the Cleveland Cavs in exchange for the 17th overall draft pick, who turned out to be 6-foot-6 forward Kevin Loder. Lacey went to the Nets for still another forward, 6-foot-5 Mike Woodson, plus a 1982 first-round draft pick, who would be LaSalle Thompson.

Thus it was a much different Kings team that finished fourth in the Midwest in 1981-82, out of the playoffs. There were also changes in the Kings' management, as Joe Axelson returned as general manager, and ownership, as three of its corporate partners, Leon Karosen, Paul Rosenberg and Bob Margolin, now shared the boardroom.

Thompson began his six-season Kings career in 1982-83, as the team got off to its best-ever start, an 8-3 record. Veteran Joe C. Meriweather was now the starting center, gaurd Larry Drew and forward Eddie Johnson its leading scorers at 20.1 and 19.8 points per game respectively.

Rebounding was way off as Johnson, the team leader, only pulled down 6.1 per contest. The Kings languished in midseason, then surged again for a 13-3 ending, resulting in a 45-37 regular-season, good enough to tie the Denver Nuggets for second place in the Midwest; however, the Nuggets took the playoff berth on the strength of a better conference record.

More changes occurred in 1983-84 as a group of six Sacramento businessmen purchased the team for cash plus assumption of $10.5 milion in debts. The team remained in Kansas City for the next two seasons, however. They again tied the Nuggets in the regular season, but this time it was for third place at 38-44.

Given the vagaries of the NBA playoff system, both teams played in the postseason, the Kings falling to the Lakers in a 3-0 first-round sweep. On the final day of that series, coach Fitzsimmons resigned to take the head coaching job with the Spurs.

The new coach was Jack McKinney, formerly the Indiana Pacers' head, but he only lasted nine games, eight of which were losses, before Phil Johnson returned, winning 30 for an overall 31-51, last-place team record. The team's last game in Kansas City was played on April 14, 1985; two days later, the NBA board of governors unanimously allowed a move to Sacramento.

Wayman Tisdale

Sacramento

Still playing in the strong Midwest Division, the Kings finished fifth in 1985-86 with a 37-35 record, finishing with a 28-23 late season after a dismal 9-22 start. They slipped into the playoffs, but were swept by the Rockets in three games, in none of which was the margin of victory less than eight points. It was to be the Kings' last postseason appearance through 1992-93.

However, the local fans were enthusiastic, selling out the season at 10,333 per game in the Sacramento arena, which was rededicated the ARCO Arena as the Atlantic Richfield Company entered into a ten-year sponsorship contract with the club.

The Kings' inaugural year on the West Coast was to be one of their better campaigns of the late 1980s and early 1990s, as the coaching combination of Phil Johnson and midseason replacement Jerry Reynolds took the team to 29-53, a .354, fifth place performance. Sadly, the Kings would not exceed that number of wins through the 1992-93

season, and when they did, in 1991-92, it only brought them last place. These were years of struggle.

Team management brought in a succession of head coaches: the great Bill Russell, in 1987-88, went 17-41, after which Reynolds finished out the season and served in 1988-89 and part of 1989-90.

The veteran, much-traveled head coach Dick Motta, formerly of the Bulls and Dallas Mavericks, coached for much of 1989-90, all of 1990-91, and some of 1991-92. Rex Hughes stepped in, early in 1991-92, and his 22-35 record for that partial season was a noticeable improvement.

What remained strong about the Kings was their fan support. Attendance was high; the average home game in 1992-93 was played in front of 17,317 fans—37 more than ARCO Arena's official capacity. It was the ninth best home attendance average in the NBA, compared with the team's 24th-best won-loss record.

The fact that the Kings were a high-scoring team—sixth-best in the league in 1992-93, with a 107.9 average—pleased fans, although defense was a weakness. The Kings in that ssame season gave up the second-most points in the league, 111.1 per game, better only than the Mavericks.

Hopes remained high too. Good draft position allowed the Kings to acquire talented young players. Kenny Smith, a guard from North Carolina, was on the all-rookie first team in 1987-88, though a hand fracture ended his season in April.

On June 27, 1989, center Pervis Ellison became the first number-one overall draft pick in franchise history; superstar center Moses Malone and veteran forward Wayman Tisdale were other key acquisitions that year. Unfortunately, medical problems, as well as contract disputes on Ellison's part, prevented either player from becoming the answer to the Kings' prayers down the middle.

In June 1990 the Kings made four first-round draft picks, the first time in history an NBA team had done so. They were forward Lionel Simmons, who made the first all-rookie team and was runner-up for Rookie of the Year in 1990-91, leading the Kings in rebounding; guard Travis Mays, who made the second all-rookie team; seven-foot center Duane Causwell; and forward Anthony Bonner.

All but Mays would still be on the roster in 1992-93. Causwell, in 1991-92, set a franchise record for blocked shots with 215. Bonner ran into bad luck at first as he broke his foot three times in his first two seasons, but he played in pain and rebounded well.

After the 1990-91 season, the Kings acquired veteran crowd-pleaser Anthony "Spud" Webb, the 5-foot-7 dunk artist, from the Hawks in a trade for Mays; Webb's 7 assists per game were to lead the club in 1992-93. They drafted Syracuse forward Billy Owens in the first round, then traded him to the Golden State Warriors for the outstanding 6-foot-5 shooting guard Mitch Richmond , a second player, and a 1995 first-round pick.

Consistently averaging 22 or 23 points per game in his three seasons with the Warriors and

AP/Wide World Photos

Dick Motta

his first with the Kings, Richmond promised to be the cornerstone of a future renaissance. Rookie guard Walt Williams, at 6-foot-7, added depth and strength, and 1993 first-round draft choice Bobby Hurley, who had led a great Duke team to the NCAA championship, was looked to as the point guard of the future.

The team had new ownership to go with its new players, for on April 6, 1992, the Kings and ARCO Arena were purchased by a group of five businessmen headed by Managing General Partner Jim Thomas. They also had a new coach in Garry St. Jean, who had spent a dozen years as an assistant with the Bucks, Nets, and Warriors.

Bringing hopes for pressure defense and fastbreak offense to his first assignment as a head coach, he won 25 games and lost 57 in 1992-93, a record consistent with the preceding few years.

Sources

Books

Berkow, Ira, *Oscar Robertson: The Golden Year, 1964,* Prentice Hall, 1971.

Carter, Craig, and Sachare, Alex, editors, *The Sporting News NBA Guide, 1992-1993 edition,* Sporting News Publishing Co., 1992.

Cousy, Bob, with John Devaney, *The Killer Instinct,* Random House, 1975.

Dickey, Glenn, *The History of Professional Basketball Since 1896,* Stein and Day, 1982.

Hollander, Zander, editor, *The Complete Handbook of Pro Basketball 1993,* Signet, 1992.

Hollander, Zander, and Sachare, Alex, editors, *The Official NBA Basketball Encyclopedia,* Villard Books, 1989.

Lazenby, Roland, *The NBA Finals,* Taylor Publishing Co., 1990.

Neft, David, S. and Cohen, Richard M., *The Sports Encyclopedia 1891-1989: Pro Basketball,* second edition, St. Martin's Press, 1989.

Sacramento Kings 1992-93 Media Guide/Yearbook.

Taragano, Martin, *Basketball Biographies,* McFarland & Co., Inc., 1991.

Periodicals

Newsweek, February 23, 1970; December 23, 1970; November 20, 1972.

Sport, April, 1979.

Sports Illustrated, January 26, 1970; October 16, 1972; December 18, 1972; October 15, 1979; February 18, 1980; April 4, 1980; October 20, 1980; April 20, 1981; November 9, 1981.

—*Richard Cohen* for Book Builders, Inc.

SEATTLE SUPERSONICS

Professional basketball's first tenant in the Northwest, Seattle began playing in 1967-68, the same year that the rival American Basketball Association opened for play.

The SuperSonics methodically set to putting together the team that would lose in the NBA Finals to Washington in year 11 of its existence and then defeat the Bullets a year later for their one and only NBA Championship in the Sam Schulman ownership period.

The Sonics' level of success has soared and plunged like the aircraft industry headquartered in Seattle. They showed improvement from year one through year five, dipped 21 wins in year six, and improved each of the next two to gain in year eight the franchise's first playoff berth with the team's second winning season. The Sonics leveled off in year nine, but dipped four wins the next season.

In 1977-78 Lenny Wilkens came to the rescue for the second time to get the Pacific Division's third-place team to the seventh game in the finals.

In 1978-79 the team won out over Washington in five games.

The 1980s also proved to be up-and-down for the Sonics. The Championship season was followed by a division second place 56-26 mark in 1979-80. Seattle then dipped 22 wins the next year, rebounded for a 52-win campaign in 1981-82, and then went into a slide to 48, 42, and 31 wins, ending the Wilkens Era and bringing on Bernie Bickerstaff. The former longtime Bullets assistant matched the 31 wins in 1985-86 and then fashioned improvements of 8, 5, and 3 wins in the next three seasons before a 41-41 finish out of the s in 1989-90 helped him obtain the general managership of the Denver Nuggets.

On came Hall of Famer K. C. Jones, who had taken Boston to its last title in 1986. After a 41-41 first year and an 18-18 start in 1991-92, Jones was out. Four games later, George Karl arrived from Spain to go 27-15 the rest of the way and pilot the Sonics to a 55-27 mark in 1992-93, endowing the team with promise for a return to late 1970s prominence.

In the Beginning

Awarded an NBA franchise, the first in the Pacific Northwest—and along with fellow expansion member San Diego (Rockets) the third and fourth NBA teams on the West Coast—on December 20, 1966, Seattle quickly adopted SuperSonics as the team nickname in tribute to the prominent aircraft industry in the cosmopolitan city. The Seattle Coliseum also quickly became home. Opened April 21, 1962, to house the State of Washington's "World of Tomorrow" for that year's World's Fair, it cost $4.5 million and has been operated by the city of Seattle.

The NBA's second straight year of expansion was also notable for being future Sonic Coach Bill Russell's second year as coach of the Boston Celtics, with Boston winning the title. The Sonics received 15 players in the expansion draft including St. Louis Hawks coach Richie Guerin, who declined to come to Seattle inasmuch as Al Bianchi was going to coach the team. Of the 14 others, nine would actually play for the Sonics, joined by draft picks Al Tucker (first round), Bob Rule (second) and Plummer Lott (fifth).

The Sonics played a wide-open game, ranking third in NBA scoring (118.7), but last in defense (125.1); they were only 8th in field goal and free-throw shooting. They just took more shots than anyone else. Walt Hazzard was fifth in NBA assists and led the team in scoring to rank seventh in the NBA (1894, 23.7) based on points scored.

Rule was 19th (1484, 18.1) in scoring and combined with veteran forward Tom Meschery for more than 1600 rebounds. The team's final 23-59 mark, their worst ever, beat out San Diego for fifth in the West. Hazzard represented the team in the All-Star Game. Rule and Tucker made the All-Rookie Team.

In 1968-69, expansion occurred again with Milwaukee and Phoenix joining the NBA. In the expansion draft to stock the teams, the Sonics lost

George Wilson to the Suns and Bud Olsen and Bob Weiss to the Bucks. The Sonics made some trades before and during the season. Walt Hazzard was sent to Atlanta for Lenny Wilkens in October. The rights to Richie Guerin were moved to Atlanta for Dick Smith a month later so Guerin could come out of retirement.

At the end of January, John Tresvant was acquired from the Royals for Al Tucker, while Erwin Mueller came from Chicago for cash and a draft pick. In the College Draft, the Sonics picked Bob Kauffman (first round), Art Harris (second), Al Hairston (fifth) and Joe Kennedy (tenth) who made the team. Harris was on the All-Rookie Team.

Seattle improved seven wins but finished ahead of only seventh-place Phoenix in the West as San Diego went from 15 to 37 wins and Bob Rule led the offense and was fourth in NBA scoring (1965 points, 24.0) while All-Star Game pick Wilkens was second in NBA assists (8.2) and ninth in scoring (1835, 22.4). Overall, NBA scoring dropped with Seattle seventh offensively and 12th defensively, narrowing the scoring margin.

Player-Coach Wilkens for 1969-70

Al Bianchi departed as coach after the season and Lenny Wilkens became player-coach of the Sonics. He was the NBA's lone black head coach as Bill Russell retired following his 11th championship in 13 Celtic seasons in 1969. Guards Lucius Allen (first round, third pick) and Lee Winfield (third round) were the only draft picks to stick. In September, Bob Kauffman was dealt to Chicago for veteran Bob Boozer and Barry Clemens.

Twelve days into the season, Art Harris was traded to Phoenix for Dick Snyder, and a week later Erwin Mueller went to Detroit for a second-round pick. In mid-season, John Tresvant was sold to the Lakers. The Sonics improved another six wins to fifth place, winning ten of their final 15 games. They lost the last slot to Phoenix, which improved 23 wins with the addition of Connie Hawkins from the ABA, despite losing the coin

TEAM INFORMATION AT A GLANCE

Founding date: 1967

Home court:
Seattle Coliseum
190 Queen Anne Avenue North
Seattle, WA 98109-9711
Phone: (206) 281-5800

Seating capacity: 14,132 (standing room only capacity: 14,692)

Team colors: Green and gold
Team nickname: SuperSonics
Logo: Seattle cityscape

Franchise record	Won	Lost	Pct.
(1967-1993)	1069	1024	.511

NBA Championships (1): 1978-79
NBA Conference Titles (2): 1977-78, 1978-79
NBA Division Titles (1): 1978-79

flip to Milwaukee for Lew Alcindor (later Kareem Abdul-Jabbar). Wilkens and Bob Rule went to the All-Star Game. Wilkens led the NBA in assists (9.1) with the best total (683) of his career. Rule was seventh in NBA scoring (1965 points, 24.6), and Snyder was fifth in field goal shooting (.528). Shortly after the season, forward Don Kojis was purchased from the Rockets.

Buffalo, Cleveland, and Northwest neighbor Portland were awarded franchises for 1970-71, and the Sonics lost Dorie Murrey and Joe Kennedy to the Blazers. In mid-September, Lucius Allen and Bob Boozer were traded to Milwaukee for Don Smith and cash. The big story of the season, however, came December 30 when owner Sam Schulman defied the NBA's 4-year college eligibility rule and signed Spencer Haywood, the first

"hardship" player, a year before, away from the Denver Rockets.

He gave the 1968 Olympic hero—who played one year of junior college ball at Trinidad, Colorado, and one year at the University of Detroit—a reported 6-year, $1.5-million deal. In 1969-70, Haywood had led the ABA in scoring (30.0) and rebounding (19.5), was Rookie of the Year, and All-Star Game and regular-season MVP.

Haywood was unhappy with the three contracts he had signed in the ABA, which included annuity payouts starting at age 40 or 41. The Sonics had lost top draft pick Jim Ard, a center, to the ABA. Bob Rule was injured after four games and out for the year. Other draft picks Pete Cross (949 rebounds), Jake Ford (5 games), and Garfield Heard (6 ppg, 5 rebounds per game) were of varying help.

Lenny Wilkens, whose uniform number 19 was the first retired by the Sonics, served the franchise in three distinct capacities. He was acquired first as a player for the 1968-69 season. A year later he was player-coach and spent three seasons in that role.

The Sonics traded Wilkens to Cleveland in 1972, and after five more years—including two as a Cleveland player, one as a Portland player-coach, one as Portland's coach, and one out of basketball—Wilkens returned to the Sonics 22 games into the 1977-78 season with the team at 5-17. He took the team to a 42-18 mark the rest of the way and to the seventh game of the NBA Finals before losing to Washington.

A year later, the Sonics won the NBA Championship in five games over the Bullets with Wilkens deserving the Coach of the Year Award for the effort. In all, Wilkens, who began his career with the St. Louis Hawks in 1960 and played 15 NBA seasons, coached Seattle for ten-plus seasons with a 478-402 record. He left the Sonics after the 1985-86 season to spend the next seven years coaching Cleveland with five winning seasons. He resigned there after the 1992-93 season and was hired shortly thereafter to coach the Atlanta Hawks.

A nine-time All-Star Game pick, including three times with the Sonics, when he earned 1971 Game MVP, the soft-spoken Wilkens was generally in the shadow of others as a play-making guard, a player-coach who won, and a coach whose best work took a back seat to "one-year wonders." But he will forever be remembered in Seattle for his two stints as coach and the 1979 NBA Championship.

Haywood averaged 20.6 points and 12 rebounds in 33 games. Everywhere he went, he was met by protests or left off the program. One team introduced him as "an ineligible player." He had been the subject of lawsuits when he signed with the ABA and continued to be for a few years in the NBA.

With all of that, the Sonics improved to 38 wins but finished ten games shy of a spot in the 1970-71 season. The NBA went to a 4-division alignment, and the Sonics were placed in the Pacific with the Lakers, Warriors, Rockets, and Blazers. Wilkens was second in NBA assists (9.2), and

Dick Snyder was fifth in field goal (.531) and free throw (.837) shooting. The Haywood signing overshadowed Wilkens's selection as All-Star Game MVP on a game-high 21 points in 20 minutes off the bench.

A furor erupted in Seattle and Phoenix after the 1971-72 season, when the Sonics won 47 games and the Suns won 49, and neither made the eight-team (four per conference) playoffs. In the East, teams with 47, 44, and 42 wins made the playoffs. This did not change until 1974-75, when ten teams qualified. The Sonics lost the last five games of the season, eight of the last nine, and nine of the last 11 to fall shy of the first playoff slot.

After 20 games, Bob Rule was traded to Philadelphia for cash and a pair of second round picks. Spencer Haywood scored (26.2, fourth in the NBA) and amassed rebounds (12.7) like an All-Star. Lenny Wilkens had a career-high 766 assists but lost the NBA title to Jerry West by a margin of one-tenth of a percentage point. Dick Snyder was fourth in NBA field goal (.529) accuracy.

The Sonics outscored their opponents for the first time ever (a 38-point margin). The key draft picks were Fred Brown in the first round and second-rounder Jim McDaniels, who played for ex-Sonic Tom Meschery with Carolina of the ABA, but jumped to the NBA after the All-Star break in time to play 12 games. Seattle settled with Carolina on him for $400,000. Attendance jumped 1,800 a game to 11,107.

In the off-season, Seattle gained a third ABA player who jumped to the NBA. John Brisker, represented by L.A.-area agent Al Ross, like Spencer Haywood and Jim McDaniels, signed August 8. The next day Don Kojis and Pete Cross were traded to Kansas City-Omaha for Jim Fox and future considerations. Two weeks later, Lenny Wilkens and Barry Clemens went to Cleveland for Butch Beard. Ten days into the 1972-73 season, the Sonics dealt Garfield Heard and a third-round pick to Chicago for Kennedy McIntosh. Tom Nissalke, a 1970-71 NBA assistant at Milwaukee and a 1971-72 ABA coach in Dallas, was hired as coach, but was fired with the team at 13-32. Bucky Buck-walter went 13-24 the rest of the way, but the 26-56 mark was fifth in the Pacific and 21 games off the pace.

Haywood played in his second straight NBA All-Star Game and was third in NBA scoring (29.2) and tenth in rebounding (12.9). He made the All-NBA First Team for the second straight season. Jim Fox ranked fifth in field goal accuracy, (.515) and Dick Snyder was seventh in free throw shooting (.861). First round pick Bud Stallworth contributed, but second-rounder Joby Wright was not a factor nor was McDaniels. Second-rounder, Brian Taylor, signed with the ABA Nets.

Bill Russell Arrives to Coach

Bill Russell, who had been an ABC-TV analyst and Los Angeles radio talk show host, returned to coaching in 1973-74 with the Sonics. Dick Gibbs came from K.C.-Omaha to complete the Kojis/Cross-Fox deal of the previous summer. Butch Beard went to Golden State in return for Walt Hazzard, who is now known as Mahdi Abdul-Rahman.

First-round choice Mike Green was lost to ABA Denver, and no other draft pick makes the team, but free agent Donald (Slick) Watts remained and was second on the team in assists and steals, a new NBA statistic.

All-Star Game performer Spencer Haywood was ninth in NBA scoring (23.5), sixth in rebounding (13.4), and ninth in blocked shots (1.41), a new statistic. Dick Snyder rated seventh (.866) and Freddie Brown ninth (.863) in NBA free throw percentage. The Sonics managed a 36-46 record, third in the Pacific Division and 11 wins shy of a berth. Brown set a single-game scoring mark of 58 points at Golden State March 23.

With the division expanded by one team per conference for 1974-75, the Sonics' 43-39 record would have made it under the old format. They went in as the fourth seed, thanks to a season-ending 7-game winning streak, and ousted Detroit in the best-of-three first round, 2-1. Seattle in turn bowed to eventual NBA Champion Golden State in six games in the West Semifinals.

Spencer Haywood played in his fourth and last NBA All-Star Game. He finished ninth in NBA scoring (22.4). Slick Watts was fourth in NBA steals (2.32) and seventh in assists (6.1). Fred Brown emerged as a scorer with his 21.0 average ranking 14th. First-round pick Tom Burleson, a 7-foot-2 center, rated eight in blocked shots (1.87) and made the All-Rookie Team.

Before the 1975-76 season began, Bud Stallworth was lost to New Orleans as the NBA added a 17th team via expansion. Dick Snyder was traded to the Cavs for a first round pick. Archie Clark was acquired from the Bullets for Dick Gibbs and a third-round draft choice. Five Seattle draft picks—

Burleson, Leonard Gray, Talvin Skinner, Dean Tolson, and tenth-rounder Rod Derline from Seattle University—had made the roster in 1974-75.

A second straight 43-39 record produced a second straight Sonics spot in 1975-76. Thanks to wins in the final two regular-season games, the Sonics went in as the second seed in the West over the Suns with a first-round bye and home court advantage verses the Suns. But Phoenix prevailed in six games. The Suns got a breakthrough win in game two and won all three home games by 11 or more points. The Suns expended a lot of energy in winning 11 of the last 15 games.

In the month before the season, the Sonics made three deals. Archie Clark was sent to Detroit for a 1978 first-rounder in September. Two days before the season opener, Herm Gilliam came from Atlanta for a draft pick, and Jim Fox was swapped to the Bucks for a pick with cash involved in both deals. The next day, Spencer Haywood was traded to New York for a 1979 first-rounder and cash. A month into the season, veteran Mike Bantom was acquired from Phoenix for cash.

Freddie Brown took over as the scoring leader. His 23.1 average was fifth in the NBA, and he was fifth in free throw shooting (.869). But Slick Watts was a major story as he led the NBA in both assists (8.1) and steals (3.18), one of four players ever to turn the trick. Tom Burleson was seventh in blocked shots (1.83) and added 15.6 points and 9.0 rebounds. Draft picks Frank Oleynick and Bruce Seals contributed, as did veteran free agent Willie Norwood. Brown made his only All-Star Game appearance and Watts was on the All-Defensive Team.

In Bill Russell's final season as coach, the Sonics slipped to 40-42 and missed the playoffs, which had been expanded to six teams per conference due to the ABA-NBA merger on June 17, 1976, by four wins.

After grabbing Indiana's Bobby Wilkerson in the first round and Pepperdine's Dennis Johnson in the second round of the draft, the Sonics were still dealing. They sold Herm Gilliam to Portland and bought LaRue Martin in a separate deal. Two

months into the season, Leonard Gray is sent to the Bullets for Nick Weatherspoon.

The Sonics' offense became more balanced, improving by nearly a point per game, but dropping 9 from ninth in the 18-team league to 18th in the 22-team loop. Fred Brown fell out of the top 20 scorers to 17.2 and Tom Burleson tumbled to 9.7 points, 6.7 rebounds, and 1.4 blocks.

Brown was fifth in free throw percentage (.884) and Slick Watts, a solid 13-point scorer, was second in assists (8.0) and third in steals (2.71). Russell's 4-year mark was 162-166. His major failing was that he didn't have a Bill Russell in Seattle as he did in Boston.

Lenny Wilkens Returns as Coach

Lenny Wilkens's return as Seattle coach—he retired as a player in 1975 and was let out at Portland at the end of the 1975-76 season—was delayed until the Sonics sank to 5-17 under Bob Hopkins, Bill Russell's assistant and cousin, who had succeeded him. The team proceeded to go 42-18 the rest of the way to finish 47-35 and third in the Pacific Division with the fourth seed.

The Sonics caught fire in the playoffs, dropping the Lakers, 2-1, in the first round, blazing Portland, 4-2, in the Western Semifinals and nudging Denver, 4-2, in the West Finals. Seattle had the home court edge over 44-38 Washington, but the Bullets won in seven games. An arena conflict caused the Sonics to give up some momentum as game two was moved to Washington and game four sent to Seattle. Seattle won game three on the road and lost game four at home in overtime. Washington's 35-point win in game six gave them all they needed to win game seven in Seattle, 105-99. However, a foundation was laid.

Five transactions before mid-season solidified the Sonics. Gus Williams was signed as a free agent from Golden State to lead Seattle in scoring (18.1) and rank second in NBA steals (2.34). John Johnson was acquired from Houston for a pair of second-round picks. Wally Walker came from Portland's 1977 title team for a pair of picks. Mike

Green was sent to San Antonio for picks. Jack Sikma was the number one pick. Slick Watts was peddled to New Orleans for a 1981 first round choice.

Back in May, Tom Burleson, Bobby Wilkerson and a pick were sent to Denver for Paul Silas, Willie Wise, and Marvin Webster, who was ninth in rebounding (12.6) and blocks (1.98). Freddie Brown was steady and rated third in NBA free throw accuracy (.898). The team was built around defense, rating second in points allowed (102.9) while scoring 104.5.

Kingdome Home

After calling the Seattle Center Coliseum home for the franchise's first 11 seasons, the Sonics elected to move to the massive Kingdome for the 1978-79 season. It was a move calculated to take advantage of the team's 1977-78 success after Wilkens returned as coach.

The Sonics and Detroit Pistons, who moved from downtown Detroit to the Pontiac Silverdome some 32 miles north at the same time, were the only NBA teams in large, domed arenas that were built for football but accommodated basketball. The Houston Rockets played some doubleheaders in the Astrodome in the late 1960s and early 1970s before the Summit was built, but no team had ever moved uniforms, lockers, and basketballs to a cavernous stadium before.

The Sonics had farmed out games to Eugene, Oregon, Tacoma, Washington, and Vancouver, British Columbia, to moderate interest. They had also played front ends of twin-bills in Portland. Now the team would have more than 40,000 seats available and a team capable of setting a season attendance record of 18,225 in 1978-79 and a better total of 21,725 in 1979-80 that would stand for almost a decade.

Seattle's bid to get back to the NBA finals was helped in June when Tom LaGarde came from Denver for Seattle's 1978 first-round pick. Then free agent Marvin Webster signed with the Knicks in late August, and in early October the Sonics received a 1979 first-round pick and $450,000 in compensation.

In between, Dick Snyder returned as a veteran free agent with the Sonics giving up two second round picks as compensation. In mid-season, Dennis Awtrey came from Boston for a 1979 first round choice. The Sonics wound up with a franchise-best 52-30 record, second-best in the NBA to Washington's 54-28 mark.

The Sonics gained a first round bye and eliminated the Lakers in five games in the Western Semifinals. Seattle then closed out Phoenix in seven games after bowing at home in game five and then staying alive with a 106-105 win at Phoenix in game six. In the finals, Washington had the home court advantage. The Bullets won game one, but Seattle took the next four, including the decisive game in Washington to win the NBA title, its only one. Dennis Johnson was the Play-off MVP.

Wilkins put together a very flexible and interchangeable seven of Jack Sikma, Gus Williams, Dennis Johnson, Fred Brown, Shelton, John Johnson, and Paul Silas. Joe Hassett, Dick Snyder, Wally Walker, and Dennis Awtrey played lesser roles. LaGarde played just 23 games. Brown, third in free throw shooting (.888), Sikma, fifth in rebounding (12.4), and Williams, eighth in steals (2.08) were the team's lone NBA leaders. Sikma was named to the All-Rookie Team. Dennis Johnson, Jack Sikma, and the coaches went to the All-Star Game.

Seattle was even better during the 1979-80 regular-season at 56-26, which was second in the Pacific Division to the Lakers and fourth-best in the NBA. Gus Williams ranked 11th in NBA scoring (22.1) and fourth in steals (2.44). Jack Sikma rated fifth in rebounding (11.1), and Downtown Fred Brown won the NBA's newest statistical category, 3-point shooting (.443).

The team got help in the draft with the number 6 and 7 picks James Bailey and Vinnie Johnson. Fourth-rounder James Donaldson took his 7-foot-2 body to Europe for a year. Dick Snyder retired, Dennis Awtrey went to Chicago, and Joe Hassett headed to the Pacers. Bailey and a healthy Tom LaGarde become parts of the nine-man rotation.

Jack Sikma joined Seattle as the team's 1977 first round pick out of tiny Illinois Wesleyan just in time to fit into Coach Lenny Wilkens's seven-man playing rotation, which delivered the franchise's seven-game 1978 NBA Finals run and the 1979 NBA Championship.

Sikma played in NBA All-Star Games each of his first seven seasons and was a perennial top 10 rebounder and free throw shooter. He also had a distinctive turnaround, sling-shot jumper that opposing players always felt they could block, but he scored consistently. Sikma, whose Sonic number 43 was retired during the 1992-93 season, played nine seasons in Seattle before going on to Milwaukee for five more years. He retired after the 1990-91 season.

Sikma toyed with the idea of one more year out West in 1991-92 but rejected it and settled in as a Sonics TV analyst in 1992-93. His career included 17,287 total points (15.6), 10,816 rebounds (9.8), 1,162 steals, 1,048 blocks and 3,488 assists in 1,107 games. He scored 14.3 in the playoffs with 9.3 rebounds in 102 games. He led the NBA in 1987-88 free throw percentage (.922) and was a 1982 Second Team All-Defensive pick.

In the playoffs, Seattle ousted Portland, 2-1, in the first round, and Milwaukee, 4-3, in the West Semifinals. The 60-win Lakers scored a 4-1 Western Finals Series victory behind L.A. rookie Earvin "Magic" Johnson. The dream of repeating was done, and on May 21 free agent Paul Silas signed to become the Clippers' player-coach. He never played again, but Seattle got a 1985 second-rounder as compensation. A week later, LaGarde went to the new Dallas Mavericks in the expansion draft. Again the coaches, Sikma and D.J., plus trainer Frank Furtado were All-Stars.

Williams Sits Out Year, Sonics Sag

Gus Williams sat out the entire 1980-81 season in a contract dispute, and the Sonics sagged to a 34-48 record in the Wizard's absence. Seattle finished sixth (last) in the Pacific Division. Dennis Johnson had already been traded June 3 to Phoenix for Paul Westphal. In late July, the Marvin Webster case was modified, and Seattle's 1981 number one pick went to the Knicks.

Westphal and Jack Sikma made the All-Star Game. Westphal played just 36 games, however, and Lonnie Shelton played just 14 games due to injury. Sikma, Fred Brown, James Bailey, John Johnson, and second-year guard Vinnie Johnson, the team's best offensive rebounder at 6-1, carried the load for Seattle. First round pick Bill Hanzlik, European returnee James Donaldson, and December trade pickup Armond Hill also helped, but the chemistry wasn't there. Sikma's 10.4 rebounds rated fifth in the NBA, Seattle's only ranking.

Gus Williams resigned at the June 1981 NBA meetings outside Boston and Seattle heaved a sigh of relief. He went on to make the All-Star Game with Jack Sikma, and a healthy Lonnie Shelton was voted to the 1982 All-NBA First Team and received the Comeback Player of the Year Award (an honor that has since been discontinued). The Sonics bounced back to a 52-30 record, second in the Pacific to the Lakers and fifth in the NBA.

In the playoffs, Seattle whipped Houston, 2-1, in the first round, but could not get past San Antonio, bowing 4-1 to Midwest champion San Antonio. Danny Vranes and Mark Radford, the team's first and second round 1981 choices, made the team. James Bailey was sent to the Nets for Ray Tolbert; Vinnie Johnson went to Detroit for Greg Kelser; and Phil Smith came from the Clippers for Armond Hill.

Williams ranked seventh in NBA scoring

(23.4) and seventh in steals (2.15). Sikma was second in rebounding (12.4) and tenth in free throw shooting (.855). 1979 draft pick Johnny Moore, cut that pre-season, led the NBA in assists (9.6) at San Antonio. Ex-Sonic Joe Hassett was tenth in 3-point shooting (.332).

The Sonics tried to retool for 1982-83 by trading for David Thompson and sending their 1982 first round pick and the rights to free agent Wally Walker to Denver, but a month after the mid-June deal the NBA special master ruled that a team could not trade a player's right of refusal. Walker was returned to Seattle, and on July 20 Denver selected Bill Hanzlik to complete the trade.

In the preseason, Walker was shipped to Houston for a draft pick. The Sonics slipped to 48-34 and fell a notch to third in the Pacific. This time, they went out in the first round of the playoffs in a 2-0 sweep by Portland, which finished just two wins back in the regular season. Gus Williams cut back his scoring to 20.0 but ranked sixth in NBA assists (8.0) and seventh in steals (2.28). Jack Sikma was fifth in rebounding (11.4) and tenth in free throw accuracy (.837). Sikma, Thompson, and Williams played in the All-Star Game in Los Angeles.

Chambers Acquired in Multi-Player Deal

Seattle made two big off-season trades to try and reverse its won-lost record and recoup attendance, which declined 4,270 to 14,024 in 1982-83. On June 27, Lonnie Shelton went to Cleveland for a 1983 second-rounder and cash. The blockbuster came August 26, when after signing James Donaldson to a 4-year contract, the Sonics sent him along with Greg Kelser, Seattle's 1984 first pick, and other considerations to the San Diego Clippers for Tom Chambers and Al Wood.

Chambers was reunited with college teammate Danny Vranes. Reggie King then came from Kansas City the day before the season began for a future pick. However, the Sonics slipped to 42-40, still third in the Pacific Division and attendance

slid another 3,122 to 10,902 in the Kingdome.

Dallas, in its first trip, ousted the Sonics, 3-2, with a 105-104 home win in game five. David Thompson signed a one-year contract extension in mid-January, but played only 19 games in this, his final season. Jack Sikma was sixth in rebounding (11.1) and eighth in free throw shooting (.856) and played in the All-Star Game.

Gus Williams ranked third in steals (2.36) and seventh in assists (8.4) in his last Sonics season. Draft picks Jon Sundvold (first) and Scooter McCray (second) made the team. Just before the season began, Barry Ackerley of Ackerley Communications purchased the team, ending 16 years of Sam Schulman ownership.

Seattle made still one more bid to shake things up in the 1984 off-season by shipping Gus Williams to the Bullets for Ricky Sobers and the right to Tim McCormick, the second trade for the 7-foot center, who was picked 12th by Cleveland in the draft that June 19th. Five weeks later, Steve Hawes, obtained 17 months before from Atlanta, said he would go to Italy. In the pre-season, Gerald Henderson came from Boston for a 1986 first round pick. The Sonics sank to 31-51, worst since 1972-73, and finished fourth (in a tie) in the Pacific Division.

The team's sag was underscored by the fact that no player finished among the NBA statistical leaders. Jack Sikma was selected for his seventh and final All-Star Game berth. Attendance fell more than 3,500 to 7,399 per game and the team announced that it would leave the Kingdome and return to the Seattle Center Coliseum. At season's end, Coach Lenny Wilkens resigned; in all, he had piloted Seattle to a 478-402 record.

Bickerstaff Comes to Renovated Coliseum

In 1985-86, the Sonics returned to a refurbished Seattle Center Coliseum. The Sonics and the City of Seattle spent more than $2 million to upgrade seating and install a new floor and scoreboard to bring the new capacity to 14,252. On June

20, 1985, longtime Bullets assistant Bernie Bickerstaff was hired as head coach.

The 1985 draft brought Xavier McDaniel, who would make the All-Rookie Team. The Sonics, however, needed to win the season finale to match 1984-85's 31-51 record and beat out Golden State for fifth place in the Pacific Division. Once again the Sonics were shut out on the NBA statistical leader boards. A number of minor moves brought little help. The season low came when a leaky roof produced the first game postponed due to rain in NBA history; the game was concluded the next day, January 6.

During the 1986 off-season, 30-year-old Bob Whitsitt was brought in from the Sacramento Kings as president and general manager. On July 1, 9-year Jack Sikma was traded to Milwaukee with a pair of second round picks for 5-year center Alton Lister and the Bucks' 1987 and 1989 firsts. The draft the previous week had brought second-round pick Nate McMillan. On July 23, Seattle acquired Dale Ellis from Dallas for Al Wood. On September 29, Seattle sent Tim McCormick and Danny Vranes to Philadelphia for Clemon John and Philly's 1989 first round pick. The next day, Seattle claimed Maurice Lucas on waivers and acquired John Long from Detroit for two draft picks. Two days later, Long was sent to Indiana for two reserves.

On the court, Seattle improved to 39-43 and returned to the playoffs as attendance improved for the second straight year to 8,692. The Sonics, after being blasted at Dallas, 151-129, in game one, won the next three, including game four, 124-98, to win the first round. Seattle then won the first two games at Houston in the West Semifinals and eliminated the Rockets in six games.

The bubble finally burst as the eventual champion Lakers swept the West Finals, 4-0. Ellis was voted Most Improved Player, Bernie Bickerstaff was named Coach of the Year, and Tom Chambers played in the All-Star Game and won its MVP Award. Ellis (24.9), Chambers (23.3), and Xavier McDaniel (23.0) ranked 8-12-13 in NBA scoring. McMillan was seventh in NBA assists (8.2) and Lister rated fifth in blocked shots (2.40).

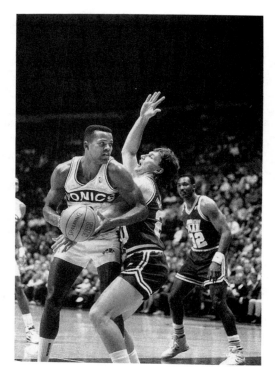

AP/Wide World Photos

Dale Ellis

With a base to build on, Seattle improved to 44-39, garnering the third-place spot in the Pacific Division and gaining the seventh seed in 1987-88. Denver eliminated the Sonics in five games after the teams swapped home-court upsets in Games 2 and 3. Attendance rose dramatically to 12,008 per game.

President Bob Whitsitt set the tone for more off-season dealing on draft day, when the Sonics sent fifth pick Scottie Pippen to the Bulls for 7-foot center Olden Polynice. During pre-season Sam Vincent and Scott Wedman were acquired from Boston for a future draft pick. Maurice Lucas signed with Portland as a free agent. At the trade deadline, Vincent was traded to Chicago for Sedale Threatt.

Derrick McKey, the team's other 1987 first, made the All-Rookie Team. Dale Ellis finished seventh in NBA scoring (25.8) with Xavier Mc-Daniel 14th (21.6) and Tom Chambers 18th (20.4). McDaniel appeared in his only All-Star Game. Ellis was 9th in three-point shooting (.413) and Nate McMillan ranked sixth in assists (8.6) and eighth in steals (2.06). In mid-season, Ellis set an NBA record by converting two 4-point plays at Sacramento.

The 1988-89 season brought more improvement in Bernie Bickerstaff's third season as head coach with a variety of player moves before the 47-35 season and another third-place Pacific Division finish. Before the draft, reserve guard Kevin Williams was lost via expansion to the Miami Heat.

On draft day, the Sonics obtained Michael Cage in a three-way deal with the Clippers and 76ers. Seattle sent draft pick Gary Grant and a 1989 first in the deal. On July 6, Tom Chambers signed with Phoenix as the NBA's first unrestricted free agent. Later guards John Lucas and Avery Johnson were signed as free agents and Bob Whitsitt then locked Dale Ellis and Nate McMillan into long-term deals.

Again, attendance climbed, reaching 12,920 per game. Ellis played in his only All-Star Game and won the All-Star Saturday Long Distance Shootout; he was also voted to the post-season All-NBA Third Team.

In the playoffs, Seattle eliminated Houston, 3-1, in the first round but was swept by the Lakers, 4-0, in the West Semifinals. Ellis was third in NBA scoring (27.5) and second in 3-point shooting (.478); Cage ranked 10th in rebounding (9.6); and Nate McMillan was fifth in assists (9.3). The Sonics made news when two players' wives got into a post-game fight.

In the 1989 off-season, Xavier McDaniel signed a new five-year deal, the Sonics lost Jerry Reynolds to Orlando in the Expansion Draft and maneuvered ahead of the College Draft. The Sonics obtained Brad Sellers from Chicago for the 18th pick in the draft, then received Golden State's 16th pick for Seattle's own in 1990.

On Draft Day, Seattle took Dana Barros (16th pick) and Shawn Kemp (17th). Kemp had not played at Trinity JC after leaving Kentucky. In August, the Sonics got their number one player back from Golden State in exchange for Alton Lister.

Before training camp, Barros and Kemp signed long-term pacts and veterans Michael Cage, Derrick McKey, and Olden Polynice signed contract extensions. The Sonics could manage just a 41-41 record for fourth place in the Pacific Division and missed the s as attendance dipped for the only Coliseum season since the team's return to 12,244.

Injuries kept Dale Ellis out of 27 games, Xavier McDaniel missed 13, and Sedale Threatt was absent from 17. Michael Cage was 9th in rebounding (10.0), the team's only ranked player. In the fourth game of the year, Seattle lost in quintuple overtime, a 4-hour, 17-minute, 155-154 battle at Milwaukee.

AP/Wide World Photos

Shawn Kemp

Another Celtic Hall-of-Famer Appears

When Bernie Bickerstaff concluded his 4-year, 161-167 tenure as head coach to become Denver's General Manager, the Sonics turned to former Celtic Hall-of-Famer K.C. Jones, who had coached at Washington and Boston and won the 1986 NBA title with the Celtics. In the draft, Seattle selected Gary Patton with the second overall pick and later signed him to a six-year contract. Avery Johnson was dealt to Denver in the pre-season for a 1997 second-rounder.

Early in the season, Xavier McDaniel was traded to Phoenix for Eddie Johnson and first round picks in 1991 and 1993. In the week before the February trade deadline, Seattle acquired All-Star sixth man from Milwaukee for Dale Ellis and Benoit Benjamin from the Clippers for Olden Polynice and 1991 and 1993 first round choices. Both newcomers signed contract extensions.

The Sonics, however, still managed no better than a 41-41 record and fell to Portland in the first round of the s, 3-2, with the home team winning every game. Pierce (.913) and Johnson (.891) wound up third and ninth in NBA free throw shooting, while Benjamin was eighth in rebounding (10.3) and ninth in blocks (2.07).

George Karl Returns From Spain

In the 1991 draft, Seattle selected 7-foot-2 "project" center Rich King and just before training camp began, traded Sedale Threatt to the Lakers for three second round choices (1994, 1995 and 1996). With the team off to an 18-18 start, K.C. Jones was fired as coach and Assistant Bob Kloppenburg went 2-2 in the interim while President Bob Whitsitt was arranging for former Cavaliers and Warriors Coach George Karl to return from Madrid, Spain, to take over the team.

The Sonics went 27-15 to wind up 47-35, fourth in the Pacific. The Sonics averaged 14,313, thanks to four 30,000-plus Kingdome crowds for Boston, Chicago, the Lakers and Portland. Ricky Pierce, who challenged Calvin Murphy's record of 78 consecutive free throws with 75 straight from November 15 to December 11, ranked third in free throw percentage (.916). Michael Cage was fifth in field goal percentage (.566), and Dana Barros led in three-point percentage (.446).

In the playoffs, Karl and the Sonics out-dueled mentor Don Nelson and the Warriors, 3-1. In the Western Semifinals, Seattle fell to Utah, 4-1. It was felt the Sonics had come of age.

In George Karl's first full season in Seattle, 1992-93, the Sonics surged to a 55-27 record, second in the Pacific Division and equalling the NBA's fourth-best mark. Thanks to four more Kingdome games, attendance climbed to 15,774, and the Sonics planned a future Kingdome move for Coliseum renovations as plans for a new arena remained stalled.

In the playoffs, Seattle advanced with a 3-2 first round victory over Utah after facing elimination in game four. In the West Semifinals, Seattle advanced 4-3, with a 103-100 overtime win in game seven. The Sonics took Phoenix to seven games in the West Finals after facing elimination a game earlier.

The November 25th pickup of Vincent Askew from Sacramento for a second round pick was helpful, but Bob Whitsitt's key deal was acquiring Sam Perkins from the Lakers for underachieving Benoit Benjamin and the rights to unsigned 1992 first-round pick Doug Christie, a Seattle-born hoopster who played collegiately at Pepperdine in the L.A. area. Perkins was the one Sonic to improve his scoring and rebounding averages in the playoffs over the regular season.

SOURCES

BOOKS

Carter, Craig, and Alex Sachare, *The Sporting News 1992-93 NBA Guide,* The Sporting News Co., 1992.

Hollander, Zander, editor, *The NBA's Official Encyclopedia of Pro Basketball,* 1981.

Hollander, Zander, editor, *The Pro Basketball Encyclopedia,* Corwin Books, 1977.

Hollander, Zander, and Alex Sachare, editors, *The Official NBA Basketball Encyclopedia,* Villard Books, 1989.

Sachare, Alex, and Dave Sloan, editors, *The Sporting News 1991-92 NBA Register,* The Sporting News Co., 1991.

Sachare, Alex, and Mark Shimabukuro, *The Sporting News 1992-93 NBA Register,* The Sporting News Co., 1992.

Seattle Supersonics Media Guide, Seattle Supersonics, 1992.

Welts, Rick, *Seattle Supersonics Media Guide 1976-77,* Seattle Supersonics, 1976.

PERIODICALS

NBA News, vol. 47, nos. 9, 30, 36, and 37, 1992-93.

Index

A

B

E

F

G

L

M